Berlin and its Culture

BERLIN
AND ITS CULTURE
A Historical Portrait

Ronald Taylor

Yale University Press
New Haven and London

Set in Bembo
Printed in Italy

Library of Congress Cataloging-in-Publication Data

Taylor, Ronald, 1924–
    Berlin and its culture: a historical portrait/Ronald Taylor.
    Includes bibliographical references and index.
    ISBN 0–300–07200–7
    1. Berlin (Germany)—Intellectual life. 2. Politics and literature—Germany—Berlin—History. 3. German literature—Germany—Berlin—History and criticism. 4. Enlightenment—Germany—Berlin. 5. National socialism and art—Germany—Berlin. 6. Art and state—Germany. 7. Socialism and art—Germany—Berlin. I. Title
DD866.8.T39 1997   97–24401
943'.155—dc21   CIP

A catalogue record for this book is available from the British Library.

10 9 8 7 6 5 4 3 2 1

For Brigitte

From what I hear, the inhabitants of Berlin are such a brazen lot that gentility gets one nowhere. If one wishes to survive in their company, one has to develop a thick skin and sometimes be prepared to deal quite roughly with them.

(Goethe to Eckermann, 4 December 1823)

CONTENTS

PREFACE

The title of this book conceals a dilemma, or a series of dilemmas. It proceeds in historical sequence but it does not aspire to be a history. Its focus is the activity of, and in, a city but that activity, like that city, is only part of a larger whole. I have tried to capture the cultural spirit of Berlin in successive ages but the discussion has inevitably encroached from time to time on other, broader fields. In particular it has sometimes been hard to avoid a certain arbitrariness when it came to deciding where cultural history ends and social history begins.

Nobody's interests would have been served, it seemed to me, by a narrative so detailed that it would have amounted to a catalogue of names and works of writers, painters and musicians, some known, many barely so, who contributed at one time or another to the Berlin cultural scene. Rather, from behind a conventional conception of what constitutes culture – literature, philosophy, painting and sculpture, the theatre, music, the decorative arts – I have located a series of historical periods and set out to identify the characteristic nature of the city's culture within those periods, setting the political and social scene on each occasion.

A periodisation derived from political history is not necessarily transferable, as it stands, to the events of culture. Nor, for that matter, do the critical moments in the evolution of one art necessarily coincide with those in the other arts. Each art obeys the laws of its own inner nature and responds to the outside world in its own terms. But I have aimed to make each period, that is to say, each chapter, into a more or less self-contained context, sustained by the momentum that governs the individual arts within it. How this momentum persists through the centuries can then be traced through the individual discussions of painting, literature and so forth in the chronological sequence.

In the company of capital cities such as Paris, London and Madrid, Berlin is a late arrival on the European scene. The *Kleinstaaterei*, the particularism, characteristic of German political history meant that different parts of the country developed in different ways, above all with different priorities, and Berlin, centre of the Hohenzollern kingdom of Brandenburg–Prussia, long lagged behind other German territories in the cultural league. In the early centuries of its existence, through Middle Ages and Renaissance, it has only token manifestations of culture to offer. With the advent of the Enlightenment, however – surely no accident – begins the surge of activity which sweeps like an ever-swelling flood down to modern times.

The flood does not flow evenly, for it is governed by political and economic determinants. Thus, to change the metaphor, the exuberance of the culture of Berlin in the 1920s is choked by the onset of Nazism, which left fifteen years of cultural desolation behind it at the end of the Second World War. That Nazi 'culture' cannot simply be ignored. But nor can one bear to give it the attention demanded by the spectacular years of the Weimar Republic that preceded it – or, for that matter, of the turbulent post-war years that follow it.

These post-war years may appear to have received more than their fair share of attention in the book. But on the one hand they are fifty of the most agitated and agonising years in the life of Berlin, while on the other we are confronting during these years not one Berlin and one German culture but two, each with its own art, its own literature, its own architecture – its own ethos. That this last chapter in the book is twice as long as the others is only a reflection of the historical reality and its cultural consequences.

One ever present problem in a book of this kind, and one which I cannot have resolved to everybody's satisfaction, is whom, and what, to include and what to leave out. Men and women important in their own right but whose relationship to Berlin belongs in the category 'they came, they saw, they left again', are not among my witnesses unless they throw a special light on the city's cultural life. At the other extreme artists who may have lived their entire life there but without impressing their names either on the city or on the history of their art have also been left aside. In between lies the range – wide enough, in all conscience – that stretches from great figures who spent significant parts of their life there – Lessing and Hegel, Schinkel and Mendelssohn, Menzel and Fontane – to the important minor artists who contributed to the cultural personality of the city while drawing from it an enrichment of their creative imagination. The criterion is reciprocity, illustrated by a selective, not an exhaustive approach to their works. Lesser figures, indeed, their energies more or less completely absorbed by their time and place, often tell us more about that time and place than their greater contemporaries.

My story ends in 1990, year of the formal demise of the German Democratic Republic and the restoration of national unity. To speculate on the cultural options facing a single, politically united Germany has not formed part of my brief. Moreover, a discussion that starts by focusing on Berlin quickly turns into a discussion on Germany as a whole. The brief Postscript reviews some of the problems that reunification has brought in its train but it can only point to some of the old things which that reunification has destroyed and hint at some of the new possibilities it has opened up. Not only physically but emotionally and intellectually Berlin in 1997 is a building site. The culture of the Federal Republic of Germany Mark Two has only just begun.

The suggestion for a book on this subject came from John Richard Parker, of MBA Literary Agents. To him, as to Robert Baldock, Candida Brazil, Kevin Brown and Sheila Lee of Yale University Press, who saw the book on its way, and to Peter James, who copy-edited the manuscript so skilfully, I should like to express my sincere thanks. A warm thank-you too to my good friends Frederic Reynold QC and David Harman for casting a stern and knowledgeable eye over parts of the manuscript. And I also owe a particular debt of gratitude to William Abbey, librarian of the University of London's Institute of Germanic Studies, who helped me locate valuable sources of information in the Institute's holdings and also lent me books from his private collection.

A grant kindly made by the British Academy enabled me to collect textual and pictorial material at first hand in Berlin and elsewhere.

My profoundest thanks, however, must go to my wife, who not only processed the entire manuscript but also brought her own knowledge of Berlin to bear on my text, and in particular on the choice of illustrations. I could not have written the book without her.

R.T.

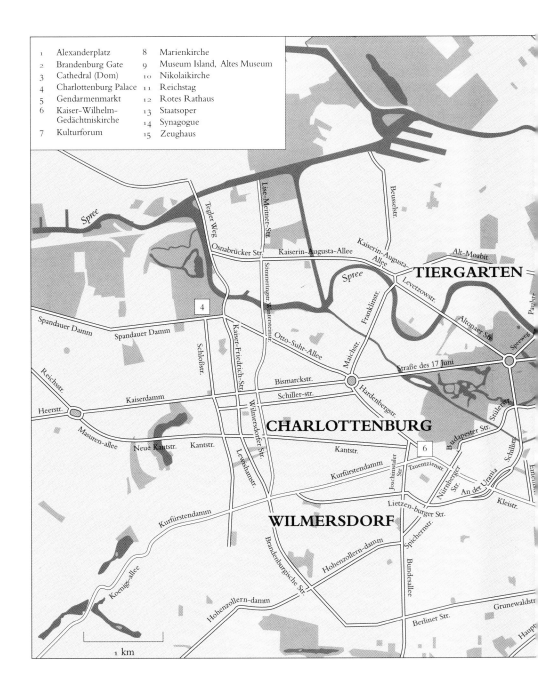

1	Alexanderplatz	8	Marienkirche
2	Brandenburg Gate	9	Museum Island, Altes Museum
3	Cathedral (Dom)	10	Nikolaikirche
4	Charlottenburg Palace	11	Reichstag
5	Gendarmenmarkt	12	Rotes Rathaus
6	Kaiser-Wilhelm-Gedächtniskirche	13	Staatsoper
7	Kulturforum	14	Synagogue
		15	Zeughaus

TIERGARTEN

CHARLOTTENBURG

WILMERSDORF

1 km

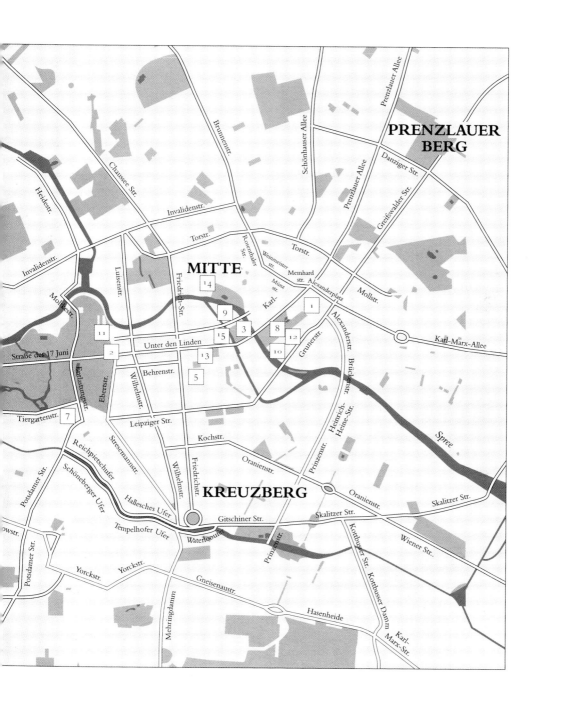

PREHISTORIC AND MEDIEVAL TIMES

Beginnings

Some 20,000 years ago, after the millennia of the glacial period, the ice and snow released its grip on northern Europe and withdrew to the Arctic ice cap. The melt water of the receding glaciers carved out valleys in the landscape, and as the earth warmed, settlers began to return to the lands from which their predecessors had been driven 40,000 years before by the southward march of the ice. The tundra with its hordes of reindeer gave way to a climate and vegetation which supported elk, boar and red deer in and around the glacial valleys, and by the ninth millennium BC stone-age man was leaving his mark on the environment. One such valley is that through which the River Spree flows today, meandering its unhurried way northwestward through the centre of Berlin to its junction with the Havel, thence onwards to the Elbe as it surges towards Hamburg and the North Sea.

Fragments of bone and primitive tools, such as flint axes and arrows, continue to be found in the Spree–Havel area and contribute to the picture of a people of hunters and gatherers. The marshy nature of the terrain also suggests the early development of fishing, while a stag mask discovered in the Berlin region in 1953 implies that, beyond their economic value, animals were invested with supernatural qualities which found expression in religious rituals.

In the course of the third millennium BC nomadic tribes moved into northern central Europe from the southeast, bringing with them an economy characterised not by primitive hunting and fishing but by the radical new operations of land cultivation and animal husbandry. A stronger sense of community developed. Huts of wattle and daub were built, cows, sheep, goats and pigs were kept, cereals, peas, beans and other leguminous plants cultivated, wool and flax woven for clothes in place of the skins worn in earlier ages.

Poor in raw materials, the Spree–Havel area came late to the knowledge of how to fuse metals and produce bronze. Likewise the succeeding iron age, dated among the Celts of southern central Europe from about 1000 BC, did not penetrate to the Germanic tribes of the Spree–Havel area until around 600 BC. Bronze fibulae and other decorative objects unearthed in the region show strong Celtic influence – indeed, they may not be the work of Germanic craftsmen at all but direct imports from the Celtic lands to the south.

The dawn of the Christian era brings the earliest historical records of Germanic tribes living in the flat, sandy plains to the east and north of the Elbe – Caesar's commentaries on the Gallic War and Tacitus' *Germania*. These tribes were driven westwards in the course of the mass migrations between the third and fifth centuries, and their lands taken over by Slavs. In the area now occupied by Berlin and its surrounding villages two Slav tribes established themselves, the Hevelli and the Sprewanes, so called after the two rivers by which they settled.

Little is known about the culture of these tribes. They practised a basic agriculture – cattle rearing, cultivation of the land, together with poultry- and bee-keeping – but had no sense of ethnic political unity, and sparseness of population in a geographical region of remote access and scant natural resources hampered economic and social progress. Nevertheless they retained possession of these middle-Elbian territories through 500 years of fluctuating fortunes until finally conquered and Christianised by the Saxons.

In 922 the Saxon King Henry the Fowler captured the Hevelli capital of Brennibor – later Brandenburg. Bishoprics were founded there and in Havelberg, at the junction of the Havel and the Elbe, in 948, and in Meissen and Magdeburg in 968. Sporadic revolts persisted but by the beginning of the twelfth century all substantial resistance had been crushed. Albrecht von Ballenstedt, a count of the Ascanian dynasty nicknamed the Bear, was personally enfeoffed with the territory by the Holy Roman Emperor Lothar III, and the whole area, roughly corresponding to the later province of Brandenburg, core of the state of Prussia, became German territory once and for all (Ill. 1). Symbolic of the role and status of the Slavs in the eyes of their

1. Silver bracteate struck *c.* 1150 for the wedding of Albrecht the Bear, Margrave of Brandenburg.

Berlin and its Culture

Germanic colonisers is the designation of them in early Latin documents not as *slavi* but as *sclavi* – an associative etymological equivalence akin to the modern use of the name 'vandal' or the phrase 'young Turk'.

Not that the Slavs have vanished without trace. Apart from the flourishing ethnic enclave of the Sorbs in Lusatia, southeast of Berlin, they have left their mark on the modern German vocabulary in loan-words which the colonisers found it convenient to adopt – words like *Grenze*, 'frontier', *Kürschner*, 'furrier', originally 'fur coat', and *Dolmetsch(er)*, 'interpreter'. Even more striking is the mass of place-names and proper names ending in the Slav suffixes *-itz* (Chemnitz, Wandlitz, personal names like Leibniz), *-in* (Berlin, Stettin, Schwerin) and *-ow* (Treptow, Machnow, Bülow). Leipzig and Dresden are Slav names, so, in a piquant irony, is Potsdam, symbol of Germany at its most determinedly Prussian.

Steadily extending their influence over a span of almost 200 years, the Ascanian Margraves of Brandenburg established a large and powerful principality. Its heartland was the Middle Mark, the region lying between the Elbe and the Oder, but it also reached out west of the Elbe into the Old Mark, with the towns of Stendal and Salzwedel, and eastwards into Polish territory beyond the Oder, almost as far as the Vistula (the New Mark).

That there was more to the Ascanians – the name derives from Aschersleben, the family castle in the shadow of the Harz Mountains – than a compulsive desire for territorial conquest can be seen in the person of Margrave Otto IV, who died in 1308. Given the sobriquet of 'Otto with the Arrow', he figures among the distinguished Minnesinger whose work is preserved in the famous fourteenth-century collection of poems known as the Manesse manuscript. He may not be the greatest of medieval poets but the very fact that his poems were considered worthy of inclusion in this most prestigious of anthologies is its own testimony, and his contemporaries pay tribute to his virtues. An illuminated miniature in the manuscript depicts him playing chess with his lady.

There had been Slav towns – fortified settlements dominated by the resident prince and his officials – in the Mark Brandenburg before the German colonisers arrived. But now they were greatly enlarged beyond their primitive origins and each given the civic rights and privileges to enable it to develop manufacture, trade and other preconditions of economic prosperity. The surrounding soil was light and sandy, which later led the Mark Brandenburg to be scornfully dubbed 'the sand pit of the Holy Roman Empire'. The only natural resource available in plenty was timber, used not only for houses but also for the boats that transported goods along the many natural waterways.

While economic progress in the medieval Mark Brandenburg was centred in the towns, the development of culture lay with the Christian monasteries. Despite the work of the Irish and English missionaries in the early eighth century, heathenism prevailed in the Frankish Empire until the time of Charles Martel (d. 741) and his grandson Charlemagne. After Charlemagne's final subjugation of the Saxons in 804 the whole of Germany became nominally Christian, with the power of the new Emperor and his new religion endorsed by the authority of the Papacy. This dualism of Church and state,

2.   Ruins of the monastery church of Lehnin. Painting by Eduard Gaertner, oil on canvas, 1858.

expressed in the antithesis of spiritual power and temporal power, the world of the flesh and the world of the spirit, hung over political, religious and cultural life as it evolved through the Middle Ages.

The intellectual power-houses of the new religion and of the new culture that accompanied it were the monasteries. The greatest of these in the Mark Brandenburg was Lehnin, a Cistercian foundation some thirty miles west of Berlin, established in 1180, where no fewer than fourteen members of the Ascanian dynasty were buried (Ill. 2). Under the guidance of the brethren from their mother church in France, the Cistercians took over the new Gothic architecture of pointed arches and vaulting but built with bricks made from local clay and loam, rather than with the granite blocks scattered across the once glacial landscape. Known as *Backsteingotik*, 'red-brick Gothic', this became the characteristic architectural style of medieval Brandenburg as far north as the Baltic coast.

Monasteries were also the educational establishments of the day, giving instruction in the Seven Liberal Arts and copying in their scriptoria not only Bible commentaries, sermons and other religious material but also the secular Latin texts used in the educational curricula. In the sphere of day-to-day living they introduced new techniques of drainage and irrigation which enabled fruit and vegetables to be cultivated where nothing had grown before, and also planted vines.

Unmistakable as the cultural achievements of the monasteries are, one cannot ignore the pragmatic community of interest that linked the men of God with the men who wielded the sword of subjugation and territorial aggrandisement. As Christianity confronted paganism, so Germans confronted Slavs. The more land accrued to the monasteries, the broader became the

4

base for missionary activity. *Pari passu* the more extensive the Christian influence, the tighter the political grip of the colonisers.

The two worlds, the religious and the political, came together in that most characteristically medieval of organisations, the Order of Teutonic Knights, one of the several such militant bodies born of the Crusades. In 1226 the Knights, called to help in the forcible Christianisation of a Slav tribe called the Prussians, colonised not only the areas known up to 1945 as East and West Prussia but most of the territory now occupied by Lithuania, Latvia and Estonia. Compared with the Ascanian, and subsequently Hohenzollern, occupation of Brandenburg, the extent of this territory was modest. But as the colonising forces coalesced and new alliances were forged, so the Knights bequeathed both to their German neighbours and to the subject Slavs a concept henceforth inseparable from public life in the successive German states that have inherited these lands – the concept of a centralised political authority based on absolutist principles. The ideal of service was paramount, the corporate values of the authority exclusive. Moral duty was pursued with religious zeal. It was a combination of values enshrined at the heart of the public philosophy that was to sustain the composite state of Brandenburg–Prussia and its successors as they evolved over the coming years.

The Twin Towns: Berlin and Cölln

For centuries before the arrival of the German colonisers the West Slav tribes of the Hevelli and Sprewanes had been sparsely settled in the area between the rivers Havel and Spree. The terrain is generally low-lying and marshy but north and south of the Spree two elevated areas rise which the successors of Albrecht the Bear, foraging from their principal base in the town of Brandenburg, occupied around 1230. Flowing gently northwestwards, the Spree was readily fordable at this point.

Two factors favoured the development of a settlement here. One was the convenience for movement and trade of the waterway system itself: the Spree joined the Havel at Spandau a few miles ahead; the Havel flowed into the Elbe; and the Elbe, one of Germany's great rivers, flowed 200 miles across the north German plain, past trading centres like Wittenberge, Lüneburg and Hamburg, before draining into the North Sea. At the same time here was a convenient ferry-point on the west–east trade route from Magdeburg, on the Elbe, via Brandenburg, Spandau and Köpenick to the Oder crossing at Frankfurt. Other lines of communication ran north to Stettin and Danzig, south to Leipzig. It would also be useful to have a place where goods in transit could be transferred from river to road and vice versa. So the twin towns of Berlin and Cölln came into existence, the former on the east bank of the Spree, the latter on the west.

But precisely when, we do not know. Both are assumed to have been granted civic status in the 1230s. The earliest known documentary evidence of the existence of Cölln is a reference to a cleric 'Symeon de Colonia', 1237; the same priest is mentioned as *Probst* (provost) of Berlin in 1244, and in 1247 a *Schulz* (bailiff) called Marsilius is also recorded as holding office in Berlin. All this suggests that Berlin and Cölln were both established towns by this time with a degree of formal administration, founded as part of the Margraves' policy of urban settlement in the Mark Brandenburg.

However, Berlin must have been older than this. Incorporated in the fabric of the present Nikolaikirche are remains of the stone walls of a Romanesque basilica dating back to about 1220. Even more: this basilica was built over a former Christian cemetery from which remains of over seventy graves were uncovered during excavation work in the 1950s. Since these burials were spread over a number of years, and a building would hardly have been erected above a series of graves until a decent period had elapsed, the existence of a settlement here could be posited for as long ago as the late twelfth century. The specific appellation 'town', however, does not occur until 1251, when, together with Spandau and Brandenburg, Berlin was granted freedom from tolls on its trade within the Mark Brandenburg as one of various urban privileges allowed by the feudal overlords.

Both Berlin and Cölln are Slav names in Germanicised forms. Berlin is derived from an old Slav word meaning 'sluice gate'. Collen (Köllen), 'an island in a marshy area', would denote what people on the other side of the water saw. The eighteenth-century writer Friedrich Nicolai recorded that in his day the inhabitants used the definite article, *das Berlin*, when referring to their city. It would be nice to believe that the bear on the city's coat of arms gave his name to the place but that is unfortunately only a whimsical piece of folk etymology.

Much of the rising prosperity of the two marshy settlements derived from the right granted to them by the Margrave to raise tolls on goods transferred here from road to waterway. Iron goods, salt and wine came in from Thuringia and fish from the Baltic, while grain was sent to the north, with timber from the forests of the Mark. Buying up Flemish cloth tax-free for their own use, merchants developed a textile industry and exported their finished products. Unblessed by nature, Berlin built its economy on trade and commerce, on an instinct for how to capitalise on an imposed set of material circumstances. Not for nothing was the first church built in Berlin dedicated to St Nicholas, patron saint of traders and mariners.

On the east bank of the Spree, close to the crossing-point, grew up the 'Olde Markt', later – and still – called the Molkenmarkt, with its associations of trade in cheese (*Molken* = 'whey'). When the original ferry gave way to a bridge, a dam was built and water mills installed, adding another source of income to the rapidly developing town. The crossing thus came to be called the Mühlendamm, the name it has borne ever since. Growing independence and self-confidence also expressed themselves in the construction of a semicircular wall to enclose the town. Cölln, on the other side of the Spree, later followed suit with its own surrounding defences. Remains of the Berlin town wall can still be seen, close to those of the former Franciscan monastery and to the site of the Hohes Haus, the residence built by the Margraves of Brandenburg for their use when they stayed in the town.

The Middle Ages

The 'Olde Markt', heart of old Berlin, is dominated by the Nikolaikirche

3. Nikolaikirche. Painting by J.H. Hintze, oil on canvas, 1827.

(Ill. 3), the oldest surviving building in the city. As it stands today, the church displays, largely in restored form, the various phases of its chequered history. The oldest part, going back to the stone basilica of the early thirteenth century, is the massive three-zone granite base at the west end on which the towers rest. This basilica gave way between 1260 and 1280 to a red-brick Gothic hall-church with a central nave and two aisles, for which in 1378 a new choir was begun; after many delays, caused *inter alia* by the great fire of 1380, which almost completely destroyed the town, the building was completed in 1470, with a single spire. It survived in this form until the late nineteenth century, when, as part of repair and restoration work, it was decided to raise a second spire to balance the first. This was the form in which the church was reconstructed in the 1980s after being bombed in 1944 and after the years of neglect that followed.

Today, its Gothic vaulting rebuilt and the interior redecorated in the bright colours that had adorned the building in medieval times, the Nikolaikirche is a museum devoted to the early history of Berlin and to the story of the church itself. Among its artistic treasures on display are fragments of fifteenth-century wall painting, funerary monuments going back to Reformation times and individual items of skilled craftsmanship associated with the church, such as fragments of old altar carvings and wrought-iron objects salvaged from the wartime destruction.

Perhaps a few decades older than the Nikolaikirche, also a piece of *Back-steingotik*, is the ruined Klosterkirche, the church of the brotherhood of Franciscan monks who established themselves here, close to the town wall, in 1249. The monastery buildings, which housed a famous grammar school from

the time of the Reformation down to the Second World War, are no more. But the shell of the church, a mid-thirteenth-century basilica with a polygonal choir added a century later, survived the bombing of 1945. The nobility of the vaulting can now be appreciated only from pictures but the superb west arch and some window tracery are still *in situ*.

What the Nikolaikirche was to the 'Olde Markt', the Marienkirche became for the 'Nye (New) Markt', a second centre of commercial activity which arose in the mid-thirteenth century half a mile or so further north. Begun around 1270 and completed early in the following century, the Marienkirche (Ill. 4) is among the most impressive surviving examples of red-brick Gothic. A building of striking dimensions, much of its fabric was destroyed in the town fire of 1380, then rebuilt on the foundation of the old hall-church, with various additions. The base of the west tower was built in the fifteenth century, and the elaborate neo-Gothic spire raised at the end of the eighteenth century by Carl Gotthard Langhans, architect of the Brandenburg Gate.

When the citizens of Berlin built their first church, they had invoked divine blessing by dedicating it to the patron saint of their activities as fishermen. Now they turned their eyes to the heart of the Christian religion and offered their second church to the Virgin Mary. In the same spirit they dedicated the nearby Heilig-Geist-Kapelle, a hospital chapel in red-brick Gothic still standing on the Spandauer Strasse, to the Holy Ghost.

Berlin and its Culture

Marienkirche.

4. (*facing page*)
Exterior view.

5. (*right*) Chalice,
silver gilt, *c.* 1270.

6. Bronze font,
1437.

The interior of the Marienkirche, cool and sober, dominated by its lofty fan and stellar vaulting, is rich in works of art – paintings, carvings, funerary monuments. Among the oldest are an elaborate, beautifully executed gilt chalice in late-Romanesque style, set with precious stones, dating from around 1270 (Ill. 5), and a bronze font dated 1437 (Ill. 6). The well-to-do burghers of the town – administrators, merchants, guildmasters – served the churches well by commissioning such items, as well as votive memorials and altarpieces, from local artists and craftsmen. Members of the Blankenfelde family, for instance, an influential Berlin clan of financiers and civic dignitaries whose house stood in the shadow of the Marienkirche itself, are commemorated in a set of votive panels depicting the Crucifixion, with members of the family grouped round the foot of the cross (Ill. 7).

By far the most famous of the Marienkirche's treasures, however, are the frescoes of the Dance of Death. Covering a length of over twenty metres along two walls of the vestibule like a continuous frieze, the paintings depict a linked series of twenty-eight scenes. In each scene a member of a particular station in the society of the day, both clerical and secular, is being led by the figure of Death in a *danse macabre*; below each scene is a dialogue in rhymed couplets between Death and the figure in question – not, as one might expect, in Latin but in Low German. On the pillar in the angle of the wall, dividing the clerical from the secular figures, is a fresco of the Crucifixion.

7. Votive painting of the Crucifixion with members of the Blankenfelde family, artist unknown, oil on wood, 1505.

8. Scene from the Dance of Death frescoes in the Marienkirche, c. 1485.

Painted in the wake of the plague of 1484, the frescoes are a public reminder of the transience of life, a visual parallel to the literary Dances of Death, half dialogue, half drama, that were performed at that period. Death was everywhere at hand. *Memento mori* – repent while there is yet time. Nor is Death any respecter of persons: neither wealth nor learning can give protection or guarantee redemption, and all ranks are depicted here. This Dance of Death carries a social as well as a personal message (Ill. 8).

Although Cölln developed more hesitantly than Berlin, in constitution and social structure as in matters of individual civic rights and the administration of justice, it had common interests with its larger partner and a shared history. Above all the two towns had joint concerns in matters of defence. Of both practical and symbolic importance, therefore, and a herald of future amalgamation, was their conclusion in 1307 of a defence pact to protect their borders against the marauding bands of disaffected gentry and others in the Mark Brandenburg, which the Margraves found it difficult to control.

As Berlin had first grown around the old Molkenmarkt, so Cölln had its core in the Fischmarkt, a few hundred yards west of the Spree crossing, on the road leading to Teltow. And as Berlin had dedicated its first church to its traders, so Cölln, showing its own priorities, invoked St Peter, patron saint of fishermen. But of the various Petrikirchen erected here, down to the nineteenth-century neo-Gothic church which was largely destroyed in the street-fighting of 1945 and finally removed in the 1960s, nothing remains. Only the old name Petriplatz recalls the days when Cölln's parish church stood here.

Also buried beneath twentieth-century concrete, close to the site of the first royal palace of 1443, is the monastery founded by the Dominicans in 1297. After the Reformation the monastery was dissolved and the monastery chapel turned into the first Berlin cathedral church.

In 1319 the line of Ascanian Margraves died out. From 1324 to 1373 the Mark Brandenburg was in the hands of the Bavarian family of the Wittels-bachs, and from 1373 to 1411 of the Luxemburgers. But these dynastic changes mattered little to the twin towns as they grew steadily in self-confidence.

9. Illuminated miniature of Virgin and Child from Berlin *Stadtbuch*, end of the fourteenth century.

Symbolic of that confidence was the institution in 1397 of an historical record of the joint town council's official financial and legal dealings over the previous hundred years. This *Stadtbuch*, as it is called, is a fascinating document, both linguistically and in terms of the social history it embodies. As well as the text, in a distinctive Low German dialect, it contains two intercalated religious miniatures painted shortly before 1400. The work of an accomplished hand, in which Bohemian influence has been surmised, these are the earliest paintings known to have been done in Berlin (Ill. 9).

Even the devastating fires that destroyed most of the wooden houses of Cölln in 1376 and in Berlin in 1380 were only temporary setbacks to the towns' advance. In the course of the fourteenth century they acquired a number of outlying villages, now familiar Berlin suburbs, like Reinickendorf, Stralau and Pankow. By 1400 they had a combined population of between 6,000 and 8,000. This left Brandenburg, Spandau, Stendal and other rivals well behind. From 1369 they issued their own coinage.

By the dawn of the fifteenth century the signs were, despite internal frictions between the classes – patricians, guilds, plebeians – of a gradual consolidation of autonomy within the two towns and a consequent burgeoning of local pride, education and cultural life. A certain stability also seemed to be heralded by the installation in 1411, at the behest of the Emperor Sigismund, of Friedrich von Nürnberg, scion of the house of Hohenzollern, as ruling prince. A few years later, after beating off attacks on his authority by freebooters and rival factions, Friedrich was rewarded by the Emperor. He was invested with the Mark Brandenburg as his fief and granted the hereditary title of elector. Brandenburg–Prussia was to remain in Hohenzollern hands for 500 years, until its disappearance from the map of Europe in 1918. But it was a stability on the rulers' terms. Berlin and Cölln concluded their formal union in 1432. They had yet to learn that their territorial master saw them, not as independent bodies within his lands, but as the future capital of his unified kingdom.

THE AGE OF THE
REFORMATION

There could be no clearer sign of the annexionist intentions of successive Electors of Brandenburg than the decision by Friedrich II, nicknamed 'Iron Tooth', in 1443 to build himself a palace in Cölln. Brick by brick, over the eight years it took to complete, the townsfolk on both sides of the water faced implacable proof of their subjugation. The Elector took over their town hall, set up his own administration and withdrew many of their hard-won privileges, above all the right to raise tolls for handling goods at the Mühlendamm bridge, their main source of income. He even brought in workers, administrators and craftsmen from other parts of Germany, and the influence of native craft-guilds began to crumble. The wealth produced in the town went no longer only to the town but also into the Elector's coffers. Berlin was to become a capital, not a free city.

A colourful description of the place was given by the humanist theologian Johannes Trithemius, Abbot of Sponheim, whom the Elector Joachim I invited to visit his court in 1505. 'The people here', wrote Trithemius,

> are good-natured but ignorant and uncouth. They take more pleasure in feasting and carousing than in acquiring knowledge. Rarely does one come across a man who has any interest in learning. They deal with each other in a rough and ready fashion which seems to be part of their nature, and they enjoy sitting around and having a tipple . . .
>
> At the same time they are diligent churchgoers. They celebrate the feasts of the saints with deference and devotion and observe with the utmost conscientiousness the fasts imposed upon them. Their attendance at mass is all the more devout for the fact that they were the last of the German peoples to be converted to the Christian faith.

Perhaps we may wonder whether the burghers of the time were really so indolent and inebriated. At all events the Elector himself was soon to show an intention to raise the cultural standards of his court. And that the intention would have more than private consequences was a reality he was prepared to accept. The Hohenzollerns may have been authoritarian throughout their history but with a few prominent exceptions they were also both cultured and realistic, like the Berliners they governed.

Elector Joachim I, Margrave of Brandenburg from 1499 to 1535, bore the cognomen Nestor, the Greek warrior renowned for his wise counsel. Earlier

Hohenzollern Margraves had flattered themselves with the names Achilles and Cicero, pointing to the world with which, allowing for a little poetic licence, they wished to be associated. But Joachim did have a touch of the humanist about him. He had had a learned education at the hands of clerics, had read the Latin classics, and engaged an astrologer to inform his Berlin court in 'scientific' terms about the state of the cosmos and its influence on the affairs of men.

Joachim I's most substantial memorial is the university which he founded at Frankfurt an der Oder in 1506, the first university in the Mark Brandenburg. Some fifty miles east of Berlin, Frankfurt was an important outpost both politically and economically which it was in the Elector's interests to develop. German scholars returning from Italy with the new humanist values of the Renaissance became teachers at the university, where particular value was attached to the training of lawyers, a class of experts increasingly in demand as the social and economic complexities of the community multiplied. The influence of Frankfurt grew even more rapidly after the Reformation, when it joined the group of universities – Wittenberg, Halle, Leipzig – prominent in the dissemination of Lutheran doctrine.

The growth in literacy promoted by the Hohenzollerns also had practical consequences for the German language in Berlin and in the Mark Brandenburg as a whole. The basis of the modern standard language – the written language of commerce, of law, of administration, of literature and everything else – is a form of High German known as East Middle German, an amalgam of linguistic features from Saxony, Bohemia, Franconia and adjoining areas. But the Mark Brandenburg is in Low German territory, whose dialects were both a hindrance to mutual comprehension and a mark of cultural backwardness. Business dealings with the increasing numbers of merchants from High German-speaking areas, and the growing numbers of administrators brought into Berlin by the Elector from such areas, forced the adoption of the 'proper' language and thus unwittingly, though gratifyingly, helped to prepare the ground for the cultivation of literature.

The Culture of the Court

The Protestant theologian Karl Barth once described how he felt on unexpectedly finding himself in the role of a reformer. It resembled, he said, the experience of a man ascending a spiral staircase in the pitch-black darkness of a church tower. Feeling his way with outstretched hand, he found himself grasping a rope and was taken aback when he heard the clanging of a bell. The man in the tower might have been Martin Luther, sounding the bell to herald the Reformation.

For Luther could not know what forces he was unleashing when he posted his ninety-five theses on the door of the Schlosskirche in Wittenberg on 31 October 1517. It was not his intention to found a new 'reformed' Church. Nor did he at that moment have the broad mass of the population in mind – his theses were, after all, in Latin. Still less did he aim to kindle the flames of social discontent that were to ravage Germany in the Peasants' War seven years later, or to anticipate the revolutionary Twelve Articles of 1525.

Yet all this and more is packed into the age of which Luther is the embodiment, an age of individualism and aggression, and ultimately of rebellion and violence. By translating the word of God into the homely German of the common man, Luther took the interpretation of the Christian message away from the Papacy, its priests, its saints and its prescriptions, and put it in the hands of the individual and his conscience. Likewise the ruler of each independent German state, by extension, was invited to free himself, whether on moral and religious grounds or for political reasons, from the authority of Rome. Hence the regionalist doctrine of *cuius regio eius religio*, by which the religion of each state – the old (Catholic) or the new (Protestant, as the Lutheran reform was known after 1529) – became that of its ruling prince.

Wittenberg, though belonging to Saxony, lay in the bishopric of Brandenburg but Elector Joachim I remained faithful to Pope and Emperor. He declared Luther a heretic and banned his writings, sensing in them, not without reason, a threat to established authority. However, with the centre of the Reformation only fifty miles from Berlin, the new ideas could not be held at bay for long. In 1539 Joachim II, a powerful ruler who had succeeded his father four years earlier, announced his endorsement of the new religion. Brandenburg became compulsorily Protestant, which it has remained ever since. All the land and possessions of the Church accrued to the Elector as both head of state and head of the new Church. And this new Church, preaching the submission to the will of one's lords and masters which was at the heart of Luther's social philosophy, joined the hereditary ruler, the army and the bureaucracy as the fourth pillar of the political and social establishment.

10. Elector Joachim II's palace in Berlin, painting by Abraham Begeyn, oil on canvas, 1690 (copy *c.* 1850).

11. Elector Joachim II by Lucas Cranach the younger, oil on wood, 1551.

Education also had its role to play in the expansionist policies of Joachim II. A ruler captured by the spirit of the Renaissance, and recognising how to bring to bear upon it the forces liberated by the Reform, he set about training an elite in schools under his direct control, men who would eventually administer the affairs of Church and state to the greater glory of God and the Mark Brandenburg.

Joachim II's grandest effort to establish himself as a Renaissance prince of the north – an effort which more or less emptied the Hohenzollern treasury – was the construction of a lavish new palace between 1538 and 1540 (Ill. 10). Determined that this should be in the most up-to-date style, the Elector turned his back on the local red brick and commissioned an architect from neighbouring Saxony, one Caspar Theiss, to design him a massive building in sandstone. A large central courtyard served for entertainment and occasions of state, and a raised walkway led across to the chapel of the former Dominican monastery, now dissolved, which became the new cathedral church under the Elector's direct patronage. Gilt and silver monstrances, jewel-studded chasses for the preservation of holy relics, gold crosses set with precious stones – such treasures, many of them the work of Saxon craftsmen, now found a home in the royal chapel.

Of the many artists commissioned by Joachim II both for portraiture and for the decoration of his Berlin palace, the most famous was Lucas Cranach the Elder, court painter at this time to the Elector of Saxony, who did a portrait of Joachim I in 1529. His son, Lucas Cranach the Younger, painted Joachim II a few decades later (Ill. 11). Both pictures now hang in Joachim II's hunting lodge, the Jagdschloss Grunewald, in the western suburbs of Berlin, which was built by Theiss two years after the completion of the new palace.

Architecture is the ideal medium for the public demonstration of personality and authority. Like sculpture in public places, it is permanently on show, and Joachim II's new palace was the most palpable means of putting the Electorate of Brandenburg on the cultural map. But, as well as commissioning paintings and other works of art, Joachim seems to have been the first of his line to promote the interests of music.

Musical activity at the time focused on three contexts, discrete in some respects but with shared interests in others: the electoral court, the Church and the burgher community. The court inevitably had the first and last word on the subject. A document of 1465 on the organisation of the cathedral church mentions the presence of five choirboys; in 1536, the year after his accession, Joachim II created posts for a cantor and succentor. Then in the 1540s he took the decisive step of instituting a band of a dozen instrumentalists, predominantly brass and percussion, to perform both in the church and in the palace. A *Kapellordnung* of 1570 gave the musicians official status and makes mention of singers and instrumentalists under the direction of a Kapellmeister – virtually a small chamber orchestra which accompanied services in the church and entertained the Elector and his guests in the palace.

12. Relief of St Bernhardin of Siena, wood, polychrome, second half of the fifteenth century. Artist unknown.

13. Leonard Thurneysser: frontispiece of scientific treatise, coloured woodcut, 1585.

Tenors and basses joined the boy choristers, and by the early 1580s stringed instruments had been added, putting the combined forces in a position to perform contemporary vocal and instrumental music brought in from the Netherlands, France and elsewhere. Some of these musicians also came from England. An inventory of pieces in the choir's repertory in 1582 is dominated by the works of the great Flemish composers of the day – Josquin des Pres, Lassus, Willaert and Cyprien de Rore.

The so-called Lutheran Mass consisted of numbers sung by the choir, initially in Latin but increasingly in German – Introit, Kyrie, Creed – and the hymns, sung by both choir and congregation in German, in which the brass players of the court band also joined. The boy choristers for the parish churches – Nikolaikirche, Petrikirche and Marienkirche – were drawn from the town's two oldest schools, the grammar school in the former Franciscan monastery in Berlin and the Gymnasium in Cölln. In charge was a cantor who also conducted the congregation in the singing of the hymns and was expected to compose music for use in both church and school.

The Christian Church, indeed, was from the beginning a Church of song. Like the Psalms, the items of the liturgy were sung to the melodies of Gregorian chant. In the Middle Ages metrical hymns increasingly found their way into divine service, many of them contrafactures of secular folksongs, and formed the core of the earliest Protestant hymnals. Both spirtually and institutionally the Protestant Church, home of the chorale – the religious song sung by the whole congregation as an act of corporate worship – is thus inseparably bound to the world of folksong. At the same time it is a union triumphantly embodied in the figure of Martin Luther himself and a living symbol of the Protestant appeal.

Secular music in the community at large is the Cinderella of these three realms of activity. That the Elector did not, however, completely ignore the interests of his subjects is seen from a provision in the *Kapellordnung* of 1570 that, if his band were not required in the palace on a Sunday, it should perform for the public in one or other of the town's churches. From the resources of the town itself came the buglers, whose duties had begun with sounding the hours from the towers of the town wall and who now assembled to play for dances and celebrations in the street. They also found themselves in demand at weddings and parties given by wealthy patricians and guildsmen. It was at this popular level, too, that folksong, the heritage of the lowest and highest classes alike, was most vigorously cultivated. One need look no further than the modern Protestant hymnal to see how much folksong has contributed to the German musical tradition.

In one way or another all this activity is a product of the energy released by the Reformation. Much in Luther is still medieval, as indeed much in Germany at the time was medieval. That is what the historical retrospect conveys. But in his time, and above all in his place, he was a revolutionary force, felt as such no less in the realm of culture than in that of religion or politics.

Encouraging as an account of such musical life may sound, Berlin still had a lot of cultural ground to make up. Other German states had more to offer than Brandenburg. Saxony had important centres in Dresden, Halle and Leipzig, all of which received a powerful stimulus from the Lutheran chorale; the court of the Emperor Maximilian I in Vienna had Heinrich Isaac in its service; Heinrich Praetorius was in Hamburg, Leonhard Lechner, a pupil of the great Lassus, had been at the Franconian court in Nuremberg and was later put in charge of musical activities at the Hohenzollerns' ancestral seat of Hechingen in Swabia. Berlin could not yet attract musicians of this calibre, let alone produce its own comparable home-grown composers.

Of greater cultural interest to the sixteenth-century court than the musician was that character who straddled the dividing line between medieval and modern, as sixteenth-century Germany itself did – the alchemist. In 1571 the science, pseudo-science, scholarship and charlatanism of this feared and respected profession, whose most famous representative at the time was the man known as Paracelsus, came to Berlin in the person of the Swiss magician Leonhard Thurneysser.

Thurneysser, a much travelled man who had in his time worked as a goldsmith, a surgeon's assistant, a soldier and a mining prospector, had recently written a book, in Latin, on the natural history of the Mark Brandenburg.

In it he claimed that precious stones were waiting to be dug up in nearby villages and that the sandy river bed of the Spree contained a high concentration of gold. Elector Johann Georg, who had inherited the exchequer that had been emptied by his father's expensive tastes, set Thurneysser up in a laboratory in a wing of the old Franciscan monastery which now housed the grammar school, and waited anxiously for him to discover the philosopher's stone.

Diagnosing diseases from urine specimens sent to him from all over Europe, dispensing herbal tinctures and potions, plotting the movements of the heavenly bodies and reading the future on the basis of their conjunctions, Thurneysser held a position of great influence in an age highly susceptible to the claims of magic and the powers of the occult. It may be only a legend that Martin Luther threw his ink-well at the devil when the fiend crept up to tempt him, but the Reformer believed, like his age, in a personal devil no less real than a personal God, and magic, whether black or white, was a very real force.

But Thurneysser the scholar and scientist left a remarkable practical monument to himself in the shape of his printing press. With his own paper mill, his own joinery and his own foundry for casting lead type, he produced sumptuous volumes of his own and others' works, with elaborate allegorical frontispieces and bindings and hand-coloured illustrations, quoting in the original from Greek, Hebrew, Arabic and other languages. Signing himself as 'physician to the Elector of Brandenburg', Thurneysser gave gratifying publicity to his patron's court, for his volumes became known throughout Europe. An anonymous wood-carving of the late fifteenth century in the Marienkirche portrays St Bernhardin of Siena, vicar general of the Franciscan order, with the family of the donors at his feet. In his left hand the saint is holding an open book which bears the inscription: 'Thurneisser hat mich neuw gemacht Do ich war alt und gar voracht Anno 1584' ('Thurneysser made me new, When I was old and much neglected'). It is an attractive souvenir of a man who, among his other achievements, seems to be the earliest Berlin conservationist and art restorer known to us by name (Ills 12 and 13).

Elector Joachim II's commitment of Brandenburg to Protestantism in 1539 led over the following decades to a strengthening of his central authority within the community of Protestant states around him – Saxony, Brunswick, Mecklenburg. The political weight of Luther's teaching lay on the retention of the status quo, the preservation of the existing stratification of society and the acceptance of the structure of authority which is the practical expression of that stratification. 'Render unto Caesar the things that are Caesar's,' preached the great Reformer. The Elector was delighted to let Luther do his work for him. And as the power of the central administration grew, the peasants, who had enjoyed a certain independence, declined into serfs, the towns found their scope for autonomous action usurped, and the influence of the estates in the *Landtag* (provincial diet) was whittled away. All this was clamped into legal position by the creation of the *Staatsrat*, a council of state which, under the presidency of the Elector himself, laid down state policy and ensured that the necessary bureaucracy was in place to carry it out. It all sounds very 'Prussian', as we might say, and evocative of the absolutism that was to come.

Another characteristic of the Prussia that was to come can be identified during this time, a characteristic of central significance for the cultural climate in the Electorate. In 1613, largely for reasons of personal conviction, Johann Sigismund left the official Lutheran faith of his Electorate and turned to the stricter regime of Calvinism. He needed nobody's permission. But, equally, he could not carry his people with him in what has been called 'Berlin's second Reformation'. When he authorised the removal of paintings, sculptures and other decorative features from Berlin churches to reflect the guilt-laden austerity imposed by Calvinism, the Berliners revolted, even going so far as physically to attack Calvinist preachers.

Two years later the Elector had to admit defeat. Quarrels between Lutherans and Calvinists continued and were often as virulent as those between Lutherans and Catholics, but Johann Sigismund conceded the right of his people to remain the Lutheran Protestants they had been for almost a century. Though in one sense a product of necessity, it was also an exercise in tolerance. As the poet Schiller was to put it: 'In that dark age of superstition Berlin was the first to light the flame of rational freedom of religion, which was both a necessity and a cause for praise.' But economically and culturally the territory was still backward, an agricultural domain locked into an unyielding struggle with its harsh climate, its poor soil, its marshlands and its acres of forest. Without a discipline of toil and sweat even survival would have been uncertain, let alone progress. And as for Berlin, the electors may have had their fine Renaissance palace there but their decision to establish their university in Frankfurt an der Oder had hardly contributed to the intellectual self-esteem of Berlin. It was to be another 200 years before the Berliners could claim their own university.

Yet people of different races and classes continued to arrive from outside to produce, in the situation so familiar in Berlin itself, an amalgam of peoples – Germans and Slavs, Sorbs and Prussians, later Scandinavians and Huguenots. By 1600 the population of Berlin–Cölln had reached some 12,000. New trades had arisen to serve the increased numbers of aristocracy and court bureaucrats, and moves were made to build on land to the west, beyond the Cölln city wall, in the area near what is today the Hausvogteiplatz. The Elector also had the marshy area north of the palace drained and turned into an orchard.

But development overall was slow and further hindered by outbreaks of the plague in 1576 and 1598–9. An acknowledgement of the rising need for education came with the conversion in 1574 of the old Franciscan monastery into a boys' grammar school, the Gymnasium zum Grauen Kloster, which quickly found itself providing instruction to 600 pupils in Latin and Greek, divinity and philosophy, with a smattering of German and history. Senior boys were expected to converse in Latin; any boy caught lapsing into German received enough strokes of the birch to discourage him from repeating the offence. The churches in the town – Nikolaikirche, Petrikirche, Marienkirche – also had their own schools. It was an age which sensed that there was much to learn.

The Reformation and Literature

By his teaching, but even more through his practical energy, Luther had liberated the word. Salvation is through the Word of God, he preached; without the Word the true meaning of faith has no substance. His translation into everyday German, first of the New Testament in 1522, then of the complete Bible in 1534, was the work of a scholar but it was not directed to scholars. It was done for the common man, to whom God could now speak in the comforting language of the fireside.

Luther's German hymns, thirty-six in all and still the backbone of the Protestant hymnal, reinforced the Bible message in their own blunt, direct, uncompromising manner and imprinted themselves more deeply on the mind with each Sunday singing. There is genuine poetry in Luther's hymns – and, indeed, in the prose of his Bible. But it is applied poetry, not poetry for its own sake.

Likewise his melodies. Luther, 'the nightingale of Wittenberg', as Hans Sachs picturesquely called him, was profoundly musical. He knew and admired the polyphonic masses and motets of Josquin des Pres and the great Flemish composers of the day. That this was music from a Catholic context did not matter: music was music. He was himself a singer and recorder player. Nothing epitomises his character and purpose more completely than the rugged, four-square melodies of hymns like 'Ein feste Burg' and 'Vom Himmel hoch'. 'Text and notes, accent, melody and manner of performance', he wrote, 'should all grow out of the mother tongue and its inflections.'

On this resolutely practical foundation arose a homely, vigorous Protestant literature in a variety of genres – dramas, verse satires, fables, anecdotes – all characterised by their moralising manner. The main centres of sixteenth-century German literature lay in Saxony, Franconia and above all Switzerland, but the Elector Joachim II's adoption of the Protestant communion in 1539 also marked the release of creative literary forces in Berlin. From 1541 dates the earliest known drama written and performed in the town – a morality by one Heinrich Knaust with the characteristically didactic title *Ein seer schön und nützlich Spiel von der lieblichen Geburt Unseres Herrn Jesu Christi* ('A Very Fine and Beneficial Play on the Gracious Birth of Our Lord Jesus Christ'). Moreover this is not just a spoken drama, in which certain parts were taken by the boys of the Cölln Gymnasium; it also contains music. One would hardly invoke the word opera but Knaust's work must at least be seen generically as an early Singspiel, like the works of the Englische Comödianten later in the century.

Nothing more seems to be known about Knaust than that he was headmaster of the Cölln Gymnasium at the time his play was published. About other men of letters who contributed to the awakening intellectual life of Berlin in the mid-sixteenth century we are better informed.

A typical Reformation figure in his blend of polemical preacher, humanist and popular author is Johannes Agricola. Born in 1494 in Eisleben, Agricola became a student of Luther's at Wittenberg and was present when his master made public his Theses. He wrote a Latin drama in 1537 in praise of the Czech reformer Jan Hus, and in 1540, impressed by his qualities, Joachim II appointed him both court preacher in Berlin and Superintendent of the Protestant Church for the whole of the Mark Brandenburg, posts he held until his death in 1566.

Strict Lutheran though he was, Agricola took a progressive line on social questions which gives him a particular interest. Basing his stance on the theology of a God of love and forgiveness, not of fear and punishment, he sought to subsume religious differences in a movement which would put an end to the feudal exploitation of the common man. Even before the Peasants' Revolt of 1525 he had published a Dialogue between a devout Protestant peasant and a follower of the social revolutionary Thomas Müntzer – the first man in Germany to issue what we would call a charter of human rights. Ostensibly so far apart, the two protagonists end by making common cause to confront what they see as the burning issue of the day: 'What shall we do to get rid of the tyrants?' The tract has a remarkably modern ring.

Agricola is chiefly remembered today, however, as the author of what he entitled *Dreihundert gemeine Sprichwörter, der wir Deutschen uns gebrauchen und doch nicht wissen, woher sie kommen* ('Three Hundred Common Proverbs Which We Germans Use Without Knowing Whence They Come'). The title does the work an injustice. For, far more than a mere assemblage of familiar sayings, it consists of a collection of pithy and colourful anecdotes, little tales and fables, each devised to illustrate the moral message of the proverb in question. Medieval didactic literature, Biblical allusions, classical legends, historical events such as the famous victory of the Teutons over the Roman legions in the year AD 9 – all this is grist to Agricola's mill. Like many of his age, he is a writer who has learnt the art of instructing while at the same time entertaining.

An equally uncompromising contemporary of Agricola's – it was not an age for wearing velvet gloves – was the much travelled Erasmus Alberus, also a pupil of Luther's and also court preacher to Joachim II. Where Agricola took the freely invented prose anecdote as his medium, Alberus chose to versify Aesop's Fables in the rhyming *Knittelvers* couplets in which most of the satirical and dramatic literature of the sixteenth century is couched. His collection, with a title that leaves no doubt about what mattered most – *Das Buch von der Tugend und Weisheit, nämlich neunundvierzig Fabeln* ('The Book of Virtue and Wisdom, Being 49 Fables') – was published in 1534.

Alberus is less versatile than Agricola but in his chosen genre, exploiting the scope for humour and repartee which the talking, anthropomorphised animals of fable give, he shows himself a witty observer of human foibles. A down-to-earth realist, he adds to his scene-setting a joyful mass of everyday detail, of characters and circumstances of his time and place, which leave us with attractive sociological insights into contemporary conditions and an awareness of areas of social criticism.

Independence of mind also characterises the satirist and dramatist Georg Rollenhagen, the liveliest and most modern of these Berlin writers caught up in the wake of the Reformation. Born in Bernau, north of Berlin, he spent most of his life as a schoolmaster, enjoying wide respect among princes and scholars but declining all invitations to take up a position at court for fear of surrendering his intellectual freedom. 'The Rollenhagens are not suited to court life,' he explained.

But few were better suited to exposing and ridiculing the pretensions, the weaknesses and the wrongdoings of their fellow-men. This Rollenhagen did with great verve in two works in particular. One is a drama in rhyming couplets on the subject of Dives and Lazarus – *Vom reichen Manne und armen Lazaro*, published in 1590. Rollenhagen finds his starting-point, in common with so many writers of his age, in Luther's Bible. Like the Lutheran pastor unfurling his sermon on his chosen text, Rollenhagen elaborates the story in St Luke's Gospel with an entertaining mêlée of invented subsidiary characters in order to teach that the privileges of the rich cannot survive death and that it is the deserving poor who will find favour in heaven.

Rollenhagen's other memorable work is a satirical epic in 10,000 rhyming couplets known as *Froschmäuseler*. Published in 1596, this immense poem has as its point of departure the *Batrachomyomachia* ('Battle of Frogs and Mice'), a Greek mock epic once attributed to Homer, in which the heroes of the Trojan War are replaced by frogs and mice who fight out their differences in a parody of the *Iliad*. By locating his poem in the Harz Mountains, Rollenhagen makes his readers – or listeners, for one imagines the work being recited, section by section, before largely illiterate audiences – feel that the fantastic world of these events lies not in some remote quarter of the universe but in their own homeland. This homeland, moreover, was recognisably north Germany, where the tradition of the beast epic had reached the height of its popularity a century earlier in the tale of Reynard the Fox.

Entertainment value and familiarity with the genre were thus assured. But it was, of course, entertainment with an ulterior motive. The frogs and the mice behave in ways calculated to evoke ridicule and mirth, whatever their position in the hierarchy. By all means laugh at others, says Rollenhagen, but learn to laugh at yourself as well. Man is a social being and must be judged in his social context, a Protestant context of responsibility for one's actions. The most drastic of these actions are those that lead to war, and, once the mocking laughter at human frailty and pettiness has died away, Rollenhagen delivers an onslaught on the immorality and irrationality of settling differences by armed conflict. Maybe the common man listened. His rulers did not.

The Visual Arts

Renaissance man looked eagerly upwards and outwards, optimistic and confident, full of the joys of knowledge and human enterprise. Reformation man looked soberly inwards, earnest, sometimes almost grim, in his Christian morality and his pursuit of salvation. Yet shared by both, at a time when the feudal social order of the European Middle Ages was cracking under the pressure of an emergent bourgeoisie, was a growing awareness of the stature of the individual personality, coupled with a realisation of the need for knowledge of the objective world and for the means to manipulate that world to one's own ends. The onward march of urbanisation, the development of elementary manufacturing processes, the extension of communications, the emergence of a class of civil servants for the administration of new social responsibilities as the power of the German principalities grew – these liberating forces could not but leave their mark also on the visual arts, especially in the new Protestant states. Without losing its function to instruct and educate, art was also acquiring, or perhaps restating, the impulse of aesthetic enjoyment.

Architecture responded most bluntly, perhaps least 'artistically', to the new demands. 'The only reason for building churches', wrote Martin Luther, 'is in order that Christians may come together, pray, listen to the sermon and receive the sacraments. When this reason no longer exists, such churches should be pulled down, like other buildings that have no more use. Sound, medium-sized churches with low vaulting are best.' It is both a philosophical and a practical criterion. On the one hand an assembly of worshippers consists, not of a hierarchy of priests and people but of a single family gathered together for a common purpose. On the other, the function of this family worship can only be fulfilled if the word of the preacher, which is also the word of God, can be properly heard by all the believers present. The architectural philosophy of the sumptuous medieval cathedral, symbol of the heavenly Jerusalem, gave way to that of the hall-church – a simple, unpretentious, rectangular room with nave and aisles of equal height, its straight, flat walls uncluttered with side chapels, niches and statuary. This simplicity, in its turn, prescribed the limits within which the activities of painters and sculptors could be accommodated.

Since the Reformers, like Luther himself, saw art as an adjunct to the Word, rather than as an autonomous activity with its own self-justifying values, the subjects of paintings were expected to be taken from the stories and texts of the Bible – the Last Supper, the Lord's Prayer, Adam and Eve, the Day of Judgement, the various miracles and parables. The aim was the reinforcement of the Lutheran dogma by the immediate impact of the visual image.

14. Gold jewellery, sixteenth–seventeenth century, found 1956–8 during excavations in the Nikolaikirche.

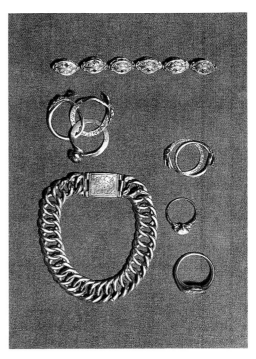

Berlin and its Culture

A characteristic painting in this genre, done in Berlin in the mid-sixteenth century, hangs in the sacristy of the Marienkirche. It is one of a number of works in the church by Michael Ribestein, an artist appointed to the Berlin court by Elector Joachim II in 1539. Ribestein's picture portrays, as a didactic exercise, the successive tenets of the Apostolic Creed – God the Creator, with Eve being born from Adam's rib, the Annunciation and the birth of Christ, His descent into hell, the Holy Catholic Church and so on. Dominating the scene is the Crucifixion, with Mary embracing the cross on the one side and the Roman soldier offering Christ a sponge filled with vinegar on the other. Resurrection, Ascension and Last Judgement have their place in the top of the picture. The composition may be arbitrary and the execution naive but the picture is an interesting product of its age, with fascinating realistic detail in its programme.

Belonging to the same tradition of parallels between scenes from the Bible and the realities of the present is a seventeenth-century *Last Supper* in the village church of Kaulsdorf, on the eastern fringes of Berlin. Here, instead of Christ and his disciples sitting at the long table, the predella portrays a set of local Protestant worthies celebrating the Eucharist with Him. As a motif, it is an extension of the *Last Supper* done for the palace chapel in Dessau by Lucas Cranach the Younger, in which Christ is flanked, not by the twelve apostles, but by Luther, Melanchthon and other leading Reformers. The Cranach painting and the Kaulsdorf predella share the same explicit message – that it is those of the Protestant faith who are the true heirs of Christ and the chosen defenders of His teaching.

Sculptors as well as painters were finding their skills in increasing demand for the florid commemorative statuary with which well-to-do burgher families honoured their dead. Among the elaborate tombs in the Marienkirche, pride of place belongs to that of the Berlin lawyer Jakob Flaccus and his wife (1562) by Hans Schenck, court sculptor to Joachim II. It shows a characteristically Protestant programme. Its principal motif is the Last Supper, presented, however, not as an occasion of solemnity and calm but as a scene of movement. In the centre the landlord holds aloft a platter with the Paschal Lamb which he offers to Christ, sitting on the left. Behind him a servant carries a loaf of bread. In the gallery above a chandelier is being put into place. It is a work full of urgency and vitality, like the silver and bronze medallions that Schenck made of Luther, Melanchthon and various German princes, including his own Elector.

The growing number of elaborate funerary monuments from the latter half of the sixteenth century, in the Marienkirche and elsewhere, is a direct consequence of the custom of burying distinguished members of the community in the church itself. In reformed churches the numerous side altars characteristic of Catholicism were done away with, together with their attendant paintings and sculptures of the Virgin Mary and the saints, their elaborate crosses and other furnishings. The vacated side chapels were then converted into family vaults on which carvers and sculptors lavished their attention. Apart from their intrinsic aesthetic qualities, these monuments, like cemeteries, are a repository of social history and social values and a barometer of movements in social taste.

Artistry on a smaller scale, invested in a secular rather than religious context, is revealed in personal items of gold jewellery discovered in the course of excavations in the Nikolaikirche during the 1950s. Among them were various gold rings, including a double love-ring or engagement ring of 1528, together with a gold bracelet with chased clasp. The individual sections of the love-rings have clasps in the form of hands, which link together when the ring is closed (Ill. 14).

A humbler survivor from the handicrafts of the period is a glazed earthenware drinking vessel in the form of a bear (the emblem of Berlin) with two cubs, bearing the date 1562 (Ill. 15). A homely but accomplished piece, possibly commemorating some special occasion, it bears witness to a growing skill in the manufacture of encaustic ware. It may have few pretensions to being great art but it has its own convivial contribution to make to the image of mid-sixteenth-century culture in Berlin.

15. Drinking vessel in the form of a bear, glazed earthenware, 1562.

THE CONSOLIDATION
OF PRUSSIA

Energetically as Elector Joachim II strove to raise the prestige of his court in the comity of German states, by the time of his death in 1571 Berlin had made few inroads into the cultural deficiencies that left it trailing behind Dresden, Nuremberg, Augsburg, Munich and other towns. The Renaissance had come to Brandenburg but proven to be an expensive luxury. The exchequer was bare. Joachim's successors, Johann Georg and Joachim Friedrich, spent the rest of the century adding new territories to the Hohenzollern collection. By far the most significant of these acts of annexation came in 1618, when Elector Johann Sigismund became formally invested with a reluctant duchy of Prussia, thereby marking the birth of what was to become the great European power of Brandenburg–Prussia. But this still lay a few years hence.

In the decades preceding the outbreak of the Thirty Years War Berlin – indeed, Brandenburg as a whole – was already in a state of decline. New trade routes passed it by and the fact that the Elbe and the Oder, Brandenburg's most important lines of communication, reached the sea in the territory of other states, was proving increasingly troublesome, both politically and financially.

Chronicles record that in 1576 almost 4,000 people died in the twin towns during an outbreak of the plague. Morality and a sense of civic propriety also seem to have been victims of deteriorating standards. A decree promulgated by Joachim Friedrich in 1603 issues a stern warning against an apparently flourishing trade in prostitution and widespread fornication and instructs all members of the clergy to identify and report any offenders among their flocks. Miscreants who persist in their unclean ways, warns the Elector, are to be made known to the palace authorities, 'in order that We may graciously consider further appropriate measures'. It came as a vote of no-confidence in Berlin–Cölln when, soon after the beginning of the war, the panic-stricken Elector Georg Wilhelm bolted and set up his court in Königsberg, 400 miles away.

Culture and War

By 1570 or so literature had slid into a state of stagnation. Reformation drama had spent its force, and the level of tolerance for the absorption of naive didactic fables and the like had been reached. As so often in German literary history, a revival had to be generated from without. The *commedia dell'arte* arrived from Italy, and towards the end of the century bands of strolling players came eastwards from the Netherlands and Brabant.

But a far greater impact was made by visitors from England. Originally part of the retinue of English aristocrats fighting in continental wars, the wandering theatrical troupes that came to be known as the Englische Comö-dianten had their German heyday in the early years of the seventeenth century. More important than the actual plays they brought with them – mangled versions of Shakespeare, Marlowe, Ben Jonson and other popular English dramas of the day – were the stage effects of the Elizabethan theatre and the highly developed skills of the English professional actor. At the beginning their performances, both for the court and for the public, were entirely in English, the players depending on pantomime and crude humour to attract their audiences and convey the meaning of their words. Whatever the subject of the play, the principal character was invariably the clown, dubbed 'Hans Wurst' or 'Pickelhering'. Gradually the actors introduced gobbets of broken German into the performance, calling also on local talent to help out in minor roles.

It was not long before imitators saw their chance. German troupes sprang up wherever the new entertainment had proven particularly popular. Many English actors stayed in Germany and made themselves indispensable to the permanent theatres that more and more princes were establishing in their courts. The Thirty Years War dampened enthusiasm for these developments as increasing sums were taken from state coffers for military purposes but troupes continued to visit throughout the war, and two volumes of *Englische Comödien und Tragödien* were published in 1620 and 1630 .

Particularly active in north Germany, as well as in Holland, was one John Spencer, whose players almost came to be regarded as the Brandenburg troupe-in-residence for a time under Joachim Friedrich and Johann Sigis-mund. From the electoral account-books it emerges that the members of the troupe, nineteen actors and sixteen musicians, received not only money for their efforts but also payment in kind, including, by Johann Sigismund's express command, new suits of clothes of high-quality fabric. Although engaged principally for the pleasure of the court, they also performed for the townsfolk in town halls and market squares, particularly on public hol-idays and special occasions.

The Comödianten led a peripatetic existence by choice, and it is not sur-prising to find that John Spencer moved on after a while. Johann Sigismund, however, engaged a series of successors, the last a troupe of eighteen actors and musicians especially recruited in England at the Elector's behest in 1617.

Much in these plays was improvisation, and since no one beyond the leader of a company would be even mildly literate, little was written down. The primary intention was to entertain, although there remained a didactic element carried over from Reformation and humanist drama.

Nor was the English cultural invasion confined to the stage. The remark-able increase in the size of the court band under Johann Sigismund owed a great deal to the importation of musicians from Elizabethan England, musi-cians steeped in the glories of Byrd, Morley, Dowland and a host of others.

Most of the string players in Johann Sigismund's enlarged orchestra were Englishmen, among them the composer Walter Rowe, who was appointed violist and court musician in 1614 and spent the rest of his life in the court's service.

In its early days the court orchestra, in so far as it deserved the name, had been dominated by brass instruments – a military band, in the tradition of its practical origin in the field of battle and the sounding of formal calls. Such music was formulaic and severely limited, to say the least. But the arrival of string players brought untold new possibilities, above all in the development of melody and thence of counterpoint. In 1619 the English violinist and composer William Brade was appointed Kapellmeister to the Berlin court – the first time an instrumental player, not the director of the choir, had been put in charge of the Elector's music.

One of a group of English musicians who, both as performers and composers, greatly advanced the cause of polyphonic instrumental music in Germany, particularly for strings, Brade has his niche in musical history as an early composer of dance music – collections of galliards, pavanes, voltas and other contemporary dances. They are written for a five-part chamber ensemble, predominantly strings but, he added, 'adaptable at will for all musical instruments'. The convivial and relaxed spirit of his music owes much to its folksong melodiousness, combined with lively rhythms and entertaining harmonies, which, one would like to think, were well received by the courtiers.

From Bartholomäus Praetorius, a contemporary of Brade's and a cornettist in the court band, comes a similar collection of five-part *Newe liebliche Paduanen und Galliarden*, published in 1616 – predecessors, like Brade's, of the dance suites that reached their full glory in Bach and Handel. In Germany as a whole over one hundred such publications of dance music appeared between 1601 and 1628, ten years into the Thirty Years War. Between 1629 and 1648, when the war ended, the figure fell to a mere fourteen, and of Johann Sigismund's once proud orchestra of over thirty only seven now remained. The struggle for physical survival had become a full-time occupation.

The great war, or set of wars, that broke out in 1618 and ravaged Europe for the next thirty years meant different things to different men. In terms of great-power politics it was essentially a struggle for European domination between France, i.e. the Bourbon dynasty, and the combined forces of the Holy Roman Emperor, i.e. the Habsburgs, and Spain. Initially Germany – that is, the hundreds of German principalities concerned only with their own territorial interests and with no common political aim to pursue – was not involved.

But the vacuum left by this particularism, which was intensified by the religious antagonisms provoked by the Reformation, could not be expected to survive for long. One little German state after another was dragged into the conflict on either the Catholic or the Protestant side, until the Habsburgs were finally defeated. Under the terms of the Peace of Westphalia in 1648 the political sovereignty of the principalities was reiterated and with it the principle of territorial fragmentation which was soon to issue in the period of princely absolutism. The progressive prospects offered by the Reformation had been dashed. What the Germans had experienced over these thirty years was a public war fought out on their territory by foreign powers with private agendas, plus a civil war of their own. When the war started, the total population of Germany, it is estimated, was some 16 million. Thirty years of war reduced it to 6 million.

This decimation was due only in part to the actual fighting. It had been total war, felt by the whole community, as troops of all nationalities pillaged their way through town and countryside. Agriculture, industry, trade and commerce were set back decades, perhaps a century. The peasants lost their crops and their livestock, the townsmen their markets and their livelihood. Only the princes, the territorial rulers, emerged from the war with their position intact, their control more secure than ever.

Less quantifiable but no less penetrating, leaving scars that took even longer to heal, were the psychological consequences of seeing a homeland turned into a battlefield. Resentment turned into resignation, forbearance into despair. Human life was cheap, men and women expendable. Whichever turning one took, death could be expected to lurk round the corner. 'Memento mori!' and 'Vanitas vanitatum vanitas!' cried the men of the cloth, Reformers and Counter-Reformers alike. The Lord was visiting his displeasure upon a wicked and sinful people, and culture was a luxury few could contemplate and even fewer afford.

Berlin had its share of suffering. Wallenstein, commander of the imperial armies, set up his headquarters in the Elector's palace and stationed 40,000 men in the town. Powerless to resist, the citizens managed to save their streets from becoming a battleground only by paying whatever levies were

16. Renaissance porch of the so-called Ribbeck House in the Breite Strasse, 1624. The oldest surviving secular building in Berlin

Berlin and its Culture

demanded of them. Before the war Berlin had some 8,000–9,000 inhabitants, a third of whom perished in four outbreaks of the plague between 1626 and 1637. By 1640, when it fell to the twenty-year-old Friedrich Wilhelm to extricate Brandenburg from the conflict, the population had dropped to a mere 6,000. The Renaissance palace was in a state of decay, over a third of the 1,200 houses within the joint city walls were abandoned, and the settlements that had grown up outside the bastions had all but disappeared. Hardly the basis for a revival of culture (Ill. 16).

The Age of the Great Elector

17. Equestrian statue of the Great Elector by Andreas Schlüter, bronze, begun 1696, unveiled 1700. Originally on the Kurfürstenbrücke (today Rathausbrücke), now in the courtyard of Charlottenburg Palace.

'Celui-ci a fait de grandes choses.' Such was Frederick the Great's pithy epitaph on his great-grandfather (Ill. 17). And, indeed, it was hard to recognise in the Brandenburg that the Elector Friedrich Wilhelm, the Great Elector, bequeathed to his successors the Brandenburg that he had inherited from his father in the final years of the Thirty Years War. In 1640 he came into possession of a collection of territories of varying sizes and characters, each controlling its own affairs through its own political and social institutions. By 1688, when he died, he had more or less completed the construction of the unified Hohenzollern state we know as Prussia, with its capital in Berlin.

Nor does his fame rest only on his politics. He was also determined to make Prussia a cultural power. Under his aegis an enthusiastic programme of housebuilding was launched in Berlin. Two new urban districts, Friedrichswerder and Dorotheenstadt, extended the town westwards, and the famous avenue later called Unter den Linden was laid out. He had the sandy streets cobbled and instructed that they be regularly cleaned. Concern for safety and greater freedom of movement led to the appointment of the first municipal night-watchman in 1677 and the installation of street lighting in 1679 (Ill. 18).

But the Great Elector's overriding concern was to make his state militarily strong. Berlin was turned into a garrison town – the last thing it needed. The joint town council of Berlin–Cölln, accustomed to deciding its own civic priorities, now found itself subject to the yea or nay of a military governor. As if this were not enough, the Bürgermeisters of the twin towns might even be nominees of the Elector himself, who, as a devout Calvinist – his citizens as a whole remained faithful to Lutheran Protestantism – took every opportunity to put those of his own persuasion into positions of authority. Truth to tell, the Great Elector did not like the towns. He preferred the company of the aristocracy and the landed gentry to that of the burghers, and turned to commoners such as lawyers and doctors only under *force majeure* or on occasions when he sensed a practical advantage.

Two such occasions, however, stand out, moments of decision which had a profound influence on the economic and cultural life of Prussia, but especially of Berlin. The first came in 1671, when the Habsburg Emperor expelled the Jews from Vienna. Speculating that their skill in financial matters might

18. Town plan of Berlin and Cölln by Johann Gregor Memhardt, engraving, 1652.

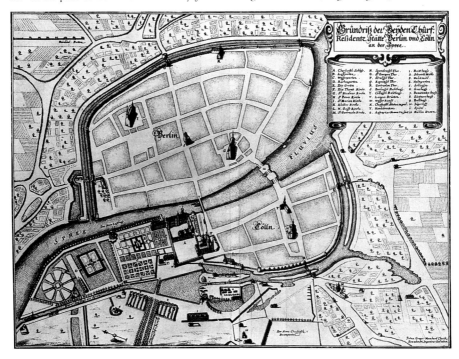

Berlin and its Culture

improve the economic health of his country, the Elector invited fifty of the leading Jewish families to set up their businesses in Berlin with the status of *Schutzjuden*, 'protected Jews'. Thus the first Jewish congregation in the capital came into being.

As with the Jews, so with the Huguenots. In 1685 King Louis XIV of France revoked the Edict of Nantes, which had granted freedom of worship to the Protestant Huguenots, and 800,000 fled their country. Many took refuge in England, in Switzerland and in Holland. Others, on the personal initiative of the Great Elector, found a welcome in Brandenburg.

It was an inspired but calculated gesture. For the new immigrants were skilled and educated – better educated than the majority of their hosts. Even the poorest could read and write, at a time when over 50 per cent of the inhabitants of Brandenburg were still illiterate.

But it was above all in the crafts and new manufacturing skills which they brought with them that the Huguenots' huge contribution to the Brandenburg economy lay, in particular to the prosperity of the capital. Paper and printing, soap and linseed oil, watches and optical goods, millinery and all aspects of textile production, tailors, bakers, goldsmiths, pharmacists – these are only some of the new areas of expertise in which they established themselves. Characteristic of their combination of artistic sense and practical vision was the foundation by Pierre Mercier of the first workshop in Berlin for the manufacture of tapestries, a process which Mercier later also set up in Dresden.

Thrifty, industrious, pious, content with modest dwellings for their families, the Huguenots set about developing Berlin in the way the Elector envisaged, settling in particular in the recently created community of the Dorotheenstadt. A number had been officers in the French army before they left, and now transferred their allegiance to the Elector; others joined later, until by 1688, the year Friedrich Wilhelm died, Huguenots made up more than 15 per cent of the total military strength and almost 20 per cent of the population of Berlin as a whole. 'They have brought abundance and prosperity to the city', wrote the eighteenth-century traveller Baron Karl Ludwig von Pöllnitz, 'and made it one of the finest in Europe. To them we owe our factories, our police, our weekly markets and many of our cobbled streets. It was they who gave us the taste for arts and sciences, and by curbing our uncouth manners, they enabled us to stand comparison with the most enlightened nations.' A glance at the French Huguenot names in the current Berlin telephone directory shows how permanent is the imprint left, after three centuries, by a single decision of the Great Elector.

What he did for the politics of his state, the Great Elector also did for its culture. To be sure, he had had predecessors who were at pains to raise the cultural status of the court in individual spheres but no one had set out with such determination to advance systematically the interests of the arts and crafts as a whole and promote the advancement of knowledge. He was a serious collector of *objets d'art* from all over the world, in particular chinaware from the Far East, and set aside rooms in his palace for their display. He also encouraged the study of Oriental civilisations, especially Chinese, by scholars in Berlin and at the University in Frankfurt an der Oder – a byproduct of the interest in the Far East that he had developed during his early years in Holland. The Netherlands, indeed, were the main formative influence on the development of his cultural tastes and standards.

In what was still a firmly feudal society the personality of the individual overlord counted for much, and a change of ruler could mean a radical change of direction in military, political, cultural or any other policy. But no Elector could disguise the fact that in the seventeenth century Berlin lived almost entirely on art conceived and produced elsewhere, above all in the Netherlands. Here, in a world of prosperity and self-confidence sustained by the possessions of empire, the extrovert forms of Baroque dominated. Allegorical paintings and reliefs of classical and Biblical subjects appeared alongside richly sensuous still lifes, portraits and architectural paintings, examples of which found their way to Berlin.

But it was above all in the physiognomy of his royal capital, as it shook off the debris of the Thirty Years War and began its inexorable rise to power and wealth, that the Great Elector left his public mark. Turning to Dutch artists, designers and architects, he laid the structural foundations of the city which grew into the Berlin of modern times. There was already a geographical affinity between the flat landscape of the Netherlands and the sandy plains of the Mark Brandenburg, and the simple, direct lines of the Dutch urban scene were readily assimilated.

Johann Gregor Memhardt, architect of the 'fortress Berlin' that the Elector had ordered, was engaged to build further extensions to the already sprawling Royal Palace, and later to extend a second Hohenzollern palace at neighbouring Potsdam in the same Netherlandish Baroque style. This new building, in its turn, created the need for gardeners, sculptors, painters, designers and craftsmen of all kinds.

Potsdam, indeed, began its rise to cultural glory at this time. There had been a fortress here at a crossing over the River Havel since the Middle Ages but, unlike Berlin, little to promote its growth as a commercial or manufacturing centre. With the example of Louis XIV's Versailles before his eyes, the Great Elector set about developing Potsdam into a satellite court, a country residence with fine hunting where the day-to-day administration of the state could be laid aside for a while. The Elector was a lover of gardens, and by laying out parks and encouraging the cultivation of orchards and nurseries, he drew the general population into his plans for a more beautiful and more prosperous Potsdam. The produce of local vineyards is even said to have been exported to England in the succeeding years.

When Memhardt died in 1678, Friedrich Wilhelm appointed as his successor Johann Arnold Nering, an architect of Dutch extraction who had already worked in Berlin. Much of what Nering built has been destroyed but three proud examples of his work still survive to be enjoyed in Berlin today. First, it was he who made the basic designs for the royal residence which became the Palace of Charlottenburg. Then, fulfilling a cherished dream of the Great Elector's, he planned and initiated the great Zeughaus (Armoury) that dominates the entrance to Unter den Linden, in its completed form the greatest surviving Baroque building in the city. Finally there is Nering the town-planner. In 1688 the Great Elector's successor, Friedrich III, gave orders for the further extension of his capital. The first addition to the twin-town unit of Berlin–Cölln had been Friedrichwerder, west of Cölln but still within the town fortifications. Also westwards, north of Unter den Linden but outside the walls, lay Dorotheenstadt, named after the Great Elector's second wife and constituted in 1674. Now, pressing still farther westwards, south of the axis of Unter den Linden, Friedrich III added a third community, Friedrichstadt, which Nering laid out in a grid pattern still clearly in evidence today. These were the five corporate bodies that united in 1709 to form the single administrative authority (*Magistrat*) of Berlin.

The Culture of a Capital

Berlin was gradually approaching the moment, as the struggling, strife-torn seventeenth century moved into the self-confidence of the eighteenth, when it acquired the status of a true royal capital. Presiding over this surge of energy for almost seventy-five years, the span of their combined reigns, were just two men – Friedrich Wilhelm the Great Elector and the Elector Friedrich III, later King Friedrich I of Prussia.

But looming over this activity, and constraining to a considerable degree its cultural manifestations, were two forces. One was the ruler's political ambitions in the name of Brandenburg, and the extent to which culture needed to reflect those aims – put bluntly, to extol the name of Hohenzollern through visible displays of wealth and influence. The other was the pressure emanating from the Protestantism which had been the religion of Brandenburg since 1539.

The Italian Renaissance, as an intellectual force, had had only a stunted influence in Germany, and then rather in Catholic than in Protestant states. The Thirty Years War drained the country of energies that would otherwise have been free to absorb the full inspiration of Renaissance art and literature, while the Counter-Reformation left north Germany almost untouched. Moreover, the centres of Baroque literature in seventeenth-century Germany, whether Catholic or Protestant, are anywhere but in Brandenburg. Silesia claimed the key figure of Opitz, the German Boileau, together with the poets Angelus Silesius and Friedrich Logau and the most accomplished of German Baroque dramatists, Andreas Gryphius. Literary societies, after Renaissance models in Florence and elsewhere, sprang up in Nuremberg and Strasbourg, while the greatest German novelist of the time, Grimmelshausen, author of that superb picaresque story of life during the Thirty Years War, *Simplicius Simplicissimus*, was a native of Hessen. It was left to Berlin to claim one of the most moving religious poets of the age, a poet in the rugged national tradition that owes nothing to the Renaissance – Paul Gerhardt.

Gerhardt was a Lutheran pastor who was appointed deacon at the Nikolaikirche in 1651, where he wrote a religious poetry of unmatched poignancy and serenity. Here are hymns in the tradition of Luther, forthright, open-hearted, cast in the mould of the German folksong and addressed to the simple citizen as he struggles to pick up the pieces of his shattered life after the years of war. In Gerhardt's *Geistliche Andachten*, published in 1667, are to be found some of the most famous of German hymns – 'O Haupt voll Blut und Wunden', set by Bach in the *St Matthew Passion*, or the sublime trust in God expressed by 'Nun ruhen alle Wälder'. It is a Christianity close at times to pantheism, an expression of thanks to God for the beauties of nature and the divine love embodied in those beauties, and a call for man, in joy and optimism, to put his faith in higher things.

Yet Gerhardt's hymns, like Luther's, would never have penetrated the German Protestant consciousness as they did had it not been for their melodies. It was Gerhardt's good fortune to have as colleague at the Nikolaikirche the organist and composer Johannes Crüger. Crüger was a prolific composer and the influential author of a theory of music and a singing tutor containing interesting discussions of national and foreign vocal styles current at the time. But he survives today only as the compiler of the most important early Protestant hymnal and as a composer of hymn tunes second in their genre only to those of Luther.

Crüger's influence on musical life in Berlin, both in policy and performance, went well beyond the confines of the Nikolaikirche. At one time the Great Elector had a plan to put him in charge of the music at court, seeing him as a man who might marry the native German tradition, the world of his subjects, with the foreign influences, above all from France and Italy, that were rapidly coming to dominate taste and fashion at court. Crüger had the catholicity of outlook to succeed. But he was never given the chance.

The war over, a sense of well-being and optimism began to return, and with it a demand for entertainment, both at court and among the townsfolk at large. This coincided with the extensive cultural programme – large-scale building projects, the importation of artists and craftsmen from abroad – initiated by the Great Elector in the latter part of his reign and continued by his successor. The growth in population also formed part of the equation. More suburbs were springing up outside the town walls, and by the turn of the century Berlin, inside and outside the walls, had some 30,000 inhabitants. Over the coming generation the figure almost doubled.

Presiding over this expansion and over the attendant consolidation of the status of Berlin as a royal capital was the Great Elector's second son Friedrich, who succeeded his father in 1688. His reign, culturally as politically, was built on a love of pomp and display, the most appropriate historical demonstration of which marked the moment when, in 1701, in Königsberg, he crowned himself King in Prussia. Unlike Paris or Vienna, Berlin had no extensive aristocracy which could add its own contributions, financial and cultural, to the activities of the court itself. All the more keenly, therefore, did the King feel that the well-being of his state rested entirely on his own shoulders. As King Friedrich I he reigned until 1713, unifying under his sovereignty all the Hohenzollern possessions in Germany. Henceforth the nobles, burghers and peasants of these lands became subjects of the Prussian king, soldiers in the Prussian army and victims of the Prussian civil service.

A bitter but telling comment on the values that prevailed at the King's court came from his Queen, Sophie Charlotte. Shortly before her death in 1705 she noted: 'I am about to die, thereby doing everything for His Majesty of which I am capable, in that I am not only lifting from his shoulders a burden that he always felt in my presence but also offering him the opportunity to mount a lavish funeral. This, given the taste that he is prone to demonstrate, will be the most important consideration for him.' Friedrich I as he liked to see himself is portrayed in a ceremonial painting done in 1701, immediately after his coronation, by Samuel Theodor Gericke, one of the many portrait painters, from Germany and abroad, appointed to the Berlin court to immortalise the dignitaries of the day.

Political absolutism, reflected in public displays of power and authority, found its natural extension in cultural absolutism – to be more exact, in the new King's determination to make his court the equal of that of Louis XIV of France. In 1696, following the examples of Paris and Rome, he founded an Academy of Arts, charged with training native artists, builders and craftsmen for the rapidly growing number of tasks hitherto largely the prerogative of skilled immigrants. Four years later, also in the wake of foreign models, he created an Academy of Sciences, for the presidency of which, through the influence of his Queen, he succeeded in attracting no less a figure than the philosopher Leibniz.

The Berlin Academy, which later became the Prussian Akademie der Wissenschaften, embraced an impressive range of disciplines, ranging from mathematics and astronomy, through physics, chemistry and medicine, to language and literature. Stress was laid not only on the observation of the natural world and on scientific calculation but on the practical applications of knowledge, which is also to say on the integration of intellectual activity into the processes of day-to-day life. The findings of biology, for example, were put to the service of agriculture. In 1716 the Academy acquired an Anatomy Theatre, where medical students were instructed not just in the structure and functions of the human body but also in how to tend the sick and wounded. From this there developed a few years later the oldest and most famous of Berlin hospitals, the Charité. The French name acknowledges the extensive role played in the Academy by the Huguenots.

Buildings and Handicrafts

Standing on the Schlossbrücke, the bridge that crosses the western arm of the Spree, and looking westwards down the dead-straight avenue of Unter den Linden towards the Brandenburg Gate, one surveys a panorama of buildings which have shown a remarkable power of survival. A stylistic blend of German, French and Italian, they were built between 1700 and 1850, the period of the consolidated, absolutist Prussian state, to constitute what has become known as the 'Prussian style'.

Spanning, as it does, a century and a half of agitated history, the term 'Prussian style' cannot have one single, unchanging meaning. Nor are its features exclusively the creation of architects and artists, for a succession of Prussian kings insisted on the incorporation of their own visions and practical requirements in the finished artistic product. But the 'Prussian style' – a graver, more austere Baroque than that of France or Italy – does have a starting-point. It is the first and grandest building in Unter den Linden, the Zeughaus, or Royal Armoury, the work of various hands but above all of Andreas Schlüter.

Schlüter was first and foremost a sculptor. Born around 1659, he had worked in his native Danzig and at the Polish court before being invited to Berlin by Elector Friedrich III in 1694. His primary task, like that of other

court servants, was to contribute to the public manifestation of power and majesty that gave tangible expression to the rise of the Prussian monarchy – a rise as evident in the massive increase in the size of the army as in any demonstration of aesthetic ambition.

Were Schlüter to have confined himself to his original calling, he would still be remembered as one of the most outstanding German sculptors of his day, an artist who brought the forms of Italian high Baroque to Berlin. But only five years after his arrival in the Mark Brandenburg he found himself appointed director of the royal building works in succession to Nering.

Pride of place among the buildings to which Schlüter was required to devote himself belonged, naturally, to the Royal Palace. The Renaissance building of 1538, with its various accretions, had fallen into a state of increasing disrepair during and after the Thirty Years War, and between 1698 and 1706, on the basis of Schlüter's designs, a new palace was built, the largest Baroque building north of the Alps. It survived until the end of the Second World War, when, though damaged, it could have been restored. But the communist rulers of East Germany blew it up in 1951, and no innocent visitor would now know where Schlüter's masterpiece once stood.

Nevertheless contemporary prints have survived that convey the exuberant splendour of Schlüter's original plan, and pre-war photographs record the majesty of both exterior and interior (Ill. 19). A particular glory was Schlüter's interior courtyard, set round with cornices and balustrades intended to receive statues. Here as elsewhere, the driving force behind Schlüter the architect is Schlüter the sculptor. The main staircase of the palace, designed around 1700, was reckoned among the noblest such features from the Baroque age (Ill. 20), showing not only a derivation from Italian high Baroque but also marks of the French Baroque of Louis XIV's Versailles.

Now a Museum of German History, the Zeughaus was commissioned by Friedrich III both as a royal arsenal and as a building to house the accumulated spoils of Hohenzollern wars. It was conceived on a huge scale. Far

The Elector's Palace.

19. (facing page) Schlüter's design for the Berlin palace, c. 1702. Etching by P. Schenck after a sketch by S. Blesendorf.

20. Main staircase.

larger than its function required, it was to all intents and purposes a second palace. Schlüter's prime responsibility lay in providing sculpted decorative features to the interior and exterior façades and other parts of the building – not mere accretions but integrated figures and motifs which expressed in themselves the consolidated function of a building devoted to the needs and purposes of war. To the external façades Schlüter applied sculptures of casques and crests appropriate to a public display of military valour and of Hohenzollern victories in the field. But for the inner courtyard he depicted the other side of war – a series of reliefs of dying warriors, their stone features

21 a and b. Dying warriors by Schlüter, in the courtyard of the Zeughaus, sandstone, 1696.

convulsed in pain, images of searing intensity, amounting almost to humanitarian, even political statements. These twenty-two masks in sandstone are among the greatest works of Baroque sculpture, with an expressive intensity, directed at an universal theme, which 300 years have done nothing to diminish (Ill. 21). Impressive as other surviving works of Schlüter's are – the bronze equestrian statue of the Great Elector (see Ill. 17), the pulpit in the Marienkirche – none matches the power and pathos of these suffering heroes.

Schlüter may have been the only genius to put his gifts at the disposal of the Elector–King but the rapidly growing prestige of the new monarchy demanded a veritable army of craftsmen, engravers, architects, sculptors and painters to decorate the rooms of the new palace. Some painters were even appointed to work only in specific areas – the Dutchman Willem Frederick van Roye for his still lifes and Paul Carl Leygebe as 'court painter of battles and landscapes'. Portrait painters, many of whom also taught at the Elector's Academy of Arts, were particularly in demand.

Among developing arts and crafts particular interest attached to porcelain. Since the opening of the trade route to the Far East in the sixteenth century, European countries – Holland, England, France, Germany – had become fascinated with the art of China and Japan. Chinoiserie was highly congenial to Baroque taste, and a thriving trade developed in the import of Chinese and Japanese porcelain. The Great Elector had already set an example by amassing a large collection of exotic artefacts, and the trend grew through the eighteenth century, reaching its bizarre climax when the King of Saxony bartered a whole regiment of his dragoons for a hundred items of chinaware from the collection of King Friedrich Wilhelm I of Prussia.

The heyday of Berlin china did not arrive until the foundation of the first manufactory in 1751. But as early as 1680 a Dutchman called Pieter Fransen van der Lee had set up a works in Berlin for the production of fayence ware – Delft porcelain, as it was known – and a second followed in 1699, also on Dutch initiative. Until displaced in the affections of the aristocracy and the wealthy burghers by finer china, these fayences were highly prized for their Oriental forms and designs in the blue and white tones characteristic of the exotic originals. For this reason the emphasis in the early stages lay on the production of large, highly decorated pieces to grace the rooms of palaces and villas or to be displayed in individual thematic collections. Later, as designers and decorators turned their attention to the more delicate and subtle possibilities opened up by the use of china clay, fayence ware became more utilitarian and found its way into humbler households (Ill. 22).

Parallel with the emergence of this new interest in pottery and china ran a remarkable development in the manufacture of glass. But with a key difference. For, whereas the process of fayence manufacture had been imported from abroad, credit for the new techniques in glassmaking lay with one remarkable man, a German, employed by the court of Brandenburg. His name was Johann Kunckel.

Kunckel had started life as an alchemist at the Saxon court in Dresden. Becoming aware of the superstitious futility of what he was doing, he took up the serious study of the physical sciences and became a teacher of

22. Fayence vases from the factory of Cornelius Funcke, Berlin, first third of the eighteenth century.

23. Ruby glass teapot by Johann Kunckel, *c.* 1679–93.

experimental chemistry at the University of Wittenberg, where he came to the attention of the Great Elector. In Brandenburg the manufacture of glass was a state monopoly. The Elector saw in Kunckel the man to consolidate this monopoly and he set Kunckel up with his own furnace on the Pfaueninsel, an island in the River Havel, close to Potsdam. Nature had been anything but generous to Brandenburg in matters of soil quality and natural resources but sand and wood were available in profusion, and there were already three glassworks in production in the Mark before Kunckel arrived in 1678.

By summoning Kunckel to his service, the Elector hoped to raise the quality of his native glassware to that of the famous centres in Bohemia and Silesia, and Kunckel devoted his efforts to the production of various kinds of crystal and other glasses of exceptional quality. This was glass as an *objet d'art* for the privileged elite, not a utilitarian product for the masses. The goblets, vases and so on then passed from the Potsdam works into the hands of the engravers, who decorated them with likenesses of the Prussian royal house, family crests, scenes from classical mythology and other motifs (Ill. 24). Today Kunckel is best remembered for his coloured glasses, especially his so-called ruby glass (Ill. 23).

24. Glass incised with depiction of two lovers, signed H I (Heinrich Jäger?).

44

The pursuit of craft activities such as china and glass production, cabinet-making and furnishing, and the weaving of textiles and tapestries, was increasingly taking place in independent studios and workshops outside the context of the medieval craft guilds. In their early days the guilds had done much to raise the standards of goods produced, and had guaranteed those standards through the application of strict labour practices and firm control of the market. At the time this control had operated in the interest of producer and consumer alike. But as the range of handicrafts multiplied, especially under the stimulus of the new skills and energies brought into Brandenburg by the Huguenots, so the introverted policies of the guilds led to inflexibility and economic inadequacy. The future lay with the encouragement of individual initiative, the investment of resources with which to expand the volume and variety of production and satisfy the new demands. In a word, the need was for the development of a capitalist economy.

The prime mover in this expansion was the royal court, which included not just the grand new Baroque palace in Berlin but also the various smaller residences in the environs – the palaces of Köpenick and Oranienburg, for example. The finest of these 'suburban' houses, and the one that made the greatest demands on artists and craftsmen, was the Versailles-inspired Charlottenburg Palace built for Queen Sophie Charlotte, wife of King Friedrich I. Begun by Nering, the construction was taken over by the Swedish architect Eosander von Göthe in 1701, and despite later additions it is the hand of Eosander that one sees today in the forecourt and *corps de logis*, with its façade surmounted by the Baroque splendour of the dome. Queen Charlotte made her palace a centre of the arts, above all music, during the few years she held court there, and the rooms – including a theatre in the grounds for the performance of opera – had to be equipped and decorated accordingly, essentially in the French style which represented the height of fashion (Ill. 25).

While Charlottenburg and its humbler companions gave a direct stimulus to the production of all kinds of works of art, wealthy merchants and businessmen were increasingly in a position to follow the royal example. That the possession of elaborate *objets d'art* may have been prompted by considerations of prestige rather than aesthetic conviction is incidental. The works were produced and acquired, and the world has cause to be grateful. It was this demand-fuelled economy that led directly to such enterprises in and around Berlin as the glassworks of Kunckel and the fayence manufactory of Gerhard Wolbeer. Turners, joiners, cabinet-makers and other workers in wood were also continually needed, their products ranging from parquet flooring, doors and panelling to ornate picture frames and lacquered furniture (Ill. 26).

Gold- and silversmiths, too, were busy, the overwhelming majority of them Huguenots who brought with them French techniques and tastes. Chandeliers, mirrors, candlesticks and other interior fittings were obvious outlets for their skills, also silver cutlery, items of personal adornment, costume decoration and jewellery in general. A conversation piece by Paul Carl Leygebe (c. 1710) of the King and Queen and their inner circle at a smoking party in the so-called Drap d'Or Chamber of the Royal Palace in Berlin gives an impression of a characteristic social occasion in intimate surroundings where the crafts of the day can be admired (Ill. 27).

25. (*above*) Charlottenburg
Palace, built in several stages
between 1695 and 1790.

26. Lacquer coin cabinet
by Gerard Dagly, *c.* 1701–14.

A considerable quantity of silverware has survived from a quite different source, namely the Church. As the scars of the Thirty Years War healed, so thoughts turned to restoring and re-equipping the churches which had suffered years of neglect. A rising population created a need for new churches. Furthermore, when new villages or towns were established, it was frequently the King's custom to symbolise his blessing on the new settlements by presenting the local church with silverware for ritual use – altar crosses, patens, chalices.

Prime examples of new churches established under Friedrich I are two prominent buildings which still dominate the skyline of the Friedrichstadt, the district immediately south of Unter den Linden – the French Church and its pendant, the German Church.

The two churches stand on opposite sides of the market square called the Gendarmenmarkt, after the Gens d'Armes cavalry regiment which had its stables here. The French Church, begun in 1701 by Louis Gayard as a counterpart to the Huguenots' church at Charenton and completed in 1705 by Abraham Quesnay, was built for the immigrant Huguenot community. It is a plain, centralised structure with a gallery and with semicircular conchs on the north and south sides. The German Church was begun in the same year to a design by Martin Grünberg but took three years longer to complete. It too is a centralised structure with conchs.

What immediately strikes the eye, and what inseparably links the two churches, are the two identical late Baroque-classicistic towers – classical porticos on three sides, with an abundance of applied statuary, surmounted by

27. *Frederick the Great's Fraternity of Smokers in the Berlin Royal Palace*, oil on canvas by Paul Carl Leygebe, *c.* 1710.

elaborate domes. However, these domes, built to designs by Karl von
Gontard, were in fact not raised until seventy-five years later, in an age domi-
nated by French classical taste. Both churches were gutted by fire during the
Second World War but have since been rebuilt.

Music and the Stage

At this time, and for 200 or more years to come, spoken drama and plays-
with-music – operas, Singspiele – existed side by side in one and the same
theatre, together with ballet and other forms of stage entertainment. The
Englische Comödianten, with their Pickelhering plays and their impro-
visatory, *commedia dell'arte* manner, were still in some demand, and German
troupes had followed in their footsteps.

By all accounts the entertainment provided by such companies served a
multitude of interests. The Church, however, was always suspicious of theatre
and of the footloose folk associated with it. The Pietists in particular, similar
to the Puritans in the severity of their outlook, brought their Calvinist strictness to bear on the situation, and Philipp Jakob Spener, Provost of the Nikolaikirche and leader of the Berlin Pietists, protested to the King. 'The
annoyance they [troupes of strolling players] cause is clear for all to see', he
complained, 'and persons of elevated station who were present took offence
at many things in the performance.' The players had ignored warnings to
moderate their language, Spener went on, 'so that there is no other way of
dealing with this public nuisance and of retaining a sense of honour before
God than by banning it outright'.

But tastes were becoming more sophisticated. At the same time the range
of festive occasions celebrated at court was broadening. Balls and masquerades catered for the urge to self-projection and display and led to performances of pastoral scenes, ballets and pantomimes, in which the courtiers
themselves sometimes took part. Visiting dignitaries from other courts, who
needed to be suitably impressed, offered convenient stimuli for the composition of such works, and poets and composers were retained for the purpose.

When the Crown Prince Friedrich Wilhelm, later King Friedrich Wilhelm
I, married Princess Sophie Dorothea of Hanover in Berlin in 1706, the most
adventurous of these early productions was mounted – an allegorical
Singspiel interspersed with ballet scenes called *Beauty's Victory over the Heroes*,
libretto by Johann von Besser, court master of ceremonies, music by August
Reinhard Stricker and Gottfried Finger, two members of the court
orchestra. To complete the team of celebrities engaged, the sets were designed
by the court painter Friedrich Wilhelm Weidemann, and the auditorium and
stage laid out by Eosander von Göthe (Ill. 28). A few years earlier, in 1690,
a Singspiel called *Der Scherenschleifer* ('The Knife Grinder'), also to a text by
Besser, had been given – the first recorded performance in Berlin of a
German opera.

Among those commissioned to attend the Crown Prince's wedding celebrations was a troupe of French actors, forty men strong, led by George du
Rocher. Rocher's men were given a long-term engagement in the town
which committed them, on the basis of a repertoire of French plays and

Sieg der Schönheit
über die Helden.
Vorgestellet
In einem Ballet und Sing-Spiel;
Bey Vermählung
Seiner Königl. Hoheit
Fridrich Wilhelms/
Kron-Printzens von Preussen/
Mit
Der Durchlauchtigsten Printzeßin
Sophia Dorothea/
Aus dem Chur-Hause Braunschweig-
Lüneburg.
Im December des 1706. Jahres.
Cölln an der Spree/
Druckts Ulrich Liebpert/ Königl. Preuß. Hof-Buchdr.

28. Title page of Singspiel *Sieg der Schönheit über die Helden*, performed before the Royal court in Berlin in 1706.

ballets, to give two performances a week for the court, principally in Berlin but also in Oranienburg, Köpenick and other summer residences. On other weekdays they had permission to play in a public theatre set up in the rear of a large Renaissance house belonging to one of the court chamberlains, and to charge for admission. Performances at court, on the other hand, cost nothing to the privileged circles entitled to attend them.

Thus the advance of French cultural values, soon to become irresistible, finally made itself felt in a court which, as much for political as any other reasons, had persisted mainly with things German. It was, for example, in particular for the performance of contemporary German music – the concertos and suites of Telemann at its head – that Friedrich I expanded the court band into a proper orchestra. An entry in the court accounts for 1712 records an outlay for twenty-seven musicians – eleven violins, two violas, five cellos, four oboes (who doubled on flutes), four bassoons and cembalo – while brass and percussion from the Royal Trumpeters could supplement these forces when necessary. A member of the King's music staff whose name later became more familiar in London than in his native Berlin was Johann Christoph Pepusch, arranger of the music for John Gay's *The Beggar's Opera* in 1728.

Very different were the emphases set by Queen Sophie Charlotte in her own court of Charlottenburg (Ill. 29). Here, in the woods to the west of the

29. Sophie Charlotte, second wife of King Friedrich I of Prussia by Gedeon Romandon, oil on canvas, c. 1690. Charlotte initiated the establishment of the Prussian Academy of Science, and Charlottenburg Palace bears her name.

town, this cultured lady, who had grown up in the refined Hanoverian court and experienced at first hand the culture and intellectual life of France and Italy, set about creating her own cultural centre. A constant flow of intellectuals and artists came to her palace from all over Europe, the most famous among them the philosopher Leibniz.

Her greatest love, however, was music, above all Italian music. She organised vocal and chamber music recitals of works by contemporary Italian composers – Alessandro Scarlatti, Stradella, Corelli – and promoted performances of modern Italian operas by Giovanni Buononcini, Ariosti and others. The young Telemann remembered hearing her play the harpsichord continuo in a performance of Buononcini's opera *Polifemo*.

But the Charlottenburg Palace as a centre for the arts was a hothouse bloom, created and tended by one person alone. It perished with the Queen's early death in 1705 after a mere six years. The King could not match her vision or her culture and was in any case preoccupied with affairs of state in Berlin, where he could insist on his preference for home-grown German opera.

Berlin and its Culture

Cultivation of the native German musical tradition rested to a large degree, as it had done since the Reformation, on the development of forms that grew out of the Lutheran chorale. The finest of these, the third composite vocal form to emerge in the Baroque period alongside opera and oratorio, is the church cantata, composed to Biblical and other religious texts, which reached its height in Buxtehude and Bach. The cantata became the staple fare of Protestant church choirs, taking its place in the repertoire alongside the motets, songs and oratorios of earlier north German masters such as Schütz and Michael Praetorius. But none of these masters seems to have had any personal links with Berlin, nor did the great organ composers of the day, like Pachelbel and Froberger, whose works must have been played in Berlin churches.

Friedrich I, first King of Prussia, died in 1713. As a ruler, he had built energetically, extravagantly, on the firm foundations that his father, the Great Elector, had laid. He left behind him a state infinitely more powerful, more self-assured, more cultured. And even if that culture were dominated by things French, starting with the French language, his concern had been to raise the cultural status of the Prussian world, not just to imitate for the sake of imitation, however fashionable. He confirmed the reputation for religious and intellectual tolerance which the Great Elector had already gained and he made Prussia the foremost Protestant state in Europe.

All this had cost a lot of money, and frugality was not a word in Friedrich I's vocabulary. Two recent outbreaks of the plague had seared their path through the population. A revolution was perhaps inevitable, a revolution that turned a scene of optimism and adventure into thirty years of cultural darkness. It was the achievement of one man: King Friedrich Wilhelm I, called, not for nothing, the 'Soldier King'.

Spartan Interregnum

'It is almost as difficult to believe that Frederick I and Sophie Charlotte could have such a son as that the son could be the father of Frederick the Great.' The historian's sense of wonder – the words of J. A. R. Marriott. Converting incredulity into argument, Marriott goes on: 'The twenty-seven years of his reign completed at a terrible price the work of the Great Elector; and in the evolution of Prussia they have their indisputable place as the period in which all the most unlovely and forbidding qualities of Prussianism were scourged into the kingdom.'

While pondering what was 'difficult to believe' about Friedrich Wilhelm I, Marriott might have conceded that it is also difficult to be fair to him. He was crude, self-righteous, brutal, with 'the mentality of a drill-sergeant', as the phrase had it – to many, a monster *tout court*. He was also a devout Christian, patriotic, diligent, mercilessly insistent on loyalty, obedience and other 'forbidding qualities of Prussianism', as Marriott calls them. He lived for one thing and one alone – the army. He saw the greatness of Prussia – his Prussia – as synonymous with the greatness of the army – his army. Within a few years, by recruiting methods which do not bear humane examination, he doubled the number of men under arms. Friedrich I had left a

30. Portrait of a Potsdam Grenadier, probably by Georg Lisiewski, oil on canvas, c. 1735.

force of some 30,000 men. When the Soldier King had finished with it, his army counted 90,000. Barracks, uniforms, training grounds, the ordnance and other weapons, ammunition, not to speak of the victualling of such masses of cannon-fodder – all this came to devour nearly 80 per cent of the state's revenue (Ill. 30).

A lawyer, one H. G. Klose, who visited Berlin in 1731 and had known the town in the good old days, described the change in his *Berliner Briefe*:

> If one wishes to picture to oneself the Berlin court today, one has to realise that the present government consists merely of generals and high-ranking officers, who make up the entire royal household. No longer does one see sumptuous dresses trimmed with gold and silver braid, as under the previous monarch – no servants with cockades of long ostrich plumes, no retainers in splendid livery, no magnificent carriages as at other courts. Now everything is military.

Prominent among the victims of the new regime were the arts. One of the King's first acts was to dismiss most of the painters engaged by his predecessor and cut the salary of the few – chiefly portrait painters – he retained. Since buildings were to become purely functional and erected as economically as possible, the visions of imaginative architects and sculptors were abandoned as superfluous luxuries. Eosander von Göthe, Queen Charlotte's architectural guru, lost his position and went back to Sweden. Schlüter entered the service of Tsar Peter the Great. Even the long-serving Johann von Besser, court poet, librettist of court operas and master of ceremonies to Friedrich I, was declared redundant.

Musicians fared no better. The excellent orchestra that Friedrich I had built up was disbanded, the only players retained, characteristically, being the trumpeters. Music, for Friedrich Wilhelm I, meant military bands as the expression of his philosophy of Prussian statecraft, and Church music to take care of his piety and his insistence on a muscular Christianity. The concerts that used to take place in the Berlin court or at Charlottenburg were a thing of the past. The only oases of culture left were the amateur recitals in Monbijou Palace – the charming Baroque residence by the Spree (all trace of it has now vanished) where Queen Sophie Dorothea, the Soldier King's wife, held court – or the private chapel of Margrave Christian Ludwig, for whom Bach wrote his Brandenburg Concertos.

Opera, that effeminate, unrealistic, useless creature imported from irrelevant Romance cultures, had no chance of survival. For French ballets like those performed to the command of Friedrich I by George du Rocher, and the Italian entertainments by Ariosti and his like mounted in his Queen's palace at Charlottenburg, the Soldier King had neither taste nor time. Indeed, his tolerance of the stage reached little beyond entertainment at fair-ground level, an activity which did not provoke thoughts on human conduct, on society, on morality or other potentially subversive subjects. The Church was in general as opposed to the theatre as before, and His Majesty was delighted when theorists like Martin Heinrich Fuhrmann, cantor at the Friedrichwerder Gymnasium, confirmed his prejudices by publishing works attacking the influence of opera on Church music.

At the same time he welcomed public performances by the troupe of strolling players managed by Johann Carl von Eckenberg, the legendary 'strong man' who led a team of 'English, Dutch and Italian tightrope walkers, acrobats and bareback riders, together with a large company', as a playbill of 1738 announces. To round off their display, Eckenberg's playbill continues, they will perform a new work entitled *The Kingdom of the Circumcised in the Kingdom of the Living*, which, to judge from its subtitle, was a piece of anti-Semitism much to the taste of a contemporary audience – and, apparently, of the King himself, who bestowed on Eckenberg and his troupe the proud title 'Company of the Royal Court'.

After the dismissal of so many painters, sculptors, designers and decorative artists whose careers had been built on an ostentation that had collapsed overnight, and in the shadow of a dark cloud of officially sponsored anti-intellectualism, the two Royal Academies founded at the end of the previous century sank into a sorry state. Official subsidies were withdrawn. Subjects of study in the Academy of Arts for which the need had been rudely interrupted – tapestry weaving, jewellery, embroidery and other pursuits of luxury – dropped out of the curriculum. Painting came to mean portraits –

of the King, of his family, of his courtiers, of his armies. Friedrich I's Academy of Sciences was reduced to a training college for field surgeons and medical orderlies. Investigation and research became alien notions – what mattered was a healthy army. When Leibniz, president of the Academy since its inception, died in 1716, Friedrich Wilhelm I demonstrated his estimation of intellectual values by appointing as Leibniz's successor Baron Jakob Paul Gundling, a drunken servant of the royal household and the butt of all manner of crude jests among the courtiers.

The Soldier King has had an almost entirely bad press. Yet towards the end of his reign signs appear of what look suspiciously like achievements from which his people drew genuine benefit. He doubled the revenue of his state and corrected the imbalance between expenditure and income that he had inherited from his pomp-loving predecessor. He accumulated substantial savings in the royal treasury in order to make Prussia financially self-dependent. And in the best tradition of his grandfather he offered asylum to the thousands of Protestants driven out of Austria by the Archbishop of Salzburg in 1731 – the historical episode in the background of Goethe's epic poem *Hermann und Dorothea*.

In one sense all this was its own justification. But Friedrich Wilhelm I's Calvinistic piety led him to take one step further, the step that led from the parade ground to the Church, where the union of Prussianism and Christianity could receive divine blessing. He now had garrison churches built for both Berlin and Potsdam, the latter a particularly important piece of Prussian church architecture in the tradition of Schlüter (both churches were destroyed in the Second World War). Prominent secular buildings which owe their existence to the King's town-planning initiatives include the Crown Prince's Palace on Unter den Linden, converted into a Baroque residence for the future Frederick the Great in 1732, and the adjacent Princesses' Palace, built a year later.

Musical culture may have withered under his rule but the Soldier King did not entirely neglect the visual arts. Gobelins and other tapestries continued to be manufactured, some in newly founded factories. In 1720 the King removed a number of paintings from Prussian palaces in the Netherlands, formerly belonging to the house of Orange, and had them hung in Berlin, works by van Dyck, Frans Wouters and Rubens among them. And although many found their services dispensed with overnight, a basic staff of competent artists was retained, with responsibility for the royal collections and for carrying out court commissions – Paul Carl Leygebe (see Ill. 27), Friedrich Wilhelm Weidemann and the Italian Carlo Francesco Rusca, famed throughout Europe for his portraits of royalty. With remarkable foresight the King also renewed the appointment of the most accomplished of these portrait painters, Antoine Pesne, a Huguenot who served three successive Kings of Prussia, reaching the height of his powers under Frederick the Great. In his last years, *mirabile dictu*, the Soldier King even took up painting himself, making copies of works in the royal collections and doing at least one known self-portrait.

Friedrich Wilhelm I may not have been a Maecenas. Yet neither was he quite the cultural ogre that popular history has made him. Three days before he died in 1740, he said to his son: 'I have put the state and the army in order.' This achievement, at least, cannot be denied him.

THE AGE OF ENLIGHTENMENT

Fridericus Rex

'I have put the state and the army in order.' But the Soldier King's achievement had demanded its price, a price paid in economic terms by a failure to recognise the need for a comprehensive industrial policy for his kingdom, and in cultural terms by a systematic neglect of the claims of the artistic spirit. His successor certainly found the army 'in order', and he quickly put it to the use for which armies are intended. A state deprived of cultural sustenance, however, was emphatically not 'in order'. Under the rule of the Frederick who came to be known throughout Europe as 'the Great', Prussia, and with it Berlin, was to become a very different place.

But a place of contrasts. Conflict was already prefigured in Friedrich's genetic constitution: his father a Prussian martinet, rough, puritan, choleric, with horizons strictly German; his mother a Hanoverian princess, sister of King George II of England, cultured, gentle, tolerant, a lover of the arts and inspired by the civilisation of France. Thesis and antithesis emerge with chilling inevitability: war and peace, crudity and delicacy, bigotry and tolerance, things German and things French. At times he could behave in a manner most unbecoming to a monarch. 'He broke his flute, a few days ago, on the head of his favourite hussar', wrote James Harris, British plenipotentiary to the Prussian court, 'and is very liberal in kicking and cuffing those employed about his person.'

Having in 1741 profitably absorbed Silesia into Prussia by an act of naked aggression, the man Voltaire dubbed the 'Solomon of the North' turned his back on the Berlin Palace and retired to Sanssouci, his summer residence outside Potsdam. Here, where he always felt happiest, he philosophised, wrote poetry, plays and treatises on the conduct of warfare, worked on his *Mémoires pour servir à l'histoire de Brandenbourg* and other projects, composed music and played the flute (Ill. 31).

He also ran the state of Prussia. As the 'first servant of his people', as he called himself, he felt responsible for everything that went on in his kingdom. He rose at three in the morning in summer, four in winter. From then until midday he received reports from his generals and civilian officials and dictated instructions on the conduct of the day's affairs. After lunch he signed letters and decrees. The rest of the day was devoted to the pleasures of mind and spirit, sometimes in solitude, sometimes in company – a conversation

31. Frederick the Great by Joachim Martin Falbe, oil on canvas, 1752.

with Voltaire, a discussion with his learned circle on art and literature, a musical soirée. 'It was Sparta in the morning', said his French guest, 'and Athens in the afternoon.'

With the Seven Years War (1756–63) Frederick consolidated the position of Prussia in Europe once and for all. In 1740 his army had consisted of 90,000 men. At his death in 1786 it totalled over 200,000. That was Prussia as Sparta.

Prussia as Athens was to find expression in the creation of a complex of buildings surrounding a great open square at the eastern end of Unter den Linden – the 'Forum Fridericianum'. This grand project, dominated by the desire for a revived Royal Academy, never functioned in the way Friedrich had intended but its constituent parts still stand – the Opera House (see Ill. 34); Prince Heinrich's Palace (now the Humboldt University); the high-Baroque building for the Royal Library (known to Berliners, from its curved façade, as the 'Commode'); and St Hedwig's Cathedral, erected for the Catholic community in Berlin and modelled on the Pantheon in Rome.

Impressive as these individual projects are, imposing a personality on the development of the heart of the capital, they yield precedence to the architectural complex which must be considered Friedrich's greatest achievement as designer and patron – his summer palace and estate of Sanssouci, outside

32. Potsdam-Sanssouci façade, 1745–7.

Potsdam, built 1745–7. Here, on a terraced hillside covered with vines, he drew up plans with his favourite architect Georg Wenceslaus von Knobels-dorff for a residence in which he could cast off the burdens of government and live, if only for one blissful moment, 'sans souci', carefree (Ill. 32).

The Rococo palace of Sanssouci has a majestic setting, looking out over terraces and down a tree-lined avenue. The interior is a riot of Rococo deco-ration, in the fabric of the rooms as in their paintings, sculptures and other accoutrements (Ill. 33). Further buildings and landscape features were added over the following years – a picture gallery, grottos, a Chinese tea house, with numerous items of sculpture disposed around the gardens. Finally, in 1763, the King called on Knobelsdorff to design a second, larger palace for representative state purposes – the Neues Palais, in late-Baroque style.

The town centre of Potsdam, including its royal palace, was destroyed in the Second World War. But Sanssouci, its buildings and its gardens, has survived – a tribute to the political will and artistic vision of one man. Frederick the Great did not represent his age. He was his age.

So there is Friedrich the designer of estates and gardens. There is also Friedrich the musician, by all accounts an excellent flautist and the composer of flute concertos and sonatas, marches, cantatas, arias and operatic libretti. Above all there is Friedrich the Enlightenment *philosophe*, reviver of the old Academy of Sciences into an 'Académie Royale des Sciences et Belles-Lettres de Prusse', for whom the profession of *belles-lettres* embodied the highest of human aspirations. Most of what he wrote is all but forgotten. One work, however, is not – his essay *De la littérature allemande*, published in 1780.

Usually regarded, with misplaced condescension, merely as the admission by an elderly Francophile of his inability to comprehend the genius of Shakespeare

33. Sanssouci, music room *c.* 1745. The pianoforte is by Gottfried Silbermann.

and to grasp what English models could do to inspire a contemporary German literature, *De la littérature allemande* is in reality far more. Point by point it surveys the predicament of a backward German culture as seen by an intellectual of the European Enlightenment, identifying causes and prescribing solutions. Without a properly developed language, says Friedrich, capable of the subtleties of argument and expression essential for clarity of meaning, no true discourse, no worthwhile literature can emerge. French and Italian, like classical Greek and Latin, have this quality, and the literary results lie before us; German, as yet, does not. But by imitation of the best models in the culture closest at hand – Corneille, Racine, Boileau, Montesquieu, La Fontaine – German can learn how to refine its tongue, acquire a sense of the highest literary values and establish a true foundation for its own national culture.

To be sure, Friedrich has the limitations of outlook of the man of the Enlightenment. He could not reconcile the 'abominable plays' of the unruly Shakespeare with the disciplined pattern of French drama and the classical unities. He fulminates against Goethe and the Shakespeare-inspired crudities of his 'detestable' play *Götz von Berlichingen*, which to his horrified gaze was leading German literature in a ruinous direction. But with the optimism proper to the man of reason he is convinced that, once set on the right path, Germany can find its own salvation. The elevation of Prussia through the imitation of France. The dichotomies persisted to the end.

During the forty-six years of his reign Frederick the Great turned Prussia from a German principality into a European power. He bequeathed many noble buildings to his capital, brought back the painters, the sculptors, the musicians and the decorative artists. The man in the street, on the other hand, profited little. His reality was of open sewers in the pot-holed streets of the

Berlin and its Culture

city, where 'even by the royal palace', a traveller recorded, 'piles of human and animal excrement were to be found, subjecting passers-by to the most unpleasant of smells'.

Perhaps not surprisingly, therefore, the great man's death left the citizens both cold and relieved. 'There is a deathly silence but no mourning', wrote the French statesman Mirabeau, who attended the royal funeral in the Marienkirche:

> People seem benumbed without showing grief. Not a face but does not wear an expression of relief, of hope. No sign of regret, no sighs, no words of praise. Is this the reward for so many successful battles, so much glory? Is this how a reign must conclude that has lasted for almost half a century? The people were all longing for the end – now they are all congratulating each other.

In his will the King had stipulated that he should be buried beside his dogs. His successor naturally refused to do such a thing. But it was a request perversely characteristic of the lonely, misogynous monarch.

Friedrich stood for the concept of enlightened despotism. His Prussia, above all his Berlin, became a bastion of religious tolerance and freethinking. But the cultivation of this enlightenment left the rarefied atmosphere of the court and passed into the hands of the emergent middle class. Aristocracy gave way to meritocracy. At the end Friedrich was overtaken by history, by the reality that the days of extravagant royal palaces and an indulgent court-dominated culture, of a Prussia – a Germany – in the cultural shadow of the *ancien régime* of France, were gone for ever.

The Spirit of Enlightenment and the Power of the Word

However enlightened the 'enlightened despot' Frederick the Great may have been, the intellectual movement known as the Enlightenment – the German *Aufklärung* – coincides with, and itself bears a responsibility for, the decline of the feudal class system and a dramatic rise in the influence of the middle classes. These processes are accompanied by an abbreviation of the power of orthodox religion and dogma and the growth of manufacturing processes. Man now stands in the centre of things as the master of his own fate, the rational and empirical study of whom will yield true knowledge of the universe and the power that flows from that knowledge. The eighteenth century is a pedagogical age, the age of the liberation of the individual personality and the individual moral conscience. In Kant's well-known words: 'Enlightenment is man's emergence from his self-inflicted state of minority.'

To the traveller from foreign parts the physical prospect of Berlin towards the end of the eighteenth century offered a bewildering medley of contrasts. 'There are fine broad streets', noted the writer August Friedrich Julius Knüppeln in 1798,

> which the feeble human gaze can hardly take in. The Friedrichstadt, in particular, is well and symmetrically built, and the present King [Frederick the Great] has done everything possible to make this quarter of the town outstandingly fine. In

contrast there are dingy alleys such as one usually only finds in country towns – so dark and narrow that when a coach drives through, pedestrians have to stop and wait until it has passed. And there is so much dirt that one gets a very bad impression of the royal capital . . . with its poor, propped-up houses, its desolate, unbuilt squares, with great piles of dung in front of the doors and the citizens showing in their features marks of extreme poverty.

Approaching the Brandenburg Gate and Potsdam Gate, on the other hand, one feasts one's eyes on fine streets and even finer houses and villas built in the latest style and to a variety of tastes, above all in the Leipziger Strasse, which is the most beautiful I have seen for a hundred miles around . . .

The streets are full of shops and covered stalls – the whole of the Mühlendamm Bridge, with the Jägerbrücke and the Königsbrücke [both since removed], is covered with tradesmen's stands selling decorative items made of silk, linen and wool, together with other trinkets and adornments. Many such stalls are run by Jews.

A bustling scene, the product of enterprise and energy. Not all observers, however, found the natives congenial. 'In general', wrote the diplomat James Harris in a despatch to the Foreign Office,

the Prussians are poor, vain, ignorant and destitute of principle; had they been rich, their nobility could never have been brought to serve as subaltern officers with zeal and ardour. Their vanity makes them think they see their own greatness in the greatness of their monarch. Their ignorance stifles in them every notion of liberty and opposition, and their want of principle makes them ready instruments to execute any orders they may receive, without considering whether they are founded on equity or not.

And as for Prussian morals, 'the men', Harris told a friend, 'are constantly occupied how to make straightened [sic] circumstances support the extravagance of their life. The women are harpies, debauched through want of modesty rather than through want of anything else. They prostitute their persons to the best payer, and all delicacy of manners or sentiment of affection is unknown to them.'

Freedom of investigation means little if the results of that investigation cannot be freely disseminated. As Gutenberg's invention of movable-type printing had providentially preceded Luther's translation of the Bible, so Frederick the Great met the spirit of the *Aufklärung* with the virtual removal of censorship of the printed word within his kingdom. Broadsheets, both printed and handwritten, had circulated since the early decades of the seventeenth century. But the *Königlich privilegierte Berlinische Zeitung* – which later became the famous *Vossische Zeitung* – was the only newspaper in Berlin until, on his accession, Frederick the Great encouraged the foundation of two more. He took a great interest in these papers, sometimes sending them items of his own.

These items were not always what they seemed. On an occasion in 1767 the King enquired what was the main subject of conversation among his citizens. He was told that they feared another war with Austria. Irritated by this news, he sent the paper a detailed report of a disastrous hailstorm that had just struck Potsdam, causing immense damage. In a trice the hailstorm became the leading topic of conversation, especially in Potsdam itself, where nobody knew anything about a hailstorm. When the trick was revealed, some people were amused, others indignant. Either way the King had succeeded in getting them to talk about something other than the danger of war.

A basic educational thrust was directed towards the achievement of a German language that should be acceptable for literary expression while also narrowing the gulf between the elevated usage of learned circles and the limitations of an unlearned readership. And since this readership was drawn from the growing middle classes, with an urge to become better educated, the exercise of this common language became a bond that united them in their advance towards a collective personality. Only a few decades earlier Leibniz, president of the Berlin Academy of Sciences, had still written mainly in Latin and French.

There was a striking rise at this time in publishing and bookselling (both trades customarily lay in the same pair of hands). Though still well behind Leipzig, Halle and Frankfurt am Main, Berlin, aided by its liberal press laws, experienced an upsurge in publishing in the middle of the eighteenth century that lifted it above older established centres like Strasbourg and Cologne. The leading figure in this dynamic development, with Moses Mendelssohn and Lessing one of the great triumvirate of the German *Aufklärung*, was Christoph Friedrich Nicolai.

Nicolai, son of a Berlin bookseller, is a character – one of many – whose rationalist limitations are readily identifiable yet no less readily transcended by his importance in his historical context. He was always looking to educate taste, to point to what in poetry, painting, music and the other arts was worthy of imitation as German culture strove to make up some of the ground that separated it from its more advanced neighbours. But it could not be otherwise. Even Lessing still talked in terms of imitating foreign models as the way to inspire the advance of German literature – the vital decision was to choose the right models. At all events Nicolai's journal *Bibliothek der schönen Wissenschaften und der freien Künste*, launched in 1757, and still more persistently the 268 numbers of his *Allgemeine Deutsche Bibliothek* (1765–1806), put before the public an encyclopaedic set of essays, reviews and commentaries from various hands with a persuasive authority that could not but impress its age.

The challenge of the Enlightenment in Berlin found its purest philosophical expression, however, in the noble figure of Moses Mendelssohn, the first emancipated Jew in the history of German culture.

Frederick the Great, who stood for the rationalistic freedom of all religions, shared with his subjects a far from enlightened attitude towards the Jews. His decree of 1750 created a sub-class of *Schutzjuden*, 'protected Jews', who had to buy this inferior social status from the state, receiving permission to remain in their own self-governing communities in the shadow of the town walls, unintegrated and unloved. A privileged few, through skills in medicine, finance and wholesale trade, gained positions of influence in the state but the mass, forbidden to carry on a trade or to own land, could only scrape a living as pedlars or pawnbrokers. The Jewish community in Berlin in the mid-eighteenth century amounted to a little under 2,000 – a figure similar to that of Amsterdam and Vienna – out of a total population, including soldiery, of about 140,000.

Moses Mendelssohn, son of a Jewish schoolteacher in Dessau and grandfather of the composer Felix Mendelssohn-Bartholdy, first lived through this dichotomy, then transcended it. His family spoke only Hebrew. Laboriously he taught himself German, then Latin, Greek, English and French, making clear his determination to leave behind the hermetic world of Jewry for an experience of the intellectual world of the Gentiles. As the German protagonists of *Aufklärung* railed at the intolerance and bigotry of the clerics, so progressive Jews attacked the rabbinical tradition as perpetuating the isolation of the Jews and impeding their social and intellectual advance.

Mendelssohn put forward no new philosophical system, nor did he claim to have redrawn the map of knowledge. The last twenty years of his life – he died in 1786, a few months before his King – he spent in metaphysical reflection on the meaning of natural religion and the implications of a natural morality. The value of a religion, he maintained, lay in its influence on human conduct, not in any claim to the possession of an exclusive, revealed truth. One must acknowledge a plurality of religious truths to accommodate the needs and traditions of different individuals and peoples. This is the meaning of Boccaccio's parable of the three rings which Lessing used in his play *Nathan der Weise*, the hero of which embodies the wisdom and integrity of Mendelssohn himself. The directness and lucidity with which he pursued his arguments had already earned him the name of the 'German Socrates'.

But in the end Mendelssohn's central concern remains the fate of his own people in their historical context. True, the appeal for tolerance goes out to the rulers. But the oppressed too have their responsibility if hurtful prejudice is to be broken down and the rational ideal of a common humanity established. 'I can give no wiser advice to the house of Jacob than this,' wrote Mendelssohn in his last work, *Jerusalem, or On Religious Power and the Jews* (1783): 'Make your peace with the customs and with the constitution of the country to which fate has brought you. But also stand fast in the religion of your forefathers. Bear these twin burdens as courageously as you can'.

Through the activity of men such as Nicolai, Moses Mendelssohn and Lessing – who still awaits us – the cultural star of Berlin, city of the German Enlightenment, moved into the ascendancy. Yet if on the one hand there was a cultural scene that rested on the pillars of a noble *Aufklärung*, there was another contemporary reality of a very different kind that stimulated its own mode of literary utterance – the reality of war, as experienced in Frederick the Great's Silesian campaigns. An emerging consciousness of a Prussian role in European history, coupled with a declaration of homage to the monarch who had established that role, found literary expression in lyric poetry, the most famous collection of which was Gleim's *Preussische Kriegslieder von einem Grenadier* ('Prussian Army Songs of a Grenadier'), published anonymously in 1758.

For most of his career Johann Wilhelm Ludwig Gleim took his place among the so-called Anacreontic poets, imitators of classical models, whose chief representative as far as the Berlin of Frederick the Great was concerned is Karl Wilhelm Ramler, the 'German Horace'. But for one short moment, moved by letters from the battlefront written by a young Prussian officer and filled with a passionate devotion to his King, Gleim stepped out of the idyllic Anacreontic world and into the arena of brutal military reality. Here was a world of life and death, of comradeship and sacrifice, a world that the poet himself had experienced and about which he wrote with all the honesty and directness of the folksong. Indeed, the *Kriegslieder* were originally published with accompanying melodies, and it is of the common man and to the common man that Gleim writes.

As the *Preussische Kriegslieder* speak for the grenadier as he goes into battle for his King, so the King himself is apostrophised in odes by patriotic poets of Gleim's circle. At times, no doubt, such poetry sprang from calculated self-interest. More often it represented an honest, almost spontaneous response to the personality and achievements of a man whose greatness no one would gainsay. Such a poet, remarkable as one of the few women writers of the time, was Anna Luise Karsch.

Far from being the product of circumstances that would presuppose a sympathy with the values of royalty, Anna Karsch was the daughter of a peasant and innkeeper in a village on the Silesian border. A natural talent for poetry brought her to the attention of Baron von Kottwitz, who took her in 1761 to Berlin, where her odes earned her the title of the 'German Sappho'. Gleim, Moses Mendelssohn and Lessing all expressed amazement at the poetic facility of a woman with no formal education and from the most humble of backgrounds.

No doubt circumstances were largely responsible for inducing Anna Karsch to produce reams of uncritical verse in the fashionable Anacreontic mode, and the praise from above must have made her feel like a court poet in all but name. But in private moments she turned to the village life of her childhood and the joys of the countryside, writing heartfelt lyrics on subjects of common concern and on such politically sensitive issues as war and its aftermath. The 1760s, indeed, spawned their own patriotic songs inspired less by appeals to bravery and military glory than by the dark side of war, its cost in terms of human life and suffering.

But the Gleims and the Karsches of this world, interesting as they may be as products of their age, fade into the background in the presence of Lessing.

Gotthold Ephraim Lessing is one of the giants of German cultural history. When he arrived on the scene, the German language was still struggling for full recognition as a vehicle for the expression of high intellectual and spiritual values, and German literature was still searching for a personality from among the confusion of foreign models being recommended for imitation. By the year of his death there were on display Goethe's *Götz von Berlichingen*, *Werther* and the first version of *Faust*, Winckelmann's epoch-making *History of the Art of Antiquity*, Schiller's revolutionary drama *Die Räuber* and Kant's *Critique of Pure Reason*.

Son of a Protestant pastor, Lessing was born in Saxony, went to school in Saxony and studied at the Saxon universities of Leipzig and Wittenberg. But from the moment he set foot in Berlin in 1749, determined to make his name there as a writer and as a literary reviewer, the Prussian capital became his spiritual home. However many times he left it, usually under the cloud of professional frustration, he always returned.

He established his literary reputation in the early 1750s by publishing, in quick succession, firstly a collection of poems, essays and comedies under the simple title *Schriften*; secondly, the opening part of an extended series of articles on the theory and practice of drama, published as *Theatralische Bibliothek*; and thirdly, *Miss Sara Sampson*, the first *Bürgerliches Trauerspiel*, or domestic tragedy, in German literature, and a landmark in the history of the German theatre.

Current thinking held that the true model for German drama to follow was French classical tragedy, the modern repository of Aristotelian principles. Lessing emphatically and polemically disagreed. Conceding the pre-eminence of Greek tragedy, he argued that far more congenial to the spirit of German culture than the formal Alexandrines of Corneille and Racine is the free, more natural style of English drama, with the mighty figure of Shakespeare at its head. 'After the *Oedipus* of Sophocles', he wrote, 'no dramas exercise more power over our emotions than do *Othello*, *King Lear* and *Hamlet*.'

Moreover, advancing into modern times, Lessing points out that English dramatists, in the genre of 'domestic tragedy', have proven that drama can be generated equally in contexts of everyday middle-class life as in the distant world of monarchs and courtiers. Gone, too, is the need to use literature as a medium of moral instruction. Spectators of a drama must be directly moved by the events they witness, events with which they can identify. Thus: 'If a tragedy does not have the aim of bringing tears of pity and humane sympathy to the eyes, then it has no aim.'

But Lessing was not the man to leave the matter as a statement of theoretical principle. Taking his lead from George Lillo's drama of common life, *The Merchant of London* (1731), which he may well have seen performed in Berlin, he set about writing his own domestic tragedy. He gave it an English setting, upper middle-class English characters and an English title – *Miss Sara Sampson*.

The story, sentimental in the way the public of the time liked such things, tells of an elopement brought to a tragic end by jealousy and evil. By the end of the play Sara has been poisoned by her fiancé's former mistress and her fiancé has stabbed himself over her dead body. The sequence of actions is engineered rather than self-generated, the dialogue is more cerebral than spontaneous, and not even the heroine has, for us, the natural blood in her veins that would make her a living character.

Judged by the criterion of 'bringing tears of pity and humane sympathy to the eyes', however, *Miss Sara Sampson* was an overwhelming success. At the first performance in 1755, wrote Ramler from Frankfurt an der Oder to Gleim, the audience 'sat and watched for three-and-a-half hours, sat as silent as statues, and wept'. Everywhere it was the same story. Even in Berlin, whose citizens were anything but sentimental, it had audiences riveted to their seats, and no one, reported Gleim, left the theatre dry-eyed.

Further critical works punctuated Lessing's sojourns in Berlin through the later 1750s. To his last stay in 1765 we owe two of his most important works – an essay on aesthetics which he called *Laokoon* and the play *Minna von Barnhelm*.

In his *Laokoon*, a major piece of Enlightenment aesthetics, Lessing sets out to examine, through comparison of the classical Laocoön sculpture with

Vergil's description of the same scene in the *Aeneid*, what distinguishes the means proper to the visual arts – the arts of space – from those germane to literature – an art of time. Rationalist aestheticians were at pains to keep each art form within its proper limits: the one art must not be allowed to trespass on the preserve of the other but must follow the inalienable laws of its own nature. Only thus can the purity of art be ensured.

Today, when the tendency is rather to cross the boundaries between the arts, or deny the existence of any such boundaries, Lessing's concern may seem irrelevant. Even in its own terms *Laokoon* sometimes led to unreasonable conclusions, such as the denial of the validity of descriptive poetry – the grafting of an art of space on to an art of time. But it did help to clear the critical air by stripping the veneer of cultural fashion and social pressure from the work of art and focusing attention on the creative process itself.

The last work that Lessing wrote in Berlin, the wittiest and most entertaining of all his plays, was *Minna von Barnhelm* (1767). Set against the background of the Seven Years War, it exists on a number of levels. As a comedy of character and a comedy of intrigue, it tells how, after a series of misfortunes and misunderstandings, a Prussian officer and his Saxon fiancée are finally united. As socio-political drama, brimming with allusions immediately recognisable to the audience of the day, it lays out the social realities of the war – the ruthless Prussian occupation of Saxony, the misery of wounded soldiers, the shameless duplicity of police informers, the tensions in a society where the values of the aristocracy and the officer class are giving way to those of the bourgeoisie.

Finally, as a patriotic drama, written at a time when there was as yet no 'Germany' in a political sense, it calls for the cultivation of a national consciousness in a unified German fatherland presided over by the King of Prussia, Frederick the Great. A symbolic step towards this union is the final reconciliation in Lessing's play between the two main characters, Minna, the warm, emotional Saxon lady, and Major von Tellheim, the stiff, rationalistic Prussian officer. Practical difficulties and personal shortcomings now overcome, they regain the happiness intended for them, a happiness in which the audience delightedly shares.

In 1770 the restless Lessing made his final move – to the position of librarian to the Duke of Brunswick at Wolfenbüttel, where he died in 1781. 'I cannot tell you how desolate his death has left me,' Herder wrote to Gleim. 'It is as though all the stars suddenly faded while a wanderer was out walking, leaving only a dark, cloudy sky.'

Lessing, 'the founder of modern German literature', as he has been called, not only opened up a whole new set of directions in drama, in aesthetic criticism, in religious thought. Incorruptible, polemical, a man who called a spade a spade, he revolutionised the profession of letters and with it the status of literature. In the past writers had been in the service of a king or prince and their work had been conditioned by the needs and circumstances of their patrons. Now, with literary journals and the liberating power of independent publishing houses at his disposal, the writer's bonds of dependency began to drop away. The middle-class author spoke directly to a middle-class public. And because that public was becoming increasingly concentrated in the towns, it was only the towns that provided the economic and social conditions in which the free-lance author could – but might not – survive. Given the rise of Prussia and the dramatic growth of its capital to a population of 150,000 by 1786, the year Frederick the Great died, Lessing's constant returns to Berlin become a natural way of life.

Yet in the end even Lessing had to abandon the vagaries of a journalistic career for the security of the Wolfenbüttel library. 'A tame horse is kept in a stable, is fed, and has to do his master's bidding,' he wrote, with his customary bluntness. 'A wild horse is free to roam the plains – but perishes in hunger and misery.' We can at least be grateful that his 'stable' in Wolfenbüttel gave him the peace and protection he needed for his final statement of rationalist humanitarianism – the noble blank-verse drama *Nathan der Weise* ('Nathan the Wise'). Progress – material, intellectual but above all moral – is built into the human condition. Faith in that progress, in the education of the human race, sustains the earnest optimism that makes Lessing the most encouraging, most humane spokesman for the German *Aufklärung*. It is no accident that in 1945 theatres all over a defeated and demoralised Germany should have reopened their doors with *Nathan der Weise*.

The Theatrical Scene

The Berlin theatre in the age of Frederick the Great presents an image of confusion, of uncertainty, of stuttering beginnings and frustrated hopes. Much of the confusion derived from a collision of interests. Drama was in competition with opera for both royal and popular approval. The King's preference for Italian and French opera, hitherto unconditional, began to make room for the vernacular Singspiel. Even the familiar struggle between the rationalist reformers and the old *commedia dell'arte* tradition of harlequinades and Hans Wurst plays had not yet been resolved, and the Protestant Church, Lutherans and Calvinists alike, still looked on the theatre with ill-disguised suspicion.

In 1745 a well-known troupe from Leipzig led by Johann Friedrich Schönemann came to Berlin in the hope that the King would give his support to a serious German-language theatre. Among the pieces in his repertory Schönemann had a German version of Coffey's ballad opera *The Devil to Pay*, a successor to John Gay's *The Beggar's Opera*.

Nothing could have been more alien to the King's taste. To make matters worse, the public performances in the town hall also fell flat, and Schönemann became just one more of Berlin's theatrical victims. 'Despite all efforts to change the situation', he complained, 'the great majority of people still remain attached to the old abuses and improprieties.' The 'old abuses and improprieties' were flourishing at that very moment in the comic performances of the leading Hans Wurst actor of the day, Franz Schuch, who set up his open-air stage on the Gendarmenmarkt in 1754 and enjoyed a popular success which no other theatrical enterprise of the time could rival. But things were about to change – and radically.

It was a change which, as so often in the performing arts, forced itself through by a coincidence of energies pressing towards a common goal. From one side came theatrical producers and policy makers resolved to gain for their medium a new level of respect; from the other came superior material on which to base this rise in status. From the fusion of these two interests then emerged a third element, the solid physical expression of the intellectual aspirations which had given it birth – the purpose-built commercial theatre as a bricks-and-mortar reality.

This reality took the form of a timber-frame building in the courtyard of a house in the Behrenstrasse, behind Unter den Linden, built in the 1760s with an auditorium to hold between 700 and 800 spectators – Berlin's first permanent theatre. The dramatic material to perform on this and other contemporary stages had arrived in the form of serious adaptations of Shakespeare and translations of other English plays but above all with Lessing, then, a little later, with the young Goethe and the young Schiller. Finally, two men of the theatre now appeared on the Berlin scene, actor–managers, with a vision of how to create a new theatrical experience out of their new opportunities – Carl Theophil Döbbelin and Heinrich Gottfried Koch.

Döbbelin was already a familiar figure in Berlin when in 1768 he struck sensational success with his production of Lessing's *Minna von Barnhelm*. A few years later Koch and his troupe arrived in Berlin from Leipzig and capitalised on Döbbelin's success. He mounted the first Berlin performance of Lessing's domestic tragedy *Emilia Galotti* in the Behrenstrasse theatre in 1772, then, two years later, launched a sensation. An announcement appeared in the *Berlinische Priviligierte Zeitung*:

> Today the Koch company of German players will perform, by gracious permission of His Majesty the King of Prussia, a completely new drama in five acts, diligently put together in a highly original and unusual manner by a learned and skilful author: *Götz von Berlichingen mit der eisernen Hand* ['Götz von Berlichingen with the Iron Hand']. The work is said to be conceived in the Shakespearean vein.

For good measure, and knowing what would guarantee a full house, the paper added: 'Included in the play is a gypsy ballet.'

The headlong pace of Goethe's drama, the sense of abandon and the right to unfettered self-expression in the spirit of *Sturm und Drang*, a hero not from classical sources but from the national past, a thrilling historical moment to make one proud to be German – an amalgam of such elements made up what the age saw as 'the Shakespearean vein'. The King was disgusted and deeply offended. Lessing, champion of Shakespeare but not of this Shakespeare, was angry. The public were swept off their feet.

In 1775 Döbbelin bought out Koch's company and carried on where *Götz von Berlichingen* had left off, adding *Othello*, *Hamlet* and contemporary English plays to his repertory, as well as sundry Singspiele. Schiller's *Die Räuber* ('The Robbers') was cheered to the echo in 1783, as Goethe's *Götz* had been nine years earlier.

Variety was of the essence. The public pressed for more and more new works, a demand made the more difficult to satisfy by the custom of having a double bill most evenings – usually a drama or a Singspiel followed by a ballet, but sometimes even two dramas in succession. In an average season Döbbelin would put on a new production, in whatever genre, every two or three weeks.

The death knell of French theatre in Berlin – indeed, of the dominance of French culture as Frederick the Great understood it – had sounded. While Koch and Döbbelin were promoting commercial theatre for the public, the King was still trying, with a band of desultory and unreliable players, to keep the French performances going in his Berlin palace and at Sanssouci. In 1774, the year before Döbbelin's production of *Götz von Berlichingen*, he had even had a new theatre built on the Gendarmenmarkt as a Prussian Comédie française. It lasted a mere two years, and finally, in 1778, having lost both his illusions and his interest, the King dismissed the entire troupe, ostensibly on financial grounds, since yet another war with Austria was looming, but secretly relieved to be finally rid of his unruly *comédiens*. For the next eight years the building stood empty.

The World of Music

The dividing line between spoken theatre and music theatre does not run straight. The defining parameters – drama purely of the spoken word and drama in which every word is sung – are evident. But between them lie many possibilities: music to accompany dramatic text and underscore dramatic action; music, vocal or instrumental, introduced as interludes between acts and scenes; or spoken dialogue interspersed with musical numbers, as in the line from Singspiel to musical.

Singspiel was opera in the vernacular. Like any art form it had its conventions, as the public had its expectations. But it was home-grown, and the artistic gestures and sophistications it had evolved were German gestures and sophistications, both linguistic and musical. The necessary distance between the created work of art and the audience that approached it is still there but the degree of exoticism and irrationality – to use Dr Johnson's epithets characterising the genus of opera – is reduced to a minimum.

On the other side of town, artistically speaking, though in geographical terms merely a few minutes' stroll, stood the institution which represented throughout the reign of Frederick the Great a very different ideal of opera and a very different set of artistic values. That institution was the Royal Court Opera, today called the Deutsche Staatsoper.

From the days when, as Crown Prince, he had conceived the grandiose complex of the 'Forum Fridericianum', Friedrich planned a large, free-standing building for the southern side of the cobbled avenue that ran from the royal palace through the Tiergarten to the Palace of Charlottenburg – later the 'royal mile' of Unter den Linden. Although the primary function of the building was to be that of an opera house, it was also intended as a venue for ceremonial occasions and had therefore to convey an appropriate dignity and splendour.

No sooner had Friedrich succeeded to the Prussian throne than he set about putting his plan into action. To carry through the project he called on Knobelsdorff, one of the four great architects – Schlüter, Langhans and Schinkel are the others – who between the end of the seventeenth century and the middle of the nineteenth gave Berlin its unique Prussian physiognomy.

34. Royal Opera House, built by Knobelsdorff 1741–3. Etching by Johann David Schleuen, *c.* 1748.

The site of the new opera house just west of the town bastions had been chosen by the King and was not open to discussion. But it was a builder's nightmare. The whole of Berlin is built on sand, the sand of the Mark Brandenburg, and the marshy terrain near the Spree adds its own dangers. The larger the building, the greater the problems, and this was to be a structure some sixty-five metres long and twenty-five metres wide. Knobelsdorff may well have glanced across at the Royal Palace from time to time, remembering how thirty-five years earlier, in the days of Friedrich I, Schlüter's north-east tower had threatened to collapse and been dismantled piece by piece.

'This is one of the longest and widest theatres in the world,' claimed the proud architect in his report on the finished building. 'It resembles a magnificent palace, free on all sides, with enough space surrounding it to accommodate a thousand carriages with ease.' After an astonishing construction time of less than two years, and in spite of numerous unhelpful interventions and changes of mind on the monarch's part, the theatre opened on 7 December 1742 (Ill. 34).

It is an impressive building. Above its dominant external feature, the classicistic portico, is a programme of sculptures and bas-reliefs depicting Apollo and the Muses of Comedy and Tragedy, with statues of Sophocles, Euripides, Menander and Aristophanes flanking the entrance itself. But through that entrance lies a different world. Clear, classicistic lines give way to the ornaments of Rococo, concessions demanded of Knobelsdorff and his designers by contemporary taste. Everything was on a grand scale, as befitted the setting. The music historian Dr Charles Burney, who visited Berlin in 1773, was full of admiration. 'The theatre', he wrote in his *The Present State of Music in Germany, The Netherlands and United Provinces*, 'is insulated in a large square, in which there are more magnificent buildings than ever I saw, at one glance, in any city of Europe.'

In order to make sure that the world drew the appropriate conclusions about the relationship between Apollo, the heroes of Antiquity and the man who had erected this temple in their honour, the frieze on the portico was inscribed 'Fridericus Rex Apolloni et Musis'. With suitable pride and ceremony, in the presence of His Majesty and his ministers, the Royal Opera opened with a work which showed at once where the King's musical sympathies lay and what his artistic policy was going to be – a *dramma per musica* called *Cleopatra e Cesare* by Carl Heinrich Graun, court composer and the new opera house's first Kapellmeister.

As for Friedrich the supreme culture of the spoken word was French, so his ideal of the sung word was the *opera seria* of Italy. Like Hasse, Fux and others, Graun had studied in Italy and brought back the Italianate style of composition which the King demanded. To complement this he had recruited Italian singers and dancers to join the company in Berlin, the most famous of whom was the Venetian beauty known as 'La Barbarina'. This lady, wrote a contemporary source, 'had a remarkable effect particularly on the male members of the court and the aristocracy, by virtue not only of her exceptional skill as a dancer but also of her beauty and her physical charms'. Voltaire, well aware of Friedrich's homosexual leanings, remarked snidely: 'The King was a little in love with her because she had the legs of a man' (Ill. 35).

The season ran usually from November to March. On three days of the week there would be performances of grand opera; banquets, masquerades and other social festivities were held on the other days. Graun now had a substantial orchestra of some forty players and was able to mount two new productions a year, with four male singers (including castrati) and four female singers to take the solo roles. The chorus numbered twenty-four. The choice of works, inevitably, was the King's: many of them were by Graun himself, who knew what his master wanted – *Ifigenia in Aulide*, *Phaeton*, *Armida* and others on classical subjects. Also in the repertory were Pergolesi's *Adriano in Siria* and Hasse's *La Clemenza di Tito* (to the same libretto by Metastasio used by Gluck and Mozart).

The Royal Opera House had been built by the King, the costs of every production were met by the King, the salaries of the singers, dancers and orchestral players were paid by the King, and the day-to-day maintenance of the building was financed by the King. It was a shrine to Apollo and the muses, dedicated by a man deeply responsive to the arts. But it was also a symbol of a Prussian ruler's new-found mission and status.

To be sure, there was social segregation in the auditorium – the boxes in the first two tiers were for ministers, while officers and soldiers of the garrison stood in the pit and the general public occupied the third tier. But provision had been made for all except the lowest classes. The King himself sat with his courtiers in two rows of fauteuils immediately in front of the orchestra. Admission was free to all, although, as Lessing complained in 1750, tickets did not always find their way into the most deserving hands. 'His Majesty', Lessing reported, 'wants everybody, except those of the common masses, to be admitted to the theatre, especially visitors to the city. But the Royal will is not observed as it should be. One sees the best boxes occupied by degenerate trollopes while highly respectable folk are often being turned away at the door with the most offensive of remarks.'

35. The dancer Barbara Campanini ('La Barbarina') by Antoine Pesne, oil on canvas, c. 1748.

At the beginning of the Seven Years War there were hopes that the opera might be kept going but a succession of disasters intervened. The King needed his funds for the war and stopped investing in the luxury of grand opera. In 1759 Graun died. Finally, the following year Russian and Austrian troops bombarded Berlin and grenades landed on the opera house, putting an end to all activities.

By the time peace returned in 1763, the world had become a different place. The Italian singers had gone home. The incongruity of Italianate opera in a Prussia filled with patriotic pride became increasingly apparent, and that the enterprise still lay in the sole hands of the King prevented an evolution towards a broader-based artistic policy. Developments were taking place in opera – German opera – in Hamburg, Brunswick and elsewhere in northern Germany which showed a path that led away from the alien Italianate manner. To cling to the old values and the old composers was to atrophy – which had virtually happened by the time when, in 1776, Reichardt was appointed Kapellmeister.

The career of Johann Friedrich Reichardt is a microcosm of the musical culture of an age of transition. From a comfortable middle-class background in Königsberg, much travelled throughout Europe, counting Kant, Goethe, Moses Mendelssohn and Herder among his acquaintances, Reichardt had been engaged by Friedrich to breathe new life into the moribund operatic tradition of Graun and Hasse – a static medium for vocal and visual display, devoid of dramatic conflict and tension. But Reichardt had seen the powerful new operas of Gluck in Paris, which he wanted to perform in Berlin and which he took as models for his own works. The King found Gluck unacceptable. Relations with his Kapellmeister became strained, and Reichardt turned to other fields of composition, above all Lieder, of which he wrote well over a thousand in the course of his career.

Always in search of new fields to conquer, and resigned to the King's inflexibility, Reichardt had returned to Berlin from Paris with a plan for a series of 'Concerts spirituels' on the Paris model, at which vocal and instrumental music by Handel, Haydn, Reichardt himself and others was performed. These recitals, launched in 1783, would be interesting enough in themselves as being among the first, if not actually the first, open public concerts in Berlin. But they have an added interest in that Reichardt also provided written commentaries on the characteristics of each item – programme notes, in effect. For Reichardt is a man of the Enlightenment. Art is not a pastime or a distraction but a medium of education, a means to intellectual emancipation. As such, the work of art has to be not merely enjoyed through the emotions but comprehended through the intellect, and the listener's mind has to be prepared accordingly.

The opera house was now in a state of terminal decline, the object of increasingly destructive criticism, even scorn. The King withdrew almost completely from his capital to the rural retreat of Sanssouci, where his spirit found comfort. For the last five years of his life he did not set foot in his opera house.

'Only the French know how to create comedy, only the Italians can sing, and only the Germans can compose.' The opinion of Frederick the Great. He might have added: 'And only the Germans can perform.' For the cultivation of instrumental music had held a position of special esteem in the culture of the King's court from his days as Crown Prince onwards. In his palace at Rheinsberg he had an orchestra of seventeen musicians – flute, horn, harp and strings – which played contemporary works by Handel, Telemann, Hasse and others, including the Crown Prince himself, and was under the direction of Kapellmeister Graun. After becoming king, Friedrich doubled the size of the orchestra and appointed the two men whose names have become most closely associated with the musical culture of his court. One was Johann Joachim Quantz, the King's flute teacher, composer of hundreds of sonatas for his royal master's favourite instrument and the author of the earliest authoritative treatise (1752) on that instrument. The other, a figure whose career spans the Baroque-cum-Rococo decades that separate the world of Bach and Handel from that of Haydn and Mozart, was Carl Philipp Emanuel Bach.

Second eldest son of Johann Sebastian Bach, Emanuel was formally engaged by the Crown Prince Friedrich in 1738, at the age of twenty-four, and became chief harpsichordist to the new King two years later. He remained in the service of the Prussian court for almost thirty years – 'service' being a word to take literally, for in status musicians were treated no differently from the other domestic servants. Despite frequent demands he never received a salary to match that paid to Graun or Quantz, and in 1768, bitter at his treatment, he left Berlin to succeed Telemann as music director of the five principal churches in Hamburg, where he died in 1788.

C. P. E. Bach lived in, and through, an age of transition. As an intellectual he shared the spirit of rationalism in the company of men such as Ramler, Gleim and Lessing in the debating society called the Monday Club. Thought had first to be given to the purpose of music, as of all art, and only then to the act of composition itself. Music, he maintained, had to reflect human nature. It was a language of the emotions, a mirror of the emotional world of man, with the power, through the purification of human passions, to bring about a heightened state of inner contentment. Art is thus a means to an end, to the ethical objective of a virtuous man, and this should be as firmly in the mind of the performing musician as of the poet, the actor or any other artist. 'In subdued and sad passages [the performer] must himself be subdued and sad,' wrote C. P. E. Bach in his *Treatise on the True Art of Keyboard Playing* of 1753. And if art is to serve a higher moral purpose, one has not only to understand what that purpose is but also to be able to explain how one proposes to achieve it.

The very different musical world in which Carl Philipp Emanuel had been brought up unexpectedly returned one day in May 1747. The Berlin *Spenersche Zeitung* for 11 May reported: 'We learn from Potsdam that Herr Bach, the famous Kapellmeister from Leipzig, arrived last Sunday with the intention of savouring the delights of the excellent music rendered at the royal court.' When Johann Sebastian Bach – for it was he – presented himself at Sanssouci, the newspaper went on,

> His Majesty at once gave the order to admit him. As Bach entered, the King went over to the fortepiano and without further ado did personally play a theme which he thereupon required Kapellmeister Bach to treat in the form of a fugue. Said Kapellmeister succeeded so felicitously in this task that not only was His Majesty disposed to declare his most gracious satisfaction but also the entire company present was overcome by a sense of wonderment.

After his return to Leipzig Bach wrote a number of further contrapuntal exercises on the King's theme and dedicated the whole collection to him as *Das musikalische Opfer*.

Emanuel Bach's large output – oratorios, passions and other Church music, songs, symphonies, keyboard concertos and sonatas – is not poor in the contrapuntal techniques of which his father is the world's greatest master.

But even more patent is the new expressive purpose, the pursuit of emotional utterance, which these techniques are made to serve. Especially in the slow movements of his concertos and sonatas a surge of emotion rises on the melodic line, the quality the Germans call *Empfindsamkeit*. Melody is seen as a parallel to speech, following the rules of verbal syntax and expression. Emanuel Bach writes in his *Treatise* of the 'speaking passages' in his music – flowing melodies winding their way above a pattern of subtle harmonies and modulations.

What, finally, of the monarch of Sanssouci himself? A patron of the arts, yes, but far more than just the beneficiary of other people's handiwork. Both as composer and performer the King stood in the centre of the court's musical activities – in the music room at Sanssouci, in the Palace of Charlottenburg, or wherever he happened to reside. He even took his beloved flute with him on his military campaigns and practised in his tent in the evenings.

Indeed, although this was private music-making for his own pleasure and that of his courtiers, the King behaved as though he were waiting to go on stage. 'I could distinctly hear His Majesty practising *solfeggi* on the flute, and exercising himself in difficult passages previous to his calling in the band,' recorded Dr Charles Burney of his visit to Sanssouci in 1772.

Burney had generous praise for his royal host's playing. 'His Majesty executed the solo parts with great precision,' he wrote. 'I was much pleased, and even surprised with the neatness of his execution in the *allegros,* as well as by his expression and feeling in the *adagio.*' For the orchestra Burney had harsher words, writing disparagingly of 'the Berlin school, where *pianos* and *fortes* are but little attended to, and where each performer seems trying to surpass his neighbour in nothing so much as volume'.

Friedrich's repertory came from two sources: the 300 or so concertos and sonatas written for him by Quantz, which he played in rotation, and his own sonatas, over a hundred in number. There is a great deal of charming and accomplished music in these sonatas, especially in their slow movements, whose delicacy has something in common with the paintings of Watteau which the King so admired. Four concertos for flute and strings, in an attractive, forthright style akin to Vivaldi, have also survived, together with sundry arias composed to be inserted into operas by Graun. The royal example led to a great rise in the popularity of the flute in middle-class households, a rise comparable to that of the piano in the following century.

'Never criticise the compositions of a Royal Highness,' Brahms is said to have observed waggishly: 'You do not know who may have written them.' This particular Royal Highness needed no proxy.

As emotional and easy-going as his uncle had been intolerant and unyielding, yet sharing his love of music, Frederick the Great's successor, Friedrich Wilhelm II, confirmed Reichardt as his Kapellmeister with a generous salary and with *carte blanche* to compose and perform his own operas. The new King also broadened the scope of court music by appointing to his entourage Luigi Boccherini, whom he had met while Crown Prince and who remained in his service until the King's death. The interior of Frederick the Great's opera house, which had fallen into dilapidation, was replanned and re-equipped by Langhans and in 1788 the new theatre was inaugurated with the première of Reichardt's *Andromeda*. Alongside this and other Gluck-inspired works in Italian, Reichardt wrote incidental music and Singspiele for the recently opened Nationaltheater (later Schauspielhaus) on the Gendarmenmarkt, where first Döbbelin, then Iffland held sway.

The Nationaltheater, indeed, was slowly becoming a centre of musical life. Operas by Grétry, Paisiello and Martin y Soler were added to the repertoire, and in 1789, during a visit to the city, Mozart honoured the place with his presence at a performance of *Die Entführung aus dem Serail* – a performance, according to a contemporary report, which caused him a certain amount of irritation. A few days later he was invited to play before Friedrich Wilhelm II in his town palace. The King was an accomplished cellist, and two years earlier Haydn had dedicated his six string quartets Op. 50 to him. Following in Haydn's footsteps, Mozart, after his return to Vienna, wrote his own set of three 'Prussian' quartets for the King, with prominent cello parts. But he never set foot in Berlin again.

Reichardt too, a restless character with a gift for offending his employers, was close to leaving Berlin. During a three-year leave of absence in the years following the French Revolution, visiting London, Paris and other European capitals, he became involved in the liberal politics of France and published a book in praise of the republican constitution. The moment he returned, the King dismissed him, and, although later reinstated, he never regained his former influence.

Reichardt's music is rarely heard today. The scores of most of his operas and Singspiele have been lost, leaving Lieder – direct, unpretentious strophic settings in a conventional idiom – as the main source of our knowledge. When Goethe's novel *Wilhelm Meisters Lehrjahre* was published in 1795, it contained Reichardt's melodies to eight of the poems in the book. Goethe disliked Reichardt the man – Schiller called him 'insufferably aggressive and impertinent' – but approved of him as a song-writer whose settings 'convey a sense of the universal'.

From the middle of the eighteenth century the cultivation of music in prosperous private houses and the formation of amateur music societies flourished as never before. The demand grew for instruments, text books and printed music. In 1783 Johann Carl Friedrich Rellstab opened Berlin's first music shop, incorporating a lending library, where he sold harpsichords, clavichords, fortepianos, violins and other instruments, as well as sheet music printed on his own press. 'Besides the court orchestra and the various establishments maintained by other members of the royal family,' noted Nicolai in his *Beschreibung der Königlichen Residenzstädte* of 1769, 'Berlin can boast a great many private musicians and connoisseurs of music.'

The Church gave its own performances of masses and oratorios. Here again we meet the ubiquitous Carl Heinrich Graun, director of the Royal Opera. Graun's oratorio *Der Tod Jesu* ('The Death of Jesus'), first performed in 1755 by an amateur ensemble with Carl Philipp Emanuel Bach playing the harpsichord continuo, remained the most popular piece of Passion music in Berlin for years to come. It may be no *St Matthew Passion* but its arias have a melodic appeal and its polyphonic choruses a dramatic power – much of it derived from a richness of harmony – which make its success no surprise. It even withstood the competition of Handel, whose *Judas Maccabaeus* was performed in 1774 and *Messiah* in 1786 – the latter a spectacular Berlin première, with an orchestra of 180 and a choir of over one hundred. 'The intention was to emulate the recent performance in London,' wrote the court historian Anton Balthasar König. 'Berlin wanted to demonstrate that it was in no way inferior to the English capital.'

The Visual Arts

What a prospect opens up when the traveller enters through the Potsdam Gate, the Brandenburg Gate or the Halle Gate! Broad streets stretching farther than the eye can see, houses built after the best designs of the greatest Italian architects, avenues lined with tall lime-trees, palaces, public squares, monuments and buildings – all this induces in the new arrival a most agreeable sense of amazement . . .

Even more astonishing, as one passes through the Brandenburg Gate, is the sight of the pedestrians on the avenue of Unter den Linden, with its magnificent buildings. At the far end are the library [the 'Commode'], the Catholic Church [St Hedwig's Cathedral], Prince Heinrich's palace [today the Humboldt University], together with the bridge by the Zeughaus and its statues, the Zeughaus itself, the palace of the Crown Prince, then finally the Cathedral on the left and the Royal Palace on the right, a monumental and majestic building which stands apart, superior to all the others. All these pure masterpieces of architecture offer themselves to one's gaze as it ranges the length of the Linden avenue, near and far.

Such was the impression made by Berlin on a Dutch visitor in 1788. Others looked a little deeper, beyond the royal building programme, to devel-

36. *Unter den Linden*, etching, tinted, by Johann Georg Rosenberg, 1780.

37. Ermeler House, interior, 1760–62.

opments in the culture of the middle classes. Anton Balthasar König wrote in 1792:

> Bankers, merchants and Jews were beginning to make ostentatious use of their newly acquired wealth. They bought houses that had formerly belonged to leading figures in the state and had them furnished and decorated according to their own taste. Libraries and collections of paintings were installed that had cost large sums of money. Gardens were laid out, statues erected, together with grottos and other features which attracted the eye. They commissioned likenesses of themselves and their children and decorated the walls with them. And in order to give the appearance of being men of taste, they invited artists to dine at their table.

One way for Frederick the Great to put his immortal mark on his country was by military conquest and territorial aggrandisement. Another was by the erection of monuments to symbolise the power of the state and perpetuate the memory of his own eminence. When outsiders saw themselves confronted by the cumulative results of the urban extension projects of the Great Elector, of Friedrich I, first King of Brandenburg–Prussia, of the Soldier King and now of his son Friedrich II, they could be in no doubt about what view this state of Prussia took of itself. The street scenes through which the people strolled and rode in their capital are beautifully captured in the contemporary paintings of Carl Traugott Fechhelm and the tinted etchings of Johann Georg Rosenberg (Ill. 36).

Nor was it only buildings erected in response to the royal command that made a statement about rising prosperity. Merchants and manufacturers built their own extravagant town houses. One such house to have survived is the so-called Ermeler House. Originally standing in the patrician Breite Strasse, behind the Royal Palace, it was designed around 1760 by Friedrich Wilhelm Dieterichs, architect of the Princesses' Palace in Unter den Linden, for a supplier of military equipment to the King. The interior was lavishly decorated in late-Baroque and Rococo style: particularly elegant was the spiral staircase, in gilded wrought iron, that led from the vestibule to the ornate banqueting hall on the first floor (Ill. 37).

Buildings call for interior decoration and for contents. Open spaces such as gardens and public squares are invitations to landscape design and statuary. Frederick the Great, who refused to sanction a public monument to himself, was the first to have statues erected in homage, not to royalty but to distinguished servants of the state. At the corners of the Wilhelmplatz, for example, he set marble figures of four victorious generals from the Silesian Wars, two of them by Jean-Pierre Antoine Tassaert, superintendent of the King's sculpture studios. An interesting stylistic feature of these two statues is that the generals are portrayed wearing the regimental uniform of their command, complete with tricorn and sword – in other words, contemporary and realistic in aspect and consciously modern in artistic manner. Twenty or thirty years earlier a Prussian general would have been shown as a Roman commander, wearing toga and sandals.

The public squares of Berlin and the promenades of the Tiergarten park were for the sculptor like a void waiting to be filled. Friedrich Wilhelm I, true to form, had felled the trees in the Tiergarten over a large area of what had originally been the private hunting ground of the Electors of Brandenburg and turned it into a parade ground. Knobelsdorff had begun to 'recivilise' it in the early years of Frederick the Great's reign, erecting pavilions and summer-houses in secluded corners and lining the avenues with statues, most of them copies of Roman originals. The greater part of Knobelsdorff's conception vanished early in the following century, however, when the entire Tiergarten was redesigned by Lenné.

The grounds of Sanssouci, by contrast, have retained their original layout and offered from the beginning a magnificent opportunity for sculptural display. The native Baroque tradition descended from the great Schlüter had been wavering for some time and busts and statues had been imported from abroad, particularly from the Netherlands, when the need for such pieces arose. Now, under the stimulus of the new challenge, local Berlin sculptors, led by Friedrich Christian Glume, rose to the occasion and peopled the paths and bowers of the park with their figures. Glume himself, an amazingly prolific sculptor whose father had been a pupil of Schlüter's, left a number of classical figures and mythological scenes and was also responsible for most of the applied statuary on the façade of the Sanssouci Palace.

But it is not in works created for open-air display, or in the lavish exteriors of palaces and public buildings, that the exuberance of 'Friderician Rococo' makes its most powerful impact. That precedence belongs to interiors.

No other realm of activity illustrates more vividly the contrast between the Spartan, army-dominated years of Friedrich Wilhelm I and the intellectual, art-loving world created by his son. And nowhere is the *joie de vivre*, the sense of emotional release, the enthusiasm of artistic commitment more triumphantly demonstrated than in the interiors of Sanssouci.

For the banqueting hall beneath the central dome of Sanssouci Palace Knobelsdorff made a design of columns and niches, producing what the King described as 'a free reproduction of the interior of the Pantheon'. Otherwise Knobelsdorff left the interior designs in the hands of Johann August Nahl, the royal 'Directeur des ornements', who had already supervised the interior decoration of a new wing that Knobelsdorff had added to Charlottenburg Palace. In Sanssouci Nahl, together with the Hoppenhaupt brothers and other craftsmen, was responsible for the most perfect ensemble of private rooms in the palace – the recital room, the study and the library (Ill. 38). The 'Friderician Rococo' of Sanssouci Palace, its exterior and interior alike, is of evident French derivation. But it is a lighter, more airy Baroque than that of south German palaces and churches and expresses that sense of relaxation and serenity which its master sought within its confines.

For the wall panelling and gilding, the chairs, tables, bureaux and count-less other items of furniture needed for this extrovert flourish of a Rococo art-for-art's sake, the King recruited the best craftsmen he could find from all over Germany and abroad (Ill. 39). In one area, however, Berlin was to demonstrate that it could produce an indigenous school of craftsmen equal

38. The library at Sanssouci, designed by Johann August Nahl, c. 1745.

39. Escritoire by David Röntgen, 1779.

to the best that any other town in Germany could offer. That was in the craft of chinaware.

Strenuous efforts had been made all over Germany since the sixteenth century to discover the secret of porcelain. In 1709, in Dresden, a Saxon alchemist called Friedrich Böttger announced to his King that he had solved the problem. The following year, under royal patronage, a factory was set up in Meissen which produced the first pieces of what the world has come to know as Dresden china.

But the secret could not be kept for long. In 1751 a Berlin textile manufacturer, Wilhelm Kaspar Wegely, got hold of the formula and was given permission by the King to set up his own factory. Wegely's enterprise, however, fell victim to the economic difficulties caused by the Seven Years War, and in 1763 its assets were bought by the state. Only now, as the market for luxury goods returned, with a monopoly of production in the hands of the state of Prussia and under the eagle eye of the King himself, could the Royal China Works – Königliche Porzellan-Manufaktur (KPM) – embark on its successful challenge to the supremacy of Meissen.

Until the end of the eighteenth century the products of the KPM were directed unashamedly at the upper classes. Indeed, successive Kings of Prussia were among the factory's best customers, ordering specially designed table-ware, ornaments and figures for the royal palaces and as gifts to foreign dig-nitaries. As activity expanded to incorporate a humbler market, so simpler, cheaper ranges were developed, though without sacrificing the quality asso-ciated with the famous blue sceptre, which has remained the KPM trade-mark to this day.

As the tastes and wishes of Frederick the Great manifested themselves in architecture, in sculpture, in garden design, in the whole range of decor-ative arts, so also, finally, were they expressed in painting, the court art *par excellence*.

For the kings, princes, dukes and other landed aristocracy of the age, the collection of works of art served a number of purposes. On the one hand it was an economic investment. At the same time it was a demonstration of an awareness of intellectual and aesthetic values, coupled with a sense of history. Finally, it surrounded members of the court and their guests with the objects of beauty which completed the sense of luxury and well-being that permeated their social life.

Frederick the Great was heir to all these circumstances. But beyond this the paintings he collected and commissioned show a strong personal predilection for particular subjects and artists. In his Rheinsberg days and in the early years of his reign, when the French influence was at its height, he turned to the painters of the age of Louis XV. Captivated by the idealised, Arcadian portrayal of balls, *fêtes champêtres* and the theatrical world of the Comédie française, above all by Watteau, the King sent his agent to Paris to buy up whatever he could find.

But his taste was soon to change. Visiting relatives in Holland in 1745, he became enthusiastic about the paintings of Flemish and Italian Baroque masters. He sought out works by Rubens and his school, and a letter written in 1754 gives specific instructions for the purchase of paintings by Titian, Paul Veronese, Jordaens and Correggio 'at respectable prices . . . attractive, large gallery paintings'.

To house the new acquisitions the King commissioned a new gallery – like the Palace of Sanssouci itself, a single-storey Rococo building with a central dome. The glory of the gallery is its interior, a bright, long hall, the unbroken vista framed by the columns supporting the dome, with richly stuccoed ceiling and a flourish of plastic ornamentation. The Seven Years War delayed the completion of the building until 1763, by which time many paintings were already waiting to be hung. A catalogue compiled in 1770 lists 168 pictures, 96 of them from the Flemish school and 65 by Italian masters.

Not that one should idealise the historical reality of the period, for pre-cious works of art could sometimes be preserved in alarming conditions. 'Nothing gets cleaned or swept,' complained a visitor to the gallery in the

40. Anna Dorothea Therbusch, self-portrait, oil on canvas, 1761.

Berlin palace. 'The windows have not been washed for years and in many places the glass is missing. In wet weather the damp penetrates everywhere and ruins everything. If one wipes the paintings with a cloth, a torrent of water pours down.' Conservation was apparently not the Prussian court's strong point.

As to assemble a collection of Old Masters was to demonstrate taste and status, so equally was the engagement of resident court painters. And as his measure of cultural value was French, so it was to France that Frederick the Great looked in the first instance for artists who would both paint to command and train a school of German acolytes in their own traditions. It was his great good fortune to inherit from his father just such a man, one of the leading Berlin painters of the eighteenth century – Antoine Pesne.

Berlin and its Culture

41. Scene in the Tiergarten by Jakob Philipp Hackert, oil on canvas, 1761.

42. View of the Lustgarten with Royal Palace, Cathedral and Zeughaus by Carl Traugott Fechhelm, oil on canvas, 1785.

Pesne was born in Paris in 1683. After a stay in Italy in his twenties he was invited to Berlin in 1710 and appointed court painter by King Friedrich I the following year. His particular charge, which was at the same time his special skill, was to paint portraits of courtiers in their full finery and historical scenes from the lives of successive Hohenzollern rulers. Even the Soldier King realised the value of such a man to his court, and Pesne was one of the very few artists and musicians not summarily dismissed when he came to the throne.

But it was to be in the era of Frederick the Great, both as Crown Prince and as King, that Pesne's career reached its climax. To the continuing demand for portraits – of distinguished commoners as well as of the aristocracy – were added commissions for mythological and allegorical canvases and ceiling paintings for the palaces of Rheinsberg and Charlottenburg, as well as for the town palace in Potsdam and for Sanssouci. The brilliance of his colours and his attention to detail were ready grounds for Pesne's success (see Ill. 35). When he died in 1757, he was buried with great ceremony in the crypt of the German Church on the Gendarmenmarkt, where Knobelsdorff too had been laid to rest.

In one sense developments in art at court were responses to a set of self-contained circumstances. The court was its own world and generated its own momentum. At the same time the values that prevailed at court set the tone for other classes to follow. As the King and his courtiers posed for their likenesses by court painters, so members of the prosperous bourgeoisie followed suit, displaying their portraits on the walls of their elegant mansions in the fashionable districts of Berlin. Taste in interior decoration as a whole accepted the same stimulus, so that it would have been difficult to distinguish, at a glance, between a room in one of the King's palaces and, say, the banqueting hall of the Ermeler House, as furnished in the 1760s (see Ill. 37).

Private collections of paintings and etchings grew in importance, and with them the activities of art dealers. In 1786 there were in Berlin forty such collections. Publishers too were issuing volumes of prints and engravings for educational and study purposes. A spirited interplay developed between artist and purchaser, in which not only the reputation of the artist but also the nature of the subject matter came into the reckoning. Portraits, landscapes, animals and still lifes, mythological scenes, townscapes and historical pictures – these were among the genres represented. When in 1788 Friedrich Wilhelm II announced a competition for the best works in these individual classes, he granted pride of place not, as one might have expected, to portraiture but to history painting. His particular predilection was for scenes from the history of Brandenburg–Prussia, an area in which, strangely enough, Frederick the Great had shown a dwindling interest.

Over 300 representative works were put on display at the first exhibition of the Academy of Arts held in 1786, a few months before Frederick the Great's death. Among the portraitists of the age two names, besides that of Pesne, stand out. One is Anna Dorothea Therbusch, a rare case of a woman artist who overcame the prejudices of her time so convincingly that she was commissioned to do a portrait of Prince Heinrich, younger brother of Frederick the Great. A visit to Paris led to her election to the French

Academy, after which she proudly signed her pictures 'Peintre du roy de France' (Ill. 40). The other is Anton Graff, a subtle portraitist both of royalty and of *Aufklärung* intellectuals, among them Lessing, with a special gift for portraying women.

Director of the Academy at the time of the 1786 exhibition was a Berliner born and bred, Christian Bernhard Rode, whose work covered an extraordinary range. On the one hand he provided to commission the historical and allegorical paintings in the classicistic manner to which the court attached so much value, among them a long series of works depicting the history of Brandenburg. At the same time he was a prominent religious artist, designing funerary monuments for Berlin churches and cemeteries and painting large canvases on Biblical subjects, a number of which hang in the Marienkirche in Berlin.

At the other end of the spectrum from the world of portraiture and classicistic allegorisation stands the material world, the 'world outside'. The earliest known 'portrait' of the town of Berlin, by an unknown artist, dates from 1646, the time of the Great Elector and the Thirty Years War. Isolated etchings and drawings illustrate the growth of the town over the following hundred years but from the 1770s onwards the painstaking reproduction of prominent streets and buildings, with characteristic scenes of people going about their daily round, becomes a special artistic concern. Sometimes these views merge with landscape, as in a series of scenes of the Tiergarten, closely observed and sensitively executed, by Jacob Philipp Hackert (Ill. 41).

Depiction of the streets, the palaces, churches, houses, bridges and other features of the inner city become increasingly popular in the last quarter of the eighteenth century. For most painters it represented only one sphere of activity among many but one family made it the centre of their activity and left a whole collection of beautifully executed oils. These were the Fechhelms, who came to Berlin from Dresden shortly before the Seven Years War, bringing with them the influence of the contemporary Venetian school, above all that of Bellotto, Canaletto's nephew, who had been commissioned to paint views of the Saxon capital. Interesting in the work of Carl Traugott Fechhelm, as of his father and his brothers in Berlin, is the modification of the perspective in order to accommodate features which the painter considered important but which were not strictly visible from his chosen vantage-point. His manner is that of realistic observation but at the same time he has a vision of what his composition needs in order to convey a realism of atmosphere in which human figures also have their role to play (Ill. 42).

The growth in the popularity of townscapes has partly to do with an obvious sense of pride in the achievements of the capital of Brandenburg–Prussia. But on a more pragmatic level it was accompanied by the development of techniques of coloured print-making, which meant that the public for whom an oil painting was impossibly expensive could now afford a print which was to all intents and purposes a comparable original. Art was reaching deeper into the population.

Related to the Fechhelms in style and intent is the artist, originally a designer of sets for the Royal Opera, who most effectively opened up this world of coloured prints in late eighteenth-century Berlin – Johann Georg Rosenberg (see Ill. 36). Far from emerging by whim or to individual order,

Rosenberg's prints reflect the stages of a comprehensive plan for a set of four overall views of the town with twenty coloured prints of the most important locales. The attention to detail is remarkable. The aspect of individual streets, the variations of house type from one district to another, the design of doors and windows, the decoration of façades, the trees, the public water-pumps – here, as in Hackert's paintings, is a visual framework for the reconstruction of social history.

Equally revealing is Rosenberg's presentation of human figures. Before his time one might have seen the occasional associative character – fishermen in a boat on the Spree or soldiers parading in front of the Royal Palace. Rosenberg now fills the foreground with men and women – children and animals, too, if the scene calls for them. All is carefully and soberly recorded. The urban scene has become an integrated ensemble of architectural features and a human presence. The figures have no psychology and have barely progressed beyond the status of objects. The step towards a fully social art, the depiction of men and women of all classes at work and at play, in factories and drawing-rooms, in luxury and poverty – the contemporary human condition, in a word – was waiting to be taken. The artist who took that step was Chodowiecki.

Born in Danzig in 1726, Daniel Nikolas Chodowiecki went to Berlin when he was seventeen and hardly left the city again. Virtually self-taught, he first made himself a living by painting miniatures on enamel ware which he sold to the Huguenot merchants among whom he chose to live. Seeking to extend his range, he turned to painting conversation pieces in the manner of Watteau and conventional historical and allegorical pictures. But only in

43. *Frederick the Great Reviewing His Troops,* engraving after Daniel Chodowicki, 1778.

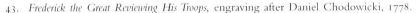

44. *Family Outing* by Daniel Chodowiecki, etching, 1775.

the 1750s did he discover the talent for drawing and etching which brought him success and made him one of the finest of all German graphic artists (Ill. 44). He left over 2,000 etchings and over 4,000 drawings. He also involved himself in the promotional work of the Academy, playing a major part in its reorganisation in 1786 and its annual exhibitions, and succeeding Rode as director in 1797.

Chodowiecki's world was the everyday, middle-class, urban world that surrounded him, the world of the man in the Berlin street and of the activities that took place within it. Nothing escaped his gaze. What that gaze revealed he converted into a realistic image, always penetrating, sometimes humorous, never aggressive – an art of sympathetic documentation. Even royalty is brought into the world of common experience. His famous engraving of Frederick the Great reviewing his troops (Ill. 43) portrays the ageing King, not as a towering superman but as the short, unheroic figure he was, 'Der alte Fritz', as he appeared to his contemporaries. But if there is no heroizing, neither is there any vilification. Chodowiecki's reality of the moment was a careworn Prussian monarch astride his horse, an objective *reus actus*.

The contemporary world is vividly brought to life in a series of drawings which he made on a journey from Berlin to Danzig in 1773 – domestic life, scenes at an inn, the state of the countryside. His shrewd humour also runs through a set of etchings depicting the ways in which various gentlemen of the time – an officer, a clergyman, a philanderer, a miser – make their proposal of marriage to the lady of their choice.

Even more influential in spreading Chodowiecki's fame than individual etchings and drawings were the illustrations he provided for books, almanacs, calendars and the like. Almost single-handedly he made Berlin the centre of book illustration in Germany. Goethe, Shakespeare (*Hamlet*,

Macbeth), Cervantes, Rousseau, Richardson's *Clarissa*, Sterne's *Sentimental Journey* – these were among the authors and works his etchings helped to popularise. So inseparable from the works did his illustrations become that editions without them seemed strangely incomplete. His virtuosity performed the same service for Johann Basedow's great educational *Elementarbuch*, an encyclopaedia of knowledge for use in the elementary schools of the time, in which Chodowiecki's amazing variety of illustrations made pages of verbal description superfluous.

When Goethe paid his one and only visit to Berlin in May 1778, he chose a highly eclectic group of people to meet – the painter Anton Graff, the poetess Anna Luise Karsch, Moses Mendelssohn and Chodowiecki. 'He is an artist I hold in the highest esteem,' said Goethe. True, it is art on a small scale. But like other great art on a small scale – Shakespeare's sonnets, the songs of Schubert and Hugo Wolf – it has the perfection that comes from truth to the nature of its genre.

ROMANTICISM

Prussia and the French Revolution

When a great leader dies, leaving behind him a political structure formed in his own image, the problem of continuity, ideological and administrative, can assume alarmingly destructive proportions. What the identity of system and ruler had united threatens to fall apart, 'the centre cannot hold'.

On the death of Frederick the Great in 1786 occupation of that centre passed to his nephew, Friedrich Wilhelm II, a benevolent, self-indulgent ruler well disposed towards the arts but incapable of presiding over the affairs of state. In the space of little more than a decade the old order had collapsed, not only in Prussia but in the whole of Germany. Partly this had to do with the familiar rivalry between Prussia and Austria, partly with their pursuit of self-centred, particularist policies that ignored the common interests of the German states as a whole. Above all, however, it had to do with the events on the other side of the Rhine – with the French Revolution, with the subsequent resurgence of France and with the wars that became the expression of that resurgence.

The political soil on which the Revolution grew in France was very different from that in Germany. While France was a metropolitan nation, Germany consisted of a congeries of disparate, autonomous territories, some Catholic, some Protestant. Political and social conditions made it unthinkable that the inspiration of the French Revolution could instantly have toppled the ruler of even the smallest of these territories. Especially in Protestant lands, Prussia at their head, the legacy of Luther had required an acceptance of the social hierarchy as a valid structure that not only generated an unconditional respect for authority but also, since the system exists with the implicit approval of God, invested that authority with an aura of religion. Frederick the Great, who saw royal power as human, not divine, and a monarch as subject to the law, like all mortals, had established his 'benevolent despotism' on just this assumption.

In return for this institutionalised politico-social inertia, however, the ideas and ideals that nurtured the Revolution penetrated all the more deeply into the intellectual realm. Liberty, equality and fraternity were not calls to the barricades but abstract concepts for philosophical investigation. With such ideals before them, ideals both rationalised and romanticised, German intellectuals saw in the French Revolution a personal liberation, a demonstration of the defeat of arbitrary power and the victory of a *Rechtsstaat*.

Behind the political rallying-cry of liberty lay the assumption of individual moral freedom, the acknowledgement of each man's right to self-expression and the full development of his own unique personality. The *Aufklärung* had pursued this aim through the liberation of the faculty of reason, based on the assumption of a rational universe and on the conviction that rational man was man at his most fully human. The inevitable reaction against this led away from the known to the unknown, from the rational to the emotional, from the analytical to the imaginative. Nature was no longer a mechanical construct operating according to laws waiting to be discovered but a wild, mysterious, awesome force to which we can only submit. Some call this force God, others are content to leave it as Nature. These trends find their spiritual home in romanticism.

The philosophical foundations of German romanticism were laid by Kant. Kant's epistemology rests on a dualism between noumena, or *Dinge an sich*, the ultimate essences of things which are beyond our experience, and phenomena, the experiential forms through which alone we can have knowledge of 'things in themselves'. In this transcendental concept of an ultimate reality beyond the reach of empirical knowledge romantic thought found its philosophical inspiration.

Thus by seizing on the concept of the ultimate unknowability of *Dinge an sich*, romantic writers could deny the exclusive rights of access to objective truth claimed by rationalism and seek the roots of knowledge buried in the subjectivity of the individual ego. Self-expression became a duty and the experiences of the heart took precedence over the operations of the mind. Dreams, mystical experiences, the irrational and mysterious, the symbolic world of religion – these became the new sources of inspiration as the limitations of rationality grew increasingly oppressive. 'Romanticism was a manner of thinking based on the mentality that believes in miracles,' wrote Henri Brunschwig.

Ironically, it was to be in Berlin, when the moment came, that the flame of literary romanticism would be kindled: ironically, because only a decade or two earlier the Prussian capital had stood at the forefront of the rationalist *Aufklärung* which the new young cultural revolutionaries now claimed to have consigned to history.

The Holy Roman Empire of the German Nation expired in the summer of 1806. Successive rulers of Prussia had done nothing to save it. Two months later Napoleon Bonaparte destroyed the Prussian army at the battle of Jena and on 27 October rode through the Brandenburg Gate and took up residence in the King's Berlin palace. The court of the new King, Friedrich Wilhelm III – the 'Citizen King', as he liked to be known – had already fled to Königsberg. The Berliners meanwhile were singularly phlegmatic about the fate of their country, and, as far as the demands of the French army of occupation would allow, went about their business as though little had changed. The official injunction of the day – a famous slogan that has since acquired an infamous history of its own – was 'Ruhe ist die erste Bürgerpflicht': 'The citizen's first duty is to stay calm.' The political fortunes of a humiliated Prussia had struck rock-bottom.

Yet almost at once they began to recover. In concrete terms it was a recovery based on a total recasting of the social framework, the abolition of serfdom and the establishment of a pattern of elected local government. The chief architect of these reforms, the name most readily associated with the political rebirth of Prussia, was Baron von Stein. But equally vital was the spiritual dimension, the appeal to that very force which two decades earlier had been unable to penetrate the entrenched realities of the Prussian state – the force of nationalism, released spiritually by the French Revolution and politically by the Napoleonic occupation. The most inspiring statement of this new position came from the man who was to become the first professor of philosophy at the University of Berlin, one of the most influential figures in the cultural history of nineteenth-century Germany – Johann Gottlieb Fichte (Ill. 45).

The significance of Fichte resides, on the one hand, in his statement of the extreme position of subjective romanticism, and on the other in the transference of this idealistic *Ich-Prinzip* to the realm of the state, that is, to a corporate German nationalism. By abolishing the Kantian dualism of noumena and phenomena, and thus the distinction between the material world and a realm beyond that world, Fichte turned what Kant had used as an epistemological demarcation into an assertion of absolute subjective freedom. The primacy of the subject was established and knowledge of the self became equated with knowledge *per se*.

Fichte's application of his solipsist philosophy to the broader realities of contemporary history and politics created a coincidence of interest between

45. Pen and ink sketch of the philosopher Johann Gottlieb Fichte by Johann Gottfried Schadow, 1814.

the ego of the individual and the ego of the *Volk*. Like Hegel after him, Fichte believed that it was the destiny of the German nation to demonstrate to the world the virtues of moral regeneration and self-sacrifice to the achievement of national ideals. From this faith emerged Fichte's famous *Reden an die deutsche Nation* ('Homilies to the German Nation'), starting-point of the recovery of Prussian self-respect and of the fateful doctrine of the autocratic, all-demanding, all-powerful state.

Fichte delivered his fourteen *Reden* at the Berlin Academy in the gloomy winter of 1807–8, under conditions of considerable personal danger. The city was under French occupation and it was no moment to be whipping up patriotic emotion. The intellectual *Zeitgeist*, too, posed difficulties. 'It was the peculiar feature of the Germany which Napoleon overran', wrote the London political review the *Round Table* in 1914,

> that her greatest men were either indifferent, like Goethe, to the violent upheavals of the period, or else, like Beethoven, moved rather by the abstract ideas evolved in revolutionary France than by any German patriotism. The ideal of that Germany was art and culture, not patriotism. Its vital forces were turned to the production, not of political efficiency or military leadership, but of Kant's *Critique of Pure Reason*, Beethoven's Ninth Symphony and Goethe's *Faust*.

Since, therefore, it is in matters cultural that Germany is pre-eminent, it shall be through culture, says Fichte, that she achieves the power to become a powerful nation state. Conversely, without that political power culture cannot flourish. Culture, moreover, is a unity, an organic whole in which – and nowhere else – the individual has his subject role to play. In passionate language Fichte invokes 'the consuming flame of that higher patriotism which conceives the nation as the embodiment of the Eternal'. For those whose psyche is attuned to such an idealist message, the course of duty is plain. Those who do not yet understand that message, which enshrines a moral categorical imperative no less absolute than that of Kant, must be taught it.

Thus to the overriding demand of loyalty to the German Fatherland is added the need for a comprehensive pattern of education. This need was met, on the one level, by Wilhelm von Humboldt's reform of the Prussian school system, involving the establishment of the Gymnasien and Real-schulen which have served Germany so well to this day. As an accompaniment to this, and in a sense its proud consummation, came the foundation in 1809 of the University of Berlin.

Paradoxically, it was to France, her tormentor, that Prussia owed her swift return to greatness. From the Revolution came the liberal ideals that spelt the end of arbitrary monarchic rule and the unchallenged privileges of the aristocracy, and the establishment of forms of government in which the people had a direct say. Had France not crushed and humbled her, Prussia would never have had to discover the resilience, the moral and spiritual fibre, first to cast off the Napoleonic yoke, then to assert herself as the leader of the movement towards national unification.

In February 1813 the Berliners greeted the Cossack cavalry as they drove the remnants of Napoleon's shattered army westwards after its disastrous

Russian campaign. The following month Friedrich Wilhelm III declared war on France, and the War of Liberation began. A year later allied troops marched into Paris, and it was all over.

'Romantische Poesie'

In May 1798 there appeared in Berlin, as the latest in an eighteenth-century tradition of such publications, a journal called *Athenaeum*, edited by August Wilhelm Schlegel and his younger brother Friedrich.

The *Athenaeum* proclaimed nothing less than a cultural revolution, a revolution captured in one word – 'Romantic'. The universal power with which the Schlegel brothers and their collaborators invested this magic word was stated with the categorical authority of a manifesto in the first number of the journal:

> Romantic literature is a progressive universal literature. Its mission is not merely to reunite all the separate genres of literature, linking literature with philosophy and rhetoric, but to merge poetry with prose, inspiration with criticism, the poetry of art with the poetry of nature. It seeks to make poetry living and social, and life and society poetic . . . Only romantic literature can, like an epic, become a reflection of the whole of life, an image of its age . . .
>
> Romantic literature is to the other arts what intellect is to philosophy, what social intercourse, friendship and love are to life. Other kinds of literature are whole, finite, and can be analysed in their wholeness. But romantic literature is in process of becoming – indeed, its essence lies in the very fact that it is in an eternal state of becoming and can never be completed.

On programmatic utterances such as this, derived from the solipsistic philosophy of Fichte's *Wissenschaftslehre*, rests the movement of German literary romanticism. The sentient ego is not just a means but an end, not a mode of experience but experience itself. Everything that is, is in the ego and for the ego. And as the capacity of the ego is infinite, so is reality also infinite, and any move to curtail that infinity in the name of 'objective' perception and analysis is condemned to the status of unreality. Where, in the familiar scheme of polarities, the classic view acknowledges objective truth, the drawing of lines of demarcation in matters of moral and philosophical decision as well as in the realm of aesthetics, the romantics plead for an idealistic totality, child of a free, uninhibited imagination responding to the absolute urges of artistic creativity. This is the framework within which Goethe delivered his famous diagnosis of romanticism as 'weak, sickly and morbid', while the world of classicism was 'sound and strong, blithe and fresh'.

The breeding-ground for the ideas that found their way into the *Athenaeum* lay in the debating societies and literary associations which met in the houses of the intellectual Berlin bourgeoisie. The most prestigious, frequented by Lessing, Ramler, Nicolai and other leading *Aufklärer*, was the Monday Club, founded as early as 1749. A few years later a Wednesday Club, more exclusive and more snobbish, was founded, followed by a Greek Society towards the end of the century.

But outshining these establishments in influence and popularity were two literary salons, cultural coteries founded on the contemporary Parisian models of Madame de Staël and her predecessors, and presided over by two cultured and stimulating Jewesses. The older of the two salons was that of Henriette Herz, where Fichte, Friedrich Schlegel, the turbulent theologian Schleiermacher, the composer Reichardt, the sculptor Schadow and distinguished foreign visitors were to be found. An atmosphere generated partly by the enjoyment of conversation, partly by a desire for self-betterment, and dominated by the idealised cultural and philosophical authority of Goethe, enveloped the proceedings. Members of the aristocracy rubbed shoulders with commoners, for the impulse to knowledge did not stop at the barriers of class. Even the royal princes, children of King Friedrich Wilhelm III, were taken to the Herz residence in the Neue Friedrichstrasse to watch the scientific experiments performed by Marcus Herz, Henriette's husband, one of the most distinguished physicians of the day.

Equally influential was the salon of Rahel Levin, later the wife of the officer and diplomat Karl August Varnhagen von Ense. Rahel, like Henriette Herz and other Jews of intellectual pretensions, found herself at odds with her Jewishness and used the activities of her salon to help her assimilate into the European intellectual tradition. Her touchstone of literary and philosophical values was Goethe, with whose lonely figure of Mignon, in *Wilhelm Meisters Lehrjahre*, she identified and in whose pantheistic humanism she found hope for the advancement of mankind.

Rahel opened her first salon in the Levin family home in the Jägerstrasse in 1790, when she was barely twenty. Among her early guests were Alexander and Wilhelm von Humboldt, Friedrich Schlegel, Schleiermacher and the novelists Jean Paul, Friedrich de la Motte Fouqué and Clemens Brentano. Kleist put in an occasional appearance but the milieu was not to his taste. The aristocracy, on the other hand, felt much at their ease. Prince Louis Ferdinand, the King's nephew, an accomplished musician and a man of broad culture, was a regular visitor, so, too, were a number of foreign diplomats accredited to the Prussian court.

But the defeat of 1806 brought these delightful proceedings to an abrupt end, and by the time Rahel launched her second salon after the War of Liberation, Berlin had become a different place. Of the array of romantic literati from pre-war times only Fouqué still lived permanently in the city, and from speculations on philosophical and aesthetic matters the centre of interest had shifted to political and social issues raised by the war and its aftermath. Writers in the romantic tradition for whom such issues were not paramount, like Chamisso and E. T. A. Hoffmann, had no dealings with Rahel's salon, preferring the atmosphere of convivial wine taverns and coffee-houses for their conversation.

The tendency of romantic literature as preached by the contributors to the *Athenaeum* was from the beginning towards a religious mode of experience. Appeals to mysticism; invocations of the Christian Middle Ages; delight in the divine beauty of nature but awe at her mysterious, sometimes destructive power; above all the cultivation of a metaphysic of music which would make that most profound of the arts a direct objectification of the force that drives the universe: values like these cannot but be subsumed, ultimately, under the designation of religious.

Two Berliners, their names inextricably linked, embody in their individual ways the kind of literature to which such an aesthetic gave rise. The one, who survived into his eighties and whose robust literary activity spanned half a century, was Ludwig Tieck. The other, who had nothing that could be called a career and who died a pitiful death at twenty-five, was Wilhelm Wackenroder.

Tieck, with his keen critical faculty and immense energy, his perception of what the new romantic culture encompassed, and his ability to convert these insights into literary form, makes contact in one way or another with almost all the motive forces behind the German romantic movement. Friedrich Schlegel once unkindly described him as 'a rough, very ordinary man who happens to have a highly developed talent'. But this talent produced remarkable results. One of the earliest of these was his exploitation of the fairy-tale, a literary form that lives in a world half real, half magic, where the supernatural and mysterious are more real than the physical and the rational because they are symbolical of a higher, ultimately religious truth. Its origins buried in an unfathomable past, the fairy-tale is touched with the spirit of the infinite, its meaning valid for all time. Art, like religion, is an allusion to that infinity, an experience of that meaning. Indeed, art, philosophy, religion, nature are all facets of a single entity, interchangeable realms within a divine cosmos.

To show what modern modulations were possible in this mythological world of fairy-tale, Tieck published in 1797 a collection of stories fusing the supernatural elements of the fairy-tale world with the psychological realities of day-to-day life. The most gripping of these stories is *Der blonde Eckbert* ('Eckbert the Fair'). Starting on the familiar plane of 'normal' human morality, it presents a chilling sequence of events which slip in and out of the paranormal world of suspended causality and potential destruction, until reaching their frightening climax in a revelation of incest, murder and madness.

Investigating another genre, Tieck turned to the heuristic power of art and its relationship to life in a rambling novel, *Franz Sternbalds Wanderungen* ('The Wanderings of Franz Sternbald'), published in Berlin in 1798. Taking its lead, like all novels of its kind, from Goethe's *Wilhelm Meister*, Tieck's story follows the career of a young painter who sets out to discover the works of the great Italian and Flemish masters and to achieve personal fulfilment through the reconciliation of life and art. In its way, the novel is a plea for the restoration of a lost Golden Age when the conflicts of the modern consciousness had not yet begun to tear the oneness of life apart.

This sense of the unity of life, a devotion to the Middle Ages and the Renaissance, and the interpretation of art as a religious experience link Tieck with the strange, ethereal figure who for one flickering moment was the guardian of the romantic philosophy of artistic creation – Wilhelm Wackenroder.

Few are the men of letters whose importance rests on so slender an *oeuvre*. He was born in the same year, 1773, as his friend Tieck, and went to the same Berlin Gymnasium. At odds with his domestic environment and with the demands of a professional career, the fragile, overwrought Wackenroder lived only for art and died in the struggle to reconcile the irreconcilable, art and life.

The fantastic title of the only collection of essays and reflections to appear during his lifetime not only says more or less all there is to be said about Wackenroder but also juxtaposes the basic terms of transcendental romantic idealism: *Herzensergiessungen eines kunstliebenden Klosterbruders* ('Effusions from the Heart of an Art-loving Friar'). The unrestrained expression of emotion; art as the experience that releases that emotion; the attribution of this experience not just to a man of religion but to the anchorite who has abandoned the material world for the contemplation of higher things: here is a repository of romantic values and an epitome of the romantic faith.

The focus of Wackenroder's artistic perceptions in his *Herzensergiessungen* is the Renaissance – Leonardo da Vinci, Michelangelo, Raphael, Dürer. The greatest European art was religious art, art *ad maiorem Dei gloriam.* Therefore the artist – painter, sculptor, poet – and the priest are one.

But one art has so far been left out of the equation, an art that reaches beyond the symbolism of carved and painted images, beyond even the appeal to mind and emotion made by the poet. 'Through words we hold sway over the entire globe,' says Wackenroder's Klosterbruder. 'But words cannot convey to our souls the invisible reality that hovers above us.' So, if words fail, how can we experience this higher truth, this 'invisible reality'? The romantic answer is: through music.

Of all the arts music is the furthest removed from material reality. It creates, and lives in, its own abstract world of consonance and dissonance, a world not subject to the public logic of rational experience or to the interpretation of objects or ideas. It offers a direct experience of ultimate, timeless reality to which the representational arts, employing the finite forms and language of human sense-perception and human thought, can never attain. But they try. Novalis' *Hymnen an die Nacht* is poetry for music's sake, a tonepoem in six intense, brooding sections. Tieck prefaced his play *Die verkehrte Welt* ('The World Upside Down') with a prologue which he called 'Overture – Andante in D major', orchestrating the text that follows as though it were a musical score. The supreme statement of this 'progressive, universal' romanticism – to use Friedrich Schlegel's definition – in discursive terms that match the totality of the demand comes in the philosophy of Schopenhauer. Its triumphant, all-consuming expression in music itself is the *Gesamtkunstwerk* of Richard Wagner.

Wackenroder's contribution to this world lay in his creation of the character of Joseph Berglinger, a Kapellmeister into whose mind he put his own thoughts on music and its divine cosmic function. Two fragments of a biography of Berglinger – that is, of a fictionalised autobiography of Wackenroder himself – conclude the *Herzensergiessungen*, and in the only other published work of Wackenroder's, the *Phantasien über die Kunst* ('Fantasies on Art'), his *alter ego* is made to reflect in a series of essays on a life devoted to music. That the power of art must prevail is never in doubt for the romantics. But it is a victory that demands as its price the renunciation of earthly happiness and the acceptance of alienation from 'normal' life, even to the point of paranoia.

In a famous lecture given during the last weeks of the Second World War, Thomas Mann identified in the German national character an inward-looking propensity derived from 'the musicality of the German soul'. 'The

relationship of the Germans to the world is abstract and mystical, i.e. musical,'
he said. And as to romanticism: 'What else is it but an expression of that
inwardness which is the finest characteristic of the Germans?' Nietzsche
closed the circle in the same terms. 'I fear', he said, 'that I am too much of
a musician not to be a romantic.' Suddenly there is much more at stake than
the mere history of a literary revolution.

Programmatic literary romanticism was launched in Berlin. But Berlin could
not hold it. Not only did the *Athenaeum* circle move almost immediately to
Jena but poets born in the Prussian capital saw no good reason to commit
themselves to it for life. Some outsiders were attracted by its reputation as a
centre of intellectual activity, others by the spirit of the War of Liberation,
scenting the trail of political liberalism and national pride. But few stayed for
long, while others came only late in their careers, when the wave of romanticism had passed. 'Like philosophy and painting', wrote the novelist Jean Paul
sardonically, 'literature in Berlin can only put down its roots in sand.'

One Berliner who remained faithful to the city for a significant part of
his career is the aristocratic Ludwig Achim von Arnim. Remembered today
almost solely for the most famous collection of German folksongs, *Des
Knaben Wunderhorn* (1805–8), which he edited in Heidelberg with his
brother-in-law Clemens Brentano, Arnim returned to Berlin and embarked
on a series of imaginative short stories. His wife, Bettina, later an affectionately remembered author in her own right, had a salon in Berlin, a rival to
that of Rahel Levin. But even this could not keep Arnim in the city. After
fighting with the Prussian army in 1813, he retired to the family estate in
the Brandenburg countryside and stayed there for the rest of his life.

Two gems of romantic storytelling from Berlin at this time have a special
charm. Both are the work of descendants of aristocratic French families and
both live in the romantic no man's land where reality fades into fantasy, the
material into the supernatural. One is Friedrich de la Motte Fouqué's *Undine*
(1811), the tale of a water-sprite who seeks to acquire a soul by marrying a
human. The other is Adelbert von Chamisso's *Peter Schlemihls wundersame
Geschichte* ('The Wondrous Story of Peter Schlemihl', 1814), the sinister, Faus-
tian story of a man who sells his shadow to the devil in return for riches,
lives to rue the bargain and spends his life wandering the world, telling his
moral tale.

Never again did Chamisso capture the magic of *Peter Schlemihl*. Indeed,
he had the wisdom not to try, accepting, as many of his romantic contemporaries were unwilling to do, that the nature of his literary genius predis-
posed him to be a miniaturist. Later, in response to a world that was changing
before his eyes, he turned to a lyric poetry focused on the social reality
around him. He was the first to confront in his verse the unhappiness of the
urban working class and the feudal landlord's abuse of power over his serfs.
He even addressed a poem to the newly invented railway locomotive – the
'steam stallion', he called it.

It was in these smaller literary forms – lyric poem, short story, fairy-tale
– that the romantic impulse was at its most natural and therefore most aesthetically satisfying. Since the universe was seen as infinite, and life as
dynamic – not being but eternally becoming – any attempted imposition of

an order or a pattern was artificial and arbitrary, an unnatural inhibition, in art as in life. True reality can be apprehended only through the fragmentary and the incomplete. Love, nature, beauty are infinite: our experience of them comes as a flash, a precious moment of insight. But to collect these moments and to try to arrange them in order – and *a fortiori* in causal sequence – can only falsify reality. All such subjective moments, whoever the person to whose experience they belong, are, in the literal sense of the word, equivalent.

One literary casualty of this philosophy is the novel. The novel *qua* genre implies a planned sequence of events, whether in a known social context or in a world of allegory, directed towards a moral outcome, a pattern for which certain material is selected and other material excluded. But this offends against the doctrine of romantic literature as 'progressive' and 'universal', in Friedrich Schlegel's sense. The formlessness of Schlegel's own infamous novel *Lucinde* and the meanderings of Novalis' uncompleted and uncompletable *Heinrich von Ofterdingen* show how the genre takes its revenge.

A similar fate befalls the drama. Drama rests on the principle of conflict, of tension. The resolution of conflict implies the assertion of one principle, one individual, over another, or, put negatively, the surrender of one side to another, whereas in the romantic aesthetic all sides claim an equal validity and an equal representation. Tieck left a handful of fairy-tale-like comedies that lie outside these terms of reference but the undramatic dramas of Arnim and Brentano are among their predictable victims.

When, therefore, one confronts in this romantic period a literature of dramatic strength, a literature of its age yet resting on timeless principles of dramatic conflict, one must suspect that it is a literature too big for conventional categorisation. So it is with the work, above all the plays, of one of the most powerful, at the same time most tragic figures in the whole of German literature – Heinrich von Kleist.

Born in Frankfurt an der Oder in 1777, Kleist served for seven years in the Prussian army, then travelled restlessly across Europe in search of a civilian role. After a period in the Prussian civil service and two years as an editor and writer in Dresden, he finally moved to Berlin in 1810. A year later he shot himself.

Kleist had arrived in Berlin with a portfolio of earlier works still in manuscript – *Der zerbrochne Krug*, *Das Käthchen von Heilbronn*, *Die Hermannsschlacht* – and in his mind were new thoughts he wanted to share with the Berlin public. To do this he created his own medium, a four-page newspaper, launched with high expectations and great publicity, called *Berliner Abendblätter*, with himself as editor and principal correspondent. It contained topical news items of national and local interest, announcements of cultural events and theatrical and musical reviews.

The initial response of the public to Kleist's paper was enthusiastic, not least because it came out daily, whereas the two existing leading Berlin papers, the *Vossische Zeitung* and the *Spenersche Zeitung*, appeared only three days a week. All sections of the reading population bought it, including the King, and such was its quality that parts were reprinted in newspapers elsewhere in the country. But the success could not last. Censorship of its political material became more irritating, the topics for discussion came to focus increasingly on Kleist's personal concerns and public interest began to flag.

The publisher complained that it was losing money and after five months it came to an end, the victim of circumstances rather than editorial miscalculation. In the course of its short life the *Berliner Abendblätter* did, however, give to the world three superb examples of Kleist's writing from the last year of his short life – a remarkable essay called 'Über das Marionettentheater' and two short stories.

In some respects the power of Kleist's mind, a savage power at times almost unbearable, is at its most intense, yet most fully under artistic control, in his narrative prose rather than in the dramas for which he is more readily remembered. His short stories centre on extreme characters or extreme situations – often the one engenders the other – and are concerned with violent, deeply disturbing, often criminal acts. They have the tension and excitement of the high-class thriller but at the same time a philosophy of the moral existence within which the terrible events follow their destructive course.

So *Das Bettelweib von Locarno* ('The Beggar Woman of Locarno'), one of the two stories serialised over a number of issues of the *Berliner Abendblätter*, tells of a woman whose ghost returns to haunt the castle of the Marquis who was responsible for her death; driven out of his mind, the Marquis sets fire to his castle and kills himself. In *Die heilige Cäcilie oder die Gewalt der Musik* ('St Cecilia or the Power of Music') the angel of vengeance descends on the gang of young vandals who have come to destroy the religious images in a convent chapel but are thwarted by the miraculous appearance of St Cecilia at the organ. This vision strikes the young men with a religious mania which causes them to spend the rest of their days as hermits in the convent, doing nothing but recite the holy offices and sing the praise of the Lord.

The subject matter is romantic, fantastic, supernatural; the manner is utterly realistic, the quivering language direct, intense, modern. The long, winding sentences and never-ending paragraphs of Kleistian syntax, unique in German literature, generate a dense, almost impenetrable atmosphere from which one finally struggles free, emotionally drained, with a tragic resolution of an overwhelming moral conflict.

The same mercilessness pervades the longest and most involved of Kleist's stories, *Michael Kohlhaas*, also completed in Berlin. An upright citizen is driven to crimes of violence in order to gain the justice due to him, and freely submits to the death penalty passed on him only after the offences he himself has suffered have been acknowledged and purged. The parallel between the injustice inflicted on a law-abiding citizen by a tyrannical overlord and the situation of Prussia under the heel of Napoleon was not lost on Kleist's readers.

In the little essay 'Über das Marionettentheater' Kleist uses the figure of the puppet, symbol of graceful, natural movement, to return to the antithesis between the intuitive and the cogitated, the spontaneous and the premeditated. In an argument recalling Rousseau, he sees man as having lost his natural purity and assurance through his exercise of the destructive power of reason. The result is an existence in disharmony, a civilisation at odds with itself. Since we cannot acquire the natural grace of the puppet, i.e. cannot regain lost innocence by regression, we have no alternative but to gather more knowledge through the exercise of our rational powers until we pass, by cyclical motion, from the finite world to infinity, to the Golden Age of legend, to the once lost state of ideal purity.

More important than to point to the fanciful assumptions and inconsistencies in Kleist's visionary argument is to view it as a utopian reconciliation of the destructive dualism in man of thought and feeling, the rational and the irrational. The characteristic romantic answer was to allow the subjective, emotional powers to flood our consciousness, to force the analytical to submit to the intuitive, the finite to the eternal. The claims of the spirit are absolute: world and spirit cannot exist side by side on equal terms. But Kleist dreams of an ultimate divine harmony in which thought and feeling, as equal realities, shall be embraced by a single understanding. The return to longed-for oneness and purity, which will mark the end of the history of the world, will have its supreme place in the same continuum as the pristine innocence of the Garden of Eden and as the partaking of the tree of knowledge that destroyed that innocence.

A practical demonstration of the happiness that will attend this reconciliation is offered by Kleist's last and greatest play, completed during the final year of his life – *Prinz Friedrich von Homburg*.

The play centres on the battle of Fehrbellin in 1675, when the young Prince of Homburg disobeys an order from the Elector of Brandenburg in the field yet succeeds in routing the enemy Swedish forces. His victory, however, is no alibi: he is court-martialled for disobedience and sentenced to be shot. Shattered by the prospect of death, he pleads in prison for his reprieve, as do his fiancée Natalie, the Elector's niece, and the whole army. But the Elector will give way only if Homburg claims the verdict to be unjust. This he cannot do, and he accepts his fate. Whereupon the Elector, satisfied that Homburg has now achieved true moral manhood, countermands the sentence of death and reunites him with Natalie.

In the character of the Prince the familiar antitheses of dream and reality, emotion and reason, the personal and the social, find an ultimate reconciliation. Starting in the natural world of his emotions, where harmony reigns – as in the puppet's state of natural grace in 'Über das Marionettentheater' – he moves into an area of conflict between his desire to live and admission of his guilt. Pursuing the path of deeper understanding, he reaches a higher state of grace and closes the ideal circle. It is, in its way, a classical, not a romantic solution, conveyed within the discipline of some of the most majestic blank verse in the German language. Seen as a whole, indeed, the progress of Kleist's work could be described as an application of romantic means to a classical end – in *Prinz Friedrich von Homburg* even a 'happy end'. But the validity of the resolution did not reach beyond the literary page. In life he saw no end but suicide.

The designation 'romantic', in its programmatic, philosophical form, may not penetrate the heart of the work of Kleist. But no word more satisfyingly describes one of the most exotic figures on the Berlin cultural stage in the early nineteenth century, one of the comparatively few German writers whose names have become familiar outside the German-speaking world – E. T. A. Hoffmann.

A native of Königsberg, in remote East Prussia, Hoffmann led an unstable, unpredictable life that itself reads like a novel. Having studied law in his home town, he worked for a time in Prussian government service in Berlin and elsewhere, but his real love was music. A self-taught composer, he became a music critic and Kapellmeister at the theatre in Bamberg, soon leaving in disgust at the cultural philistinism of the public he was expected to serve. Unable to make a living through art, he rejoined the Prussian civil service in Berlin in 1814 as a legal assessor to the appeal court and continued to sit on the bench until his death in 1822, repairing in the evening to Lutter and Wegner's wine-cellar behind the Schauspielhaus, then returning home to work feverishly through the night on the stories that made him famous.

Hoffmann combines in an extraordinary way individual aspects of romanticism which had hitherto been given an independent validity. Take, for example, the complex of themes embraced by the destructive dichotomy of art and life, based on the assumption that the two are incompatible – an assumption that Hoffmann had tried, and failed, to negate in his own life. What more poignant depiction of the agonies endured by the artist than his fragments of the biography of Kapellmeister Johannes Kreisler, his *alter ego*?

The eccentric, unsettling figure of Kreisler was an early creation of Hoffmann's who accompanied his master to the end of his life. Initially Hoffmann sets him in particular social situations to show the indignities he suffers at the hands of a culturally illiterate public. To these social cameos Hoffmann then added sundry musings and *aperçus* on music and the nature of artistic creation and published the collection under the title of *Kreisleriana*. But still lurking in his mind was the urge to draw together the strands of Kreisler's experience in a single narrative so that his final word on the life of the artist might be uttered – which is to say, his final act of self-revelation performed.

Thus emerged over the last three years of his life the unfinished novel – could one imagine it ever being finished? – *Kater Murr* ('Murr the Tom-Cat'), formally one of the most astonishing pieces of European fiction. The astonishment begins with the full title: *Murr the Tom-Cat's Philosophy of Life, Together with a Fragmentary Biography of Kapellmeister Johannes Kreisler, On Old Sheets of Waste Paper.* Murr, Hoffmann's cat, who has learnt to read and write, records his life story on the reverse side of some sheets of an incomplete biography of Kreisler that he has found lying on his master's desk. Hoffmann pretends to have stumbled across these sheets and had them published as they stand: a page of Murr's autobiography thus alternates with a page of the Kreisler story throughout the book, which comes to an abrupt stop with Murr's death.

This fanciful device conveys the overt ironical symbolism of the opposition between Murr, the animal turned pseudo-intellectual, and Kreisler, the man of the spirit. Beyond this Murr stands as a mocking image of the presumptuous confidence of the rationalist mind in the limitless powers of the intellect, to the exclusion of the intuitive and the spiritual. Hoffmann–Kreisler, the Berlin romantic, looks back at, and down on, the Berlin *Aufklärung* of the previous century.

As the outward course of Kreisler's life presents a discursive social reality, so Hoffmann uses his hero – anti-hero – as a spokesman for the romantic philosophy of music lived out by Wackenroder's Joseph Berglinger and systematised in Schopenhauer's *Die Welt als Wille und Vorstellung*. 'Art is the mediator between ourselves and the eternal universe,' writes Hoffmann. 'Our only really clear sense of the universe is through art.'

It is from these Berlin years, the last years of his life, that most of Hoffmann's famous 'tales of mystery and imagination' come (to use Edgar Allan Poe's title), stories that probe the supernatural – hypnotism, telepathy, schizophrenia, the *Doppelgänger* phenomenon, the behaviour of minds under intolerable and unnatural pressure. Character after character is driven by the uncontrollable demon within him to acts of destruction, often psychological self-destruction, sometimes even murder. Hoffmann knew the Jekyll-and-Hyde syndrome long before Robert Louis Stevenson. He is the master of the dark side of life, where man is at the mercy of forces beyond his reach and where the writ of conventional morality does not run. Incomprehension and impotence lead to madness – which is where Kapellmeister Kreisler and his fellow-victims of the regime of art re-appear on the scene.

If one were looking for a single work in which the component parts of Hoffmann's complex world combine in a grippingly modern narrative, one could well light on *Das Fräulein von Scudery*, written in 1818. It is the case history of a murderer, a goldsmith, one of the great craftsmen of his day, whose victims are those who have commissioned his works. Unable to bear the thought that his artefacts are in unworthy hands, he murders the owners and reclaims his masterpieces for himself. All this is done in the name not of material gain but of art. Moreover, although the goldsmith is as conscious of his motives as he is of his crimes, he is impelled by dark, uncontrollable forces to act as he does and can only see himself as a creature of fate.

The Faust figure of legend, the man who sold his soul to the devil, should, said Thomas Mann, have been a musician rather than a scholar, for 'music is demonic territory'. By this token Hoffmann's goldsmith in *Das Fräulein von Scudery*, too, should have been a musician. At least his creator was. That art, not life, should have the last word in a discussion of literary romanticism is as it should be.

A New Theatre

Frederick the Great had disbanded his theatre on the Gendarmenmarkt in 1778. When it reopened in 1786 there was a new king on the throne and a new spirit abroad in the Berlin court.

The genial, gregarious Friedrich Wilhelm II set great store by the arts. One of his first acts was to rechristen his uncle's old French playhouse the Nationaltheater and to give its actors the imposing title of Königlich Preussische Allergnädigst General-Priviligirte National-Schauspieler. Gone were the days of a dilettante Francophile entertainment. Theatre was now a matter of serious national concern, with a mission to address the state of public morality and public culture. The Nationaltheater became quite literally a nationalised enterprise, its funds provided by the state and its policies in the hands of trustees nominated by the King. At the 'upper' end of the repertory were *Macbeth, Romeo and Juliet, Hamlet* and other Shakespearean plays, in productions that included incidental music by Reichardt, Franz Benda and other prominent composers of the day. At the other end, more immediately welcomed by the public, were sentimental middle-class family dramas by contemporary playwrights, above all by the man who, as actor, producer and dramatist, came to dominate Berlin theatre, and with it German theatre as a whole, for twenty years – August Wilhelm Iffland.

A man of the theatre through and through, Iffland had since 1779 been an actor at the Nationaltheater in Mannheim. Enticed by a generous offer from the King of Prussia, he settled in Berlin in 1796 and took control of the Nationaltheater. Not only did he combine the functions of artistic director, producer and business manager, he also took key roles in his own plays and in the great classics of the day – Octavio Piccolomini in Schiller's *Wallenstein*, Wilhelm von Oranien in Goethe's *Egmont*, the title role in Schiller's *Wilhelm Tell* and in Lessing's *Nathan der Weise*.

Friedrich Wilhelm II died only one year into Iffland's regime but his son Friedrich Wilhelm III saw theatre-going as a gesture of identification with the activities of his people, and when Iffland pointed out that the existing theatre was now far too small for a rapidly growing public, the King readily consented to its extension. The fine new Nationaltheater, designed by Langhans for an audience of 1,800, opened in 1801.

Not that all theatre-goers deported themselves with decorum. Theatres had always been places for vanity and flirting, and the privacy of the boxes permitted intimacies that had little to do with the action on the stage. A contemporary collection of anecdotes and sketches reports an occasion when 'a certain master butcher, believe it or not, applauded the performance from his box by slapping the bare cheeks of his mistress' backside with his Herculean hand, making the whole theatre echo to the sound'. Apparently there have always been theatre-goers who are there less to see than to be seen – or in this case, heard.

Such flippancies aside, Iffland brought the Berlin theatre to a cultural eminence that it had never before enjoyed. When Schiller visited the Prussian capital the year before he died, Iffland honoured the occasion by mounting a festival of his complete plays, every performance of which the author attended. Schiller contemplated moving to Berlin from Weimar but concluded that it would be too expensive. 'There is a great measure of personal freedom there,' he wrote to his friend Körner: 'civilian life is very relaxed and music and theatre have a great deal to offer.' 'But', he added slily, 'the pleasure they give is not remotely commensurate with what they cost.'

Iffland was to reach the pinnacle of his fame a few years later, when in 1811 Friedrich Wilhelm III combined the Nationaltheater and the Royal Opera House, together with orchestra, singers, *corps de ballet*, sets, costumes and all other equipment, under one single administration, and put Iffland in charge. Iffland did not live to enjoy his position of eminence for long. But at the time this concentration of power over the artistic policies of both theatre and opera made him supremo of the largest theatrical empire in Germany.

The Establishment and the Visual Arts

The atmosphere of liberation and self-fulfilment generated in the last quarter of the eighteenth century by the American and French revolutions, then intensified by the War of Liberation of 1813–15, encompasses philosophical and literary tendencies conveniently styled romantic. These tendencies, moreover, have their contemporary parallels in English, French and other literatures, giving credence to the concept of romanticism as an European phenomenon. That the *Athenaeum*, the manifesto of German literary romanticism, had been launched in Berlin in 1798 fortified the realisation among the intelligentsia that the cultural life of their capital had a vitality equal to that of any European city.

But in the other arts at this time different values prevailed. Romantic painting, properly so called, did not reach Berlin until 1810, the year when two of Caspar David Friedrich's early works were first exhibited and the time when Schinkel did his earliest landscapes. Music was in the thoroughly eighteenth-century hands of men like Reichardt and Zelter. Beethoven's symphonies were heard shortly after their composition but *Fidelio* was performed only in 1815, and Weber's *Der Freischütz*, most romantic of operas, in 1821.

The most striking contrast between literature and the other arts at the turn of the eighteenth century is with architecture and sculpture. Literature has overcome the age of *Aufklärung* and now calls itself romantic. Architecture has left Baroque and Frederician Rococo behind and turned to classicism. Madame de Staël visited the city in 1804 and was impressed with the amount of recent new building. 'Berlin', she wrote, 'is a large city with broad, straight streets and regular in design. For the most part it has been built in recent times and there are few traces of earlier ages. There are no Gothic structures among the modern edifices and the new buildings are in no way interrupted by old ones or forced into gaps between them.'

In fact, in certain parts of the city quite a number of older buildings had survived, though these were not the fashionable districts in which visitors would expect to find themselves, especially aristocratic ladies such as Anne Louise Germaine de Staël. For her the natural historical centre of the city was the area that had grown up round the Royal Palace and Unter den Linden. Yet even here she claimed to detect a discrepant, strangely unsatisfactory relationship between the citizens and the buildings in their midst. Berlin was indeed a thoroughly modern city, she conceded, 'but nowhere does the character of the inhabitants reveal the stamp of the history of their country, and these magnificent new buildings seem destined only for convivial social gatherings and commercial purposes'.

Like his uncle, and like the son who was to succeed him at the end of the century, King Friedrich Wilhelm II had architectural pretensions. Also like them, he wanted to set his seal on his capital with the help of a leading architect of the day. Frederick the Great's mentor had been Knobelsdorff, designer of the Forum Fridericianum, of the opera house, of St Hedwig's Cathedral and of much else. In the coming century Friedrich Wilhelm III was to call on Schinkel, greatest of all Berlin architects. In between, charged by Friedrich Wilhelm II with the task of making his Berlin a neo-classical capital, came Carl Gotthard Langhans.

The classicistic movement, the formulation of whose ideals owes much to Winckelmann, united the inherited values of the aristocracy and the growing aspirations of a prosperous bourgeoisie under an aesthetic statement of harmony, grandeur and serenity. The clarity and purity of line in the noble buildings of Greece and Rome, the air of rationality and controlled power that they exuded, became the inspiration for the architecture of the present. The new King made over 5 million talers available for public buildings and monuments in the new spirit, while the well-to-do middle classes built themselves residences in a commensurate style.

A widely travelled man, then in his fifties, Langhans was invited to Berlin from his native Silesia in 1786. At the King's bidding he undertook classicistic alterations to the interiors of Charlottenburg, Bellevue and other royal palaces and extended the Nationaltheater on the Gendarmenmarkt. He was also a founder member of the influential Bauakademie, an institution established on the model of the Ecole Polytechnique in Paris for the training of architects, engineers and builders.

Appointed chief city architect in 1788, Langhans began work the same year on the monument for which he is chiefly remembered, the first classicistic structure in Berlin and the most familiar piece of architecture in the city – the Brandenburg Gate.

From the beginning Langhans knew that he was not building just a town gate. This was a prime site, not only the end of the royal mile stretching back to the Royal Palace but also the approach to the recreational delights of the Tiergarten, and beyond that to the royal palaces of Charlottenburg and Potsdam. What was needed was not a gateway but a triumphal arch, a monumental celebration of Prussian pride. So to the surfaces of the finished structure, which takes its inspiration from the Propylaea on the Acropolis of Athens, was applied an elaborate programme of symbolic sculptures and reliefs in praise of the achievements of Frederick the Great.

The Brandenburg Gate has become for Berlin what the Arc de Triomphe later became for Paris. Over its 200-year history, damaged but never destroyed, monarchs have driven through it in state, soldiers have marched through it in victory and straggled through it in defeat, and countless processions have passed under its arches. It was a rallying-point for demonstrations in the revolutions of 1848 and 1918, and for forty years its stern outlines, in a setting of bizarre, perverse isolation, marked the Cold War frontier between East and West.

No less symbolical than the Gate itself, and no less immediate a witness of the history that has swirled around it, is the quadriga that stands on its roof. It is the work of the most important Berlin sculptor since Schlüter, and one of the greatest of all German sculptors – Johann Gottfried Schadow.

Born in Berlin in 1764, Schadow learnt his craft in the studio of the court sculptor Tassaert and found intellectual stimulus in the salon of Henriette Herz, of whom he made a portrait bust which already shows the blend of realistic personal likeness and idealised, classicistic beauty which characterised his figures. In Rome, Mecca of aspiring German artists since the Renaissance, he studied at first hand the works of Antiquity from which Winckelmann had derived his aesthetic. Returning to the Berlin of Friedrich Wilhelm II, he found the new philosophy in place, namely that art was not a matter of decoration and delight, as in Rococo, but a moral medium for the exposition of humanistic and sublime ideals.

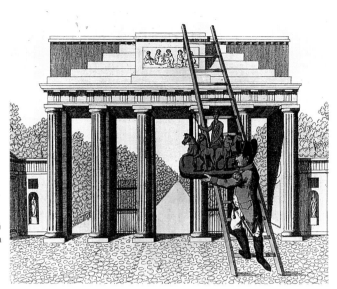

46. *The Horse Thief of Berlin, c.* 1813. A caricature of Napoleon removing the Quadriga from the Brandenburg Gate to take to Paris as booty.

Schadow was involved in the general sculptural decoration of the Brandenburg Gate from the outset. But his quadriga – a chariot drawn by four chargers and driven by the winged Victoria bearing a laurel wreath – is by far the most prominent of his contributions to the monument. The copper ensemble, some five metres high, was mounted on the Gate in 1793. In 1806 Napoleon (Ill. 46) provocatively removed it to Paris as one of the spoils of war; in 1814, to celebrate the restoration of Prussia to the Prussians, the King sent Marshal Blücher to bring it back. It was almost destroyed during the fighting of 1945 and only one of the original horses' heads survived, but it was returned to its proper place in restored form in 1958.

Familiar and famous though the quadriga is, Schadow has left greater and more beautiful works, most of them responses to specific commissions: bronze statues of Prussian generals like Zieten and Blücher, a Luther Memorial for the town of Wittenberg, a marble statue of Frederick the Great for the town of Stettin. But it is above all in gentler subjects, in the graceful, flowing lines of his studies of the male and female form and the serenity of his portrait busts that Schadow shows himself at his most noble and most moving. Of these works the life-size marble group of Princess Luise of Prussia and her sister Princess Friederike (1796) is perhaps the most beautiful. The posture of the two princesses, like their robes, is classicistic, formal; their features reflect what Schadow saw before him when they posed for him as the attractive, warm-blooded teenagers that they were. Timeless truth conveyed through an impersonal, ideal perfection that captures, but cannot absorb, the unique personal vision of living, and therefore finite, human beauty (Ill. 47).

The classicistic impulse embodied in the sculptures of Schadow and his younger contemporaries, such as Rauch and Friedrich Tieck, also made itself felt in other plastic and decorative arts. The Prussian Royal Porcelain Manufactory, the KPM, began in the 1780s to produce a chinaware decorated with motifs taken directly from Antiquity – palmettes, acanthus leaves, scrolls, triglyphs. Technical improvements in manufacture also led to the rise of a school of decorators who used the clear white surfaces to paint meticulous representations of plant and bird life, an urge to representationalism which spread in the early nineteenth century to include street scenes and familiar views of Berlin and Potsdam (Ill. 48).

Painstaking decoration of this kind found a ready application to monumental vases and similar large pieces which made ideal gifts from the King to his fellow monarchs throughout Europe, and the fame of the KPM rose accordingly. Especially popular were pieces commemorating the battles and victorious commanders of the War of Liberation. But modest practical items such as coffee and dinner services became no less desirable and affordable in middle-class circles, reflecting their pride in the city and in the country's achievements. A further stimulus to the production of the Royal Manufactory came with the introduction from England of social coffee drinking, a domestic ritual which insisted, among other things, that each guest had a cup of individual shape and with individual decoration. In such circles too the larger pieces quickly became collectors' items, the display of which testified to their owners' taste and social status.

Commemoration of personalities and events also stimulated the production of an increasing number of medallions in the latter half of the eighteenth

47. Marble statues of the Princesses Luise and Friederike of Prussia by Johann Gottfried Schadow, 1795.

48. Items of a KPM dinner service made for the royal residence on the Pfaueninsel *c.* 1790.

century. Even Friedrich Wilhelm I, the Soldier King, who took little interest in such matters, had silver medallions struck in honour of the annual parade of his Prussian grenadiers, while Frederick the Great found more humane occasions to celebrate, such as the inauguration of the war veterans' hospital in 1748.

Working in gold and silver had a tradition that stretched back to the craft guilds of the Middle Ages and had never been lost. New to Berlin at this time, however, was the production of artefacts in iron, a direct result of the patriotic surrender of personal gold and silver to help finance the war effort. Impressed in particular by the non-military uses to which cast iron was being put in Silesia and in the neighbouring kingdom of Saxony, Friedrich Wilhelm III ordered the construction of an iron foundry in the north of Berlin. Men of the calibre of Schadow, Tieck and Schinkel were called upon to produce designs for statuettes, jewellery and vases as well as for stoves, domestic furniture, candlesticks and a host of minor household utensils.

After 1815 iron came to be seen as a suitable material for commemorative monuments, especially in cemeteries, and even more especially in military cemeteries. The crosses on the graves of fallen officers in the Garrison Cemetery and Veterans Cemetery in Berlin show how decorative could be the designs achieved in a medium not immediately associated with such refinement. The skill of the Berlin foundry in filigree work and fine design was evidently beyond the reach of other workshops, for even the long-established foundries in Birmingham, unable to match the competition, imported the much sought-after 'Berlin Irons' for sale in England. Most familiar of iron artefacts in the realm of private possessions is the Iron Cross, a Prussian military award instituted in 1813 for distinguished service on the field of battle, a decoration of war made from the material of war.

The romantic movement in Germany was launched in Berlin in the final years of the eighteenth century with the declaration of an aesthetico-philosophical position. Wackenroder's *Herzensergiessungen* of 1797, followed by the 'official' journal of programmatic romanticism, the *Athenaeum*, set the tone for the new anti-rationalist view of art. Where Nature is a direct manifestation of God, Art is an indirect manifestation. God, Nature and Art are one under the divine principle. The artist is the man privileged to feel this infinite oneness and to mirror it in the finite terms of his art.

Vague and impressionistic as all this was – intentionally so – it had a far-reaching influence no less on painting than on literature. In particular Wackenroder's concentration of gaze on the Middle Ages and the Renaissance – the former against a background of national German values, the latter leading to Italy and the world of Catholicism – induced a new attitude towards the past.

As in so many areas from which the romantics drew their inspiration – reverence for artistic genius, the principle of unpredictability, the treasures of folk poetry, the worship of Shakespeare – the cult of the Middle Ages went back to Herder, whose little collection of essays entitled *Von deutscher Art und Kunst* (1773) set the romantics' agenda twenty-five years later. Here lie the

49. Explorer and scientist Alexander von Humboldt by Friedrich George Weitsch, oil on canvas, 1806.

50. *Gothic Cathedral by the Water*, by Karl Friedrich Schinkel, oil on canvas, *c.* 1813.

roots of the romantics' identification of art with religion, of Gothic architecture with German architecture, of the spirit of medieval art with the
reassertion of German national greatness. So the heroes of romantic novels
who set out on their voyage of self-discovery are artists or poets – Tieck's
Franz Sternbald, pupil of Dürer, Novalis' hazy medieval poet Heinrich von
Ofterdingen and even, in his pitiful way, Hoffmann's Kapellmeister Johannes
Kreisler.

To be sure, this medievalism did yield practical results – Tieck's transcrip-
tion of medieval love lyrics, the fairy-tales of the Grimm brothers, the study
of philology and Germanic mythology. But in its rose-hued beginnings the
romantic love affair with the Middle Ages rested on imagination and intuition
rather than on knowledge. The inroads of reality were not allowed to disturb
the reassuring serenity of the ideal. One does not demand conclusions or seek
to have the last word because there is no last word – the world is open-ended,
and the work of art, too, must be open-ended, ready to receive the beholder
into its kingdom. It is an all-embracing, quasi-religious experience, cosmic in
implication but at the same time profoundly personal.

How such values could be expressed in painting and drawing was explored
in the early 1800s by the young Karl Friedrich Schinkel. A man of extraordinary versatility, remembered in the first instance as the architect of some
of the finest and most familiar buildings in the heart of Berlin, Schinkel fell

under the spell of the romantic cult of Gothic architecture and medievalism in his twenties. Sometimes he conveyed this fascination in sketches of famous cathedrals. More often he depicted imaginary landscapes dominated by Gothic ruins, or romantic visions of Gothic cathedrals.

The all-embracing romantic philosophy of art and life finds symbolic expression in Schinkel's impressive *Gothic Cathedral by the Water* (1813–14) (Ill. 50). The great church, dominant but not oppressive, represents medieval Christianity, overlooking the ferrymen and the other townsfolk going about their business. But in the shadow of the cathedral are Renaissance houses. And on the far bank, at the water's edge, stands a classical temple. The German artists who made their pilgrimage to Italy in this age found canons of classical beauty there but the quest for 'the land where the lemon trees bloom' begins in a romantic, *Wanderlust* frame of mind. It is a scene of unity in diversity, a unity presented in the terms of transcendental romantic idealism.

A more extrovert romanticism, less encumbered with philosophical and religious interpretation, fills the stage sets that Schinkel designed for no fewer than forty dramas and operas produced in the royal theatres. Here are wild, rocky landscapes, looming Gothic castles, rushing mountain torrents and

51. Stage set (one of ten) for Mozart's *The Magic Flute*, 1815 by Karl Friedrich Schinkel. Schinkel's watercolour sketch depicts the interior of the palace of the Queen of the Night, who is standing on a sickle moon in the background.

52. *Napoleon's Entry into Berlin, 27 October 1806*, by Ludwig Wolf, chalk drawing, 1806.

brilliant colours that would have been the inspiration of any director. Unashamedly medieval romantic were his designs for E. T. A. Hoffmann's opera *Undine* and Kleist's *Das Käthchen von Heilbronn*, both produced in the Nationaltheater in 1816, while for Mozart's *Die Zauberflöte* in the Royal Opera House the same year he did a set of quite remarkably modern, at times almost expressionist designs (Ill. 51).

From the point of view of the public in Berlin, as well as of Berlin artists themselves, the discovery of the joys of romantic painting came in 1808 with the display of a picture called *Cross in the Mountains*. In 1810 two more paintings by the same artist figured in that year's exhibition at the Academy of Arts. The artist was Caspar David Friedrich.

Friedrich was already in Dresden at this time and spent the rest of his life there, a city that had listened willingly to the romantic message since the days of the *Athenaeum*. He was elected to membership of the Berlin Academy in 1810 but played no personal part in the cultural life of the Prussian capital. Berlin had in any case no school of painters at this time to compare with the Dresden School.

But both in his art and in his statements of principle Friedrich speaks the language that the Berlin romantics recognised. 'The artist is charged', he wrote, 'not with the faithful reproduction of air, water, rocks and trees but with the reflection in them of his emotions, his soul. The task of the work of art is the recognition of the spirit of nature, the complete absorption and representation of that spirit with all one's heart and mind.' The Berlin romantics could only have said: 'Amen to that.'

The relationship between man and nature re-emerges in the romantic portraiture of the age. In 1806 Friedrich Georg Weitsch, Berlin court painter in the tradition of Therbusch and Anton Graff, and a leading portraitist at the turn of the century, did a portrait of Alexander von Humboldt, who had recently returned from an expedition to South America. It shows the great explorer at work, surrounded by exotic vegetation and preparing to add a flower to his herbarium, against a distant romantic vista of the Venezuelan jungle and the Orinoco river (Ill. 49).

A step from portraiture, the individual in isolation, leads to history painting, individuals in specific contexts, pictures that describe past or present historical moments in the evocative manner of Rode and Chodowiecki (see Ill 43). Weitsch, one-time director of the Academy and a man with a fine sense of Prussian patriotism, also worked in this field, as did Ludwig Wolf, a native Berliner of a younger generation. Wolf, in particular, has left some interesting sketches of stirring historical moments through which he lived, such as Napoleon's triumphant entrance into Berlin through the Brandenburg Gate in October 1806 (Ill. 52). Subject matter such as this summarises the history of Berlin during the years dominated by Napoleon, a domination no less spiritual than military, while in stylistic terms art looks forward to the Biedermeier realism that was to accompany the social and political upsurge of Prussia and its capital through the coming century.

REALISM AND REVOLUTION

From Liberalism to Nationalism

A guide-book to the Prussian capital published in 1826 gave visitors the following information:

> Generally speaking, the Berliners live simple, temperate, modest lives. Substantial though the number of well-to-do citizens may be, the really wealthy are comparatively few, and even they are not distinguished by any excessive ostentation. True, the highest officials of state enjoy a standard of luxury commensurate with their status but nowhere does one encounter garish festivities or glittering carriages attended by hosts of lackeys. The interiors of their houses, however, reveal a considerable wealth combined with comfort and refinement of taste.

In 1815 Berlin had a population of some 200,000. By 1850 the figure had swelled to 400,000 – this against the ethnographical background of a Prussia in which a consistent proportion of over 70 per cent still worked on the land. By 1877, with the steady incorporation of outlying villages and settlements, the figure had reached 1 million.

This handful of facts contains in itself the basic statement of where Berlin – not to say Prussia and Germany – was going during these sixty years, both economically and politically. The economic scene was controlled by the onward march of the industrial revolution. In the political arena an equally irresistible force drove the country, by a tortuous path, from the *Kleinstaaterei* re-established after the defeat of Napoleon to the declaration of a national identity in 1871.

But in 1815, when the Congress of Vienna parcelled out the territories of the defunct Holy Roman Empire in post-Napoleonic Europe, such a prospect was little more than a wistful vision. In its essentials Prussia emerged from the years of French occupation politically and constitutionally unchanged. In the new German Confederation of thirty-nine states, where the voice of the conservative Austrian minister, Prince Klemens von Metternich, was the loudest, the principle of particularism – the inviolability of the princely authority of the independent sovereign states – remained intact. The years of French domination had engendered sentiments of a national German allegiance, sentiments fortified by the romantic revival of memories of a glorious German past. But such thoughts could make no progress against the entrenched reactionary interests of feudal princes whose sole concern was the preservation of the autocratic status quo, Confederation or no Confederation. As late as 1830 we find Goethe remarking to his friend Eckermann: 'There is no town or city, let alone a country, in which we can stand and categorically declare: "This is Germany." If you raise the question in Vienna, you are told: "This is Austria." And if you raise the question in Berlin, you are told: "This is Prussia." ' Nothing, moreover, contributes more to the prevention of change than an efficient state bureaucracy, behind which stands a loyal military, ready to act in the name of God. No other state could match Prussia in proudly satisfying these desiderata.

An intellectual underpinning of the political actuality was provided by the philosophy of Hegel, who came to Berlin from Heidelberg in 1818. He was appointed Professor of Philosophy at the university that year in succession to Fichte and taught there until his death in the cholera epidemic of 1831 (Ill. 53).

Whatever its relevance to other fields – metaphysics, ethics, the philosophy of history, of law and of art – Hegel's systematics had an immediate application to the political situation of the moment. His philosophy rests on the development and interaction of two basic convictions. The first is that the only true and complete reality is the whole, the absolute; the second is that reality and rationality are identical. His emphasis on the wholeness of experience puts him in the company of the Schlegels, Tieck, Schelling and other philosophical romantics of his generation, to whom the only real truth is the whole truth, and the universe indivisible. As he put it: 'One must get the thought of the universe into one's head.'

53. Distinguished Berlin intellectuals of the early nineteenth century, lithograph by Julius Schoppe, c.1830. *Clockwise from top:* Hegel; Friedrich Schleiermacher, theologian; Alexander von Humboldt, explorer and scientist; Wilhelm von Humboldt, scholar and co-founder of the University of Berlin; Christian Wilhelm Hufeland, physician and biologist; Johann August Wilhelm Neander, Church historian; *centre:* Carl Ritter, geographer.

The application to this of Hegel's second premiss, that of the identity of the real and the rational, leads to the conclusion that, as there is only one indivisible reality, so there is only one principle of rationality. Brought into the historical context of the present, this meant that that context was rational because it was real, i.e. true in its completeness, and that there was therefore no cause to try and change it.

Parallel to this ran Hegel's argument on another pressing question in the post-Napoleonic era, the question of freedom. Meaningful freedom, argued Hegel, does not consist of doing as one likes but of seeking one's role within the wholeness of the community – the state – of which one is part. By doing what the state, the supreme custodian of 'real' freedom, demands, the individual realises his own personal freedom. In effect it is a restatement of his doctrine of the subservience of the part to the whole, a doctrine eagerly embraced in later times by totalitarian regimes of both left and right.

Hegel regarded Prussia as the ideal state. The King and his officials, in grateful reciprocity, regarded Hegel as their ideal philosopher. His historical role models were men of self-assertion and power such as Charlemagne, Luther and Frederick the Great, great actors in the unfurling drama of the fulfilment of the German destiny. The dual appeal to idealism and national-ism did not go unheard in the nineteenth century.

But another and very different -ism was also stirring, an intellectual pre-occupation which made its own contribution to the eventual unification of Germany. This was the force of liberalism.

With its immediate stimulus in the Enlightenment, in the freedom of rational thought and emancipation from restrictive dogma, the moral and social tendencies assembled under the term liberalism represented the response of the educated middle classes to the political challenge of the post-Napoleonic age. Demands for freedom of thought, freedom of political and religious expression, freedom of economic activity and equality before the law could be met, they argued, only by the establishment of a *Rechtsstaat* in which a written constitution would guarantee personal and civic freedoms for all. The examples of what had been achieved by the recent revolutions in America and France showed what they meant.

Pressure for such reforms was generated with particular enthusiasm in the universities, and, indeed, already in the Gymnasien. Returning from the war in a mood for change, turning its back on things French and deter-mined to build on indigenous values, the new student generation formed associations (*Burschenschaften*) pledged to promote the ideals of honour, justice and freedom on which a new society should be built. Liberalism and nationalism, later to be at each other's throats, the former ultimately to be killed off by the latter, here make common cause. The powers that be, led by Metternich, sensed here a revolutionary danger that had to be nipped in the bud. The *Burschenschaften* were banned, political associations forbidden, education placed under police supervision, anything that smacked of 'democratic' tendencies punished.

But the movement towards German unity edged slowly forwards. The pressure of economic factors was building up. Beginning in 1819 a series of trading agreements between various German states culminated in the customs union of 1834 and over the following decades more and more states joined the union, abolishing tariffs and creating an internal free-trade area. Heavy industry expanded, and two new social classes began to emerge – on the one hand the large-scale manufacturer and trader, the capitalist enterpreneur, on the other an industrial proletariat, bringing with it the familiar social phenomena of exploitation, poverty and ghettoisation.

Friedrich Wilhelm III died in 1840, a monarch genuinely mourned by his people after a long and demanding reign. Those four decades are customarily branded an age of restoration and reaction. But he left a Prussia far surer of itself and far more advanced – in agriculture, in commerce, in the organisation of the army, in education, in civil administration – than he had found it.

Although his son was to reign for only half as long, the trials he faced were immense. No soldier, deeply religious, a believer in the divine right of kings and a convinced conservative, in the best sense, Friedrich Wilhelm IV was happiest in the company of intellectuals and artists. He eagerly joined his architects and town-planners to make his capital a more beautiful place but was ill at ease when faced with political problems. Those sceptical of his ability to come to grips with the challenges confronting his kingdom called him 'The romantic on the throne'.

Politics took pride of place in intellectual discussions of the time and there was a revival of interest in the salon. Wilhelm von Humboldt provided a new forum for such conversaziones in his recently built country villa at Tegel, on the northern outskirts of Berlin, while his wife Caroline entertained Arnim, Schleiermacher, the sculptor Rauch, the Prussian Chancellor Hardenberg and other prominent public figures at her home in the Französische Strasse. Rahel Levin and Varnhagen von Ense continued to keep open house in the nearby Mauerstrasse, and in 1827 Der Tunnel über der Spree was founded, a long-lived society which accompanied the transition from romanticism to realism

54. Stehely's restaurant on the Gendarmenmarkt. Watercolour by Leopold Ludwig Müller, 1827.

and later counted the painter Adolph Menzel, Fontane and many progressive young poets among its members.

Humbler – less pretentious, dare one say – though no less earnest, were the coffee-houses and wine-cellars. The earliest Berlin coffee-house was established in 1818, with newspapers and journals provided to encourage guests to dally awhile. The famous Café Kranzler, set up on the corner of Unter den Linden and Friedrichstrasse in 1833, carried not only the Berlin papers but also English and French journals, which were often freer and more extensive in their reportages. The area around the theatre on the Gendarmenmarkt attracted a number of establishments: Stehely's extravagant restaurant, noted for its Venetian décor and as a meeting-place for editors and writers, opened on the square in 1827, while round the corner, in the Friedrichstrasse, were Bohemian and *demi-monde* cafés of more dubious repute. Behind the theatre, with a special fame of its own, stood Lutter and Wegner's, the legendary wine-cellar beloved of the theatrical fraternity, founded as early as 1818 (Ill. 54).

But for determined groups of radicals, not only in Berlin and Prussia, not even only in Germany at large but over the whole of Europe, the time for talking was over. The Paris revolution of 1830 had already sent shock waves beyond the borders of France. Then, in February 1848, the French rose up against the regime of King Louis Philippe, drove him into exile and proclaimed the Second Republic. The flame of revolt spread through Europe like wildfire as one German state after another demanded constitutional reform, a free press, trial by jury, religious toleration and other democratic rights.

In Berlin the King lost control of the situation. After a huge demonstration in the Tiergarten on 18 March a crowd surged through the Brandenburg Gate and marched on the Royal Palace. Troops were drawn up to bar their way and shots were fired; the demonstrators set up barricades in the narrow streets of the city centre and for two days pitched battles raged. On the 21st, after making a desperate public appeal 'To my dear Berliners', the King ordered his troops to withdraw. Almost 200 civilians had been killed (Ill. 55). In a gesture of apparent reconciliation the King rode through the streets of his capital wearing an armband in the national black–red–gold colours, stopping to talk to his citizens and promising to merge Prussia into a united Germany with himself at its head.

Press censorship was abolished, freedom of association and assembly granted, the way laid open for a vigorous political life. Satirical journals enriched with caricatures sprang up, some with sober titles like *Volksvertreter* and *Demokrat*, others startling the public with names such as *Berliner Krakehler* ('Berlin Rowdy') and *Berliner Grossmaul* ('Berlin Loudmouth'). The most famous was *Kladderadatsch* ('Hotchpotch'), which pilloried the aristocracy, the generals and the clergy and preached the cause of personal freedom and German unity. By a mixture of shrewd judgement and good fortune it survived for almost a hundred years, folding only in 1944.

But the euphoria did not last. Seeing that the revolution had been suppressed in Vienna, Friedrich Wilhelm IV dismissed the ministers in his own new state assembly and, when they refused to leave, summoned his troops and placed the capital under martial law. The new National Assembly in

55. *Victims of the 1848 Revolution*, by Adolph Menzel, oil on canvas, *c.* 1848.

Frankfurt, meanwhile, a noble but premature experiment in liberal democracy, slowly but inevitably collapsed under the weight of ponderous idealistic verbiage, an inability to agree on anything resembling a coherent political policy and an ignorance of how to devise practical means of converting thoughts into actions. As one commentator put it: 'It had to teach dancing to a pupil who could not even stand.'

So the hierarchical principle prevailed, royal power was confirmed, reaction and particularism re-entrenched. When German national unity finally came, it was not through the persuasive practices of democratic liberalism but by 'blood and iron'.

Building for the State

The relationship between 'culture', however defined, and the historical, political and social circumstances from which it emerges is a complex one. Conditions may favour the cultivation of the arts or they may hinder it. Artists may rise to the challenge of their age or ignore it. The arts have their own inner momentum and may respond to self-generated pressures that pay scant heed to the world outside. To be sure, a particular interest or ideal may capture the minds of artists working in different media at one particular moment – a time of patriotic enthusiasm, for example. But the form of the response will be determined by forces within each artistic medium, not outside it.

Consequently any chosen periodisation of the historical or political continuum will not necessarily coincide with a reasonable periodisation in terms of the development of art. Movements of the *Zeitgeist*, of emphasis in aesthetic perception, or simply in fashion, do not affect all forms of artistic expression at the same time and to the same degree. Programmatic romanticism, for instance, emerges in German literature at the end of the eighteenth century and its most characteristic manifestations fall in the succeeding twenty or so years. In music, 'the most romantic of all the arts', as E. T. A. Hoffmann called it, the climax of what begins with Beethoven is not reached until Schumann, Liszt and Wagner in the middle and later nineteenth century. By this time literature has settled on quite different priorities.

The century that follows the triumphant War of Liberation offers just such a panorama of impressions, sometimes coincident, sometimes overlapping, sometimes contradictory. Berlin itself, not for the first or the last time, concealed a split personality. On the one hand it was still the conservative capital of a feudal province whose character and development rested on the personality of the ruling monarch; on the other it was a rapidly growing centre of industrial, commercial and cultural activity, of scientific and technical expertise, that was preparing for the metropolitan status waiting to be thrust upon it in 1871.

In cultural terms the so-called Biedermeier period that accompanied the Restoration over the decades following 1815 had a similar Janus-like character. Herr Biedermeier, whose name has become the designation of an artistic style and ambience, was a caricature figure from the humorous Munich journal *Fliegende Blätter*, where he is portrayed as the archetypal petty-bourgeois, respectable, lover of a quiet life, the embodiment of *Gemütlichkeit*. Furniture and interior design responded to these homely values in their own terms. Comfort took precedence over elegance; upholstered sofas and armchairs gave rooms a 'lived-in' character, with hangings in warm, plush tones. The decorative elements were drawn from a variety of sources – French Empire, occasionally classicistic, sometimes Baroque or floral – but everything was to a human scale, built for use, not for display. Sometimes beds, chests of drawers and escritoires would have strict functional lines with a minimum of decorative motifs. But the vagaries of stylistic fashion were, for the moment, less important than the convivial atmosphere in which a shared intimacy could be enjoyed by family and friends. Unexciting they may have seemed to many but the Biedermeier years brought with them a relief from the unease of Napoleonic occupation and the euphoria of liberation, an opportunity to rediscover a sense of sober reality and shared humanity.

At the same time the Biedermeier period nurtured two other interests. One was the political concern that linked the patriotic–national sentiment of 1813–14 with the liberal–national sentiment of 1848 – the concern that refers to these thirty years not as Biedermeier but as the *Vormärz*, the period leading up to the revolution of March 1848. The other leads to the cultural expressions of the new-found national confidence, the ways in which Berlin, as capital of a Prussia which had just demonstrated its military and moral superiority over an humiliated France, could celebrate its achievements in public form. What more suitable starting-point than the decoration of the city with new buildings and monuments?

Friedrich Wilhelm III, a monarch with architectural pretensions, envisaged a capital of boulevards and squares that would look like a Prussian Paris, while incorporating certain specific desires which he was determined to see fulfilled. For the execution of these plans he turned to a thirty-year-old architect, draughtsman and painter who, in line of succession from Schlüter and Knobelsdorff, was to become the greatest Berlin architect of the nineteenth century – Karl Friedrich Schinkel.

Son of a Protestant clergyman, Schinkel was born in the Prussian town of Neuruppin, in the sandy plains north of Berlin, in 1781. He studied at the Bauakademie in Berlin, made an extensive educational journey through Italy and France, and returned in 1805, at a time when talk in artistic circles was of the French Revolution and the new romanticism. This parallelism of the classic and the romantic – it was not for Schinkel a dichotomy – never left him. During the Napoleonic occupation he painted idealised Romantic landscapes with Gothic churches and ruins (see Ill. 50), then, in 1810, was appointed to the Commission for the Preservation of Historical Buildings and Monuments in Prussia, of which he remained Director until his death in 1841.

No doubt the mention of Schinkel's name recalls in the first place the Altes Museum, the Schauspielhaus on the Gendarmenmarkt and his other famous neo-classical contributions to the old historical centre of Berlin. But as well as Schinkel the architect and Schinkel the painter and draughtsman

56. Sofa by Karl Friedrich Schinkel, 1828.

there is Schinkel the designer of stage sets, of furniture and fittings, of domestic interiors (see Ills 51 and 56). And alongside all this practical activity he was quietly filling notebooks with observations and sketches intended to be brought together as a manual of architectural theory and practice as he himself had discovered and interpreted it in the course of his career.

A central characteristic of Schinkel's buildings – a quality no more to be taken for granted in a nineteenth-century architect than in one of the present day – is the respect that they pay to their environment. He did not just design a building; he designed a building in a setting. As he looked down Unter den Linden from the Zeughaus, his gaze was held by the Corinthian columns of Knobelsdorff's opera house on the left and those of Prince Heinrich's palace opposite. By filling the space between this palace and the Zeughaus with his own building, he would complete an ensemble of congruent elements. To complete his commemoration of a successful war he proposed to set statues of the victorious Prussian generals Bülow and Scharnhorst on either side of his new structure. The result, a guard-house, is the little gem of neo-classical architecture called the Neue Wache. In 1931 the interior was reconstructed as a war memorial, which it remains today.

Schinkel's Friedrichwerder Church, completed in 1830, moves from the military to the ecclesiastical, from the neo-classical to the neo-Gothic, and from stone to brick. The rediscovery of medieval red-brick Gothic formed part of the romantic revival of interest in the German Middle Ages, and one of the first to put this rediscovery to practical architectural use had been Friedrich Gilly, Schinkel's teacher at the Bauakademie. This experience was reinforced for Schinkel when he visited England in 1826 and was

57. Sketch of Friedrichwerder Church by Karl Friedrich Schinkel, pen and pencil, 1828.

deeply impressed by its Gothic cathedrals and by the chapels of Oxford and Cambridge colleges. Badly damaged in the Second World War, the Friedrichwerder Church has since been rebuilt and now houses an exhibition devoted to the work of its designer (Ill. 57).

Work directly linked to the personal requirements of the King and members of the royal family made continual demands on Schinkel's time. Between 1817 and 1822 he reworked in classicistic forms the royal cathedral as built in Baroque style by Knobelsdorff in the previous century. A few years later, at the behest of Princess Augusta, wife of Crown Prince Wilhelm, he built a palace in Babelsberg Park, outside Potsdam, a romantic, neo-Gothic fancy directly inspired by the recent restoration of Windsor Castle. Adding to the attractiveness of this palace are the surrounding gardens, laid out by Lenné and later extended by Prince Hermann von Pückler-Muskau.

Royal palaces, army quarters, churches – Schinkel was everywhere at his ease. No less did he rise to the challenge to design cultural buildings for the general public, two of which, both neo-classical in manner but by no means repetitive, still occupy prominent positions in Berlin today: the Altes Museum and the Schauspielhaus on the Gendarmenmarkt.

The Altes Museum, designed in 1822–3 for the public exhibition of the King's constantly expanding art collections, is one of Schinkel's greatest works. The broad neo-classical façade of Ionic columns looked out across the Lustgarten towards the north front of the Royal Palace. Behind the columns is a vestibule that leads to the central room in the two-storey building, a galleried rotunda modelled on the Pantheon in Rome and intended principally for the display of sculpture. The decoration of the interior of the museum was carried out by leading painters and sculptors of the day in accordance with Schinkel's conception, likewise the disposition of the various groups of allegorical and mythological sculpture mounted on prominent exterior points of the building (Ill. 58).

True, it is a building whose primary duty is to proclaim the enlightened majesty of the Hohenzollern monarchy. But it is more. It states a commitment to a humanistic ideal which the King wishes to share with his people, a statement of the principle of education through art, the great art of the classical and Christian traditions. It is art gallery, temple and educational establishment all in one.

'Through this new building the beauty of the area is made perfect, the noble Lustgarten now being closed on its fourth side in a suitably dignified style.' So wrote Schinkel to the King on presenting his designs. And indeed, although much of the Altes Museum had to be rebuilt after the Second World War, and the Royal Palace has been destroyed, one can still take in the panorama of Zeughaus, Lustgarten (the former pleasance of the Palace) and Cathedral from the top of its steps. One can even sense why Hitler, having felled the trees that used to grow here, turned the Lustgarten into a square for public demonstrations, haranguing the mob from the entrance of the museum, surrounded by the symbols of a glorious German past.

What is arguably Schinkel's most brilliant design is also among his earliest – that for the national theatre, the Schauspielhaus, on the Gendarmenmarkt. Again we confront his uncanny sense of what the location needs and what it will sustain. Langhans' rather undistinguished theatre on this

58. Schinkel's Altes Museum, engraving by C. F. Thiele, c. 1828, after Schinkel's own sketch.

prominent site, flanked on one side by the German Church and on the other by the French Church, burnt down in 1817. Working to detailed specifications laid down by the King concerning size, appearance, interior layout and above all cost, Schinkel designed a building that included not only a theatre for an audience of 1,600 but also an independent recital hall that could double as a state-room for parties and receptions. He rescued the six Ionic columns from Langhans' portico, restored the pediment above them, then repeated a pediment for the higher façade of the theatre proper behind, creating an emphatic classicistic aspect. Originally intended for opera and drama, the Schauspielhaus is now a concert hall and has been renamed the Konzerthaus (Ill. 59).

'Since 1815,' wrote the contemporary novelist Willibald Alexis,

a fine new Berlin has arisen, one whose glory is inseparably linked to the name of Schinkel. The buildings that bear his name will make that glory imperishable. Less well known, however, is how much this great artist has contributed to the improvement of general taste, even in technical matters, and the range over which his influence has been felt, from factories down to handicrafts and to the patterns used by the humblest interior decorator. Schinkel's greatest achievement is to have been the first not only to recognise and make a close examination of the splendours of Greek art but also to demonstrate how the values of that art might be applied. The path he chose was not just different – it was superior.

As Schinkel never conceived his works away from their given contexts, so also he never envisaged an architecture without sculpture. The nineteenth century was rich in sculptors, most of them pupils of the legendary Schadow, director of the Academy of Arts from 1815 until his death in 1850. It was an age not only of vigorous public and private building but also of statues

59. Schinkel's Schauspielhaus. View from the Gendarmenmarkt, wash drawing, 1821.

and monuments. Friedrich Tieck, for example, brother of the romantic poet Ludwig Tieck, was responsible for much of the classicistic programme on the exterior of Schinkel's Schauspielhaus, including the mounted figures on either side of the entrance staircase and those of Apollo and Pegasus on the apex of the upper pediment. Equally prominent are his two Horse Tamers (Castor and Pollux) on the roof of the Altes Museum.

Pride of place in the succession of Schadow, however, belongs to Christian Daniel Rauch, who quickly overtook his teacher in popular fame and made himself one of the most influential public sculptors in the whole of Germany. When the young and universally loved Queen Luise, wife of Friedrich Wilhelm III, died in 1810, Rauch was commissioned to design her tomb, a work which brought him instant success with court and public alike through its gentle realism within a cool classicistic idiom. The War of Liberation stimulated the demand for statues of the victorious military commanders to set alongside those of the generals of the Seven Years War, and Rauch, who was more at his ease in the monumental Prussian world than Schadow, was invited to submit works for the most prominent sites.

Commissions reached him, indeed, from all over Germany, among them a request for a number of busts for King Ludwig I's temple of Valhalla in Bavaria. But his masterpiece was for Berlin, a work now proudly restored to its original position in Unter den Linden after years of exile in Potsdam. This is his equestrian statue of Frederick the Great (Ill. 60).

The arguments over a suitable monument to 'Der alte Fritz' went back to the last years of the King himself, who refused to sanction any memorial to himself on the ground that it was inappropriate to honour a commander-in-chief in this way during his lifetime. Immediately the King died, discussions started again: Should he be portrayed standing or seated? As a warrior or as a man of letters? Directly and realistically, as in Chodowiecki's familiar engraving, or as a classical hero?

60. Equestrian statue of Frederick the Great in Unter den Linden by Christian Daniel Rauch, bronze, begun 1840, unveiled 1851,

In the end Friedrich Wilhelm III approved a commission to Rauch for an equestrian figure on a tall plinth which depicted famous military and civilian contemporaries of his great-uncle, together with scenes from his life and various inscriptions. Among the figures eventually chosen by Rauch from a constantly changing roll of proposals were Kant and Lessing, to represent the age of Enlightenment, and two of Frederick's ministers, Schlabrendorff and Finkenstein. The monument was finally unveiled in 1851 and a medal struck to honour the occasion, showing the statue on one side and a likeness of Rauch on the other.

Over the decade that lay between the commissioning of the monument and its erection a good deal had changed in the political mood of the city. 1848, the year of revolutions, had come and gone. Material gains in the present mattered more than military achievements in the past. Yet 'Fridericus rex' remained the Great, and loyalty remained a Prussian virtue. Rauch, in the direct realism – one might almost say Biedermeier realism – of his age, gives us both sets of values in this most magnificent of memorials. The King rides supreme, to be viewed from below. But he is not a dictator – he is borne, literally, by the enlightened generals and the great men of the German Enlightenment portrayed on the plinth that supports him.

Painting from Romanticism to Realism

The loving discovery of nature, what the romantic painter Caspar David Friedrich had called 'the complete absorption and representation of the spirit of nature with all one's heart and mind', did not relax its hold over the imagination of artists as the ethos of the age veered towards realism, even materialism. The values that had sustained German literary romanticism from Tieck and Wackenroder to Eichendorff and E. T. A. Hoffmann persisted into the late 1820s and beyond. At a time when Schinkel had turned from romanticising medieval cathedrals to designing the Altes Museum, the Schauspielhaus and other neo-classical masterpieces, Karl Blechen, one of the greatest Berlin artists of the mid-nineteenth century, was still painting Gothic ruins and majestic, awe-inspiring landscapes proclaiming the mysterious power of nature (Ill. 61).

Romanticising tendencies also took other forms. The so-called Nazarene painters who had settled in Rome, captivated by the conception of art as religion, cultivated a monumental, idealised style in portraits and religious

61. *Vallone dei Molini* (near Amalfi) by Karl Blechen, oil on canvas, 1831.

paintings over which hangs an atmosphere of didactic piety – an academic, studio-bound painting. But these works enjoyed great popularity in Prussian court circles. Karl Begas the Elder, for one, father of the sculptor Reinhold Begas, built a career on such works. Even more significant is Wilhelm Schadow, son of the sculptor, who returned from Italy to Berlin in 1819 and directed a master class in painting at the Academy of Arts. Seven years later, however, he was appointed Director of the Academy in Düsseldorf, an appointment which had the ironical result of ensuring that Düsseldorf, not Berlin, became the centre of painting in Prussia over the following decades.

A final attempt to revive the flagging fortunes of Nazarene romanticism came in 1841 with an invitation from Friedrich Wilhelm IV – himself a draughtsman and a patron of art in the service of religion – to the celebrated fresco painter Peter Cornelius to leave Munich and come to Berlin.

62. Karl Begas' portrait of his own family, oil on canvas, 1821. Begas himself surveys the scene from the far right edge of the painting.

63. *Living Room of C. F. E. Hausschild, Ironmaster* by Eduard Gaertner, oil on canvas, 1843.

Specifically Cornelius was engaged to decorate a monumental Hohenzollern mausoleum planned by the King but never built. The cartoons, however, on which Cornelius worked for the last twenty years of his life with ever diminishing enthusiasm, have largely survived – depictions of the Day of Judgement and other scenes from the Apocalypse. But the time for such art had passed.

Life was becoming what the Germans call *verbürgerlicht*, increasingly dominated by middle-class taste and middle-class values captured in the term Biedermeier, with its associations of virtuous modesty, uncomplicated frankness and 'things as they are'. Idealism was unreal and distracted men's minds from the true concerns of a useful moral life. Appeals to historical precedent, to an inspiration said to reside in great moments of history, seemed *passé*, irrelevant. Even the pride and confidence restored by the War of Liberation provided no platform from which to launch a programme of spiritual renewal. Artists looked for a new realism, based on subject matter drawn not from historical memory or from learned allegory, or even from religious parable and vision, but from the experiential world of the moment. Real were the objects chosen, realistic and objective the manner of their treatment.

Genre paintings such as domestic interiors, family scenes and social pastimes make up a large proportion of Biedermeier pictures, providing images of middle-class life which have the veracity of historical documents. True, the artist retains his personal signature, his own sense of composition and colour. But his intention is the reliable reproduction, almost photographic in

64. *Chess Match in the Voss Villa* by Johann Erdmann Hummel, oil on canvas, 1818–19.

quality, of the scene in front of him. And since the way of life he depicts is shared by hundreds of families, the paintings will be instantly traceable to their time and place, whatever variations of detail they may display, down to items of costume and the pictures on the wall. The figures, dominated by Begas *père*, in Karl Begas' portrait of his own family done in 1821 (the painter has included himself on the extreme right) exude a similar pious earnestness and sense of proper family values (Ill. 62). Painted in the same spirit is Eduard Gaertner's study, twenty years later, of the living room of a well-to-do Berlin craftsman of the time. Success in these days came on many levels (Ill. 63).

Social activities of the day also provided artists with ready material which could sometimes be treated in unusual ways. Johann Erdmann Hummel, who taught perspective and optics at the Berlin Academy, was a member of a chess club that held its meetings in the town house of the art connoisseur, Count Gustav von Ingenheim. Attending one of these evenings in 1818 – among the guests are the archaeologist Alois Hirt, the designer Hans Christian Genelli and Count Friedrich Wilhelm von Brandenburg, later prime minister of Prussia – Hummel not only captured the occasion itself but set himself interesting problems of light and shade in an optically complex and striking composition (Ill. 64).

From the social scene to the individual portrait, keenly observed and precisely reproduced, sometimes faintly romanticised – for no sitter wishes to see himself in less than the best light – but not idealised, even when the subject is from the aristocracy or the military. There was no more sober and punctilious a practitioner of this art of portraiture than Franz Krüger, dubbed, from his predilection for painting animals, 'Horsey-Krüger' – a kind of German Stubbs. Krüger painted, to the last detail, what he saw, and only what he saw. His gaze had been sharpened by years of the study of nature, of how the surface of things really looked. But only the surface. He makes no effort to penetrate the inner life of his subjects, to interpret the joys, the frustrations, the aspirations of the men – or women – of the Biedermeier world. There are no spiritual problems for the spectator to wrestle with. And if Krüger's pictures are sometimes strenuous, the strain derives not from a conflict of minds or a disharmony in the environment but from the superabundance of detail lovingly and exhaustingly applied.

Exemplary of Krüger's art, part historical chronicle, part urban vedute, are his large canvases depicting military parades organised by the King in honour of visiting foreign dignitaries. Mingling with the onlookers, Krüger made sketches of the tattoo and of the characters on display – many of whom are identifiable – then painstakingly assembled the panorama in his studio. A state visit to Prussia in 1822 by the Grand Prince Nicholas of Russia, the King's son-in-law, provided the occasion for one of Krüger's most famous pictures in this genre (Ill. 65).

65. *Parade on the Opernplatz in 1822* by Franz Krüger, oil on canvas, 1824–9.

As the first half of the nineteenth century and beyond was rich in interiors, so a taste also developed for action pictures of social life in open-air situations, which then merged almost imperceptibly into urban landscape and architectural painting. Krüger's military parades, indeed, are historical, social and architectural painting all in one.

This growing popularity of urban landscapes owed a good deal to the lead given by Friedrich Wilhelm III himself. A monarch with the popular touch, he turned away from the pomp and circumstance of history painting in favour of the modest yet colourful realism of landscape, encouraging in particular the application of such scenes to the vases, plates and other products of the KPM, the royal china manufactory. A number of the leading townscape painters of the period, Gaertner among them, served their apprenticeship under the discipline of the KPM workshops, where fineness of touch and concentration on detail were the order of the day. An adherent of the realistic school of painting, the monarch not only influenced artists to pursue a course of precise representationalism but also purchased for his own collection a large number of townscapes and panoramas done in this spirit.

With the King's death in 1840 came a change of attitude in the portrayal of street scenes. The meticulous reproduction of realistic detail in predominantly bright and uniform light conditions worked to the detriment of the poetic and specifically painterly qualities of the work of art. Precise representation omitted tension and drama and resisted the importation of anything that might attract a suspicion of individualism or subjectivism. But the 'neutral', 'photographic' portrayal of a given subject was under pressure, on the one hand from the invention of photography itself, traceable to the 1830s and 1840s, on the other hand from the artistic urge to move beyond the technical achievement of a 'faithful' reproduction of given objects.

An intriguing later work by Gaertner, a procession across the Schlossbrücke with the Royal Palace behind, which was displayed at the Academy's exhibition in 1826 and subsequently acquired by Wilhelm I, shows the painter experimenting with light effects to bring a sense of drama to the scene (Ill. 66). The threatening storm clouds cast a pall of darkness over one side of the bridge and over the jetty in the foreground, leaving the palace beyond and the Winged Victories mostly still bathed in sunlight. Citizens, boatmen, onlookers, domestic animals – the observation is as precise as ever. The occasion behind the subject matter, with puzzling details like the Union Jack fluttering from the flagpole, is still a matter for discussion. But Gaertner's principal concern is with artistic composition and dramatic effect, achieved through the use of contrasting lighter and darker tones.

Although a preponderance of townscapes tended to concentrate on the central, classical sites of the city, from the Rathaus and the Royal Palace westwards to the villas of the Wilhelmstrasse and the Tiergarten, the commercial and industrial sides of city life received increasing attention. There was as much scope, moreover, for personal interpretation of a 'real' scene of this kind as of any other. The industrialist August Borsig, for instance, commissioned Eduard Biermann, known in particular for his romantic Alpine landscapes, to do a large canvas of his iron foundry and engineering works in the north of Berlin in 1847. Realistic as the individual parts of the work seem, the smoking chimneys remorselessly testifying to Borsig's success,

66. View of the Schlossbrücke and Royal Palace by Eduard Gaertner, oil on canvas 1861. The bridge was designed by Schinkel.

Biermann's brief was clearly to produce an apotheosis of manufacturing industry, whatever liberties needed to be taken with the *actualités*. The garden and terrace in the foreground imply the presence of a benevolent employer sharing the site with his workers. But Borsig's family villa was actually some miles away. The individual parts of the picture are true – the sum of those parts is not.

The Literature of Realism

The passing of Napoleonic Europe, the War of Liberation and the Congress of Vienna had left in Germany – and not only in Germany – the feeling that a new epoch had dawned, bringing challenges that had to be faced in new ways. The philosophical romanticism of the early decades of the century had something closed, something exclusive about it. It had preached an idealistic message of the primacy of the subjective self, of the oneness of man and nature, of art as a self-justifying act of religious worship. Now, in a changed world, such hermetic values seemed unreal and evasive. The new world was open, expanding, at the mercy of science. The demand went out for education, for social change, for a set of values through which man could feel some control over his environment. The writer should be, not a wistful aesthete but a communicator and interpreter of information, a mediator between events and the public.

Not that the old values disappeared overnight. The lyric poetry of the age of Biedermeier showed the variety of the conflicting influences at work. The warm, comfortable *Gemütlichkeit* of middle-class family life engendered a conservative lyricism of familiar themes – the love poetry, nature lyrics, reflective 'God-and-the-World' poetry that had been part of the unbroken literary tradition that went back to classicism and even Baroque. The emphasis lies on the personal and the private; no scene, no occasion was too humble to be treated in verse, usually simple, rhymed strophic forms. The realistic and the descriptive merged to stimulate the genre of the ballad, popular with poets from Heine to Mörike, from Uhland to Annette von Droste-Hülshoff.

To many, however, such poetry of the status quo did not meet the challenge of the time. Political realities intruded. Events abroad such as the Greek struggle for independence and the Polish uprising of 1830 brought wider ideals to the fore, and poets such as Georg Herwegh and Hoffmann von Fallersleben (author of 'Deutschland, Deutschland, über alles') picked up the themes of the patriotic poetry inspired by the War of Liberation – the poetry of national freedom, of the pride of the *Volk*, of the good fight under God.

As its population and prosperity grew, nineteenth-century Berlin had a stream of new realities with which to grapple. In this it did not differ from other German cities growing under the stimulus, and confronted with the tensions, of industrialisation – or differed only in degree. But until Fontane and Gerhart Hauptmann in the last decades of the century Berlin produced hardly a single major writer – albeit in an age when the German writers who warrant the description 'major' can in any case be counted on the fingers of one hand. Few outsiders, moreover, were attracted into the city at the time. Of the unchallenged 'greats' of the period, Büchner, most gripping of dramatists, never went near Prussia, nor did Mörike, most moving of lyric poets. Conrad Ferdinand Meyer and Jeremias Gotthelf clung to their beloved Switzerland, Stifter to his native Austria. Grillparzer visited Berlin on a tour of Germany in 1826, found the people 'more pleasant than I had expected' and the political climate agreeably relaxed, but shuddered at the prospect of having to spend a week in the place and longed to be back in Vienna. Gottfried Keller spent five significant years in Berlin in the early 1850s – to which we shall return. But he then went back to Zürich and never left his homeland again.

Which leaves Heinrich Heine.

So restless a life did Heine lead, and so short-lived were most of his attachments, that his works can often as well be claimed for one place as for another. 'A real poet conveys the spirit, not of his own age but of all ages,' he said. 'A real poem is therefore always a mirror of every present moment.' He stayed only two years in Berlin, a footloose law student in his early twenties, recently sent down from the University of Göttingen for duelling, while living a privileged life on an allowance from a rich Jewish uncle. But they were years of vital importance to him, years in which he refined his lyrical voice and sharpened his critical pen. Probably Berlin gave him more than he gave Berlin. But with Heine things tended to be like that.

Arriving from Hamburg in 1821, Heine quickly ingratiated himself into intellectual circles. He introduced himself to E. T. A. Hoffmann's fraternity at Lutter and Wegner's wine-cellar and charmed his way into the salon of Rahel Levin, home of emancipated Jewry and liberal causes. Here this 'short, slight figure, fair-haired and pale, with not the slightest distinguishing mark in his features', as Rahel described him, suddenly found himself in the company of philosophers such as Fichte and Hegel, the explorer Alexander von Humboldt, writers like Chamisso and Fouqué. His first collection of poems was published in Berlin at the beginning of 1822. A year later came a volume containing his two tragedies, *William Ratcliff* and *Almansor*, together with the intercalated poems of the *Lyrisches Intermezzo*, a collection which includes 'Im wunderschönen Monat Mai', 'Ein Jüngling liebt ein Mädchen' and others of his best-known lyrics.

This is the Heine everyone knows, especially every lover of Lieder, the poet of deceptively artless trifles, expressions of emotional situations with which everyone can identify, cast in a simple, folksy form that cunningly conceals the workings of a sophisticated mind. The little four-line strophes lie scattered around like nuggets, ready-formed, to be picked up and admired as spontaneous creations of genius. Revelling in the pain of love rejected or love betrayed, they are in reality the products of repeated filing and polishing, of a restless intelligence that calculated and refined its purposes with more than half an eye on market forces and current critical taste.

Yet there is also, and always would be, the political Heine. A merciless critic of the political and social backwardness of his country, he eventually found the press censorship imposed under the Carlsbad Decrees of 1819 an intolerable curb on free expression and went into exile in Paris in 1831. Before this moment came, he had some observations to make – perceptive, pungent observations, both pertinent and impertinent – on the Berlin scene. These are his *Letters from Berlin*, published as a series of articles in the *Rheinisch-Westfälischer Anzeiger* in 1822.

It would be hard to imagine a more entertaining, more facetious, more prejudiced guide to the Prussian capital than Heine. One of the perils of a perpetually ironical manner is not to be recognised when one is not being ironical. But between Heine's ironical lines there are delightful glimpses to be had of the social and cultural life of the time, glimpses that would not be caught from a more sober source. There is a vignette of the theologian Schleiermacher thundering from the pulpit, an hilarious account of rival factions arguing over the relative merits of the operas of Weber and Spontini, and inside information on why Hoffmann's satirical novel *Meister Floh* had been banned by the censor.

And if one were wondering why a recent masterpiece of drama written in Berlin, Kleist's *Prinz Friedrich von Homburg*, had never been performed there, Heine had been behind the scenes and found the reason. It was, he says, because a certain noble lady, a descendant of Kleist's eponymous hero, felt personally insulted by the unheroic way the Prince was portrayed in the play, and had succeeded in having it suppressed ever since – 'a work virtually written by the spirit of poetry herself'. Heine describes it as 'worth far more than all those farces and baubles that our theatres dish up for us every night like scrambled eggs'.

After a surfeit of these 'scrambled eggs' Heine left the city in the summer of 1823 and went back to his parents in Lüneburg. But not without a characteristically sardonic *au revoir*:

Verlass Berlin, mit seinem dicken Sande
Und dünnen Tee und überwitz'gen Leuten,
Die Gott und Welt, und was sie selbst bedeuten,
Begriffen längst mit Hegelschem Verstande . . .

('Leave Berlin with its thick sand and thin tea and its population of know-alls who have long comprehended everything under the sun, including their own significance, through Hegelian logic . . .')

Still attached to Rahel Levin, Heine returned to Berlin on a few brief visits in the late 1820s, now the celebrated poet of the *Harzreise* and the assembled *Buch der Lieder*. In 1829 he met the young Felix Mendelssohn-Bartholdy there and was present at Mendelssohn's famous performance that year of Bach's *St Matthew Passion*. But by this time Germany had virtually lost him to Paris.

As an observer of the social and political scene — he left three times as much journalism as poetry — Heine found his subject matter in the reality around him. So did those of his younger contemporaries, with whom the age frequently associated him, who went under the name of Young Germany.

Less a school of writers than a loose association of malcontents for whom the old romanticism was out of date and a new, outspoken social realism the demand of the moment, the Young Germans soon fell foul of the censor. Their most spectacular martyr, the leader of the group, was Karl Gutzkow, a remarkable and in many respects paradigmatic figure, a Berliner by birth and education but, as one of the first German writers to live entirely by his pen, forced to move wherever he could find work as a dramaturge or journalist.

Nowadays more read about than read, Gutzkow had his great moment of public glory in 1835 with *Wally, die Zweiflerin* ('Wally the Sceptic'), an irreverent novel which brought its author a ten-week jail sentence for immorality and blasphemy. Immoral was the heroine's claim to sexual liberation; blasphemous was the scepticism expressed in the novel of the value of Christianity and the relevance of the doctrine of revelation.

Today nobody will raise an eyebrow. But the authorities in an age of Restoration saw it as an attack on the very fabric of society. Here was not only a challenge to established religion, or a discussion, under the seditious influence of the French socialist Saint-Simon, of the taboo topic of the emancipation of the flesh. Here was nothing less than a plea for the social and sexual equality of women. *Wally* was immediately banned, and with it the subversive works of all the other Young Germans, including, for good measure, Heine's.

It was a moment that epitomised the age of realism, in its substance as in its concept of literary form. Gone were the days of a rounded, romantic ideal or of the classical humanism of the age of Goethe, objective and demonstrable. The unity of the subjective ego had lost its credibility. A rapidly growing readership was demanding a focus upon the 'real' world in an age of flux. Established distinctions seemed invalid, because the configurations that had given those distinctions their validity had themselves changed and the concept of nature, invariably invoked, had become broader, less uniform, less cohesive. The Age of Art, as the Young Germans put it, had given way to the Age of Action. Conventional forms were no longer able to encompass the new liberal reality, either personal or political, and new genres would be needed, serving a realistic literature accessible to the public yet resting on a genuine aesthetic.

Thus in his gigantic, nine-volume novel *Die Ritter vom Geiste* ('The Knights of the Spirit'), published in serial form in 1850–1, Gutzkow chooses as his point of departure the recent 1848 Revolution. Through a complex web of human relationships, involving all social classes, Gutzkow shows how his characters, from the nobility to the working class, come to terms with the effects of the revolution and with each other – this is the realistic dimension of the novel. Then, through the reforming zeal of his central character, he creates an intellectual elite, like a masonic order, devoted to resolving social conflict and forging a new unity in a spiritually regenerated nation.

The raw material of Gutzkow's work may be society but *Die Ritter vom Geiste* is not what readers of Dickens or George Eliot or Thackeray expect of a social novel. His characters have not the inner strength to carve out their own destinies or to influence the society to which they belong. Instead, in what seems a typically German convention, familiar since the eighteenth century, they are made to receive their justification from without, from a superimposed programme of ideals brought in to perform an intellectual rescue operation. The interest of the novel lies rather in the parts than in the whole.

It also lies in the original narrative technique – since exploited in modern novels and in film – of what Gutzkow called *Nebeneinander*, 'one next to the other'. Instead of the *Nacheinander*, 'one after the other', of conventional story-telling, event following on event, Gutzkow juxtaposed the discrepant manifestations of the social and political reality of a given moment to present, as a simultaneity, the realistic totality of that moment. He himself compared these tranches of reality with a series of cross-sections through a mine shaft. It is an image that would characterise the work of others in the Young German movement, like the novelist and dramatist Heinrich Laube. But there was little to hold the group together beyond a sense of personal rebellion and opposition to the political establishment. Berlin, moreover, assumed no greater importance for its activities than any other city.

The Stage

For whatever reasons, from the end of the romantic period to the eruption of naturalism in the last decades of the century, the stage held little or no attraction for writers in Berlin. Not that there were no effective and popular dramatists at work in the German-speaking lands during these years. Vienna, above all, had a flourishing tradition led by the almost classical figure of Grillparzer in the 1820s. Gutzkow and Laube, their radical Young German years of protest behind them, later made it their preferred domicile, while the dialect comedies and farces of Raimund and Nestroy, both of them actor–playwrights, served the 'popular' end of the market.

Of the three most gripping realist dramatists of the period, none had any relationship to Berlin worthy of the name. The unhappy Grabbe, short-lived writer of historical tragedies with striking points of reference to contemporary social and political circumstances, visited the city just once, as a student agitator. Hebbel's first play, *Judith*, had its première in the Berlin Schauspielhaus in 1840 but this was due only to the fortuitous personal influence of Tieck: Hebbel had no connection with Berlin and was not present to witness the success of his tragedy.

As to the third, one of the greatest of all German dramatists, Georg Büchner seems never to have given the Prussian capital a moment's thought. A revolutionary in his native Hesse, than a political refugee in Strasbourg and in Switzerland, he saw only one of his plays published, and none was performed during his lifetime. Berlin discovered him only fifty years later, when his message reached an audience better prepared to understand it. It is no coincidence that this was the time, the 1880s, when a school of new young dramatists – Hermann Sudermann, Frank Wedekind, above all Gerhart Hauptmann – established itself in Berlin, confronting the personal and social predicament of the common man in a spirit of naturalism.

Since 1811, in the days of Iffland, the Royal Opera House on Unter den Linden and the Schauspielhaus on the Gendarmenmarkt had been under one management, which gave a strong-minded administrator great power to influence public taste. During the golden years of Count Brühl, Iffland's successor, a rich and varied programme was on offer: European classics such as Shakespeare and Calderon, modern masterpieces by Goethe, Schiller and Kleist, together with less sophisticated but enormously popular swashbuckling melodramas and blood-and-thunder historical plays, like those on the Hohenstaufen dynasty by Ernst Raupach, the most immediately successful of Berlin dramatists in the mid-nineteenth century.

But Brühl's two royal houses, conservative in policy and jealous of their monopoly, were already insufficient to meet the potential demand, especially at the popular end of the repertoire, and in 1824, in a converted building on the Alexanderplatz, the first private theatre in the city opened its doors. The brain-child of a successful horse-dealer called Friedrich Cerf, the first in a long line of Jewish impresarios in Berlin, the Königsstädtisches Theater had room for an audience of some 1,500. It offered a mixture of classical drama, light comedies and operas, for some of which the romantic painter Carl Blechen did the sets. Especially popular were the works of Rossini, a popularity assured by the engagement of the young prima donna Henriette Sontag, who conquered the hearts of the Berliners with her charm and artistry in *L'Italiana in Algeri* and other contemporary works.

When Henriette left the company, however, much of the theatre's glamour went with her. Ambitious attempts to broaden the repertoire brought the enterprise to a state of almost constant debt, which Friedrich Wilhelm III equally constantly met out of state funds. For the urge to raise the status of Berlin among the cities of Europe – even among the capitals of the other German states – involved encouraging, and if necessary subsidising, public cultural activities, and the King's support of theatre had its political as well as its altruistic side.

Still the demand for theatres grew. In 1843 an immense winter garden was built near the entrance to the Tiergarten by a Breslau entrepreneur called Joseph Kroll. Here there were to be concerts three or four times a week, together with masked balls and other entertainments for what the King, in his decree making the prestigious site available for Kroll's establishment, called 'the educated public of Berlin'. In 1850 a theatre was added to the complex, offering farces and light entertainment, with the occasional serious play and opera. Flotow's *Martha*, for example, was put on, together with *Zar und Zimmermann* and other works by Lortzing.

But a succession of bankruptcies and false starts, the occasional fire and other setbacks dogged the 'Kroll' over the years. Moments of revived glory, attracting international prima donnas such as Adeline Patti and Désirée Artôt in the 1860s, could not save it and by the end of the century its demise as a private institution was a foregone conclusion. It was taken over by the state as a second opera house and survived as such until 1931.

Alongside such large-scale enterprises as the Königsstädtisches Theater and the 'Kroll' there emerged in the mid-nineteenth century small troupes of actors and musicians who set up their stalls in taverns and, in summer, in outdoor restaurants and other popular spots. Here they played *Volksstücke* – lowbrow comedies with familiar city types as characters, making free use of dialect and off-the-cuff humour, aggressively realistic and blatantly calculated to appeal to the earthier emotions. The scope for improvisation in such plays and sketches was immense, and allusions to contemporary personalities and events would constantly be slipped into the dialogue, sometimes to the disapproval of an ever-vigilant censor, always to the delight of a chuckling audience. This satirical presentation of characteristic proletarian figures from the city scene reached a fine art with Adolf Glassbrenner, who in ballads and anecdotes, sketches and plays, created a whole world out of such types and made a fortune from the spectators' eagerness to spend ten pfennigs in order to laugh at themselves.

Music in the Nineteenth Century

Music, like drama and dance, is an art of performance. It matters less where the music played and the dramas acted originate than that there are competent players to perform and interested audiences to watch and listen. Centres of creative activity, like Vienna at the time of Haydn, Mozart, Beethoven and Schubert, may become pre-eminent but whereas the enjoyment of a piece of architecture, or a sculpture, or a painting is confined to the unique location in which it happens to be, a piece of music can be experienced in as many places as musicians can be found to perform it. And since it is only through performance that a composer can make his work known, he will seek out the accessible towns and cities – sometimes even the countries – that promise the greatest publicity.

There is thus a natural link between the performing arts and socio-economic circumstances. From the patronage of kings and princes at one end of the historical scale to the commercial pressures of modern concert-giving at the other, musicians have taken their wares to the most profitable markets. Seen from the other end: seats of power, whether a medieval court or a modern industrial and political centre, vie with each other for the services of leading artists. And as the performing artist needs a public for his spiritual and economic survival, so the place that can offer him such a public will both raise its cultural prestige and share in the material reward.

Such is the situation of Berlin in the nineteenth century. Apart from Mendelssohn, who spent his youth there, none of the century's great German-Austrian composers – Beethoven, Schubert, Weber, Schumann, Liszt, Brahms, Bruckner – felt moved to make a home in the Prussian capital. Even Wagner, with his Teutonic patriotism, his cult of power and his love of extravagance – qualities much at their ease here – can hardly be imagined as part of the Prussian landscape, with a Festspielhaus in Berlin rather than Bayreuth. But no less than a host of others, great and small, Wagner was at pains to ensure that Berlin got to know his music dramas, especially after it became the imperial capital in 1871.

At the very beginning of the century the Berlin romantics – Wackenroder, Tieck, Novalis – had put forward a cosmology, later reinforced by E. T. A. Hoffmann and Schopenhauer, which perceived the world as an aesthetic phenomenon to be apprehended, in its essence, through music. But the romantic music that was to embody this philosophy came from anywhere other than Berlin. Hoffmann's starting-point was Beethoven – in Vienna, like Schubert and Brahms; Schumann's romanticism was born in Leipzig; Liszt divided his creative life between Weimar, Budapest and Rome. And Wagner, the arch-romantic, composed his music dramas wherever his restless life led him – Dresden, Zurich, Munich, Bayreuth. But never Berlin.

As the nineteenth century opened out in the wake of the French Revolution, and as the inspiration of the revolutionary ideals received joyful national confirmation in the War of Liberation, so forces had been released whose onward march through the century was irresistible. As well as their obvious political and social manifestations these forces had their cultural dimension, and nowhere did the differences of opinion over matters cultural declare themselves more openly than in opera.

In the early nineteenth century there were two houses playing opera in Berlin. One was the Royal Opera House on Unter den Linden, where Italian and later French works were given; the other was the Schauspielhaus, originally called the Nationaltheater, on the Gendarmenmarkt, primarily a theatre for spoken drama but also the home of the Singspiel. When Brühl took over from Iffland in 1814, he led the opera to new heights, giving a clear indication of his policies by mounting the first Berlin performance of Beethoven's *Fidelio* in 1815, only a year after its première in Vienna. He followed this the next year with E. T. A. Hoffmann's recently finished *Undine*, a great success at the time but now only a collector's item. When the Schauspielhaus burnt down in 1817 during a rehearsal of Schiller's *Die Räuber*, the impetus was temporarily lost, but four years later the theatre reopened in Schinkel's superb new design with Goethe's *Iphigenie*, followed a few weeks later by the first performance of Weber's *Der Freischütz*.

Brühl's predilection for German opera could not but damage the fortunes of the French and Italian opera in the Royal Opera House. It also annoyed Friedrich Wilhelm III, whose tastes favoured just such works. To redress the balance he created a new post of 'General Music Director' and appointed to it Gasparo Spontini, an Italian working in the Paris Opéra, whose work he had heard on a recent visit to the French capital. Brühl, on the other hand, wanted to see Weber in the post, so did the Berliners at large, who no longer had much sympathy for the ostentations and artificialities of the Franco-Italian school. So the battle lines were drawn: home-grown German versus a foreign import, Weber versus Spontini.

As in most such contrived rivalries, one of the parties becomes cast, with historical hindsight, as a figure either manifestly inferior as an artist or morally dubious as a person, or both, to the point where he is either ignored or despised. Who is prepared to look at the case of Piccinni, thrust into an artificial role as an opponent of Gluck? Who knows Salieri other than as an unsavoury rival of Mozart? What was at stake in the Parisian *guerre des bouffons*? So while the world knows and respects Weber, it has all but forgotten Spontini, on whom were heaped the negative characteristics that cling to a potential loser.

In fact Spontini was an accomplished all-round musician who did a great deal for Berlin music during his twenty years in the capital. He had gone in 1803 from Naples to Paris, where his success, nurtured by the patronage of the Empress Joséphine, made him one of the foremost composers of opera in Europe. In 1819 Friedrich Wilhelm III enticed him to Berlin with the promise of an influence equal to that of Lully at the court of Louis XIV, and Spontini celebrated his arrival with a gala performance of his most recent work, *Olimpie*, based on a tragedy by Voltaire.

Spontini had an imperious, aristocratic air about him and kept his orchestra on a short rein. 'I conduct not with my hands but with my eyes,' he said. 'My left eye is for the first violins, my right eye is for the seconds.' This discipline undoubtedly helped to raise the orchestra's standard, while Hoffmann welcomed him to Berlin as a composer worthy to be seen in the company of Handel, Hasse, Gluck, Mozart 'and all those masters who coin their works only from the purest, most precious metals'.

A synthesis of Italian and French elements, with its dramatic characterisation derived largely from Gluck, Spontini's operatic work draws its effectiveness from large-scale choruses, triumphal marches, ballets and similar expansive movements rather than from intimate solo numbers. The overall effect could be powerful but a study of the details reveals little subtlety and the harmonic vocabulary is limited – inevitably so in a context dominated by slow-moving displays of pomp and majesty. French taste liked things that way. So did the King. But the public, as they were to demonstrate a few weeks later, rose to a different kind of opera.

Spontini did try to make his music more German. In 1829 he began work on an opera set in the German Middle Ages called *Agnes von Hohenstaufen*, to a libretto by Ernst Raupach. It was a work of Wagnerian proportions which took eight years to complete and has never been published. Spontini's duties as superintendent of music for the royal household required him to compose occasional choral and orchestral pieces for weddings and other royal functions, while as conductor of the Royal Opera he supervised a repertoire that ranged from Gluck and Mozart to Rossini's *Barber of Seville* and *The Thieving Magpie*, Marschner's *Hans Heiling*, Bellini's *Norma* and works by Spohr, Auber and Cherubini.

But he never fully assimilated to Berlin ways. The death of Friedrich Wilhelm III in 1840 removed his main source of support, and when the new King released him from his contract, he went back to Paris, a figure whose moment had passed. The symbolic event that marked the passing of that moment was one of the great occasions in the musical history of Berlin – the first performance of Weber's *Der Freischütz*.

Born in north Germany, Carl Maria von Weber led a restless life, moving from one court to another – Munich, Frankfurt, Prague, Vienna – in search of a satisfactory position as Kapellmeister, with opportunities to perform his operas, orchestral and chamber music. Berlin knew him since 1812, when he arrived to conduct his one-act opera *Abu Hassan*. He met E. T. A. Hoffmann, Rahel Levin and her husband Varnhagen von Ense and other prominent members of the intelligentsia but the musical establishment was suspicious of his originality, and Iffland, director of the royal theatres at the time, showed little interest in him. Back in the city three years later, he hopefully offered the King a cantata called *Kampf und Sieg* ('Struggle and Victory'), which, like Hoffmann's *Battle of Leipzig* and Beethoven's 'battle symphony', *Wellingtons Sieg*, dramatised the events and emotions of the war against Napoleon. But His Majesty merely sent his gracious thanks. His real musical tastes lay elsewhere and he was already negotiating to engage Spontini.

In Brühl, however, the cause of German music found a new champion. He had come across Weber's work on a visit to the Saxon court in Dresden and determined to promote it in Berlin. Dresden was at the time something of a cultural backwater compared with Berlin, so with *Der Freischütz* completed and awaiting production, Brühl had little difficulty in persuading Weber to launch it in the Schauspielhaus.

In the Singspiel tradition, the musical numbers interspersed with spoken dialogue, *Der Freischütz* captures the contemporary romantic taste for the supernatural and the exotic already invoked in Hoffmann's *Undine* and Weber's own *Abu Hassan*. From a world of magic hidden in the depths of nature emerges a sinister story with its roots in the Faust legend, the story of the man who makes a pact with the devil. The fairy-tale world of the forest, scenes of mystery and intrigue, the tension generated by a sense of impending disaster – such material inspires Weber to a dramatic music of utter originality, an originality residing to a large extent in the orchestration. Coupled with this are the folk-like melodies, unmistakably German in idiom, whose charm and immediate appeal made them the hit tunes of the day. In no time the whole piece had become national property.

The first performance, on 18 June 1821, showed what to expect. 'As early as four o'clock', wrote Julius Benedict, a pupil of Weber's and his first English biographer,

I joined the crowd besieging the theatre, and when, two hours later, the doors were opened, I was literally carried into the pit by the surging human wave. Many Iron Crosses were to be seen, and the students of the university mustered in large numbers. Frau von Weber was in a pit box with William Beer [brother of the composer Meyerbeer] and his wife, while E. T. A. Hoffmann, Professor Lichtenstein [Professor of Zoology at the University], Heinrich Heine and a host of literary and musical aspirants, among them little Felix Mendelssohn, with his parents, occupied boxes and stalls.

Berlin and its Culture

The King and his court were not represented. But it made no difference. Weber had never experienced anything like it. 'The enthusiasm was unbelievable,' he wrote in his diary. 'The Overture and the Volkslied ['Wir winden dir den Jungfernkranz'] had to be repeated, and of the seventeen numbers, fourteen were greeted with tumultuous applause. *Soli Dei Gloria*'.

Weber returned to Berlin in 1825, the year before his death, to conduct his *Euryanthe*. But the Berliners did not warm to the work – a continuous web of music and dramatic action, a long way from Singspiel. It 'lacked tunes', they found, and its departure from the familiar number-form had a disorienting effect. They could not know that they were on the road that led to Richard Wagner.

Spontini had failed to achieve what Friedrich Wilhelm III had employed him to achieve, namely, to make the Berlin opera the equal of that in Paris. He was dismissed in 1841, and again the call went out to the French capital for a General Music Director who would accept the challenge on behalf of the new King, Friedrich Wilhelm IV, a monarch who set great store by the arts and sciences. The call was heard by one of the greatest operatic composers of the day. True, he had learnt his craft in Italy, had imbibed the spirit of Rossinian *bel canto* and had chosen to establish himself in Paris, writing immensely successful operas to French libretti. But – and this is what really mattered to the King and his advisers – he was a German. He had even been born in Berlin, and his family, owners of a flourishing banking business, were much respected in the city. He was born Jakob Liebmann Beer but called himself Giacomo Meyerbeer.

Berlin's introduction to Meyerbeer had been a sensational performance of *Robert le Diable* in 1832 with an orchestra of 112 and a proverbial 'cast of thousands', including twenty-two horses. As so often with Meyerbeer's operas, the spectators were swept off their feet, leaving the critics to carp and sneer – some of their hostile criticism, one suspects, generated less by the musical evidence than by resentment of Meyerbeer's earlier desertion of Berlin for Paris and by the fact that he was, and remained, a Jew (Heine and Mendelssohn, among many, converted to Protestantism).

Accustomed to Parisian standards, Meyerbeer did his best to raise the level of the Berlin opera, on the one hand by bringing in some of his leading soloists from Paris, on the other by patiently but insistently rehearsing his orchestra and chorus until he was satisfied. For their part his musicians had good cause to be grateful to him for persuading the court exchequer to raise their salaries to a level that better reflected their worth. After the royal command performance of *Les Huguenots* in 1842, given a few weeks before his official appointment as General Music Director, he donated his entire fee to his singers and players.

In addition to performing the standard repertory of Mozart, Gluck and Weber, he considered it to be 'the moral duty of the royal opera', Meyerbeer wrote to the King, 'to present every year a number of operas by contemporary German composers'. He therefore included in the repertoire works by Spohr and Flotow and arranged for Wagner to conduct the first Berlin performance of *Der fliegende Holländer* in 1844.

Meyerbeer's own contribution to modern German opera was *Ein Feldlager in Schlesien* ('An Encampment in Silesia'), based on an episode from the life of Frederick the Great. Like Spontini's *Agnes von Hohenstaufen*, the choice of subject matter from the German national past was a gesture towards his Prussian patron, and he went to great lengths to assemble a spectacle opera of the kind he knew was expected of him. Yet for all the realism of his operatic style and the majestic originality of his orchestral effects, Meyerbeer concentrated his musical attention on the singers, and to ensure the success of his new piece he invited Jenny Lind, the 'Swedish nightingale', to come from Paris to sing the title role.

No expense was spared. The King himself was even rumoured to have had a hand in the libretto devoted to his illustrious ancestor. But to no avail. 'The audience expressed the unanimous view that it was an inferior and boring piece of work,' wrote Varnhagen von Ense in his diary. Whether the embarrassed monarch thought the same is not recorded.

Although born a Berliner, Meyerbeer never felt fully at his ease in the city, and after three years he asked to be relieved of his post. Apart from the *Feldlager in Schlesien*, those three years had yielded only occasional pieces for the royal household and a few songs, including settings of Heine. It was a poor harvest. The moment he returned to Paris, things changed. He set to work on a new text by his faithful librettist Eugène Scribe, and a few years afterwards offered to the Parisian public *Le Prophète*, the most spectacular of his invariably spectacular successes. The legendary 'Berlin air', from which many claimed to draw their spiritual sustenance, only brought Meyerbeer to the point of suffocation.

Hand in hand with the public growth of the performing arts in the nineteenth century went the spread of amateur music-making, which itself sometimes merged into the professional sphere as standards rose. Vocal and instrumental groups were formed to perform partly for their own pleasure, partly for that of assembled families and acquaintances in the tradition of *Hausmusik* (Ill. 67). And if aspirations outgrew these domestic confines, the performers would constitute themselves as a society and embark on a public career. The earliest of these societies, the model for similar bodies that sprang up all over Germany, was the Berlin Singakademie, a choral society founded under royal patronage in 1792 and directed from 1800 onwards by Carl Friedrich Zelter (Ill. 68).

Only a minor figure in the history of music, Zelter meant a great deal to Berlin. A dyed-in-the-wool Berliner, a master builder by trade, he taught himself the theory and practice of music in his spare time, joined the Singakademie and began to compose. In 1796 he published his first collection of songs and sent a copy to Goethe, a number of whose poems were included in the volume. It marked the beginning of a lifelong friendship between the two men, whose correspondence, as a source of insights into Goethe's mature philosophy of art and life, is barely less revealing than his conversations with Eckermann. Zelter became his favourite composer. In composing songs, Goethe wrote to him, 'it is a matter of inducing in the listener the mood set by the poem. Show me who else has achieved that as perfectly as you.'

From taking over the Singakademie until his death in 1832 Zelter devoted himself to the activities of his institution and to the musical life of Berlin. He organised a chamber orchestra to accompany his singers and later

67. Lyre piano by Johann Christian Schleip, Berlin, c. 1840.

founded an independent male voice choir (*Liedertafel*) which also, in its turn, became a prototype for the whole country. A staple part of the choir's repertoire was the music of the so-called Berlin Lieder School – strophic songs suitable for amateur groups, many of them by Reichardt and by Zelter himself.

Zelter was teacher, chorus master, musicologist and impresario in one and viewed the various strands of his activity as parts of a single comprehensive musical exercise, theoretical and practical. What more natural, therefore, that when the University of Berlin was founded in 1809 Friedrich Wilhelm III should appoint him Professor of Music. The importance of the Singakademie itself for the cultural life of the city received emphatic recognition in 1827, when the King presented the society with a new recital hall – a charming piece of neo-classicism based on a design by Schinkel and set in a grove of chestnut trees off Unter den Linden. Since its reconstruction in 1952 after war damage it has been called the Maxim Gorki Theatre but to Berliners it has always been 'Zelter's Singakademie'.

From the beginning the society had a generous supply of modern cantatas, sacred and profane, and other choral works to perform on a regular basis, among them Zelter's own. There were also individual occasions to cherish, such as a performance of Mozart's Requiem in the Marienkirche with an augmented complement of 115 singers. Specially written for the

Realism and Revolution

68. Singakademie Concert Hall, lithograph by Ludwig Eduard Lütke, c. 1840.

Liedertafel was a group of settings of Theodor Körner's patriotic poems by Carl Maria von Weber, who sought out the company of Zelter and the Singakademie on his visits to the city and was always given a warm welcome.

But a growing awareness at the turn of the century of the music of earlier ages, a process in which a new breed of music historian played an important role, revealed a treasure of hitherto neglected music. The world of Baroque was rediscovered, above all the music of Bach and Handel. The Singakademie rehearsed Bach motets, the B minor Mass and the St John Passion in the early years of Zelter's regime, and performed Handel's *Samson* in 1819 and *Alexander's Feast* in 1824. *A cappella* groups like the Royal Court and Cathedral Choir discovered their own repertory of older music, while Baroque chamber music was also being taken out of the drawer and dusted down.

It was an irresistible movement. In its practical aspect it opened up a whole new repertory to sing and play. At the same time it restored a sense of historical continuity and revived the conception, fostered by the thinkers of the Enlightenment, of the unity of the aesthetically beautiful and the morally good. Its supreme demonstration came on 11 March 1829 with an historic performance in the Singakademie's new concert hall of Bach's *St Matthew Passion*, composed exactly one hundred years earlier. The conductor, and the young man responsible for the entire occasion, was Zelter's most famous pupil – Felix Mendelssohn-Bartholdy.

Mendelssohn is one more of those, both before his time and after, whom Berlin attracted but could not ultimately hold. Yet for thirty years of his short life Berlin was his home and the centre of his intellectual and musical world. Born into a prosperous Jewish banking family – by 1823 Abraham Mendelssohn and Co. was the third largest bank in the city – he had no financial worries and was able to wander wherever his privileged genius led him.

As rich as the material circumstances of the family was its cultural pedigree. Felix's grandfather was Moses Mendelssohn, leader of the German Enlightenment and protagonist of a liberal philosophy which united the values of Christian civilisation with those of the Judaic tradition. The assimilatory process was continued by Moses' daughter Dorothea, who married the romantic writer Friedrich Schlegel and by whom Felix was initiated into the great cultural issues of the day. Prodigiously gifted, he began at twelve to study composition with Zelter, who insisted on taking the boy to Weimar to play to his friend Goethe. Goethe was amazed. Here was a second Mozart. 'What this little man is capable of in improvisation and sight-reading is simply incredible,' he exclaimed. By the time he was seventeen, Mendelssohn had composed five string symphonies, chamber music and songs, the priceless Overture to *A Midsummer Night's Dream* and an opera called *The Wedding of Camacho*, based on an episode in *Don Quixote*, which was given one public performance at the family's expense in 1827 but did not survive the critics' disdain.

Bach fugues and other contrapuntal works made up a large part of the music on which Zelter based his teaching, and the *St Matthew Passion* was one of the priceless scores he had in his possession. It had not been heard in public for decades. The plan to resurrect it came, however, not from Mendelssohn himself but from his friend, the actor Eduard Devrient. When they finally persuaded Zelter to make the Singakademie available for the occasion, Mendelssohn turned excitedly to Devrient and cried: 'To think that it has been left to you, an actor, and me, a Jewish boy, to revive this greatest of all Christian music!' He was barely twenty at the time.

The *St Matthew Passion* of 11 March 1829 has gone down in history. The choir numbered 400, with the normally modest orchestra augmented by musicians from the opera and the royal household. The reception was overwhelming. Not that the audience heard only what Bach had written, or even all that he had written, for Mendelssohn cut some of the numbers in the interest of dramatic tension and embellished the instrumentation to meet contemporary taste. For over a hundred years audiences all over the world loved it that way. Today's purists would have had apoplexy.

A few weeks after this triumph Mendelssohn, a much travelled man, paid the first of his many visits to England, playing and conducting his own and others' works, including the first performance in Britain of Beethoven's Emperor Concerto. As a conductor, he favoured the contemporary practice of unifying the movements of a symphony or concerto by adopting a more or less consistent *moderato-cum-allegro* and *mezzo forte*. It was an expression of a balanced, rounded personality, the generous, helpful man for whom no one had a bad word.

Mendelssohn was everywhere *persona grata*, especially in Berlin, the city he always regarded as his own. He took it as something of an indignity, therefore, when on Zelter's death he was not appointed to direct the Singakademie. In 1835 he went to Leipzig as conductor of the famous Gewandhaus concerts, and, without giving up his permanent residence in the Leipziger Strasse in Berlin, impressed his personality on the musical life of the busy Saxon city over the coming ten years.

But Berlin soon called him back. As part of his plan to reorganise the Academy of Arts as the cultural centre of Prussia, Friedrich Wilhelm IV put forward a proposal in 1840 to divide the Academy into four schools – architecture, sculpture, painting and music – each with its own director. The school of music would virtually become an independent conservatoire, training young musicians and giving public concerts. With Meyerbeer about to take over the opera, and Mendelssohn as General Music Director at the Academy, also on hand to write incidental music for productions at the Royal Theatre, the musical supremacy of Prussia, argued the King, would be unchallengeable.

But the grand design never left the paper. Perhaps the whole ethos of Berlin – a down-to-earth, rationalist, 'Voltairean' city at heart, as Georg Brandes called it – was unconducive to such a project at the time. With no role to fulfil, and hardly consoled by the award of the 'Pour le mérite', the highest civilian decoration the King could bestow, Mendelssohn returned to Leipzig, city of Bach. There, in 1843, under the auspices of the King of Saxony, he founded the conservatoire that should have had its home in Berlin.

From his final years came the Violin Concerto – 'the best-loved of all concertos, the heart's jewel', the violinist Joseph Joachim called it – and the oratorio *Elijah*, which he conducted at Birmingham in 1846. He died the following year, only thirty-eight years old. He had drawn his fame from all over Europe, and all Europe mourned his death, London and the English royal family as deeply as any.

Mendelssohn's swan-song for Berlin had been the completed incidental music for *A Midsummer Night's Dream*, written in 1842 – the music of an elegant romantic imagination held in the mould of a classical mind. At the same time he led by example the movement to rediscover the music of the German classical past and to bring to public concert-going an enhanced historical and aesthetic awareness. Perhaps it is proper, after all, that although he was neither born there nor died there, it should be in rationalist–romantic Berlin, in the cemetery of the Protestant Dreifaltigkeitskirche, that he found his last resting-place.

Compared with other important German cities – Munich, Vienna, Frankfurt – let alone with international centres such as Paris and London, Berlin had an embarrassingly underdeveloped public musical life at the beginning of the nineteenth century. Reichardt had instituted 'Concerts Spirituels' on a subscription basis in 1783, given by a partly amateur, partly professional band of instrumentalists and singers. Inspired by Reichardt's surprising success, the publisher and music dealer Carl Friedrich Rellstab, father of the well-known and much feared critic, launched a series of 'Concerts for Connoisseurs' four years later. But they were isolated ventures.

Concerts such as these took place in the ballrooms of large hotels or in the salons of mansions belonging to aristocrats like Prince Radziwill or prosperous burghers such as the banker Herz Beer, father of the composer Meyerbeer, where *Hausmusik* had long been part of the family's way of life. Famous during the 1820s were the Sunday concerts conducted by the boy Mendelssohn in the garden pavilion of his family villa in the Leipziger

Strasse. Such occasions, however, could never be more than exclusive, semi-private affairs. Indeed, a lack of suitable concert halls was one of the forces that hampered the development of music for a wider public. True, concerts of religious music were given in the city's large churches, such as the Klosterkirche and the Marienkirche. But even the famous Singakademie, founded in a private house in 1790, became a focus of Berlin musical life only after being provided with its own concert hall in 1827, with seats for over a thousand.

It was an audience with its own special character. 'For the visitor from Paris', wrote Berlioz in his memoirs, after attending a performance of the *St Matthew Passion*, 'the reverence with which a German audience listens to such a work has to be experienced to be believed. Each person follows from a copy of the text: not a movement anywhere, no whisper of approval or dis-approval, no applause. One is not at a concert – one is in church.'

Provision for public concerts had begun to improve when, with the per-functory consent of Friedrich Wilhelm III, the recital hall in the Schau-spielhaus advertised a series of subscription concerts in 1805 arranged by Bernhard Anselm Weber, court Kapellmeister and Music Director of the opera until the arrival of Spontini in 1820. Weber set the tone for his con-certs by opening the season with a performance of Mozart's *Requiem*, while other members of the royal orchestra followed Weber's lead, arranging their own programmes of choral, chamber and symphonic music both in the Schauspielhaus and in the homes of the wealthy. A season of concerts in 1821 included Handel's *Samson*, together with music by Gluck, Haydn, Mozart, Carl Maria von Weber, Hummel – who played one of his own piano concertos – and many now forgotten composers.

Since the orchestra was virtually out of commission from 1806 until the liberation in 1814, musicians came to rely on such private initiatives for their survival. The King had fled to Königsberg with his court before Napoleon's triumphant entry into Berlin, and stopped financing his theatres and their personnel. It was left to Iffland, director of the two state houses, to extract what funds he could from the occupying French authorities to keep his actors and musicians together.

Concert programmes at this time did not have the concentration on a few complete works to which the twentieth century has become accus-tomed. Concerts were also much longer. Individual movements of sym-phonies and concertos would be taken out of their context and interspersed with operatic arias and choral items to create a mélange of items of diverse character. A choral and orchestral concert in Kroll's concert hall to mark the King's birthday in 1849, for example, consisted of no fewer than fourteen items, ranging from Beethoven's Fifth Symphony (complete) through pieces by Spontini, Mendelssohn and Rossini (the overture to *William Tell*) to popular marches, polkas, waltzes and folksong arrangements. The literal view of a musical text that we now take for granted was in any case not charac-teristic of the nineteenth century. When Mendelssohn conducted his first symphony in London in 1829, he did not play the score as written and printed but replaced the 'official' Scherzo with that from his recently com-pleted Octet, clearly without offending any conception of the spiritual unity of the work.

Of lasting influence on the course of Berlin musical life was the foundation in 1826 of an amateur orchestra calling itself the Philharmonic Society. Its leader, Eduard Rietz, was a violinist who had led the court orchestra for a number of years but fallen out with Spontini. In a few years Rietz turned his players into one of the best bands in the city. It accompanied the Singakademie in its concerts of church music and formed the core of the orchestra that Rietz led at Mendelssohn's performance of Bach's *St Matthew Passion*. Ensembles like Rietz's helped the orchestra of the Royal Opera to keep alive the tradition which later in the century became firmly established in the Stern Academy and the state conservatoire (Hochschule für Musik).

Rising economic prosperity was making Berlin an increasingly attractive port of call for actors, singers, musicians and performers in all fields, and the more vigorously the city promoted its cultural life, the greater the interest shown by artists in making their impression on the place. It was a well-trodden path. Mozart had played before the court of Friedrich Wilhelm II in 1789, and Beethoven in 1796. With the nineteenth century came the virtuoso performer. Among the earliest was the demonic violinist Paganini, who on one of his hectic European tours in 1829 played before the Prussian royal family and gave eleven public recitals, six in the Schauspielhaus, the others in the opera house. The 1830s saw a procession of visits from dazzling pianists, some of them child prodigies, like Clara Schumann, others, like Thalberg, Moscheles and Kalkbrenner, established virtuosi and composers. Technical brilliance, not to say ostentation, was the order of the day. And no artist shone more brilliantly than Franz Liszt.

Determined to conquer Berlin with his playing as he had already conquered Vienna, Dresden, Leipzig and a host of other cities, Liszt arrived at Christmas 1841 and stayed for three months. As had been his custom elsewhere and as etiquette required, he played privately before royalty and aristocracy but also gave over twenty public concerts, almost half of them for charity. His triumphs were so overwhelming, his presence so charismatic, that for the ten weeks of his stay the name of the King of Prussia seemed to be not Friedrich Wilhelm IV of Hohenzollern but Franz Liszt. His portrait was exhibited all over the city, while elegant ladies displaying cameos with his likeness screamed and jumped up and down at his concerts in a display of mass hysteria worthy of a pop concert.

This may not suggest great discernment on the part of the public, but Berlioz, who visited the city in the same year as Liszt, was vastly impressed with the quality of the music he heard. To be sure, performances at the Royal Opera tended to be ill-disciplined and poorly attended but the orchestra was larger than that of the Paris Opéra and its brass superior (if anyone knew about brass, it was Berlioz). 'Were I to describe in detail all the musical riches of the royal city of Berlin', he wrote in his memoirs,

> I would never finish. Few if any capitals can boast treasures comparable to these. Music is in the very air. One breathes it in theatres, in churches, in the street, in public parks – everywhere. For everyone respects music in Berlin, rich and poor alike, clerics and soldiers, the common people and the King. The monarch

above all brings to the cultivation of music the same passion as he devotes to science and the other arts, which is saying a great deal . . . Hence the attraction that Berlin holds for great artists, and the remarkable popularity of music in Prussia.

On the express wish of Friedrich Wilhelm IV Berlioz paid another visit to Berlin in 1847, on his way back from Moscow, to conduct a performance of his *Damnation of Faust* at the Royal Opera. The King promised Berlioz half the receipts from the occasion and entertained him two days later at Sanssouci, almost as though hoping Berlioz might be enticed to Berlin on a more permanent basis. But Berlioz did not return.

Quite different was the experience of Wagner when he came in 1841 to conduct his *Fliegender Holländer* in the Schauspielhaus. At the first performance utter silence followed Act One. But Acts Two and Three were greeted with enthusiastic applause, from which Wagner concluded that he had scored a success. At the second performance the overture produced some tentative clapping, which was immediately met by a counterblast of hissing. From then on everything was received in utter silence.

The baffled Wagner received an explanation of this curious behaviour a few days later. The public waited, he was told, until the critics, led by Ludwig Rellstab, had delivered their first-night judgements in the following morning's papers. Subsequent audiences then knew how they were expected to react. Rellstab and his cohorts had delivered a dismissive verdict on the opening night of the *Holländer*, and the audience at the second performance behaved as they were expected to.

When he returned six years later to rehearse and conduct his *Rienzi*, Wagner found that little had changed. He still failed to attract the interest of the King and had the misfortune to be completely overshadowed by Jenny Lind, who had a series of guest appearances in the city at the time and monopolised the attention of the opera-going public. The critics had not softened their hostility towards him, nor did audiences find anything new to admire. 'After the third act', wrote the playwright Charlotte Birch-Pfeiffer, 'masses of people just left the theatre, as I did. Like me, they quite literally could not stand it any more.' Officialdom made amends by electing Wagner an external member of the Akademie der Künste in 1869. But when the *Ring des Nibelungen* finally reached Berlin in 1881, it was performed, not in the Royal Opera House and with royal approval but in one of the city's new private theatres and by a visiting company. There was nothing the Berlin public liked more, his hosts told him, than to go to the theatre to see something new and unfamiliar with the fixed intention of booing it off the stage.

Dispiriting, almost insulting, as Wagner found this criticism, the role of the critics could not be dismissed as an offensive irrelevance. Neither could their competence. Berlin did not have, like Vienna, an educated musical public with a sense of history, an audience who knew what to look for and could distinguish between good and inferior music. Berlin critics had first to guide and instruct before the concept of appreciation could have any relevance. Even an event like Mendelssohn's revival of Bach's *St Matthew Passion* could, of itself, have only a limited effect. Indeed, its very novelty gave it the quality of an experiment, and to evaluate an experiment demands sophistication and a firm background of knowledge. But if Berlioz's testimony is to be believed, these qualities were only waiting to be awakened. A knowledgeable and sophisticated public was being moulded.

THE SELF-ASSURANCE
OF EMPIRE

Power and Pride

Berlin continued to extend its territorial limits. Suburbs like Moabit and Wedding, with parts of Schöneberg and Tempelhof, were incorporated, giving the city in 1861 a total area of sixty-five square kilometres. House-building boomed, so did land and property speculation. Sumptuous villas were built for the new wealthy bourgeoisie, along with *Mietskasernen* ('rented barracks') for the masses – tenement blocks still characteristic today of parts of the inner city, with impressive façades but dingy courtyards and dark, poky rooms at the back. Factories sprang up as more and more steam engines were installed. On the heels of Borsig and Siemens came the electrical giants Telefunken and AEG (Allgemeine Elektrizitäts-Gesellschaft), chemical concerns, textiles, publishing and many other trades and industries.

Achievements in engineering and applied science were matched by advances in basic scientific and medical research. Helmholtz, Professor of Physics at the University, founded the science of acoustics and invented the ophthalmoscope; Heinrich Hertz discovered electromagnetic waves; Rudolf Virchow, 'the father of modern pathology' and also a liberal politician later elected to the Reichstag, was treating patients in the Charité hospital and introducing vital reforms in public health.

In the humanities too the University of Berlin, which became the largest university in the country before the end of the century, boasted many distinguished names. Jakob Grimm, philologist, grammarian and cultural historian, held a chair there from 1841 until his death in 1863; Wilhelm Dilthey, cultural anthropologist, was professor of philosophy during the last twenty years of the century, and the sociologist Max Weber lectured there. Most outstanding of all was the succession of great historians, from Barthold Niebuhr, Leopold von Ranke and Theodor Mommsen down to Friedrich Meinecke.

All around were the physical proofs of progress. Loan banks such as the powerful Berliner Handelsgesellschaft were established to encourage investment in industry. New museums and picture galleries, cafés, beer-cellars, music halls – everywhere were signs of the need to provide for the edification and entertainment of a rapidly growing population with a multiplicity of tastes.

The transformation was not lost on Karl Marx, for one, when he visited the city in 1861. 'Anyone who saw Berlin ten years ago', he wrote, 'would not recognise the place today. What used to be a parade-ground, rigid and regimented, has turned into the buzzing centre of German heavy industry.' That same year Friedrich Wilhelm IV died. One of the first acts of his successor, Wilhelm I, later Kaiser of the new German Reich, was to appoint as prime minister a man whose name was synonymous with Prussian and German politics for the next thirty years. That man was Count Otto von Bismarck.

Perverse as it may seem, given his ultra-conservative image and his concern to perpetuate the supremacy of the Junker aristocracy, Bismarck's pragmatic genius found in the ideals of 1848 the means both to the achievement of his conservative goals and to the creation of a Germany acceptable to the German people. 1848 had rested on a dual principle – liberalism and nationalism. The one needed the other. Bismarck now drove a wedge between them and jettisoned the former. The nationalist urge, he realised, had gained a momentum of its own and could be appealed to in its own terms, for its roots penetrated deeper into the people's consciousness than those of liberalism and democracy (Ill. 69).

The final, crucial three steps of Bismarck's strategy followed in quick succession. In 1866 he engineered the Seven Weeks War, at the end of which Austria had ceased to be part of Germany and Prussia held territorial dominion over the whole of north Germany from the Rhine to the Baltic. The following year the North German Confederation was formed, with Bismarck as its Chancellor and Berlin as its capital. Lastly came the victory over the old enemy, France, at whose hands the Germans had suffered so many humiliations over the centuries and which had fought stubbornly to the last to perpetuate the principle of German particularism.

Karl von Clausewitz, Prussian general in the War of Liberation, wrote: 'There is only one way for Germany to achieve political unity, and that is by the sword. One of the states will have to subject all the others to its will.' What arose in 1871 as the German Reich was in reality a Prussian Reich, dominated by the Prussian aristocracy and Prussian traditions and with the Prussian capital now also, through no ambitious intent of its own, the capital of a whole new country (Ill. 69).

Culturally too the emphasis moved from the regional to the national. Patriotic lyrics accompanied the Prussian, Bavarian and Swabian troops into battle, reminding them that they were embarked on the physical demonstration of a spiritual unity long apparent in the realm of culture. 'National unity would not have been attainable', wrote no less a person than Bismarck, 'if the embers had not been glowing beneath the ashes. What fanned the flames? German art, German science, German music, not least the German Lied. We have never had particularist music: there has never been Saxon music or Prussian music. When a Lied was composed, nobody worried where it came from – it was simply a German Lied.'

The phenomenon of national oneness rapidly made itself manifest in new structures of commercial and social life. Accompanying the mechanisation of industry came the development of the railway network, including the S-Bahn (*Stadtbahn*), a four-track elevated railroad running through the city from east to west. The urban canals were extended and construction of an underground sewerage system began in 1873. This and much more in the field of

69. Sketch of Bismarck by Adolph Menzel, watercolour, 1865.

public works was financed out of the billions of marks exacted in reparations from a defeated and humiliated France after the war of 1870–1.

In the year the war ended, Berlin had a population of 800,000. By 1890 it had grown to over 1½ million. Hundreds of joint-stock companies were set up to share in the expansion, and the financial world's image of itself was made plain for all to see in the ornate façades and interiors of the burgeoning new banks. Newspapers and journals multiplied in a new mass demand for information – and no Germans have developed a keener political awareness, especially over the last two centuries, than the Berliners. The city's origins as a colonial outpost, the poverty of its natural resources, its constant exposure to migrational movements, the shallowness of its spiritual and cultural roots, now finding itself thrust willy-nilly into the role of capital of a new-born Reich with over 40 million inhabitants – all this has promoted a taste for scepticism and a faculty of political improvisation. Berliners found themselves tarred by other Germans with the brush of 'Schnodderigkeit', an unflattering quality of brusqueness and off-handedness flecked with emotional coolness, and after a few decades of rule from the new Reich capital words like 'superficial', 'conceited' and 'vulgar' were being heard. Nobody seemed to love the place – not even the Berliners themselves.

Anti-urban sentiments came to the surface as the dehumanising grip of industrialisation tightened. Harking back to the romantic idealisation of nature as the heart of beauty, a source of solace and emotional regeneration, young people wandered among the forests and lakes around Berlin in the *Wandervogel* movement that worshipped the great outdoors – more precisely, the great German outdoors. In its historical context the movement was an innocent manifestation of the ideal of *mens sana in corpore sano* and of a face-to-face communion with nature of an earnest, peculiarly German kind at which others incline to smile. But, summoning memories of the cult of gymnastics fostered at the time of the War of Liberation, it also lent itself to involvement in the sometimes distasteful politics of nationalism, and the Pan-German movement found it a useful ally. A sinister legacy eagerly seized upon by totalitarian regimes, it was rediscovered by the Nazis in their propaganda for the Hitler Youth, then by the communist East German regime after the Second World War.

In politics the Berliners were natural Social Democrats (the Social Democratic Party was founded in 1875). The pace of industrialisation ensured the irresistible growth of the urban proletariat, anti-monarchist by instinct and now driven into conflict with the combined 'Prussian' forces of the old Junker class and the new capitalist managers. Money talked, and the captains of industry, secure in their villas in Charlottenburg and the Grunewald, rode roughshod over the public interest in their pursuit of prosperity, while in northern suburbs the emergence of a proletarian underclass led to slums and the social problems associated with them.

In foreign affairs tension was generated by national imperialist pressure and the industrialists' drive for overseas markets, in principal rivalry with Great Britain and France. At home the stage was being set for the confrontation between the conservative alliance of Junkers, Prussian civil servants and the moguls of industry and commerce on the one hand and the forces of liberal democracy on the other. Whether victory went to the old order or the new, the whole of national and international life would feel the impact. The war of 1914 brought the first part of the answer; the peace of 1918 brought the second.

Civic Glories

Friedrich Wilhelm IV, who came to the throne of Prussia in 1840, showed himself from the beginning to be no less devoted to the arts than his father. A personal friend of Schinkel's from his days as Crown Prince, he shared the great architect's historicist taste both for the classicism of the Altes Museum and for the romanticism of the turrets and spires of the palace at Babelsberg. His broad sympathies extended to all the arts, stimulating his sense of mission to create in Berlin a centre of culture unrivalled in Germany. Philosophers like Schelling, poets like Friedrich Rückert, the painter Peter Cornelius, Felix Mendelssohn-Bartholdy – few stayed for the rest of their lives but that they came at all was a tribute to the King's personal initiative. The state of near-insanity in which he spent the last four years of his life was a sad reward for his labours on his people's behalf.

Schinkel died in 1841, only a year into the new King's reign. But his pupils ensured that his neo-classical spirit should persist. One particularly appropriate site for a demonstration of the Schinkel heritage was the area behind the Altes Museum, the northern part of the island held between the two arms of the Spree.

In the 1820s the King had acquired the huge collection of Italian and Netherlands paintings belonging to the English businessman Edward Solly, the jewel of which was the Ghent altarpiece, *Worship of the Lamb*, by the van Eyck brothers. Some of these works already hung in the Altes Museum. But a second gallery was urgently needed, a need met, at least in part, by the Neues Museum, built 1843–6 by Schinkel's versatile pupil Friedrich August Stüler. A covered overhead walkway linked the two museums so that visitors could pass freely from one to the other. Only fragments of the rich interior of the Neues Museum survived the war of 1939–45 but it is to be rebuilt within the overall plan to reunite the museums that had developed independently in East and West Berlin since the end of the war.

Some twenty years after the Neues Museum a third gallery arose on this same tract of land, known today as the 'Museum Island' – the National Gallery. Again it was a typical piece of Berlin classicism by Stüler; again it incorporated ideas sketched by Friedrich Wilhelm IV himself; and again it was a product of necessity – in this case to create, as desired by the benefactor, a businessman called Wilhelm Wagner, a new museum of modern art to house a large collection of contemporary paintings he had bequeathed to the monarch in 1861.

Stüler's design is for a raised temple-like structure with a vestibule of Corinthian columns surmounted by a decorated pediment, on the apex of which stand personifications of Painting, Sculpture and Architecture. Dominating the entrance at the junction of the two symmetrical stone staircases is an equestrian statue of Friedrich Wilhelm IV by Calandrelli, while reliefs

70. National Gallery, built to plans by F. A. Stüler, 1866–76.

and decorative sculpture allegorise the historical development of German art. But the gallery was not completed until 1876, long after the death both of its benefactor and of its architect, and five years into the reign of Kaiser Wilhelm I. What had been launched in praise of Prussia now became a shrine to the new German Reich, to the 'holy German art' of Wagner's *Meistersinger* (Ill. 70).

Traditionally commissions for works of art had come from the King and the aristocracy. From the middle of the century architects and artists increasingly sought their work among the ennobled bourgeoisie, the industrialists, the financiers and others who were riding on the wave of economic prosperity. New classicistic façades were applied to older residences. Portraits, statues and busts were commissioned to proclaim the sitter's social status, and elaborate classicistic funerary monuments to ensure the immortality of that status in death.

As the leading architect of the day, Stüler found himself in demand from all quarters. As well as numerous private commissions he received requests from the Protestant Church for new places of worship and the municipal authorities ordered statues of distinguished civic dignitaries. Perhaps his supreme achievement, however, lies in his contribution to one of the most striking buildings in the whole of Berlin – the New Synagogue in the Oranienburger Strasse.

The full emancipation of the Jews in Prussia was decreed in 1812. No longer official outsiders, they eagerly sought to assimilate, and at the same time contribute, to the culture in which they lived. Some of them had even helped man the revolutionary barricades in 1848. The first modern synagogue in Berlin, in the old Jewish quarter round the Grosse Hamburger Strasse and the Auguststrasse, was consecrated in 1714. The Enlightenment and later the French Revolution drew the Berlin Jews into the nineteenth-century reform movement, and as their numbers grew, so did the need for a larger synagogue. The commission was given to Eduard Knoblauch, whom Stüler replaced a few years later, and the building was completed in 1866 – the largest synagogue in Europe at the time, with two organs and seats for a congregation of 4,000.

Synagogue architecture embraces a multiplicity of forms, the choice depending to a critical extent on whether a particular congregation follows a traditionalist or reformist path in its ritual. Local Christian influence – one aspect of the desire to assimilate – could show itself, for example, in a preference for an elongated structure of nave and aisles over a central plan that focused on the podium from which the Torah was read. For all Stüler's sumptuous Moorish decoration of its interior, inspired by the Alhambra, the New Synagogue in Berlin adopts this 'assimilatory' ground plan, with the Torah displayed like an altar at the far end of the nave.

But externally, with its great iron-framed golden dome in romantic, orientalising style, flanked by minaret-like towers, the eclectic synagogue proudly declares its uniqueness. Here is no modest place of worship for a community content to merge into the generality but a statement by an imaginative architect of the personality of a high-profile people. Representatives of the municipal authority and members of the Prussian government, led by Bismarck, attended its consecration. Ruined and unused since its destruction by the Nazis in the Kristallnacht pogrom of 9 November 1938, it was restored and reopened in 1995 (Ill. 71).

Also unique among Berlin buildings of the 1860s, in a totally different idiom though equally a symbol of growing importance and authority, is the large new city hall, built in Berlin red brick and known as the 'Rotes Rathaus'. The Berlin municipal authority, the *Magistrat*, had had its seat on this spot, the corner of an important intersection of north–south and east–west streets, since around 1300. Nering had extended the building at the end of the seventeenth century but by the mid-nineteenth century it had become inadequate for dealing with the affairs of a city of over 400,000 inhabitants and was pulled down in 1865 to make room for the present building. A city architect, Hermann Friedrich Waesemann, incorporated in his design sketches already made by Schinkel and others, and the building was finally occupied in 1869.

Instead of the classicistic forms that dominated both the public and private buildings of the time, Waesemann adopted an Italian neo-Renaissance style using clinker as his basic material. The four wings enclose three courtyards, and the rectangular complex occupies a complete block within

71. New Synagogue in the Oranienburger Strasse, built by Eduard Knoblauch and Friedrich August Stüler, 1859-66. Painting by Emile de Cauwer, oil on canvas, 1865.

the surrounding streets. A complex terracotta frieze runs round the entire building between the first and second storeys, carved by various sculptors and depicting scenes from the history of Berlin and Brandenburg.

Relations between the municipal council and their Prussian overlords had rarely been cordial, and especially since the events of 1848 the Berliners' characteristic liberalism and blunt independence created a more or less permanent state of friction with the forces of conservatism and authoritarianism. The building of the new city hall now offered a golden opportunity for the provocative display of civic autonomy. Its tower, almost one hundred metres high, even had the effrontery to be taller than the dome of the Royal Palace itself (Ill. 72).

Such was the speed at which Berlin was expanding – expanding arbitrarily and at random, with no overview either in time or in space – that little thought was taken for the morrow. The characteristic *Mietskasernen*, accommodating a maximum of bodies in a minimum of space, went up all over the city to cater for the growing proletariat. In their wake came the attendant social and cultural infrastructure – stores, schools, hospitals, churches, taverns and places of entertainment. Their needs met locally, people clustered in individual communities and established the identity of their own *Kietz*, their own 'patch', with little inclination to contemplate a broader scene.

Not everyone saw this as desirable progress. 'I loved the old Berlin,' wrote the actress Caroline Bauer in 1870,

> that modest, harmless, provincial little Berlin that had a mere 193,000 inhabitants in 1824, no gas, no railways, no water supply, no sidewalks, and just two theatres and two newspapers. A cobbler's apprentice getting a hiding from his master, or a man flying a kite, or an overturned horse-and-cart used to provide entertainment

72. Rotes Rathaus, built to plans by H. F. Waesemann, 1861–79.

for hours . . . But as for this second half of the century, this metropolis with its dazzling gas lamps in the streets, with its two dozen theatres, the roaring of steam engines, a feverish pursuit of riches, a philosophical nihilism and pessimism – it all fills me with disgust.

One man who set out to head off this dehumanisation by designing parks and open spaces, oases of peace where people could refresh their tired spirits, was the landscape gardener Peter Joseph Lenné. Carrying the official title of Director of the Royal Gardens since 1822, laying out the grounds of palaces in Berlin and Potsdam, planting trees, shrubs and flower beds in prominent sites in the city, Lenné virtually turned himself into a town-planner. But a town-planner with a difference, a man who started from human and environmental considerations, from the well-being of the people as a whole, a designer who anticipated the garden-city movement of the twentieth century. Despite the upheavals of the intervening years the basic design of the Berlin Tiergarten today, including the Zoological Gardens, is still Lenné's.

Conscious that not only the fashionable west but also the sprawling industrial suburbs of east and north Berlin needed their own recreational areas, Lenné persuaded the *Magistrat* to plan for the reinvigoration of body and spirit. Grass and play areas alone were not enough: Lenné also wanted to see fountains, statues and architectural features to raise aesthetic awareness and convey for the common man something, albeit in miniature form, of life in the gardens of an aristocratic summer palace. The Volkspark in the working-class district of Friedrichshain, laid out in the 1840s by Lenné's pupil Gustav Meyer, with the famous fairy-tale fountain and other free-standing sculptures added some decades later, shows what he intended.

The immense growth of public and private building through the mid-nineteenth century was a reflection of economic expansion. Not that there was no limit on how much a project could be allowed to cost. Friedrich Wilhelm III had enjoined Schinkel to salvage and reuse as much material as possible from the old burnt-out Schauspielhaus while executing his new design in 1818, and the Jewish elders had from the beginning laid down a firm maximum figure for their New Synagogue. But whatever sums of money changed hands, and whatever questions of taste and purpose were involved, the relationship between patron and artist was direct, almost uncomplicated, the reflection of a straightforward agreement between two parties.

With the proclamation of the German Reich in 1871 came a new consideration. Whereas the context had been in the first instance that of the rising metropolis, then perhaps, but by no means necessarily, that of the Prussian state, it had now acquired a national dimension. There were new political realities to represent, new national values to cultivate, a new urban personality to express. What more natural than to promote an architecture – or architectures, since there is more than one way of doing these things – which makes that personality explicit and visible to all?

The need to make a point, the current political point, manifested itself in all walks of life and in an eclectic mixture of historical styles – Italian and Netherlandish Renaissance, the late Gothic of the Netherlands and Germany,

73. Ballroom in the Siemens family villa, 1875.

Baroque, even Rococo, all, however, infused with a spirit of pride, assurance and Prussian efficiency. The villa built 1875–8 for the Borsig family in the Wilhelmstrasse, flanking the Tiergarten, is in the style of a late Renaissance *palazzo*. The Siemens' mansion in Charlottenburg, on the other hand, has a contemporary ballroom whose interior combines Renaissance features with formal classicistic motifs reminiscent of Schinkel (Ill. 73).

Commercial building offered a similar self-confident range of options. The Reichsbank announced its presence with a massive pseudo-Renaissance fortress built 1869–76 by Friedrich Hitzig, who had designed the Stock Exchange ten years earlier. And if the exterior could be appropriately grave and impressive, the interior could be overwhelming, not to say intimidating (Ill. 74). The power of money had to be given its fitting image.

For all their aristocratic pride and dignity, the façades of both the Reichsbank and the Stock Exchange still have a lightness of touch, an aura of genuine quality within their historic idiom. Later finance houses in the Berlin banking quarter of the Friedrichstadt become heavy and overbearing, often as a consequence of a preference for ponderous facings of rustic masonry. When monumental pilasters and other neo-classical detail came to be mounted on this heavy base, the result could be an unbeautiful oppressiveness which some would unkindly call Prussian. But they are inalienable features of the Berlin landscape.

Reichsbank and Stock Exchange were destroyed in the Second World War. On the other hand a number of houses in the Behrenstrasse, the 'street of banks', like those built for the Dresdner Bank in 1887–9 and for the Berliner Handelsgesellschaft in 1899–1900, were so solidly constructed that they survived.

Berlin and its Culture

74. Interior of the Reichsbank, 1892–4.

75. Atrium of Wertheim's departmental store, designed by Alfred Messel, 1897–1904.

76. Anhalter railroad terminus, historical photograph, 1882.

Other activities directly involved in the rise of the economy found their own building styles through which to express their values, styles frequently evolved in conjunction with the use of new materials. One of the city's earliest department stores (1898–1900), that of Hermann Tietz in the Leipziger Strasse, was a four-storey structure in iron, glass and stone, with a façade decorated in fashionable art-nouveau style. Even more spectacular, built in the concrete that subsequently became standard for such stores, was Wertheim's (1896–1906), the Harrods of Berlin, a technical sensation in the revolutionary opulence of the ways in which it displayed its goods, with glass-roofed courtyards, crystal chandeliers, mosaics, gilded terracottas and an ornate façade over 300 metres long (Ill. 75). Railway termini, on the other hand, tended to Italian Renaissance forms in brickwork, with details taken from Florentine and Roman *palazzi* (Ill. 76).

Little of this is left to be enjoyed today. One proud monument to the cultural energies of the final decades of the century has, however, survived, the last of the art galleries to be built on the 'Museum Island' – the Kaiser-Friedrich-Museum, renamed in 1956 Bode Museum, after its founder (Ill. 78).

Building on this marshy sliver of land had always been a nightmare because of the instability of the sandy soil and the shallowness of the water table. The construction of the Altes Museum had already caused problems. But the royal collections were continually growing and had to be accommodated. During his years as crown prince, Friedrich III, a sad figure who died of cancer only three months after becoming Kaiser in 1888, had assumed responsibility for activities on the Museum Island, and from his discussions with the scholar and art collector Wilhelm Bode, at that time an assistant to the director of the National Gallery, came the thought of a new museum.

The triangular site at the northern tip of the island is a challenge for any architect. Two of its sides are flanked by the waters of the Spree and the third abuts the tracks of the city's elevated railway, the S-Bahn. The waves created by the passing barges, the vibration of the rattling trains, the humid atmosphere – hardly ideal conditions. But the museum is still there, although facing a changed future through reorganisation and the transfer of parts of its collection to the new Kulturforum near the Tiergarten.

Its squat dome emphasising the importance of its position, the neo-Baroque features of its bowed façade looking out across the river, the stately Bode Museum was built to plans by Ernst von Ihne, who a few years later designed the Prussian State Library on Unter den Linden. The interior is no less impressive, in particular the neo-Renaissance entrance hall and staircase beneath the main dome, with Ihne's skilful division of the irregular floor area of the building into a series of exhibition galleries. From the beginning Bode conceived the gallery as a Renaissance museum, and numerous structural and decorative features of the rooms, brought in from other sources, were made to form integral parts of the interior. But the unity of Bode's vision has now gone, probably for ever.

Given the symbolical significance of the year 1871, given also the identity of interest with which Kaiser Wilhelm II bound Church and state to each other, and both to himself, the architectural values of the new Empire reach a climax in two buildings, one secular, one ecclesiastical, which reflect the view that the new establishment took of itself. One is the Reichstag. The other is the Cathedral (Berliner Dom).

The 397 deputies elected to the first Reichstag in March 1871 had no purpose-built premises at their disposal and for over twenty years the assembly met in the converted building that used to belong to the Prussian

77. Reichstag building by Paul Wallot, 1884-94, with Begas' bronze and granite Bismarck Memorial, 1897-1901, now in the Tiergarten. Photograph 1925.

Royal Porcelain Factory. A competition was eventually launched for a proper parliament building, and in 1883 Paul Wallot, an architect with no close ties to Berlin either before or after, submitted the winning design. But after modifications of one kind or another, a number of them demanded by the Kaiser himself, it was to be 1894 before the deputies could move into their own house.

Heavy yet impressive in a monumental, high-Renaissance style, richly embellished with sculptural decoration, its glass dome a proud tribute to technological progress and new materials of construction, the Reichstag makes a clear statement of function. That function, moreover, with the surrounding historical events and associations, was made the more explicit by the symbolic layout of the surrounding area as a whole. Formerly called the Königsplatz (now Platz der Republik), used as a parade ground under Friedrich Wilhelm I, the square was redesigned by Lenné as a recreational area, in the centre of which the Siegessäule, the 'Column of Victory', was erected in 1873. Then, between 1897 and 1901, Reinhold Begas' elaborate Bismarck memorial took its place in front of the steps leading up to the neo-classical portal of the Reichstag. The whole composition was a celebration of the birth of a nation – its grand new parliament, the father of that nation, and the military victories by which nationhood had been won. Severely damaged, first in 1933 when the Nazis set fire to it, then during

78. The Museum Island: Bode Museum, Pergamon Museum, National Gallery, Neues Museum, Altes Museum.

Berlin and its Culture

79. View of Kaiser-Wilhelm-Gedächtniskirche from Tauentzienstrasse. Photograph, 1906.

the Second World War, the Reichstag building is being reconstructed to become once more the meeting-place of the German parliament in 1999 (Ill. 77).

No less self-assertive in its own way is the Berlin Cathedral, built over an eleven-year span, 1894–1905, to designs by Julius Carl Raschdorff, an architect already known for his work on the Technische Hochschule (now Technische Universität) in Charlottenburg and for his recently completed mausoleum in Potsdam for Kaiser Friedrich III.

Soon after his accession Wilhelm II launched a church-building programme, one prominent result of which was the neo-Romanesque Kaiser-Wilhelm-Gedächtniskirche (1891–5), whose ruined spire, looking down the Kurfürstendamm, has become one of the most familiar sights in Berlin tourist literature (Ill. 79). But the occasion called for something grander, more imperial. There had been a church in the Lustgarten, north of the Royal Palace, since 1750, when Jan Boumann the Elder executed a design by Knobelsdorff. Schinkel had carried out modifications in the 1820s but Friedrich Wilhelm IV, in a changed political and social climate, looked for a totally new building. He could reach no agreement with his architects, and not until the new empire had achieved a degree of consolidation was the decision taken to pull down the old Baroque cathedral and build anew (Ill. 80).

Maybe what arose in its place would not readily be called beautiful. But it is impressive in its pompous way, and its plan highly unusual. To reflect the Kaiser's philosophy of Church and state, the cathedral had to be both public place of worship and Hohenzollern mausoleum. To this end Raschdorff designed a structure in three parts – a general church beneath the dome, an apse-like Hohenzollern mausoleum-cum-chapel (now destroyed) and a private chapel for weddings, baptisms and the like. An

80. Cathedral (Berliner Dom), built by Julius Raschdorff 1894-1904.

eclectic composition of Italian Renaissance and Baroque elements, surmounted by four corner towers and with a central dome above the body of the church, both exterior and interior of the cathedral have a profusion of sculptural decoration – Biblical scenes, Jesus and the disciples, statues of Reformers – carried out by leading artists of the day. The interior of the dome and the vaults is decorated with frescoes and mosaics which, when added to the other monumental features, give the interior an atmosphere of grandeur yet also of sobriety.

The mausoleum chapel, together with the crypt below, was the private domain of the Hohenzollerns. Here Wilhelm II assembled over ninety sarcophagi of members of his house, going back to the Elector Johann Cicero of Brandenburg, who died in 1499. The Great Elector lies here with his wife Dorothea, so do Friedrich I, first King of Prussia, and his Queen Sophie Charlotte, both in elaborate gilded Baroque sarcophagi designed by Schlüter. These survived the Second World War, though many of the others did not. Bombs and shells also wrought havoc on the fabric of the church itself but all has since been restored for public use.

Sculptors of Empire

As in architecture, so in sculpture – the same urge to make a public statement about the present time and the present place, the same pleasure, shared
by artist and public alike, in the commemoration of the great and the good,
the same sense of expansion and optimism. Memorials were erected in plenty,
especially to Kaiser Wilhelm I and to Bismarck. The effect could be anomalous and mildly ridiculous. During a tour of Prussia in 1907 the French
journalist Jules Huret reported:

> There are two things that strike a visitor the moment he leaves the station. One
> is the huge number of electric streetcars speeding along the streets. The other is
> a statue of Kaiser Wilhelm I or Bismarck. At the beginning I used to keep count
> of these statues and collect postcards of them, in spite of the fact that there was
> little difference between one blackened bronze figure and another. But I soon
> gave up. There were too many.

The most extravagant plan for a display of statuary in the German capital
came from Wilhelm II himself. To honour the city 'and to celebrate the glorious past of our noble Fatherland', as he put it, he planned to construct an
avenue of marble figures in the Tiergarten, near the Siegessäule. 'These
figures', the Kaiser went on, 'are to be the rulers of Brandenburg and Prussia,
beginning with the Markgraf Albrecht the Bear and ending with Kaiser
Wilhelm I.' Not only that, but to accompany each royal figure there were
to be two busts of distinguished contemporaries whose achievements in war
and in peace reflected glory on the monarch in question. Frederick the
Great, for example, was flanked by Field Marshal Schwerin and Johann Sebastian Bach, Friedrich Wilhelm III by Blücher and Freiherr von Stein (Ill. 81).

It was a preposterous undertaking – thirty-two monuments laid out along
the two sides of the 400-metre-long avenue, the Siegesallee, twenty-seven
sculptors receiving commissions for individual figures, most of them impres-
sively mediocre. Proudly inaugurating the finished work in 1901, Wilhelm II
stated a position that has not lost its relevance over the intervening century.
'I wanted to show the world', he said, 'that the most satisfactory means of
fulfilling an artistic purpose is not by forming committees or announcing
competitions but, in the manner tried and tested in Antiquity and in the
Middle Ages, by direct contact between patron and artist.'

He concluded with carefully chosen words that convey a great deal of the
spirit which runs through the much maligned *Gründerjahre* (the 'foundation
years' of Empire) and the era that followed:

> Art should help to educate the people, as well as offering the lower classes the
> opportunity, after a day of toil and strain, to restore their strength through contact
> with ideals. Grand ideals have become the permanent possessions of us, the
> German people . . . It is we, above all other nations, who are called upon to
> cherish, to nurture and to perpetuate these great ideas.

Once again we are in the world of 'holy German art', viewed not from
Bayreuth but from Berlin. The German people, who received a new Reichstag

81. Statues in the Siegesallee, designed 1901. Photograph, 1912.

building only a few years before, are the God-given custodians of cultural and spiritual values, while the Kaiser himself assumes the role of a latter-day Medici prince. And what better way for school-children to learn the history of Brandenburg–Prussia than by being taken on a guided tour of the Sieges-allee, each monumental station of which has a stone bench on which the passer-by can sit to contemplate his hero and reflect on his deeds?

Wilhelm II's Berliners, always at hand with an irreverent designation, and not blind to the discrepancy between the Kaiser's idealisation of history and the undistinguished neo-Baroque statues before their eyes, dubbed the walk the 'Puppenallee', 'Dummies Avenue'. But they accepted it. After all, a park bench is a park bench.

In 1938, as part of Albert Speer's recasting of the city centre, the entire complex of monuments, together with the Siegessäule, was moved one kilo-metre westwards and centred on the Grosser Stern, in the middle of the Tiergarten, where the column has since stood. Despite damage to individual figures the avenue as a landscape feature survived the Second World War, only to be destroyed in 1947 by a directive from the Allied Control Council, who saw it as a symbol of the Prussianism they wanted to forget – and wanted the Germans to forget.

The nineteenth-century cult of the public monument inevitably produced a preponderance of effigies of royalty and grandees of state. But since the time of Rauch, descendant in the classical line of Schadow and the most influential of nineteenth-century Berlin sculptors, a middle class growing in self-confidence had turned increasingly to honouring not inherited status but intellectual achievement, those from their own ranks who had created the nation's scientific and cultural wealth – Goethe, Kant, Lessing, Wilhelm and

Alexander von Humboldt. From Rauch's studio, as well as from the lecture halls of the Academy of Arts, where Rauch had taught from 1811, came a school of apprentices and pupils who, working in the spirit of their master's realistic humanism, dominated the sculptural scene in Berlin for the rest of the century.

Some are remembered for individual works. August Kiss did a famous bronze *Mounted Amazon* for the entrance to Schinkel's Altes Museum, which gained him the reputation of being the best sculptor of horses in Berlin. The extravagant gilded bronze *Winged Victory* atop the Siegessäule, nine metres high, is the work of Friedrich Drake, whose marble statue of Friedrich Wilhelm III, one of the finest of its kind, stands in the Tiergarten below.

By far the strongest personality among sculptors in the latter half of the nineteenth century, however, a lad who had entered Rauch's studio as a seventeen-year-old apprentice at the moment when his mentor's great equestrian figure of Frederick the Great neared completion, was Reinhold Begas.

Begas was the master of neo-Baroque. Like many young artists, he spent a period in Rome, finding his inspiration there not in the relics of Antiquity but in Michelangelo. Back in Berlin he began to move from the cool nobility and rationality of Rauch's humanism towards a more emotional, more sensuous manner which, originally a purely aesthetic impulse, later found itself being drawn into the context of nationalistic sentiment.

A number of Begas' works, including wonderfully expressive portrait busts, can be seen in Berlin today, though not all his open-air pieces occupy the sites originally chosen for them. His statue of Alexander von Humboldt still

82. Neptune Fountain by Reinhold Begas, bronze and granite, 1891.

guards the entrance to the university in Unter den Linden, where it was erected in 1883. At the Grosser Stern, transferred from its original, conceptually proper position in front of the Reichstag, stands his last great work, the Bismarck Memorial (1897–1901): Bismarck as superman, his deeds allegorised by the figures surrounding him – Atlas bearing the weight of the world, Siegfried forging the sword with which to slay his enemies, a Sibyl reading the book of history in which the Iron Chancellor's achievement is foretold. More appealing, perhaps, is Begas' earlier figure of Schiller in front of the Schauspielhaus, capturing the poet not as classical moralist but as passionate idealist.

Begas' most familiar piece, passed every day by thousands crossing what is now a vast open space in the heart of imperial Berlin, is his Neptune Fountain, originally sited in the Palace square (Ill. 82). Commissioned by the city fathers as a gift to Wilhelm II and formally presented to him in 1888, it has its conceptual origin in the fountains of Rome. In the centre sits Neptune surrounded by four voluptuous river goddesses symbolising Rhine, Elbe, Oder and Vistula, with an attendant programme of tritons, putti and aquatic creatures. It is a work bubbling over with enthusiasm and confidence, as much an expression of the pride and optimism of its age as statues of royalty and the celebration of feats of arms. Indeed, the arts in general, and above all the visual arts as media of public display, were to become no less the beneficiaries of national expansion and success than the social world and the spheres of industry and commerce. Gone were the days when the enjoyment of art was the privilege of the cloistered few.

Painting and the Social Scene

Nowhere did the growing pleasure in art show itself more explicitly than in the foundation of museums and art galleries. Discovery, collecting and display went hand in hand. Archaeological expeditions to Greece and Asia Minor from the 1870s onwards brought back new treasures, among them the famous so-called Pergamum Altar and the Market Gate of Miletus, for which a special museum was later built. In 1880 Heinrich Schliemann uncovered the treasure known as the Gold of Troy and donated it to the state. The Crown Prince Friedrich Wilhelm and his English wife made their own contributions to the Berlin museums but most of the exhibits came from wealthy private collectors.

On the heels of the collecting of works of art came public discussion of the collected items – art criticism – and the development of a commercial market. Private galleries arose for the display and sale of artists' work. It was in one such private venue, the gallery of Fritz Gurlitt, that the first German exhibition of French impressionists was held in October 1883 – to the general disapproval, incidentally, of the critics. The acquisition of paintings was becoming a desideratum for more and more of the population, who, however, also needed to be made aware of criteria of quality and taste – a situation not lost on contemporary artists looking to capture a share of the market. Not a few chose their subject matter with an eye to a particular class of potential purchaser, from the Kaiser downwards.

A perfect embodiment of the public and private aspiration of the art world of the *Gründerjahre* and the Wilhelminian decades, in both their aesthetic and commercial aspects, is Wilhelm Bode, founder of the museum now named after him. Scholar, collector, administrator of energy and vision, Bode joined the staff of the National Gallery in 1872 as a young man of twenty-seven. The European galleries he had seen, despite the wonderful treasures they contained, seemed to him like soulless repositories, works exhibited out of their historical and geographical context, in stylistic confusion, and thus deprived of the full impact he knew they should make.

He thus conceived the idea of a museum in which the paintings, sculptures, furniture and so on of a given period and style should be brought together to provide a concentrated experience of that style – German Gothic, for example, or Italian Renaissance. Since neither the Kaiser nor the aristocracy could or would finance such a plan, Bode set about encouraging members of the well-to-do bourgeoisie to invest in works of art to fulfil his purpose, whereby they would receive both the approval of a grateful monarch and the public respect due to patrons of culture. With the uncanny instinct of the expert Bode himself directed the course of the purchases, also contributing works from his own collection.

His efforts were crowned when the foundation stone of the Kaiser-Friedrich-Museum, as it was originally called, was laid in 1898 and Wilhelm II ceremonially opened the building in 1904. The Second World War and its aftermath played havoc with the collection that Bode had built up and much has gone for ever. But the building still stands in his memory (Ill. 83).

83. Wilhelm von Bode by Max Liebermann, oil on canvas, 1904.

By the middle of the nineteenth century Berlin had set itself firmly on the artistic map. It may not yet, like Dresden, have produced a painter of the stature of Caspar David Friedrich, or caught the spirit of Biedermeier with the conviction of a Carl Spitzweg in Munich or of a Ferdinand Waldmüller in Vienna. But in landscape, genre and history painting, portraiture, architectural painting, and in styles diversely defined as classicistic, romantic, Biedermeier or realistic, Berlin claimed its share of attention. And if one had hitherto missed the name of a supreme artist, one genius who would express like no other the *Zeitgeist* of over half a century of German, and especially Berlin, life, that lack was about to be remedied. In 1830 Adolph Menzel arrived in the city.

Rarely can there have been an artist who exhibits such a discrepancy between personality, upbringing and mode of life on one hand and fame and influence on the other. Born in Breslau in 1815, Menzel was already making chalk and ink sketches as a child. Thinking to put him through a course of training at the Academy, his father took him to Berlin. But he remained obstinately autodidactic. 'I refused to have anything to do with teachers', he said, 'and the only word our language has to describe my approach is naturalism.' A few years later, equipped with his home-grown 'naturalism', he embarked on the seventy years of his active career – a tiny, gnome-like figure in glasses who moved in company as rarely as he decently

84. *Room with Balcony* by Adolph Menzel, oil on canvas, 1845.

Berlin and its Culture

85. *The Rolling Mill* by Adolph Menzel, oil on canvas, 1872-5.

could, and when he did, then in such a way as to be scarcely noticed. He is captured in a ballroom scene painted by Anton von Werner in which the Crown Prince Friedrich commands centre stage; the diminutive Menzel, characteristically, lurks diffidently at the side, almost out of the picture (see Ill. 86). In the evenings he would be found in one or other of his regular haunts — Huth's restaurant, Frederich's wine-bar or the Café Josty on the Gendarmenmarkt — not to carouse, argue and tell stories, like Hoffmann at Lutter and Wegner's, but just to watch and sketch the goings-on around him. Otherwise his only regular excursions from his chosen solitude were the Sunday meetings of the literary club, the Tunnel über der Spree. But when he died in 1905 at the age of eighty-five, now His Excellency Adolph von Menzel, honorary citizen of Berlin and Breslau, the only artist to be awarded the Prussian Order of the Black Eagle, the Kaiser himself walked behind the coffin on its journey to the grave. Yet to the end the little man insisted that, for all his success, he was 'of a thoroughly plebeian cast of mind'.

Menzel began his career as a book illustrator, providing hundreds of drawings and engravings in the tradition of Chodowiecki for a biography of Frederick the Great, then for a special edition of the King's writings themselves. Frederick remained an object of fascination for him throughout his life — not in a spirit of adulation but as the historical figure around whom life at the time revolved.

Masterly and socially revealing as his drawings were — and he was sketching as tirelessly at the end of his career as at the beginning — it is Menzel's paintings that display at its most impressive the originality which makes him the greatest of German realist painters. His subject matter was drawn from reality and his techniques were employed to uncover the full nature of that reality. For reality is not merely a matter of surface impressions and empirical evidence: it is in the inner reality, accessible through empathy and – in the broadest sense – love that the profoundest truths reside. 'Not everything meticulously and painstakingly copied from nature is true to nature,' he once wrote. It is a standpoint that Menzel shared with his French contemporary Courbet, whose art he greatly admired.

As one committed to painting everything he saw, in his own phrase, Menzel had a range of subjects that embraced, then went beyond, all the areas on which his contemporaries lavished their efforts, from history painting to Biedermeier interiors, from romantic landscapes to compositions of the industrial city, from family portraits to contemporary political events. To the complex of works centred on Frederick the Great, for example, belongs his beautifully executed conversation piece of the King playing the flute to his guests at Sanssouci. The realism is pervasive, the result of years of study of the minutiae of the King's habits and circumstances. The members of the company can all be identified – sitting at the harpsichord, for instance, is Carl Philipp Emanuel Bach. Technically the picture is a study in illumination, the candle light from the sides and from the chandelier above shining on the brightly dressed courtiers and casting a sophisticated pattern of shadows. Impressionism before its time.

At the other end of the social scale is his simple but moving Biedermeier study of his own living room in the Schöneberger Strasse, the curtain fluttering in front of the balcony door, the wall reflected in the mirror, the spontaneous, gentle, lived-in reality of a world at one with itself (Ill. 84).

But Menzel knew that the world outside was not at one with itself. The revolution of 1848 was enough to prove that. Initially he sympathised with the revolutionaries but his painting of their coffins on public display in the Gendarmenmarkt (see Ill. 55) is a statement of human frailty, of the inability to live up to proclaimed ideals, not the declaration of a political stance. As the revolution disintegrated into fragments of unfinished business, so Menzel could not find the will to apply the few brushstrokes that would have turned the *infinito* into a completed work.

Impressive in a different way but also an essay in the tensions generated by a changing society is Menzel's famous later painting of work in a rolling mill. When exhibited in 1875, *The Rolling Mill* caused a sensation. Here was a totally new area of attention – industry, to most a quite inappropriate sphere in which to seek material for artistic treatment. Again basing his composition on the play of light, here the contrast between natural daylight and the glow of molten metal, Menzel depicts the dangerous conditions in which these workers earn their sweaty living, surrounded by the heat and the pollution of the manufacturing process. But he is only recording what he has seen. Working conditions may well border on the intolerable but this is not the naturalist's cry of protest, still less a declaration of solidarity with the working class (Ill. 85).

While retaining in subject and style the characteristics of what generally passes as 'realism', Menzel's younger contemporaries in the 1880s and 1890s exhibit two markedly divergent tendencies. The one set store by what could be called the conventional values of the *Gründerjahre* – a sense of national pride and personal achievement, respect for history and traditional ideals, a conception of art as a force for the promotion of personal and social morality. Against this stood those who were suspicious of a Reich forged by blood and iron, indignant at the exploitation, the poverty and the criminality generated by the pitiless pressures of industrialisation and committed to an art of social comment, art, ultimately, as an agent of social change.

Representative of those in the conservative camp, content with the traditions of monarchy and the comfortable feeling of stability that it conveyed, was Anton von Werner, director of the Berlin Academy's art school and the authoritative academic painter of the day. Royal portraits and the representation of important historical moments were his *métier* – the proclamation of the Empire in the Palace of Versailles in 1871 or the opening of the Reichstag by Wilhelm II in 1894. As historical documents, accurate and technically correct, they have their interest; as works of art they are dry and formulaic. Had Werner arrived on the scene a few years later, he would have been a court photographer rather than a court painter (Ill. 86).

Conservatism could, however, take livelier forms. As the industrialisation and commercialisation of Berlin life surged on, with old buildings being pulled down and communities broken up in the name of what was – and is – euphemistically called 'development', voices were heard lamenting the loss of past beauties. A movement arose, inspired by the need for a historical record, by a sense of civic pride, and not least by aesthetic considerations, to preserve these corners of 'Old Berlin' for posterity.

86. *Crown Prince Friedrich at the Ball in 1878* by Anton von Werner, oil on canvas, 1889. The diminutive figure of Adolph Menzel is standing by the entrance on the right.

The *ne plus ultra* of an art pledged to a naturalistic, 'photographic' reproduction of reality is photography itself. Berlin and Munich were the German cities in which technical research into the magical new medium was furthest advanced, and it was in Berlin, in the early 1860s, that a man called Friedrich Albert Schwartz appeared who was to use the invention to create a new art-form.

F. A. Schwartz has his place in this context because, while carrying out the technical task of recording the panorama of his city, he put his skill and his instincts, to no less a degree than the academic painters around him, at the service of composition, balance and other aesthetic criteria. Palaces, churches, shopping streets, railroad stations, river scenes, quiet corners – from the 1860s to the turn of the century Schwartz combed the city for his material, developing a predilection for rooftop views and other unusual perspectives. By focusing in certain directions from an elevated viewpoint, he discovered that he could demonstrate, better than at ground level, the differences in social class revealed by the different quality of the houses. By the end of his life he had a flourishing business in a succession of portrait studios and laboratories in the Potsdamer Platz and other fashionable locales and had received the royal patent as court photographer to Prince Karl of Prussia, the Kaiser's brother.

Veneration of the urban heritage had both a positive and a negative aspect. For the preservation of the historical record *per se* there could be nothing but

87. *View over the Spree* from the cycle 'Old Berlin' by Julius Jakob the Younger, water-colour on paper, 1885.

Berlin and its Culture

88. *The Mother* from the cycle
'Dramas' by Max Klinger,
etching, 1883.

gratitude, and that there were many picturesque vistas and idyllic corners to be cherished could not be gainsaid. Working in a spirit not unlike that of Schwartz, Julius Jacob produced in the latter half of the century over a hundred oils and watercolours, lovingly executed, to preserve the memory of 'Old Berlin' as truthfully as he could (Ill. 87). At the same time there was also a danger of sentimentality, of seeking refuge from an unsettling present in a romanticisation of the past. Jacob, one senses, lives on the impressionistic fringes of such a tendency.

But life was not standing still. The onward march of mechanisation and industrialisation brought unwelcome new tensions in its train, new social problems, new terrors and inhumanities. As contemporary naturalist dramatists were centring their plays on the sordid, kitchen-sink conditions of proletarian life, and lyric poets like Arno Holz deliberately cultivated the distasteful, unpleasant realities which fashionable literature avoided, so Berlin painters were recording their own responses to the new world, often seeking out the grim moments from which others, in fear or embarrassment, had averted their gaze.

Thus Max Klinger, moved by what he saw in the capital in the 1880s, made a powerful series of engravings under the title 'Dramas' – scenes of human tragedy provoked, he makes clear, by the living conditions of the proletariat. One harrowing scene, *The Mother*, taken from the records of a

89. *Railroad Tracks in the North of Berlin* by Franz Skarbina, chalk and watercolour on paper, *c.* 1895.

criminal trial, is described by Klinger in his own words: 'A family made destitute by domestic quarrels. The husband, a drunk, abuses his wife and child. In despair the woman jumps into the river with her child. The child drowns. The mother is indicted for murder and attempted suicide but acquitted.' Klinger's engraving tells the story in stark detail (Ill. 88).

Equally unmistakable in its social meaning, a meaning made the more insistent by the understated manner of its presentation, is the work of Franz Skarbina, who was born in Berlin and died there but spent considerable periods in France and Belgium. Here, from originally seeing himself as a realist painter in the line of Menzel, he came under the influence of the impressionists, painting Parisian street scenes with a sense of colour and illumination that brought him immediate popularity. Back in Germany in the late 1880s, he treated Berlin in the same spirit, showing a predilection for the tramps and other downtrodden characters on the urban scene.

Characteristic of Skarbina at his best, and of the whole movement of art as social realism, is the large painting of a night-scene which he called *Railroad Tracks in the North of Berlin* (c. 1895). The soulless industrial scene, however, uncannily brought to life by the distant lights that punctuate the monochrome darkness, is not the real subject. The centre of attention rests on the anonymous couple hurrying across the bridge, the bent, weary railwayman on his way to the night shift, anxiously followed by his wife, prisoners of the industrial system. It is not a piece of anti-capitalist propaganda. But there can be little doubt where Skarbina's sympathies lie (Ill. 89) – or those of Hans Baluschek, whose many studies of proletarian life led the poet Richard Dehmel to describe him as 'the quintessential painter of Berlin at its most characteristic' (Ill. 91).

Also from the world of impressionism, alongside Skarbina and Baluschek the most accomplished of the painters of the Berlin scene but without their tone of social criticism, is Lesser Ury. Decisively influenced by studies in France and Belgium, like Skarbina, Ury made his individual mark in his scenes of Berlin life painted in different seasons, at different times of day, in rain and shine, therefore in different lighting conditions, both natural and artificial. The fashionable locales were his preferred subjects – Unter den Linden, Friedrichstrasse, Café Bauer, Potsdamer Platz, above all at night, with the fascinating effects produced by the interplay of the fixed street lights and the moving lamps of horse-drawn trams and cabs. Ury's works have all to do with atmosphere, the atmosphere of the moment (Ill. 90).

90. *Nollerndorfplatz at Night* by Lesser Ury, oil on canvas, 1925.

91. *Women Scavenging Coal* by Hans Baluschek, oil on canvas, 1901.

Ury, Skarbina, Baluschek, the landscape painter Walter Leistikow, the young Max Slevogt, who lived in Berlin from the turn of the century to the outbreak of the First World War, powerful late impressionists like Max Beckmann and Lovis Corinth (Ill. 92) – these and others, artists of otherwise divergent interests and commitments, found common cause in the so-called Berlin Secession of 1898 and the breakaway movements that followed.

Founded, not under a prescriptive manifesto but as a free association of artists who 'seceded' from the official artists' association, the Verein Berliner Künstler, in order to mount their own exhibitions of 'alternative art', the Secession gave a platform to all topics and all styles. An impressionistic delight in the spontaneous interplay of light and colour, in the countryside as in the town, linked the activities of many painters. But there was also room for politicised art – the early work of Heinrich Zille and Käthe Kollwitz – and for allusive, symbolical tendencies from the world opened up by the speculations of Sigmund Freud. Nurtured in this atmosphere of freedom and experiment, the art of the expressionists, above all, was to flourish in the early decades of the new century.

Although the Secession was an open, undogmatic organisation, it did have an elected president, a man who symbolised the progressive qualities in contemporary art while retaining his individuality as one of the finest painters of the age – Max Liebermann.

Born in Berlin in 1847, a 200-per-cent Berliner who was never heard to speak anything but Berlin dialect, Liebermann spent a number of years in

Holland and elsewhere, returned to Berlin in 1884 and stayed for the rest of his long life there, with a studio near the Brandenburg Gate. In 1920 he was elected president of the Prussian Academy of Arts and held this position, a revered public figure, until forced to resign in 1933 as a Jewish perpetrator of 'degenerate' works. 'I couldn't eat as much as I'd like to throw up,' was his immortal response to the Nazis. He died in 1935, before the worst of the pogroms started.

As the nineteenth century drew to a close, the position of Munich as the leading art centre in Germany was being increasingly challenged by Berlin, where powerful forces were at work undermining the authority of academic, 'establishment' painting. In the wake of the provocative exhibition of works by Eduard Munch in 1892 came the foundation of the XI, a group of painters led by Leistikow, Skarbina and Liebermann, who acted as catalysts in the introduction of the methods of impressionism into German art, above all in portraits and landscapes (Ill. 93). The movement became more emphatic with the formation of the Berlin Secession and for a few brilliant years the three leading German impressionist painters – Max Liebermann, Max Slevogt and Lovis Corinth – were all working in Berlin. Others came

92. *The Blinded Samson* by Lovis Corinth, oil on canvas, 1912.

93. *The Cabbage Field* by Max Liebermann, oil on canvas, 1912.

and went, caught up for a while in the excitement of what was happening. But Liebermann never left.

With the arrival in Berlin of the 'Brücke' painters from Dresden in 1910, the days of impressionism as a force in the land were numbered. The growing extremisms in society and an incipient tendency to violence, never far below the surface in modern Germany, created an atmosphere in which the refinements and delicacies of impressionism did not reach the heart of things. The Great War made the argument unanswerable. Max Beckmann and Lovis Corinth were only two of those who turned their backs on impressionist values and became masters of the new expressionism (Ill. 92). Liebermann could hardly be unaware of the political and artistic revolution taking place outside his door but it did not penetrate his work. With him the restful landscape of pre-war times is still the restful landscape of post-war inflation and poverty. The younger expressionist generation, speaking for the thousands who were left on the battlefield or were tasting the bitter fruit of defeat, saw things differently.

The Literature of Society

It is often the minor figures, those whose voice is barely audible beyond the age which it addresses, that tell us the most about that age. So precise is their focus on the characters and events of the world around them that their creative energy is totally absorbed in the instant.

One such instant in nineteenth-century Germany was the revolution of March 1848 – or, more precisely, the decades on either side of that revolution, which produced a surge of political poetry. Prussia had a tradition of such poetry going back to Gleim's *Prussian Grenadier* songs from the Seven Years War; Arnim published a collection of earthy, popular war poems (*Kriegslieder*) in the shadow of Napoleon's victories of 1806, while, as Napoleon's defeat in the War of Liberation approached, Körner and Ernst Moritz Arndt welcomed in ringing tones the rising spirit of patriotic pride and the political advances that the fighting heralded.

Now, thirty years later, the promotion of the national interest again captured the imagination. Some of the poetry devoted to this cause was frankly conservative, seeking to consolidate the values of the restoration and appealing to a conception of the Fatherland as a spiritual ideal blessed by God. Others, progressive patriots such as Georg Herwegh and Freiligrath, took a political stand, seeing the situation in social terms governed by the forces of the industrial revolution. Herwegh and Freiligrath both led restless lives, pursued by the censor of one state or another for expressing 'extreme' views. A spiritual comrade-in-arms, born in Berlin, a resident of Berlin most of his life and buried in Berlin, was the attractive figure of Adolf Glassbrenner.

Part journalist, part poet, part cartoonist, Glassbrenner presents a comic yet acute picture of the life of the lower classes in Berlin – as Zille was to do in the next century – creating satirical characters out of the coachmen, street traders, hurdy-gurdy men and loafers that made up the street scene in the poor neighbourhoods. He makes himself the spokesman for the underprivileged, publishing poems, dialect comedies, anecdotes and drawings in a succession of popular journals, casting the caricaturist's ironical eye over the social inequalities suffered by his beloved Berliners. Like Herwegh, but gentler, less savagely socialistic in tone, he saw the defeat of 1848 as a mere temporary setback and tirelessly pursued his liberal line until his death in 1876.

By that time another wave of political poetry had swept across the country. But 1871 was not 1848. The upper and middle classes had made common cause on the basis of shared economic and political interests, and a patriotic poetry now sang of the unity of the new Empire, not of the social circumstances that divided it. Pressure grew to take politics out of poetry and to appeal to the individual, not the collective. Patriotic poetry was no longer, as in the War of Liberation, against something – French dominion – but for something – the new Fatherland. But the same poetic forms and the same poetic imagery accommodated both.

Earlier in the century the novel-reading public had eagerly awaited the 'cross-sections through a mine shaft', as he called them, in the social novels of Karl Gutzkow, one-time *enfant terrible* of the Young German fraternity. Equally popular in their day were the social novels and short stories of Friedrich Spielhagen, an immensely successful younger contemporary of Gutzkow's.

Spielhagen is barely remembered today, a minor figure in an era rich in minor figures. Even the romantic aristocrat and would-be social reformer Bettina von Arnim, author of the charming *Briefwechsel Goethes mit einem Kinde* ('Goethe's Correspondence with a Child') and of *Dies Buch gehört dem König* ('This Book is Meant for the King') – a passionate appeal for the banishment of social injustice in the Prussian kingdom – has become little more than a footnote in literary history.

Holding to a faith in science and the industrial process on one hand and to utopian, Lassalle-inspired visions of human society on the other, Spielhagen writes of and for the middle-class world in which he lived. Born in Magdeburg in 1829, he came as a student to Berlin, where he spent most of his long and productive life and where he died, still read and enjoyed, in 1911.

In the earliest of his multi-volume novels, *Problematische Naturen*, also his most popular and most frequently reprinted, the hero, who has fought on the barricades in 1848, finds himself unable to express his personality in society as it exists yet is disillusioned with the ideals of the revolution. There is little action in the novel and little development of living characters. In return we are given a great deal of intellectual discussion on the issues of the day, which the middle-class readership, anxious to educate itself and to find its role in a fast-moving world, eagerly relived in its own terms. The five volumes of Spielhagen's *Hammer und Amboss* ('Hammer and Anvil') envisage a desperately optimistic solution to the problem of how the apparently incompatible interests of masters and workers can be reconciled. But by the time of *Sturmflut* ('Storm Tide'), published in 1876, he sees disaster looming for the new Reich, a disaster foretold in the Stock Exchange collapse of 1873, the 'storm tide' of the title.

What Spielhagen has before his eyes is the Berlin outside his window, a world of optimists and pessimists, of both honourable and ignoble men, the privileged and the exploited, all caught up in the tensions of an industrial society whose demands threaten to rob man of his humanity. He identifies the conflicts between the classes but has an almost sentimental faith in the power of reason, based on a recognition of common interests, to overcome them. At the end of *Hammer und Amboss* the workers offer to rescue their heroic new employer from bankruptcy by forgoing their wages; he, on his side, makes them all partners in the firm so that they can share in its subsequent prosperity. In the last analysis we are facing a very German solution, in literature, to a set of social problems, a solution that calls, not for change in the material environment but for the ethical education and spiritual renewal of the individual. Against a world seen in such terms of sweet reason and common humanity the Marxist ideology of the class struggle could make little headway.

Something of an oddity among Berlin novels in this age of realism is the wistful, rambling *Die Chronik der Sperlingsgasse* ('Chronicle of the Sperlingsgasse') by Wilhelm Raabe, a writer who has been forced into the shadows by Stifter, Gottfried Keller and Fontane but re-emerges from time to time to make his own original demand for attention. He was not a native Berliner, and he spent most of his life elsewhere, chiefly in the small-town world which was his natural habitat. But for two years he lived in the old Spreegasse in Berlin – the 'Sperlingsgasse' of his title – conjuring out of his experiences a first novel rich in scenes from life in his historic little street.

Raabe, who was only twenty-six at the time, writes as an old man recording his reminiscences of friends and neighbours who have since moved away or died, the 'chronicle' enabling him to combine, with a minimum of formal constraint, a fictional narrative with a realist's reflection on the world in which his characters move. There are tinges of melancholy romanticism in the book, and everything takes place in a very intimate Biedermeier world of quiet satisfaction. But success has its price, and Raabe's sympathies are often seen to lie with those – the underprivileged, the misfits, the neglected – who cannot pay that price. Material progress is a fact but Raabe will not allow a facile materialistic optimism to sweep all before it. There is a negative as well as a positive realism. 'After all', runs the opening sentence of his novel, 'it is an evil age in which we live.' Evil or otherwise, it was an age as susceptible to the appeal of the pessimistic philosophy of the recently discovered Schopenhauer as to the ebullient materialism of Feuerbach, Lassalle and Karl Marx.

There is one attractive little writer, however, immensely popular in his day, who chose not to make a monumental tragedy out of life but to retreat into a charming, idyllic gently humorous world inhabited by a sunny, smiling character he called Leberecht Hühnchen.

Hühnchen was the creation of one Heinrich Seidel, a civil engineer who turned to writing only in the latter part of his life. In a series of anecdotal cameos, originally published individually between 1880 and 1893, then gathered into loose collections, Seidel creates an 'alternative' world, governed neither by the high-flown socio-political rhetoric of the day nor by the selfish pursuit of wealth and fame but by simple kindness, honesty and naive goodness. 'He possessed the gift', says Seidel of his anti-hero, 'of sucking honey from every blossom, even poisonous ones.' Like the romantic idealist of Eichendorff's *Aus dem Leben eines Taugenichts* ('Memories of a Good-for-Nothing'), Hühnchen takes as his motto 'God's in His Heaven, all's right with the world' – though a glance without his rose-coloured spectacles would have shown him that it was not.

Gutzkow, Spielhagen and Raabe, each in his own way, all took direct issue with the social conditions of their time, meeting head-on the problematic realities that clamoured for attention. As the example of Gutzkow and other Young Germans had shown, the heavy hand of the censor was always poised to fall on the overly explicit expression of views felt to question received values. But whatever the repressive conditions, writers always find ways of getting the better of their masters by recourse to stratagems such as parable, allegory and other poetic devices in which to cocoon their message. Under the pressure of such circumstances there now emerged a sub-genre which was to meet just this need and at the same time capture an enthusiastic public – the historical novel.

That enthusiasm was kindled by Sir Walter Scott. Scott had already played his part in Anglo-German literary relations by translating Bürger's ballads and Goethe's drama *Götz von Berlichingen*. Now it was for the Germans to convert the pageantry of the romantic Waverley Novels into their own terms – a revived awareness of their historical heritage, a pride in the achievements of the present and a confidence in the fulfilment of their national destiny.

The first and most influential Berlin writer to 'naturalise' the Scott novel was Wilhelm Häring, who wrote under the pseudonym of Willibald Alexis. Alexis achieved fame overnight with two historical novels, published in the 1820s, which he had the temerity to describe as 'free translations of two unknown works by Sir Walter Scott'. These he followed with a series of realistic novels set in various periods of the chequered history of Brandenburg–Prussia. Starting in the fifteenth century with the rivalry between the twin towns of Berlin and Cölln and their scuffles with the Elector, he worked his way down to the time of the Napoleonic Wars and the recent revolution of 1848. Though Alexis came from Silesia, Berlin was both his spiritual home and the heart of his literary subject matter, and he is part of the Berlin scene in a way that others who happened to spend time there – novelists like Theodor Storm and Paul Heyse, the poets Friedrich Rückert and Ernst Moritz Arndt – are not. He worked on a number of liberal journals until publicly rebuked by Friedrich Wilhelm IV for expressing opinions considered injurious to the state. His last twenty years were spent in rural retirement in Thuringia, where he lived just long enough to see the creation of the Second Reich.

The immense popularity that Alexis' novels enjoyed at the time rested on their satisfaction of both a desire and an opportunity that he identified in his public. The desire was for a picture of their past, illustrated by a lively narrative of characters, historical and fictional, whose lives combined to create a reality of their own. The opportunity was for a demonstration of parallels between the world of the past and the society of the present, parallels which revived thoughts of an ideal moral world that held promise for the future and at the same time exposed the shortcomings of life at that moment. Such a hidden agenda could be smuggled past the censor as pieces of historical reportage but readers would readily draw the critical conclusions that the author intended.

Thus in *Ruhe ist die erste Bürgerpflicht, oder vor fünfzig Jahren* ('The Citizen's First Duty Is to Keep the Peace. Or: Fifty Years Ago'), published in 1852, Alexis appears on the surface to be describing the demoralised Prussia of 1806, its armies humiliated by Napoleon and Berlin occupied by French troops. Society is rotten through and through: the King can think of nothing better than the defeatist injunction which Alexis takes for his title. But his subtitle invokes the present. Four years after the abortive revolution of 1848 the people have again been betrayed by their leaders. In the five volumes of his novel, originally published in serial form, Alexis surveys the whole gamut of social classes, from court and aristocracy through the Berlin salons of the intellectual middle class to the common soldiery. In the last analysis it is a novel about Berlin itself, a nineteenth-century panorama not unworthy of a place in the company of its great twentieth-century successor, Döblin's *Berlin Alexanderplatz*.

A very different piece of fiction in an historical framework, living by its own order of realism and its own set of moral values, is Eichendorff's *Das Schloss Dürande* ('Château Durande', 1837).

In terms of his literary career Joseph Freiherr von Eichendorff has an ambiguous relationship to Berlin. He was a Silesian aristocrat by birth and returned to spend his last years close to his birthplace. One of the greatest of German lyric poets, he owed his poetic awakening to the romantic folksong movement of the early nineteenth century, and most of his best-known poems, together with that little jewel of romantic fiction, *Aus dem Leben eines Taugenichts*, were written in Heidelberg, folksong capital of Germany. But he spent the years 1831 to 1844 in Berlin as a Prussian civil servant in the Ministry of Culture with responsibility for Roman Catholic affairs, including education, and it is to this period that *Das Schloss Dürande* belongs, together with a number of essays on ethical and cultural matters.

Like Tieck, former arch-romantic in Berlin now writing his own style of realistic short stories in Dresden, Eichendorff has turned from a private world of aesthetic idealism and fancy to a scene dominated by the realities of social pressure and historical movement. As a member of the aristocracy, he belongs to a class whose time has passed, like the Durande family in pre-revolutionary France of whom he writes. He cannot welcome the events of 1789 but nor can he disclaim an historical responsibility for them. Since he neither will nor can deny his allegiance to the class into which he has been born, he sees his task as the rescue of the ethical and religious values by which he himself has always lived. For the revolutionaries, as he portrays them, are an ill-disciplined rabble incapable of furthering the cause of civilisation. At the end of Eichendorff's vividly told story the château is in flames and the characters round whom the events revolve have all perished.

From the viewpoint of a Gutzkow, a Spielhagen, even of an Alexis, Eichendorff stands for a reactionary romanticism no longer of relevance. He is not 'socially critical', not 'realistic' enough. But *Das Schloss Dürande*, like the collection of his poems published in the same year, responds to a reality on a different level, a reality that derives from the unchanging power of nature and, beyond that, from the immanent presence of God. It is a reality as genuine as the reality of social change or of material progress. The crucial difference is that it rests on faith in God rather than on confidence in man. Perhaps this is one way of generalising the distinction between the age of romanticism and the age of realism.

There remain two of the greatest German writers of the age of realism who illustrate, through their relationship to Berlin and Brandenburg, the two extremes of a passing but significant acquaintance and a life-long devotion – Gottfried Keller and Theodor Fontane.

Swiss by birth, Swiss by political and emotional allegiance, Gottfried Keller's customary place in literary history is in the company of Conrad Ferdinand Meyer and Jeremias Gotthelf as the leader of the great trio of nineteenth-century Swiss poets and novelists. But at a sensitive moment in his career he spent six years in Berlin, years that changed the course of his life. No doubt Berlin was more important for Keller than Keller was for Berlin. Nevertheless the city fathers did later consider it appropriate to recall his stay there with a plaque on one of the houses where he lived. (It happens to be the wrong house but they meant well.)

Keller was a man of false starts. After a fatherless upbringing and a desultory education he left Zurich for Munich hoping to become a landscape painter. Two years later he was back in Zurich, penniless and unfulfilled. Then, in 1850, he received a scholarship to study theatre in Berlin. The theatre was not his *métier* but the time he spent in what he called his 'house of correction' by the Spree released his personality as both man and artist. He enjoyed Berlin theatres, especially the farces with their political ad-libbing, but avoided literary circles like the Tunnel über der Spree, preferring to take long walks through the city and size up with a painter's eye the reality around him. Brought up with the Alps on his doorstep, he considered that the flat landscape of the Mark Brandenburg weakened the mind and made people unproductive, and that his imagination too would dry up if he stayed.

In his twenties Keller had explored his withdrawn, somewhat uncongenial ego in the subjectivity of lyric verse; now, at thirty, he set out to objectify his experience. With the help of an advance from a trusting publisher he stayed in Berlin long enough to lay the foundation of a literary reputation that has never faltered. Before returning to his native Zurich, which he never left again, he converted the events of a hitherto inadequate life into the novel *Der grüne Heinrich* ('Green Henry') and wrote the short stories that make up the first volume of *Die Leute von Seldwyla* ('The Folk of Seldwyla').

Der grüne Heinrich stands in a line of 'artist novels' that is peculiarly German and which includes Goethe, Novalis, Tieck, Mörike, later Hesse and Thomas Mann. Life and art are portrayed as enemies, success and happiness in the one as incompatible with fulfilment in the other. Or, like Heinrich Lee, the autobiographical hero of *Der grüne Heinrich*, he may fail in both life and art. The strength of this long, rambling work lies in its poetic yet mercilessly realistic presentation of a succession of human situations in their political, social and ethical implications. The realism gains in intensity, moreover, from the unyielding materialism which Keller had absorbed from the teachings of Feuerbach. This materialism, in its turn, reinforces the sense of pessimism and tragedy that hangs over Heinrich's life, thwarting his attempts to make something of himself and stifling his hopes for some lasting emotional attachment to relieve his loneliness. When chance puts a fortune into his pocket and he sets out for home to share his good luck with his mother, it is only to find that she is being buried that very day. Life has lost its purpose, and he too dies a few days later. In a second version Keller derived a more positive conclusion from his materialist philosophy and granted his hero a modest degree of self-fulfilment in a government post from which he could serve the community.

As a natural next step from the episodic manner of *Der grüne Heinrich* there followed the succession of short stories in which Keller's poetic realism is perfectly displayed, the first collection of which, under the title *Die Leute von Seldwyla*, belongs to his Berlin years. Even if he had left nothing more than these five little pieces – the equals of gems of earlier nineteenth-century storytelling such as Chamisso's *Peter Schlemihl*, Eichendorff's *Taugenichts* and the stories of Kleist and Hoffmann – Keller would have secured his memory in literature. Creating an imaginary village community, he satirises the lives of the Swiss petty bourgeoisie in a vein now comic, now tragic, with a deterministic directness and honesty which show that it is not just a sleepy, narrow-minded Swiss village that he had in his sights but mankind in general, as he had come to know it and suffer at its hands.

Yet despite what seems a stern conceptual framework there is in Keller a great deal of affectionate romantic characterisation and narration which has led him to be seen as a master of 'poetic realism', a peculiarly German form of nineteenth-century fiction. His painter's eye takes in all around him; his view is comprehensive, not selective, and his style is correspondingly loose, associative, almost epic. It makes for an unusual narrative manner which charms some but which others find frustrating.

Only slowly did Keller's works make their mark on the German public. Further collections of short stories appeared after his return to Zurich, including a second volume of tales about his fictional village of Seldwyla, and he continued to write until a few years before his death in 1890 – Swiss to the core and fêted at the end as a national hero. But without Berlin it might have been a different story.

And in the case of Theodor Fontane, finally, in whom the nineteenth-century German social novel finds its supreme expression, without Berlin and all it stood for there would have been no story at all. In fact until 1878, when at almost sixty Fontane published his first novel, there literally was no story. It is one of the most remarkable cases of late development in the annals of literature (Ill. 94).

Up to that point Fontane had a merely local reputation as a journalist and travel writer, and in some circles as a minor poet, especially of ballads. Of Huguenot descent, born in the Mark Brandenburg north of Berlin in 1819, he found his way as a young man into the café life of the city and joined the mildly liberal literary club Der Tunnel über der Spree, where Geibel, Storm, Heyse and other poets were occasionally to be found, along with Prussian officers and the intellectual bourgeoisie. Always a viewer of

94. *Theodor Fontane* by Max Liebermann, lithograph, 1896.

situations in the round rather than from a committed standpoint of his own, he had difficulty in negotiating the 1848 Revolution, being drawn to its liberal, idealistic message on the one hand but anxious to preserve a peaceful, ordered society on the other. Asked in later life whether he favoured the ideal or the real, he replied – 'The diagonal.'

After a period in the 1850s as a foreign correspondent in London, Fontane embarked on an attractive series of accounts of his rambles through the Brandenburg countryside, published under the title *Wanderungen durch die Mark Brandenburg*. He also recorded his experiences as a correspondent in the three Prussian wars, then left regular employment behind and devoted the last twenty years of his life to writing novels and short stories.

By the time of his death in 1898 a different wind was blowing. Wilhelmine Germany was under attack from the young naturalists caught in the spell of Ibsen and Zola, and the society of which the seventy-year-old Fontane wrote was slipping into history. Yet Fontane himself kept an open mind on the modernist movement at the turn of the century, and, as drama critic of the *Vossische Zeitung* for twenty years, vigorously pleaded the case for Ibsen and for the naturalist dramas of the young Gerhart Hauptmann.

Fontane is the novelist *par excellence* of German social realism, one of the few German writers to find a place in a European tradition – the tradition of the social novel of George Eliot, Dickens and Thackeray, of Balzac and Flaubert, of Tolstoi and Dostoevsky. Like Keller, he began his literary career as a poet but diagnosed in himself an inability to speak with the clear voice of an inner poetic ego – he felt at his ease, he confessed, rather 'when saying things through one or other of the characters I have invented'. His gaze misses nothing in the world of which he writes or in the psychology of the characters in it. 'Realism embraces life in all its richness, the greatest and smallest things alike,' he said.

Of Fontane's sixteen novels, all of them built round Prussian characters, the earliest had a historical setting and showed an indebtedness to 'the Walter Scott of the Mark Brandenburg', Fontane's Berlin contemporary Willibald Alexis. From *L'Adultera* (1882) onwards, however, down to his late masterpiece *Effi Briest* (1895), the location is Berlin, the time is the present, and the problems are those of contemporary society, above all the relationship between the sexes, both inside and outside marriage.

But although each of his novels has a nub of problems that seek resolution, and although these problems in themselves reveal what exercised people's minds at the time, Fontane's eye is focused on his characters. Where their actions and interactions lead, there he follows. His works are not designed to a master plan of formal devices and dramatic climaxes but explore an open landscape of personal and social psychology, quietly, objectively, lovingly. He is as free of sentimentality as of grand, passionate gestures, sympathetic but often also ironic, like a true Berliner. Truth, moreover, lay for him in the unpretentious moment, the unconscious detail. Small is beautiful. 'The grand style', he declared, 'amounts to a neglect of everything that really interests people.'

Since there is so much detail to be found along the way, Fontane's narrative pace is gentle, unhurried. He has no case to make, is reluctant to apportion blame, seeking to understand all in order to forgive all, and to reconcile, as in his political views, the apparently irreconcilable. So in the fraught situation of adultery that underlies *L'Adultera*, an offence that leads to the virtual ostracism of the offending couple by those who used to be their friends and social equals, the offended husband not only forgives his erring wife but blesses her new-found adulterous happiness, and the social equilibrium is restored.

A similar status quo prevails after the strains of class conflict have run their course in one of Fontane's richest novels, *Irrungen, Wirrungen* ('Trials and Tribulations'). A familiar format of the doomed love between a man and a woman from different social classes provides a frame for a vivid tapestry of scenes showing the confrontation of conventions and expectations characteristic of Kaiser Wilhelm I's new empire. In the meetings of the Tunnel über der Spree in Berlin Fontane had made the acquaintance of Prussian officers and knew their code of conduct and ways of thinking. As a journalist, then as a writer of travelogues, he had rubbed shoulders with men and women from all walks of life, in peace and war, in the city and in the countryside. Putting the levels of experience together, he tells the story of the love of a young Junker for a gardener's daughter. The Junker knows – so does the girl, so does the reader – that, although their love will not perish, it can never take precedence over his loyalty to family and class. As he makes a 'suitable' match with a young lady of his own standing, so the girl finds happiness in a marriage at her own level. There is no great tragic sacrifice in the name of an ill-starred love. In his cool, conversational style Fontane moves among his social groupings in carefully identified surroundings, smiling here, chiding there.

To be sure, Fontane's chosen milieux are those of the ruling classes. He does not seek direct confrontation with the problems of the growing proletariat or what the naturalists of the day called 'the social question'. For a picture of life seen through the eyes of the lower classes at the turn of the century, and of the horrors of Berlin as an urban Leviathan, one must turn to a work like *Das tägliche Brot* ('Daily Bread') by Clara Viebig, an immensely popular woman writer of the period.

But, although he may focus on the better-off, Fontane is far from assuming the moral superiority of those circles, and the unquenchable love that the humble girl in *Irrungen, Wirrungen* is called upon to renounce has an unconditionality that her Junker lover cannot equal. Nor does the aristocracy escape uncriticised in one of Fontane's last and greatest novels, the tragic *Effi Briest* (1895), in which the theme of adultery, as handled in refined society, returns to claim the mind and body of the offending heroine, as the unyielding social code demands its price.

Effi Briest, a companion to Flaubert's *Madame Bovary* and Tolstoi's *Anna Karenina* in the context of the European social novel, tells of a loveless marriage, a wife's infidelity, the claims of emotional fulfilment and their frustration under the unyielding norms of Prussian social convention. But Fontane's story presents a far more subtle picture than that of a black-and-white confrontation between personal passion and social expectations. Resigning herself to her prescribed marriage, the heroine at least welcomes the prospect of security and a comfortable life; later she discovers how unimportant such things are compared with a profound human relationship. She also realises that love is not a natural part of the code by which her class lives. That class is doomed, its conventions – the conventions of the Second Reich – soon to disintegrate. But, to the extent that she accepts the consequences of those conventions, Effi is a willing victim of her situation and dies resigned to her fate. Fontane, wherever his sympathies lie, is not about to launch an impassioned campaign on her behalf. Rather, in his cool, wise, measured manner, frequently through gripping dialogue, he lays open the forces that carry in themselves the seeds of their destruction. The society from which these forces emanate, one is made to feel, has not long to live.

Fontane died at his desk, quietly and unobtrusively, in 1898, aged seventy-nine, and was buried in the Huguenot cemetery in Berlin. He had never been an author with mass appeal but fame caught up with him, and four years earlier he had been awarded an honorary doctorate by the university. Until the end he was a familiar figure on his daily round through the Tiergarten and along the banks of the Spree. 'He was born to be the "old Fontane"', wrote Thomas Mann, 'and *he* will live. The first sixty years of his life were, almost consciously, merely a preparation for the last twenty. His life seems to teach that only being prepared for dying is truly being prepared for living.'

Social Theatre

In the theatre, as in so many other fields, the year 1871 marked the arrival of a new self-confidence and the release of a new enthusiasm. Two years earlier new laws in Prussia liberalising trade and professional activities had removed the last vestiges of restrictive practices surviving from medieval times. With a permit from the police authorities any adventurer could set up a new theatre, although in practice many so-called theatres were little more than corners or rooms in inns and taverns set aside for popular music-hall entertainment by proprietors who sensed a welcome opportunity to increase their turnover.

While being compelled to offer what audiences were known to want, directors of larger theatres often sought to manipulate public taste both as an exercise in education and in the interests of variety. Some were uncannily successful in bringing visiting companies to their theatres with performances that became landmarks in the history of the Berlin stage. The most sensational of these companies was that of the court theatre in Meiningen, which played Shakespeare, Kleist and Schiller in what later became, and still is, the Deutsches Theater. Berlin audiences had never seen such lavish productions, such elaborate sets, such detailed realism, such crowds of extras on the stage. Critics, Fontane at their head, put their own weight behind the efforts to create a new, more demanding public. In 1883, nine years after the first visit of the Meiningen troupe, Adolph L'Arronge, owner of the Deutsches Theater, mounted his first season of German classics – Lessing's *Minna von Barnhelm*, Goethe's *Iphigenie auf Tauris*, Schiller's *Kabale und Liebe* and *Don Carlos* – and almost overnight toppled the venerable Schauspielhaus from its unchallenged pre-eminence. Under Otto Brahm, then Max Reinhardt, and since the 1930s under a series of pressures no less political than artistic, the Deutsches Theater has never forfeited its prestige in the theatrical life of Berlin.

Meanwhile at the splendid Victoria-Theater near the Alexanderplatz, Rudolf Cerf, son of the founder of the Königsstädtisches Theater, engaged an Italian company for a season of operas by Donizetti and Verdi, during which *Rigoletto* and *Ernani* were heard in Berlin for the first time. In 1880 Cerf's successor, Emil Hahn, brought the Weimar Court Theatre to the Victoria-Theater with the first complete performance in Berlin of Goethe's *Faust*. The following year an even grander event took place – four complete cycles of Richard Wagner's *Der Ring des Nibelungen*, given by Angelo Neumann's ensemble from Leipzig. Kaiser Wilhelm I set the royal seal of approval on both composer and theatre by attending the final performance of *Götterdämmerung* in person. But the royal presence could not disguise the economic realities, and ten years later the Victoria-Theater was pulled down to make room for a road-building scheme.

On the other hand the years on either side of 1900 also saw the foundation of a number of theatres which still survive today. The Theater des Westens, near the Zoologischer Garten, with its elaborate Renaissance façade, goes back to 1896, the original Theater am Schiffbauerdamm, home of the Berliner Ensemble, even to 1892. The westward thrust of avenues like the Kurfürstendamm, prime symbol of the expansionist confidence of Empire, opened up new possibilities in the district of Charlottenburg, where the modernist Schiller-Theater was built in 1906 and a second opera house in classicistic style, the Deutsches Opernhaus (later called the Städtische Oper and now the Deutsche Oper), in 1912.

These two Charlottenburg theatres symbolised in their architecture two opposing schools of thought on the contemporary function of the theatre. Traditional attitudes adhered to familiar historicist principles which saw the theatre as an agency for the promotion of moral values through the greatest dramas that the world has to offer. Particularly in the decorative features of its interior the Deutsches Opernhaus reflected the philosophy that, as a solemn temple dedicated to art, it should manifest those forms which have proven their timeless qualities through the centuries.

For the sponsors of the Schiller-Theater the emphasis lay elsewhere. Their aim was to introduce great art to the man in the street who had until now not been able to afford it. To express this philosophy, the Schiller-Theater had an auditorium consisting of a single raked bank of seats, with no boxes and no upper tiers. The audience confronted the stage action *en bloc*, united in their enjoyment of a shared experience.

Social changes, above all those promoting a wider access to education and culture for the 'fourth estate', brought with them organisations and initiatives which carried further the idealistic programme of the Schiller-Theater. Under the auspices of the Social Democratic Party a Volksbühne (People's Theatre) movement was launched in 1891 which succeeded in raising the funds for its own theatre in an unfashionable area near the Alexanderplatz. Although from the beginning it took the occasional socialist dramatist, like Emil Rosenow, under its wing, it had at the time no thought of turning theatre into an instrument of political agitation, as Piscator and Karlheinz Martin were to do ten years later. Its repertoire included the familiar German

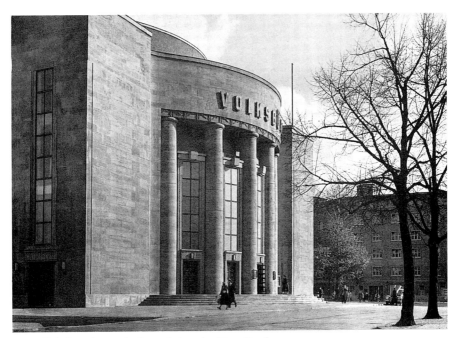

95. Volksbühne theatre, built to designs by Otto Kaufmann, 1913–15.

classics but also broke a lance for the exciting new naturalist dramas of Gerhart Hauptmann and Frank Wedekind, together with the challenging works of Ibsen and Bjørnson, Gorki, Tolstoi and Gogol (Ill. 95).

There are a number of familiar truisms about the development of nineteenth-century Europe – its secularisation, its optimism, the growth of the processes of industrialisation and urbanisation, the stratification of society, a sense of rising personal aspirations but also of constricting social pressures. Truisms they may be but they are no less true for that. Against this background Berlin had by the last decades of the century become a microcosm of the opportunities and frustrations, the confidence and the disillusionment that made up common experience, and as *Reichshauptstadt* it had a place in the sun which it would never lose.

Through the nineteenth century the pace of theatre-building in Berlin had been gradually quickening, less to accommodate vibrant new plays than to satisfy a rising demand for places of entertainment. Suddenly, in the 1880s, three factors combined to cause an explosion. The first was the availability of the new theatres themselves; the second was the influential presence of critics and theorists, men professionally involved in the promotion of the city's culture. The third force was, so to speak, the explosive charge itself, a blast that shook the Berlin stage to its foundations – a blast called naturalism.

The socio-economic scenario against which naturalism emerged was governed above all by the emergence of a proletarian underclass whose living conditions made a mockery of the rising wealth the industrial process was designed to produce. The middle classes secured their comfortable existence and made common cause with their natural allies, the Prussian bureaucrats and the officer caste. Particularly powerful during the years of Bismarck's ascendancy and the *Gründerjahre* which followed was the awareness that Germany was now a world power and could display a military presence commensurate with that status.

In philosophical terms the age was caught in a current of determinism, materialism and anti-clericalism. Nietzsche pronounced God to be dead. Darwin and Karl Marx had presented their models of natural and social evolution in which inner laws relentlessly worked their way through, free from divine intervention. Nothing transcended matter. Man was not a creature of God but a product of his environment and ultimately its victim. Dogma has become meaningless, the idealist tradition of the nineteenth century played out. The age of socialism is dawning.

Feeling themselves charged with an anti-Wilhelmine mission to become the pioneers of change, groups of young writers mounted the literary barricades. Some dealt in theories and manifestos, mocking a shallow and exhausted bourgeois literature incapable of meeting the needs of the modern age, and proclaiming a new, naturalist ideal of art resting on a faith in materialism and democratic humanism. Such were the brothers Heinrich and Julius Hart, journalists who, like others of their generation, saw that Berlin would inevitably become the rallying-point for the new movement and launched a cultural journal there in 1882 with the suitably aggressive title *Kritische Waffengänge* ('Critical Crusades'). Taking for granted the supremacy of drama among literary genres in the contemporary situation, they argued that the moment demanded a national people's theatre which should lay out the vital conflicts, personal and social, that the age had to confront.

Others, rather than theorise, clothed the new values in poetic form from the outset. An urban lyric poetry of protest emerged, like that of Arno Holz, which painted naturalistic portraits of the sordid conditions of working-class life. Holz is an angry young man from a working-class background, impatient and scornful of whatever he sees as having outlived its relevance. The world of the *Mietskaserne*, the hurdy-gurdy man, the end of the factory shift, the pleasure-seekers in the Friedrichstrasse – a feast of new, urban subject matter presented itself, often celebrated in new, free poetic forms. For Holz, whose idol was the political Heine and who set himself in the 1848 tradition of progressive poets such as Fallersleben and Georg Herwegh, opposed not only the social policies of Wilhelmine Germany but also its aesthetic values, and saw the *Volk* as a revolutionary force no less in the arts than in politics.

A greater poet than Holz, and one of the most interesting figures in the naturalist literature of *fin de siècle* Berlin, was the conflict-ridden Richard Dehmel, friend and fellow-crusader both of the Hart brothers and of Arno Holz. The interest and the conflicts are already present in the components of his biography – an upbringing in idyllic rural surroundings south of Berlin, a classic father–son conflict of generations, a commitment as a young man to the life of the metropolis and a powerful eroticism overlaid by a piercing intellect and an unyielding political consciousness. In the shadow of Nietzsche Dehmel laid claim to the uninhibited right of self-fulfilment, free of social and moral restraints – the tortured world to which 'Erwartung' belongs, a poem that has reached a wider public as the background to Schoenberg's *Verklärte Nacht*.

Almost in direct opposition to Dehmel the passionate poet of the erotic self is Dehmel the intellectual protagonist of the cause of the working class, the torch-bearing poet who deals not in mere sympathy, or even in human tragedy, but in political conviction and the inevitability of revolution. A social comment on the life of the working class, Dehmel's verse shares a world with the contemporary engravings of Max Klinger (see Ill. 88).

To the radicals of his age, and to himself, Dehmel stood on the side of history. History has taken a different course. But the imagery of the birds who enjoy their freedom, as man, too, will one day enjoy his, has an appeal to any caught in a condition of oppression which time will surely change:

> *Nur Zeit! wir wittern Gewitterwind.*
> *wir Volk.*
> *Nur eine kleine Ewigkeit;*
> *uns fehlt ja nichts, mein Weib, mein Kind,*
> *als all das, was durch uns gedeiht,*
> *um so kühn zu sein, wie die Vögel sind.*
> *Nur Zeit!*

> ('Just time. We sense the storm,
> We people.
> Just a little eternity.
> We lack nothing, my woman, my child,
> save all that prospers through us,
> to become as bold as the birds.
> Just time.')
> (from Richard Dehmel, 'Der Arbeitsmann')

Literary clubs such as Durch! and Der Tunnel über der Spree, journals such as the Hart brothers' *Kritische Waffengänge*, studies in the new naturalist aesthetic by Arno Holz and others: there was no lack of theatrical advice on how to set dramatic literature on a new course. Nor was there a shortage of theatres. The need now was, on the one hand, for modern plays that would exemplify the new values, and, on the other, for a kind of steering committee, a body of men prepared to put their weight behind the concept of a 'new' theatre and present these plays in concert as a coherent experience.

The decisive move came in 1889. A group of writers and critics, led by Maximilian Harden and Otto Brahm, drama critic of the *Vossische Zeitung*, met in a Berlin restaurant and founded the Freie Bühne, an organisation pledged to offer the public serious dramas dealing with the moral and social problems of the age. The title was taken from the naturalist Théâtre-Libre in Paris, whose recent performances, above all of Ibsen's *Ghosts*, had shocked the French theatre-going public in a way that the Freie Bühne now hoped to repeat in Berlin. In the first number of a journal founded as a critical accompaniment to their productions, Brahm made the group's aims explicit: 'We are setting up a "Free Theatre" for modern life. At the centre of our activities stands Art – a new Art that looks reality and contemporary life straight in the eye . . . Writ large on the banner of the new Art, inscribed in gold letters by the leading minds of the day, is just one word – Truth. It is Truth, Truth in every walk of life, that we demand and after which we strive.' Learning what was afoot, Fontane and others hastened to assure Brahm of their support, and Samuel Fischer, founder of the famous Fischer-Verlag, offered to publish the new dramas.

The Freie Bühne opened its first season in September 1889 with a performance of Ibsen's *Ghosts* in the Lessing-Theater. The cast was drawn from other ensembles in the city, and Brahm supervised the production. Since its first performance two years earlier *Ghosts* had been banned in Berlin but in a well-worn stratagem the Freie Bühne described the occasion as 'private', for members only, thus taking it beyond the censor's reach. Other works in the repertoire for this and the following season included Zola's *Thérèse Raquin*, Tolstoi's *The Power of Darkness* and Strindberg's *The Father*, as well as Arno Holz's and Johannes Schlaf's *Die Familie Selicke*, the *locus classicus* of German naturalist drama, in which stock components – poverty, the ruined marriage of a drunken father and a careworn mother, a downtrodden daughter forced to abandon her hopes of happiness, the tragic death of a child – are magnified to the point of parody. Holz and Schlaf, pointing to the typicality and inevitability of the situation and to the stuttering, ungrammatical, earthy language they adopted, would have called it 'Truth'.

But the greatest triumph of the Freie Bühne lay not with Ibsen or any other foreign author, or yet with the shocking *Familie Selicke*. It came with the second of its productions, an unknown play by an unknown writer living on the outskirts of Berlin. His name was Gerhart Hauptmann, and his play, *Vor Sonnenaufgang* ('Before Sunrise'), became a *succès de scandale* that made him famous overnight. Simultaneously it both set the seal on naturalist drama as the most vital form of contemporary theatrical expression and established Berlin – once and for all, one is tempted to say – as the theatrical capital of Germany.

Hauptmann is a strange case. An amazingly prolific writer of novels, short stories, poetry and plays over the fifty years of his active life, he was celebrated throughout almost all of this time as one of the greatest, if not the greatest, living German writer. A handful of his forty or so plays, mostly from his prodigious early years, have a firm place in the repertoire of every modern German theatre, and the short story 'Bahnwärter Thiel' ('Thiel the Line-Man'), from the same early period, is a gem of realist–naturalist fiction. But Hauptmann is not a Kleist, or a Büchner, and unlike his Scandinavian forebears Ibsen, Bjornson and Strindberg, he has made little impact outside his native country.

Yet in many ways Hauptmann *is* naturalism, in his settings, his themes, his characters, his language. Born in Silesia in 1862, he came to Berlin in 1884 and in a flurry of activity wrote the best-known and most powerful of his dramas during the comparatively few years he spent there – *Einsame Menschen* ('Lonely People'), *Die Weber* ('The Weavers'), *Der Biberpelz* ('The Beaver Pelt'), *Fuhrmann Henschel* ('Henschel the Drayman'). In 1912 he was awarded the Nobel Prize for Literature – the year after Maeterlinck, the year before Rabindranath Tagore. He experimented with the techniques of surrealism and the Neue Sachlichkeit of the 1920s and was to be found in the company of leading politicians and intellectuals during the years of the Weimar Republic. But, like many proud of the national cultural tradition, he displayed an ambivalence towards the Nazis that cast a shadow over his last years, and his 'Yes' in the plebiscite of 1933 to approve Hitler's accession as Führer and Reichskanzler left many hoping it could be put down to senility. He died in 1946 in his Silesian homeland – which had just become Polish territory – and was buried in his retreat on the Baltic island of Hiddensee.

Vor Sonnenaufgang is exemplary, full-blooded naturalism, frenzied, at times to the point of the grotesque, especially in its language. Its characters, inhabitants of a Silesian mining village, stand for adultery, cruelty, alcoholism, attempted incest and suicide; social conditions are governed by forces of industrial capitalism which have brought corruption and injustice into the conduct of human affairs and set the haves against the have-nots. It is a scene of unremitting gloom broken only by the optimistic socialism of one character, and even his optimism shrinks before the prospect of the woman he loves becoming a dipsomaniac. In the event she kills herself in despair. It is Hauptmann's prime naturalist theme – man trapped in his own helplessness, at the mercy of a brutal environment and dominated by a wild longing to escape.

The play violently divided its first-night audience. As one half hurled insults at the stage, the other half cheered, and only with difficulty did the actors fight their way through to the end. But press reviews and the reception of later performances showed who had won the battle. Brahm had proven the political power of the modern theatre. 'For me', he said, 'theatre is not just theatre but a vehicle of literary agitation – and the most powerful there is.' For his part, Hauptmann, who denied that true art could be didactic – 'Art that moralises is not art' – had demonstrated the function of drama in his own aesthetic terms, in an age that looked to the advance of scientific knowledge for the achievement of a just and peaceful society. For art, says Hauptmann, goes deeper, seeks eternal truth, 'aims to express the purest essence of a chosen object, thus investing it with universal validity'.

Hauptmann's most famous play, *Die Weber* ('The Weavers', 1891–2), invokes this validity for the class struggle. Based on the revolt of the Silesian weavers in 1844 against their intolerable living conditions, and originally written in Silesian dialect, it has little by way of a formal plot, nor is its action directed towards the evolving fate of a few principal characters, still less of a single hero. The 'chosen object', to quote Hauptmann's own words, is the people in their collective struggle to free themselves from their poverty, a struggle for which one can see only a pessimistic outcome. For although there is a character in the play – one of the weavers themselves – who makes a tentative appeal to a Christian ethic of earthly suffering in exchange for happiness in the world hereafter, even he is not free from thoughts of vengeance, and at the end he is killed by a stray bullet when troops are called in to put the riot down. Death may bring something to an end but it does not solve anything. At the same time there is no doubt where Hauptmann is pointing his 'J'accuse'.

Unlike that of *Vor Sonnenaufgang*, the première of *Die Weber* in 1893 went off surprisingly peacefully. 'There was no division into rival factions, no fighting', reported the *Berliner Börsen-Courier*, 'only earnest attention everywhere, coupled with appreciation and delight.' Brahm, who became director of the Deutsches Theater in 1894, made *Die Weber* the centrepiece of his naturalist repertory and gave it almost one hundred enthusiastic performances during his first season. Court and Junker circles, not unexpectedly, saw it as a seditious influence, and the following year Wilhelm II cancelled his annual subscription for the royal box at the Deutsches Theater in protest. But by this time Brahm and his theatre had become too firmly integrated into the social and cultural life of Berlin for the Kaiser's complaint to have any effect, either on Brahm's reputation or on the theatre's finances. In fact, as usually happens in such cases, the popularity of the offending work and its author only increased.

Treading a well-worn path from Silesia to Berlin, Hauptmann sought and found fame in the capital. Half of his major naturalist plays, however, are located in, and have recourse to the dialect of, his homeland; the others take place in or near Berlin, two of them – *Rose Bernd* and *Die Ratten* – in the Berlin of the working class.

The latter, a tragi-comedy set in a tenement building and dating from 1910, is an interesting counterpart to what was at the time the most sensational single success in all naturalist drama – Hermann Sudermann's *Die Ehre* ('Honour', 1889). At the centre of Sudermann's play stands, not a set of characters living out their conflicts in the *Mietskaserne* where they live, but the tenement itself in all its oppressiveness. Class is set against class in direct, if melodramatic style, giving the audience an intensified experience of their own reality, an experience which is at the same time an exercise in social criticism projected, as it were, from the heart of those social conditions themselves. But it is not a call to arms. Its language, despite its recourse to dialect, has not the peremptory roughness and deliberate crudity of the programmatic naturalist. Its streaks of sentimentality make it suspect to some, yet they show what the theatre-going public of the time flocked to see.

Sudermann, who also wrote novels and other dramas, did not have the staying-power of Hauptmann, and the remarkable reception given to *Die Ehre* has cast him as a one-work writer. But it is a memorable work nonetheless.

Slowly but surely Berlin was drawing creative and performing artists from outlying provinces into its sphere of influence. They enjoyed what it had to offer and used its attractions to further their careers. Sudermann, a native of East Prussia, was one of the few who came and stayed. Hauptmann gave up his house there at the end of the century and returned to Silesia. Frank Wedekind, who was writing his scandalising sexual dramas in Munich at the same time as Hauptmann was conquering Berlin, joined the Deutsches Theater as an actor in 1904 and played in a number of his own dramas, as well as in cabaret. It was the broadminded Deutsches Theater, too, that first put on his *Frühlings Erwachen* ('Spring's Awakening'). But Wedekind had always disliked the conception of a German Empire dominated by Prussia, and he stayed in the capital only a few years. Likewise Strindberg, whose European reputation, with those of Ibsen and George Bernard Shaw, had been launched in the Prussian capital, hovered round the Berlin theatres at this time, albeit without any prospect of staying.

In no field of culture were the pickings richer, the urge to impress more irresistible, than in the theatre. Otto Brahm, his work supported by the forces behind the *Volksbühne* and similar popular movements, had laid the foundations of a theatrical culture that not only absorbed the German classics but also identified the challenges thrown down by dramatists of the moment. Brahm was a critic, a man of the word, whose priorities began with the literary text. And critics, from Fontane to the most respected, most feared of them all, Alfred Kerr – also a Silesian émigré – could make or break the reputation of a playwright or an actor at will.

What the Berlin stage now needed, however, was not a man of the word. It was a man of the theatre. That man arrived in Berlin from Salzburg in 1894 as an actor in Brahm's company. Ten years later he took over as director of the Deutsches Theater itself, by that time Germany's leading theatre. His name was Max Reinhardt. But his story is a matter for the twentieth century.

Music for the People

After restless decades of conflicting artistic tastes and policies in the operatic life of the capital, with the King, his music director, the administrators of the royal theatres and the public rarely seeing eye to eye, there followed in the middle of the nineteenth century a welcome period of consolidation, presided over by the new general administrator of the royal theatres, Botho von Hülsen. Hülsen, a young guards officer with a passion for the stage, seemed at the time an unusual choice for the post. But his sense of order and discipline was much to be welcomed, and the standing of the Berlin opera rose steadily during the thirty years of his stewardship.

Above all, although the repertoire could not but be dominated by Italy and France – Donizetti, Adam, Auber, Rossini, Gounod's *Faust*, Bizet's *Carmen*, Verdi's *Rigoletto* and *Il Trovatore* – modern German works were increasingly making their mark. Most of these German composers are totally unknown today. Others survive by a single work, like *The Merry Wives of Windsor* by Otto Nicolai. Nicolai came to Berlin as court Kapellmeister in the revolutionary turmoil of 1848 and conducted the première of *The Merry Wives* the following year. His death a few weeks later at the age of thirty-eight robbed the city of a musician who could have contributed a great deal to its musical life.

Ballet too was growing in popularity. Dance scenes had been an integral part of French opera since Lully, and the royal Prussian opera that followed the French line, including the Parisian works of Gluck, needed a *corps de ballet* alongside its singers and orchestral players. Rank and file dancers could be recruited locally but for star choreographers and ballerinas eyes turned again to Paris or to a fashionable Italian court. Wilhelm I, especially after his translation from King to Emperor, was even more insistent than his predecessors on establishing the criteria of his capital as a cultural metropolis. For their part, actors, singers, dancers and others in the world of the performing arts found both material reward and artistic satisfaction in the stimulating atmosphere that the Kaiser offered them.

Wilhelm II, who succeeded his father in 1888, was no less determined than his predecessors to assert his will in the cultural field, especially over the activities of his royal theatres. He knew what he liked. More importantly, he knew what was good for his people, and made sure that they got it. Opera after opera bore the superscription 'By His Majesty's Command', many of them patriotic in substance or sentimentally folksy in musical idiom, most dying a natural death in the season of their first production.

As an example of what he had in mind, the Kaiser commissioned Leoncavallo, composer of the immensely popular *Pagliacci*, to make an opera out of an historical novel by Willibald Alexis called *Der Roland von Berlin*. Alexis' story, set in fifteenth-century Brandenburg, embroiders an historical episode in which the Elector Friedrich II asserts his authority over the rebellious citizens of Berlin who were fighting to retain their civic independence.

Why the Kaiser found the historical analogy of Alexis' novel attractive is clear enough, and he had a predilection for the contemporary *verismo* operas of Leoncavallo, Mascagni and Puccini, which were hugely popular at the end of the nineteenth century. For a time, indeed, performances of *Pagliacci* and *Cavalleria rusticana* outstripped those of any other work in Berlin. But the Kaiser's choice of Leoncavallo, Italian through and through, to compose this Prussian opera seemed bizarre in the extreme, a judgement only confirmed by the stubborn failure of the work to make any impression on the public. Even critics whose newspapers were expected to defer to His Majesty's taste could find little good to say about it, and *Der Roland von Berlin* has taken its place among other ephemeral extravagances by Berlin 'outsiders' – Spontini's *Agnes von Hohenstaufen*, Meyerbeer's *Feldlager in Schlesien* – written to project the fame of the Hohenzollern dynasty.

Eminently unmemorable though such pieces may be, they ministered to a penchant for loudness and showiness characteristic of public taste in the Wilhelmine era, and had a contagious effect on production policy as a whole. External glitter mattered more than conceptual intelligence. Or as the actor Eduard von Winterstein remembered the situation: 'It was far more important to display real-life costumes than real-life emotions.'

In the more substantial aspects of its repertoire the Berlin opera increasingly showed the internationalism to be expected of a capital city. Humperdinck's *Hänsel und Gretel* (1894) was a national favourite but equally popular were Saint-Saëns' *Samson et Dalila* (1901) and Puccini's *Madame Butterfly* (1907), with leading soloists drawn from other German opera houses and from abroad – Frieda Hempel, the American soprano Geraldine Farrar, Caruso, the Russian bass Chaliapin. The range of works on offer, particularly at the lighter, more popular end of the repertoire, was further extended when Hans Gregor opened his Komische Oper in the Friedrichstrasse in 1905, where Bizet's *Carmen* became a great favourite. An even greater success was Offenbach's *Tales of Hoffmann*, given its German première in the Komische Oper in 1905 and performed almost 500 times in the years leading up to the First World War.

The role of conductor was acquiring a new importance. In the early years of the century the composer usually conducted his own works – Weber, Spontini, Meyerbeer, Wagner – and, as far as Berlin was concerned, only during the times when a strong creative personality was in residence did performances reach an acceptable standard. Since Meyerbeer left in 1845, or, at the latest, since Heinrich Dorn's departure in 1868, the Royal Opera under Hülsen had had no firm-minded Kapellmeister to impose his authority on the proceedings. But a new breed of musician was about to take over – the full-time conductor, with the charisma to mould a performance to his personal vision. The first to claim this role was Felix Weingartner, appointed to the Royal Opera in 1891 from Mannheim, a showman who ushered in a new age by conducting for the eye as well as for the ear. Weingartner's unostentatious successor Richard Strauss, on the other hand, using a restrained technique of minimum gestures, conducted for the music (see Ill. 96).

In one function or another – as First Kapellmeister at the court opera, as the Kaiser's General Music Director, as conductor of the symphony concerts – Strauss had a stormy relationship with Berlin that lasted for twenty years. Launching his reign in 1898 with *Tristan und Isolde*, followed the year after by the first performance of *Die Fledermaus*, he quickly established his authority. But he also came to Berlin as a composer. *Don Juan*, *Tod und Verklärung*, *Till Eulenspiegel* and other of his famous orchestral pieces were already in his portfolio, and why should he not expect to see his operas performed in the theatre where he had been appointed to conduct?

But the conditions he laid down in 1901 for his latest opera *Feuersnot* were rejected by the theatre management as unreasonable, and the Kaiser considered parts of the libretto insulting to Prussian morality. The offended Strauss retaliated by denying the Prussian capital the right to stage any future premières of his works. Such was the success of *Feuersnot*, first in Dresden, then in Vienna, that its performance in Berlin became only a matter of time. But Strauss did not withdraw his embargo, and Berlin had to sit and watch while one after another of his operas were premièred elsewhere.

The conservatism of public taste also laid restrictions on what Strauss could afford to perform. He feared that Schoenberg, for example, for whom he had secured a teaching post at the Stern Conservatory in 1902, would cause problems. 'Your compositions', he wrote apologetically to Schoenberg, 'from the point of view both of their intellectual content and of their sound, are so bold and experimental that for the time being I dare not play them before a more than conservative Berlin public.' The composer Max Butting explained what Strauss meant by 'more than conservative'. 'The public here', wrote Butting drily, 'is from the beginning suspicious of any music written by a composer who is not even dead yet.'

Wilhelm II, who found Strauss' operas both musically and morally degenerate, made a rueful observation about the Kapellmeister he had been proud to welcome to his court. He felt, he said, as if he had been suckling a serpent at his breast. When the Berliners learnt of the Kaiser's remark, they christened Strauss 'the Imperial Breast Serpent'. In any case they needed no antidote for the Straussian venom. They revelled in it. The climax of their delight was reached with *Der Rosenkavalier* in 1911, despite the bowdlerisation of Hofmannsthal's libretto by an ever-zealous Prussian censor.

Far from an air of authoritarianism, Strauss as conductor conveyed an aura of tolerance which verged on the perfunctory. His rehearsals were usually straight run-throughs. Once, rehearsing his tone-poem *Don Juan*, he unexpectedly broke off and asked his players to repeat a particularly tricky passage.

96. *Richard Strauss* by Max Liebermann, oil on canvas, 1918.

The result was little better. 'Just once more, if you will.' When the third time was still unsatisfactory, he lost interest and told them to play on. 'Let them practise it at home,' he muttered.

The city's orchestral tradition, meanwhile, reaching back to the Philharmonic Society of 1826 and built on by the Stern Conservatory and the Hochschule für Musik, reached its apogee in the foundation of the Berlin Philharmonic Orchestra in 1882.

This great orchestra owed its existence, not exactly to chance but at least to a surprising combination of circumstances. A military bandsman from Silesia called Benjamin Bilse had founded a professional light orchestra with which he had phenomenal success all over Europe in the 1860s. On the establishment of the Empire Bilse was invited to bring his band to Berlin. He leased his own concert hall in the Leipziger Strasse and after a single season had established his Saturday and Sunday concerts as popular events in the social calendar. In an informal atmosphere middle-class audiences sat at tables drinking beer or chocolate, the women knitting while nursing their children on their lap. 'As the music started up', recalled Gerhart Hauptmann, a regular visitor in his younger days, 'the waiters did not stop serving but brought the food and beer in on tiptoe, communicating with the customers only by sign language.'

Under such circumstances the customers' enjoyment not unexpectedly demanded its aesthetic price. 'Having provided oneself with a ticket for the appropriate sum', reported a contemporary source, 'one can listen one day to the oratorio *The Death of Jesus*, on another to the *Death of Abel*, but every evening without fail to the lingering Death of Music, which, however, has no desire to die.'

After a few years of serving up music under such conditions many of Bilse's musicians began to grumble and in 1882 three-quarters of them left to form their own 'Philharmonic Orchestra'. Coincidentally the court orchestra of Meiningen, under their conductor Hans von Bülow, had been invited that same year to perform in Berlin. With Bülow came Brahms. Most of the concerts were devoted to Beethoven, performed with an intensity the Berliners had never before experienced. On one evening Brahms played his Second Piano Concerto with Bülow conducting; the following evening the roles were reversed in Brahms' First Piano Concerto. The orchestra played standing: only thus, maintained Bülow, could they bring the necessary energy and concentration to their playing. This, said the renegades of the new Philharmonic Orchestra, was the sort of musical experience that deserved to be offered to Berlin.

Two years later Bülow, former husband of Cosima Wagner and champion not only of Brahms but also of Wagner and the 'New Music' in general, returned to Berlin and showed the catholicity of his taste by conducting pieces by the twenty-year-old Richard Strauss and the twenty-one-year-old Felix Weingartner. Here was proof, if proof were needed, that Bülow was the man for Berlin. For five years, from 1887 to 1892, he conducted the new Philharmonic Orchestra to packed houses in the Philharmonie, the orchestra's concert hall that had once been a roller-skating rink, playing works from the whole classical and modern repertoire. His short, vigorous gestures carried his players along with him by sheer intensity, and he conducted everything from memory. When challenged on this, he replied: 'One must have the score in one's head, not one's head in the score.'

The concerts of Bilse's time had tended to be long-drawn-out affairs, with something for everybody, from the sublime to, if not the ridiculous, at least the mundane. Bülow brought in radical changes, reducing the length of his concerts and building the programme round one substantial work, usually a symphony. Above all he discarded everything second-rate, however popular it had become and whatever special local reasons there might have been for its inclusion. 'There is good music enough', he explained, 'and it needs me more – unfortunately – than does the other.'

As standards of performance rose and the repertoire widened, so the knowledge and power of discrimination of audiences grew, establishing an interrelationship beneficial to both sides. 'Bülow once rightly said', wrote the music critic of the *Berliner Tageblatt*, 'that each member of the public, taken individually, is a . . . (I would prefer not to repeat his expression), but that the public as a whole is a damnably clever fellow.'

From some fifty or so public concerts a year in the 1860s the figure reached well over a hundred by the 1870s. New concert halls were built – the Mozartsaal on the Nollendorfplatz, which concentrated on modern music, the Beethovensaal, the Bechsteinsaal and others. The importance of the following morning's reviews in the newspaper rose correspondingly, and a new breed emerged – the agent–impresario, a broker between music and market.

The early conductors of the Berlin Philharmonic Orchestra after Bülow followed each other in quick succession. Then, in 1897, came Artur Nikisch, the first of the great triumvirate – Wilhelm Furtwängler and Herbert von Karajan were the others – whose combined regimes covered almost a century of sustained magnificence. Reserved in his movements, Nikisch seemed to cast a spell over his players, then withdraw from the proceedings and allow the spell to work its own magic. 'He does not conduct', said Tchaikovsky, 'but it is as if he surrenders himself to some mysterious sorcery . . . You hardly notice him.'

In the context of the light music from which Bilse's breakaway orchestra had originally come, a great following attended the open-air concerts given by military bands, which much impressed Berlioz on his visits to Prussia. Part of their appeal rested on the sheer spectacle of the occasion – soldiers resplendent in their regimental uniforms, the flamboyance, the impressive discipline and the patriotic pride. Yet the public's enjoyment was not allowed to be frivolous. Military music was not just entertainment, it was an expression of noble sentiment, and a band concert was a statement of Prussian virtues. 'Military discipline and respect are to be observed with the utmost strictness on such occasions', stated a royal edict, 'and any persons indulging in improper behaviour or interrupting the music in any way will be punished.'

The programmes of these concerts were cunningly devised. After an operatic overture by Mozart, Verdi or Meyerbeer, followed by assorted marches and polkas, came an item of battle music in the tradition of Beethoven's *Wellington's Victory*, appealing to the more questionable side of patriotic emotion and even provoking children to re-enact the battle with sticks and stones. Other occasions were more pacific. As the popularity of these concerts grew, and with it the number of establishments that sensed the economic potential of the situation, bands from outside were invited to visit the city. Johann Strauss *père* brought his waltzes and polkas from Vienna in the 1840s, and his son, on a wave of enthusiasm for things Austrian and Hungarian, arrived towards the end of the century with the 'Blue Danube', 'Vienna Blood' and other evergreens. In 1900, during his first tour of European cities with his own band, John Philip Sousa played a programme of American music at Kroll's establishment, introducing German audiences to his operettas and marches and also bringing with him an Americanised form of the polka called the cake-walk, which quickly made its mark in European cabaret.

From stimuli such as these was born a piece of characteristic *fin de siècle* light entertainment – the Berlin operetta. Pageantry and sentimentality, a growing taste for dance (Isadora Duncan set up a ballet school in Dahlem in 1903), an aura of carefree happiness captured in the infectious melodies of popular songs sung and whistled all over town – it was an irresistible cocktail. Paul Lincke, the 'Berlin Johann Strauss', composer of *Berliner Luft* and *Frau Luna*, was the great name, the Metropol in the Behrenstrasse the great theatre. Then came Jean Gilbert with *Polnische Wirtschaft*, and Friedrich Holländer, the revue and film music king, composer of the song that made Marlene Dietrich famous, 'Falling in Love Again'.

At the other end of the spectrum of public musical life lay the cultivation of musical education. Critics such as Rellstab and Adolf Bernhard Marx were doing much to form popular taste, exerting an influence certainly more beneficial than those who had felt the lash of their tongues, like Wagner, would admit. New music journals were being founded to review both performances and published new music. Marx was appointed professor at the university, marking the establishment of music as an object of academic study, while scholars began to mine the archives of the Royal Library in search of treasures from earlier ages. At the same time performers were finding their needs met by private bodies. These were few in number and limited in scope in the early decades of the century, like Spontini's school for training recruits to the orchestras of the royal theatres. But after the violinist and conductor Julius Stern arrived from Paris in 1846 and four years later founded the conservatoire that bears his name, their number quickly increased. The orchestra and choral society that Stern also created gave the first complete performance of Beethoven's *Missa solemnis* in 1856, an occasion in musical history to be put alongside Mendelssohn's historic performance of Bach's *St Matthew Passion* in 1829. Five years after helping to found the Stern, Theodor Kullak, a music teacher at the Prussian court, left to form an academy of his own, which by 1880 had a thousand students and a complement of one hundred teachers, while in 1895 Karl Klindworth and Xaver Scharwenka merged their rival piano academies in a powerful single institution.

In response to the change of atmosphere that followed the events of 1848, the King had issued a decree laying down the function of art in the community and envisaging teaching institutions to which the people at large would have access. But the noble thoughts never rose above the status of pious hopes. Not until 1869 did the state become directly involved in the education of young instrumentalists, the year the King commissioned Joseph Joachim to found a state conservatoire, the Hochschule für Musik, under the auspices of the Prussian Academy of Arts.

It is a chastening thought that only at this moment, in a rapidly expanding city of a million inhabitants, poised to become the capital of a new empire, did Prussia acquire a state-run institution in which to educate its performing musicians. Paris had had its Conservatoire de Musique since 1795, Vienna its Konservatorium der Gesellschaft der Musikfreunde from 1817, London its Royal Academy of Music since 1822. All that Berlin had hitherto been able to point to was Friedrich Wilhelm IV's abortive attempt to install Mendelssohn in the Academy of Arts in 1841.

Mendelssohn, in fact, provided the link between Joachim and the Berlin Hochschule, for it was in Mendelssohn's conservatory in Leipzig that Joachim received the musical education which turned a child prodigy into a mature musician. One of the great solo violinists of the day, Joachim had worked under Liszt in Weimar and at the court of King George V of Hanover but although spending much time on the international concert circuit, both as soloist and with his quartet, he retained his post as director of the Berlin Hochschule until his death in 1907.

A number of people, Wagner among them, hoped that Joachim, like Hans von Bülow, would use his position to promote the cause of the New Music of Liszt, Berlioz and himself. But it was not to be. Joachim proved himself a musical conservative who concentrated on the classics, especially Beethoven, both in the policies of the Hochschule and in his own repertoire as performer. The classical tradition, as he saw it, now lay in the hands of his friend Brahms, whose music, with that of Schumann, he did much to promote. Brahms, who played in a solid, straightforward manner the very opposite of that of the Lisztian school of keyboard gymnasts, gave two recitals in Berlin in 1868, including in his programmes Schumann's *Etudes symphoniques* and his own Handel Variations.

Distinguished directors such as Eugen d'Albert and Franz Schreker followed Joachim at the Hochschule, and prominent figures joined the teaching staff – Max Bruch and Humperdinck for composition in the early decades, later the musicologist Curt Sachs, pianists like Artur Schnabel and Edwin Fischer in the 1920s, Paul Hindemith as professor of composition and many other famous names. Add to this the ceaseless flow of visiting virtuosi – pianists such as Clara Schumann, Anton Rubinstein, Busoni and Saint-Saëns, the violinists Ysaÿe, Sarasate, Emile Sauret, Karel Haliř, not to speak of the foreign singers who saw their chance here – and there emerges a picture of an exciting new metropolis offering a boundless range of opportunities to those with the initiative to grasp them.

Berlin could finally count itself a focus for the interpretation of music, music as a performing art, a centre for the activities of the music industry. Not until after the coming war would it be able to boast a comparable assembly of composers. Once into the 1920s, however, now the cultural Mecca of the country, Berlin became home for a concentration of creative musicians – and not only musicians – the like of which it had never known before and has never known since.

THE YEARS OF
THE WEIMAR REPUBLIC

A Republic for an Empire

The demise of the long-lived Hohenzollern monarchy and the short-lived Wilhelmine empire in 1918 was not a sudden, unforeseeable catastrophe but the final eruption of a malignant growth already discernible at the birth of the Second Reich in 1871. Forged in blood and iron, that Reich perished in blood and iron.

In 1914 spirits were riding high. Patriotic pride filled the country with a warm glow, spreading the reassuring conviction, from the industrialists to the intelligentsia, from the army to the proletariat, that Germany was embarking on a just war. But it was not long before an anti-war sentiment began to spread, informed by a sober appraisal of the surrounding realities. Bread rationing was introduced in Berlin in 1915 and soup kitchens appeared on the streets. Anti-war strikes were called in Berlin factories in 1917. More and more voices asked what, and who, the man in the street was fighting for. After America entered the war in April of that year and the Romanov dynasty was toppled a few months later, the anti-war mood enveloped all but the generals. When 1918 opened with Wilson's Fourteen Points, promising reconciliation and the establishment of a new international order based on cooperation, not rivalry, defeat in war, by now a foregone conclusion, seemed nothing to fear. On the contrary, the sooner it came, the better.

The last few familiar events followed in rapid succession. At the end of October the Kaiser fled to Holland. On 9 November he abdicated. The same day the Social Democrat Philipp Scheidemann, later Foreign Minister, appeared on a balcony of the Reichstag and proclaimed the establishment of a 'great German republic' to the milling crowds outside. Two days later the Armistice was signed. The monarchy was dead – Long live the Republic. 'This is more than just a lost war,' wrote the architect Walter Gropius, who shared this moment in Berlin. 'A world has come to an end.'

Elections for a new world were held two months later and a National Assembly convened, with the Social Democrats as the largest party. The atmosphere in Berlin was still tense, with a danger of violence from the extreme right or the extreme left – or both. In order to formulate the new republican constitution, the Assembly therefore decided to meet in Weimar, city of Herder, Goethe and Schiller, seat of classical humanism, whose symbolic auspices would be uniquely favourable.

Unlike the German defeat of 1945, which left the whole of Germany physically and psychologically shattered, the war of 1914–18 ended in a mass of confusions. For the army nothing had changed. They had not lost the war on the battlefield, they had been 'stabbed in the back' by defeatist republican politicians at home. Liberals of Social Democrat persuasion saw the possibility of evolution into a democratic republic, while radicals of the left scented the air of revolution. A bewildered bourgeoisie, with little chance under the monarchy to develop a political consciousness, felt itself to be the prime victim of events as it faced the years of inflation which were to wipe out its hard-won prosperity in a flash. And overhead, like a predator waiting to pounce on its prey, lurked the Treaty of Versailles, whose traumatic consequences – economic, political and psychological – seemed to threaten the very survival of the nation.

This fragmentation made for a dangerous domestic situation, especially in Berlin, where political extremism came to feel very much at home. How much became menacingly evident with the murder of Karl Liebknecht and Rosa Luxemburg in 1919 and the Kapp Putsch of 1920. The enthusiastic reorganisation of local government, made necessary by the incorporation of outlying areas that had formerly controlled their own affairs, brought its own polarisations. Districts became socially stratified – Tiergarten, Wilmersdorf and Zehlendorf belonged to the better-off, Wedding and Prenzlauer Berg to the industrial proletariat, and the cultural infrastructure reflected the distinction.

Dangerous and divided it may have been, but thousands found the attractions of Berlin irresistible. Many came as unashamed economic migrants, part of the swell of movement from the countryside to the cities that had not let up since the earliest days of industrialisation. The census of 1910 recorded a population for Berlin, as then constituted, of 2 million. By 1920, in the newly defined Greater Berlin, it had reached almost 4 million. Of the $2\frac{1}{2}$ million in employment, 46 per cent were blue-collar workers – heavy and precision engineering, electrical goods, textiles – and 26 per cent white-collar workers, including civil servants.

Physically the city was a depressing sight. 'It bore the marks of the war that had been lost,' wrote the dramatist Carl Zuckmayer in his autobiography. 'The people were irritable and bad-tempered, the streets dirty and full of crippled beggars, soldiers blinded in the war or with their legs shot off, while men and women in elegant shoes or bootees walked hurriedly past.'

Yet the thousands who came – not only Germans but also foreigners with their own personal agendas, like Christopher Isherwood, Vladimir Nabokov and Marc Chagall – knew what enticed them. 'Berlin had a taste of the future about it', said Zuckmayer, 'and as a result people were only too willing to put up with the cold and the dirt of the place.'

In a spirit of 'anything goes' writers, journalists, actors, painters, musicians all found their way here in the course of the 'Golden Twenties'. Congregating in restaurants and establishments like the Romanisches Café in the shadow of the Kaiser-Wilhelm-Gedächtniskirche, and the Café des Westens – irreverently dubbed 'The Megalomaniacs' Café' – on the Kurfürstendamm, they embarked on endless discussions about the nature of the new society and how their art should respond to it. Independent spirits though they were, they all welcomed the collapse of the monarchy, and, at a time when most cultural activity was heavily politicised, they would all call themselves republicans in one sense or another.

The sharpest and wittiest vehicle of the intellectual left-wing cause during the 1920s was *Die Weltbühne*, a weekly journal containing fiction and poetry, social comment and political satire, often written by men responsible for the texts of the political cabaret songs characteristic of the age. Under the editorship of Carl von Ossietsky, who died in a Nazi concentration camp in 1938, *Die Weltbühne* became the rallying-point for an astonishing variety of writers, Marxists and non-Marxists alike, who saw in some form of socialism the young Republic's only hope of survival. From Thomas Mann to Karl Kraus, from Walter Benjamin to Alfred Döblin, from Ringelnatz to Erich Kästner — the list of its contributors is as endless as the nuances of their political and artistic personalities are infinite. Until banned in 1933, it shone like a beacon for thousands who, whatever their differences, regarded themselves as progressives and took their bearings from the lead that it gave.

More exclusively political a creature than these, a moral firebrand whose name remained unshakeably synonymous with *Die Weltbühne* throughout the 1920s, was Kurt Tucholsky — essayist, critic, cabaret writer, novelist, author of some of the most entertaining social and political commentary in the German language. Like most journalism, it is bound to the age with whose problems it deals, and assumes an awareness of those problems. But Tucholsky — a native Berliner, Jewish, with a doctorate in law, a member of the Independent Social Democratic Party but never a communist — had the ability to generalise current issues and give his articles a relevance that reached beyond their immediate context, mocking human foibles and exposing social iniquities with a polemical wit worthy, at its best, of association with Heine, even with Lessing. Militarism, German nationalism, right-wing bias in the administration of justice and the suffocating petty-bourgeois mentality of the country's political leaders were among his favoured objects of hate.

After Hitler's seizure of power Tucholsky fell silent. 'We must see the situation for what it is,' he wrote in bitter resignation to the dramatist Walter Hasenclever. 'Our side has lost. The only decent thing a man can do is to withdraw from the scene.' He sought exile in Sweden, where, in 1935, in a state of morbid depression and despair, he took his own life.

At the opposite end of the political spectrum from *Die Weltbühne* were forces that based their programme for national renewal on an appeal to patriotic Prussian values and the ideals of *Volk*. Some of these forces appealed to a specious nationalism that was not above invoking the reactionary militarism that the lost war had discredited. Other groups, such as the Catholic Centre Party and the German People's Party, led by Gustav Stresemann, represented a respectable conservatism which had its legitimate appeal to those afraid of the implications of left-wing radicalism. But the roots of Weimar democracy, whether gauged from the left, the right or the centre, were painfully shallow and could not withstand the storms that were soon to break over them.

Once the nightmare of the early post-war inflation years had passed and a new stable currency had been introduced at the end of 1923, the optimism that accompanied the foundation of the Republic, whatever the political frictions within it, began to come into its own. The Social Democratic city council embarked on a programme of public works dominated by plans for new housing estates designed by architects like Bruno and Max Taut. Social institutions – schools, hospitals, libraries, leisure facilities – would follow. Wages rose steadily and the social security system, founded by Bismarck half a century earlier, was extended, most notably in the field of unemployment benefit. In foreign affairs Germany gave every indication of having become a good European neighbour and was admitted to the League of Nations in 1926. Stability within and peace without seemed guaranteed, the future under control.

That future had only three more years to run. 'We have been living on borrowed money,' said Foreign Minister Stresemann to the Reichstag in November 1928. 'If a crisis were to develop and the Americans called in their short-term credits, we should face bankruptcy.' A year later they did. In October 1929 the Wall Street stock market collapsed, precipitating the Great Depression. At the beginning of that year Germany had 1 million unemployed. By 1930 the figure was over 3 million, and by 1932, 6 million. It was too much for the fragile Republic to bear. The politics of extremism took over and in January 1933 Hitler became Reichskanzler.

Berlin was a microcosm, often in characteristically intense, not to say sensational form, of what was happening in the country as a whole. Unfamiliarity with the workings of democratic institutions bred procedural uncertainties, a nervous anxiety which bordered on the hectic. For many it still embodied the noble conservative values that had entitled it to become the capital of imperial Germany in 1871. As an industrial and commercial power-house, an insatiable devourer of labour, it had grown receptive to the demand for social reform in the name of the underprivileged. Anti-democratic forces of the left and right, in the councils of the nation but also on the streets, squared up to each other. The Weimar Republic was tearing itself apart. When Hitler and the National Socialists offered to put the country together again, the people gladly accepted the offer, and paid the price.

But, before that moment of trauma dawned, a brilliant flourish of cultural activity lit up the years of the Republic, activity that reflected the intense, frenetic, polarised world of post-war Germany, in the intense, frenetic, polarised life of its capital city.

Architecture in the 1920s

When the monarchy collapsed, it dragged down with it the triumphantly nurtured pride in imperial achievement that had dominated public life. There was nothing left to be proud of, no meaning to the celebration of past victories, no prospect of a glowing future. The self-confident, self-glorifying piles erected during the *Gründerjahre* and the Wilhelmine age now stood like massive exercises in incongruity and irrelevance, almost in shame, incompatible with the ethos of the new society. The detritus of an inward-looking nationalism had to be swept away and minds opened to the ideas being aired in the international exhibitions that were an important part of the architectural scene in the twentieth century.

97. Church of St Martin, Berlin-
Kaulsdorf, designed by Josef Bachem,
1929-30.

Dominant among these ideas, already in circulation in the immediate pre-
war years, was functionalism. Gone was the concept of an architecture in
which a basic structure was erected and ornamentation then applied to it as
an aesthetic afterthought. Façade and decoration now became part of the
structure itself. The form proclaimed the function, an aim pursued in particular through the consistent use of modern materials, above all concrete
and glass. No less amenable to this treatment, a traditional stylistic feature in
north German architecture, was clinker, a particularly hard, dark brick widely
used at the time in Berlin buildings ranging from churches to power stations (Ill. 97).

Behind this concept of unification stands the philosophy of the Deutscher
Werkbund, an association of artists, craftsmen and industrialists founded in
1907 'to promote the fruitful cooperation of arts, crafts and industry to the
benefit of all' – a kind of technological *Gesamtkunstwerk*. As builders and
engineers were to strive after beauty as well as efficiency, so artists and
craftsmen – between whom there was no distinction – were engaged to decorate the interior of railroad cars and ships and to share in the design of
household appliances. One of the earliest examples of functionalist architecture in Berlin is Peter Behrens' turbine factory of 1909 with its flat, unen-
cumbered surfaces (Ill. 98).

When the Werkbund restarted after the war, different priorities had
emerged. German soldiers returning from the front could hardly expect
'homes fit for heroes to live in' but the housing situation was catastrophic.
The Werkbund became increasingly political, and its idealistic vision of co-

operation between art and industry retreated in the face of the old suspicion, born in theories of the class-struggle, of the motives of factory owners
and capitalists in general. Well-known private architects like Erich Mendelsohn designed exclusive houses in functional style for the well-to-do but
there was also an urgent need for low-cost housing for the masses. This
turned the architect into a town-planner, with an obligation, willingly shoul-
dered, both to build the largest number of dwellings in the shortest possible
time and to devise a concept of urban living, a social model to embrace the
domestic and leisure life of self-contained communities within the city whose
needs have been anticipated and provided for. So housing estates developed,
planned with the full acknowledgement of an urban reality dominated by
mechanical and industrial interests.

Parallel to this in the 1920s ran the so-called 'garden-city movement'. As
the Werkbund shared the philosophy of the English arts-and-crafts movement of the previous century, so the garden-city movement also acknowledged English antecedents. Offering an escape from modern industrial
society, it envisioned the creation of picture villages as idyllic retreats which
would promote peace of mind and a sense of neighbourliness among those
who could afford to live there. The comfortable middle-class Berlin suburb
of Zehlendorf was chosen as one suitable district for such settlements. English
influence is also unmistakable in the magnificent villas and country houses
built from pre-war times through the 1920s by Hermann Muthesius.

Housing estates for the less privileged were planned on rather different
lines. Here the key figure is Bruno Taut, an uncompromising architect
whose successive allegiances stretched from a radical, visionary, utopian
expressionism at one extreme to a functional, eclectic neo-classicism at the
other. Taut was not merely a designer of buildings but a prolific writer, for
whom any discussion of architectural form and theory had meaning only

98. AEG turbine factory, designed by Peter Behrens, 1909.

99. Horseshoe housing estate in Berlin-Britz, designed by Bruno Taut and Martin Wagner, 1925-7.

in relationship to the nature of the society which it both served and helped to create. Starting with a fanciful vision of a purified mankind symbolised by the transparent beauty of glass, the modern medium which re-establishes contact with the medieval Gothic cathedral, he propounded an industrial architecture that would achieve its purpose through the creation of beauty alone. Functionality, symbolised by the modern building materials of iron, concrete and glass, would be absorbed into an ideal aestheticism, to be cultivated in a mystical secret society which Taut and his colleagues called the Glass Chain.

Faith in a vision, as so often, led down the path of coercion, and soon Taut is found talking of a 'great building plan . . . that must be hammered into the minds of the public by all available means'. Not surprisingly, he saw socialism as the natural political framework for the realisation of his ideas, and, when it came to the actual construction of social housing, the Social Democratic administration of the city gave its support.

Whereas the Werkbund, with whom Taut had been associated before the war, had envisaged a union of arts, crafts and industry as equal partners, Taut saw the arts assembled under the leadership of architecture. This gave architecture the power, and the right, to define the collective life of the community – almost to create that community, which should comprise workers and tradesmen, shop assistants and white-collar staff alike. Taut was appointed design architect to the trade union housing organisation in 1925, and from this position of influence built estates in the Berlin districts of Britz, Zehlendorf and Tegel which still stand as a tribute to his vision (Ill. 99). The rows of dwellings in his Horseshoe Estate in Britz (1925–7, with Martin Wagner), using straight lines, standardised blueprints and mechanical

100. Einstein Tower in Potsdam, designed by Erich Mendelssohn, 1920-1.

rather than traditional building methods, have an organic functionalism designed to reflect Taut's utopian concept of human togetherness in a shared environment, in which trees and grassy areas have a vital role to play. Taken together, Taut's various housing projects in the city provided no fewer than 10,000 dwellings.

Unlike Hamburg and Frankfurt, where a relatively uniform, consistent policy prevailed in the style of large-scale building projects, Berlin offered a variety of styles reflecting a variety of social philosophies on what sort of community should be created. In contrast, for example, to the squat, three-storey blocks of Taut's enclosed Horseshoe Estate, though equally expressive of its age, Hans Scharoun designed for the industrial suburb of Siemensstadt a series of assertive, almost forbidding four-storey blocks (1932) arranged in parallel lines between swathes of grass.

Individual public buildings showed a similar variety. One of the most striking and most famous pieces of architecture in the Berlin area from the years of the Weimar Republic is the so-called Einstein Tower on a hill outside Potsdam, an observatory which houses an optical telescope specifically designed to verify Einstein's general theory of relativity. Embodiment of 1920s expressionism, the tower, both exterior and interior, was designed and built in 1920–1 by Erich Mendelsohn. How far Mendelsohn was ahead of his time emerged when his plan for a building entirely in reinforced concrete was found to outstrip the technical ability of the construction industry to put it into effect. In the event only the base and entrance were done in solid concrete, leaving the tower itself to be built in brick with a concrete facing. At a stroke – and it is a remarkable building – Mendelsohn became the most famous architect in the city (Ill. 100).

101. Clubhouse on the Berlin Avus, designed by Edmund Meurin, 1923.

102. Protestant church
on the Hohenzollernplatz,
Berlin-Wilmersdorf,
designed by Fritz Höger,
1930-3.

Expressionist tendencies of a different kind shade into the functional lines of Neue Sachlichkeit in Edmund Meurin's Avus Club House of 1923, a building whose exterior conveys little about its use (Ill. 101). Indeed, an increasingly common trait of architecture in the 1920s and 1930s is the application of certain features and techniques – glass and external illumination, for instance, as well as individual predilections in details of ornament – to buildings irrespective of their function. Emil Fahrenkamp's Shell House by the Landwehrkanal (1931) does not reveal to the quizzical gaze whether it is an office block or an apartment house, or both, while without its campanile Fritz Höger's Protestant church on the Hohenzollernplatz in Wilmersdorf (1932) could be taken for a warehouse, a generating plant or a railroad station (Ill. 102).

Expressionist Art

As the war of 1914–18 only set an official seal on changes manifest in the spirit of public life long before the first shots were fired, so the culture of Empire had long splintered under the pressure of successive modern movements. The Berlin Secession of painters led by Max Liebermann and Walter Leistikow went back to 1898. In 1910 Liebermann led a New Secession, appealing to a broader public than that satisfied by the academic art of meticulous representationalism based on a limited subject matter, and calling on an impressionistic delight in the brilliance, the colour and the vivacity of movement in nature and in scenes of human happiness. There was no one, single 'secessionist style' – just a common scorn for the irrelevance of the academic realism of court-approved painters such as Anton von Werner, with their backward-looking glorification of the monarchy, and a common demand for freedom of self-expression.

This freedom could nevertheless lead to a community of interest among artists who, though stylistically divergent and working in different media, addressed a common set of circumstances and shared a view of the social function of art. Thus a concern with the life of the lower classes united three important artists, all of them born elsewhere but all drawn to Berlin at the turn of the century and all inseparable from the cultural life of the city throughout the 1920s and beyond – Heinrich Zille, Käthe Kollwitz and Hans Baluschek.

Zille is one of those artists so closely identified with the milieu in which they lived that their work is in danger of not reaching beyond the confines of that milieu. With his working-class family he came to Berlin from Saxony as a boy, taught himself to draw and paint and devoted his life to sketching, often with a bitter humour, 'his' Berlin – sickness and poverty in the slums, the corner pubs where the men met at the end of their shift, a Sunday family outing, the prostitutes of the Friedrichstrasse, cabaret scenes. As snapshots of the social scene it is an art – an 'art of the gutter', Kaiser Wilhelm II called it – that stands in the line of Chodowiecki and, earlier, of Hogarth.

Zille was a master of the broad, rapid, telling brushstroke, the single, subtle pen line, which led him to be dismissed as little more than a gifted cartoonist. But his claims went beyond this. He was one of the earliest artists

103. *The Iron Cross* by
Heinrich Zille, lithograph,
1916.

to identify himself openly with the political cause of the working class and
to believe that art could be used as an instrument of social change. In practice, however, in a perverse irony, he was taken up, enjoyed and exploited by
the very middle classes whose dissolution he awaited. As the homely symbol
of Berlin's corporate personality, he watched helplessly while his name was
taken in vain to promote Zille liqueurs and Zille cigarettes, while to popular
Zille Dances came, not the proletariat and the poor of Zille's world, but
well-heeled patrons pretending to be such. His gentrification became complete when in 1924, five years before his death, he was given the title of
professor and elected to membership of the Academy of Arts (Ill. 103).

The appeal and reputation of the work of Käthe Kollwitz, like its subject
matter, is as universal as Zille's is local, and her upbringing in Königsberg
was as comfortably middle class as his was desperately proletarian. But
nothing could distinguish them in their commitment to socialism and to art
as an agent of socialist policy. 'I want to have an effect on this age', she said,
'when people are so bewildered and in need of help.'

Käthe Kollwitz began her career as a graphic artist at the turn of the
century with essays in social criticism in the line of Max Klinger, filled with
anger at the plight of the Berlin working class. But although the bulk of her
work is in the form of etchings, lithographs and woodcuts, the comparatively few sculptures that she left, executed mainly in the 1930s but the products of thoughts and emotions lived with for years before, epitomise her art
at its most moving. The central experience underlying these pieces – and
not only these pieces – is death, above all death in war, seen through the
eyes of a woman who has brought life into the world. Here is no quest for
beauty and the sensuous pleasures of life. Seldom does she smile, rare are her

Berlin and its Culture

Käthe Kollwitz

104. *(left)* *Pietà*, bronze, 1938.

105. *Revolt*, etching, 1902.

moments of happiness and serenity, for the struggles of man against capitalist exploitation and imperialist war can only bring a smouldering sorrow.

She lived with that sorrow, the sorrow of a mourning mother, from 1914, when her eldest son was killed in the First World War, until the end of her life in 1945. For almost twenty years she sought to sublimate her emotions by working on two granite figures, *The Father* and *The Mother*, for a military cemetery in Flanders, finally erected in 1932. The spiritual essence of her emotions on this terrible complex of realities is captured in her moving *Pietà*, a larger version of which stands in the war memorial of Schinkel's Neue Wache in Unter den Linden. Death itself, in a spirit of resignation, almost of savage yearning, is also the subject of a set of late lithographs with a frightening power and intensity that set her among the most gripping artists of the age of expressionism (Ills 104 and 105).

No less moved by the social scene around him was Hans Baluschek, a Silesian immigrant from Breslau with a view of society shaped by Zola, Ibsen and Strindberg. He joined the directorate of the Berlin Secession in 1913 and spent much of his energy raising the public consciousness of art until the Nazis put an end to his activities in 1933.

Unlike Zille and Käthe Kollwitz, and unlike Max Klinger, spiritual father of all three, Baluschek worked not only in small-scale graphic forms but also in oils and water colours, and often in large formats. Berlin gave him his

106. *Pariser Platz in Berlin* by Oscar Kokoschka, oil on canvas, 1926.

107. *Friedrichstrasse*, by
Ernst Ludwig Kirchner, oil
on canvas, 1914.

subject matter – street scenes, the industrial landscape, episodes in the
domestic and working life of the lower classes, depicted with a relentless
realism based on an intense human sympathy and carrying an insistent social
message. Industrialisation has bred hardness of heart, and the prosperity of
the bourgeoisie has been bought with the degradation of the workers. In
order to illustrate these themes from various naturalistic angles, Baluschek
grouped works in cycles focused on a particular topic, such as the world of
the railway locomotive, symbol of the power of mechanical progress, and its
impact on social life, or the cycle called 'Victims' – studies of drunkards,
prostitutes, the poor, the sick, those whom that 'progress' has turned into
outcasts.

In 1905 a group of young painters in Dresden – Ernst Ludwig Kirchner,
Erich Heckel, Karl Schmidt-Rottluff, joined the following year by Emil
Nolde and Max Pechstein – constituted themselves as Die Brücke, an anti-
establishment movement opposed to realism and facile representationalism
and claiming the romantic rights of subjective self-expression, of primitive
emotionalism and unfettered creativity. A few years later, drawn by the
vibrant life of the metropolis and by the opportunities for exhibition and
publicity that it offered, they had all found their way to Berlin. Here, in
1910, there appeared the first number of an avant-garde journal that launched

the new movement on a grand scale, a forum for the provocative new philosophy of art, with an appropriately vigorous title – *Der Sturm*, the gale. The following year, with a different metaphor but conveying the same dynamism, *Der Sturm* was joined by *Aktion*. The philosophy of art they propounded, valid no less for literature than for the visual arts, received the name expressionism.

'Expressionism believes in the all-possible,' declared the critic Friedrich Markus Hueber. 'It is the philosophy of utopia. It puts man back in the centre of creation, giving him the power to fill the void as he chooses, with lines, colours and sounds, with plants and animals, with God, with space and time, with his own ego.' An old, sick world is dying, a world of social and moral decadence, of a false rationality, of war. In its place will come the primacy of the individual personality, the cult of spontaneous self-expression, of protest, of irrational outburst, the extreme state of mind foretold in Munch's agonised painting *The Scream*, exhibited as early as 1902 in a show mounted by the Berlin Secessionists.

Plunging into the hectic life of the city, Kirchner, Nolde, Kokoschka and their fellows responded with bold, slashing strokes and colours to the characters and the atmosphere they encountered (Ill. 106). Kirchner, in particular, who also did many unpeopled townscapes of squares, houses and waterways, makes the nervous rhythm of the street scene his world, as the

108. *Self-portrait* by Erich Heckel, coloured woodcut, 1919.

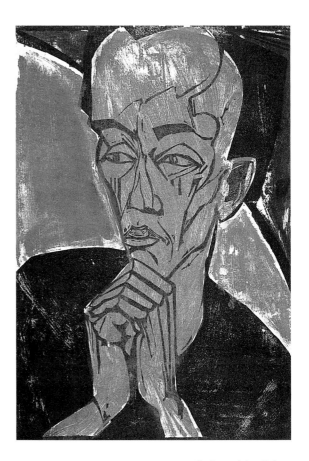

109. *Fallen Man* by Wilhelm Lehmbruck, bronze, 1915-16.

elegant *demi-mondaines* are pursued down the infamous Friedrichstrasse by a posse of potential customers (Ill. 107). The strong vertical linearity recalls the techniques of the wood-cut, a medium in which the Brücke painters in Berlin found a keen satisfaction, with elongated forms that evoked a comparison with medieval Gothic sculpture (Ill. 108).

Kirchner, like other Brücke artists, was also a sculptor, one who prided himself on his anti-academic stance. The nineteenth-century tradition of representational sculpture in Berlin was still strong, sustained by such far from academic artists as the immensely popular Georg Kolbe, whose decorative realism, above all in studies of the female form, sustained a career that began before the First World War and ran through the whole of the Second. Kolbe portrayed psychological man. The expressionists portray existential man, man in a feverish, agitated world where the concept of beauty expands to embrace deprivation, insecurity and anxiety, and where the idealisation of the object

110. *Triad* by Rudolph Belling, birchwood and mahogany, stained and polished, 1924.

gives way before the subjective intensity of the expression. Caught between rebellion and resignation, with neither strength nor will to face the world, his head held in his hand, the expressionist man of Wilhelm Lehmbruck symbolises the human condition in the war years and their aftermath (Ill. 109).

There was a dichotomy embedded in the attraction exerted on artists by the city. On the one hand, in material terms Berlin had become the leading cultural centre in Germany, a serious rival to London and Paris. It was *the* place to live and work, offering a scene of incomparable richness and diversity. No small part of the credit for this belongs to the enterprise of art dealers such as Paul Cassirer, who were prepared to risk exhibitions of progressive painting and sculpture, certain only that they would raise a storm of indignation in conservative circles. Ernst Barlach, one of the greatest of expressionist sculptors, otherwise with only intermittent contacts to Berlin, admitted that he owed his 'discovery' to Cassirer, and the avant-garde of eastern Europe – Moholy-Nagy, Naum Gabo, El Lissitsky – also flocked to the German capital.

The urge to experimentation in a revolutionary post-war atmosphere took particularly striking forms in the plastic arts. Where some, such as Käthe Kollwitz, stay with the social tragedy of the human condition, others explore a conceptual, abstract line, setting themselves problems posed by the nature of sculpture itself. Rudolf Belling, a member of the left-wing Novembergruppe, pursued the implications of a philosophy that saw sculpture, not as objects in space but as constructs embracing space, making space part of the sculpture. In Belling's *The Triad*, for example, three female figures in polished wood, symbolising architecture, painting and sculpture, dance in a circle to enact the concept of the *Gesamtkunstwerk*. Such works often deal

111. Family grave in the cemetery of Berlin-Stahnsdorf by Max Taut and Rudolf Belling, concrete, 1920.

Berlin and its Culture

112. *Revolution* by Ludwig Meidner, oil on canvas, 1913.

in abstract shapes behind which lurks a cogitated programme and purpose hardly traceable from the piece itself (Ill. 110). On the other hand a striking arched concrete structure raised by Max Taut in 1920 above a family grave in a Berlin cemetery shows how such expressionist forms could also be put to the fulfilment of a practical task (Ill. 111).

Even before the war artists had sensed a rising brutalisation of life. Frightening visions of the world ahead are the series of *Apocalyptic Landscapes* painted by Ludwig Meidner in 1913 – urban and rural scenes shattered and splintered, houses tottering, trees uprooted, human figures fleeing from the scene in panic. The coming turbulence in human society, domestic as well as international, is foretold in Meidner's large canvas *Revolution*, depicting the savage fighting at the barricades led by a wounded figure bearing the revolutionary banner, his face contorted with pain and anger in the 'expressionist scream' as the world around him is shot to pieces (Ill. 112). This is not revolution as an heroic act, the fulfilment of world purpose, but revolution as destruction, the Moloch of the city consuming its own children as the cataclysm approaches (Ill. 118).

The Great War itself was the dominant event in the life of a whole generation, and artists found in it a host of human, and inhuman, themes. Sometimes these derived directly from the circumstances of war itself – the callous realism of Max Beckmann's scene in the morgue, or of Otto Dix's engraving of a body caught in the barbed-wire entanglement (Ill. 113). Other works combine the brutality of the moment with a savage view of the post-war

113. *Body Caught in Barbed Wire* by Otto Dix, etching, 1924.

future, like Kirchner's self-portrait as a soldier blinded and with his hand shot off, fearing in his vision of a naked woman that he has become impotent (Ill. 114). By contrast a proud, not to say triumphalist war memorial by Fritz Klimsch depicts a youth emerging from the flames of defeat, sword in hand, eager to resume the fight for the future. The gloom-and-doom philosophy was by no means shared by all.

With the end of the war came the demise of the degrading world which, the expressionists proclaimed, had long been staring at its destruction. Together with the Futurists, the Cubists, the Surrealists and other modernist factions, they had been united in what the poet Gottfried Benn described as 'a basic urge to destroy so-called reality, to pierce relentlessly to the heart of things'. Now the need had changed. There were consequences to be faced, conclusions to be drawn. Sated with this high-flown utopianism, artists turned from the conceptually ideal to the physically real, from the expression to the object. 'The object has primacy', declared Otto Dix, who found many frightening ways, including the technique of montage – the juxtaposition of discrepant 'objects' instead of the creation of organic form – to show how much reality the concentration on the object could be made to bear. Constructivist experimentation also seemed inappropriate to a period when the new Republic was apparently establishing a firm economic and political order. The term *Neue Sachlichkeit*, neo-realism, or the 'New

114. *Self-Portrait as a Soldier*
by Ernst Ludwig Kirchner, oil
on canvas, etching, 1924.

Objectivity', came into use, embracing a variety of sometimes conflicting
tendencies but retaining both a sense of social, often political obligation, an
engagement with modern technology and an aesthetic commitment to a
functional formalism found at its most powerful in the artists and teachers
of the Bauhaus in Weimar.

Attention shifted from the rights of 'expression' to the skills of craftsmanship, to practical order and sober everyday values conveyed by a technical perfection particularly at its ease in the plastic arts. Sculptors took a cool
look at the realities around them – objects, animals, individuals. An age of
commissioned portrait busts and statuettes returned, now extending, in these
democratic times, to such heroes of popular culture as Beniamino Gigli, Max
Schmeling and Marlene Dietrich (Ills 116 and 117). The cult of the
graceful, healthy human body, expressed in the pre-war work of Kolbe, is
picked up, a cult which a few years later slid with frightening ease into the
world of 'Strength through Joy' and the eugenic body worship of the Nazis.
Welcome as the sobriety and objectivity of Neue Sachlichkeit had been as
a relief from the noisiness of the expressionists, by 1930 it had begun to slip
back into the conservatism of the German classicistic tradition, which had
never completely disappeared.

Berlin offered as many forms of reality as anyone could absorb, depicted
in as many styles. Groupings of artists emerge with their own programmes

115. *The Card Players* by
Otto Dix, oil on canvas,
montage, 1920.

of topics for treatment and their own new interests of style and technique.
Berlin being Berlin, politics stood in the centre of things – politics German
style, rich in strident extremism, poor in the skills of patient argument and
compromise. Not by chance did the Novembergruppe, a German Association of Radical Painters and Artists, as they described themselves, choose their
name for its echoes of the Russian Revolution of November 1917 and the
Berlin Revolution of November 1918.

More radical than the Novembergruppe, both in their philosophy of the
contemporary situation and in their artistic response to it, were the so-
called Dadaists, who brought to the art scene a startling approach as penetrating and revolutionary as it was short lived. Anarchist in tendency,
Dadaism denied the validity of bourgeois social reality as constituted,
declaring it meaningless, riddled with contradictions, worthy only of
ridicule and parody. Life consists of heterogeneous, discrepant, random
components which can be assembled, dismantled and replaced at will. So
can human beings, for this is the age of the machine, of man-as-machine.

116. *The Boxer Max Schmeling* by Rudolf Belling, bronze, 1929.

117. Ernesto de Fiori at work on a portrait bust (stucco) of Marlene Dietrich, 1931.

118. *The City* by George Grosz, oil on canvas, 1916–17.

'This evening', says the widow Begbick in Brecht's comedy *Mann ist Mann*, 'we are reassembling a man like we reassemble a car, and he doesn't lose a thing in the process.' 'What's the point of the mind in an age that will run its mechanical course anyway?' asked Raoul Hausmann, theorist of the Dadaist movement.

So the role of the artist in this world of the absurd is not to pretend to express a coherent, original personality but just to cobble together whatever discrete elements come his way. He is not a unique creator of organic wholes, rather an assembler of bits and pieces, a manufacturer of a jumbled simultaneity of objects, symbols, thoughts and emotions existing, Freud-like, on different levels of consciousness. Hence the collages of men like John Heartfield and George Grosz – assemblages of objects, newspaper clippings, photographs, arranged to achieve maximum shock and often offence (Ill. 115).

Since the elements in parody or satire, or any distortion of 'reality', must be individually recognisable in their own right, the step from the technique of montage to a fully painted realism is a small one. A political *engagement* directed to the exposure of a post-war society polarised into privileged and under-privileged, and to the portrayal of the degrading elements in that society, gripped many artists (Ill. 119). None responded more uncompromisingly than George Grosz to the contrasts that were part of everybody's experience in the streets – the crippled ex-serviceman, still in uniform, trying to sell matches and boot-laces on a street dominated by the self-centred and heedless bourgeoisie (Ill. 120).

119. *Park Bench in Wedding* by Otto Nagel, oil on canvas, 1927.

Expressionism, Dadaism, Constructivism, Neue Sachlichkeit, November-gruppe – convenient as it may be to discuss artists in such terms, according to where the main accents of their work seem to fall, they only denote tendencies, or temporary allegiances. An artist may shift his position, or a once influential -ism quickly disappear. The alleged boundaries between one trend and another are usually blurred, and what one critic categorises as 'Berlin Secession' another may call 'expressive realism'. Or one may arrange by political affiliation, by social-critical intent, or simply by subject matter.

Yet whatever the terminology, there remains a common 'feel' about these works, an air that immediately betrays the time and place to which they belong. Their raucous tone, their thrusting, often deliberately offensive manner, their black-and-white view of the world and their claims to own the one, single Truth – the Weimar Republic died of such things.

The Expressionist Word

'Once you had Berlin, you had the world,' said Zuckmayer. Writers, actors, artists and critics who might otherwise never have exchanged a word, rubbed shoulders with each other at social gatherings in the villas of public figures like the industrialist Walter Rathenau and the diplomat Count Harry Kessler. Max Liebermann, Gerhart Hauptmann, Hugo von Hofmannsthal, Max Reinhardt and the actors of his ensemble were to be found here. Rilke took up residence in the city for personal reasons over various periods before and during the war but found it an uncongenial place. 'My God, what a world of shoving and pushing,' he wrote, likening its aggressiveness and its Prussianism to the violent emotions conveyed by an expressionist painting. Hofmannsthal met Richard Strauss here after a performance at Reinhardt's

Deutsches Theater, a meeting which led to *Elektra* and the four other operas on which the two men collaborated.

From a totally different intellectual and spiritual world came the isolated figure of Ernst Jünger, protagonist of an anti-democratic authoritarianism and writer of powerful novels glorifying the comradeship and the cathartic, even erotic qualities of war. Jünger moved to Berlin in 1927 at the height of his journalistic campaign for an anti-rational, anti-liberal 'New Nationalism' and stayed until 1933. Equivocal in his attitude towards the Nazis, he developed a dislike of city values irrespective of the Berlin political climate and retreated to the south German countryside, railing against what he called 'the benumbed, mechanical, almost drugged mentality' of the urban masses – but not before he had made a characteristic call in *Der Arbeiter* ('The Worker', 1932) for the formation of a new intellectual elite to govern the state, an elite to whose commands the individual must bow.

What to Jünger was unnatural and oppressive about Berlin came to Franz Kafka – such were its Protean attractions – as a liberation, if only briefly. Leaving his bourgeois occupation and the provincialism of Prague behind, enticed by pre-war memories of the city, he arrived in Berlin in the autumn of 1923. With inflation raging at its height, it was a moment to be leaving the city rather than joining it. His meagre pension barely allowed him to survive the winter, and the only work he started during his six-month stay was the story *Der Bau*, the last of his animal allegories. He died three months later.

Berlin had the fascination of a huge consumer outlet – too big to ignore but not an object of affection, and certainly not the almighty authority before which all others must bow the knee. Its roots were shallow, its success, even its intentions, governed by the values of the short term. Hofmannsthal, one of the many who had reason to be grateful to Berlin but could never warm to it, summed up the paradox:

> Berlin is not *the* capital. No native of Munich, or Stuttgart, or Hamburg will regard Berlin as his capital. But it is an overwhelmingly large German city, which embraces everyone who enters it with a power that cannot be resisted – not so much an urban entity as an epoch. What counts is today's world, and only today's world.

Hofmannsthal, Jünger, Rilke, Kafka – these and more came from all corners of the German-speaking world, looked, stayed a while, then left again. But others in the post-war years came and stayed for good – at least, for as long as the political situation allowed them to. 'I belong to Berlin,' declared Alfred Döblin, a doctor from Stettin, author of the most famous of German novels from the 1920s, *Berlin Alexanderplatz*. Bertolt Brecht from Bavaria belonged to Berlin too, so did Gottfried Benn from Mecklenburg, Johannes R. Becher from Munich, Ernst Toller from Poznan, Arnold Zweig from Silesia and many more. Much of its appeal derived from its reputation for non-conformism and political liberalism. It is no accident that many of the intellectuals attracted there, in company with native Berliners like the inimitable Kurt Tucholsky, engaged directly in political activity or wrote a strongly politicised literature, or both.

Expressionism, both as an aesthetic movement and as an existential mood, dominant in the decade 1910–20 and into the early years of the Weimar Republic, belonged to youth, a youth in revolt. The oldest writers, like Döblin and Georg Kaiser, were in their thirties when the First World War broke out; the majority were of an age to be sent to the front, and many died in action. In social terms the protest was against the sordid phenomenon of modern industrial society and its destruction of human dignity. The aesthetic protest took the form of a rejection of the conceptual and the expository in favour of the spontaneous and the instinctive. The so-called 'objective reality' which surrounds us – that is to say, the degrading state of unnatural oppression to which capitalism has brought us – is not true reality at all: 'real' reality is the inner, spiritual reality of the act of expression, in this case the expression of protest. Yet, for the protest to claim validity, the object has to be preserved. Hence the expressionists' specific love–hate relationship to the city.

Literature created in this spirit – and expressionism finds its way no less into music, film and dance than into art and literature – takes all forms. There are anti-war novels (Arnold Zweig's *Der Streit um den Sergeanten Grischa*), novels on contemporary society (Döblin's *Berlin Alexanderplatz*; Fallada's *Kleiner Mann, was nun?*), anti-war plays (Günther Weisenborn's *U-Boot S4*; Ernst Toller's *Hinkemann*) and the breast-beating, apocalyptic dramas of Georg Kaiser's *Gas* trilogy. But the essence of the expressionist mood is at its most concentrated in the realm of lyric poetry. For here, in a few lines of explosive verse, are captured both the objects of the expressionists' burning hate and the sense of desperate enthusiasm, of *Rausch*, intoxication, which generated their poetic energy. Sometimes they shriek at us – the 'expressionist scream', the agony conveyed in Munch's frightening picture. At others they regard the coming cataclysm with nihilistic detachment, as though they were mere spectators of their own destruction.

The range of extreme reactions to an extreme situation is encompassed in an anthology of verse published in Berlin by the poet Kurt Pinthus in 1920 under the title Janus-like *Menschheitsdämmerung* – 'The Twilight of Mankind' but also 'The Dawn of Mankind'. In his preface Pinthus describes it as 'a collection of passions and emotional shocks, the yearnings, happinesses and sufferings of an age – our age'. The sense of perdition conveyed by such a title, at a moment when Germany was smarting under defeat in war and when Spengler had recently reinforced the message of irreversible decay in his perversely popular *Decline of the West*, had an immediate appeal. European culture was lurching inexorably into totalitarianism, domination by technology and the cult of relativity. 'There are no eternal verities,' said Spengler.

So Pinthus chose to open his *Menschheitsdämmerung* with a chilling poem called 'End of the World' by Jakob van Hoddis, following it with Georg Heym's 'Umbra Vitae', a set of strophes on the transience and meaninglessness of life couched in the rhetorical style of the Baroque poets with whom the expressionists claimed an affinity. Some poets throw up their hands in passionate despair of the human condition, wallowing in their cosmic helplessness. Others rail at the cruelties and miseries of the city, symbol of manmade suffering and monument to the false gods worshipped by earlier generations, but cannot resist its fatal attraction. Some join Johannes R.

Becher in seeing the situation in overtly political terms, with the Russian Revolution of 1917 as the inspiring hope for mankind, while gentler voices, like that of Franz Werfel, appeal to the humanistic, sometimes religious values that bind men together. Common ground is the recognition of the evils of the present. Utterly discrepant are the visions of the future that will overcome those evils.

There is an air of collectivity about this expressionist lyric poetry, and only a few of the twenty-three poets represented in *Menschheitsdämmerung* have a substantial independent reputation – Becher and Gottfried Benn, Franz Werfel and Georg Trakl. In a sense the themes and passions that bind them are of greater significance than their individual responses to those themes. Stylistically and emotionally, too, they share a literary and spiritual heritage, the heritage of Nietzsche, who sought all possible means of expressing the depths of his subjective being, 'obliterating the content in the interest of the expression', as Benn put it. In Nietzsche they found the high priest of the irrational, the charismatic prophet with an inflammatory message, a spiritual leader whose disciples saw themselves as an elite and whose coruscating, intoxicating language – Hölderlin and Kleist brought a similar inspiration – was the liberating ideal they adopted. 'It is impossible to write poetry since Nietzsche as one used to write it before him,' said the naturalist dramatist Johannes Schlaf.

Though not to be counted unreservedly among the expressionists, there is an affinity, through words like 'leader', 'charisma' and 'elite', between them and an esoteric, almost cabbalistic figure who also emerged from beneath the shadow of Nietzsche – Stefan George. The centre of his own hermetic world, surrounded by a circle of acolytes and with no desire to be accessible to the masses, George published slim volumes of strikingly original verse preaching a private poetic utopia governed by the power of irrationalism, mysticism and the authority of the poetic principle. In Berlin and elsewhere he attracted for a while a number of remarkable writers and scholars to whom his anti-democratic message had a particular appeal at the time of what they saw as a republic with no sense of national cohesion. The intellectual world at large saw the 'George Circle' as a body of precious, otherworldly cranks. But their call for obedience to a messianic 'Führer', their reactionary politics, their rejection of rationalism and their xenophobia brought them perilously close to the Nazi orbit.

George himself, who died in 1933, was no Nazi. But, like Nietzsche – and, in a different way, like Wagner – he forces one to face the question of whether a writer may not, after all, bear a responsibility for the misuse of his work by later generations. If a message can be perverted, may there not be an element of perversion in the message from the beginning? George's last volume of poetry, published in 1928, was called *Das Neue Reich*. 'If ever God raised a man to the status of prophet by fulfilling his prophecies', wrote Walter Benjamin, 'that man was Stefan George.'

As different from George and from the expressionists of *Menschheitsdämmerung* as one could imagine, yet no less characteristic of the contrast-ridden Weimar years, was the satirical verse written for cabaret. Like the cinema, in some ways the most representative artistic genre of the 1920s, cabaret has its roots in the social, political and cultural life of the time. But, whereas cinema is a mass medium, cabaret is a refined, intimate milieu that rests on the talent of the individual. In the German-speaking world – Munich, Vienna, but above all Berlin – satirical social comment has always been a staple ingredient of cabaret, going back to Max Reinhardt's Schall und Rauch and other pre-war establishments. Here, in those days, one came across Wedekind, Morgenstern, Otto Julius Bierbaum and others performing their own material.

After the war the tone became more mordant, the content of the chansons and the political sketches – by radicals such as Walter Mehring, Kurt Tucholsky and Erich Mühsam – more aggressive. Like all satire, their material presupposes a recognition of what is being satirised, and where the subject matter is a passing situation or a personality whose actions are over and done with, the very topicality of the satire restricts its attraction, even its intelligibility, to later generations. There are two poets, however, who at one time or another wrote such cabaret material but whose reputations rest on more durable foundations. One is Hans Bötticher, who called himself Joachim Ringelnatz, an attractive figure now satirical and superficial, now sentimental and sympathetic, an embodiment of the contradictions of commitment and detachment, sincerity and disillusionment so familiar among the intellectuals of the Weimar Republic. The other is Bertolt Brecht.

As his older expressionist contemporaries talked of idealistic visions of a New Man, a 'revaluation of all values', in Nietzsche's phrase, so Brecht kept his eyes on the here and now, on the materialistic reality of the relative, not the spiritual ideality of the absolute. Man was part of nature, subject to the same in-built processes of change. Art was a natural part of life and the language of poetry must derive from a corresponding matter-of-factness – a language appropriate to the practical world of Neue Sachlichkeit in which things were 'as you saw them', not the hysterical, overheated prosody of *Menschheitsdämmerung*.

Brecht, born in Augsburg, came to Berlin in 1921 from an uncongenial Munich. The Bavarian capital had long been a cultural Mecca for many. But its reactionary political climate drove the radically minded away, among its victims Heinrich Mann and Lion Feuchtwanger, both of whom sensed the implications of Hitler's attempted coup in 1923 and also moved to Berlin. Brecht aimed to conquer the theatre there, and it is first and foremost as a dramatist that the world thinks of him. But his influence as a poet went deeper.

For Brecht poetry, like all art, is communication: 'All great poems have the quality of documents.' Artist and public face each other on the same material and spiritual plane, in the tone and atmosphere of everyday life, the only life there is. Brecht's first published volume bore the mock liturgical title *Bert Brechts Hauspostille* – a 'domestic breviary' of fifty poems, most of them either ballads or balladesque in character, together with a selection of the tunes to which they are to be sung. The Swiss writer Max Frisch described how, at 'An Evening with Brecht', the would-be proletarian *enfant terrible*, with his steel-rimmed spectacles and ubiquitous leather jacket, would sing from his breviary as he strummed his guitar – a domestic cabaret turn, Weimar style.

But this is not art as entertainment. Like the contemporary *Gebrauchsmusik* of Hindemith and Kurt Weill, music as a practical commodity, it is a poetry that feeds directly into life. 'This collection of homilies', writes Brecht in his introductory instructions on how to treat his poems, 'is intended for the reader to use. It is not meant to be soaked up mindlessly.' The reader must be prepared to work for its meaning.

Within the generally regular stanzas of the *Hauspostille*, as of poems in later collections from the 1920s, Brecht's diction is plain and dispassionate, yet emphatic and gripping, the rhythm crisp yet free, with a deliberate avoidance of decorative elements – a kind of lyrical anti-lyricism. 'As a dramatist, this man has considerable talent,' wrote Tucholsky in 1928. 'As a poet, he has even more.' The poetry that Brecht was to write when he returned to Germany from exile after the Second World War showed how right Tucholsky was.

Berlin and the Novel

'In der Asphaltstadt bin ich daheim,' runs a line in one of the best-known poems in Brecht's *Hauspostille* – 'My home is in the asphalt city.' A later collection carried the title 'Primer for Town Dwellers'. One cannot imagine him – or Döblin, or Heinrich Mann, or Feuchtwanger, or Erich Kästner, or Tucholsky, or any other writer who made Berlin what it was in this age – living anywhere else. The culture of the Weimar Republic – exciting, overwrought, challenging, decadent, call it what one will – is an urban culture. Love it or hate it – preferably both – the city was the ambient reality with which one had to come to terms. There is no nostalgia for past glories, no romantic pining after verdant meadows and the mysterious forests of legend. Life is the present – the life of the individual, of society, of the new nation and of the still newer state. Describe it, politicise it, allegorise it – Brecht's asphalt city of Berlin remains the central, dominant reality.

Poetry could compress spiritual and conceptual meaning. Drama presented case-histories, individuals *in extremis* fighting to survive the tragedy of circumstance. It was above all the novel, however, that could encompass the wealth of social and historical data from which writers fashioned their works, and the latter years of the Republic, a fleeting moment between emergence from one catastrophe and disintegration into another, saw a flurry of novels animated by the social scene of the present and the recent past.

Most penetrating of the events of recent memory was the war – the defeat and the carnage that had preceded it. Many had believed the promises of imperial glory and now felt indignant. Some also felt defiant. Others welcomed the collapse of the monarchy and looked forward eagerly to an age of republican democracy. Those for whom the army still represented the noblest values refused to believe that there had been a military defeat at all, while others condemned war altogether and became pacifists.

The late 1920s saw the publication of a number of novels that joined issue with the subject in contrasting ways. The two most famous, embodying totally incompatible philosophies of war and military values – Remarque's *Im Westen nichts Neues* ('All Quiet on the Western Front') and Ernst Jünger's *In Stahlgewittern* ('In Storms of Steel') – have no links with Berlin. Others, however, by writers who made their home in the capital and committed themselves to its radical political causes, are no less powerful in their individual ways and express a pacifist tendency shared by many. Such are Heinrich Mann's *Der Kopf* ('The Head'), Ludwig Renn's *Krieg* ('War') and Arnold Zweig's *Der Streit um den Sergeanten Grischa* ('The Fight Over Sergeant Grischa').

Heinrich Mann, left-wing elder brother of the conservative Thomas, and no less prolific a novelist and essayist, left Munich for Berlin in 1925. Like those of many novelists at this time, his works have a greater interest as social history than as literature. But where the focus of his attention is a central character rather than a set of circumstances, a character from whose career the circles of the social scene radiate, he has created memorable personalities – like the fawning careerist of *Der Untertan* ('The Toady'), whose unscrupulousness illuminates what Mann saw as the corruption that ran through the chauvinist society of the Wilhelmine age. Also focused on that age is the satirical novel *Professor Unrat,* his only work to have reached a wider public, albeit less in its own right than through *The Blue Angel,* the film which launched the career of Marlene Dietrich in 1930. But *Professor Unrat* was written as early as 1905, long before Mann took up residence in Berlin. The encroachment of associations with the Berlin cabaret world and the sexual mores of the 1920s in the film is a piece of cinematic licence.

Der Kopf, on the other hand – the title stands for politicians and conservative intellectuals – is a *roman à clef* that sets out to describe how the capitalist society of imperial Germany brought the country to war. Complex and expansive, like most of Mann's novels, it carries an implied plea for pacifism as a positive virtue to set against the evil of war. But the double suicide with which the story ends only symbolises Mann's inability, shared by many at the time, to envisage how history might have taken a different course.

The novel-reading public of the Weimar years made Heinrich Mann one of the most popular writers of the day. But as a Marxist he set little store by the politics of the Republic. He was elected President of the Prussian Academy of Arts in 1931, forced by the Nazis to resign two years later and spent the rest of his life in exile, first in France, then in the USA. Many Marxist exiles quickly returned to East Germany at the end of the war to help build socialism. Thomas Mann also went back to Europe. Heinrich, for whatever reasons, stayed. He died in California in 1950 but the following year his ashes were brought to Berlin and interned in the old Dorotheenstadt cemetery where Brecht, Dessau, Hanns Eisler, Wieland Herzfelde and other cultural heroes of the German Democratic Republic also lie. It is a more fitting resting-place for him.

Pacifism from the inside, as one might call it, informs Renn's remarkable novel, *Krieg.* The man calling himself Ludwig Renn writes a war diary as one who enlisted in the army as a private in 1914, filled with patriotic zeal. In reality, 'Private Renn' was a Saxon aristocrat, Arnold Vieth von Golssenau, who had come through the war as a company commander. Assuming the persona of a common soldier in the trenches, he coolly records, as though sending back despatches to a newspaper, the day-to-day course of the war, his conversations with his comrades, the cold, the hunger, the pain, and in the end the pointlessness of it all. Men are the actors in the drama but the driving force is war itself, war seen not in terms of right and wrong but as the death rattle of capitalist imperialism. The story is thus given a meaning that surpasses the individual fates of the men who are caught up in it.

Krieg makes a further point which did not escape its enthusiastic readers in 1928. Private Renn goes into the war in a spirit of buoyant optimism, convinced of the justice of the national cause. He is in good company. Many distinguished scholars, scientists and artists – Max Reinhardt, Gerhart Hauptmann, the Nobel Prize winners Wilhelm Röntgen and Max Planck – put their names to a declaration in 1914 supporting the German General Staff and the invasion of Belgium. Prussian values and modes of thought died hard. But as Renn's novel takes its course, the irrelevance of those values, and the civilisation that rested on them, becomes all too evident. It is as though Renn has explained to his readers the meaning of these last four years.

The third of these works set in the 1914–18 war is one of the finest of all twentieth-century German novels. Arnold Zweig's *Der Streit um den Sergeanten Grischa* describes the last months in the life of a Russian prisoner-of-war in the hands of the Germans. Caught trying to escape, Grischa is taken for a spy and sentenced to death by a military tribunal. When he proves that he is not a spy, another tribunal declares the sentence unjust. The 'conflict' in the title of the novel then develops between the old Prussian military code, rigid but just, and an arbitrary jurisdiction derived from the temporary exigences of martial law. Grischa becomes a helpless victim of the conflict. Finally, by decree of the German High Command, he is shot.

An anti-war novel on the grand scale, rich in vivid realistic detail, *Grischa* owes its literary position to its thematic richness and the insights into the moral problems facing a society rent by conflict and on the point of collapse. On the one plane there is the epic of Grischa himself, the classic 'little man' turned into a scapegoat by forces he is powerless to influence. At the same time Zweig invests much subtlety in the conflict between these forces themselves, presenting the Junker officer caste not as an emotionless, monolithic body of automata but as a community which has to reconcile within itself conflicts between the past and the present, between a stubborn adherence to a narrow, iron-hearted code and the recognition of a humanitarian ethic. And from the background – this is 1917 – come the rumblings of the Russian Revolution, symbol of a future that will sweep away this age of decadence and false morality.

In these novels of Heinrich Mann, Renn and Arnold Zweig, the Great War is not a backdrop but a subject in its own right. Likewise the society of the post-war years, torn by the mutually destructive influences of militarism and pacifism, idealism and cynicism, is a Pandora's box of motifs from which the novelist assembles his social picture. The economic recovery after the post-war inflation was a short success story waiting for a long disaster. Violence was becoming a way of life as Nazis and communists settled their scores in the street. Unemployment and criminality soared, social unrest grew and a sense of nervous insecurity gripped the country.

These are the historical realities in the background of one of the most popular novels of life in the decaying Weimar Republic, a work showered with praise by Hesse and Thomas Mann, which has sold millions of copies, been translated into twenty languages and twice made into a film – *Kleiner Mann, was nun?* ('What Now, Little Man?') by Hans Fallada.

Fallada's 'little man', Johannes Pinneberg, is a Berlin shop assistant, a white-collar worker with middle-class pretensions but in reality a member of an under-class no better off than the proletariat, who at least have their trade unions to help preserve their solidarity. As the economic situation at the end of the 1920s deteriorates, Pinneberg, with a young wife and child to support, is dismissed for trying to invoke the sympathy of a well-to-do customer for his predicament. While his wife struggles to feed the family by working as a seamstress, Pinneberg joins the ranks of the unemployed, at a time when one out of every three workers is on the dole. Unwittingly caught up in a political demonstration, he is set upon by the police as an agitator and made to realise that poverty is not just misery but a crime. At the end he can only ask: 'What now, little man?'

But poor Johannes Pinneberg does have an answer to his question. To be sure, it is only a personal answer, for there is no universally valid answer to his situation, and Fallada does not believe in the class struggle or world revolution, but an answer nonetheless. It is love – specifically love between man and wife. Sentimental it may be, in the face of the crushing realities of Pinneberg's existence and as the Nazi storm is about to break. But readers grasped it as a precious scrap of personal consolation in an age of institutionalised intolerance and strident sloganising, when the fate of the individual counted for nothing.

Politically active contemporaries expressed dissatisfaction at the absence of any firm socio-political standpoint on the author's part. 'Am I a reformer?' Fallada retorted: 'Or a teacher? No – I am a describer.' He described what he saw, what his thousands of readers saw, with a compelling realism and narrative power. In another social novel, *Bauern, Bonzen und Bomben* ('Peasants, Bosses and Bombs'), he chronicles the intolerance, hatred and violence that tear a small-town community apart under the vicious regime of a corrupt local government – the kind of situation the Nazis were at that very moment preparing to move in on. Not for nothing – his real name was Rudolf Ditzen – did he adopt the pseudonym of Fallada, the horse in the Grimms' fairy-tale, whose head went on speaking the truth after its death.

There was no shortage of novels about Berlin in the early 1930s. Some concentrated on the political implications of a disintegrating society – how, as in F. C. Weiskopf's racy story *Lissy oder die Versuchung* ('Lissy, or Seduction'), the Nazis gathered support by promising to restore law and order and by reinvoking the sense of national pride to which they knew the masses would respond. Erich Kästner, by contrast, author of the ever-popular *Emil and the Detectives* and of satirical texts for Berlin cabarets, wrote a novel called *Fabian: Story of a Moralist*, in which he holds up a mockingly distorting mirror to the perversions and inequities of Weimar society – a kind of literary counterpart to the caricatures of George Grosz. The then immensely popular Lion Feuchtwanger, too, a close friend of Brecht's, whom he followed from Munich to Berlin in 1925, and one of the many Jewish refugees who later found a new home in California, wrote a powerful trilogy of novels under the title *Der Wartesaal* ('The Waiting-Room'), a concept symbolising the fateful course of German history in the image of a place where people were anxiously waiting for a better future. But none of these novelists achieves the vividness and poignancy of Fallada.

Except one, author of the Berlin novel to end all Berlin novels – Alfred Döblin and his *Berlin Alexanderplatz*.

To trace the life of Döblin – from his Jewish origins in Stettin, through his years as a neurologist on Berlin's proletarian east side, his exile in 1933 in France and later in the United States, to his return to West Germany after the war and his death there in 1957 – is to review a panorama of German history in the first half of the twentieth century. And to follow his literary career from the expressionism of the early 1900s – he was a co-founder of the revolutionary Berlin journal *Der Sturm* in 1910 – through socialist, psychological and aesthetic phases to the Roman Catholicism in which he ended his days, is to survey the whole gamut of intellectual pressures and attractions of these years.

On the one hand Döblin spoke the language of 'art for the people', of a culture in which control is wrested from the hands of a self-protecting bourgeoisie. At other times he was at pains to assert the sacred autonomy of the poetic imagination, distinguishing between true literature and production-line works of fiction for the masses. It was a familiar conflict among left-wing intellectuals at the time, caught, as they were, between the demands of their own creative ego and statements about the proper role of the artist in society.

Franz Biberkopf, former truck driver and jail-bird hero of *Berlin Alexanderplatz*, lives out the same experience on his own level, recognising what needed to be changed in his society but shrinking from actions that would bring those changes about. 'When the time is ripe, and if it suits me,' he reflects, watching a group of political demonstrators march by, 'I'll join in. Man has the gift of reason – it's only cattle that move in herds.' It might almost be Brecht speaking.

'The terrible thing that was Biberkopf's life', as Döblin called it, is quickly told. Newly released from prison after serving a sentence for murdering his girlfriend, Biberkopf at first tries to go straight but quickly lapses back into the company of burglars, pimps and other criminals in the seedy Berlin quarter where he lives. He is thrown out of a car while trying to escape from the police and loses his right arm. Arrested again for complicity to murder, he is sent to a mental asylum, where he finally begins to put the pieces of his wretched life together. On his discharge he is given a job as a janitor at a small factory by the Alexanderplatz, which is the last we see of him. 'We may expect', says the novel, 'that he will make a better fist of his life this time.'

Each of Döblin's major works of fiction emerged as a concretisation of ideas he had already expressed in postulatory, theoretical form. *Berlin Alexanderplatz* demonstrates the working of a world held in tension between two warring but inseparable principles – a positive, constructive principle and a rival, negative principle of decay and disintegration. Biberkopf is basically a 'good person', earnestly set on becoming a reformed character when he leaves jail. But the cards are stacked against him. Döblin's professional experience in a working-class area had brought him into contact with criminal and near-criminal elements and led him to conclude

120. *Kurfürstendamm* by George Grosz, oil on canvas, 1925.

that, as he put it, 'no hard and fast line could be drawn between criminality and non-criminality, and that the society that confronted me was riddled with criminality'. Although the novel hopes that Biberkopf will 'make a better fist' of things in the future, Döblin hardly encourages us to put much money on it.

The scenes of life in the Berlin underworld are what made *Berlin Alexanderplatz* a best-seller and a powerful film. But its fascination and originality come as much from its style and manner – one moment naturalistic, the next expressionist or surrealist, as description dissolves into action, sometimes logical, sometimes incongruous, sometimes freely associative in a bizarre stream of consciousness, owing much to Freud. James Joyce's *Ulysses* and John Dos Passos' *Manhattan Transfer*, which had both appeared a few years earlier, also lurk in the shadows. It is picaresque novel, study in psychopathology, social and political commentary, moral *Bildungsroman* and other things besides, with a dazzling pandemonium of aesthetic techniques to match. There is no common denominator that will subsume its extremes and its paradoxes. But then, neither is there in the Berlin from which its life-blood comes.

Theatre in the Weimar Years

In 1894 Otto Brahm, director of the Deutsches Theater in Berlin, the leading theatre in the German-speaking world, attended a performance of Schiller's *Die Räuber* in Salzburg. He was struck by the unknown twenty-one-year-old actor in the role of Franz Moor and offered him an engagement on the spot. Ten years later, after running a succession of Berlin theatres to the accompaniment of an ever growing reputation as a producer, this young actor was to take over the Deutsches Theater himself. Not only that. Instead of leasing it, like most producers, he bought the entire theatre outright, complete with sets, furnishings and other contents. It was characteristic of Max Goldmann – the man who called himself Max Reinhardt.

After abandoning his Berlin cabaret Schall und Rauch in 1902, Reinhardt launched his first theatre with plays by Strindberg, Oscar Wilde's *Salome*, Wedekind's *Erdgeist* and Maxim Gorki's *The Lower Depths*, works with a strong naturalistic content to which, through his sets, costumes and original use of lights and colours, he added a particular atmosphere of his own expressionist creation. The following year he also took control of the theatre in the Schiffbauerdamm, where he had great success with Maeterlinck's *Pelléas et Mélisande*, Oscar Wilde's *A Woman of No Importance* and Shaw's *Candida*.

Finally, in 1904, he won his greatest prize, the Deutsches Theater, where his lavish productions set new standards of theatrical illusion and attracted new mass audiences to the experience of serious drama, the classics and the moderns, German and foreign alike. Leading actors and actresses – Eduard von Winterstein, Alexander Moissi, Friedrich Kayssler, Lucie Höflich – hastened to put themselves at his disposal, especially for Shakespeare, the Greek tragedians and the German classics but also for Strindberg and Wedekind, Büchner and Hofmannsthal. Zuckmayer and the young Brecht were among his dramaturges. Max Slevogt, Lovis Corinth and Eduard Munch designed sets for him, and even the grand old man of German painting, the irascible ninety-year-old Adolf Menzel, was coaxed out of his studio to advise on matters of costume. Hofmannsthal became Reinhardt's literary adviser, forming an association broken only by Hofmannsthal's death in 1929.

But Reinhardt had not finished. Always linking size and intensity, he held to a belief that, by employing a multiplicity of means in a lavish spirit neo-romantic in its uninhibited demands, the theatrical experience would be at its most irresistible. Big is beautiful. For some time he had been eyeing a nearby building with a huge arena, formerly a circus, with seats for 3,000. Here he saw the chance to realise a dream to bring classical drama to the mass audience which he foresaw the theatre would soon have to serve. In 1910, revelling in the scenic and lighting effects for which he had become famous, he mounted an opulent production there of *Oedipus Rex*, and later of *Hamlet*, to show what he meant. In 1919, its auditorium magnificently rebuilt by Hans Poelzig as an exercise in expressionism, the theatre passed into Reinhardt's possession and was formally rechristened the Grosses Schauspielhaus. (Known latterly as the Friedrichstadtpalast, it stood until 1980, when its foundations were discovered to be subsiding, and the whole building was pulled down.) Reinhardt's mammoth open-air productions in public settings like the Rathausplatz in Vienna and the

Parvis Notre-Dame in Paris expressed the same philosophy of theatrical production.

After the war, in changed economic circumstances, Reinhardt began to lose interest in his Berlin enterprises and spent more time in his native Austria, where, with Hofmannsthal and Richard Strauss, he was co-founder of the Salzburg Festival in 1920. As 1933 approached, he knew that Europe was no place for a Jew, and he left first for Paris, then for the United States. His famous production of *A Midsummer Night's Dream* in the Hollywood Bowl in 1934 has joined the annals of theatrical history.

Reinhardt's career, including the establishment and encouragement of a drama school to ensure that his principles outlived him, had its roots in the pre-war years, in the monarchist world of the court theatres on one hand and private commercial enterprises on the other. The generation of producers and directors that followed, moulded by the war from which they had just emerged, was pitched into a world of mutilated ex-soldiers and hungry children, a world of inflation and talk of revolution, in which shouting and shrieking seemed the natural way of expressing oneself, whether in life or in art.

Grasping the new social and political reality, there emerged in the 1920s a breed of directors, penetrating of mind and politically committed, who were to impose their personalities on the dramas of passion and protest that new young writers were offering them, as well as on the works of the classical repertoire. As the novel opened up the riches of recent and contemporary history, so the drama offered a public outlet for the release of the anger and the visionary abandon that held the new generation in thrall. To convert the passionate words on the page into passionate experience in the theatre required the no less passionate conviction of the director. The result, for the years of the Weimar Republic, was a theatrical life of untold originality and excitement.

In 1919 Leopold Jessner, a producer who had worked in Hamburg and Königsberg, was appointed director of the Schauspielhaus on the Gendarmenmarkt, formerly a royal theatre, now the property of the Prussian state and renamed the Staatstheater. Jessner's first production, Schiller's *Wilhelm Tell*, made him the undisputed but far from uncontroversial champion of expressionism in the Berlin theatre. For Jessner all theatre was political because it reflected the way in which the dramatist came to terms with his age. And because subsequent ages have to discover for themselves the surviving validity of each work, the producer has to set the governing idea behind the work in the centre of his interpretation. He cannot give himself over to the creation of some theatrical mood or illusion, or to an explicit concentration on character.

This 'thinking-man's theatre' underpinned the expressionist tendency to abstraction and the characteristic typification of the *dramatis personae* in the works of contemporary dramatists – men and women identified not by personal names but as simply 'The Father', 'The Son', 'The Wife'. Similarly Jessner demanded sets reduced to a minimum, with a handful of formalised, almost anonymous items on the stage – prominent among them the famous 'Jessner staircase' – inviting symbolic interpretation.

A convinced Social Democrat, who saw his Staatstheater as an institution for the whole population, Jessner played a European repertoire that struck a balance between the classical and the modern, on the one hand Shakespeare, Goethe, Schiller, Kleist and Büchner, on the other Ibsen, Shaw, Strindberg, Gerhart Hauptmann, Wedekind. Towards works being written in his presence, as it were, by dramatists such as Kokoschka, Brecht and Zuckmayer he showed, surprisingly perhaps, a certain reserve, reluctant to expose his theatre to the danger of being seen as a laboratory for testing experimental material.

One who had no such fears, because experiment was the very life-blood of his theatre, was the formidable Erwin Piscator, a man who polarised Berlin theatrical life in the 1920s. Arriving from Königsberg in 1920, Piscator became a protagonist of 'proletarian theatre', the stage as an agency of political agitation, playing to steadily dwindling audiences of uncomprehending workers in trade union halls and beer-cellars.

Then, in 1924, in the Berlin Volksbühne, Piscator's Proletarisches Theater gave the first performance of a play with the generic title of 'epic drama'. The play itself, *Die Fahnen* ('The Banners'), a dramatisation by Alfons Paquet of the Chicago anarchists' trial of 1886, is unimportant. But here was a totally new form of theatrical experience, a kind of dispassionate reportage, a multimedia assemblage of heterogeneous episodes, some spoken, some sung, some projected by camera on to a screen as still or moving pictures – in short, the antithesis of everything the European tradition had come to recognise as logical, homogeneous, consistently motivated 'dramatic drama'. 'The theatre should not just play on the audience's passions', wrote Piscator, 'but deliberately appeal to their reason, invoking not elation, inspiration and emotional abandon but understanding and knowledge.' Brecht, characteristically, succeeded in making the world believe that it was he who had invented non-Aristotelian 'epic' drama. It was not the only thing the acquisitive Brecht 'borrowed' from Piscator and others.

As Max Reinhardt had founded a drama school to enshrine his principles and methods, so Piscator's own Theater am Nollendorfplatz became a centre of attraction for men and women sympathetic to his aims – the architect Walter Gropius, later director of the Bauhaus, the satirical artist George Grosz, Brecht, actors like Max Pallenberg, Oscar Homolka and Helene Weigel. A method of 'objective acting' also emerged from the Piscator studio to reinforce the concept of 'epic drama' and the enterprise was further enriched by incidental music. In common with other producers Piscator had his resident composer and conductor, one Edmund Meisel, for this purpose but 'outside' composers such as Kurt Weill and Hanns Eisler also provided music for his productions.

Reinhardt, Jessner, Karlheinz Martin at the Volksbühne and at Piscator's Nollendorfplatz theatre, Piscator himself, Brecht – directing talent in the 1920s offered an *embarras de richesses*. Like musicians and other performing artists, theatre directors have at their disposal the entire world literature in their field. The challenge is to their powers of interpretation, their urge to uncover – critics will say invent – a modern relevance in works from another time and place. The classics can thus have their contemporaneity restored to them – not in the manner in which Sophocles was contemporary to fifth-century Athens, or Shakespeare to Elizabethan London, for we cannot feel or understand with the faculties of the past, but through the demonstration of their modern validity. To this extent a director may be content to devote most, even all of his attention to masterpieces of the distant or recent past, casting only an occasional glance in the direction of the angry young poets and dramatists of the moment. That one could make revolution with the classics as effectively as with a protest drama on which the ink was barely dry had been scandalously demonstrated by Jessner in his inaugural production in the Staatstheater of Schiller's *Wilhelm Tell*, a democratic – Social Democratic – statement in the name of freedom and on behalf of the new Republic.

But there were also contemporary plays, plays expressionist both in sub-stance and in manner, albeit mostly by writers with only loose associations with Berlin. Their themes are close to those treated in novels of the period – the war, the despair of the post-war years, presentiment of coming social disaster. Their tone, hysterical, importunate, the product of a mind almost out of control, has the same mixture of urgent intolerance and passionate cyni-cism that fills the lyrical pages of *Menschheitsdämmerung*. The underlying real-ities are strong but the creative mind has a collective, rather than a personal quality – again as in *Menschheitsdämmerung*. Max Reinhardt's post-war pro-ductions of such works as Reinhard Göring's war drama *Die Seeschlacht* ('The Naval Battle') and Reinhard Sorge's expressionist extravaganza *Der Bettler* ('The Beggar') caught the despairing mood of 1917 and 1918 but could not rescue their authors for posterity.

The experience of the Volksbühne during and after the war shows the pressures and counter-pressures, the relationship – in reality the gulf – between the theatre that audiences attended and applauded and the politi-cally loaded theatre to which ideologues often wanted to subject them. Early on in the war the governing body of the Volksbühne, faced with declining receipts, offered its theatre to Max Reinhardt, who brought with him from the Deutsches Theater his productions of Shakespeare, the German classics and Gerhart Hauptmann. The Volksbühne audience applauded wildly. They went to the theatre to be entertained, not lectured, and responded sponta-neously to the power of dramatic spectacle. Only in the course of the 1920s did the political aspirations of the Volksbühne movement reassert themselves, as new protest plays, long in showmanship, short in literary value, thrust themselves into the foreground – protest against the war and what had led up to it, against the betrayal of the younger generation by their elders, against the immorality of a self-centred materialism.

From this almost anonymous background there emerge in the 1920s two dramatists with highly individual voices, both of the wartime generation, both from the provinces but committed to, and earning their reputations in, Berlin, both of radical left-wing views, both soon to be driven out of Germany by the Nazis. The age saw them as rivals in the establishment of political drama. One is Ernst Toller. The other is Bertolt Brecht.

Toller was an idealist and a born revolutionary, a martyr for those who shared his political convictions, a thorn in the flesh of those who did not. As a student, he agitated against the war and for his support of the Soviet-style Workers' Council in Munich was sentenced in 1919 to five years' imprisonment, during which time he wrote four of the five dramas on which his reputation rests. Shown copies of these plays, Piscator and Karlheinz

Martin sensed a remarkable talent and mounted performances of them at the Volksbühne and elsewhere. So, when he emerged from jail in 1924, Toller found that he had become one of the most talked-of young playwrights of the day.

Toller's dramas chart an agonised path from hope and vision to despair and cynicism. In the first, *Die Wandlung* ('The Transformation'), he shares the optimism of those expressionists who look to build a new world based on the true inner humanity of man. By the time of *Masse-Mensch* ('Mass-Man') the following year he has concluded that the masses are not yet ready to achieve revolutionary ends, and reinforces this bitter perception in *Die Maschinenstürmer* ('The Machine Wreckers'), a play based on the English Luddite uprising of 1815, which poses the classic revolutionary dilemma: to use violence is to betray the ideals of the revolution but not to do so is to condemn the revolution to failure.

A few days before the first performance (1922) of *Die Maschinenstürmer* in the Grosses Schauspielhaus in Berlin the Jewish Foreign Minister of the Republic, Walter Rathenau, had been assassinated. Fired by the passionate language of Toller's drama and by the knowledge that the author was in jail, the audience in the huge arena turned their applause into a political demonstration against violence and the nationalist–militaristic enemies of the Republic. 'It was an occasion the like of which scarcely any German theatre can have witnessed,' wrote Alfred Kerr, doyen of Berlin drama critics, in the *Berliner Tageblatt* the next morning.

The best known, and in some ways most terrifying, at times most unpleasant but most powerful of Toller's dramas is *Hinkemann* (1924), the story of a working-class man who returns from the war with his genitals shot away. First pitied by his wife, then mocked and rejected, he is reduced to performing a distasteful circus act in order to survive at a time when wounded ex-servicemen are ten a penny. An anti-war play as well as a savage demonstration of man's inhumanity to man, the pall of darkness is barely lifted throughout the three acts. Hinkemann's wife, her spirit broken, no longer able to understand what has been going on, kills herself. At the end Hinkemann himself – a latter-day Woyzeck, Büchner's archetypal victim – is left alone on the stage with his wife's body, fashioning a rope for his own suicide. 'Any day can bring the kingdom of Heaven', he muses, 'any night, the end to the world.' The end of Toller's world came in 1933. A Jew and a communist sympathiser, he fled to London, then to New York. A few days before the outbreak of the war he hanged himself.

Toller carried a burning message. His tone has the expressionist's stridency, his language is deliberately offensive, coarse to the point of parody, tragically comic in its exaggerations. 'In times of violent social conflict the theatre will reflect this conflict,' he wrote. Such was the man and such were his times. He knew that another war was waiting to happen.

Brecht, five years younger than Toller but still one on whom the Great War left indelible scars, had his own experience of expressionism, an experience that he released into the grotesque amoral, asocial monster at the sordid centre of his first play, *Baal*. Shot through with the spirit of Büchner – to Brecht the greatest of all German dramatists – *Baal* was an outburst of protest that Brecht had to get out of his system in a suitably violent way.

From then on his passion, no less intense, simmered in more controlled conditions, the impact of his message made only the more powerful by the steely sense of intellectual purpose, but also of inescapable irony, that holds his dramas in its grip.

Already in his second play, *Trommeln in der Nacht* ('Drums in the Night'), Brecht took total control of the stage. It is a companion piece to Toller's *Hinkemann*, the story of a pathetic non-hero returning from the war to a sordid petty-bourgeois world of duplicity and cynicism in which his fiancée has left him for another man and where much vaunted ideals turn out to be so much hot air. 'Do you expect my flesh to rot in the gutter so that your ideal can find a place in heaven?' shouts the disillusioned homecomer. So when the moment of decision comes, he turns his back on Karl Liebknecht and Rosa Luxemburg and opts for a comfortable life with his former fiancée, who has decided to go back to him. Brecht himself, supreme egoist in all things personal and professional, would have done the same. *Trommeln in der Nacht*, which earned Brecht the Kleist Prize for Drama in 1922, gave him a position in the public eye which he never lost.

Berlin, which he made his permanent home from 1924, was Brecht's milieu, the city he loved to hate. He sought out its seedier industrial corners, preferred to drink in bars frequented by pimps and prostitutes, went to football and boxing matches, wrote advertising copy and sleeve notes for gramophone records – activities to open up as wide and ostentatious a gulf as possible between himself and 'literature', including those who practised it. He carefully cultivated the pose of the workers' poet, having his shabby clothes, in which he appeared to have slept, made to measure by a tailor in his native Augsburg.

In 1928 *Die Dreigroschenoper* made him and his composer Kurt Weill sensationally famous overnight. He may have had little affection for Berlin but he needed the unique facilities that it offered, not least its shrewd, irreverent, sophisticated public, the bourgeois public that squealed with delight as it watched its values being murdered night by night on the stage of the Theater am Schiffbauerdamm.

John Gay's *The Beggar's Opera* of 1728, Brecht's starting-point, pillories the eighteenth-century aristocracy by equating their predatory mode of life with that of the underworld. Retaining Gay's plot but transplanting it to the age of Victorian capitalism, Brecht makes his target the bourgeois society that first created, then sustained, this underworld. Change the system, abolish poverty, and a proper moral society will follow. 'Erst kommt das Fressen, dann kommt die Moral,' as Mackie Messer, Brecht's Macheath, elegantly puts it – 'Grub first, morals later.'

The Brecht–Weill *Dreigroschenoper* was the most intoxicating theatrical success of the 1920s. In Berlin alone it ran for a year, and within a week of opening in August 1928 had been booked for over fifty theatres in Germany. Gramophone companies rushed to sign up the stars of the show and bring out records of the songs and ensembles. People hummed and whistled the tunes as they walked down the street, and a '3-Groschen bar' opened in Berlin, playing only '3-Groschen' music. Time-bound it may be, but if one had to choose one work to characterise the Berlin of the 1920s at its headiest and most sophisticated, that work would have to be the *Dreigroschenoper*.

This capitalist world of Brecht's imagination returned two years later as the centre of attention in *Aufstieg und Fall der Stadt Mahagonny* ('Rise and Fall of the City of Mahagonny'). Mahagonny is everywhere and nowhere: it can be Berlin or, since the play is set in America, any archetypal American city. Kurt Weill, who wrote the music — the work is in reality a three-act opera — described the story as 'a parable of modern life in which the principle character is the city itself'. It is a mocking presentation of society in which everything and everybody has its price, and the cardinal sin, for which the principal male character is executed, is to have no money. In the end Mahagonny goes up in flames.

Up to this point Brecht's political stance could be described in terms barely more specific than 'anti-capitalist' or 'radically left-wing'. But he was moving towards a more formal Marxist position, and in a group of so-called *Lehrstücke*, 'didactic plays', written on either side of 1930, he set out to illustrate the working of Communist Party dogma in given situations. In the most subtle of these pieces, *Die Massnahme* ('The Measures Taken'), a young comrade is seen to obstruct the work of the party by giving way to his humane instincts and helping the oppressed labourers. Called to account, he confesses his guilt and is 'liquidated', like the victims of Stalin's show trials. On the surface the collective orthodoxy prevails: the Party is always right. But the voice of the young comrade and his common humanity cannot be completely suppressed. Whatever one's loyalty to the cause, there is an inalienable personal morality that takes precedence. It is a scenario that attended Brecht, a born survivor, throughout his career. Hand-in-hand with this Marxist-oriented drama, promoting a rational understanding of events, not an emotional involvement in them, went Brecht's concept of 'alienation', *Verfremdung*, and the theory of non-Aristotelian 'epic' drama first put into practice, in an equally politicised context, by Piscator. Since the function of art was to change the world in accordance with Marxist principle, audiences must be made to think rather than feel, make decisions rather than ponder motives.

Brecht was one of the many intellectuals who did not take the threat of Nazism seriously. Hitler will quickly disappear from the scene, they said. 'There is no greater crime than to leave,' added Brecht. In February 1933, the day after the Reichstag fire, he left. His exile took him to Switzerland, France, Scandinavia and finally California. He returned to Europe in 1947 and settled two years later in East Berlin, where he died in 1956, a world figure with a reputation far greater than when he had left.

In the familiar terms of tendencies of the *Zeitgeist* the Brecht of the 1920s belongs to the Neue Sachlichkeit that reflected the material consolidation of the Weimar Republic. Some dramatists who a decade or so earlier had shared in the screaming excesses of expressionism, revelling in a world of apocalyptic visions and extremes, like Georg Kaiser, now found a new and calmer voice in psychological drama or in comedy. Statements on the condition of man and the state of the cosmos gave way to a concentration on practical, manageable issues and the observation of human foibles, personal and social. Carl Zuckmayer, who had launched his dramatic career in 1920 with a typical piece of expressionist excess, conquered the Berlin stage with a succession of earthy comedies, most famous of them the ever popular *Hauptmann von*

Köpenick, a riotous satire on militarism, bureaucracy and blind obedience to authority. Everybody knew, friend and foe alike, where Zuckmayer was looking. The Nazis huffed and puffed but Zuckmayer's little corporal-turned-captain had their measure. Audiences were allowed to continue laughing until the beginning of 1933, when the curtain came down. Zuckmayer joined the exodus of intellectuals, writers, actors, artists, musicians and others who suddenly found their activities banned and their livelihood taken away. The time for comedy was over.

Cinema

To survey the literature, the painting, the architecture, the music and the other arts of Berlin is to look at a part of a larger whole, a part of the culture of a nation. Capital city it may have become but it was only one cultural centre among many in the German-speaking world. Writers and painters came and went, leaving us to complete the story of their careers elsewhere. Novelty, fashion or the prospect of common causes attracted one moment, left apathy the next.

But not with film. Down to 1945 the history of the Berlin cinema is to all intents and purposes the history of German cinema itself. Following Max Skladanovsky's exhibition in Berlin in 1885 of what he described as his 'theatre of living photographs', cinemas sprang up all over the city. Audiences flocked to what they saw as a fascinating extension of the entertainment world of cabaret and music hall into new realms of illusion. In the years before the First World War many of the movies shown – romances, chase films, suspense films – came from France and Denmark but there were also early German comic masterpieces by Ernst Lubitsch which drew packed houses.

Convention dates the serious history of the native German film from *The Student from Prague*, made in 1913 and starring Paul Wegener, an actor of Reinhardt's. Wegener, with Conrad Veidt and others, was responsible for leading the film away from sensationalism and facile amusement into the realm of theatre. This he achieved through a sophisticated technique of gesture and facial expression which set a benchmark for the whole film industry and guaranteed the dominance of the silent film for the next fifteen years, well after the 'talkie' had been invented. Many resented the intrusion of sound but were at the same time so convinced of the artistic superiority of the silent medium that they saw no threat to its survival.

Film, like journalism – but unlike literature or painting or music – stands in a peculiarly direct relationship to the mentality of the society to which it belongs. For one thing it is a synthetic product, the creation not of a single but of a collective mind, and therefore the agreed outcome of deliberations from a wealth of different angles – a *Gesamtkunstwerk*, in its own way. At the same time, as a mass medium governed by basically commercial criteria, it depends for its success on mass appeal and must move with, as well as help to create, the tastes of the mass market. And never, ironically, did the cinemas enjoy a greater popularity than during the post-war years of hunger and deprivation.

In a way that literature never could, film in these expressionist years of protest and experiment, novelty and self-projection, captured that market. The *locus classicus* of expressionist film is Robert Wiene's *Cabinet of Dr Caligari*, made in 1919, with Conrad Veidt in the title role. Here is the demonic, nightmarish world of the expressionist imagination, peopled by psychotic characters at the end of their tether. No less starkly expressionist are the asymmetrical designs of the décor and the jagged lighting effects, technical masterstrokes that imposed their authority on one film after another while giving *Caligari* a cult status it has never lost. It is a total cinematic experience – drama, architecture, lighting, camera work – a closed, almost claustrophobic world which holds its characters captive. All these early films were made in the studio, where the director created a hothouse environment into which no natural features from the outside world would be allowed to penetrate. The audience are no less prisoners of the action than the players.

Indeed, the demands made by *Caligari* and its successors on their audiences were considerable. Emotions were subjected to a relentless battering, the mind held in constant agitation. To be sure, the film industry also had its lighter, less expressionistic side, with guaranteed popular appeal, such as costume extravaganzas and the historical films of Ernst Lubitsch (*Madame Dubarry, Anna Boleyn*), with spectacular crowd scenes that picked up the contemporary reality of street demonstrations. But it is in the wake of *Caligari* that the most striking achievements of silent German cinema lie. Their expressionism also extends to their scripts. The most important scriptwriter

121. Scene (with Conrad Veidt) from the film *The Cabinet of Dr Caligari*, 1919–20.

of the day, Carl Mayer, adopted the passionate, staccato diction of dramatists like Georg Kaiser and added to the fatalistic context the resentful tone of a post-war generation that rejected the social and moral values of their fathers. Expressionism even found its way into the make-up room, where all manner of bizarre visages were created.

The two greatest heirs to the *Caligari* tradition through the 1920s are F. W. Murnau and Fritz Lang, the former remembered for his horror movie *Dracula* (1922) and his *Faust*, in which the fully mobile studio camera was used for the first time. Lang came to film not from the theatre but from the visual arts and architecture, and his slow-moving style enabled him to convey as much meaning through his multi-dimensional sets as through the actions of his characters. His *Nibelungen* epic, a monumental mixture of inspired showmanship and sensational Kitsch, with its atmospheric décor and its fire-spitting dragon, is an archetypal expressionist artefact.

Lang's abiding fame in the early history of German, that is Berlin cinema, rests on *Dr Mabuse, der Spieler* ('Dr Mabuse, the Gambler') and the futuristic *Metropolis* (1927). In its subject matter of crime, hypnotism and insanity, as well as in its surrealist décor of sharp angles and abstract contrasts, heightened by the lighting techniques of chiaroscuro, *Dr Mabuse* follows closely in the footsteps of *Caligari*. *Metropolis*, on the other hand, is a frenzied exercise in excess – a statement of the class conflict between masters and workers, of the theme of robots and humans, of the final victory of truth through the mediation of love, all brought together in a fantastic vision of the future. It is a measure of its technical brilliance – its shots of mass movements, of the labourers at work on the robots, of the city submerged under the rising waters – that *Metropolis* has survived the farrago of nonsense that passes for its script. In 1931 Lang returned to earth, so to speak, with the thriller *M*, bringing his technical wizardry to bear on the exciting new medium of talking pictures, which had made its belated German début in 1929.

As in the mid-1920s the expressionist mood of self-centredness and extro-vert gesturing in the arts gave way to Neue Sachlichkeit, a realism drawn from the material world of an observed environment, so film makers too stepped outside the private world of their studios in search of public realities. *Pari passu* the excesses of expressionist acting gave way to a greater naturalism, as they do in Walter Ruttmann's remarkable social documentary *Berlin: Symphony of a City*. Taking a day in the life of the city in the spring of 1927, from the arrival of an overnight train in the early morning to a fireworks display above the dark streets in the evening, Ruttmann offers, not a narrative continuum but a montage of cross-sections arranged in the terms of the film maker's socialist vision – realism and supra-realism in one. This was the age when the techniques of photo montage were also being exploited in other contexts – by John Heartfield in the pursuit of political aims and by Piscator in his multi-media productions in the Theater am Nollendorfplatz.

A more thoroughgoing analytical realism, applied to extreme dramatic situations and states of mind, was brought to the screen by G. W. Pabst in a number of films that explored in particular the female psychology – works such as *The Love of Jeanne Ney* and *Pandora's Box*, the latter an adaptation of Wedekind (the influence of Freud is never far away). With his striking attention to realistic detail, his use of close-ups and the concentration of his camera on the facts of the physical environment, Pabst was out not to elicit gasps of wonder from his audience but to draw them into the sequence of events he was presenting. In 1930 he joined the early makers of talkies with *Western Front 1918*, a powerful denunciation of war to set alongside Remarque's novel *All Quiet on the Western Front*, published a year earlier.

With the arrival of the 1930s came more and more films in the cause of social criticism, counterparts to contemporary novels and dramas centred on conditions at the time of the depression and the imminent collapse of the German attempt at social democracy. At the same time the use of film as an instrument of psychological representation, sometimes with a realistic, sometimes with a romantic tinge, emerges in famous pieces such as Josef von Sternberg's *The Blue Angel* (1930), an early example of the film that rides roughshod over the literary work on which it is based but becomes a brilliant achievement in its own right.

Shortly afterwards Sternberg joined the procession of directors and actors – Ernst Lubitsch, Fritz Lang, Murnau, Pabst, Peter Lorre, Oscar Homolka, Conrad Veidt – who left Berlin for Hollywood, some for professional reasons, some as victims of racial persecution, many as both. As in so many walks of life, from atomic physicists to poets and musicians, Germany's loss was America's gain (Ill. 121).

Short and Sharp: The Music of the Weimar Decade

1918. The Second Reich, pride of 1871, had collapsed and the new Republic, flying the black–red–gold flag of the 1848 Revolution, had been proclaimed. The royal opera houses, theatres and museums had become the property of the Prussian state. Now a new policy for the arts was needed for a new democracy and a new democratic capital.

Charged with formulating such a policy and putting it into practice was the new Prussian Ministry of Science, Arts and National Education. In a changed constitutional situation political interests came to the fore, and when the Social Democrats gained an overwhelming victory in the Reichstag elections of January 1919, the direction of the new cultural policy became clear: culture belonged to the people.

As in the other arts, so also in music the post-war years invited a politicisation of activity. On the one hand there developed, in the shadow of the Volksbühne movement, a pressure for the extension of musical experience to 'the common man' – in consumer terms, a widening of the market. At the same time opposition to pre-war values, and the society from which they came, took aesthetic form in the aggressive promotion of a modern music that lived by a different philosophy.

The two tendencies could be found linked in a single organisation such as the Novembergruppe, an association of artists and musicians, among them the composer Max Butting, the conductor Hermann Scherchen and the critic Hans Heinz Stuckenschmidt, who saw music as an activity directed towards the enlightenment of their fellow-men and the enrichment of their lives. One composer who came to Berlin in 1925 with a mission to write music in the spirit that would serve the cause of revolution was Hanns Eisler. A pupil of Schoenberg's in Vienna and from 1930 Brecht's preferred musical collaborator, Eisler is comparatively rarely played today but the choral works he wrote for workers' massed choirs, to politically charged texts, made a great impact at the time and still have something of the primitive appeal of a familiar work like Orff's *Carmina Burana*.

Responsibility for musical life in the new Prussia was put in the hands of Leo Kestenberg, a Social Democrat of considerable influence over the cultural policies of the Weimar years. It was Kestenberg who appointed Franz Schreker as director of the Berlin Hochschule für Musik in 1920 in preference to Humperdinck, the students' and teachers' choice, and who invited Busoni to take a master class at the Academy of Arts the same year. And on Busoni's death in 1924 it was Kestenberg who appointed Schoenberg as his successor.

Besides this control over state institutions of learning, and thus over educational strategy in general, Kestenberg's brief covered the two state opera houses – the Staatsoper on Unter den Linden and the Kroll Opera on the renamed Platz der Republik – and the Schauspielhaus, now Staatstheater, on the Gendarmenmarkt. With firm ideas on the function of opera in the new society, Kestenberg assembled a team of musicians and administrators willing to promote the kind of programme he had in mind. Based on the native classics – Mozart, Weber, Lortzing, Wagner – the proposed new repertory also included a substantial number of works by contemporary composers, ranging from Richard Strauss, Humperdinck and Puccini to more strenuous works by Busoni, Pfitzner and Franz Schmidt. For the period between 1919 and 1932 as a whole the statistics of the Staatsoper show that the most popular work was *Cavalleria rusticana*, followed by Richard Strauss' *Salome* and Puccini's *Madame Butterfly*. True to the philosophy of his party, Kestenberg, an early activist in the Volksbühne movement, also encouraged the Staatsoper to give popular performances at popular prices in order to widen the appeal of opera. In the same spirit the opera house orchestra (Staatskapelle) gave Sunday-morning concerts in the Schauspielhaus which attracted growing audiences.

In 1920 the regular symphony concerts of the Staatskapelle were conducted by the thirty-four-year-old Wilhelm Furtwängler, who took over the Berlin Philharmonic Orchestra two years later. First Hermann Abendroth, then Bruno Walter followed Furtwängler at the Staatskapelle. In 1923 Erich Kleiber was appointed musical director of the Staatsoper itself, in 1925 Walter went to the Städtische Oper in Charlottenburg and in 1926 Klemperer took over at the Kroll Opera. The first Berlin Music Festival was held in 1929, with Toscanini and Richard Strauss among the visiting conductors.

Furtwängler, Walter, Abendroth, Kleiber, Klemperer – the most brilliant German conductors of the day jostling each other within one square kilometre. It could only have happened in Berlin. And it could only have happened when it did.

The Staatsoper mounted many controversial modern works during the Weimar years – Busoni's *Doktor Faust*, Kurt Weill's *Royal Palace*, Janáček's *Jenůfa*, Milhaud's *Christophe Colomb*. None of these, however, could match the expressionist masterpiece which had its première in 1925 under Erich Kleiber

– Alban Berg's *Wozzeck*. The public was already prepared for a challenging experience but not for the fighting that broke out in the auditorium between rival groups of supporters and protesters at the end of the performance. The following day the battle was continued by the critics in the columns of their newspapers, pro and contra divided as much on political as on musical grounds. For Wozzeck, the pathetic anti-hero at the centre of the nineteenth-century play by Büchner which Berg set, is an archetypal victim of war, sadism and social injustice, who symbolised for the expressionist poets and dramatists of the time all that was wrong with the world. It was a challenge that middle-class conservatism, busily establishing a new material prosperity, did not particularly want to hear. Berg's atonal music alone would have been enough to undermine their smugness. Allied to Büchner's searing drama, its intensity becomes almost unbearable.

Meanwhile the Kroll Opera, only a few hundred yards away from the Staatsoper, was going its own independent way. Amalgamated with the Staatsoper in 1895, it had fallen into disrepair during the war but was rebuilt in 1924 under the watchful eye of Kestenberg, who had his own plans for the house. To put them into effect he appointed Otto Klemperer, then at Wiesbaden, as General Music Director with a brief to mount progressive productions that would do away with the unnatural and artificial practices of conventional opera and attract a new kind of audience.

Not unexpectedly, 'difficult' modern works such as Stravinsky's *Oedipus Rex* and Schoenberg's *Erwartung* figured prominently in the repertoire. But no less difficult proved to be the radically deromanticised, sometimes politicised versions of familiar eighteenth- and nineteenth-century classics in the cool, detached spirit of Neue Sachlichkeit. Modern artists were invited to design sets and costumes and let their own experimental urges loose on the stage, arousing more horrified indignation than gratified approval. In the end, having acquired the reputation of being a hotbed of outspoken left-wing modernisers, and this being a time of national retrenchment, the Kroll had its funds withdrawn. It gave its last performance – Mozart's *The Marriage of Figaro* – to a packed house in the summer of 1931.

The story of the Kroll Opera in the 1920s mirrors the cultural history of the Weimar Republic itself – its hopes, its achievements, its failures, its collapse. The talk was of revolution, the tone dogmatic, extremism became a way of life and a mode of thought. But by the end of the decade the revolutionary élan had spent itself. The public wanted to keep the theatrical and musical conventions they had grown used to, precisely because they were the same public as before, not some new proletarian entity disposed to welcome displays of ideological experimentation. Composers turned away from aggressively modern subject matter for their operas and went back to history. By 1931 the Kroll had itself become history.

The answer to the question, What happened to the impressive Kroll building afterwards? – the auditorium held an audience of 2,300 – is as bizarre as that to many other questions asked about Berlin. In 1933 it was taken over as the chamber where the emasculated German parliament met after the Reichstag building had been set on fire by the Nazis. Here the elected representatives of the people signed away the Germans' democratic rights and handed the country over to Hitler. Here, in other words, Germany voted to become a dictatorship. By then Kestenberg and Klemperer, like all 'non-Aryan' intellectuals and artists, knew that their days in Germany were numbered. Many had already left.

Today the whole area is grassed over and nothing remains to remind the pilgrim into history of where the famous Kroll Opera once stood.

If post-war Vienna, in the person of Schoenberg and his circle, had the more important composers, post-war Berlin had the more exciting intellectual life, and with it a rapidly expanding scope for the performing arts. Musicians with established reputations could be enticed to the German capital to perform and to teach; students would follow the famous names to their chosen institutions, whose reputations would rise accordingly. Franz Schreker is a case in point – an interesting Viennese composer whose operas stand between the expressionist Richard Strauss of *Salome* and *Elektra* and a spare, contrapuntal manner akin to that of the neo-classical Stravinsky – who became director of the Hochschule für Musik in 1920.

An even bigger capture was Busoni. Italian by birth, cosmopolitan by temperament, Ferruccio Busoni had had his principal home in Berlin since the end of the nineteenth century. A Protean figure who defies classification, Busoni had an international career as one of the great piano virtuosi of his day and was also a conductor whose concert programmes in Berlin contained many first performances in Germany – Debussy's *Nocturnes*, Delius' *Paris*, Sibelius' Second Symphony and *Pohjola's Daughter*, Nielsen's *Four Temperaments* and many others. He wrote a treatise on the aesthetics of music and published an edition of the keyboard works of J. S. Bach. Above all he left a handful of compositions – operas, works for orchestra, piano music – among the most original of their time.

That his music, which culminates in the opera *Doktor Faust*, is comparatively rarely heard, is as he would have wished. It is esoteric music, the work of an aristocratic figure who believed, as he put it, 'that there has to be a great barrier between the public and the work of art'. It was an undemocratic message, unwelcome to many and at odds with the 'music-for-all' philosophy fashionable in Social Democratic circles. The intellect rules, and the listener has to work hard. Busoni's orchestral textures are too intense – almost, one might say, too expressionistic – for the concept of Neue Sachlichkeit to be invoked but the cerebral nature of his music, the concentrated application of means to ends, brings it into the context of an age determined not to lay itself open to the charge of being 'romantic'. If only, one feels in the superb *Doktor Faust* and elsewhere, he could have 'let himself go', allowed more spontaneous emotion into his music. But then he would no longer have been Busoni.

Like the contemporary poet Stefan George, also an autocratic figure with a view of art as lofty and exclusive, Busoni needed around him a circle of disciples to receive his ideas. What his students gained – among them the twenty-year-old Kurt Weill – lay not so much in the acquisition of skills and techniques as in the sharing of the experiences of an inspiring mind.

Busoni died in 1924. Taking his place in the Academy's master class came no less a figure than Arnold Schoenberg, the most challenging, most important – which is not to say the greatest – composer of the modernist twentieth century. Born in Vienna, eight years younger than the man whose place he took, Schoenberg had had brief experiences of Berlin in 1901 and again in 1911, when he taught at the Stern Conservatoire, but his base, centre of the so-called Second Viennese School, was the city of his birth. From here, in the five years or so before the outbreak of the First World War, had come the revolutionary atonal pieces that shook the musical world. The piano pieces Op. 11, the melodrama *Erwartung*, the song settings from Stefan George's *Das Buch der hängenden Gärten* – exercises in musical expressionism, counterparts to Schoenberg's own paintings from the same years, and companions, within the modernistic *Zeitgeist*, of Picasso and James Joyce – all this lay ten years back and more.

In 1922 Hermann Scherchen performed *Pierrot Lunaire*, and Furtwängler conducted the Five Orchestral Pieces Op. 16 at a Berlin Philharmonic Orchestra concert the same year, while the codification of Schoenberg's so-called 'twelve-tone technique' was first embodied in pieces written in 1923. The Berlin Academy was well acquainted with the revolutionary credentials of the man they appointed the following year.

Not that Schoenberg's way was immediately seized upon as the only path forward – the contemporary music of composers as diverse as Stravinsky, Bartók, Prokofiev and Kurt Weill is enough to show that. And although there have been many composers in successive generations who have taken the serial twelve-tone method as a springboard for their creative activity, it is little closer to claiming a unique validity today than it was at the time of its invention. It leads to a markedly cerebral, almost rational music, abstract in tendency and thus described as 'expressionist', with disjointed melodies and discordant harmonies, as far removed as possible from the sensuousness of impressionism and romanticism.

This anti-romanticism, a natural ally of the Neue Sachlichkeit of the mid-1920s, was a natural expression of the age and shared above all by the younger generation, the protesters against the discredited values of the past. It compelled a radical rethink of the theory and practice of music – and not only music. One could acknowledge Schoenberg as a driving force without becoming a Schoenbergian. In fact, although Schoenberg did not stop his students from using the twelve-tone method, he did not teach it in his classes but based his methodology on the classics. Never did he claim to hold the key that would unlock all doors, and his personal tastes in modern music reached from Bartók to Charles Ives, from Shostakovich to Gershwin. As he once observed, there is still a great deal to be said in the key of C major.

Schoenberg stayed at the Academy until 1933, when as a prominent Jewish purveyor of 'degenerate' music, he was forced into exile. He died in Los Angeles in 1951. During these eight years in Berlin he wrote the one-act opera *Von heute auf morgen*, the third string quartet and the Variations for Orchestra (1926–8), all twelve-tone works. Above all he began work on his masterpiece, the opera *Moses und Aron*, most of which, however, was written outside Germany.

In 1925 Schoenberg joined the Academy in Berlin. This was the year of the first performance of Alban Berg's *Wozzeck* in the Staatsoper. And it was the year the twenty-five-year-old Kurt Weill wrote the work that brought

122. Manuscript of the 'Moritat' of Mackie Messer from the Brecht-Weill *Die Dreigroschenoper*, 1928.

him to the fore in contemporary German music – the expressionist one-act *Der Protagonist*.

Weill, son of a Jewish cantor in Dessau, joined Busoni's master class at the Academy of Arts in 1920 and quickly made a name for himself as the self-sure young composer of 'difficult' music in a non-tonal style that put him in the avant-garde company of Schoenberg, Hindemith and, at times, Stravinsky. After a few earlier, smaller pieces, he wrote a formidable violin concerto in 1924, then set about turning Georg Kaiser's black expressionist tragedy *Der Protagonist* into an opera, a harsh, unyielding work in a thoroughly modern idiom of which he had made himself master. A few years later he wrote a companion-piece, this time a comedy, also to a text by Kaiser, called *Der Zar lässt sich photographieren* ('The Tsar Has His Photograph Taken').

Then, apparently set on this modernistic musical course, he met Brecht one evening in 1927 in a Berlin wine-bar, and the whole direction of his life changed. A famous collaboration between poet and composer followed, a collaboration for ever associated with *Die Dreigroschenoper*, the most perfect epitome of its time and place (Ill. 122).

It is, of course, not 'real' opera at all. Like *The Beggar's Opera*, it is a play with interjected songs, songs branded through and through with Weill's trademark – a fiendishly clever blend of sentimentality and spikiness, like the Berliners themselves, that creates its own jazzy world of delicious decadence.

Jazz filled the air of the 1920s. At an unsophisticated, consumer level, it offered relief from the recent traumas of war and inflation, rousing the Golden Twenties to dance their way, light-heartedly, light-headedly, through the world of their Americanised society. For the 'serious' composer it offered a novel assortment of melodic and above all rhythmic elements that they could use to invigorate their music in moments of frivolity or ironic detachment – moments which Weill, one among many, was adept at exploiting.

Die Dreigroschenoper embodies the second, 'post-modernist' Weill. In the few years left before the Republic collapsed, a third Weill had just time to show himself – a Weill devoted as ever to music theatre but now absorbed in full-blown opera. In 1929, also with Brecht, came what is in many ways his masterpiece – *Aufstieg und Fall der Stadt Mahagonny* ('Rise and Fall of the City of Mahagonny'), a formally 'conventional' number opera of recitatives, arias (including the popular 'Alabama Song' and its fellows), duets, ensembles and orchestral interludes. Also fully fledged opera is *Die Bürgschaft* ('The Pledge'), first performed in the Städtische Oper in Berlin in 1932. Nothing symbolises more strikingly Weill's versatility, and at the same time the bewildered public admiration that he must have provoked, than the discovery that, while *Die Dreigroschenoper* was still playing to full houses in one part of the city, a double bill of *Der Protagonist* and *Der Zar lässt sich photographieren* was being performed in the Städtische Oper. Was this really one and the same man, people wondered?

A month after the Reichstag fire Weill escaped from Germany while he still could, finding a new family home with Lotte Lenya in New York and a new musical home on Broadway. That was the fourth and final incarnation of the chameleonic Weill – the Weill of musicals. He died in 1950, a mere fifty years old, an American citizen and proud to be so.

Obedient to the spirit of the progressive company he kept, Weill always had his mind on opening the experience of art to a wider public, cutting short its confinement to a privileged middle-class elite. He did not see in music, as Brecht saw in literature, a means of changing society but he always emphasised the social dimension of art and the artist's social responsibility, and a didactic streak ran through him no less than through Brecht. The didactic intent also extended to music for children, who could be introduced to an ideological principle through the text and at the same time given a direct musical experience. The Brecht–Weill *Jasager* ('Yea-Sayer'), called a 'school opera', does just that.

This is practical music-making, crisp and to the point, in the spirit of Neue Sachlichkeit, a functional music focused on the needs of society, employing calculated, impersonal means the antithesis of the emotional, self-projecting manner of romanticism. In its critical detachment and its rejection of emotional involvement, Weill has created the musical correlative of Brecht's epic drama – gestic music, as he called it.

It is also to the world of Neue Sachlichkeit that the last of the important composers working in Berlin in the years of the Weimar Republic belongs – Paul Hindemith.

Born near Frankfurt, Hindemith was offered a position as teacher of composition at the Berlin Hochschule für Musik in 1927 at the age of thirty-two. A distinguished viola player, he was already seen as a leader of the

German avant-garde, adopting a cool, anti-romantic style dismissed by some as mechanical and soulless, greeted by others as an intellectual challenge to clarity of thought and purpose. 'A composer today', Hindemith maintained, 'should write only if he knows the purpose he is writing for. The days of composing for the sake of composing are probably gone for ever.' To accompany this radical philosophy he promoted an ideal of active participation in the musical act, an accessible music for performing amateurs, an ideal that would restore the eighteenth-century unity of composer, performer and listener. Hence the use of the term 'neo-classical' to characterise this music; hence too the extensive use, by Hindemith himself and others, of a contrapuntal style that requires the involvement of a set of performers all on an equal footing, a style that also takes account of the fashionable idioms of jazz. In its turn this movement led away from the production of opulent, large-scale orchestral canvases in the Strauss–Debussy mould to a preoccupation with more austere forms such as trios, quartets and chamber groups in general, as well as with choral music, genre *par excellence* for the participation of amateurs.

Such was the philosophy on which Hindemith had staked his reputation in the earlier 1920s. His compositions, along with those of other *enfants terribles*, featured regularly in the international festivals of modern music at Donaueschingen and Baden-Baden, taking their place in the distinguished company of Stravinsky, Milhaud, Alban Berg, Bartók and others. In the year before coming to Berlin he had completed his largest work to date, the opera *Cardillac*, based on E. T. A. Hoffmann's story *Das Fräulein von Scudery*.

Like the precise, clinical outlines and textures of his own music Hindemith demanded from his students at the Hochschule clarity of purpose in the pieces they wrote – who was going to perform them and who was going to listen to them. This philosophy led to the invention of the term *Gebrauchsmusik*, 'music for use', which has become a Hindemith trademark – a counterpart to the philosophy of form and function that informed the activity of the artists and craftsmen of the contemporary Bauhaus.

A characteristic piece of such music from Hindemith's early years in Berlin is *Wir bauen eine Stadt* ('Let's Build a City'), a successor to the Weill–Brecht *Jasager* written the year before. But this 'school opera' was not only to be performed by schoolchildren, it was also created by them, in cooperation with Hindemith – the work of a socialist-style collective proceeding by criticism and emendation, further criticism and further emendation, until a final state of satisfaction, or exhaustion, was reached.

Alongside this and other *Gebrauchsmusik* Hindemith, a very private man, continued to write substantial works for symphony orchestra. Although he did not hold radical political views, and was not a Jew, the Nazis distrusted him. In 1934 a radio ban was put on his works. But he let another three years of Nazism go by before realising the impossibility of his position. In 1937 he resigned from the Hochschule and decided to leave the country, almost unobtrusively, to make a new home in Switzerland. Most of his contemporaries – Schoenberg, Eisler, Weill, Dessau, Křenek and the rest – did not have the luxury of choice.

NAZI BERLIN

'Ein Volk, Ein Reich, Ein Führer'

Perhaps the cruellest paradox in the short life of the Weimar Republic is that what was politically so inept, so depressing and ultimately so tragic should sustain so varied and so brilliant a culture. That culture was nationwide. But Berlin had become its centre. As Zuckmayer said, 'Once you had Berlin, you had the world.' And once you lost Berlin, you lost the world.

The Weimar world and its capital were lost in the Reichstag elections of September 1930, when the National Socialist vote rose from a paltry 800,000 to almost $6\frac{1}{2}$ million, against a background of 3 million unemployed. Two years later it had become $13\frac{1}{2}$ million votes and 6 million unemployed. In January 1933 Hindenburg appointed Adolf Hitler Chancellor of Germany. But democracy had already been dead for over two years. The Nazis were left just to mutilate the corpse.

Yet the murder had not taken place secretly or reluctantly. Hitler's aims had been public knowledge since *Mein Kampf*, published ten years earlier. The Nazi ideology – the creation of the Grossdeutsches Reich, the eugenics of the Master Race, the eradication of the Jews and all the other obscenities – was an open book, there for all to read. Parliament, said Hitler, was only a means to an end – the end being 'the liberation of the German Volk'. That sounded highly desirable to the millions who decided that the National Socialists were the party to vote for.

Nor dare one overlook the intellectual circles that regarded Nazi barbarities as temporary excesses in an otherwise sound political programme, or who saw the whole movement as an aberration that would soon burn itself out. 'Let it run its course,' said former Foreign Minister Baron Neurath nonchalantly, as late as 1934. 'In five years nobody will remember it.' 'We'll just wait for the storm to blow over,' Döblin reassured his friends, as he set out for the Swiss border in 1933.

In the beginning it was mainly the political opponents of Hitler who left. The Reichstag fire of February 1933 became the pretext for rounding up left-wing intellectuals like Carl von Ossietzky, editor of *Die Weltbühne*, the poet Erich Mühsam and the dramatist Friedrich Wolf, whose fate led Brecht, Anna Seghers and Ludwig Renn to draw the obvious conclusions. As Hitler consolidated his power and anti-Semitic measures became more vicious, the number of Jewish refugees grew, though many Jews, too, patriotic shopkeepers and tailors, found it impossible to believe, until it was too late, that their own and their rulers' interests were not the same. In 1933 Berlin had a Jewish population of some 200,000. By 1945 only 5,000 were left – though even this tragically small number seems a miracle.

Between 1933 and the beginning of the Second World War over 1,300 writers and poets left their German homeland for a new life in foreign and often unwelcoming countries. Some had established reputations that assured them at least of recognition – Brecht, Arnold Zweig, Thomas and Heinrich Mann, Stefan George, Feuchtwanger, Stefan Zweig, Georg Kaiser, Franz Werfel. The majority – small-town journalists, critics, free-lance writers – had lost their livelihood when freedom of expression died.

The loss to music was perhaps even greater, from the famous – Schoenberg, Weill, Eisler, Bruno Walter, Otto Klemperer, Erich Kleiber – to the anonymous rank-and-file Jewish musicians in the country's great orchestras. Max Reinhardt, Piscator, Fritz Kortner, Peter Lorre, Fritz Lang from theatre and film; George Grosz, Feininger, Gropius and Mies van der Rohe in art and architecture; Freud, Einstein, Max Born, scholars such as Erich Auerbach and Ernst Cassirer – the list is endless and the effect of their flight on German cultural life immeasurable. 'You have brought with you everything of that Germany which we love and respect,' wrote Romain Rolland in welcoming the exiles. 'You bring the spirit of Goethe and Beethoven, Lessing and Marx.'

So what was the spirit they left behind? In one sense it was the same spirit that they had taken with them. Whatever the anti-human doctrines of fascism, those who had plotted their intellectual course from the fixed points of Goethe and Beethoven, and felt no immediate compulsion to leave their country, continued on their traditional path. The idealist tradition of the nineteenth century had lost none of its validity. Unpleasant though some of what was going on outside might be, one could learn to come to terms with it and take refuge in the inspiration of great minds. The architect Mies van der Rohe, for example, and even the maligned composer Paul Hindemith felt under no personal threat in 1933 and considered it entirely possible that the new authorities would leave them to pursue their careers with little interference. Even the Jews left in Germany retained their right of association in the Jewish Cultural League founded in 1933, which published, albeit after Nazi scrutiny of its contents, a newsletter devoted to Jewish matters. The Nazi bureaucracy oversaw events with the disciplined intensity they had inherited from their Prussian forebears, with Berlin slipping back into the authoritarian ways it had not forgotten since the days of Empire.

So there arose a state within a state. On the outside was the repressive dictatorship that defined every aspect of public life and demanded obedience to every official prescription. By the summer of 1933 virtually the whole structure of constitutional government had been dismantled. Political parties, trade unions, industry – all had been banned, subverted, bribed or coerced into cooperation in the first stages of *Gleichschaltung*, the subsumption of all aspects of national life under the central directives of the National Socialist Party. The individual mind was sucked into the same vortex and the sense of new allegiance to the *Volk* personalised by an individual attachment to the charismatic Führer himself. Loyalty, service and unity – traditional Prussian virtues – would restore national pride and power. In the Reichstag elections of November 1933 there was only one party to vote for, and almost

90 per cent of the electorate (less in Berlin, to the Berliners' credit) voted for it. By the time they realised what they had voted for, it was too late.

But this outer shell was in reality a sham. To be sure, millions hailed Hitler as their economic saviour, the leader who cured unemployment overnight and restored the nation's self-esteem. And there were thinking men who for one reason or another found it not just expedient but even acceptable to make their peace with their surroundings. But many, too, sheltered behind the noble traditions of the past, clinging to the spirit of Goethe and Beethoven, as Romain Rolland had called it. Turning, or trying to turn, a blind eye to the inhuman realities around them, they convinced themselves that the times called rather for the private presentation of the good than the public condemnation of the evil. The boldest spirits, who would not keep silent, paid the ultimate price.

The Nazi Canon of Literature

Berlin remained the administrative centre of the country, and it was in the capital that the Nazis established the bodies that would supervise the execution of their policies. To coordinate control of the media of culture Hitler charged Joseph Goebbels, Minister of Education and Propaganda, with the formation of a Reichskulturkammer, a censorship office with seven departments individually responsible for literature, radio, theatre, film, music, the visual arts and the press. An idea of what to expect came early in 1933 when leading liberal members of the Prussian Academy of Arts were expelled and others resigned. Thomas and Heinrich Mann, Ricarda Huch, Werfel, Georg Kaiser, Schoenberg, Franz Schreker, Käthe Kollwitz – these were only the most famous. To drive the point home a ceremonial bonfire of 'non-Aryan' books took place in front of the university library, at which the works of Jewish, left-wing and other 'un-German' writers, from Heine to Freud, from Heinrich Mann to Ossietzky and Tucholsky, were thrown into the flames. 'Those who start by burning books', wrote Heine a hundred years earlier, 'end up by burning people.'

Not surprisingly there was little difficulty in filling the vacant places in the Academy with more tractable members. Most were opportunists anxious to further their careers by producing the kind of literature the regime wished to promote. But the situation also threw up the occasional example of a respected and influential figure who, for reasons not easy to discern, came out in open support of the Nazis in a way that subsequently damaged his reputation beyond repair. Such a figure, an object lesson in intellectual failure in the face of totalitarianism, was Gottfried Benn.

Long resident in Berlin, a leading expressionist lyric poet from the decade of the Great War, one of the many who owed their *Weltanschauung* and their passion to Nietzsche, Benn had always had a high profile. Obsessed in the early 1930s with the threat posed by international communism and disgusted, almost gleefully, with the failure of democratic republicanism, he demanded political solidarity, a restoration of national pride, an appeal to inspiration and charisma and the acceptance of a concomitant measure of authority. This he made public in 1933, voluntarily and under no pressure, in a Berlin radio talk called *The New State and the Intellectuals*. The state, he said, recalling Hegel, mattered more than the individual: liberalism and internationalism were over, and the future, biologically as well as spiritually and intellectually, lay with the National Socialists. Small wonder that he had difficulty in clearing his name after the war.

At no time did the National Socialists produce anything that might be graced with the name of an aesthetic. Censorship took care of the negative aspect of national policy, ensuring that nothing subversive or critical of Party orthodoxy saw the light of day. Writers who overstepped the mark could be expelled from the official writers' union, the Reichsschriftumskammer, or forbidden to write, or simply arrested. Publishers were given black lists of banned works and authors, libraries were told what they could and could not distribute, and bookshops what they could and could not sell. With the newspaper world under the control of Goebbels' Ministry of Propaganda, the system was virtually impenetrable. To seal it completely, the cultural autonomy enjoyed by the individual provinces up till 1933 was abolished and policy decreed centrally from Berlin. All in the name of the German *Volk*.

The associations of this magic word reach back into the nineteenth century, and the Nazis knew it. It invoked the romantic world of folksong, of Germanic legend, of the divine power of nature, coupled with a longing for national political unity, so long delayed, finally won in 1871 and now, under Hitler, triumphantly restated. As an idealistic concept *Volk* was both inclusive and exclusive: inclusive in that it represented the summation of characteristics inherited and shared by a given people, here the German people, as decreed by fate and the facts of creation; exclusive in that this body of characteristics is unique to its heirs and cannot be shared by those of other racial origins. The Jews, therefore, cannot belong to the German *Volk*, since their roots lie elsewhere. Membership of the German *Volk* is in the blood, and physical expression of this belongingness is the occupation of the German homeland – hence the phrase *Blut und Boden*, 'blood and soil', as a metaphor for what was at stake.

To inculcate *Blut und Boden* values in the minds of their captive population, the Nazis adopted a dual strategy. One line of attack, the obvious one, was to promote contemporary literature in their chosen image, works compounded of crude sentimentality and primitive nationalism, with an optimistic, honest-to-God morality calculated to be irresistible. Sometimes writers of a religious cast of mind could be induced to recognise Hitler as the embodiment of a national resurgence that would bring an automatic solution to the social problems facing the country. The cult of the Führer, indeed, had from the beginning a mystical, religious aura about it, like his impact on the assembled thousands at mass rallies of the Party. Other writers revived the war novel, which allowed the values of comradeship and self-sacrifice to be portrayed as the noblest virtues to which a man can aspire.

To complement approved literature by living writers Goebbel's Ministry of Propaganda put out directives on how the literature of the past was to be interpreted. The greatness of National Socialism, it was argued, was prefigured in the great 'Aryan' culture of earlier ages; the onus lay on the present to discover these points of reference and arrive at a proper understanding of what tradition and historical continuity mean.

As a necessary prelude to this, Jewish writers had to be removed from the scene, chief among them Moses Mendelssohn, founder of the German Enlightenment, and Heine, target of the Nazis' most vituperative attacks. Nor did the anti-Semitic crusade stop at Jewish writers themselves. Endless researches were conducted into the company kept by non-Jewish authors, and if they were found to have Jewish friends, the incriminating fact was made public. The reputations of Friedrich Schlegel, Schleiermacher and the others who frequented the salons of Rahel Levin and Henriette Herz in the early nineteenth century could be subtly undermined in this way.

One of the early victims of perversely selective interpretation was Schiller. *Wallenstein*, for example, was treated as a military spectacular and a swathe of glorious Prussian history, while *Wilhelm Tell* emerged as a demonstration of the assertion of the popular will. Goethe was less easy to pervert but even here a trawl through his works led to slogans like 'Goethe the Nature Lover' and 'Goethe the Pagan Hedonist', which could be directly referred to the Nazi cult of a healthy body in the great open air, or made to reinforce the anti-Christian groundswell of the movement. No less easily wrenched from its context was Goethe's concept of organic growth, evolution under the pressure of in-dwelling, inalienable forces, which was taken to imply a belief in the *Volk* and its right to self-perpetuation.

The romantics, too, were rich in *Volk* values. The joys of nature in Eichendorff; national political sentiment in Fichte, Kleist and Hölderlin; folksong and the folk-tales of the Grimm brothers – all this could be readily pillaged.

A very special ally was Nietzsche, with his scorn of culture, his 'will to power' and his vision of the *Übermensch*, all couched in his intemperate, inflammatory language. The Superman became magnified into the Master Race, and a sub-human class of *Untermenschen* created. And what better endorsement of the policy of the removal of the Jews than the anti-Semitic tirades of Richard Wagner, defender of the concept of *Volk* and trustee of a truly German art in his noble *Meistersinger von Nürnberg*?

As the Reichsschriftumskammer controlled the written, so the Reichstheaterkammer controlled the spoken, literary word. The emigration of Jewish actors and producers had left the theatre in a parlous state. The Theaterkammer took over control of the leading theatres in the city, dismissed the remaining Jewish personnel, installed its own nominees in positions of authority and established its own repertoire of plays. Berlin became something of a theatrical shop-window in which the regime could show the world how assiduously it cared for the nation's cultural heritage.

At the beginning regulations made for state and municipal theatres had not applied to the private institutions that survived. But from 1934 all theatres were put under a single regime and the process of *Gleichschaltung* made complete, because, as the decree put it, 'theatre must be regarded as an agency of the nation's education'.

It proved surprisingly (unsurprisingly?) easy to find men of stature willing to work to the requirements of the new regime. Gründgens became director of the Schauspielhaus in 1934, Heinrich George took over the Schiller-Theater, and the once revolutionary Karlheinz Martin, the Volksbühne. Hermann Göring, Minister President of Prussia and titular head of all Prussian state theatres, observed drily: 'It is easier to turn a great artist into a decent National Socialist than to make a great artist out of a humble Party member.'

Whereas genuine men of the theatre may have controlled the productions themselves, the decisions on what to perform were taken in the offices of the Party. The theatre, in a German tradition that went back centuries, was seen as a medium of education as well as a place of entertainment, so the aim had to be mass audiences in full houses. On the one hand were hack plays on historical, *Blut und Boden* or anti-Semitic themes, dispensing a homespun morality and an heroic patriotism. On the other stood such German classics as could be manipulated to serve a nationalist cause, like Kleist's *Die Hermannsschlacht* or Hebbel's *Nibelungen*. Other classics were banned – Lessing's *Nathan der Weise*, for instance, because of its noble Jewish hero, or Gerhart Hauptmann's *Die Weber*, which exuded pessimism and gloom at a time when the workers needed positive motivation. *The Merchant of Venice*, by contrast, was the perfect vehicle for conveying the unpleasant features of international Jewry, although the number of foreign works performed was deliberately restricted.

Hardly to be characterised as drama, yet an invocation of the *Volk* in dramatic form, were the bizarre events called by the Nazis *Thingspiele* – mass open-air pageants, part military tattoo, part pseudo-religious ceremony, with patriotic speeches delivered by characters in costume and with massed bands and choirs leading an audience of thousands in an act of state worship. Special areas in open country were laid out for these celebrations. One such, an arena built on the model of a Greek theatre and holding 20,000 people, was erected in 1936, the year of the Berlin Olympics, on the edge of the Grunewald in Berlin to a design by Speer and is still in use today for pop concerts and other mass spectaculars.

The cinema was subjected to the same pressures. Film was the mass medium of the day, cheap and permanently on offer in a way that theatre could not match, and its influence as a means of communication was too great to be left to chance. Goebbels saw it as an instrument of education 'at least as influential as the primary school', as he put it. Besides that, the technical skills that had been developed in the studios at Babelsberg, on the outskirts of Berlin, in the days of great pioneers of the silent film like Murnau and Fritz Lang gave the Nazi film industry a flying start. And although that industry was a German industry, producing German wares for a German market, its technical excellence bolstered the nation's reputation around the world.

Gleichschaltung of the cinema mirrored that of the theatre. In the early years occasional films from abroad with Jewish actors in starring roles found their way into prominent cinemas; the result was usually a public reprimand in the next day's newspapers and the film's withdrawal. When the British film *Catherine the Great* was shown at the Berlin Capitol in 1934, the Nazis engineered a rent-a-crowd demonstration of protest against the Jewish star of the film, Elisabeth Bergner, who had left the country the previous year and found asylum in England. The banning of further performances could then be presented as the official response to popular clamour, accompanied by a display of feigned indignation at this attempt by the Jews 'to creep back into the German film world by the back door'. By the Nazis' own figures, before 1933 'non-Aryans' made up some 50 per cent of all filmwriters and 40 per cent of directors – a situation that could not be tolerated.

Films made under National Socialist auspices, both before and during the Second World War, followed predictable lines. Nature films in praise of German mountains and German forests, domestic soap operas acted out by smiling village communities enjoying healthy minds in healthy bodies, adventure stories to illustrate the virtues of German courage and German heroism – all the trappings of the *Blut und Boden* world were there. The spirit was idealist, the manner realist. This was no time for vague exhortations and misty visions. Nor was personal interpretation welcome, let alone criticism, and pressure could be brought to bear on even the best-known names not to step out of line. The great Emil Jannings, after being warned for questioning official edicts, was eventually prepared to go on record as saying: 'Art has always served practical needs, and it is the function of cinema, as the most powerful medium of dramatic expression, to promote by its choice of subject matter a sense of national community.'

Since this national community, the *Volk*, could conveniently be addressed by identifying and stigmatising those who were not *Volk*, an important 'educational' role fell to anti-Semitic films like *Die Rothschilds* (1940), a grotesque chronicle of the rise of Nathan Rothschild from ghetto con-man to international banker – two occupations shown as differing only in degree of mendacity. The Berlin *Lokal-Anzeiger* hailed it as 'a parallel to the historical conflicts being played out in our time'.

Even more infamous is the Nazi version of Feuchtwanger's novel, *Jud Süss* (1940), a racist remake of the film produced in England in 1932 with Conrad Veidt in the title role. This presented the hero in too favourable a light for the Nazis to tolerate. What Goebbels wanted was a monster who would stand as a perverse embodiment of everything Jewish, a character against whom the whole population could be incited to vent their rage. This is precisely what the director Veit Harlan gave him. Harlan's *Jud Süss*, like the other anti-Semitic films of the time, played its own part in the preparation of the ground for the 'Final Solution to the Jewish Problem' in 1942. Harlan stood trial after the war for crimes against humanity but was acquitted for lack of evidence.

The kind of popular hero the regime had in mind to promote was portrayed in films such as *Hans Westmar, Einer von vielen* ('Hans Westmar, One of Many'), a dramatisation of the life of the thug and Nazi martyr Horst Wessel, and *SA-Mann Brand*, a primitive, sentimental concoction of anti-communism, devotion to the Hitler Youth, street violence and self-sacrifice to the Führer. 'The day of national awakening has arrived,' concluded the *Völkischer Beobachter* in its review of *SA-Mann Brand* in 1933: 'Germany has been set free.' Quite what Germany had been set free from was a question few cared to ask, the less so as the freedoms around them were being inexorably reined in. But through its pursuit of escapism and its revelation of inspiring achievement film could bring excitement into humdrum lives, enhance a sense of personal and communal well-being and intensify the feeling of devotion to the Führer.

Nothing conveyed this mood more spectacularly than the documentaries commissioned by Hitler from Leni Riefenstahl, a Berliner through and through. *Triumph of the Will*, a record of the Nazi rally in Nuremberg in 1934, employed a battery of thirty-two cameras and a crew of 120 to choreograph a mammoth display of the unity and ambition of the Nazi movement. The contentment of family life, a happy and healthy younger generation, the cooperation of soldiers and workers, with Hitler presiding over the resurgence of the *Volk* like a Wagnerian hero to the accompaniment of massed bands and choirs – such was the pageant that Riefenstahl offered her Führer. A similar extravaganza, a worship of the body beautiful, accompanied the Berlin Olympic Games of 1936, overwhelming the senses with sheer visual power while appealing at the same time to the aesthetic consciousness.

However strenuously Riefenstahl later protested her innocence of any intention to glorify the Third Reich, the impression her revolutionary films leave is hardly one of professional exercises carried out by a dispassionate technician. Admiration of the how cannot disguise the nature of the what.

'Whether 'tis nobler in the mind . . .': The Literature of Inner Emigration

Hitler's accession to power on 30 January 1933 – by legal means, as he never failed to insist – caught democratic Germany unawares. The choice was a stark reality: to stay or to leave – though for the humble many the financial implications made it no choice at all. Writers who insisted on their right to speak openly could do so only from a place of safety outside the country. Those who stayed knew that they could survive only by avoiding attention. They met secretly with their fellows, circulating their work by underground channels, while some offered neutral material for publication, knowing that one injudicious word could bring the Gestapo to the door. A mutual suspicion grew up between those who left and those who stayed. The former believed, like Thomas Mann, that anything written in Nazi Germany could not but be tainted by its poisonous environment and should be pulped. Those who stayed accused Mann and his like of deserting them and claimed that they alone, preservers of their spiritual integrity through the years of the Nazi tyranny, were entitled to speak for Germany after the war. Sometimes the antithesis was put the other way round, those who spent the Nazi years in their homeland being portrayed as having by their presence alone given tacit support and comfort to the regime.

Such issues still provoke argument, largely because they quickly merge into that historical complex of personal, social and political problems that make up the 'German question'. But there did survive during these years a literature that refused to conform to Nazi *Gleichschaltung* and in various skilful ways kept a humanistic morality and a sense of common decency alive. It is the literature of what has come to be known as 'inner emigration'.

If his material existence were assured, a writer could withdraw more or less completely from the literary scene and survive in silence. Another might content himself with harmless essays and reviews for specialised readerships; bolder spirits could risk their careers, even their lives, by seeking outlets for surreptitious criticism. Inner emigration took many forms. It was never a movement, and the nearest it came to describing anything beyond a variety of personal initiatives was in terms of a shared political or religious allegiance, or a predilection for certain literary forms.

As the centre in which the organs of state power were concentrated, from the Reichskulturkammer to the Gestapo, Berlin was the last place where any writer would stay who had it in mind to publish independent literature. In the 1920s journalists and men of letters had flocked here in search of the stimulus and excitement it offered. Now the dead hand of dictatorship and despotism lay across the city. Professional associations had been disbanded or reconstituted with a compliant body of Nazi sympathisers, like the Preussische Akademie der Dichtkunst. The best hope for survival lay in escape to remote areas of the countryside, where many had already chosen to live and where one was not confronted with the characteristically brutal architecture being put up in the name of the Thousand-Year Reich.

Hans Fallada, author of *Kleiner Mann, was nun?* and an archetypal urban novelist, bought a farmhouse in rural Mecklenburg and tried to put from his mind what was going on in the country by continuing to write novels focused on social life in the Republic that the Nazis had murdered. A born storyteller, he left on his death in 1947 two semi-autobiographical, semi-documentary novels on life in the Third Reich – *Jeder stirbt für sich allein* ('Each Man Dies His Own Death') and *Der Alpdruck* ('The Nightmare') – which describe how men struggled to preserve their humanity in an inhuman environment and how they could face the world after the terror had passed.

The career of Erich Kästner, also a Berlin novelist of the Weimar Republic, shows how fickle the ways of the Nazis could be. A phenomenally successful writer in the early 1930s, especially of children's books, he was in Switzerland on the fateful 27 February 1933 when the Nazis set fire to the Reichstag building, and could have stayed abroad. Instead he returned to Berlin 'in order to be an eye-witness', as he put it, convinced that Hitler would soon be swept aside. Suspicious of his foreign connections, the Gestapo interrogated him on several occasions, and his *Three Men in the Snow* had to be published in Zurich. At the same time his plays were still being performed, the film of *Emil and the Detectives* was shown without criticism and he was even invited to write screenplays for the UFA film company. After the war, an honoured figure with a legendary reputation, he went back to his first love, writing satirical texts for Die Schaubude in Munich, the first post-war German cabaret.

A very different 'inner emigrant' was the expressionist poet and herald of the Third Reich, Gottfried Benn. Regarded with distrust by the Nazis, who were always suspicious of intellectuals, he retreated step by step from his fascist position. When in 1936 he published a selection of his poems, including items displaying an ugly, expressionist, 'un-German' imagery, the Reichsschriftumskammer expelled him. The rest of the Nazi era, including the war, he spent as a medical officer in the army. When he returned to Berlin in 1945, he resumed his literary career as poet and essayist in a nihilistic mood that met with a ready response from the disillusioned post-war generation.

Still of interest in this context is Benn's essay of 1943 'Zum Thema Geschichte' ('On the Subject of History'), in which he puts forward a diagnosis of Nazism not as a single demented outburst but as a product of incompatible forces endemic to the German national character. Provincialism and a dreamy subjectivism confront a passionate yearning for national self-expression and an iron determination to achieve it. It is the old antithesis of subjective and objective, of the centrifugal and the centripetal, the old romantic dilemma that haunted the nineteenth century.

Fallada, Kästner and Benn endured the Third Reich by what might be called empirical means – individual strategies devised on an *ad hoc* basis and centred on personal survival. Others sustained themselves through faith in an ideology, sometimes political, sometimes religious. Günther Weisenborn, who had lived in Berlin after the success there of his anti-war play *U-Boot S4* in 1928, became an active member of the communist resistance. Jailed in 1942, he was set free at the end of the war and honoured the anti-Nazi resistance movement in a moving collection of documents from the years 1933 to 1945 published as *Der lautlose Aufstand* ('The Noiseless Insurrection').

An even more vital source of inspiration and solace than politics in these days of darkness was religion. Under the guise of writing a literature of a religious or allegorical nature a number of bold spirits ventured to write poetry and fiction whose true meaning, camouflaged under deliberately misleading external features, carried a message of hope for those who knew where to look for it. The censor could sometimes be amazingly obtuse, and works saw the light of day which one would have expected only to find circulating secretly among friends or to have resulted in the author's arrest.

Two such works, spiritually related, are *Der Grosstyrann und das Gericht* ('The Great Tyrant and the Court of Justice') and *Am Himmel wie auf Erden* ('In Heaven as on Earth') by Werner Bergengruen, a Christian writer who lived in Berlin during the Weimar years and the first half of the Nazi period. Superficially they are both exciting historical novels. The latter, set in sixteenth-century Brandenburg, centres on the conflict between the Elector Joachim I and his people at a moment of crisis which threatens the survival of the state. *Der Grosstyrann*, set in an imaginary Italian court at the time of the Renaissance, portrays the temptations facing those who wield power and the guilty credulity of their victims, a combination that produces a society which only a return to Christian values can save from destruction. What begin as political issues are resolved as religious issues.

But the courageous parallels to the Germany of the day, starting with the warning that the Tyrant himself will eventually have to answer before God for his deeds, can hardly be missed. At the same time Bergengruen would have us accept a corporate guilt for the whole of mankind. No one will escape the day of judgement.

Christian values, absolute in their demands and boldly confrontational in their contemporary relevance, also permeate the tragic figure of Jochen Klepper, remembered for his classic novel *Der Vater* ('The Father'). The hero of this historical romance – it is hardly a biography – is King Friedrich Wilhelm I, father of Frederick the Great, whom Klepper invests with Christian virtues at odds with the authoritarian, militaristic qualities that the Nazis identified in a Prussian leader. Klepper was removed from the

Reichsschrifttumskammer in the year *Der Vater* was published, an honour shared by Reinhold Schneider, Bergengruen and others of the dwindling number of non-conformist writers who dared to put pen to paper. Over the ten years before his suicide in 1942, as he struggled to keep his Christian humanitarianism alive while his Jewish wife and her daughter waited for the extermination camp, Klepper kept a diary. Published posthumously in the 1950s, it is one of the most moving personal documents to come out of these years of the Nazi tyranny.

To some even more moving, given the circumstances of its genesis and the improbability of its survival, is the literature of concentration camp and prison, represented in Berlin by the *Moabiter Sonette* of Albrecht Haushofer. Haushofer's was an extraordinary career. An academic, an expert in political geography, he became a foreign policy adviser to Rudolf Hess, Hitler's deputy, was appointed Professor of Geopolitics in Berlin in 1940 and acted as a consultant to the German Foreign Ministry until 1941. Then he suddenly changed direction, withdrew from his work for the regime and joined the Christian resistance. Dismissed from his chair, he became a party to the plot of 20 July 1944 to assassinate Hitler and was sent to Moabit prison to await sentence. A few days before the end of the war an SS lynching mob broke into the prison and shot him. When his body was discovered, he was clutching in his hand a manuscript of poems which have come to be known as the Moabit sonnets – calm yet intense reflections on his past life, on prison, on the great figures of history and culture, on the future of mankind, all in strict sonnet form, from which they receive a discipline which could alone sustain them.

A Revolution Cast in Concrete: The Nazis and Architecture

It is tempting to see culture as coming to a fateful end in Berlin – indeed, in Germany as a whole – in 1933 and struggling uneasily to its feet in 1945. Many, from the most diverse of motives, would like to pretend that the intervening period represented an uncharacteristic and unique aberration, a product of circumstances so extreme and bizarre that they could not possibly recur. One moment Berlin is a cultural Mecca, the next it is the capital of barbarism.

The National Socialist revolution brought with it a 'revaluation of all values', in Nietzsche's phrase, which, as far as the dissemination of culture was concerned – the publication of literature, the exhibition of works of art – drove the old values underground. The Reichskulturkammer determined what was culture and what was not. One either conformed or withdrew into one's shell.

In an age of dictatorship and *Gleichschaltung* the architect will be under pressure to express through his designs the image that the regime has of itself and the values that it wishes to see put on public display. But he can work within such circumstances less precariously and under less tension than, say, the writer, who deals in ideas. Matters of form, construction, materials and the other constituent elements of architecture are handled in their own internal terms and challenge the architect's skills *sui generis*. He proceeds from the conditions of his commission but he need not share the beliefs of his patron. As a composer may write a mass without being a Catholic, so an architect can build a block of government offices or a sports stadium in the 1930s without being a Nazi. Indeed architecture and music, the two archetypal non-representational arts, find themselves side by side at the extremity where the arts of space and time meet.

There was, moreover, a good deal in the Nazi programmes to which many architects felt they could directly respond in professional terms. The Party prided itself on being both national and socialist. Men of national, conservative leanings could pursue traditional goals, aiming to achieve that sense of national unity which the Weimar Republic had manifestly failed to engender. Those for whom the word 'socialist' pointed the way forward, like the descendants of the Werkbund movement of arts and crafts, and those sympathetic to the Bauhaus ideals and the trends of European modernism, found an attraction in working towards an objective, functional architecture for the people *en masse*. The Nazis, for their part, had little difficulty in adopting this approach to their populist vision of the interests of the *Volk*, while from the early years of the regime a not inconsiderable number of teachers in colleges and university departments of architecture were prepared to endorse the Nazis' cultural policies.

The National Socialists had no theory of architecture – merely a collection of assorted prejudices held together by pseudo-historical references and analogies. Party ideologues such as Alfred Rosenberg, an architect by training and author of *The Myth of the Twentieth Century* – a work second in importance in the Nazi pantheon only to *Mein Kampf* – defined the current cult of monumentalism as a modern synthesis of the classical, the Gothic and the Germanic. Like a great war – to use the Prussian imagery beloved of the Nazis – it unites the nation, proclaims its destiny and symbolises its march into the future with a confidence equalled only by Antiquity and the Renaissance. 'Our buildings serve to consolidate our authority,' said the Führer. An architecture for its own sake had no place here.

Although the Nazis aimed at a pattern of architecture based on the heroic values of *Volk* and Fatherland, the various available styles were disposed in a hierarchy. At its head stood a monumental neo-classicism, with its axiality and its symmetry, its columns and porticos, the style prescribed for official and public buildings. The associations it wished to capture were the grandeur and authority of Greece and Rome – not only the inspiration of other totalitarian capitals of the time, like Rome and Moscow, but also the world from which countless communities in the United States had drawn the style of their civic buildings.

At the same time the neo-classical idiom enabled the Nazis to demonstrate their rejection of 1920s modernism in the name of the noble tradition that led back to Schinkel. In 1934 a competition was held for a new Reichsbank building behind the former royal palace in Berlin. The prize went to Mies van der Rohe for an uncompromisingly modernist design which Hitler refused to sanction. Instead he gave the commission to a hack architect, Heinrich Wolff, who produced an oppressive piece of neo-classicism that could stand as a prototype for 'totalitarian architecture' wherever totalitarianism ruled. It is a cruel architecture that crushes the spirit and compels submission. Hitler's first personal architect, Paul Ludwig Troost, who saw himself as a latter-day Schinkel, left examples of such work in the Nazi stronghold of Munich – the Haus der Deutschen Kunst, for instance – but not in Berlin.

Firmly committed to Berlin, on the other hand, was Troost's successor in Hitler's affections, still one of the more interesting and controversial figures among Nazi leaders – Albert Speer. Speer built little – he was more a town-planner and choreographer of public displays like the Party rallies in Nuremberg. But his megalomaniac designs, incorporating Hitler's own sketches, for a completely new city centre have a gruesome fascination. He planned a new north–south axis through the metropolis, seven kilometres long, which would intersect the existing east–west axis on the line of Unter den Linden near the Brandenburg Gate. The new axis, a site for ceremonies and parades, is dominated by a triumphal arch and by a huge Pantheon-like Grand Hall, to be the largest building in the world. Here was the new heart of the Thousand-Year Reich, a capital to be called Germania. All functionality and practicality have gone; only monumental architectural rhetoric remains, a rhetoric of world domination, of total war. It seems somehow appropriate that Hitler should have appointed Speer Minister of Armaments Production in 1942, and that the Nuremberg War Crimes Tribunal should have sentenced him to twenty years' imprisonment in 1945.

As the classical mode was considered appropriate for the institutions of the state, so housing developments, Hitler Youth hostels and other community centres were designed in traditional, folkloristic styles that echoed the *Blut und Boden* philosophy of attachment to the soil. 'In the beginning was the farmhouse,' said Troost – a rural symbol of patriotic devotion and a demonstration of both practical and aesthetic unity with its surroundings. A model of this devotion in a private dwelling was Göring's convivial hunting lodge Carinhall, in the woods north of Berlin, a ranch-like building with hewn oak beams and wood panelling, perfectly matched to its environment and frankly declamatory of its function.

Functionalism, displayed in predictable ways derived from the industrial processes of mass production, defines the third style in the Nazi hierarchy. A few fragments of this standardised testimony to the spirit of the Third Reich still survive in Berlin – Göring's Air Ministry in the Wilhelmstrasse (1935–6), designed by Ernst Sagebiel, who also did Tempelhof Airport; a wing of Goebbels' Ministry of Propaganda designed in 1933 by Speer (Ill. 123). A kind of poor man's classicism, found in representative buildings like Speer's new Reich Chancellery (1938–9) as in government offices and industrial buildings, it is a style which, ironically, looks with one eye in the direction of the glass-and-concrete modernism which Hitler ostentatiously rejected, while retaining a clear view of the authoritarian associations of monumentalism. Perhaps the two were not as far apart as they pretended.

At all events the architecture of Berlin between 1933 and 1945 drew extensively on the vocabulary of the Weimar era, which was itself no stranger to the investment of particular forms and styles, national and international, with ideological meaning. It is an architecture that cannot be abstracted from the historical continuum. At the same time it is one more paradigm of that so characteristic German phenomenon – the politicisation of art.

123. Model based on Albert Speer's vision of Berlin as a new metropolis, 1942.

Painting and Sculpture

'The spiritual renewal of the nation has led to the urgent reconsideration, in the visual arts as in other fields, of what constitutes the essence of the German personality . . . By calling on the evidence of earlier centuries, we can give support to the aspirations of our own age and establish their relevance in the overall historical scene.'

Pompous yet sinister words like these, uttered in 1935 by a prominent art historian of the time, convey the sort of future that faced artists in the Third Reich. The Reichskammer der bildenden Künste, responsible not only for painters and sculptors but also for decorative artists, draughtsmen, art dealers and teachers, registered its compulsory members and laid down the Party line. 'Only when the artist has become an indispensable contributor to the creative processes of the nation can one call his position a healthy one,' pontificated the President of the Chamber.

It quickly became evident what this sophistry meant. Art had to be naturalistic, objective and optimistic. Franz Marc's *Tower of Blue Horses* was rejected because horses are not blue. When Göring saw Leistikow's painting *Grunewald Lake*, he said: 'I am a huntsman and I know that the Grunewald does not look like that.' The banner of *Blut und Boden* was raised and painting and sculpture required to concentrate in an appropriately declamatory style on the subjects that reflected the values of the Master Race – happy workers on their farms, the joys of motherhood, the cult of athletic prowess, the naked warrior striding into battle for the Fatherland, men of the SA on the march.

Massive statues were carved of muscular heroes defiantly facing the future; in contrast allegorical paintings sought to project a contemporary meaning

124. *The Party* by Arno Breker, bronze, 1939.

while cultivating stylistic links with Baroque. Nudity was taken as the expression of a primeval classical idealism but often turned into a smirking eroticism. This was the speciality of Adolf Ziegler, Hitler's 'court painter', whose prurient obsession with the female nude earned him the sobriquet of 'The Master of the German Pubic Hair'.

Most of the works of art done under the Nazi aegis are hack material by forgotten artists likely to arouse little more than horrified mirth today. One name, however, does stand out – that of the sculptor Arno Breker. Leaving behind a romantic representationalism derived from Rodin, Breker recognised the opportunities stimulated by the rhetoric of the National Socialist message and committed his talents to the unity of the political and artistic will. He soon became Hitler's favourite sculptor, grounding his success in a calculated relationship between a piece of sculpture and its immediate surroundings – the monumental male and female athletes for the Berlin Olympic Stadium, for instance, and the political figure *The Party* for Speer's New Reich Chancellery in 1939, which embodies stylistic features both classically naturalistic and, in its flowing dynamism, Baroque (Ill. 124). At the same time it is an art which, for all its consummate skill, lives perilously close to the frontiers of Kitsch.

Those whose art did not conform – those, that is, who had for racial or political reasons not already fled the country – faced a bleak future. In 1937 the modern section of the Berlin National Gallery was closed and many of its abstract, non-naturalistic paintings, engravings and sculptures removed. Some were sold abroad to museums who knew great art when they saw it – Van Goghs, Gauguins, Cézannes, Braques, Picassos and other modern masters. Much was simply destroyed. Museums in the rest of the country were raided and a selection of the offending material put on public display, first in Munich, than in Berlin and other cities. 'Degenerate Art' the show was called, works of post-impressionists, expressionists, Dadaists – Liebermann, Kirchner, Beckmann, Kollwitz, Kandinsky, Schmidt-Rottluff and a host of others, all branded as specimens of 'cultural Bolshevism', negative in their attitude to the brave new Nazi world.

Indeed, the custodians of this world went on, not only were these works the very denial of what the age needed, they besmirched the national honour. Otto Dix, for example, had served in the trenches in the Great War. He returned haunted by the horrors he had seen and did a series of etchings depicting, not heroic German soldiers marching into battle but wounded men in agony, men with their arms and legs blown off, a soldier on leave ogling the prostitutes parading along a city street. Could such an insult to the cream of the nation's youth be tolerated?

But crowds flocked to this wonderful display of decadence, not, as the organisers claimed, in order to vent their scorn on the exhibits but out of sheer delight and because they feared this would be their last opportunity for a long while to see these masterpieces. Parallel to this show the Reichskammer also put on display, at another venue, paintings and sculptures in the

125. *Proclamation* by George Kolbe, bronze, 1937.

officially approved 'healthy' German idiom from which people were expected to derive their scale of values. But for every one visitor to this vulgar so-called Great German Art Exhibition sponsored by the Nazis, three enjoyed the products of degeneracy. A sophisticated public like the Berliners did not need to be told what to enjoy or what was good art and what was bad.

Kirchner sought refuge in Switzerland, Beckmann in Holland, Kokoschka and John Heartfield in London. Mies van der Rohe, who tried to keep the Bauhaus alive as a private institution in Berlin after its dissolution in Dessau in 1933, left for America, along with George Grosz, Feininger and Gropius. Max Liebermann, the grand old impressionist, died in Berlin in 1935 and was spared the worst.

But many stayed, sharing with the writers of the 'inner emigration', if not the determination, then at least the hope that they could survive without compromising themselves. Some older, established figures, like the sculptor Georg Kolbe, could keep aloof from Nazi ideology while working in an Hellenistic style that still brought them official commissions (Ill. 125). But once the Nazi pressure had gone, Kolbe revealed an uninhibitedly human-istic spirit in his moving figure portraying liberation from war and terror. A group of thirty- and forty-year-old sculptors who would have no truck with the regime – Gerhard Marcks, Joachim Karsch, Ludwig Kasper, Hermann Blumenthal – found communal refuge in Käthe Kollwitz's studio in the Klosterstrasse, working clandestinely in styles that made no concessions to Party directives (Ills 126 and 127). There was still a private gallery or two in

126. *(left) The Harmonica Player* by Joachim Karsch, bronze, 1938.

127. *The Swimmer II* by Gerhard Marcks, bronze, 1938.

128. *The Watchmen* by Karl Hofer, oil on canvas, 1936.

Berlin prepared to exhibit and sell the works of such artists, and this, coupled with the occasional private sale, tided them over the years of oppression.

The sanctions that the state could bring to bear on its politically and artistically 'unreliable' citizens, as it called them, were considerable. A man could be dismissed from his position at an art school and forbidden to teach elsewhere. He could be banned from exhibiting his works in public. Most devastating of all, he could be prohibited from painting or modelling at all, even in the privacy of his own studio. Not infrequently the police would raid his home to ensure that the order was being observed.

At the same time the system was riddled with inconsistencies. Paintings might be impounded yet the artist left working on a public commission. A ban might be lifted for no apparent reason. Or a classic 'degenerate' artist like Max Beckmann, forbidden to paint, could change his medium and begin to produce sculpture without interference. Corruption and sheer inefficiency had their role to play in Nazi Germany as in any totalitarian state.

A fearless opponent of the regime, of whose rise and fall he had frightening visions years before the nightmare became reality, was Karl Hofer (Ill. 128). Making no effort to conceal his opposition to the National Socialists, either in his paintings or in print, Hofer was dismissed in his fifties from the Berlin Hochschule für bildende Künste and, along with Oskar Schlemmer, was one of the first artists forbidden either to exhibit or to paint. His studio was bombed in 1943 but he survived to help re-establish the Hochschule after the war.

Where Hofer was the visionary, the harbinger of a destruction to come, Otto Nagel painted a Berlin – his Berlin, for he was the complete Berliner – on which the bombs were already falling (Ill. 129). A politically committed artist in the tradition of Zille and Käthe Kollwitz, Nagel joined the German Communist Party at the time of its foundation and devoted his life as painter and draughtsman to the working classes and their urban surroundings. Banned from painting in 1934 – a ban he ignored – repeatedly arrested and interrogated by the Gestapo, he spent a number of months in the concentration camp of Sachsenhausen. Many of his works were lost or destroyed during the war but he became a much honoured figure in post-war East Berlin, where he took on a number of official roles and where he died in 1967.

Most of Nagel's portrayals of working-class scenes date from the 1920s, the years of inflation and uncertainty in the struggling new republic. These are the people in the proletarian district of Wedding among whom he grew up – marketeers, postmen, washerwomen, children, vagrants – depicted keenly, powerfully but affectionately (see Ill. 119), even where social conditions could have justified rage. His solidarity with the workers becomes insistent in sketches of the misery and despair that accompanied the mass

129. View of the cobbled Friedrichsgracht and the Spree by Otto Nagel, oil on canvas, 1941.

130. *The Hitler State* by Magnus Zeller, oil on canvas, 1938-9.

unemployment of the early 1930s. After 1933 he turned to sketching the streets, shops and houses of working-class north Berlin, then, after 1940, to recording the corners and alleyways of the oldest parts of the city round the Petrikirche and the Klosterstrasse. But not just out of casual painterly interest. Berlin had already had its first air-raids and Nagel realised that the city he knew would soon no longer be there. So he began his 'race against destruction', as he called it, to sketch the historical scene before it was too late. 'One day I would paint a picture of a certain building or a certain corner, the next day it would be a pile of rubble.'

Were it not for Nagel's paintings and sketches, we would not know what these old corners of Berlin used to look like. Nor would we have such a human account of the rebuilding of the city after the war if he had not wandered among the ruins with his sketch book in the 1950s, registering what needed to be done and the people who were needed to do it.

Some of those banned from painting obeyed and found other ways to survive, daring at most to try to sell some of the works still in their hands. Some had the courage to paint in small forms which could be quickly hidden if the Gestapo paid a sudden visit, like Nagel, or like Emil Nolde, whose early membership of the Party had not saved him from the verdict of expressionist 'degeneracy' and who made hundreds of little clandestine sketches, like diary jottings, to be worked up when the danger had passed. A few, a very few, were prepared to risk all by continuing to paint anti-Nazi pictures as though nothing had happened, determined to prove to posterity that there really had been a resistance against Hitler. One such was Magnus Zeller.

A man in his mid-forties when Hitler seized power, Zeller had been a member of the Berlin Secession before the First World War. Politically he was drawn into the revolutionary camp, artistically into an agitated expressionism that played a great deal on the grotesque. When ten of his works were confiscated in 1937, he retired to a village outside Potsdam, where, heedless of the consequences, he embarked on four oil paintings allegorising the Nazi tyranny in four different sets of religious or political circumstances. The canvas called *Hitler's State* exposes, in a mass of bizarre detail, the existential absurdity and inhumanity of conditions in Nazi Germany, the Nazi ideal itself being presented as a pseudo-religion resting not on revelation but on nihilism and carrying within itself the certainty of its own destruction. The spirit of opposition could hardly be more defiantly demonstrated (Ill. 130).

Music under the Nazis

Step by step Goebbels was bringing the cultural life of the country under the complete control of his Ministry of Propaganda. 'To us,' wrote his deputy Walther Funk in 1934, 'German culture is synonymous with National Socialist culture. Once one has grasped this, one will understand why the Führer has made the arts the responsibility of our Ministry.'

So one division within the new Reichskulturkammer was designated a Reichsmusikkammer, with the responsibility of co-ordinating musical activities throughout the country. First president of the Musikkammer, to his eternal shame – this was 1934 – was Richard Strauss. Strauss found a way of resigning the following year but the stain on his honour has never worn off. Through shrewdness or political naivety – not unlike Gerhart Hauptmann in this – he survived the Nazi tyranny unharmed and shrugged off post-war recriminations about his Nazi associations more easily, though no more justifiably, than the conductor Wilhelm Furtwängler.

Although the functionaries of the National Socialist bureaucracy treated music as one art among the others, to be subjected to ideological *Gleichschaltung* with the rest, more intelligent minds – the more dangerous for their intelligence – recognised the immediacy of the power that music exercises over the emotions. Abstract, irrational, irresistible, music could spread the spiritual values of the movement more effectively than painting or literature. Hitler, who dabbled in painting and architecture and considered himself a connoisseur of musical values, would make high-flown allusions to the quasi-religious nature of art. Goebbels too, in his address to the Reichsmusiktage in 1938, showed he was well aware of what was at stake. 'The language of sound', he said, 'is sometimes more compelling than the language of words . . . Music is an art that penetrates to the very depths of the soul.'

The immediate practical function of music in the new regime was to promote the national interests of the *Volk* in two ways: on the one hand by educating people to seek out the Germanic, Nordic, 'Aryan' qualities in their nation's art; on the other by mounting a crusade against those who by definition were excluded from participation in that art – the Jews. The message was delivered in a piece of characteristic Nazi verbiage. 'The challenge facing us today', boomed Wolfgang Stumme, head of the music education department in the Hitler Youth, 'is to employ music as a living, vital, educative force that will help preserve and unify our country, to promote music as a spiritual, blood-linked form of expression and to make it a means by which our race can acquire superior knowledge and reach a higher standard of development.'

Through the Reichsmusikkammer, the Hitler Youth, the Kampfbund für deutsche Kultur and other bodies, the Nazi state administered an immense musical empire. Festivals were inaugurated, funds were made available for sponsorship of projects by town councils and workers' organisations, and competitions organised to identify budding young composers and performers. The award of medals and certificates of achievement never fails to stimulate ambition, and central control produced a consistently high level of musical performance.

As early as 1931 the Party founded its own orchestra, the Nationalsozialistisches Reichs-Sinfonieorchester, for which Hitler designed special brown tailcoats – the Führer's orchestra, as it came to be known. All the players were members of the Party. Membership of the Party, indeed, always carried advantages. Composers previously passed over would find commissions coming their way after they joined, while orchestral players and teachers were rewarded with salary increases. For leading positions membership would be taken for granted. 'Others need not apply.'

Following a decree issued in April 1933 all 'non-Aryans' automatically lost their official appointments – Schreker as director of the Berlin Hochschule, Schoenberg with his master class at the Academy of Arts, Klemperer as conductor of the state opera. Jewish singers and instrumentalists were summarily dismissed. Leo Kestenberg, whose work as official music adviser to the Prussian government during the 1920s had contributed much to the promotion of new music and the advancement of the cause of music in public life, had been removed even before the decree of 1933.

Foreign soloists could, and did, show their distaste for Nazi policies by refusing to perform in Germany. As early as the summer of 1933 the Jewish violinist Fritz Kreisler, an Austrian citizen who had made his home in Berlin since 1924, declined Furtwängler's invitation to play with the Berlin Philharmonic Orchestra in the coming season. Mentioning specifically Klemperer and Bruno Walter, Kreisler replied to Furtwängler, in sadness rather than in anger: 'I am firmly resolved not to appear again in Germany until the right of all artists, whatever their race, religion or nationality, to pursue their careers has become an irrefutable reality.' Kreisler himself was forced out of Austria by the *Anschluss* of 1938 and eventually emigrated to the United States.

Since Nazi racial doctrine required not only that Jews be removed from current public life and influence but also that their past activities be exposed as alien to the interests of the German *Volk*, the music of earlier German Jewish composers was instantly banned. That the ban would fall on contemporaries such as Schoenberg, Schreker, Berthold Goldschmidt, Weill and Korngold was obvious. But it also had to be demonstrated, with the anti-Semitic assistance of Wagner, that Mendelssohn, Meyerbeer, Offenbach and Mahler had no place in German opera houses and concert halls. It was a source of embarrassment, especially since his works had such mass appeal, that whereas Franz Lehár himself was unquestionably 'Aryan', he had married a Jewess and the libretti of his operettas were all by Jews. Equally awkward, and to be concealed as far as possible, was the fact that Lorenzo da Ponte, librettist of Mozart's *Don Giovanni, Marriage of Figaro* and *Così fan tutte*, was also Jewish.

The most complete embodiment of the values the Nazis determined to destroy was Arnold Schoenberg – expressionist, modernist, internationalist, Jewish anarchist all in one, a paradigm of what they sneeringly called 'cultural Bolshevism'. Atonalism had cut the ground from beneath the familiar structure of diatonic music, the inherited pattern of our musical experience. The result was bewilderment and chaos. With his so-called twelve-tone principle of composition Schoenberg introduced a new order into his revolution, but an order with a totally different language which expressed a totally different set of meanings. Such dissonant and discordant music could not be tolerated, undermining, as it did, the serenity of a familiar, well-ordered world and unconducive, as it was, to a sense of popular optimism and well-being. Tunefulness was the order of the day. Anything that smacked of modernism, whether German or foreign – Stravinsky, Bartók, Berg, Milhaud, Weill, Eisler and a host of others – would not get a hearing.

A musical *cause célèbre* in the Nazi era was that of Paul Hindemith, one of the leading composers of the European avant-garde in the 1920s and 1930s and a teacher of composition at the Berlin Hochschule since 1927. With a Jewish wife and a wide circle of Jewish musical friends and fellow-performers, Hindemith was a ready victim of racial smears. His dissonant, modernist, formalist compositions performed at international music festivals were held to be thoroughly unGerman – they even stooped so low, it was pointed out, as to make use of elements drawn from jazz, characteristic product of the sub-human Negro race. (European white-man's jazz was apparently acceptable, since Berlin radio, incongruously, had its own officially sanctioned dance band.)

Matters came to a spectacular head in 1934 when the première of Hindemith's new opera *Mathis der Maler* in the Staatsoper was banned. Furtwängler, who was to have conducted, published an open letter to Goebbels in the *Deutsche Allgemeine Zeitung*, objecting to the adduction of racial, national or any other extrinsic criteria for determining what is good and what is bad music. This amounted to a direct attack on Nazi racial policy, the ideological foundation of the state. Furtwängler was immediately made to resign from his official positions at the Staatsoper and in the Reichsmusikkammer, and publicly to disclaim any intention of interfering in political matters, which were the responsibility of the Führer and the Party.

When, shortly afterwards, Furtwängler conducted the orchestral symphony *Mathis der Maler* that Hindemith had assembled from the music of his opera, the audience in the Philharmonie, fully aware of the implications, rose to a man and applauded as Furtwängler mounted the rostrum. A few weeks later Erich Kleiber made a similar act of musical defiance by conducting Stravinsky's much reviled *Sacre du Printemps*, also to wild applause.

In the end Furtwängler, to whom music and its public performance meant everything, had no option but to submit. He refused to renounce his Jewish associations and tried, though with limited success, to distance himself from the Nazi regime. But controversy never left him, and he never fully salvaged his good name from the ruins of the Third Reich. As to Hindemith, realising he no longer had a future in Germany, he resigned from the Hochschule in 1937 and emigrated to Switzerland, where the opera *Mathis der Maler* finally had its first performance the following year.

For an antidote to the modernist venom the Nazis went back to the Germanic tradition of Wagner and Bruckner as carried forward into modern times – sometimes with undisguised anti-Semitic hostility – by Hans Pfitzner, of whose music Hitler expressed particular approval. Welcome too was the earthy folksiness of Carl Orff and the work of Werner Egk, Kapellmeister at the Staatsoper from 1936 to 1940 and later head of the composition section of the Reichsmusikkammer. Festive music commissioned from Orff, Egk and Richard Strauss for the Olympic Games in Berlin in 1936 conveyed a suitable sense of national pride, while pieces for military band, 'odes to the Führer' and patriotic songs for the marching masses of the SS and the Hitler Youth would always find a market.

Composers like these – Rudolf Wagner-Régeny, friend in Berlin of Kurt Weill and the Brecht designer Caspar Neher, was another – managed to live through the Nazi years by steering an unobtrusive course between protest, which would have meant arrest or worse, and a degree of conformity which could be construed as collaboration. But it could be a degrading experience. In a bitter note found among his posthumous papers Richard Strauss wrote: 'It is a sad moment when an artist of my stature has to ask some little upstart of a minister what I may compose and perform. I have joined the ranks of the domestic servants and bottlewashers and am almost envious of my persecuted Jewish friend Stefan Zweig.' (The novelist Stefan Zweig wrote the libretto for Strauss' opera *Die schweigsame Frau*, which was allowed three performances in 1935 before Zweig's Jewishness proved too much for the censor.)

It is no less sad to witness an artist of Strauss' stature writhing to retain his moral integrity while still willing to accept the patronage of the Nazis. In letters he spoke scornfully of his Olympic Hymn as 'something for the mob' but one can hardly credit that he could not have found some excuse to decline the commission if his antipathy towards the regime was as intense as he liked in private to make out. 'A man who utterly despises sport', as he described himself, he even conducted the piece at the Games when the moment came. His letters show one Strauss, his public persona conveys another. In the end he was trusted by no one, not even the Nazis for whom he compromised his honour.

The classical German repertoire of concert hall and opera house – Bach, Mozart, Beethoven, Weber, Brahms, Wagner – was untouchable, though meanings sometimes had to be adjusted. The herding together of human beings in prison like animals and the final overthrow of the tyrannical regime responsible for such crimes against humanity were aspects of Beethoven's *Fidelio* that had to be glossed over. Instead attention was focused on the sub-title of the opera, 'Conjugal Love', and the work presented as a hymn of praise to the institution of (German) marriage and the loyalty of a devoted (German) wife. That *Fidelio* is set in Spain was not permitted to cloud the issue.

Against all expectations a few contemporary operas did find their way on to the stage, among them those of Werner Egk, a man who with considerable political agility succeeded in commending himself to the Nazis without paying a post-war price. His fairy-tale opera *Die Zaubergeige* ('The Magic Fiddle'), an entertaining piece in a tonal idiom spiced with modernisms and strong rhythms, became one of the most popular contemporary works in the repertory of the 1930s. When he conducted his most important work, *Peer Gynt*, at the Staatsoper in 1938, rumbles of displeasure were heard at its occasional jazziness, reminiscent of Kurt Weill's now despised *Dreigroschenoper*. But after Hitler saw it and expressed his enjoyment, officialdom could only leave it alone. Egk had, after all, made clear in public his anti-elitist view of 'music for the people' as the composer's contribution to the cause of a resurgent nation.

The year after Egk's *Peer Gynt* Wagner-Régeny had his opera *The Burghers of Calais* performed in the Staatsoper under Herbert von Karajan, also to a warm reception. The public readily took to its undemanding but well-crafted, melodious blend of the Brecht–Weill manner and the Italian *bel canto* tradition. But the libretto by the celebrated stage designer Caspar Neher, based on Georg Kaiser's play, emphasised virtues that ran counter to the National Socialist ideology and the work was soon withdrawn.

As in any totalitarian context, the mass of the people found their various ways of arriving at a *modus vivendi*, turning inwards for comfort in the world of mind and spirit. Amateur music-making in choral and instrumental groups created bonds between people, while the repertoires of concert halls and opera houses preserved the noblest traditions and a sense of spiritual continuity. The great conductors, save Furtwängler, had left Berlin by 1935 but most of the operatic stars (fewer singers than instrumentalists were Jewish) were still there to be enjoyed – great Wagnerian singers like Frida Leider and Max Lorenz, Maria Cebotari in *Madame Butterfly*, Erna Berger in *La Traviata*, Heinrich Schlusnus as Posa in *Don Carlos*. Richard Tauber, who was still charming Berlin audiences in *The Merry Widow* and other Lehár operettas in the early 1930s, sang his last role at the Staatsoper in 1932 before ultimately finding refuge in London.

With the outbreak of war in 1939 came the progressive restriction of musical life, but not before political events had given it a stimulus from an unexpected quarter. In the wake of the Soviet–German pact it suddenly became prudent to devote attention to Russian music, which had hitherto been dismissed as 'unNordic' and devoid of national character. Now concerts of modern Russian music were hurriedly organised – Miaskovsky, Shostakovich, Khatchaturian – and the Staatsoper was enjoined to perform Glinka's *A Life for the Tsar*, Mussorgsky's *Boris Godunov* and Borodin's *Prince Igor*. But conditions soon changed all this.

The Staatsoper was almost completely destroyed during an air-raid in 1941. So great was its symbolic importance for the capital, however, that Hitler immediately ordered it to be rebuilt as a matter of public urgency. It resumed its activity until the summer of 1944, when all Berlin theatres closed. It was destroyed a second time during the last months of the war, like the Schauspielhaus, the Kroll Opera, the Philharmonie and almost all the other of the city's theatres and concert halls. When cultural activities began to emerge from the rubble, the Berliners found themselves looking at a very different world.

X

TWO BERLINS

Emergence from Defeat

In the First World War, the civilian population of Berlin, as of Germany as a whole, had suffered food rationing and other privations, and scarcely a family had not lost a father or a son at the front. But there had been no bombing, no artillery barrages, no street-to-street fighting. The foreign armies said to be the victors in the war had never occupied an inch of German territory or raped and pillaged their way through the German countryside. To be sure, there was a price to be paid in the 1920s for the defeat, a price paid in the currency of inflation, unemployment and human misery. But in 1918 Berlin neither looked nor felt defeated.

How different the end of the Second World War. The figures tell the story. When the fighting in Europe stopped in May 1945, 40 per cent of Berlin lay in ruins. Before the war it had a population of over 4 million. Now the number was little over half that, two-thirds of them women and a quarter of them over sixty. The destruction begun and continued by British and American bombers since 1940 was completed by the Russian artillery in 1945. Physically exhausted, psychologically dazed and shattered, the people found shelter where they could, in cellars, in holes among the rubble, roaming the streets in search of food and friends. The future did not bear contemplation. All that could be felt was despair and fear – despair of survival, fear of the vengeance that would be sought for the crimes committed in their name over the past fifteen years.

For two months, May to July 1945, the Russians had Berlin to themselves, time in which not only to dismantle and ship back to the Soviet Union as reparations whatever industrial plant was still usable but also to set up a communist-style infrastructure of municipal government that would consolidate their authority. After the Western allies took up the occupation of their agreed sectors, a four-power Kommandatura nominally controlled the whole city but in practice the eastern and western halves became increasingly irreconcilable as the grip of the Cold War tightened. Both sides needed to strike a balance between the visceral urge for retribution and a calculated policy of political and social re-education – questions for which East and West had starkly divergent solutions. Month by month, year by year, in economic policy, in political structure and in social intent the rival sectors became less and less like each other, more and more like their occupiers.

But culturally in these early post-war years, and sometimes even politically, as long as travel was still relatively free from restriction, attempts were being made to hold the country together by appealing to those liberal, humanistic values which the Nazis had trampled underfoot but which had sustained those of the 'inner emigration' during the years of darkness. Günther Weisenborn, a writer well known from the Weimar era and recently liberated from three years in a Nazi prison, was one of those who returned to Berlin full of confidence that the city would soon regain its identity. 'No one believed', he recalled in his memoirs,

> that the division of the city would last. Hundreds of thousands travelled to and fro every day, living, working and making love in the east and the west alike . . . It had been the Berliners, whose vision had been only slightly clouded by the bloodstained veil of dictatorship, who built up the most effective pockets of resistance to the Nazi regime. Now they were learning to test themselves, to observe and to reflect. We lived a reckless life, full of hope and with a critical eye in this strangely unnerving city, this Pompeii of the North.

A body calling itself the Cultural Alliance for the Democratic Renewal of Germany was founded a few months after the end of the war, with Gerhart Hauptmann as its president and prominent intellectuals from a broad liberal church − Ricarda Huch, Anna Seghers, the painters Otto Nagel and Karl Hofer − among its members. Two years later the Alliance organised a German Writers Congress attended by 'inner emigrants' such as Ricarda Huch, Elisabeth Langgässer and Günther Weisenborn from the 'West' and returning exiles from Moscow like Johannes R. Becher and Friedrich Wolf from the 'East'. Basic doctrinal differences, together with the undisguised opposition of the Americans, who in this age of McCarthyism not unnaturally suspected a communist infiltration of such occasions for their own ends, guaranteed that the Alliance would be short lived. But whatever the political divisions, many returning intellectuals assumed that the cultural unity of the city they had left, an organic unity obvious to all, could be restored. Indeed, only as such was there any hope for it. 'Every artist and intellectual is well aware', said Peter Huchel, East Berlin writer and editor who later defected to the West, 'that Berlin will either survive as a cultural entity or it will perish.'

Among the first stirrings of a new cultural life in occupied Berlin was the provision of a platform for the art that had been driven underground by the Nazis. 'Degenerate' expressionist paintings by established artists such as Nolde, Heckel and Pechstein, together with the realist, socially committed work of Hofer and Otto Dix − all of whom survived the war in various parts of Germany − were put on show, together with the sculptures of Ernst Barlach and Käthe Kollwitz. Unlike the self-centred mood of expressionist, Dadaist and constructivist experimentation after the First World War, a strong spirit of realism was abroad, a coming to terms with the welcome destruction of the one world and the uncertain emergence of another. 'In my pictures', said Dix in 1948, 'I am at great pains to achieve an understanding of our age, for it is my belief that above all one must have some subject matter to express, some topic to deal with.' The strong Berlin tradition of representational painting was reinforced by the re-establishment, only a month

131. *Berlin Ruins at Night* by Karl Hofer, oil on canvas, *c.* 1947.

after the end of the war, of the city's art college, the Hochschule für bildende
Künste, with Hofer as its director and Max Pechstein, Schmidt-Rottluff and
Renée Sintenis among its faculty.

But there was little great art available for the public to enjoy. Having
removed the most important exhibits to places of safety, the Nazis had closed
state museums and art galleries at the beginning of the war and used them
since then only for the occasional show. In 1945 scarcely one had survived
intact. All five on the Museum Island – the Altes Museum, the Neues
Museum, the Pergamon Museum, the Bode (formerly the Kaiser-Friedrich)
Museum and the National Gallery – were too badly damaged to house the
works brought out of their places of safe keeping, whereupon the Russians
sent them to the Soviet Union as booty. It was ten years before they could
be persuaded to return them – or most of them – to their rightful owners
in Berlin and elsewhere in East Germany, including sections of the Pergamum altar. The Altes Museum reopened only in 1966, while the Neues
Museum remained a total ruin until the 1990s, when reunification marked
the beginning of its restoration.

Some artists conceived it as their duty, in this moment of chaos and helplessness, to engage their art in the service of reconstruction, the creation of

a society that will never again allow such evil to engulf it. Others, suspicious of a view that saw art as an instrument of social policy, thought in individual and artistic terms, sometimes religious – art *sub specie aeternitatis*. But the immanent reality from which none could escape was the stifling pressure of human misery, the demoralisation of ruins. This was the shared subject matter, whether recorded as documentary evidence, like pictures of refugees fleeing the city, or as the starting-point for an ironical comment on war itself, or, as in *Ruins at Night* by Karl Hofer, who lived in the city throughout the war, as an assemblage of images in which shattered walls turn into mask-like, demonic human faces beneath a pitiless moon (Ill. 131).

As in art, so in music. What had been banned for the past fifteen years or written in exile was brought back in triumph – Schoenberg, Hindemith, Kurt Weill, Webern, together with Stravinsky, Honegger, Prokofiev, Bartók and other foreigners. Mendelssohn was heard again and Mahler, and access restored to the world of European modernism without detriment to the reassurance conveyed by the familiar tonal idiom. Among composers now free to resume the careers interrupted by Hitler were Hanns Eisler and Paul Dessau, both exiled communists, both collaborators of Brecht's and both voluntary citizens of the new East Germany after their return from the uneasy safety of the United States.

No less vital was the re-establishment of contact with the modern literature and art of Europe and America that had been kept out of sight – Eliot, Joyce, Camus and French existentialism, Ionescu, Beckett and the theatre of the absurd, the novels of Hemingway and Faulkner, the plays of Eugene O' Neill, Tennessee Williams and Thornton Wilder, the paintings of Picasso, Dali, Matisse and other 'degenerates'. As Germany under National Socialism had been made to look inward, to think in the confining nationalistic terms of the *Volk*, so now it could open itself to new influences and become part of the international scene.

The literary landscape in Germany in the immediate post-war years, far from simply mirroring the stark political reality of collapse and radical realignment, offers a confusion of vistas. The senior generation that had stayed in Germany throughout the Third Reich – Gottfried Benn, Ernst Jünger, Gertrud von le Fort, Werner Bergengruen – continued to write and publish with a striking absence of interruption. Sometimes a contemporary work seemed to define the dominant national mood of the moment. Such were Wolfgang Borcherdt's *Draussen vor der Tür* ('Left Outside'), a radio play, later a drama, of a German soldier returning from the eastern front in 1945, and Hermann Kasack's Kafkaesque novel *Die Stadt hinter dem Strom* ('The City Beyond the River'), both published in 1947. Poignant testimony to the spirit of resistance to tyranny came with the publication of Haushofer's *Moabiter Sonette* and other sombre collections of verse, while the works of those who had gone into exile now reappeared with a new aura of authority. Heine, Börne, Kafka, Hermann Broch, Hesse and others were rediscovered by a generation from whom they had been withheld. Alongside Lessing's *Nathan der Weise*, with its plea for tolerance and a humanist ethic, the most frequently performed play in post-war Germany was *Des Teufels General* ('The Devil's General'), an anti-war, anti-Nazi piece by Carl Zuckmayer, popular dramatist of the 1920s, who made a brief return to Germany in 1946 before going back to his rural retreat in Vermont.

But to the younger generation most of this writing was tainted, in ways as varied as they were inevitable, with what had happened in the last fifteen years. The recent past, not least for linguistic reasons, had to be written off – *Kahlschlag*, a clean sweep, a total clearance, was the chosen image. Writers had to commit themselves to new political aims, to seeing themselves as builders of a new society, with the clock restarted from 'zero point', the defeat of 1945. Most influential among these radical reformers were those associated at one time or another with the Gruppe 47, founded in the American Zone of Occupation by Hans Werner Richter and Alfred Andersch, and a persistent source of influence on West German literature for the best part of twenty years.

Cultural life in Berlin, despite the destruction of the city, despite the hunger and the homelessness, recovered with remarkable speed. Within a few weeks of the end of hostilities, the first buses and S-Bahn trains began to run again and the *Berliner Zeitung* appeared on the streets. The Berlin Philharmonic Orchestra, which had last played only two weeks before the fighting stopped on 2 May, reassembled on 26 May for a concert in a local cinema that had somehow escaped destruction. The programme opened, symbolically, with music that had been banned since 1933 – Mendelssohn's incidental music to Shakespeare's *A Midsummer Night's Dream*. The next month the company of the Städtische Oper celebrated the end of the war with Beethoven's *Fidelio*. In August the Brecht–Weill *Dreigroschenoper*, with Hans Albers as Macheath, was performed in the reopened Hebbel-Theater under Karlheinz Martin, while the Deutsches Theater, now left in the eastern part of the city, resumed in September with Lessing's *Nathan*, and its annexe, the Kammerspiele, in December with Shaw's *Captain Brassbound's Conversion*.

In 1946, after a harsh winter, the pace of recovery quickened. Friedrich Luft, drama critic in the line of Otto Brahm and Alfred Kerr, whose radio broadcasts were to acquire legendary status over the coming decades, reported his amazement that cultural life among the ruins was returning to normal so quickly. 'Yesterday', said Luft one day in February 1946,

> I had the opportunity to drive through the city from one end to the other. It was like a ghost town. We have got used to the debris in our own area and what we see on our way to work, but I suddenly realised how little of Berlin is left, and wondered whether we might be fooling ourselves. Then I drove past a board plastered with announcements of plays, operas and concerts. In the newspaper I found advertisements for almost 200 places which were putting on plays – in all parts of the city. I mean it. There are at least half a dozen concerts a day – in all parts of the city. Two opera houses are giving regular performances. What other city in the world can say as much?

Political cabarets, irrepressible features of the Berlin cultural scene, were springing up in various nooks and crannies, led by *Ulenspiegel*, where cynicism and mordant wit ruled – sentiments appropriate to a moment when the shattered megalomania of an evil dictatorship left the population staring into an abyss of nihilism. With Russian support the Germans in the eastern sector of the city converted the old UFA film corporation into their own DEFA organisation, took over its studios and put out the first post-war films, anti-fascist in tone and content. The western sector, which did not develop its own film industry until much later, was content at the time to show American, British and French movies heavy in entertainment value, light in intellectual substance.

An early foreboding of the direction that events were going to take showed itself in the field of education. In January 1946 the University of Berlin reopened, no longer, however, as the Friedrich-Wilhelms-Universität of Hohenzollern memory but as the Humboldt-Universität, a name rich in cultural and pedagogical associations which it still bears today. But with the change of name went a revolution in educational aims and practices. For Unter den Linden, where the university stands, was in the Soviet sector of the city, and to the Russians universities, like the rest of the educational system, were means of inculcating communist principles in the young. Determined to rebuild their sector of Berlin and their zone of Germany in the Soviet image, the Russians introduced into university curricula compulsory courses in the Russian language and in Marxism–Leninism and set about the indoctrination of the coming generation. The lines of future confrontation were already being drawn.

The only immediate answer the Western allies could find to the Humboldt University was, a few months later, to elevate the Technische Hochschule, founded in 1879 in what was now the British sector, into the Technische Universität. In 1948, by which time the Iron Curtain had fallen and the chill of the Cold War had settled over Europe, a mass exodus of students and faculty from East Berlin led to the establishment under American protection of the Free University of Berlin, which subsequently became one of the largest German universities, as well as one of the most radically politicised.

Given the confrontational situation in which Europe was left in 1945; given in particular the grotesque reality of the former German capital, divided into four parts and internationally administered by four different conquering powers, yet isolated, as an urban entity, in the middle of the Soviet zone of occupation, politics could never be kept out of the equation. Indeed, at least since the end of the First World War, virtually all intellectual and artistic activity in Berlin had taken place against a politicised background. Even a flight from the reality of politics into a world of abstraction draws its *raison d'être* from the reality on which it turns its back.

Whatever visions of an harmonious political cooperation between East and West may have circulated in the immediate post-war years were finally dissipated by the events of June 1948. In retaliation for the introduction by the Western allies of a new currency in their zones of occupation and their sectors of Berlin as the foundation for economic revival, the Russians blocked all land routes to West Berlin in an attempt to starve it out. For almost a year it was kept alive by the allied air-lift, which flew in food, fuel and clothing until the Soviet Union admitted its blockade had failed. West Germany constituted itself as the German Federal Republic (Bundesrepublik Deutschland), East Germany five months later as the German Democratic Republic (Deutsche Demokratische Republik, or simply DDR). East and

West Berlin received their separate municipal councils, each economically and constitutionally bound to their respective godfathers. East Berlin was declared the capital of the German Democratic Republic, while a quiet little Rhineland town called Bonn, birthplace of Beethoven, was pronounced capital of the Federal Republic. West Berlin was left isolated, sealed into an alien context, an outpost of the West in the middle of hostile territory.

From the beginning West Berlin had to struggle for an identity, starting on the purely geographical level. For the heart of the pre-war city was now in the East – not only the Prussian heart of the Forum Fridericianum and Unter den Linden or the former centre of government in the Wilhelmstrasse but the Museum Island, the historic churches, the commercial and entertainment districts of the Leipziger Strasse and Friedrichstrasse, the Staatsoper, the Schauspielhaus, the Deutsches Theater, the Theater am Schiffbauerdamm, the Volksbühne. All this was now in the hands of others.

By the same token, from the perspective of the East, West Berlin was a perpetual irritant. Its bright lights, its material wealth and its flourishing culture were a high-profile demonstration to the socialist world of its comprehensive superiority – economic, political, cultural, even moral. With free access to Western radio and television programmes, the chosen sources of information about events not only in the world at large but even in their own country, the citizens of the East suffered a permanent confrontation with what was being denied them. The communist government tried to conceal its inferiority complex behind authoritarianism and bluster. But no one was deceived.

Two Germanies, two Berlins. But culturally there was only one Berlin to inherit. So over the coming years, as the worlds grew further and further apart, there arose an Academy of Arts (East) and an Academy of Arts (West), a State Library (East) and a State Library (West), a National Gallery (East) and a National Gallery (West). Museum exhibits that had been stored for the duration of the war in what was now Western-occupied territory were brought out and exhibited in West Berlin, while East Berlin galleries displayed what had survived in that part of the country. A bizarre fate sometimes decreed that a picture from a national collection would turn up in the West, while its original frame was left in the East. Much was destroyed; much was pilfered, some of it in the meantime recovered. Each side had its own image of the patrimony to project.

The survival of West Berlin in the decades following the air-lift was a principle that would never be surrendered. But it exacted a heavy price. Substantial subsidies helped to keep manufacturing industries going which would otherwise have collapsed. Financial inducements were offered both to keep and to attract workers to the city, where the preponderance of older citizens made in any case for a demographic imbalance. Berlin's position as an industrial metropolis had gone, and although some well-known names remained – Siemens, AEG, Bosch – the headquarters of such firms moved to the safety of West Germany, leaving their Berlin factories with only a subsidiary role to play. To complete the vicious circle of decline and loss of confidence many families deserted their former capital for the industrial centres of the West.

East Berlin, by contrast, fully integrated into its economic hinterland, nationalised the industrial plant it had inherited from a defeated Germany and turned itself into a substantial producer of consumer goods. As West Berlin was the West's defiant eastern extremity, at the mercy of the vagaries of Soviet behaviour, so East Berlin was made the technical and industrial showcase of the Soviet bloc. Complementarily, the East German army, indoctrinated with a hatred of all that West Berlin represented, formed the westernmost contingent of the forces of the Warsaw Pact.

As the ideology of the East became ever more oppressive and the economic gulf between East and West ever wider, the trickle of refugees from communism began which was later to become a flood. A series of Soviet threats, ultimata and restrictive measures failed to dislodge West Berlin from its status as an integral part of West Germany or to panic the Berliners into mass exodus. The Berlin Wall and its 'death strip', built in 1961 through the centre of the city, stopped the flow of refugees overnight, turning East Berlin, and with it the whole of the German Democratic Republic, into one huge prison.

For almost thirty years, to the profitable delight of Len Deighton and John le Carré but to the anguish of the Berliners themselves, the prison Wall stood – until the extraordinary events of November 1989 forced the East German government out of office, led to the destruction of the Wall and the collapse of communism, and paved the way for the reunification both of divided Berlin and of divided Germany as a whole.

Out of the Ruins: The City Builds

'The bombers had carried out their task of destruction and nothing was left standing in the centre of the city. The moment had finally arrived.'

In a tone of near-euphoria Hans Scharoun, architect and head of the municipal town-planning department – a latter-day Schinkel in influence and vision – greeted the architectural challenge facing Berlin at the end of the war. What Scharoun and his partners envisaged, as expressed in the project they laid before the public in 1946, was not a return to the form of the city as it had grown since the nineteenth century, in particular since 1871, but a concept of 'the city as landscape', an organic structure of individual neighbourhoods, each consonant with its topographical, historical and cultural environment. The centre, a point of spiritual refreshment and repose on the 'arc of culture' that stretched from the old Royal Palace, past the Museum Island and along Unter den Linden to Charlottenburg Palace, was to be the Tiergarten, a restful island of nature in the midst of a throbbing social and commercial life, with the buildings of the new 'Cultural Forum' on its southeastern flank.

This vision of a series of 'city landscapes', held within a grid of freeways which the age of the automobile would soon make imperative, not only offered a diversity in unity within the city's geographical boundaries but also paid homage to history. For Berlin had not developed purposefully from a single nucleus, like a series of ever-widening concentric circles. Rather, it had grown as an agglomeration of individual villages, each with its own inner logic and dynamic, and thus with its own physical, intellectual and spiritual character. Many felt at the time that Scharoun's plan paid the necessary respect to historical realities while showing what the realities of the future would demand – in other words, that his plan was somehow instinctively 'right'.

Like the painters Karl Hofer and Heinrich Ehmsen and the sculptor Waldemar Grzimek, Scharoun thought and worked, for as long as it was still possible, in the spirit of a unified Berlin, refusing to play the East off against the West or vice versa. But the political events of 1948, followed by the official foundation of the two rival German states the year after, exposed that hope as an illusion. Accepting the consequences, Scharoun turned his back on the East and designed a variety of striking private and public buildings for West Berlin, such as the Philharmonie, the nearby Prussian State Library and a high-rise apartment block in the northern suburb of Reinickendorf (Ill. 132). Writing in 1965, at the time his new National Gallery was being constructed in the Cultural Forum complex, Mies van der Rohe reaffirmed a principle. 'Today, as for a long time past', he wrote, 'I believe that architecture has little or nothing to do with the invention of interesting forms or with personal inclinations. True architecture is always objective. It is the expression of the inner structure of our time, from which it stems.'

Precisely what constituted 'the inner structure of our time' in divided post-war Berlin was a question to which the two rival governing bodies had divergent answers, based on their incompatible views on where history was leading a defeated and demoralised people and what kind of society they were out to create. Yet in the immediate terms of urban reconstruction their basic problem was the same: how to balance the short-term need to provide a bombed-out population with some sort of roof over their heads against the claims of long-term planning, the eventual rebuilding of the city as they wished to see it. For urban renewal begins with destruction, destruction of

132. Interior of the Philharmonie Concert Hall, designed by Hans Scharoun, 1963.

what at that moment may be desperately needed. Beyond this arguments rage over what to preserve and what deliberately to destroy, arguments conducted as often in political as in aesthetic terms. Only then can designs for the future be drawn up.

The first side of the divided city to show what it saw as 'the inner structure of our time', in Mies van der Rohe's phrase, was the East. Seized by a desire to make a dramatic architectural statement to assert the personality of his state, Walter Ulbricht, the East German leader, ordered the redevelopment of a two-kilometre-long avenue recently renamed Stalinallee (now Karl-Marx-Allee). Following the model of Stalinist Moscow, blocks seven to ten storeys high were to be erected on both sides of the avenue, to accommodate apartments, shops, restaurants and other leisure facilities. Construction work started in 1950 and proceeded eastwards, culminating in 1960 at the Frankfurter Tor.

The building of the Stalinallee was a political act – architecture as a statement. The East German Socialist Unity Party's position on architectural style was to decry anything which smacked of functionalism, modernism or Neue Sachlichkeit, or which recalled the internationalism of the Bauhaus, and to talk in vague, emotive terms of drawing on 'the best native German traditions' to produce an architecture that would express 'the power of the working class'. The result could be described as a kind of 'classicistic modernism'. Modern is its response to the physical needs of the population within an overall conception of dwellings, stores and recreational areas existing side by side in a comprehensive social context – the basic principle of town-planning adopted throughout the German Democratic Republic. 'Classicistic' are the columns, pediments and other details of neo-classical ornamentation through which Hermann Henselmann, chief architect of the Stalinallee, sought to invoke associations with the Berlin historicist tradition, above all with Schinkel (Ill. 133).

Played up by the East German government as a showpiece that would demonstrate to the world what the new socialist German state could achieve, the Stalinallee has always attracted extremes of reaction. Its non-functional decorative features led modernists in the West to deride it as an example of 'wedding-cake style'. Others called it 'a gigantic rabbit hutch' or compared it with the soulless structures of the Third Reich – one totalitarian regime, after all, is much like another.

A different response came from the American architect Philip Johnson – who has returned to Berlin since reunification to oversee the redevelopment of an area around the former Checkpoint Charlie. Asked in the 1960s which buildings in East and West Berlin were most likely to survive for posterity, Johnson replied: Le Corbusier's high-rise 'Unité d' Habitation – Typ Berlin' (c. 1960) near the Olympic Stadium in West Berlin, and the Stalinallee.

Driven, not least under political pressures, to launch its own distinctive programme of reconstruction, West Berlin announced in 1953 a competition for the creation of a new Hansaviertel, a prime residential site on the northeastern edge of the Tiergarten, which had been totally destroyed in the war. The results of the competition and the completed first section of the plan, which included contributions from foreign as well as German architects, were presented to the public at a lavish international exhibition, the Interbau, held

133. Stalinallee (now Karl-Marx-Allee).

on the Hansaviertel site in 1957. In contrast to the unitarian concept of East German planners, the West broke down traditional block structures and replaced them with a dispersed arrangement of buildings set around with the natural green areas and woodlands of the Tiergarten outside.

Here in the Hansaviertel the modernists came into their own. Walter Gropius designed an apartment block, while Werner Düttmann built a new centre for the Academy of Arts and an ingenious little complex of shops and a public library in concrete, stone and glass – a loggia surrounding a central courtyard with direct access to a subway station.

One of the most prominent and most controversial buildings in post-war Berlin, the Kongresshalle, also formed part of the 1957 Interbau exhibition, though it is not strictly part of the Hansaviertel (Ill. 134). Dubbed the 'pregnant oyster' by the disrespectful Berliners, the Kongresshalle has had a turbulent history. After twenty years of use as a convention centre, part of its sweeping steel and concrete roof collapsed. Three years of deliberation preceded the decision to rebuild, and it reopened as part of the city's 750th anniversary celebrations in 1987.

Basically the Kongresshalle is the work of the American architect Hugh Stubbins, but it also owes a good many of its details to the local influence of Werner Düttmann, one of the younger generation of Berlin architects who started work after the war. Born and bred in the city, Düttmann devoted his career to its reconstruction, influencing developments even where his own designs were not involved. He played a decisive part in persuading Mies van der Rohe to undertake the new National Gallery and made public his fear, shared by many, that a city dominated by the demands of the automobile – which West Berlin was rapidly becoming – would dehumanise the environment. After his contributions to the Hansaviertel he showed his versatility in designs that ranged from office blocks to churches, from apartments to entire public squares. Congruence with the surroundings was a cardinal principle. 'Berlin is many cities,' he once observed.

Of the cluster of new buildings making up the Cultural Forum focused on the old Kemperplatz, the most impressive is the Philharmonie, Scharoun's masterpiece. The chosen site itself was already a subject of controversy – an empty, devastated area close to the ghostly Potsdamer Platz, the then silent wilderness where the occupation sectors met and concrete and barbed wire ruled. The Philharmonie's prow-like exterior made a powerful statement as visible and as unmistakable to the East as to the West, a declaration of permanent occupancy. Its complex interior is arranged, not as the conventional concert hall in which the audience confronts the stage, but with the orchestra surrounded by the listeners, on a variety of levels. 'Music in the centre', said Scharoun, '– that, put in its simplest terms, is the underlying concept of the new hall.' The superb acoustics set the seal on Scharoun's achievement.

The building of the Berlin Wall in 1961, the Four-Power Agreement on Berlin ten years later and the Basic Treaty between the Federal Republic and the DDR at the end of 1972 all served to harden the division between East and West. Anomalous and grotesque as the position of West Berlin was, a colonial island of capitalism completely walled off from its hostile communist surroundings, both sides had pledged themselves to the perversities of the status quo.

To replace the tens of thousands of East Berliners who used to cross the border every day to work in the West, workers had to be attracted from West Germany, and to accommodate them architects were called upon to design massive new estates. Such were the so-called Gropius-Stadt in the southern part of the city, named after its architect-in-chief, and the Märkisches Viertel on the northern outskirts, in which Düttmann again played a part (Ill. 135).

Both those projects extended over many years and were finally completed in the 1970s. And both, in the face of the unsavoury reputation that has attached itself to high-rise apartment blocks in general, demonstrate that attractive environments can be created for large numbers of people through a variety of imaginative designs for houses of different forms and sizes, some of fifteen storeys, others of five, with generous gardens and playgrounds interspersed. Areas of greenery take time to mature, and only now, twenty or thirty years on, can one experience the total integrated design that the planners envisioned when the project was launched.

No less controversial at the time than the development of new estates in outer suburbs were policies relating to what to preserve and what to 'redevelop', i.e. destroy, in the inner city. Not before unforgivable sins had been committed, in East and West alike, did the consciousness dawn of the need – the duty – to preserve the old historical districts which gave the city

134. Kongresshalle, designed by Hugh Stubbins and Werner Düttmann, 1957.

its character, and where necessary, to restore them. In this the weight of responsibility lay, as a result of history, more heavily on the East than on the West, since the centre of Prussian Berlin, and the cultural buildings that had arisen round it, had from the beginning been under Soviet/DDR control. Initially a rabid determination prevailed to rid the city of as many as possible of the surviving memories of dynastic Prussian rule. The decision to blow up the former Royal Palace, which, though damaged, could well have been restored if the will had been there, was a purely political act. Many historical churches, too, that could have been saved were razed to the ground as relics of religion, irritants to the leaders of a state avowedly atheist in character. The fate even of the massive cathedral, damaged but by no means critically so, hung in the balance until a start on systematic restoration was reluctantly approved in 1975.

On the other hand, driven as much by a desire to gain international prestige and publicity as by genuine cultural conviction, the East Germans did preserve and repair the Staatsoper, Schinkel's Altes Museum, the Bode Museum and many of the palaces on the lower part of Unter den Linden. Their belated coming to terms with national history in the 1980s also led to the striking restoration of two major sites in the city. One was the Gendarmenmarkt, the large open square in the Friedrichstadt dominated by Schinkel's Schauspielhaus of 1821 and flanked by the twin eighteenth-century French and German Churches. The interior of the Schauspielhaus, in particular, left totally gutted for years after the end of the war, now stands as a tribute to what restoration can achieve when given its head. The other showcase – a less happy undertaking – was the recreation of the complex of narrow, winding streets, now pedestrianised, round the medieval

135. The Märkisches Viertel housing development in the northern suburb of Wilhelmsruh, completed in the 1970s.

Nikolaikirche, the oldest surviving building in the city. A slightly embarrassing mixture of genuine restoration and 'olde worlde' mimicry – new old façades, new old cafés, new old street lamps – the finished article comes dangerously close to the ethos of a theme park.

Most of the representative new architecture of East Berlin clustered round the two new focal centres created in what had provocatively – and illegally – styled itself since 1949 the capital of the German Democratic Republic. The one, the scene of parades, Party rallies and demonstrations, was the so-called Marx-Engels-Platz, a vast open concrete space where the Royal Palace used to be. Incorporated into the otherwise unmemorable façade of the Council of State building on the south side of the square is one of the Baroque portals designed by Eosander von Göthe for the palace of King Friedrich I. In its new and incongruous environment the portal owes its presence, not, however, to any aesthetic urge but to its historical significance as the balcony from which Karl Liebknecht, in a moment of deluded hope, proclaimed a German Socialist Republic in November 1918.

The only other feature of architectural interest or quality in the square is the post-modernist Palace of. the Republic (1973–6), a multi-purpose building that used to house the Volkskammer (Chamber of People's Deputies), a conference hall and various social facilities, including a theatre. Externally it has little to commend it, and its tinted reflector glass façades are an offence to the Cathedral opposite, but its interior, decorated with paintings by contemporary artists, was an interesting exercise in architecture for the masses. Its final fate, like that of many former official buildings in East Berlin since the reunification of the country in 1990, is still uncertain.

Hub of the other centre of development in the eastern part of the city was the Alexanderplatz. As the Marx-Engels-Platz had become the ceremonial centre for state occasions, so the Alexanderplatz, formerly an area of unsavoury associations, was redesigned, pedestrianised and made into a shopping area and social meeting place. Work began in the 1960s and went on into the 1980s. To enhance the representative status of the area the brash television tower, proposed and designed many years earlier by Hermann Henselmann, architect of the Stalinallee, was finally erected near by in 1969, together with fountains and other decorative motifs. Here too there are plans afoot to bring the whole area back closer to its pre-war aspect, including tramlines across the centre of the square.

In the part of Berlin left in the hands of the West after the war there was no natural historical centre. A new focus of attention was created around the eastern end of the Kurfürstendamm, dominated by the imperial Gedächtniskirche. As in Coventry Cathedral, with which the Gedächtniskirche developed a spiritual bond after the war, the remains of the spire were left standing and a new, modern church built alongside them: a severe octagonal structure in concrete and blue glass was erected in 1961 by Egon Eiermann, with a free-standing campanile on the other side of the crippled spire. But the ruins of the buildings in the square around the church, including those of the Romanisches Café, popular haunt of artists and intellectuals in the Roaring Twenties, were rapidly cleared, to be replaced by strident tributes to the consumerism and material prosperity that accompanied the West German Economic Miracle. The Kurfürstendamm itself, its façades restored, its shops glistening, became the city's social promenade, the Unter den Linden of the West. The proximity of the Berlin Zoo – even the banal presence of the adjoining railroad station, the only mainline terminus in the western part of the city and thus a powerful symbol of its lifeline to the West – also became a factor in the equation.

As part of the celebrations in 1987 of the 750th anniversary of the city's foundation, a second international building exhibition, spread over various sites, was held to review events since the Hansaviertel exhibition of thirty years earlier. One of the principal messages that went out from the new Interbau exhibition was the need for a return to historical considerations in the reconstruction of urban communities, a need to repersonalise a city which in the early post-war years had been subjected to the tyranny of the urban throughway and the mindless destruction wrought by the urban 'developer'. Put another way: the call was for a rediscovery of tradition, a call both unfashionable and unwelcome in the shadow of defeat and through the decades when the two Germanies were having to define their characters and their public roles anew.

An object lesson in contemporary architectural thinking in such contexts emerges from the development on the southern flank of the Tiergarten, formerly an area of elegant villas accommodating government agencies and foreign embassies. The houses that survived are being, or have been, restored. Taking their cue from the historical and aesthetic *genius loci*, Rob Krier, Hans Hollein and others designed a complex of post-modern apartment blocks nestling among the trees of their leafy environment. Similar projects were promoted by the Interbau exhibition for areas quite different in character and historical associations, such as the southern Friedrichstadt – a desolate tract of land including the Berlin Museum and the ruined Anhalter railroad station – and the equally ravaged Prager Platz in Wilmersdorf.

In the context of the reunified city such projects, however imaginative, however enlightened, are like drops in the ocean when one surveys what still has to be done – and redone – half a century after the events that made it all necessary and all possible. Berlin will remain a building site far into the next century.

The Literature of the West

The physical and spiritual collapse of May 1945 left Germany, first in a state of unified, indiscriminate chaos, then, after a few years of fear and apprehension, in the grip of a partition from which there was no foreseeable escape.

Some found more in this chaos than a passing moment of horror before the return of a 'normal' optimism and serenity. The poet Gottfried Benn, whose works from the expressionist decade of thirty years earlier now gave him almost the status of a classic, returned to his home in Berlin in 1945 from service as an army surgeon and lived through the Russians' final assault on the city. In his *Berliner Novelle 1947*, surrounded by ruins, hunger, cold, despair, Benn sees the destruction of his city as a symbol of a modern age doomed to perish. 'West Germany is on the road to cultural decline because Berlin has ceased to exist.' Survival, if the word still has any meaning, can only be in an abstract, esoteric intellectual and artistic world free of any commitment to reality or the present. Such apocalyptic nihilism, like that of the cultural pessimism of Oswald Spengler's newly discovered *Decline of the West*, and like the black despair of Borcherdt's post-war drama *Draussen vor der Tür*, could not but exert a powerful appeal at such a moment.

Two states now emerged, each claiming to be the rightful custodian of the national heritage. Berlin, its four-power status crumbling almost by the day, became a microcosm of the global East–West antagonism, the Cold War.

But the confrontation between East Berlin and West Berlin was not a conflict between equals. As time went by East Berlin became more and more firmly integrated into the territory of the DDR itself as the nominal capital of that territory. West Berlin, on the other hand, surrounded on all sides by alien, virtually enemy land, had to struggle to survive. The vibrant pre-war metropolis now existed only in the mind. West Berlin was still the largest city in Germany – far larger than East Berlin – but its capital status had gone. It had become provincial, like Munich, or Stuttgart, or Cologne – in fact, had returned to its regional role of the nineteenth century before Bismarck made it the capital of empire.

DRAMA

The first decade and a half of the life of the German Federal Republic, and with it West Berlin, was a period of restoration, in culture as in politics. Theatres were quickly rebuilt and public demand for performances grew, a demand met not by new dramatic initiatives proceeding from 'point zero' but by a return to the European classics, repository of the traditional values through which Germany must inspire its moral revival. Goethe, Schiller, Kleist, Gerhart Hauptmann, spiced with imported works by Camus, Anouilh, Eugene O'Neill and Thornton Wilder – such was the basic repertory that saw the German stage through the 1950s. Towards the end of the decade Brecht also began to be played, revealing a theatre of an originality and power that no contemporary dramatist in the West could match.

This conservative policy of 'forwards into the past', expression of an officially sponsored reluctance to face the nation's Nazi history, began to unravel in the early 1960s following war-crimes trials which thrust before the public uncomfortable issues of responsibility for the acts of inhumanity committed in its name. Young intellectuals moved sharply to the left, and the arts followed suit. Traditional dramatic models like Zuckmayer were deemed incapable of encompassing present-day issues, and from its retreat behind conventions and historical precedents the drama emerged with aggressive demands for a new statement of principles and functions to which its practitioners could refer. The outcome, as political in substance as aesthetic, was the first native German form of drama to emerge after the war – documentary drama.

One of the earliest documentary dramas to reach the stage, and a classic example of the genre, was Heinar Kipphardt's *In der Sache J. Robert Oppenheimer*, produced in 1964 by Piscator in the Freie Volksbühne in West Berlin. Initiator of revolutionary political theatre in Berlin back in the 1920s, Piscator had been one of the great directors of the Weimar Republic. After the disbandment of left-wing theatre under the Nazis he went into exile and eventually found his way to New York, where he ran a drama school for the New School of Social Research. He returned to Germany after the war – not to the socialist East but to the capitalist West – and was director of the Freie Volksbühne from 1962 until his death in 1966.

Kipphardt, who left West Germany for East Berlin in 1949 but changed his mind ten years later, set out in his play to present the moral dilemma of the leading scientist behind the manufacture of the atomic bomb that destroyed Hiroshima. The work merits the description documentary to the extent that its action rests on the transcripts of the hearing by the United States government in 1954 of the case of Robert Oppenheimer and his alleged communist associations. But the proceedings of a government commission, as they stand, are not drama, and the play is not a montage of documentary material. The drama, and the specific points that the author wants to make about the moral responsibility of the scientist to himself, to science and to society, are contained in the fictional material that lies between the excerpts from the courtroom proceedings. Moreover, although 'documentary' may seem at first sight to be the equivalent of 'objective', the whole play is conceived as an exercise in political persuasion. Each piece of selected historical evidence may be factual and objective in itself but the selection and arrangement of the evidence follow the dramatist's subjective purpose.

Generically *Oppenheimer* belongs in the context of realistic didactic drama descended from Brecht's *Lehrstücke* of the early 1930s. Indeed, both in conception and production the documentary drama of the 1960s is the natural heir of the left-wing literature of the Weimar Republic. And it seemed an act of providence that Piscator, of all men, should now return to Berlin to launch the work of the new avant-garde and add to it his decades of experience of political theatre. He also brought with him all the multi-media tricks of his Weimar days, using screen projections, newspaper headlines, tape-recordings, including excerpts from speeches by Senator Joseph McCarthy himself, to intensify both the political and the moral argument. And as in the 1920s, incidental music was an integral part of the show. Brecht would have recognised what was going on.

During his last four years in Berlin Piscator made his name inseparable from the wave of politicised documentary plays that swept through the German theatre in the 1960s. The year before *Oppenheimer* he produced Rolf Hochhuth's *Der Stellvertreter* ('The Representative'), perhaps the most infamous work of its kind, certainly the first post-war German drama to command international attention, with its allegation that Pope Pius XII, through moral cowardice and his policy of non-intervention, shared a responsibility for the holocaust. Almost equally famous, and located in the same moral area, is Peter Weiss' *Die Ermittlung* ('The Investigation'), a drama cast in the form of a trial which, mirroring the proceedings of the Auschwitz war-crimes trials of 1963–5, investigates the question of personal and collective German guilt for the fate of the Jews. The scene is not one of spectators watching actors and applauding their performance but of a combined involvement in the re-enactment of an occasion aimed at eliciting a common political response. Piscator, who also put on a variety of other works at the Freie Volksbühne – *A Midsummer Night's Dream*, Bernard Shaw's *Androcles and the Lion*, Gerhart Hauptmann's *Fuhrmann Henschel* – gave *Die Ermittlung* its first production in 1965.

Documentary drama, by definition, rests on historical events and historical characters. In the context of the 1960s it represented not only a swing of critical intellectual opinion to the left but, on a broader front, the preparedness of the public to confront painful moments in the recent past. 'The strength of documentary theatre', said Peter Weiss, 'lies in its ability to take fragments of reality and combine them to form a practical model of contemporary events.'

Never resident in Berlin, choosing to make his home in Sweden, Peter Weiss was nevertheless responsible for one of the most exciting and startling events on the Berlin stage in the 1960s – the première in the Schiller-Theater of his extraordinarily titled *The Persecution and Assassination of Marat as Performed by the Inmates of the Asylum at Charenton under the Direction of the Marquis de Sade*. The title contains the plot and the dialectical argument within it. Marat is the rational revolutionary, a Brechtian figure; Sade, author of the play the lunatics perform, is the embodiment of passion and anarchy. Within the violence inherent in the situation the murder of Marat is set against the debate between individualism and the dictatorship of the asylum society – the French revolutionary situation. The characters switch from their roles in the Marat story to their real roles as lunatics. The Marat-play takes place in the framework of the Sade-play and both are transposed on to the stage of the present in a double alienation. There are songs and choruses, dance and pantomime, a total theatrical experience of interlocking fantasies, leaving the political message that revolution is always followed by dictatorship. 'With this clever and highly intelligent play', wrote Friedrich Luft, 'Peter Weiss has finally brought the interregnum of mediocrity to an end.'

A non-dialectical but no less intellectually fascinating play from these mid-1960s, part documentary, part historical, wholly realistic and political in the broadest sense, is Günter Grass' *Die Plebejer proben den Aufstand* ('The Plebeians Rehearse the Uprising'). Probably the best-known living German writer, Grass had lived in Berlin since before the Wall. Given his life-long involvement in politics, it was a natural domicile, at least for part of the time, the place where the realities of a divided nation were at their most insistent.

Grass' *Plebejer* is precisely located in time and place – Berlin, on the symbolic 17 June 1953. A director – Brecht in all but name – is rehearsing the first scene of Brecht's *Coriolan*, in which the citizens are preparing to revolt. Outside the theatre a real revolt has erupted as the workers of East Berlin take to the streets. 'Brecht', as a good socialist, should have joined the workers; instead he aestheticises the situation, acting out in art what should be acted out in politics.

The drama exists on many levels, and much of its interest derives from the interplay of ambiguities between these levels, an interplay held within the framework of Grass' attack on Brecht for his conduct on 17 June. The plebeians, for example, are at once the rebellious Roman citizens of *Coriolanus*, the actors 'Brecht' is rehearsing in his version of Shakespeare's play, and the 'real' workers outside the theatre. Two levels are those of art, the other is that of reality – historical fact – the statement of an incompatibility that has been a persistent theme in German literature through the ages. It is the problematical inadequacy that dogs the intellectual, the artist, Grass is saying – the characteristic that leads him to observe and interpret rather than participate. Brecht – the real Brecht – happens here to be in Grass' sights. But Grass too has the status of victim, and his *Plebejer* can no more escape its ambiguity than can Brecht's *Coriolan*.

Ambiguity carried to the nth degree, a categorical assertion of the meaninglessness and formlessness of existence and a consequent denial of the sense of any higher purpose in life underlay the theatre of the absurd which found its way from France (Camus, Ionesco, Beckett) to Germany in the early 1960s. Beckett was in Berlin to stage his *Endgame* and *Happy Days* in 1967 and returned to do *Waiting for Godot* at the Schiller-Theater during the Berlin Festival of 1975. But although it attracted the occasional writer, like Wolfgang Hildesheimer, the philosophy of the absurd left little mark on German drama as a whole and virtually none in Berlin, where political and 'alternative' concerns outweighed all others.

Such concerns were also the life-blood of cabaret, a characteristically Berlin medium for measuring the political temperature of the moment. One could hardly expect a return to the halcyon times of the 1920s but from the early days of recovery at the end of the war the Berliners' characteristic irreverent wit had found its way back into the world of sketch and revue, most triumphantly with Günter Neumann's radio show called – with a play on the isolation of West Berlin – *The Islanders*. In Weimar days the objects of derision had usually been individuals or particular groups in society. In later settings, like Volker Ludwig's Reichskabarett of 1965, the 'system' itself, the political establishment, came under fire in programmes devoted to single worldwide themes, such as United States involvement in Latin America. The Reichskabarett's show on this subject was called *The Guerrilla Fighter Sends His Kindest Regards*.

Political tension in West Berlin grew in 1967 and 1968 with the arrival of a culture of violent protest and demonstration, the militant student movement and the consequent Emergency Laws invoked by a state fearful for its survival. The 'street theatre' of the Russian Revolution was revived, presenting the radical opposition's view of the issues of the moment through placards, slogans, improvised sketches, monologues and the other tools of agitprop. Art becomes absorbed into politics. For as politics is the sphere of action and reality, so theatre, to be politically effective, must lose its ambience of illusion and symbolic meaning. The 'Happenings' of these years form part of the same picture – exercises in the obliteration of the distinction between theatre and reality by proclaiming reality itself to be a work of art. The perfect union has been achieved: art has been swallowed up in reality, life has become art. It is all a very laborious way of making the artist superfluous.

Nor was it only adult theatre at which such ideas were directed. A by-product of the anti-authoritarian movement of the late 1960s was the foundation in West Berlin of the Grips Theater, presenting a politicisation of fairy-tale material designed to involve children and young people in general in the process of understanding the social and political issues of the day from a declared ideological standpoint. The message matters more than the medium but the entertainment value of its revue-like productions guaranteed Grips' survival and earned it substantial financial backing from the Berlin Senate, spokesman of the capitalist society whose values it so heartily scorned. Both the finances and the scorned values are still alive and well and living in the Altonaer Strasse in Charlottenburg, a permanent feature of the city's cultural landscape.

Fringe events like Grips, street theatre and Happenings represented the politicisation of literature at its extreme, politicisation to the point where literature has virtually ceased to exist. The 1970s, in the wake of a faltering economic advance and an increasing polarity of society, turned away from the theatre of sloganising didacticism and world-changing pretensions and returned to the subjective vision, to a theatre which nurtures private fantasy and imagination rather than feeding a public political appetite. The direct recourse to subject matter from the past remains but the fate of the individual now matters more than the course of history. From an anti-American play on Vietnam (1968) Peter Weiss turned to the single mind *in extremis* – *Tolstoy* (1970), *Hölderlin* (1971) – while in 1976 Hochhuth wrote a monodrama – a two-hour *tour de force* for the actor who plays the role – on Hemingway (*Death of a Huntsman*), whom he portrays as a moral weakling who sacrifices ideals to expediency.

But the new subjectivity, fortified by the anti-establishment pressures of the past decade and by opposition to the conventional world of middle-class 'culinary' theatre, as Brecht had called it, found its keenest expression in the realm of staging and production – what became known as 'producers' theatre', as opposed to 'playwrights' theatre' and even 'theatre-goers' theatre'. One of the leading centres of this revolutionary self-justifying and self-governing new theatre in Berlin was the Schaubühne am Halleschen Ufer, under one of Germany's leading and most controversial post-war directors, Peter Stein.

After stormy episodes in Munich and Bremen, Stein, a native of Berlin, took over at the Schaubühne in 1970. The two principles on which this avowedly anti-capitalist theatre rested were that it should be free to indulge in aesthetic experiment and investigate the role of art in society, and that the company should organise its affairs as a collective. For the city of Berlin, struggling to preserve its position in the realm of the performing arts and willing to pay for it, the capture of Stein and his Schaubühne was a coup. For Stein, the Marxist with millions of marks of capitalist money in his pocket – the city met nearly 75 per cent of his budget – it meant the freedom to experiment with new forms and references of political drama with at least a temporary sense of security.

One of the collective's early aims was to use their performances to raise the issue of social, that is socialist, change. Hence their choice of Brecht's *Die Mutter* ('The Mother'), a play, based on Gorki, which follows the rise of a sense of political awareness in its central character. The 'epic acting', led by Therese Giehse, veteran of Brecht's own days and the first Mother Courage, sharpened the contours of the action, while as part of the preparation for their roles the actors were urged to familiarise themselves with Marxist writings in order to raise the level of their political consciousness.

The Schaubühne was from the beginning a contradiction in terms – an institution financed by the taxpayers of a society it was committed to undermine. By accepting state subsidies, it had tacitly acknowledged at the outset the rule of the establishment, and when it approved the plan to build it a new state-of-the-art home in the glitter of the Kurfürstendamm, which opened in 1982, the partnership was sealed.

Productions in the new Schaubühne over recent years have ranged widely, taking in Genet's *The Blacks*, Eugene O'Neill's *The Hairy Ape*, works by Maeterlinck, Euripides, Chekhov and Harold Pinter. Britain saw Stein's work in a production of Verdi's *Otello* for the Welsh National Opera in 1986. But the previous year, with little warning, Stein had parted company with his Schaubühne. Perhaps he, and they, realised that they had reached the limits of their search to present an alternative awareness that would seriously challenge the rule of the status quo.

An enterprise like the Schaubühne and the presence of a personality like Peter Stein was bound to attract young dramatists and would-be producers to Berlin, which already had a robust theatrical life. One who has made a particular name for himself is Botho Strauss, a theatre critic who joined Stein at the Schaubühne in 1971 and worked on its productions of Ibsen's *Peer Gynt* and Kleist's *Der Prinz von Homburg*.

A consciously poetic writer, Strauss shares the subjectivity of manner of Handke and Thomas Bernhard, focusing, like them, not on systems and slogans but on individuals, characters at odds with their environment and with themselves. Articulate middle-class professionals – doctors, actors, artists – emotionally unfulfilled in their isolated, alienated worlds, sit in their closed society and contemplate the hopelessness of ever making real contact with other people. It is not a theatre of plot but of characters united by loneliness. Or, as in Strauss' *Gross und Klein* ('Great and Small'), hailed by critics as the best new play of 1978, there is a single lonely character in focus – a neurotic female who wanders from one place to another searching for her husband, for her friends, for peace of mind and security, and finally finds her way to a clinic which declares her perfectly healthy and sends her away to go quietly mad on her own. In Strauss' characteristic manner the woman's progress is portrayed in a sequence of separate stations in a cinematic technique. It is an existential situation, yet at the same time typical, recurrent, open to the eclecticism that Strauss brings to bear on it. His plays of the 1980s, such as *Die Fremdenführerin* ('The Tourist Guide'), thus present situations in which social relationships and tensions cannot be depicted head-on and sequentially but only obliquely, as examples of a recurrent formula – in other words, of a myth, here the myth of Pan and Syrinx, captured in a mood both empathetic and parodistic.

Compared with the rumblings beneath the surface of life in East Germany, conditions in West Berlin during the early and mid-1980s were broadly uneventful. In 1987 East and West Berlin each organised their own programme of events to commemorate the 750th anniversary of the city's foundation, and for the following year, 1988, West Berlin was the nominated European City of Culture, an occasion marked by a mammoth programme of concerts, exhibitions, lectures, dramas and spectacles of every conceivable kind. For the first time the DDR participated in the West Berlin Festwochen, sending a theatrical troupe from Dresden and an extensive exhibition of contemporary paintings by DDR artists – a gesture calculated to show that, when it came to matters cultural, the East was fully the equal of the West.

One of the most extravagant and controversial avant-garde events of the year was Robert Wilson's production of *The Forest* in the Freie Volksbühne, a modern version of the Gilgamesh epic for which Heiner Müller wrote much of the problematical text. The 'new subjectivity' and a return to aesthetic values had begun to assert itself. At the same time Hochhuth's *Juristen* ('Lawyers') of 1979, an exposure of the legal system under the Nazis, and Kipphardt's *Bruder Eichmann*, first produced in 1983, reopened chapters of the national past which most thought had been closed, or should be left unread.

Variety and vitality were assured, and it seemed like a period of calm consolidation. Until the events of 1989.

THE POETIC SELF

In 1980 the West Berlin publisher Klaus Wagenbach compiled an anthology of post-war German prose and poetry for use in the senior grades of West German grammar schools. An indefatigable promoter of progressive literature and radical causes – it was he who issued recordings of Wolf Biermann singing his forbidden ballads in his apartment in East Berlin – Wagenbach wanted something to set against the current literary school fodder of Bergengruen, Wiechert, Carossa and other underwriters of yesterday's values. He selected texts from some thirty West German authors and ten from the DDR. Of poets from the West, only seven were resident in West Berlin. Of those from the East, on the other hand, all except one lived in their 'capital of the German Democratic Republic'.

Statistics are unsure elements for building cultural arguments. But the fact remains that, although many writers primarily associated with other genres – Grass, Uwe Johnson, Kipphardt, Wolfdietrich Schnurre – also wrote verse from time to time, West Berlin has little poetry to show after the death of Gottfried Benn that will stand comparison with Hermlin, Kunert, Biermann, Volker Braun and others living and working – at least to start with – in East Berlin. And of the steady stream of voluntary and involuntary exiles who crossed from East to West during the years of division, hardly any, beyond the occasional actor, made his home in West Berlin.

There may be few strong poetic personalities to confront but the volume of verse produced in the post-war years was considerable, and no less so its variety. Some poets pursued a contemplative, introspective line recalling the 'inner emigration' of the Nazi years, while others plunged into the emotional and intellectual hurly-burly of a society reconstructing itself from the ruins. Some sought to revive the status of the pure aesthetic utterance, others joined the movement of *littérature engagée*. Some saw poetry as didactic, others as entertainment. Some were passionate, others cool, detached, sardonic. Common to all was a sense of release from the tyranny of the Third Reich and its abuse of the German language, the restoration of the right of the individual subjective voice to be heard. The world had become a very different place since the last time there had been freedom of literary expression, and in some quarters the cultivation of a literally ego-centric lyric was equated with an escapism almost irresponsible in its time and place. Yet nothing seemed more natural than to seek to re-establish in this changed world the link between man and his environment, man and nature, traditional preserve of lyric poetry – nature as an objective reality, both as a symbol of continuity and rebirth and as a point of subjective reference for defining the human condition. For the Berlin poet that nature is the city itself, from whose desolation and suffering its children cannot wrench themselves free:

> BERLIN,
> mein ruiniertes BERLIN,
> wo anders sind wir denn ruiniert worden als in BERLIN,
> noch deine Ruinen, BERLIN, umschliessen mehr Zukunft
> als alle Düsseldorfer Versicherungsgebäude zusammen.
>
> Ich liebe dein Grinsen, BERLIN,
> die nackte Fassade,
> all' die gehäufte Vergeblichkeit in deinen Zügen,
> dein Zorn.
> die Zermürbung in deinen Gesichtern.
>
> ('BERLIN,
> my ruined BERLIN,
> where else have we been ruined as in BERLIN,
> yet your ruins, BERLIN, embrace more future
> than all Düsseldorf's insurance buildings put together.

I love your mocking grin, BERLIN,
the bare façade,
all the heaped-up futility in your features,
your rage
the exhaustion in your faces.')
                                        (from Reimar Lenz, 'BERLIN')

The energies of the 1950s went into the rebuilding of the city. Not needed as comfort or distraction, let alone as an agent of propaganda in the building of a new society, poetry sought its justification from within, from the cultivation of aesthetic values, of what made poetry poetry. Standing for opposition to the politicisation of literature, it made its own case for the joy of artistic creation, specifically for the restoration of the primacy of language and for the elevation of poetic craftsmanship. Art fills the void left by the failure of life to transcend the prevailing nihilism. Meaning is held in the magic of the poetic word and the poetic form, in the associative power of symbols and images, which leads to the self-sufficiency of what came to be known as 'hermetic' poetry. Gottfried Benn, whose aesthetic survived well beyond his death in 1956, spoke of 'the absolute poem, the poem without faith, without hope, addressed to no one, the poem made of words assembled in a fascinating form'. Only at the moment the created poem emerges as an act of craftsmanship does the lyrical self exist.

A formalistic lyric poetry of this kind had little chance of justifying itself for long in the tense political world of the 1960s. One effect of the building of the Berlin Wall, an urge felt perhaps even more intensely in the eastern part of the city than the western, was an almost spontaneous need to communicate, to share with others thoughts and experiences which the sufferings of the time made it impossible to conceal. The world is a dark place. Nature herself shares this darkness and becomes a source not of consolation and serenity but of uncertainty and menace – nature as portrayed by Peter Huchel, the East Berlin poet and editor whose collection *Chausseen Chausseen* (1963), filled with bleak images of fear and foreboding, could be published only in the West.

Not surprisingly the mid-1960s also saw the return of a realism in the service of political and social causes. From being devoted to the interests of its own closed world, poetry became an open activity again, an act of agitation directed towards revealing the contradictions and shortcomings of society. The student revolts and the Vietnam War added themes for a specific poetry of social and political protest which assigned itself the dual function of medium of enlightenment and call to arms. Folk singers like Biermann and F. J. Degenhardt have their place in this movement, and the anti-culture of the followers of Jimi Hendrix and Julie Driscoll is not far away.

But even without these extreme political dimensions this poetry speaks of the rediscovery of reality, of the tangibility of objects, however trivial, of a receptivity to the outside world and a desire to address that world. The finished poem, moreover, is to the poet an object in its own right, there to serve a purpose for anyone who cares to use it. Here is matter-of-factness, not ideology; precision of observable detail, not gentle allusiveness. Formally, at the same time, the subjective self on which the whole tradition of lyric poetry rested, from the Middle Ages through Baroque, Goethe, Hölderlin, Heine, Mörike down to the twentieth century and Gottfried Benn, is left in the background.

The shadow of the Berlin Wall fell, literally, on a colony of poets and artists who in the 1950s and 1960s set up anti-bourgeois communities in the run-down tenements of Kreuzberg. Historically Berlin had developed as an agglomeration of villages, each claiming its own character and its own loyalty. As the Prenzlauer Berg district attracted the dissidents and anti-authoritarian elements of a protest culture in East Berlin, so Kreuzberg, with its ethnic mix and its non-conformist shabbiness, the focus of 'alternative' sub-cultures but also of artists and poets of protest, became the symbol of rebelliousness in the West.

It is often rather the existence of such communities themselves than the identity of individuals within them that arouses interest. But as well as Günter Kunert, the East German poet who lived in Kreuzberg for a time after turning his back on the DDR, and the painters Karl Horst Hödicke and Reiner Fetting, the colourful personality of Günter Bruno Fuchs stands out among the Kreuzberg brotherhood. Poet, painter, wood-cutter, alcoholic, sometimes using the bizarre techniques of surrealism, sometimes the penetrating, laconic manner of Brecht, his mood provocative and aggressive one moment, melancholy and ironical the next, Fuchs became a key figure on the 'alternative' scene, a man who spoke for the rebels and social exiles among whom he had chosen to live:

> *Wenn Sie*
> *keine Arbeit finden,*
> *dann sollten Sie*
> *schlafen*
> *und überwintern. Sie*
> *haben dadurch*
> *die seltene Möglichkeit,*
> *einigen Tieren*
> *näherzukommen.*

> ('If you
> cannot find work,
> You should
> sleep
> and hibernate. That way
> you will have
> a rare opportunity
> to get to know certain animals
> better.')

From the debris of the events of 1968, among them yet another demonstration that social change will not be brought about by literature, emerged the so-called New Subjectivity of the 1970s.

In its immediate historical context the New Subjectivity represents a synthetic middle path between two extreme and now rejected positions – self-contained, hermetic poetry on the one hand and the subjection of poetry to the demands of a political cause on the other. The radical political stance of the young poet remained intact but no longer got in the way of his poetry. The subjectivity of that poetry, moreover, had little to do with the emotionalism of the familiar lyrical tradition identified in literary history but is the product of a cool reflection on the common objects and experiences of day-to-day existence, like a series of snapshots. Language and syntax are simple, matter-of-fact, non-poetic to the point of indistinguishability from prose. The poet does not raise his voice – he is, after all, writing what quickly came to be known as 'everyday poetry', natural in its formulations, realistic and subjective at the same time. 'What those poets have to say', wrote a reviewer, 'is on the lines, not between them.'

Behind the lines, however flat, natural, even spontaneous they may seem, lies a great deal of theorising. Many poets were at pains to make their aesthetic as well as their political position clear in journals and reviews, anxious that the intellectual infrastructure of their work should be properly grasped.

Most of the leading poets and critics, such as Peter Rühmkorf and Rolf Dieter Brinkmann, lived and worked in West Germany. But one characteristic figure, a child of the post-war generation decisively influenced – 'scarred' might be a more appropriate word – by the American folk- and pop-music scene, decided to settle in the anti-authoritarian world of West Berlin – Jürgen Theobaldy. Poet and critic, casting himself as the spokesman for a disinherited generation, putting a case for colloquial diction as a poetic medium, Theobaldy published in 1977 an anthology of contemporary verse which provides virtually all the raw material one needs for understanding the poetic scene in pre- and post-1968 Germany. The title of the collection alone gives symbolic expression to the subject–object antithesis that set the poetic agenda of the time: *Und ich bewege mich doch . . .* , Theobaldy called it – 'But I *do* move . . .' – invoking Galileo's 'Eppur si muove'. Theobaldy's colloquial, dead-pan tone suits Berlin. Introducing a volume of his own verse, he explained: 'These poems are for all those who travel second class in German trains, sit in the front row in the cinema and watch football matches from the terraces that are farthest from the pitch.'

As fashion swayed to and fro between literature as public political commitment and literature as private artistic concern, so an aesthetic of commonplace language in the formlessness of everyday speech was pushed aside by the return of poetic diction, rhyme, symmetry and formal literary structures. The sonnet reappears, albeit rather self-consciously, and the ode is revived, inviting the critical attention to linger on formal interest and technical virtuosity. In one sense it is an attempt to regain the past for the present, to demonstrate an historical continuum; equally it is a formal exercise in its own terms, significant at that moment as representing the philosophy of 'backwards into the future'.

In West Germany as a whole, and in West Berlin in particular, political developments bore directly on the course of cultural life, and the consolidation of the early 1980s under a Christian Democratic administration played its part in the reassertion of traditional forms and values as modernism and avant-gardism retreated. The subjective autonomy of the lyrical vision remains paramount but it finds expression within a tradition, which is to say it accepts the validity of a living history, a philosophy of continuity and a need to acknowledge the restraint imposed by the reality of the object. Günter Kunert's *Berlin beizeiten* (1987), a collection of poems each addressed to a particular location in the city, shows the quiet, unobtrusive pleasure still to be derived from lyric poetry in this vein.

This traditionalism even reaches a point where the poet is ready to reassume his eighteenth- and nineteenth-century role as visionary, *poeta vates*, embodied in the person of Hölderlin, a figure who exerted a paradigmatic fascination on poets, novelists and dramatists of the 1960s–1980s. The cool, constructionist skills of modernism are exposed in their unreal inadequacy by the warmth of an appeal to beauty, to moral values, to joys and disillusionments that can be shared with others – a conventional poetry of communication. And if he sees catastrophe threatening – a new world war, ecological disaster – the communication of the poet as prophet becomes even more urgent, the responsibility of his calling even more evident. That there was a political Hölderlin, a poet to be understood in part as a child of the French Revolution, made his relevance all the more inescapable.

Sonnet, ode, prose poem, the language of the special literary occasion and the language of everyday discourse, the questing subject and the all-powerful object, the hermetic poem and the call of the barricades, poetry as art and poetry as political act – the 1980s have them all, side by side, and, to a greater degree than one might expect, in East and West alike. Most, in that flashpoint of world affairs that was Berlin, observed what was going on, whichever their side of the Wall. Some, anxiously, resignedly, ironically observed themselves observing what was going on. Few foretold what would be going on before the 1980s were out.

THE NOVEL OF THE WEST

The condition of a nation's literature both reflects and depends on the condition of its language. While the Renaissance was enriching the rhetoric and the poetic repertoire of Italy, France and England, Germany, driven by the invasion of the Reformation, had a rough, unsubtle, unbeautiful vernacular which had only just acquired a unified written form through Luther's translation of the Bible. It was a blunt instrument for a blunt age. A craggy, rough-hewn effectiveness the literature of sixteenth-century Germany may have – beauty, sophistication and variety it has not. The German language, like the German nation-state, German historical awareness and a German sense of political democracy, was a late developer. Leibniz, scorning the language around him, wrote the *Monadology* and all his other important works in either Latin or French. And when in 1780 Frederick the Great decided to make known his thoughts on German literature, he published them, not as *Über die deutsche Literatur* but as *De la littérature allemande*.

In 1945 the German language stood at a crisis point of its own making. So perverted had it become by a regime itself perverted, so monstrous the thoughts it had been abused to express, its syntax mangled and a hideous vocabulary foisted on to it, that it had to be purified before it could be touched. 'Every single "and", every single adjective required the greatest warines', explained Wolfdietrich Schnurre. *Kahlschlag*, 'total clearance', and *die*

Stunde null, 'point zero', images created to symbolise the spiritual and cultural state of the nation, had no less relevance to the condition of the language itself. The untouchability of the language infected by the Nazis is the precondition for Adorno's much debated precept that to write poetry after Auschwitz is 'barbaric', a realisation that demonstrates 'why it has become impossible to write lyric poetry today'.

To revive the language and their aesthetic instincts writers went back to the realist novels of Neue Sachlichkeit and, beyond this, to the familiar realist tradition of the nineteenth century. The European and American modernists and existentialists to whom they had been denied access during the Third Reich revealed new patterns of language. In particular, largely as a direct consequence of the Americans' cultural policies in their zone of occupation, the Germans discovered Hemingway and the American short story, observing how an extreme detachment and objectivity of presentation, like that of a dispassionate reporter, could point the way to the recovery of their own language and literature. The most influential of post-war literary coteries, the Gruppe 47, emerged directly from this background.

Experience of the war and the German defeat provided ready subject matter for writers in the post-war years. One of the earliest, a man with the most remarkable of careers, was Theodor Plievier, author of a documentary novel *Stalingrad* (1945), based in part on his experience as a fifty-year-old war correspondent on the eastern front, and of *Berlin* (1954), a chronicle cast in the same mould, but by a man who had since become a Westerner. A native Berliner from a working-class family, Plievier served in the German navy throughout the First World War and used this experience in two revolutionary novels of the 1920s which brought him immediate success. He became the darling of the German Communist Party and spent the years of the Third Reich in the Soviet Union but came increasingly to resent the authoritarianism of the Party and defected to the West in 1947. Like those of Uwe Johnson, Martin Gregor-Dellin, Walter Kempowski, Gerhard Zwerenz and many other novelists who left the DDR before 1961, Plievier's career lies on both sides of the divide.

As the DDR had its war novels with their own interpretation of history, especially of what should follow the defeat of Nazism, so West German writers too looked critically at what was emerging from the ruins and what kind of society the Western allies would promote. *Die Geschlagenen* ('The Defeated'), for instance, a novel by Hans Werner Richter, describes bitterly how, four years after the end of the war, the Nazi mentality is far from dead and how old Nazis are finding their way back into positions of influence. Here, as many of the post-war generation were to see it, lay the roots of much that they despised and protested against in the materialistic, consumption-driven society of the burgeoning Federal Republic.

For all the talk of 'point zero', there were writers of older generations who had survived the Third Reich in 'inner emigration' and who, their moral standing intact, now brought to the literary scene a link with the honourable pre-Nazi past. The brilliant spectacle of Weimar culture had, if the truth be told, run its course before the Nazis took over the country. But there were still those who wanted to believe that they could find the trail that had petered out in the early 1930s.

Christian writers in particular enjoyed a new lease of life. Bergengruen's allegorical novel *Der Grosstyrann und das Gericht*, written in Berlin in the 1930s and now eagerly re-read as a picture of the moral depravity characteristic of all dictatorships, became one of the most popular books of the 1950s. An anti-political mood developed during the Adenauer era and 'count me out' – 'Ohne mich' – became the fashionable reaction to any thought of personal commitment or public initiative. A safe, allegorical, oblique literature, intellectually precise and well crafted, living by time-honoured aesthetic criteria, corresponded to this mood of restoration. Arno Schmidt's complex and confusing *nouveau roman* focused on a divided Berlin, *Das steinerne Herz* ('The Heart of Stone'), a jumbled montage of biographical episodes, political *aperçus*, fears of rearmament and nuclear war, and reflections on everything from nature to sex, is an example of the difficult, at times almost incomprehensible literature to which such an introspective philosophy could lead.

But such a literature could not be more than a private playground for aesthetes. After three years Arno Schmidt's first novel, *Leviathan*, had managed to sell just 600 copies. If literature was to become again part of life, the life of common experience, it would have to turn outwards and look that life in the face. This quickly led to taking sides, to the politicisation of literature; at the very least it meant responding to reality and making a coherent picture out of those responses. The earliest to do this in post-war Berlin was Wolfdietrich Schnurre.

Schnurre grew up in Berlin and returned there after deserting from the army on the eastern front shortly before the end of the war. His family home had been in the Soviet sector but as early as 1948 the restrictions being put on his freedom to publish where he chose drove him to move to the West – no farther, however, than West Berlin. 'Berlin has shaped me and determined both my nature and the way I write and think,' he said.

Although he also wrote novels and lyric poetry, Schnurre's characteristic genre is the short story. He had firm ideas on the impulse and function of literature in an age, and in a place, which was emerging from one catastrophe and shuddered at the prospect of becoming the battlefield for another. Surrounded by wartime ruins, he recalled, 'one wrote because one could not help it. One wrote out of a sense of shock and indignation. One wrote because the terrible events of the war had forced us to learn a lesson. One wrote to utter a warning.' Literature, in other words – all art – presupposes commitment: not a narrow commitment to an ideology or a political aim but a concern with humane values, with the demonstration of the humanity, and not infrequent inhumanity, of man.

This might give the impression that Schnurre deals only in disaster and cosmic gloom. But, though never less than earnest in his sober realism, he possesses an ironical humour, both of colloquial dialogue and of situation, which can make a moral point as effectively as an episode described in sombre tones. In his very first story, 'Das Begräbnis' ('The Burial'), it is God – who, as we know, was proclaimed dead by Nietzsche almost a century earlier – that is being buried, a surreal event enacted in the broadest Berlin working-class dialect by a hilarious gang of monosyllabic locals, spokesmen for the language of *Kahlschlag*. The deceased had been seriously ill for some time, said the official announcement. It poured with rain throughout the grotesque ceremony, adds the author.

Or take a later story, 'Das Manöver' ('Manoeuvres'). In the course of military exercises the commanding officer's jeep loses its way in a cloud of smoke from an artillery barrage. When the smoke clears, he finds himself surrounded by thousands of sheep. Losing his nerve, he fires recklessly into the flock, which surges round the jeep and overturns it, leaving an aged ram to attack and kill the officer himself. The arrogance of the military, the ridicule that the officer attracts by his actions, the ignominy of his end, the discomfiture of the army in the face of a flock of sheep – the motifs and their interplay are legion. The reader can make the connections for himself.

Schnurre's career has a sadder side, one that diverts attention from the individual personality to the trauma of post-war existence in divided Berlin. In story, essay, article and address Schnurre devoted himself after 1961 to a life of protest against the Wall, eventually reducing himself to a nervous condition which consigned him to hospital for eighteen months. This was not the psychotic suffering of one highly strung man. 'Wall sickness', a compound of claustrophobia, a sense of abandonment and helplessness, was an acknowledged clinical condition in both East and West Berlin in the 1960s. Schnurre almost burnt himself out over this issue. He never stopped writing – there is, after all, plenty of reality left to write about. But the sense of urgency, of compulsion, was perhaps not quite what it had been. He died in 1989 – but before he was able to see his detested Wall come down.

As the West German economic miracle worked its magic on a society of rising affluence, so a set of new social realities and problems presented themselves as stimuli for a new generation of fiction writers. Different as they were in their individual philosophical positions and literary styles, these writers shared an irrepressible need to comment through their fiction on the political tensions in their divided country, on the implications of a world governed by the mutual antagonism of the two super-powers, on the moral state of West German society and the direction in which it was moving.

In a single year three works were published which, as direct responses to their contemporary world, confronted these issues and together marked the most significant moment in the development of the modern novel in West Germany. The year was 1959. The novels were Günter Grass' *Die Blechtrommel* ('The Tin Drum'), Heinrich Böll's *Billard um halb zehn* ('Billiards at Half-Past Nine') and Uwe Johnson's *Mutmassungen über Jakob* ('Speculations about Jacob'). Böll has no part in the Berlin story, while Grass had not yet established the links that made the city his chosen domicile for a time – *Die Blechtrommel* was written in Paris. But Johnson, from the moment in 1959 when, as a twenty-five-year-old citizen of the DDR, he took the S-Bahn in East Berlin and got out in the British sector, became a figure inseparable from the literary scene of West Berlin. Here he stayed for fifteen years and published the three novels on which his reputation rests.

Yet he had no illusions about the West, where he had expected to find a greater sense of social justice to accompany the basic democratic freedoms. As prepared as Grass to indulge in open political argument, and enjoying the privileged status of one who had openly deserted the socialist totalitarianism of the East, he found congenial company in satirical non-conformists like

Wolfgang Neuss and his political cabaret in West Berlin. But never completely at his ease either in a divided city or in a divided country, though at home in the English-speaking world, he left Berlin in 1974 and spent the last ten years of his short life in the isolation of Sheerness, on the Thames estuary.

Johnson was *the* novelist of a divided Germany – especially for the divided Germans themselves. He embodied the division in himself, he wrote of characters who lived and suffered under it, and the world accepted him as its witness. West Berliners' behaviour towards the East, East Berliners' attitudes towards the West, the image of the city's split personality as seen by an outsider – such subjects, together with the never-ending succession of crisis points through which the city lived, drew him into the arena of public controversy, although he was not the man to engage in the hurly-burly of active politics, like Grass.

But, inseparable as politics were from the situations of which he wrote, Johnson believed in the autonomy of the work of art. He wrote novels in which there was a political dimension but he was not a political novelist. A novel, he wrote, is 'a version of reality, not a society in miniature or a mirror held up to the world'. Still less can it have a political function. 'A novel is not a weapon of revolution.'

Complex and challenging in style, Johnson's novels make great demands on their readers. In *Mutmassungen über Jakob* – the first German novel with the East–West divide as its subject – an East German railway worker is returning from a visit to his fiancée who has defected to the West. Walking back along the railroad tracks in thick fog, he is knocked down by a train and killed. The novel begins with his death and reviews the 'speculations' of the title over how he met his death. Was it an accident? Did he commit suicide? Was he deliberately killed and, if so, did the train come from the East or the West? The question cannot be answered, nor can the enigma of Jakob's personality be unravelled. Altogether we know less about our times, about the people around us, and about ourselves, than we pretend. 'Where reality is known only to a very limited extent', said Johnson, 'I would have no desire to portray it as better known than it is.'

Our perpetual state of uncertainty in the face of rival realities expresses itself in the complicated, multi-layered, arbitrary syntax and style of Johnson's *Mutmassungen*. Sentences are broken off in mid-stream, punctuation confuses meaning, the reader loses track of which character is conveying a piece of information, 'reality' becomes increasingly unattainable and meaningless. The same contorted, surrealist style is carried over into Johnson's *Das dritte Buch über Achim* ('The Third Book about Achim'), again a fictional biography – this time of a sporting hero of the DDR – through which he illustrates the conflicting experiences and conditions of life on both sides of the border that separates the two German states. So drastically have these two states moved apart that any hope of an understanding between them – and any hope of a proper biography of Achim – has vanished. Like the other characters in the novel, like Johnson himself, we search in vain for the real Achim of the title, on whom there have been two unsuccessful books already. There is no omniscient author waiting to put us out of our uncertainty, merely disparate fragments of truth and semi-truth that sometimes come together to form a short-lived context of meaning.

Life in West Berlin after the Second World War was dominated by politics. Its very survival, indeed, was a political balancing act. Forced into a siege mentality, the West Berliners developed a special sensitivity to the state of relations between the Soviet Union and the West, well aware of the fragility of their position. So those who chose to make it their first or even their second home – and even if in part for the financial and other concessions that the territory enjoyed – tended to do so in order to be in the forefront of the political action. Domestic politics too were intensifying, as the fortunes of the Christian Democrats waned and the country moved to the left. It was against such a politicised background that from 1960 onwards Günter Grass made his decision to live for at least part of the time in Berlin. The Berliners, he once observed, are 'perhaps the only people in Germany who have developed a political sense since the war'.

Born in 1927 in what was then German-speaking Danzig and is now the Polish city of Gdansk, Grass spent his school life under the Nazis. He was drafted into the army in 1944 at the age of sixteen, wounded the following year and ended the war as a prisoner of the Americans. Before devoting himself to literature and politics, he studied art and subsequently added striking graphic illustrations to editions of his books.

Grass stands alongside Heinrich Böll, Martin Walser, Peter Weiss and Hans Magnus Enzensberger – none of whom made his home in Berlin – as one of the influential post-war novelists and poets who believed in a politically committed literature. Politics, a sense of social awareness and responsibility and the act of literary creation are inseparable, and the writer has an obligation to address the public on the vital issues facing his world. Given the generation to which he belonged, having no responsibility for the Nazi era but being left to come to terms with it in one way or another and remove the ruins that were its legacy, Grass found in his birthplace and in the immediate past his first complex of raw material – the so-called Danzig Trilogy, consisting of the novel *Die Blechtrommel* (1959), the short story 'Katz und Maus' ('Cat and Mouse') and the novel *Hundejahre* ('Dog Years'), published in 1963. In the broad context all three portray the petty bourgeoisie of a provincial town (Danzig), as a microcosm of the society that connived at the rise and the success of the Nazis.

The grotesque, picaresque *Die Blechtrommel*, the first and still the best known of Grass' novels, was written before he developed his substantive association with Berlin. *Hundejahre*, too, a complex novel with multiple narrators (the title suggests the heat of the 'dog-days'), though written in Berlin, looks back to the fascist era, the moral bankruptcy of the Churches, the failure of idealist philosophy, and now, after the catastrophe, the embarrassed haste to brush the past under the carpet and sign up to the economic miracle. The peace of a present that has not healed the wounds inflicted by the past is a false peace. 'I prefer to keep the wound open,' said Grass.

Grass has never been silent for long, because there has never been a shortage of contemporary issues that stirred him to action. But his concentration of activity in the early 1960s, coinciding with a swell of political activity in Berlin and in West Germany as a whole, remains unique. Direct involvement in political affairs was at this time a necessary means of putting his beliefs directly to the test in the real world, not obliquely in the indulgent world of fiction, where the author's own views are not up for challenge. He beat the campaign trail for the Social Democrats and Willy Brandt and was talked of as a possible deputy to the Bundestag, even as Oberbürgermeister of Berlin. These experiences, fresh in his mind, he worked into the novel *Aus dem Tagebuch einer Schnecke* ('From the Diary of a Snail'), published in 1972, which carries the message that political and social progress, the improvement of the human lot, can only happen at a snail's pace – the process described in the political context of the time as the 'step-by-step policy'. The same non-revolutionary socialist message is woven into *örtlich betäubt* ('local anaesthetic'), in which Grass confronts the irrelevant extremism that sustained the extra-parliamentary opposition and the student demonstrations of 1967–8, out of which grew the urban terrorism of the Baader–Meinhof gang.

As a middle-of-the-road Social Democrat, Grass has inevitably garnered the criticisms both of those for whom his politics go too far and those for whom they do not go far enough. Whenever, after four or five years' work, another massive novel arrives, it is a major literary event, albeit one that meets with a mixed response. So it was in 1986, when, after the gentle, ironical love-story *Unkenrufe* ('The Cry of the Toad'), he published *Die Rättin* ('The Rat'), an apocalyptic vision of the destruction of the world in a nuclear war.

The hero of his 1995 novel, *Ein weites Feld* ('A Big Subject'), is a reincarnation of the nineteenth-century novelist Theodor Fontane as a chameleonic *apparatchik* who lives through the East German regime, then, in the confusion of the early years of reunification, changes his tune and joins the privatisation agency, the Treuhand. Fontane's career, from young liberal to reactionary, then to enlightened conservative, gives Grass the framework for another exercise in his recurrent obsession with coming to terms with the past, this time with the ramifications of the Stalinist East German past of oppression and the secret police.

Nor does the oppression stop there. For Grass, in constant anachronistic fear of the spectre of a 'Greater Germany', was a vehement opponent of the decision to unite the two Germanies in one fell swoop under terms laid down by Bonn, advocating instead a kind of confederacy which would have made possible a more humane solution of the personal and social problems involved. In practice, the behaviour of the West, as he saw it, in particular the precipitate privatisation of the entire East German economy, amounted to a takeover, one huge act of oppression and deceit. Under the Nazis people denounced Jews and liberals. Under communism, in one half of a divided country, East Germans betrayed other East Germans. Now, in a reunited Germany, informer and informed upon sit side by side, both betrayed by their bigger brother in the West. In terms of his own image and reputation, too, as tenacious as ever, Grass continues to do his best to 'keep the wound open'. It is indeed, as the Fontane character from whom Grass took his title was in the habit of saying, 'a big subject'.

After the revolutionary hurricane of the late 1960s had blown itself out, leaving the state still firmly in control of its citizens and its institutions, the attraction of political activity waned. Parties, associations and splinter groups ceased to carry conviction and the primacy of individual experiences and values began to reassert itself. From having been politicised, literature became personalised, privatised. A new subjectivity took over, an aversion from the collective, a statement of the permissive individualism that found its way into the 1980s as the philosophy of 'doing one's own thing'. It was an atmosphere also conducive to the rise of feminism, which took its lead, as far as Germany was concerned, from France (Simone de Beauvoir) and the United States (Susan Sontag).

In the context of Berlin the movement towards the depoliticisation of literature, the search for new–old subject matter and the return of the aesthetic dimension find a paradigm in Peter Schneider. Born during the Second World War, brought up in the earliest generation to know only the Federal Republic of Germany, Schneider stood in 1968 in the ranks of those who saw revolution in the streets as the precondition for the revival of literature. A few years later, after the wreckage of the revolution had been swept away, he made a complete volte-face, disclaimed the political domination of literature and returned in 1973 to the conventional art of storytelling with the novel *Lenz*.

Lenz was one of the great literary successes of the 1970s, a success almost equal to that of Plenzdorf's *Die neuen Leiden des jungen W.*, published the same year. The ultimate historical figure at the heart of the story is the eighteenth-century *Sturm und Drang* dramatist Jakob Michael Reinhold Lenz, an eccentric, unbalanced character who lived most of his life on the fringe of insanity. In 1836 Georg Büchner wrote a fragment, part documentary, part fiction, on the life of this unhappy creature, a terrifying study of a disintegrating mind which could only perceive reality as chaos. 'He did everything that the others did', writes Büchner at the end of his story, 'but there was a terrible void in him. He felt neither fear nor desire – his existence had become a burden he just had to bear.'

Schneider now relocates Büchner's story in the years of the recent student riots, converting the schizophrenic hero into an intellectual who discusses with workers and students the doctrines of Mao and the theories of cultural revolution but cannot reconcile the tension within himself, as an individual, between what his reason tells him and what his emotions urge upon him. His love for a working-class girl ends in a cul-de-sac. The abstract and the concrete are in opposition, so too are the reality of the subjective self and the demands of political commitment. 'Lenz' drifts now in one direction, now in another, ultimately finding the 'good life' in Italy – not the nineteenth-century Italy of romanticised classical ideals but the contemporary Italy of Euro-communism. The police pick him off the street and deport him as a vagrant. Asked back in Berlin what he is going to do now, he replies: 'Stay put.' Whether his learning process has led anywhere remains an open question. The book itself stands as a kind of memorial to the generation that lost its way in 1968.

Told in a flat, matter-of-fact tone of voice, with verbatim quotations from Büchner intercalated in montage style, Schneider's *Lenz* caught at every turn the mood of the author's generation. The bearded marchers of 1968, now clean-shaven servants of the state and society, recognised the gods that had failed them. Life was not the collective pursuit of some utopia but a personal Odyssey. The primacy of the subject had reasserted itself. Even more emphatically is it reasserted in a novel, once something of a cult-book, by a Berlin friend and contemporary of Schneider's, Nicolas Born, a writer who died in his early forties. Called *Die weltabgewandte Seite der Geschichte* ('The Dark Side of History') and published in 1976, it describes the author's search for his essential identity at a time of profound insecurity, by ridding himself of all personal attachments, all beliefs, all sense of society. 'Turn away from the world and inwards to yourself – and to nothing else,' is his motto, a romantic, narcissistic message eagerly grasped by a generation that rejected the concept of absolute values. No less subjective and self-centred is a wave of novels of the 1980s that focused on the father–son, father–daughter relationship, a classic context in which a writer of the present generation, like the Berliner Christoph Meckel, could return to the subject of the Nazi past via the experiences and attitudes of his parents.

Schneider returned to the theme of individual self-expression in a totally different context ten years later in *Der Mauerspringer* ('The Wall-Jumper'). There could hardly be a more thoroughly 'Berlinesque' story. In a series of cameos and anecdotes – border crossings, East Berliners trying to escape, encounters with the Volkspolizei and the Stasi – Schneider diagnoses a Wall psychology, a Wall not only on the ground but in the mind, creating a way of life for a personality beholden to neither one side nor the other. In one way Schneider is invoking, in the mid-1980s, the unified Weimar Berlin of the cherished 1920s, a wishful 'Berlin of the mind'. In another his story is an essay in the familiar German pastime of settling scores with the past, in this case the recent past which had turned into the foreseeable future. When in 1989 that foreseeable future itself became the past, and the two Germanies were able to pretend that they were one nation again, the whole process creaked once more into action. Schneider returned to examine the process of reunification and the tensions inherent within the 'Siamese city', as he called Berlin, in a series of penetrating eye-witness pieces published in 1990 as *Extreme Mittellage: Eine Reise durch das deutsche Nationalgefühl* ('An Extreme Central Position: A Journey through the National Sentiment of the Germans').

Mirroring the sobering consequences of the political consolidation of the early 1970s, and following the Basic Treaty of 1972 between the two German states, literature at the end of that decade found less in the inner-political condition of society with which to generate public passion. In return private issues of religion, psychotherapy, sex and feminism became more pressing, while those determined on agitation found international targets in nuclear energy, ecological disasters and the activities of multi-national companies.

Given the exposed situation of the divided city, stabilisation of an intolerable status quo was preferable to corrosive uncertainty. But it meant that through the 1980s East and West became more and more estranged. In the 1970s Günter Grass, Peter Schneider and others had made regular visits to fellow-authors in East Berlin but the second of the much trumpeted East–West Writers' Conferences in 1983 showed how entrenched the rival positions had become and how little the one side was willing – or, by this time, was able – to listen to what the other side was saying.

Miraculously, one side was about to collapse. The Wall did not fall, it was pushed. And Günter Grass' plebeians were not 'rehearsing the uprising' – this was the real performance.

The Literature of the East

That the two Germanies would grow ever further apart, not only politically and socially but also culturally, was inevitable. As the West eagerly rejoined the open, multifaceted European tradition, the East demanded of its artists and writers conformity with the values and practices that would promote the interests of the new socialist state. Communist ideologues laid down the lines of communication that would link the new art with the national cultural traditions of which they, no less than the West, were heirs. But access to those traditions could not be free and arbitrary. Specific points of contact had to be identified. The past, as in the Third Reich, had to be 'interpreted', cultural history – like all other history – rewritten. The function of culture was to support the onward march of socialism. All cultural activity was therefore didactic, and the custodians of Party dogma decided centrally, on political and doctrinal criteria, what literature would be published, what art exhibited, what music encouraged.

In the vanguard of the artists and intellectuals pledged to the furtherance of a socialist German state were those of the senior generation now returning from exile. Willy Bredel, Friedrich Wolf and Johannes R. Becher came back immediately from Moscow, Anna Seghers and Ludwig Renn from Mexico, the Brecht-composers Hanns Eisler and Paul Dessau from America. Then, after 'changing countries more often than I changed my shoes', as he put it – via Denmark, Sweden, Finland, the United States and latterly Switzerland – came Bertolt Brecht.

'THE PLAY'S THE THING'

Now fifty, bearing a new European reputation based on plays written in exile which Germany had never seen, Brecht arrived back in Berlin in 1948. Until his death in 1956, and beyond, his presence, and later his ghost, dominated the theatre, not only in Berlin but in Germany as a whole, the West no less than the East.

Brecht brought back with him four major plays, written between 1938 and 1945 – *Mother Courage and Her Children*, *The Life of Galileo*, *The Good Person of Setzuan* and *The Caucasian Chalk Circle*. He still believed in the class struggle, and his basic theory of epic theatre, first formulated in the early 1930s, was still in place, aimed at detaching the spectator's feelings from the emotional tumult on the stage and inducing him to pass rational, analytical judgement on the scenes he witnesses. But these plays of the war years are less bluntly doctrinaire than those he was writing during his last pre-exile years in Germany. They have a sympathetic humanitarian concern which on the one hand makes them unreliable vehicles of a revolutionary message and on the other puts them among the most freely accessible, and probably most durable, of his works.

Take *Mother Courage*, the story of a pitiful camp-follower, caught up in the turmoil of the Thirty Years War. Determined to make a living by the war, she is too stupid to learn the lessons of experience and too obtuse to grasp the baseness of her actions. War is evil, says Brecht, and those who live by war are wicked. Yet audiences have never brought themselves to withhold completely their sympathy from the shameful Mother Courage. Brecht wanted them to rise in anger to protest against war. Instead they rise in pity at the sight of the poor woman – one of the star roles (Brecht would hate the term) of Helene Weigel, Brecht's wife – with whom war has dealt so cruelly. Brecht has moved us *malgré lui*. We have let him down by reacting as human beings.

Yet the work of art, whatever its aim, must retain its integrity *qua* art. When it was suggested, after the early performances of *Mother Courage* in Berlin, that the heroine should be given a final speech in which she made the author's intentions explicit, Brecht indignantly refused. So crude a procedure would have been tantamount to admitting that he had not put his message across in the course of the play itself. At the same time the artist in him rebelled against any thought of allowing the inner being of his play to be destroyed. He was the victim – fortunately – of his poetic instinct.

Equivocation, allied to a broad streak of non-conformity and a pronounced talent for survival, took Brecht a long way. In East Berlin he realised every playwright–producer's dream – a theatre at his sole disposal in which to perform his own works in his own way, with his own chosen collaborators and his own troupe of actors, the Berliner Ensemble. And not an anonymous little building somewhere in the suburbs but the very theatre where, back in 1928, he had had the greatest success of his life with *Die Dreigroschenoper*.

Not that the Theater am Schiffbauerdamm and the Berliner Ensemble were offered to him on a plate. While recognising the reputation of its new comrade-in-arms, the Party was suspicious of the amount of artistic freedom he would demand and of the extent to which, protected by his fame, he might decide to strike out in his own direction. He was autocratic in both personal and artistic matters and had no time for bureaucrats.

Nor was he interested in half a Germany. Marxism he saw as the post-war solution for the whole shattered country, and in company with the other old-guard communist intellectuals now returned from exile, often using the periodical *Sinn und Form*, edited by Peter Huchel, as their mouthpiece, Brecht insisted on addressing all Germans. He saw the manifestation of militarism as no less offensive in the East than in the West. 'When Germany comes to be reunited', he said, '– and everyone knows it will, though no one knows when – it will not be through war.' Nor was it.

Mounted on the wall of Brecht's study in his house in East Berlin – now a Brecht museum and archive – was a slogan that read 'Truth is concrete'. Exploitation, social change, society – these are concepts, abstractions. Concrete is the individual, his problems, his fate. So whatever doctrinal propositions underlie Brecht's *Galileo*, for example, what remains uppermost in the spectator's perception is the hero's conscience-stricken fight to reconcile his genius as a scientist with his obligations to society. From the beginning the Berliner Ensemble's production of the work, with Ernst Busch in the title role, tried to minimise the danger that the audience would discover a human sympathy for Galileo's predicament. Yet as in all these late plays of Brecht's, notwithstanding his stated intentions, before or after the event, it is the personal predicament of the hero that grips and moves us, not the theoretical presentation of a social problem.

The Berliner Ensemble was more than just a troupe of actors and actresses performing under the aegis of one strong personality. It was, so to speak, the executive organ charged with communicating to the public a philosophy of man, of society, of man *in* society, of the function of art in society, of the nature of aesthetic pleasure. Playwright, actors, producer, technicians – all worked to the same ideals. One had to buy the whole package, for each item had neither meaning nor purpose by itself. Society is changeable, human nature is class-bound and also changeable, conflicts are social conflicts, events and circumstances are not linked but discrete, aesthetic pleasure derives from observation of the dialectic in action – these are the components of Brecht's didactic theatre. Every aspect of the theatrical experience, on both sides of the proscenium arch, serves the achievement of the stated aim.

The Brechtian 'method' – the word makes clear his opposition to Stanislavsky – survived through its own inner momentum for some twenty years after Brecht's death, and tours throughout Europe and overseas made the Berliner Ensemble the German Democratic Republic's most famous cultural export, alongside steroid-laden Olympic athletes. But already in the 1970s, after Helene Weigel's death, it was becoming mannered and inflexible, like any closed system that is the child of circumstances which no longer exist. Even before this their performances of Brecht had become weary, and excursions into new territory, like the documentaries of Kipphardt (*In the Matter of J. Robert Oppenheimer*) and Peter Weiss (*Vietnam Discourse*), seemed strangely halfhearted. This was in any case a time when relations between the Party and the country's artists and intellectuals were particularly strained. Apart from the occasional venture – plays by Volker Braun and Heiner Müller and twentieth-century 'classics' like Wedekind and Zuckmayer – the Ensemble stagnated through the rest of the 1970s and 1980s still devoting half its energies to fossilised productions of Brecht. After the dissolution of the DDR the theatre was put into the hands of a five-man team of men of the theatre, among them Heiner Müller. The experiment of an allegedly socialist German theatre in and for an allegedly socialist German state was over.

Brecht's brief presence in Berlin, together with the performances of his Berliner Ensemble, attracted the young literati of the DDR to the capital, the variety of whose culture far outshone what any provincial centre could offer. To claim that a survey of cultural activity in East Berlin comes close to being a survey of cultural activity in East Germany as a whole would be an exaggeration, but not a gross exaggeration. West Berlin, by contrast, was one centre among many – not even *primus inter pares*.

Brecht built on the premise that people could be educated by art, *ergo* that art could help to change society. His aesthetic derived from the concept of epic theatre – a technique with a tradition stretching back to Greek Antiquity and Sanskrit literature – and the associated principle of alienation, *Verfremdung*. Art as a vehicle of social change was a Marxist–Leninist tenet, and the Party ideologues, following their Soviet masters, saw in the public, confrontational art form of drama the ideal medium for presenting the new, socialist hero.

But in their eyes Brecht was not producing this new heroism. They envisaged a type – rather, a stereotype – of the honest, simple citizen working towards the reconstruction of his battered country in the name of the socialist Economic Plan. Brecht, as they saw him, was demanding too much freedom, laying too much emphasis on 'formalist' matters of expression and aesthetic presentation. The true ideal, and the demand of the moment, was embedded in the catch-phrase 'Socialist Realism', the defining term, Soviet in origin, of all officially approved art in the German Democratic Republic, as everywhere else in the Soviet bloc of those days. Plays set their action in the agricultural and industrial workplace, their heroes and heroines expressing sentiments conducive to the building of the new society. Prescriptive though the framework was, the occasional writer found room for humour in his dialogue, or an ironical glance at the contradictions in society between what was and what ought to be. The verse comedy *Katzgraben* (1953) by Erwin Strittmatter, author of some of the most entertaining novels to come out of East Germany during the 1950s and 1960s, allows itself a good deal of freedom in such matters. But there was no young East German dramatist to enjoy the spontaneous success that attended a work like Borchert's *Draussen vor der Tür* – a work banned in the East on the ground that it presented a specious picture of how the Germans should come to terms with their responsibility for the war and the trauma of their defeat.

Communist doctrine interpreted war as the climax of the militarist–capitalist system. War can be avoided only by changing the system, hence socialism is the only guarantee of peace. Proceeding from such principles, the custodians of Party rectitude effortlessly presented the East as the home of the good, the peaceful Germans, and their intellectuals and artists as leaders in the struggle towards the socialist Jerusalem. Black sheep could not be tolerated. The façade of unity had to be preserved. The Party was always right. Or not.

Sometimes, however, events could give the system a jolt. The death of Stalin in 1953 and the uprising of 17 June three months later brought a certain psychological relaxation. The regime even felt sufficiently confident of itself to allow the establishment of a political cabaret, Die Distel ('The Thistle') – a pale reflection of cabaret as pre-war Berlin knew it but a body of actors and singers who managed to walk a perilous tight-rope of mockery and satire throughout the DDR years without being banned. Here Wolf Biermann, later to become a thorn in the side of the regime, began his career singing his spiky political ballads. By an odd coincidence Die Distel opened in the same year, 1953, as the most famous of West Berlin cabarets, Die Stachelschweine ('The Porcupines'), led by Wolfgang Neuss.

The cruder forms of propaganda literature aimed at increasing agricultural and industrial productivity were now phased out and in the early Khrushchev era voices were heard – the voices not of dissidents but of committed socialists like Anna Seghers and Stefan Heym – protesting against the abysmal standards of the permitted literature of the day. But the Party could tighten or loosen the reins as it chose, and after the rebellions in Poland and Hungary in 1956 the concessions made to the acceptable limits of freedom of artistic expression were peremptorily withdrawn. In one way or another most of the dramas of these years stand in the shadow, conceptually, technically and linguistically, of Brecht and epic theatre, based on the dialectical exposition of conflicts and contradictions within situations and characters as the means of reaching conclusions appropriate to 'actually existing socialism', as the DDR described its social and political order.

The movement towards the equation of intellectuals and workers, and the integration of art into the realities of everyday life, were given a characteristic impulse in 1959 with the so-called Bitterfelder Weg. Taking its name from the centre of the chemical engineering industry, this 'way forward' proposed a dual solution to the problem of art and life. On the one hand, writers should spend time in the factories and collective farms, rubbing shoulders with the workers and experiencing their problems at first hand. Correspondingly the workers should be encouraged to become writers themselves, learning through the experience how the work of art comes about. Not surprisingly, the first initiative led nowhere, in spite of Party pressure. The second did have a short-lived success with the formation in industrial centres of writers' circles in which men shared with each other their concerns and hopes. But it hardly matched the Party's expectations.

Apart from the old guard – Brecht, Friedrich Wolf – drama over the first ten or so years of the DDR has left few memorable names. The pressure of conformity claimed its victims. Two young dramatists, however, who were to emerge as leading, controversial, therefore by definition interesting, figures in East German literature over the coming decades, appeared on the scene in the late 1950s and early 1960s. One is Peter Hacks – like Wolf Biermann, one of the few who crossed from the West to the East to demonstrate their political convictions. The other is Heiner Müller, a fiercely independent character with a zig-zag career, honoured by his country one moment, banned the next, yet never contemplating that he could live or work anywhere other than in the DDR. Both saw themselves as continuators, in their individual ways, of Brecht. Hacks, in particular, interspersing songs à la Brecht between the scenes, followed the master's adaptations of older plays into historical territory, using material from the past to expose, for example, the corruption of Church and state.

The authorities had nothing against such pieces. But characteristic of their almost pathological fear of anything that might stimulate an audience, in this most public of media, to think along lines unwelcome to the Party or to challenge its omniscience, was their inability to handle the sensation caused in 1965 by *Moritz Tassow*. Tassow, in Hacks' play, is a visionary socialist who in 1945 wants to press on relentlessly with the collectivisation of agriculture in the name of the people. But the blinkered functionaries of the Party have decided that the time is not yet ripe for such a step. Although they have their way in the end, they are mocked by Hacks almost as hindrances to the progress of ideal socialism and the individual's fulfilment within it. The Party was not amused.

While subsequently changing his tune, claiming that the DDR had now removed the sources of class conflict and created a society in which art could play a positive role, Hacks became something of a *rara avis* by reviving the concept of 'grand drama', a fusion of the subjective and the objective in the spirit of fantasy and poetry, transmitted through blank verse. It is an anti-Brechtian drama of linguistic virtuosity, operatic in its theatricality, with figures from classical mythology as its focus – *Amphitryon* (1967), *Omphale* (1976). The latter was originally conceived as a libretto for Siegfried Matthus, and among Hacks' reflections on literature is in fact a treatise on the nature of the operatic libretto. His plays have great wit and a great sense of theatre. Unfortunately he will also be remembered, like Hermann Kant, as an open supporter of the expulsion of Wolf Biermann from his adopted country.

At the same time as Hacks' *Moritz Tassow,* Heiner Müller, a problem child to the DDR authorities throughout his life, wrote his first play, *Der Lohn-drücker* ('The Man Who Kept Wages Down'). Cast in a Brechtian form of disjunctive, unchronological scenes, it faces head-on the contradictory situation of a factory worker serving the interests of socialism while still holding in his historically conditioned mind the thought patterns of capitalism. This is no hero of socialism of the kind the Party was looking for from its men of letters. The ideological battle has not been won. Müller presents the contradiction and leaves the audience – not the Party – to resolve it. Not surprisingly, the play was almost immediately taken off.

Dates crucial to the course of political events do not necessarily correspond to comparable moments in the realm of culture. But in a totalitarian regime, where culture is not so much a private indulgence as a tool for the achievement of political ends, the effects of a political decision will be felt by artists, writers and musicians in the pursuit of their art no less than in their daily lives.

Such a moment was 13 August 1961, when the East German leader Walter Ulbricht, with Soviet approval, ordered a wall to be built through the middle of Berlin along the sector border between East and West. Hitherto there had been supervised but relatively free travel across the city by road and rail, and between the foundation of the DDR in 1949 and this moment in 1961 $2\frac{1}{2}$ million East Germans left their country for the West. For economic reasons alone the blood-letting had to be stopped. Movement from East to West and West to East ceased overnight.

There was now only one way to look – inwards. The Wall itself entered literature as both a physical and a psychological reality, a symbol of confinement and repression but also a statement of national identity, the definitive partition of Germany, with two governments, two nationalities, two armies, two currencies, two social systems. The majority of the best-known dramatists, poets and novelists active at the time – older figures like Stephan Hermlin and Stefan Heym, the younger generation of Hacks, Heiner Müller, Günter Kunert, Sarah Kirsch and Christa Wolf – still accepted the social order under which they lived, despite the indignities to which it often subjected them. But the internalisation of their activity was accompanied by a growing subjectivity, a critical identification of conditions which were not as they should be – 'corrupt' was a word not far from their lips. To such criticism the authorities reacted with bans on publication and performance and violent public attacks on 'anarchists, modernists and nihilists' who were undermining a fledgling socialist society. When murmurs of disapproval were heard as tanks of the Warsaw Pact countries, including the DDR, suppressed the uprising in Prague in the summer of 1968, Ulbricht uttered dark threats against 'counter-revolutionary elements' among the country's intelligentsia.

Two plays dealing with the relationship between the workers and the industrial process during these years – 'production-line dramas' one might call them – reveal the internal problems, personal and economic, created by the way the country was developing. One is Heiner Müller's *Der Bau* ('The Building Site'), the other, Volker Braun's *Kipper Paul Bauch* ('Paul Bauch the Tipper').

In the centre of *Der Bau*, a play stylised in form but wholly realistic, stands a team of construction workers divided among themselves. One group is caught up in the old, bureaucratic way of doing things and makes little headway; the other, led by a progressive maverick, opposes the sterile orthodoxy and finds his own way of getting things done. The building site is Müller's image of the DDR itself, in which the bureaucratic regime is portrayed as no less alienating than the alienation of the capitalist system they were supposed to have left behind. And when the foreman says to the Party secretary: 'If I'd known I was building my own prison, I'd have put dynamite in every wall,' the audience knew what wall Müller had in mind.

Here is none of the prescribed optimism the authorities looked for. When the Central Committee of the Party demanded that the text of the play be changed to include more 'positive' content, Müller could only comply. It was the fate of all deviants, as Brecht's *Lehrstücke* of the 1930s had already taught him. Not until 1980 was it judged safe to perform the play in East Berlin, by which time Müller had become well known, though, unsurprisingly, not well understood, in the West.

The hero of Volker Braun's *Kipper*, a truck-driver in an open-cast coal mine, also suffers for his impatience to achieve here and now the life of the happy communist worker. Put in jail for injuring a fellow-worker in his reckless pursuit of higher productivity, Paul Bauch is made to learn that it is the interest and decisions of the team, not of the individual, that are paramount. He is a loner, with his own idealistic vision of communist society. But the Party bureaucracy, pledged to the concept of collective decisions and collective discipline, has no place for such men, or theatres for such plays. It posits a complete identity of interest between itself and its citizens, a relationship of serene harmony. To suggest that it might not be so is revisionist heresy, to which the Party will issue a response as depressing as it is predictable. Small wonder that an increasing number of East German writers, deprived of the opportunity to publish or perform in their own land and for the men and women of their own society, should risk the consequences of spiriting away their manuscripts to be published in the West – a West, especially a West Berlin, quick to sense every change of cultural climate in the other part of the city.

Such works found an eager readership in the West, for they were vital sources of information about life, real life – material, intellectual, spiritual – on the other side of the Wall. Hence the extraordinary success of *Die wunderbaren Jahre* ('Those Wonderful Years'), a best-selling collection of cameos and anecdotes of contradiction-ridden life in the DDR by the poet Reiner Kunze, who was forced out of the country in 1976. Smuggled back into the East by Western visitors, such books brought with them a sense of reassurance, confirmation that the West knew what was going on in the other half of Berlin and Germany, and would use that knowledge when the moment came.

That West Berlin had its own socialists was of no interest to the DDR authorities. Indeed, on the principle of 'Better the devil you know . . .', they were often happier to deal with declared opponents of socialism than with independent radicals whose liberalism challenged the Party's proprietary right to decide what was socialism and what was not. When the dialectical *Marat/Sade* play by Peter Weiss, a firm socialist and later Marxist, was performed in Rostock in 1965, the Politbureau welcomed it as a piece of progressive theatre. But when in 1970 he wrote a play on Trotsky, a taboo figure in the Soviet bloc, then one on Hölderlin, showing how the French Revolution turned into the dictatorship of Napoleon, driving Hölderlin mad, the authorities suddenly declared Weiss *persona non grata*, withdrew all his works from the repertoire and refused him entry to the DDR.

After the intransigent, scowling Ulbricht was replaced in 1971 by Erich Honecker, who remained First Secretary of the Party until his country collapsed in 1989, the atmosphere seemed to lighten. In a policy speech almost feverishly seized upon by the intelligentsia Honecker declared: 'If one proceeds from the firm starting-point of socialism, there cannot, in my view, be any taboos in the field of art and literature, whether in subject matter or in style.' 'The firm starting-point of socialism' may have been a phrase open to interpretation. But writers who saw themselves as committed socialists found in Honecker's words a relief from the constraints of the 'Bitterfelder Weg' and 'socialist realism', an opportunity to criticise openly what was not right – not truly socialist – in the administration of their society, and the chance to express their subjective artistic selves.

One work embodies this new-found freedom to perfection, a drama (also published as a short story) that brought its thirty-eight-year-old author instant success and shook the old guard of the Central Committee of the Party to the core – Ulrich Plenzdorf's *Die neuen Leiden des jungen W.* ('The New Agony of Young W.')

Inviting the parallel with Goethe's Werther, Plenzdorf's very unheroic hero is a young worker who writes a series of letters to a friend protesting against the patronising, authoritarian attitudes of his superiors. As he assembles a new invention which he hopes will impress his fellow-workers with his qualities, he produces a short circuit and electrocutes himself. An accident? Suicide, like Goethe's Werther? Or the predestined end for a man who cannot find fulfilment in society as it is?

Such open questions irritated the Party. The problem of how to treat death in a socialist society – Christa Wolf had faced it a few years earlier in her novel *Nachdenken über Christa T.* – was now one of Honecker's jettisoned taboos but the objects of Plenzdorf's criticisms and the extent of the subjective freedom to which he laid claim sorely tried the bureaucrats. Nevertheless his work survived and with it the admission – no small step in this regimented society – that there could be such a thing as a conflict of interest between individual and society, and that this too was no longer a restricted area.

When Plenzdorf's work was put on in West Berlin, it barely raised an eyebrow. Exciting and original as it was to audiences in the East, Plenzdorf's problems were not the West's problems. Friedrich Luft headed his review: 'Not for Export'.

But the relaxation could not last. Through the 1970s works were increasingly banned, authors expelled from the Writers' Union and from the Party, until in 1976 matters came to a spectacular head with the expulsion of the poet and folk-singer Wolf Biermann. It was a moment that illuminated in a flash the intellectual situation in which the whole country found itself.

Son of a Hamburg docker murdered by the Nazis, Biermann had left the West as a seventeen-year-old idealist in 1953 and thrown in his lot with the DDR, only to find, from the very beginning, that this was not what he understood by socialism. Refusing to hold his tongue, he began to write lyrics and ballads which he set to music and sang in his hoarse, croaking voice to his own guitar accompaniment, in cabaret tradition. He acquired a great following not only in the East, where audiences responded with delight to every nuance of his barbed criticisms of a corrupt, neo-Stalinist regime, but also in the West, where his records sold in thousands. Forbidden to publish or perform in public from 1965 onwards, he became the idol of potential dissidents. Unexpectedly he was allowed out of the country for a tour of West Germany in 1976, whereupon the authorities used his absence to deprive him of his citizenship overnight and bar him from returning to what he regarded to the end as his country.

Immediately almost all the leading writers, among them Stefan Heym, Volker Braun, Christa Wolf, Stephan Hermlin and Heiner Müller, signed an open letter of protest, quoting the Marxist right, even obligation, to persistent criticism of the revolutionary process and demanding Biermann's reinstatement.

Far from relenting, the authorities set out to drive unruly authors into line through public attacks and bans, even by police interrogation and arrest. At the same time they got rid of troublesome elements by allowing those to leave who found it intolerable to stay, thus effectively expatriating themselves. But most, like Biermann, did not want to leave; they wanted, by the exercise of a critical right which the regime would not tolerate, to stay and create a proper socialist state – the state, lest it be forgotten, that they themselves had promoted and served from its beginning. The intellectual world was polarised, the atmosphere poisoned, personal antipathies provoked and aggravated.

The drama, no less than the other genres of literature, bore the marks of such pressure. As novels and collections of poetry by East German authors were increasingly published in West Germany, works written in and for the DDR by men and women now no longer there, so East German plays were having their premières in West German theatres – plays not only by recent émigrés but also by vilified resident celebrities like Heiner Müller.

Müller remained until his death in 1996 the most controversial and high-profile of DDR dramatists. In a deliberately brutal, expressionist, surrealist diction calculated to shock, he turned to the exploitation of classics like Shakespeare and Molière, extracting from them a message of black pessimism about the future of a world – above all Germany, socialist or otherwise – in which there is change but no progress. Even fascism, which, the Party never tired of boasting, they had defeated in 1945, had not gone away, leaving Müller, in *Die Schlacht* ('The Battle'), to make his own gruesome contribution to the literature of *Vergangenheitsbewältigung*, the coming to terms with the Nazi past. 'My main interest when I write plays is to destroy things,' he said of his *Hamletmaschine*, destroying Shakespeare in the course of what he described as 'a self-critique of the position of the intellectual'. Decadent, anarchist, irrational, sadistic, the scent of Kafka, James Joyce and Samuel Beckett, Artaud's Theatre of Cruelty – an improbable cocktail to be concocted by a writer living among the lies of socialist realism.

Accepting the Kleist Prize in 1990, Müller said: 'The ice-age of no dialogue between minds, hearts and spirits has begun. The only escape route leads downwards, into dreams, for some into the graveyard.' It was a characteristic twin-pronged remark to a now unified, but not united country.

Formal legitimation of the theatre lay with the Ministry of Culture, though the Socialist Unity Party had the last word in policy matters. But a state monopoly over the country's theatres – in 1988, towards the end of its separate existence, there were sixty-eight, some ten of them in East Berlin – did bring advantages, both to the professionals and the public. A high level of subsidy meant that ticket prices could be kept low and an experience of theatre and opera made available to the whole of society, as well as to children and other special groups. For the performers and all those involved in the finished production, from designers and technicians to administrative staff, it meant guaranteed employment. Furthermore generous subventions made it possible to plan and mount productions with a degree of security and commitment that was the envy of countries where theatres are at the mercy of the market. On average only around 12 per cent of a theatre's income was raised from box-office sales – the state took care of the rest. In terms of its international image too the DDR needed to demonstrate its own entitlement, no less evident than that of the West, to inherit the great tradition of classical German drama. The background may have been murky, the motivation dubious, but the result could be impressive.

LYRICAL REALISM

> *Als ich wiederkehrte*
> *War mein Haar noch nicht grau*
> *Da war ich froh.*
> *Die Mühen des Gebirgs liegen hinter uns*
> *Vor uns liegen die Mühen der Ebenen.*

> ('When I returned
> My hair was not yet grey
> I was happy.
> The toil of the mountains is behind us
> In front of us lies the toil of the plains.')
> (Brecht, *Wahrnehmung* ('Perception'))

Brecht belonged to the senior generation of writers who returned to Germany after the war to help build a socialist society. The mountainous task, the overthrow of Nazism, had been accomplished – now the direct route through the flatlands beckoned. But Brecht's poetic world during these last years of his life embraced more than the direct social and political needs of the moment. He served his fellow-citizens; at the same time he served his art through a personal vision, a kind of subjective objectivity. Art, moreover, was inseparable from nature, however defined. In his lakeside retreat at

Buckow, in the woods south of Berlin, he wrote a little group of poems called the *Buckow Elegies*, lyric gems not calling on nature as conventional background or a sentimental fall-back position but weaving nature into the fabric of human existence with a deftness of touch that no contemporary could match.

National reconstruction and the building of socialism were the dominant themes of the poetry of the early post-war years in East Germany. Little of this poetry, with its clichés and its harsh militancy, has an individual voice. That of Johannes R. Becher, however, did – on occasion, at least, for his immense output also contains a good deal of chaff. Becher did not have Brecht's mastery of the taut poetic line. But he found a compensation in the adoption of classical forms such as the sonnet or the conventional quatrain of folksong association, in which technical restraints encouraged precision of expression. That content determines form is a commonplace of literary criticism. The reverse can be no less valid. With a career stretching back to the expressionist years of the First World War, Becher had a ready-made reputation when he returned to East Berlin after ten years in Moscow. Author of the DDR national anthem, virtual Poet Laureate – Brecht would have been too insubordinate for the position – Becher became the country's Minister of Culture in 1954, which he remained until his death four years later.

From the beginning – though less so in the last decades of its existence – writers in the DDR enjoyed higher prestige than their confrères in the West. This brought with it the necessity of working to the agenda that the state had laid out. Poets had to summon the young country in fulsome tones to work for the consolidation of the new social order and the fulfilment of economic plans. As there were 'production dramas' focused on the agricultural and industrial process, so there was 'tractor poetry' in praise of a socialist economy, poetry which had little chance of surviving the mood of the moment in which it was written. But although socialist realism was the prescribed dogma, there was already in the 1950s a handful of poets from the generation that had come through the Second World War for whom socialist realism, like patriotism, was not enough. Two stand out, by their contrasting personal careers as by their distinctive and influential poetry – Stephan Hermlin and Johannes Bobrowski, both of whom made their home in East Berlin after the war.

Born during the First World War, a communist from his youth, Hermlin fled Berlin in 1936. Moving through various Middle Eastern and European countries in exile, he worked with the *maquis* in France before finally escaping to Switzerland, where he was interned until the end of the war. After two years in Frankfurt he transferred his allegiance in 1947 to East Berlin, where he died in 1997. Respected in both East and West, he was a driving force behind conferences in the 1980s at which leading writers from both sides met to discuss the future of their two Germanies.

Hermlin's modest poetic *oeuvre*, intellectual to the point of esoteric, the work of a fastidious craftsman, came to an abrupt end in 1958 – essays and short stories took its place. In one respect it was a poetry increasingly out of step with the requirements of the Party as dogma hardened and tolerance declined with the intensification of the Cold War. Hermlin was pledged to his adopted state. But a declaration of loyalty did not absolve him from the specific obligation to work, and to stimulate others to work, for the tangible victory of socialism, not just to offer general moral uplift and a heightened awareness of the dialectical process. In another respect it was perhaps a poetry that could go no further, or at least, that Hermlin could take no further. Yet its importance lies precisely in that it re-establishes, through its absorption of romantic, expressionist and other elements from the historical corpus of the German lyric, a contact with the modern European tradition that would otherwise have been lost under the weight of political pressure. The regime had little use for such elitist, 'formalistic' literature, such unrepresentational language, such extreme imagery. It would have found a more natural place, ironically, in a West German context. Now, since 1990, it can be taken into the full, undivided tradition where it belongs.

Totally different in biography and personality, a lyric poet no less remote *qua* poet from the world of commonplace 'reconstruction poetry' than Hermlin but rougher, more emphatic in tone, is Johannes Bobrowski. Born in East Prussia in 1917, a soldier on the eastern front and a Russian prisoner-of-war for four years, he came to Berlin in 1949. Here he settled, both a committed Protestant and, since his return from Russia, a declared communist, as a literary editor in the publishing offices of the East German Christian Democratic Union. He died in 1965 at the age of forty-eight, but the modest output of verse and fiction of his last ten years was sufficient to bring him fame in East and West alike – which, as one who still saw Germany as one country, not two, was the way he would have had it.

At the core of Bobrowski's work lies his Baltic homeland, in one aspect the source of affectionate memories as the stimulus for a poetry of nature, but also a perpetual reminder of German barbarism towards the native Slavs, the Prussians, starting as far back as the days of the Teutonic Knights and most recently renewed by the Nazis. It was Bobrowski's way of coming to terms with the past – bold, commanding verse in free, staccato rhythms, a diction reminiscent of Brecht in its sinewy directness, and an introspective visionary intensity recalling the odes of Klopstock and Hölderlin, poets of little relevance to the DDR canon of literary values.

Bobrowski and Hermlin, with contemporaries such as Erich Arendt, back from wartime exile in South America, and Louis Fürnberg, who had found refuge from the Nazis in Palestine, belonged to a generation for whom the Second World War had been the central experience. Their seniors – Brecht, Becher, Wieland Herzfelde – had even known the First World War as well. These were all men whose minds had been cast in the mould of the class struggle and latterly in the fight against Hitler. Since the foundation of the German Democratic Republic they had helped to build on the ruins of what they had helped to destroy.

But the new generation could feel no responsibility for Nazism or for the war. They went through the war as schoolboys, some almost as children, and inherited a world for which the battle had been won by others. The national task was now one of consolidation. A new pattern of social values was being imposed, and it was this that the young poet saw when he looked around. Poetry had to serve a social function. Indeed, Party ideologues indulged in a rhetoric which virtually equated literary production with industrial production. True poetry could hardly survive in this suffocating atmosphere without incurring the charge of 'formalism', the cardinal sin in the socialist aesthetic calendar. It was a charge made the more galling by a growing awareness that the ideals the Party preached bore little relationship to the actual society they had created and on which they clamped their impervious authority. The country, glaringly but unrepentantly, was a lie.

In such circumstances the young, undeceived poet could only hold on to his art. Compared with fiction and drama, poetry addresses a small audience, and in unpropitious times the poet may be heard or read only by a closed circle of friends. Perhaps this helps to explain why, in contrast to the difficulties put in the way of novels and dramas, poetry, often written by men who were also novelists or dramatists, suffered less at the censor's hand. The young Günter Kunert, for example, direct and unsentimental in Brechtian manner, a master of the pithy pay-off line, was able to publish collections of verse in the late 1950s and the 1960s which were anything but socialistically realistic yet passed unchallenged.

Kunert and his younger contemporaries, Sarah and Rainer Kirsch and Volker Braun among them, sought a role for the subjective self in a deterministic society of prescribed parameters and accepted wisdom. They demanded the right to challenge ready-made answers, to identify a role for poetry which they could define in their own aesthetic terms. They asked questions to which the state could only give replies that were either meaningless or incriminatory. A few invoked the vocabulary of technology in their poems – the battleground where man forces his will on nature. Some sought to locate the eternal verities – love, beauty – in the new social order, envisaging personal relationships made all the more fulfilling for being consummated in socialism. Sarah Kirsch found a haven of peace in nature and in intimate love poetry. Whatever. The ego becomes both subject and object, both observer and observed, the self as poet, as worker, as preacher, as lover, or just as existential self. Poetic form is the guarantor of the honesty and authenticity of the utterance – often free verse but also traditional structures as deliberate points of reference to precedents inherited from the eighteenth and nineteenth century. There were kindred spirits among these poets, receptive to common influences, and the building of the Wall in 1961 intensified the sense of intellectual community and shared fate that accompanies any state of forced isolation. But there were no 'schools' of poets in the conventional use of the word. Each had his own furrow to plough.

Yet the individual vision could also illuminate an area of the wider context, giving glimpses of the unique circumstances of time and place in which it arose. Two otherwise very different poets of the 1960s and 1970s had this quality, both from working-class families, both deeply critical of the sham socialism of the DDR, both harassed and abused by the regime and both eventually refugees from their country – Reiner Kunze and Wolf Biermann.

Kunze, whose father was a miner, had already fallen foul of the authorities in the late 1950s, when he was a lecturer in aesthetic theory at the University of Leipzig. His first poems, like almost all his later works, were published in the West, and after 1968 his work was banned completely in the DDR for its protests against the state's degrading treatment of its citizens. At times bitter, at others quietly observant, with a great capacity for love of his fellow human beings, Kunze's is not the poetry of political protest as generally understood but a plea for humane understanding and tolerance in oppressive circumstances.

Where Kunze is intense, introspective, sometimes ironic, Wolf Biermann is aggressive, openly provocative. As a folk-singer irresistible, in the way Bob Dylan and Joan Baez are – were – irresistible, Biermann nevertheless writes a poetry that needs no melodies to support it. In its lapidary precision of language, its straight-in-the-eye honesty, it reminds us that Brecht is never far away, and behind Brecht the tradition of political lyric that stretches back through Tucholsky to Heine. Even closer, perhaps, is his spiritual affinity to François Villon, scurrilous hedonist and scourge of authority but at the same time master of a melancholy tenderness.

Biermann was consumed by the anger and sorrow that accompanies the destruction of a dream – anger at the betrayal of an ideal, at a state that immures its own citizens and sends in the tanks to crush the Prague Spring, sorrow at the passing of a vision, at the condemnation of a people to cold disillusionment. He was the symbol of a doubly divided Germany – irrevocably divided into East and West but the East also tragically divided against itself. The roots of the alienation lay painfully deep:

> In diesem Lande leben wir
> wie Fremdlinge im eignen Haus
>> Die eigne Sprache, wie sie uns
>> entgegenschlägt, verstehen wir nicht
>> noch verstehen, was wir sagen
>> die unsre Sprache sprechen
> In diesem Lande leben wir wie Fremdlinge.

> ('In this country we live
> like strangers in our own house
>> Our own language, as it
>> strikes our ears, we do not understand,
>> nor do those who speak our language
>> understand what we say
> In this country we live like strangers.')
>>> (from *Das Hölderlin-Lied*, 1967)

Après moi le déluge, Biermann might have said. One by one the intellectuals and artists who had somehow come to terms with 13 August 1961 in the hope that the German Democratic Republic might change course towards true socialism, allowed themselves to be expelled to the West. Indeed, a list of the substantial authors who stayed would be considerably shorter than one of those who left. Thomas Brasch (son of a member of the Politbureau), Bernd Jentzsch and Reiner Kunze left in the same year as Biermann, followed by Jürgen Fuchs, Sarah Kirsch and Rudolf Bahro, the actors Manfred Krug, Angelica Domröse and Eva-Maria Hagen, the producer Götz Friedrich. Jurek Becker, Günter Kunert, Rolf Schneider and Erich Loest, released for 'special visits' to the West, decided not to return. Such forced departures were preceded by harassment and persecution, often also by imprisonment, and followed by petty acts of malice towards the families left behind.

Wrenched from the habitat into which they had been born, exiled poets had to learn a whole new set of assumptions. Their natural subject matter, the data of the old, familiar everyday life, however shabby, however much of an irritant, had been taken away from them. Some found a corner for themselves in byways such as children's books. All had to make their peace with an environment not of their original choosing.

The younger generations they left behind in the DDR, those writing in the 1980s, were as uncertain and as sceptical as their émigré predecessors of where their country was going. Most trod their individual paths, and most, as before, found their way to Berlin. One group, however, has acquired a kind of corporate identity, a non-conformist collective living in the decayed Prenzlauer Berg quarter of the city, which indulged in self-conscious linguistic experiments, verbal and formal games played in a detached, matter-of-fact tone of voice. By dislocating words and reassembling them to create new contexts and surreal meanings – or non-meanings – they converted their marginalised situation into an alternative literary culture that recalls the world of Dada and the *poésie concrète* of the 1960s – and has as little chance of survival. A few of these poets even succeeded in having their work published in the West. At home they neither felt at one with the 'actually existing socialism' around them nor saw any practical alternative to it. In November 1989 that problem was solved for them. Others soon took its place.

THE NOVEL IN SOCIALISM

As in the world of drama, with Brecht, and lyric poetry, with Brecht and Becher, so too in the narrative fiction of the post-war years in East Germany – and *a fortiori* in East Berlin – recovery lay initially in the hands of those returning from years of exile. Having watched the destruction of Nazism from afar, and with it the physical and moral annihilation of what was still their country, the exiles now had to address a new generation. Best known among the returning novelists were Arnold Zweig, who had spent the war in Palestine, and Anna Seghers.

Zweig's best days were behind him. But Anna Seghers, who had already made a great impression with her concentration-camp novel *Das siebte Kreuz* ('The Seventh Cross'), published in 1942 and filmed in the USA two years later, brought back with her an unfinished story called *Die Toten bleiben jung* ('The Dead Stay Young'), which she now completed and published in 1949.

In its realistic, almost chronicle style and its anti-fascist message, *Die Toten bleiben jung* is the archetypal East German novel of the post-war years. Its action spread over the period 1918–45, it tells of the murder by army officers of a young communist during the Spartacist uprising of 1918, then of the shooting of his son at the end of the Second World War by one of the same officers, who kills himself in remorse. 'Know thy enemies' is the motto – the imperialist forces that seize power, subjugate the masses and drag the nations into war. *Die Toten bleiben jung*, made into a memorable film by Joachim Kunert in 1968, is Anna Seghers' contribution to the education and enlightenment of the young DDR citizens with whom the future of the country lies. If the lesson is not learnt, there will be a Third World War. The true meaning of words and concepts debased and perverted by the Nazis, like *Volk*, fatherland and nature, had to be restored. It is necessary to understand the nature of destruction, of war, before one can rebuild.

A classic war novel, part historical document, part kaleidoscope of eye-witness adventures, is Stefan Heym's *The Crusaders*, a chronicle of the advance of a US armoured division through Europe from 1944 to the surrender. Heym, who had escaped from Germany to the USA as a young man, served in just such a military unit. But he fell foul of the authorities for his political views, gave back his war medals and returned to East Germany in 1952, where, a socialist of ideals, he became a defiant opponent of the DDR regime. Originally written in English, *The Crusaders* became, alongside Norman Mailer's *The Naked and the Dead*, a world best-seller among war novels, a book that combines a personal experience of war and military occupation with a display of the national and political forces that would determine how the post-war world developed.

Much later Heym returned to the year 1945 in a very different frame of mind with *Schwarzenberg* (1984), again an historical novel made to carry more than an historical meaning. Its starting-point is a curious little episode from the last days of the war. Schwarzenberg is a small town in central Germany which marked the point at which the Soviet army advancing from the east was to meet the American army advancing from the west. A misreading of the map led the two armies to halt some way short of the town, leaving it unoccupied. Uncertain which side would eventually march in, the citizens took affairs into their own hands and declared an autonomous republic with their own elected officials. The extraordinary situation lasted only a week or two before the Russians took over but it provided Heym with a golden opportunity to satirise the parish-pump politics of the men and women of Schwarzenberg as they discuss how to constitute their utopia.

Like writers in the West, though usually from quite different standpoints and with quite different purposes, East German novelists constantly returned over the following decades to the recent war and its fascist ambience for subject matter, and the reception of such novels by the public showed that there was a steady market for them. Dieter Noll's massively popular *Die Aben-teuer des Werner Holt* ('The Adventures of Werner Holt'), published in 1960, describes in naturalistic detail, not flinching at violence and brutality, a young soldier's life from 1943 till the end of the war. This was the sort of book from which East German youth learnt its history – a counterpart to Remar-que's *All Quiet On the Western Front* from the First World War but heavily politicised to demonstrate the nature of the fascism the war had been fought to crush.

War and Nazism also provide the setting for one of the most enter-taining – if the word be permitted in such a context – and most skilfully written of all East German novels, Jurek Becker's *Jakob der Lügner* ('Jacob the Liar'). This is war and Nazism seen in a very particular light, for Becker was Jewish and grew up in a Polish ghetto and in concentration camps. The living conditions he describes, like the relationships between the Jews and their Nazi oppressors, are the testimony of one who was there. Yet into this fabric of cruelty and tragedy Becker weaves a personal story as comic as it is poignant. Jakob, his hero, has overheard on a Nazi radio – the Jews are not allowed such luxuries – that the Russian army is closing in, and concludes that liberation is at hand. Morale rises. He cannot disillusion his people, so he supplies encouraging news bulletins day by day, pretending the information comes from the radio. He dare not stop lying, for his people's sake. The outcome is that prescribed by history. One day lorries arrive and take the inhabitants of the ghetto to the gas chambers. The Russians are still miles away.

It is a humane story, very Jewish, full of warmth and genuine relationships, not weighed down with ideological ballast, the work of a politically and artistically courageous man. Also a successful film maker, Becker claimed his independence and had no qualms about criticising the actions of the DDR regime. His readers will not have missed the significance of a story in which the hero cannot stop lying.

Nine years after *Jakob der Lügner*, in 1976, Christa Wolf, one of the best-known East German writers, whose experience of the war was as a child and a teenager, made her own reckoning with the war and the Nazi past in her autobiographical *Kindheitsmuster* ('Patterns of Childhood'). But by now the question has changed. Christa Wolf no longer asks: How did the war come about and how was it won by heroes such as those in the novels of Noll and Anna Seghers? but: What marks has the Nazi experience left on the way the present younger generation sees the future? The past cannot just be given a dialectical explanation and put on one side as over, dealt with, but must inform the present as a living reality without which our understanding of the existential here-and-now is only partial.

Born in 1929 in an area of eastern Brandenburg which is now Polish, living since the 1960s on the outskirts of Berlin, Christa Wolf belongs to a generation which bore no responsibility for Hitler. Much of *Kindheitsmuster* is self-indulgent, an exploration of the author's ego, stylistically somewhat contrived, appealing to aficionados of the free, associative imagination, as she muses on the sixteen formative years she spent in the Third Reich. The author's subjective morality functions within a context of material conditions, some factual, others imagined, some in the past, others in the present. But living in a state that presented itself as a nation of democrats and resistance fighters, while unloading guilt on to the capitalist West, young readers in particular eagerly looked for the information carried by the strand of objective narrative in the novel – a belated confrontation with the past that would not have been possible earlier.

In the 1950s the Party line required writers to turn their attention from the anti-fascist victories of the past to the promotion of the socialist New Man of the future. 'Progressive writers', declared the Party secretariat, 'can help through their works to develop a sense of optimism and pride among industrial and agricultural workers, making them aware of the social problems connected with the fulfilment of the Economic Plan.'

The unsurprising result was a crop of predictable, conformist novels from which artistic spontaneity and individuality had been banished in the name of 'solidarity', leaving torsos of interest to no one. Wooden heroes serve only a heavily didactic purpose as they march towards the goal of dialectical understanding, protagonists of a socialist *Bildungsroman*.

The credibility of such characters had difficulty in surviving the events of 17 June 1953, when the simmering realities of life and work under socialism boiled over. Indeed, the Party's fixation on dogma and dialectic was a deliberate diversion of attention from the brute facts of life in East Berlin. An openly realistic presentation of the harshness of conditions as they really were, the state of mind of a population watching lavish prestige blocks go up in the Stalinallee while their own sub-standard houses flaked and crumbled – no such negative material could be permitted. And as far as 17 June itself is concerned, it was years before even loyal servants like Anna Seghers and Hermann Kant ventured, or were permitted, to deal with those events – the former in *Das Vertrauen* ('Trust', 1968), the latter in *Das Impressum* ('The Publishing House', 1973), both of which curtly dismiss the occasion as an act of imperialist, counter-revolutionary agitation. Stefan Heym's fascinating *Fünf Tage im Juni* ('Five Days in June'), on the other hand, the work of a man who refused to kow-tow to the regime's petty restrictions, could be published only in the West, like most of his novels.

Attempts to inject some lively authenticity into these 'reconstruction novels' of the 1950s, as they were called, led to the incorporation in the action of elements of reportage – episodes and conversations directly drawn, allegedly, from the industrial milieu in which the novel is set. The so-called Bitterfelder Weg initiative of 1959, sending writers into the factories and encouraging workers to become writers, moved in the same direction. But such pragmatically engineered constructs lacked an informing aesthetic principle, an unshaken commitment to the primacy of the poetic imagination, and they paid the price, through both their political ineffectiveness and their aesthetic inadequacy. No more successful were novels of the 1960s which, obedient to a shift in Party ideology, viewed the future rather in the intellectual terms of the nature of social change itself than through the roseate hopes of the heroic worker in his factory.

Sunday, 13 August 1961 is a date no Berliner – no German – can forget. When, at two o'clock in the morning on that day, East German soldiers started putting up barbed-wire barricades across Berlin streets at sector boundaries between east and west, and the cross-town S-Bahn and subway trains stopped, there was shock and horror – but, ironically, little surprise. This was not a strike in a totally unexpected direction – rather, a terrifyingly logical step by the East German government to put an end to the ever growing exodus of its citizens.

But in a perverse way the Wall served only to consolidate what had been evident since 1949 – even since 1945. With every year that passed, the separate existence of the East German state, the German Democratic Republic, against desperate hopes in East and West alike, became more and more undeniable, more and more irrevocable. It provided its own environment for its artists and intellectuals, and when authors set out to write about the men and women around them, it was the German Democratic Republic that set the framework. The Berlin Wall brought a new theme, a new moment of tension. It may have intensified the realities within its perimeter. But it did not change, let alone create them.

Of the many novels and short stories from the 1960s and 1970s which draw on the realities of a now hermetically sealed country, two stand out, works by two of the best-known of the country's writers – Christa Wolf and Günter de Bruyn.

Christa Wolf's *Der geteilte Himmel* ('Divided Heaven'), published in 1963, made into a film the following year, became one of the most popular of all East German novels, in the West no less than in the East. It is a clever, mildly sentimental blend of love story and social comment, with something for everybody. The romance is between a country girl and a student who has grown dissatisfied with life in the DDR and decides to defect to West Berlin. She, however, having visited him there, cannot envisage herself as part of that scene and returns home. Shortly afterwards the Wall is built, and their separation is sealed. At the end we see her trying to put her life together again after a botched attempt to commit suicide.

On the surface *Der geteilte Himmel* is the sort of East–West story directly attributable to the forcible division of the city – in the first place a brutal physical reality but with an increasingly psychological impact. Concede its economic necessity, as many intellectuals did, the Wall remained a demonstration of moral bankruptcy.

But the story went further, and controversially so. For although the heroine resists the temptations of the capitalist West, leaving her boyfriend branded as a traitor to his country, the question of the nature of human relationships in a socialist society and of the truth of subjective experience remains. The question is made the more awkward by the heroine's attempted suicide. Where is the much vaunted optimism and sense of achievement the state demanded? The unresolved dissonances and the ideological freedom that Christa Wolf allowed herself met with official disapproval. Above all the Party had not been called upon to help solve the problems posed. This independence, in a context where independence was not wanted and rarely found, is what brought the work its success.

Life and love under socialism, but also the frustrations, deceptions and lies of the society crouching behind its brave new Wall, all cleverly encompassed in an ironically probing narrative, return in Günter de Bruyn's *Buridans Esel* ('Buridan's Ass'), published in 1968. De Bruyn, a Berliner by birth, for many years a librarian before devoting himself to literature, is one of the most attractive of East German fiction writers. Standing somewhat apart, insisting on a personal view of the reality around him, he was among the signatories to the public letter of protest at the expulsion of Wolf Biermann but like Christa Wolf – though unlike Günter Kunert, Jurek Becker, Volker Braun, Ulrich Plenzdorf and a host of others – made no move to leave his country.

Taking as his starting-point Buridan's fable of the ass that found itself unable to choose between two identical piles of hay and starved to death, de Bruyn constructs a love triangle in which a comfortably placed librarian leaves his submissive wife and family for an attractive younger woman, Fräulein Broder, who offers him a chance of greater self-fulfilment. But the change to a life with her in a tenement block proves too great a strain. He cannot live up to his vision, either as a lover or as a member of society. Their love wanes, and he goes back to his wife and to his old job – a resolution portrayed not as a victory for the moral code on which family life in socialism is built but as its defeat, the failure of a man to live up to the challenge of new realities. At the same time, Fräulein Broder emerges as a strong personality who resolutely follows the path of her own development, a model of the feminine independence promoted by the state.

Described in these bare terms, the story sounds conventional, even trite. The real interest of *Buridans Esel* is as a portrait, or series of portraits, of East Berlin society in the 1960s. Leaving aside the pure entertainment value of a story well told, it can be read – and one feels the author means it to be read – as a piece of social history, describing the class structure in a nominally classless society. At one end of the spectrum are what de Bruyn disparagingly refers to as 'fat-cat communists' living in their suburban villas, careerists who have used their Party membership to feather their own nests. At the other end lies the world of those, like Fräulein Broder, who live in gloomy, cockroach-ridden tenements with insanitary communal toilets but who are the real custodians of a sense of urban identity, of the historical continuity on which alone the future can be built.

That there is such a future is an assumption of de Bruyn's. But it has to be demonstrated in the novel, through the development of those elements in society with whom it rests, a development which the writer's subjective imagination must be allowed to fashion. Gone are the days of the simple 'reconstruction novel', with its ready-made hero and its programmed didactic optimism. The 1960s embrace in literature a variety of new, independent ways of dealing with the given realities of life, raising the level of consciousness of what was at stake, initiating rather than following or reflecting, drawing on autobiographical material for both narrative and psychology, and prepared, if that is the way things are, to leave a message clouded with uncertainty, even with pessimism and tragedy.

Such a work is Christa Wolf's *Nachdenken über Christa T.* ('Reflections on Christa T.'), published in the same year as *Buridans Esel*, the year of the Warsaw Pact invasion of Czechoslovakia. Christa Wolf presents through her autobiographical heroine the tragic life and death of a young woman destroyed by the incompatibility of the legitimate claims of the members of society with the form and condition of that society. Put another way: it is a study in individuality, an account of how a woman with her own demands on life, but also with a desire to serve the society to which she belongs, is made to learn that society has little use for imaginative people of independent mind like her but is looking for docile yes-men, mindless clones who will not ask embarrassing or forbidden questions. Unable – in effect forbidden – to assimilate into the society in whose midst she finds herself, she is driven back upon herself and thereby calls the whole basis of that society into question. Christa T.'s failure to achieve fulfilment in the terms laid upon her is symbolised in the novel by her early death – apparently from leukaemia but hastened by a paralysis of the will to live. What survives is the vision of the subjective ego fighting for self-expression in an alien environment.

The implications of *Nachdenken über Christa T.* were not to the authorities' liking. Nor did its gentle yet curiously oblique style, an amalgam of narrative biography, anecdotes, diary entries, dreams, flashbacks, make for coherent, easy reading. With characteristic illogicality officialdom allowed a generous print-run for the first edition – shortage of newsprint was a perpetual source of complaint in the DDR – but took steps to see that it was hardly reviewed. At the same time they reprimanded the author, one of their star figures, for a thoroughly unsocialist-realist book.

No such reproach could be levelled at Hermann Kant, author of the DDR novel to end all DDR novels, a work in which the country found its historical achievements suitably lauded and its social principles vindicated – *Die Aula* ('The University Hall').

Kant was the darling of the East German cultural establishment right up to the demise of the country in 1990, and his career is a model of the ambitious, conformist worker-turned-intellectual communist on whom the state relied for its justification and its prestige. Born in 1926, a soldier at the end of the war and a Polish prisoner-of-war for four years, Kant became a mature student in Berlin in 1952 and later settled there as a free-lance writer. He was a member of the East Berlin Akademie der Künste and President of the Writers' Union until 1990, when his activity for the Stasi was uncovered and left him in disgrace.

Distasteful though Kant's personal careerism may have been, *Die Aula*, his first novel (1965), is both a fascinating piece of historico-social documentation, autobiographical over large areas, and a literary *tour de force*. It has no conventional plot that progressively unfurls but a single, all-embracing situation gradually filled by a succession of episodes held together by a central character. The situation is the planned reunion of a group of university students ten years after graduation; the character is the member of the group, a journalist, entrusted with the task of looking up his former friends in preparation for the occasion. The book then consists of accounts of the careers and achievements of these alumni over the intervening years. One is a black sheep who turned his back on the DDR and fled to Hamburg; the others have enjoyed the opportunities for success which socialism offered.

Die Aula, like Kant's later novels of the 1970s, bristles with the formulae and the linguistic commonplaces of the one-time DDR which now, since reunification, have a quaint, almost comical residual interest, evidence for future generations of a peculiar period in the history of the German language. It is not afraid to mock the more bizarre manifestations of an over-zealous application of Party dogma. At the same time it passes over in silence the events of 17 June 1953 and the building of the Berlin Wall. Nor is it short of the ready-made sneers at the capitalist society of the West which were second nature to a Party member.

But in its mixture of changing perspectives, flash-backs, interior monologues and other narrative techniques, as well as in its wit and the liveliness of its style, it is a skilful piece of work, and, published in both East and West editions, has sold far more copies than any other novel of the period. Kant's success caused considerable gnashing of teeth among West German critics but the élan of *Die Aula* defeated them. And apart from its qualities as a piece of racy storytelling, it has the quality of an historical record which documents how the officially sponsored young generation of those days set about building a new society which paid no respect to the bourgeois traditions of their parents. That neither that society nor the country any longer exists makes Kant's novel something of a museum piece.

The hesitant hopes roused by Honecker's 'no-taboo' speech in December 1971 led to a muted return of confidence in the right of individual choice. Ulrich Plenzdorf's *Die neuen Leiden des jungen W.*, available the following year both as short story and as drama, captured what young people in particular had missed, a role model of self-fulfilment whom an alarmingly high number said they could accept – alarming to the authorities, that is. For here the proposition is being put that the fulfilment of the individual may be found not within the system but outside it, even against it. Catching a whiff of freedom, writers began to expose in their stories specific abuses of power, such as censorship of mail and denial of professional advancement to those not in the Party.

Stefan Heym, himself a frequent victim of the authorities' capricious malevolence, found this a perfect moment to re-enter the lists. In his masterly novel *Der König-David-Bericht* ('The King David Report') he tells of a Jewish historian summoned by Solomon to write the definitive biography of his father David, a biography expected to portray the King in all his nobility and greatness. When the historian's researches reveal instead a corrupt and tyrannical ruler, Solomon accuses him of treason and condemns him, not to death but to eternal oblivion – no word he speaks or writes shall be preserved or remembered. He shall become a non-person.

Readers could hardly believe their eyes. Could the censor really have failed to recognise what this was all about? Official pressure for the falsification of history; the suppression of unwelcome truths; the punishment of troublesome non-conformists by forbidding them to publish, effectively ostracising them from the intellectual life of the country – this was not the land of Israel in Biblical times but the German Democratic Republic of the here-and-now.

Such hostile freedom of expression could not be tolerated. The state reasserted itself and darkness fell again. Dissidents were made the objects of trumped-up charges aimed at humiliating or intimidating them. One after another, by whatever means, left the ship that seemed intent on scuttling itself. Formerly the term 'exile literature' had referred to the work of those who fled the Third Reich. Now it was being used of those who had been thrown out of the East and were trying to put their careers together again in the West. For stubborn characters like Heym and Heiner Müller, writers of international reputation who refused either to leave or to be thrown out, life was made more and more difficult. Between 1976 and 1980 a further thirty of the dwindling number of members still there were expelled from the Writers' Union – the equivalent of a publication ban. Under legislation passed as late as 1979 the expression of unorthodox views could be deemed a 'public outrage' and equated with 'conduct prejudicial to the interests of the state', punishable by a long term of imprisonment.

Politically monolithic the country may have appeared but beneath the surface there was a young generation at work – those who had known neither Nazism nor war – which had no reason to be grateful to their state and harboured a nagging resentment of a society in which they felt they could not fulfil themselves. They can hardly be credited with responsibility for the events of November 1989 but in retrospect their aims were consonant with the spirit of those events. They felt alienated from their society instead of liberated by it, at the mercy of impersonal bureaucracies and dehumanising technological processes, feeling no obligation to invest in public involvement. 'As far as social commitment is concerned', said the poet Uwe Kolbe, born in 1957, 'people of my generation are keeping their hands in their laps.' They had no use for Brecht and didactic literature. Some even questioned whether, as they had always been told, everything really was possible under socialism. It was an echo of the post-war 'ohne mich' stance in the West.

The possibility of a literature freed from the constrictions of a socialist framework, located in a freer, more open society, was pursued by Christoph Hein, one of the most successful of the younger generation of playwrights and novelists. In his novel *Horns Ende* (1985), a confrontation with the Stalinist 1950s in the DDR, he uses the forces of history to reveal the political pressures at work in his own society, even daring to propose a continuity between the DDR and the Third Reich, symbolised by the Germans' subservience to authority and their craven preparedness to betray their fellow-citizens, whether to the Gestapo or to the Stasi. Hein does not see himself as a public educator, like Brecht, but he does acknowledge the writer's social responsibility, a responsibility he construes as to provoke thought and argument, above all in the causational terms of history. Writers in East Berlin surveying the national future from within the 1980s can have drawn little comfort from what they saw. By the end of the decade the country of 'actually existing socialism' had itself ceased to exist and taken its socialism with it.

Cinema

Before the war Berlin had held sway over the German film industry. Indeed, through the decade of the Weimar Republic, in silent films as in the early talkies, the story of the German cinema is virtually coterminous with the story of Berlin cinema, dominated by the UFA company. When the war ended, the UFA studios found themselves in the Soviet zone of occupation and were immediately put back into service for the production of films that promoted Soviet interests and the Soviet view of the German past, present and future. The East German regime inherited this cinematic empire, and the actors, producers, directors and technicians of the film industry returned to the UFA – now rechristened DEFA (Deutsche Film-Aktiengesellschaft) – making their own contribution to the centralisation of cultural life in East Berlin and leaving West Berlin in limbo.

Yet for a number of years after the end of the war there seemed to be a genuine prospect of a degree of cooperation between the film makers of East and West, who saw no reason to be forced into a state of artificial antagonism towards each other. Actors, in particular, found it invidious to be labelled East German or West German, and producers saw both the professional and the political advantages to be gained from pooling their experience.

One of the most expansive co-productions planned was of Thomas Mann's novel *Die Buddenbrooks*. Mann unhesitatingly welcomed the idea. 'I would have regarded it as a modest contribution to the cultural reunification of Germany,' he wrote to the DEFA a few months before he died. But the Federal German government of Konrad Adenauer, mindful of the views of the Americans, had set its face against such collaborations and the project was encouraged to collapse. The DEFA had better fortune in its dealings with the French, who were less heavily burdened with Cold War ballast and with whom a number of co-productions involving big names like Gérard Philippe, Yves Montand and Simone Signoret did come to fruition. (A film of *Buddenbrooks* was eventually made in the West in 1959.)

The first film (1946) to come out of post-war Germany – at the same time the first DEFA production – was Wolfgang Staudte's *Die Mörder sind unter uns* ('The Murderers Are Among Us'), starring Hildegard Knef and Wilhelm Borchert, a confrontation with post-war issues such as national guilt, retribution and the punishment of ex-Nazis. All films from these early years – and it is something of a miracle that any films at all could have been made in times of such devastation and chaos – had to be licensed and censored by one of the four occupying powers. This meant that, even if one hesitated to talk of propaganda at such a poignant moment, there was political control over the way the war and its aftermath were presented. Berlin was inevitably the centre of attention. In 1947 Roberto Rossellini directed an outsider's brutal view of what he found there in the semi-documentary *Germania: Year Zero*, filmed largely on location, while in the same year the DEFA issued *Strassenbekanntschaft* ('Street Acquaintance'), a feature film rich in the depiction of the moral depravity rife in the occupied capital but commissioned originally as a warning against the dangers of venereal disease.

Depravity there was, to be sure. But this was Berlin, with its irrepressible spirit of mockery and satire, and the gloom could never pervade every corner of the scene. So the following year saw the appearance of a romp called *Berliner Ballade* ('The Ballad of Berlin'), scripted by Günter Neumann, star of the West Berlin radio cabaret *The Islanders*, a show which in the cold and hungry winter of 1948 had the will and the energy to burlesque the perversions of the time, ridicule the pompous excesses of a resurgent German bureaucracy and even ridicule the political policies of the occupying powers. *Berliner Ballade* too, which takes a satirical look at the state of society as it would have appeared to a man living a century later, has much of the cabaret about it.

A similarly lighthearted account of the relationship between the occupying forces and their conquered victims was taken in the comedy *Hallo Fräulein!* (1949), in which an American officer and a young German music student act out the 'non-fraternisation' charade of the post-war years. Here, as in other films of the period from both the Soviet and the Western camp, the position of women in society becomes a topic for debate, for the war had brought women an irreversible independence and sense of equality which, particularly in the West, a male-dominated world had difficulty in assimilating.

FILM IN WEST BERLIN

In the 1950s cinema-going, and with it the number of movie theatres, was at its height. Deprived of its film-making facilities at Babelsberg, West Berlin adopted the same strategy as in other areas of culture in which it had lost its former pre-eminence of creative artists: it made itself a centre for performance and exhibition, seeking to regain some of its former kudos by providing a platform for the display to the outside world of the artistic achievements of the whole country. In 1951 the annual International Film Festival was founded, pledged 'to promote understanding and cooperation between peoples and cultures by presenting films of high quality', which has since acquired an importance equal to that of Cannes, Locarno and Venice. The 1950s also marked the high point of West German film production in the post-war years – 135 feature films were made in 1955. Since then the number has steadily declined, falling to a mere fifty-nine in 1990, the result of a complex interaction of socio-economic factors and the fluctuating status and quality of film as an artistic medium.

During this time Munich had made itself the centre of the West German film industry, the place where most of the big names were to be found – Alexander Kluge, Werner Herzog, Edgar Reitz, Rainer Werner Fassbinder. Only Wim Wenders, of prominent film makers, made his home in Berlin, which, as in its function of promoter of exhibitions, theatre and concerts, continued to establish itself as an administrative centre. In 1965, as a belated answer to the East German Film Hochschule established in 1954, the Federal government and the *Land* of West Berlin founded a Film and Television Academy in Charlottenburg for the training of directors, cameramen and other technical experts.

A key moment in the development of the cinema in post-war West Germany arrived in the mid-1960s, when a group of young film makers made a determined break with the conventional cinema of box-office values and launched New German Film, an enterprise sustained by an ambitious philosophy of experimentation, freedom from commercial pressure and political interference, and the right to compete in the international arena. Formulated at a meeting in Oberhausen of makers of shorts, the new policy came to be known as the Oberhausen Manifesto. Methodological inspiration came in particular from France – Louis Malle, Jean Resnais, Jean Renoir. Subject matter was drawn from personal relationships in contemporary West German society, the affluent *Wirtschaftswunder* society, seen through critical left-wing eyes and presented as an 'authentic' picture, owing much to the techniques of the documentary. Political pressure was also brought to bear on the newly founded Academy in Berlin, whose students wanted film to play a militant role in the context of political agitation and education.

On the heels of the proclamation of New German Film came the assurance of subsidies from public funds. This finance could not of itself guarantee quality but it made possible much that would have otherwise remained stunted and unfulfilled, and the superior product, in its turn, attracted the larger audiences required for a film's success. Without such support the success that greeted the débuts in 1966 of men like Alexander Kluge with *Abschied von gestern* ('Goodbye to Yesterday') and Volker Schlöndorff with his *Der junge Törless* (after the story by Robert Musil) would have been beyond reach. High points of West German film like Schlöndorff's version of Grass' novel *Die Blechtrommel*, and Wolfgang Petersen's two sensational successes, *Die unendliche Geschichte* ('The Unending Story') and the epic war film *Das Boot*, have all been large-budget undertakings.

In the wake of the events of 1968 there emerged one of the few groups of films specifically linked to Berlin – films dealing with the condition of the working class. *Liebe Mutter, mir geht es gut* ('Dear Mother, I'm Fine'), released in 1972 and using largely non-professional actors, plays on the tension between employers and workers during a time of recession, and was followed by further studies of the social and psychological effects of strikes, dismissal and other features of the current industrial scene. Strangely enough, despite the tension generated by successive waves of *Gastarbeiter* in the city, films centred on ethnic minorities such as the Turks make their appearance only in the 1980s, and even then, with the feature and documentary work of Tevlik Baser, not in Berlin but in Hamburg.

Thematically related to such films, however, was the work of Reinhard Hauff, now Director of the Berlin Film Academy, who portrayed an intolerant society in terms of its victims, its outsiders, especially the outsider caught up in violence. His *Messer im Kopf* ('Knife in the Head') of 1978, recalling the assassination attempt on the student leader Rudi Dutschke in Berlin ten years earlier, pursues the issue of the relationship between violence in the name of protest and the violence used by the state to crush that protest – an issue never far beneath the surface in German public life. Violence and the threat of violence is also the code by which the hero of Hauff's *Die Verrohung von Franz Blum* ('The Brutalisation of Franz Blum') has to live – the code of brutality that governs life in jail, where survival is synonymous with dehumanisation. And what goes on in jail goes on in society outside.

In 1982, with *Der Mann auf der Mauer* ('Man on the Wall'), Hauff joined the many – others are Herbert Ballmann with *Einmal Ku'Damm und zurück* ('Return Ticket to the Ku'Damm'), Peter Timm, an émigré from the DDR, with *Meier*, and Rudolf Thome with *Berlin Chamissoplatz* – who in the 1980s made the East–West confrontation the centre of their attention. With a script by Peter Schneider, whose own story *Der Mauerspringer* was published the same year, *Der Mann auf der Mauer* catches the schizophrenic confusion of the young man who, while living in East Berlin, wanted nothing so desperately as to escape to the West; now, deported to the West, he looks forlornly back across the Wall and longs to return to the East. It is his fate to straddle the border. The Wall has become a way of life.

DEFA AND EAST BERLIN

The cinema of the West had shown a reluctance in 1945 to confront the issues of recent history. Even the younger generation took time to grasp them. It was 1965 before Jean-Marie Straub faced the inter-war years with his *Nicht versöhnt* ('Not Reconciled'), based on Heinrich Böll's novel *Billard um halb zehn*, and in *Der junge Törless*, released a year later, Schlöndorff also confronted the 1930s. But the popular appeal of the Nazis had already been treated ten years earlier in *Lissy*, the DEFA film with which the greatest of East German directors, Konrad Wolf, made his début. Wolfgang Staudte's first film, *Die Mörder sind unter uns*, moreover, had faced the issue of guilt and war crimes barely a year after the war ended. Indeed, the DEFA in Babelsberg had from the beginning been given the task to do precisely this, as well as to convey the values of the socialist community of the future.

No less productive than Staudte, a communist survivor from the 1930s, was Kurt Maetzig – co-founder of DEFA and the Babelsberg Film Academy, initiator of the DDR newsreel service and maker of over twenty feature films. The suspicion that had already begun to open up between the two Germanies could not be ignored when Maetzig's *Der Rat der Götter* ('The Counsel of the Gods'), an exposé of the role of German armaments manufacturers in the growth of Nazism, was banned in the West as a piece of blatant communist propaganda.

Whereas the evils of the Third Reich had a repellent fascination that constantly stimulated the imagination, to entice an effective film from the drab realities of everyday life became an increasingly unrewarding prospect. Attention in DEFA turned to filming classics of German literature – Heinrich Mann's *Der Untertan*, Büchner's *Wozzeck*, Lessing's *Emilia Galotti*, E. T. A. Hoffmann's *Das Fräulein von Scuderi* – and to honouring the quality of national heroism, as Maetzig did in his two epic films on the communist leader Ernst Thälmann. The 1950s, indeed, saw a dramatic increase in state funding 'to stimulate the growth of a progressive German film industry', as the decree put it, and a series of important figures in the history of East German film – Konrad Wolf, Gerhard Klein, Frank Beyer, Heiner Carow – were launched on their careers.

Lissy, a film version of F. C. Weiskopf's novel on the lure of Nazism; *Sonnensucher* ('Sun-Seekers'), set in a uranium mine; *Professor Mamlock*, based on his father's drama on the fate of the Jews under Hitler; *Der geteilte Himmel*, after the novel by Christa Wolf; *Solo Sunny*, story of a Berlin pop-singer – these are some of the highly successful films made by Konrad Wolf between 1957 and his death in 1982. Son of Friedrich Wolf, left-wing Berlin dramatist of the 1920s, and brother of the East German Stasi chief Markus Wolf, Friedrich returned as a young man in 1945 from asylum in the Soviet Union. He helped to establish the East Berlin daily newspaper, the *Berliner Zeitung*, then found his way into cinema as assistant to Kurt Maetzig in his Thälmann films. For fifteen years he was President of the East German Academy of Arts, and after his death the Film Academy in Babelsberg was renamed after him. Like Willy Bredel, Johannes R. Becher and the others, including his father, who came back to build a socialist Germany, he became a pillar of the East German cultural establishment but retained a critical gaze on his society and never sank into crude propaganda. The East–West dichotomy of *Der geteilte Himmel* and the pop-music tensions of *Solo Sunny* cut deep into contemporary East German consciousness and did not pass without considerable debate.

Not, however, that other young film makers had been afraid to show the seedy side of their society, often as part of a scenario spanning East and West Berlin. Gerhard Klein, who had made the sentimental *Eine Berliner Romanze* in 1956, turned the following year to the near-criminal milieu of adolescent dropouts in *Berlin – Ecke Schönhauser*, a study in vandalism and general anti-social behaviour of a kind the authorities denied could ever exist in a socialist state.

'If it's forbidden,' they said, 'it can't exist.' Perhaps that is why they allowed *Berlin – Ecke Schönhauser* to be shown.

But Klein did not escape so lightly next time. His *Berlin um die Ecke* ('Round the Corner in Berlin') presents a desolate picture of a disillusioned and rebellious younger generation that blames its frustration on its elders. 'We are all slaves,' says the graffito daubed on the wall of their factory. The Party was horrified. 'Arrogance . . . capitalist immorality . . . absence of a sense of collective relationships . . . anarchism in the workplace' – such was the outburst provoked by the film. It was immediately withdrawn, and the final cut was shown only in 1990, after the collapse of the DDR and twenty years after Klein's death.

An equally predictable fate awaited the painter and documentary film maker Jürgen Böttcher's *Jahrgang 45* ('Born 1945'), made in the same years, 1965–6, as *Berlin um die Ecke*. Here, however, there is not grim-faced resentment and violent protest but a sense of pointlessness, an urge among the twenty-year-old generation of Prenzlauer Berg for an alternative life-style. 'Confused, frivolous and in no way representative of our social order', came the official verdict: 'the setting bears no relationship to the characteristic features of our socialist reality.' Böttcher later delivered his photographic obituary on his one-time country behind the Wall in *Die Mauer*, a documentary reflection on the gradual removal of the fortifications between Potsdamer Platz and the Brandenburg Gate from November 1989 to the end of 1990.

The irony of the fate that befell *Berlin um die Ecke, Jahrgang 45* and a few other films like them was that Klein and Böttcher, like Wolf Biermann, Manfred Krug, Robert Havemann and others who refused to be muzzled, thought themselves 'safe' in the wake of policies announced at the 11th Plenary Session of the Central Committee of the Socialist Unity Party in 1965. The Wall had stopped the flow of deserters. The quietness that followed, even if the quietness of the grave, was proclaimed to be a time of consolidation when internal problems and contradictions could be resolved by dialectical discussion. But, as many quickly discovered to their cost, this was not the invitation to frank criticism that they had been waiting for.

The Wall itself gave rise to a handful of misconceived films readily forgotten. The physical and psychological tragedies for which it was responsible were not permitted material for the film makers of the East. As the years went by, it could be accepted only for the implacable tribute to socialism that it was. Better to fill the mind, as DEFA did, with well-constructed thrillers – some of them slily located in West German society, where criminality could be implied as endemic – or with the most improbable of genres, the western, of which Babelsberg did twelve co-productions with other socialist countries in the 1960s and 1970s. The white man's invasion of North America but failure to annihilate the Indians was an inviting subject for anti-imperialist philippics. 'A synthesis of Karl Marx and Karl May', one critic called the outcome. Producers looking to deal with more substantial issues and more intimate emotions continued in the tradition of filming German classics – Lessing's *Minna von Barnhelm*, E. T. A. Hoffmann's *Die Elixiere des Teufels*, Goethe's *Werther* and *Die Wahlverwandtschaften*, Thomas Mann's *Lotte in Weimar*.

In the late 1960s, in particular after the dissident activities of Klein and Böttcher, the DEFA's fortunes were at a low ebb. Out of favour with the ideologues, it needed to reconcile the irreconcilable – acceptability to the censor, popularity with the public and innate cinematic quality. Even Konrad Wolf had to accept degrading public criticism for 'undermining the unity of the Party' but restored his reputation, and that of the DEFA, in 1968 with the autobiographical *Ich war neunzehn* ('I Was Nineteen'), a gripping account of relations between Russians and Germans in Berlin during war and occupation. Few films of the time matched its power and authority, and the DEFA's prospects rose.

They rose still further after Erich Honecker's much publicised speech at the 8th Party Congress in 1971 seemed to promise a further relaxation of controls over what could and what could not be expressed in the arts. Hitherto forbidden topics such as illegally attempting to flee the country made a bold appearance, along with cunning comedies packed with ridicule and satire of everyday life under bureaucratic socialism. Above all there was Heiner Carow's *Die Legende von Paul und Paula* (1973), to a scenario by the DEFA scriptwriter Ulrich Plenzdorf, a film that played to packed houses for months. Not without reason. For here, against a background of familiar personal and social norms, including the ideological prescriptions of an ossified leadership, was a demonstration, rich in gibes and satirical thrusts, of the right of a man and woman to happiness together without the precondition of a socialist society.

But it could not last. In 1976 Biermann was expelled and others followed, men from the film industry among them. The rule of reaction and repression returned. The DDR 'battened down the hatches', as the current metaphor had it, and they stayed battened down until the end.

Yet there were still forces at work that could not and would not be denied expression. The ruling caste had set great store by its insistence on confronting history and coming to terms with the past but was incapable of coming to terms with the present. The people were not the sheep the Party took them for, and film makers looking for the frustrations of the individual and the tensions of society knew where to find them.

Small wonder that audiences flocked in 1980 to Konrad Wolf's last film, *Solo Sunny*, to watch Sunny, a pop-singer from Prenzlauer Berg, claim her unfettered right to love, to a proper career, to acceptance in her own right, and finally – hence the title – to her own place in the sun, her own solo spot. Her world is a sub-culture of individuals seeking self-fulfilment, not a regimented socialist youth club. Sunny may not contribute much to the well-being of society but there is more to life, say Sunny and Wolf, than working on a production line or operating a check-out at a supermarket.

Although 'liberalisation' would not be the word, the occasional chink of light could be glimpsed in the 1980s, moments when some hitherto forbidden subject was allowed into the frame, or an attitude struck that suggested a streak of non-conformism. Children's films, moving in realms where the real and the imaginary are intertwined, where utopias are built and peopled with allegorical characters, offered possibilities to say one thing and mean another.

The material privileges enjoyed by Party functionaries at the expense of the rest of the population was an immediately identifiable theme woven into Helmut Dziuba's *Erscheinen Pflicht* ('Attendance Compulsory'), which was rewarded with hostile reviews and allowed only a limited public run. And although the DDR boasted that, in contrast to the Turks in capitalist West Berlin, refugees from third-world countries had no difficulty in assimilating to a socialist society, in reality they were despised and ignored, like the unhappy Chilean family in Hannelore Unterberg's *Isabel auf der Treppe* ('Isabel on the Staircase'), made in 1984.

But one must not make too much of such moments. In this same year, 1984, workers and soldiers began to erect an additional wall in the middle of the 'death strip' that divided East from West Berlin. As any official slackening of the reins was inconceivable, so too was any thought of rebellion. Either you toed the line or you lost your job – or worse.

Only a few of these later films, moreover, in so far as they dealt with the localised realities of the DDR, had a chance of survival, for later audiences could not identify the necessary points of reference. They were films for the insiders of the time. In 1975 Volker Braun wrote a story about a girl who was forced by the Party and the secret police to disclaim her love for an anti-social young man on pain of losing her job; after trying to commit suicide, she goes back to him but no one will employ her. The book, *Unvollendete Geschichte* ('Unfinished Story'), was banned as a gross slur on the integrity of the organs of state. In 1991, in conditions of 'peace', Frank Beyer and Ulrich Plenzdorf made a film of the story. There was barely a flicker of interest, let alone of anger. The non-existence of the German Democratic Republic had already begun.

Art in Socialist Realism

Soviet doctrine presented the defeat of 1945 as a liberation from fascism to be succeeded by an aggressive socialism which was the sole guarantor of future peace. No less socialist than the political and social infrastructure was the pattern to be applied to culture. The drive towards a new society demanded a healthy, optimistic, realistic art committed to the prescribed ideals. The natural leaders of the movement were those respected radical artists who had staked out their anti-fascist position in the 1920s and 1930s, had survived the Third Reich, whether in Germany or in exile abroad, and could now lay the foundations of the new cultural order – painters such as Otto Nagel and Heinrich Ehmsen, sculptors like Gustav Seitz, all three co-founders of the new Akademie der Künste in East Berlin in 1950.

But the ever-present nightmare of the ruined city had first to be overcome. As writers cultivated a *Trümmerliteratur*, 'a literature of the ruins', within the catharsis of coming to terms with the Nazi past, so the sight of heaps of rubble and the ghostly shells of blackened buildings drove artists to depict the perversion and horrors of recent German history. A forty-year-old soldier at the end of the war, a communist since the 1920s, Horst Strempel painted a large triptych in which, drawing on conventions of Christian iconography, he brings together motifs of the concentration camp, of the suffering of the children, of persecution, demoralisation and the agony of guilt – a symbolic statement of a Germany on its knees (Ill. 136).

For the same reasons that governed developments in the other arts, Berlin – East Berlin, capital of the German Democratic Republic – rapidly

136. *Darkness Over Germany* by Horst Strempel, oil on canvas, 1945-6. This is the central panel from the triptych of the same name.

became the focus of the country's activities in the visual arts. Important schools of painting and sculpture arose elsewhere in the country – Halle, Leipzig, Dresden. But the capital was the capital – one, moreover, with strong socialist traditions. A new Hochschule für bildende Künste was founded to rival that left in the West and, together with the new Akademie der Künste, provided for the training of young artists by some of the country's leading painters and sculptors. Meanwhile the Ministry of Culture and other state bodies organised exhibitions and competitions in the city both to stimulate the creative urge of the artists and to attract the interest of the public.

One of the fundamental challenges facing the founders of the new society was how to establish links with those forces in the historical heritage which could be seen – or made to be seen – as legitimate precursors of the humanist–socialist ideology. Painters looked back to portraits and landscapes by nineteenth-century realists like Karl Blechen, Eduard Gaertner and Franz Krüger. Even more striking was the resurgence of the traditions of the great Berlin school of sculpture – Tieck, Rauch, Begas – descended from Schadow. Here, in the work, first of Theo Balden, Gustav Seitz, Fritz Cremer and Waldemar Grzimek, then of the younger, wartime generation of Wieland Förster and Werner Stötzer, there arose an impressive body of sculpture in the classic, realistic line firmly rooted in the study of nature.

As among writers, musicians and intellectuals in general, so also among the ranks of painters and sculptors the new German socialist state found willing supporters whose careers, in return, the state was prepared to promote. But favour could be withdrawn as whimsically as it was granted. An artist might gratefully carry out an official commission, only to find the fruits of his labour consigned to the store-room instead of put on prominent display. In 1948 Horst Strempel did a mural for Friedrichstrasse railroad station to a commission from the Reichsbahn. Three years later it was condemned by the Party as 'formalistic' and ordered to be obliterated.

Strempel responded to the insult by turning his back on the DDR and moving to West Berlin. Others even dared to deny that the interests of art must coincide with the interests of the state. 'Art and artists follow their own path, an aesthetic path,' declared the popular Leipzig painter Wolfgang Mattheuer. 'No state can hold them back, nor can a market tie them down.' But many, like Max Lingner, painter of the tiled murals for the Ministry building in the Leipziger Strasse, bore such humiliations in silence, seeing them as the price to be paid for the establishment of a more equitable social order in their part of Germany.

In all the arts the degree of freedom allowed, in both subject matter and manner of expression, varied with the political climate and with what the Party considered to be the needs of the moment. Over the whole forty years of its existence the DDR was caught in a series of fluctuations between an unyielding Stalinist rigidity and temporary episodes of apparently liberal concession. Fully aware that it did not have the confidence of the mass of its citizens, and suffering from an unshakeable inferiority complex in the perpetual presence of its Western rival, the regime, with its Soviet Big Brother breathing down its neck, had to strike a balance between what Marxist–Leninist orthodoxy prescribed and what it could risk imposing on the population. Lenin, after all, had regarded Germany as the ideal soil for the realisation of communism.

In matters of art the cardinal sin was formalism. By this was meant any propensity to set aesthetic considerations above social function, form above social content, or to assert the independent personality over the collective image. 'Socialist realism' – naturalism, Soviet style – was the dictated manner. Work that had its roots in, say, the German impressionists and the Berlin Secession was unwelcome. As early as 1950 John Heartfield, famous left-wing Dadaist montage artist from the years of the Weimar Republic and recently returned to East Berlin from wartime exile in London, found himself the object of an 'anti-formalist' tirade. So too, at one time or another, did prominent personalities such as Brecht, the composer Paul Dessau and – before he moved permanently to the West – the architect Hans Scharoun.

With the death of Stalin in 1953 came an apparent easing of tension in cultural policy. Far from the product of any revision of doctrine, this was a reluctant tactical move by Walter Ulbricht, the East German leader, to keep hold of his position in a Politbureau where Stalinists and supporters of Khrushchev were in violent disagreement. But it brought a moment of respite to artists and intellectuals. 'Formalism' and 'internationalism' disappeared from the Party's critical vocabulary overnight, a simple realism applied to the mundane facts of everyday socialist life was no longer demanded, and the artist had the freedom to follow his individual expressive instincts. In some ways more important, membership of policy-making bodies now extended to freethinking artists who, complained an irritated Politbureau committee, 'had no connection with the task of socialist reconstruction and held modernistic views'. The most important artistic influence on these new, independent-minded painters came from Toulouse-Lautrec, Picasso and Matisse, as well as from Max Beckmann, Nolde and Karl Hofer. 'The subjects portrayed also changed dramatically overnight,' complained the same committee. 'Suddenly canvases were covered with circus clowns, waiters, alcoholics, prostitutes, cripples, cats and dogs.' It might have been the Nazis railing at the war-wounded and *demi-mondes* in the expressionist paintings of Otto Dix and George Grosz one war ago.

A test of how far the new artistic tolerance could be pushed by an artist not prepared to make concessions to officialdom was set by Waldemar Grzimek with his statue of Heine, commissioned by the Berlin *Magistrat* to commemorate in 1956 the centennial of the poet's death (Ill. 137).

Heine posed problems for the official DDR. On the one hand, as the victim of a reactionary regime, supporter of the 1948 revolution, friend of Marx, Lassalle and Engels and defender of the cause of the workers, he could be pressed into service as a forerunner of socialism. On the other hand he was an ironical romantic, a lyrical genius haunted by the fear that

137. *Heinrich Heine* by Waldemar Grzimek, bronze, 1954-6.

the individual spirit – his individual spirit – might be crushed under the weight of the mediocrity of the masses. For the purposes of commemoration the state looked for an appropriate display of heroic qualities which would enable it to bask in the reflected glory of its illustrious ancestor – Heine as inspiring optimist, a Marxist before his time.

What Grzimek gave his patrons, to their considerable discomfiture, was not a statuesque Heine holding forth to the multitude but a seated bronze figure quietly and intensely arguing with the companion on whom his quizzical gaze is fixed. Youthful, vivacious, this is an independent spirit who looks beneath the surface of things, who acknowledges that there is much ambiguity in the world and that reality is a far from simple concept. Around the plinth of the figure runs a frieze depicting scenes from Heine's life and motifs drawn from various of his poems, including *Deutschland, ein Wintermärchen*.

Heated arguments divided artists and *apparatchiks* over what should be done with the sculpture. It had originally been intended for a prestigious location off Unter den Linden, behind Schinkel's Neue Wache. But the ideological fuss now made that impossible, and two years after the event it was supposed to celebrate, it was erected on the edge of a public park in East Berlin. Grzimek himself, who had been dismissed from the West Berlin Hochschule because of his links with East Berlin, pursued the chimera of a unified Berlin for as long as any trace of reality still clung to the prospect. He retained his teaching post at the East Berlin Hochschule for a few years but drew the only possible conclusion from the events of 1961 and returned to end his career in the West.

The thaw of the early 1950s soon gave way to a new ice age. In the wake of the Hungarian uprising of 1956 and the appointment of Alfred Kurella as Party overseer of cultural policy, anything that hinted at intellectual or artistic independence was stamped on and the offenders subjected to show trials. 'Back to Socialist Realism' was now the cry, with Kurella seeing artists as educators of the proletariat, with whom they should rub shoulders in factories and collective farms in the way urged upon writers at the Bitterfeld conference of 1959. What constituted acceptable art was a matter for the organs of the state, acting in the name of the people – the Central Committee of the Party, the Free German Youth Movement, the trade unions, the Culture League – not for the artists themselves.

Nor were such bodies going to allow 'formalistic' qualities to override what they identified as lack of socialist commitment on an artist's part. The young painter Harald Metzkes, for instance, a pupil of the highly respected Otto Nagel, thought he was following the Bitterfeld line when he exhibited a large canvas based on his experience in a Berlin engineering factory, only to find himself accused of a 'shamefaced subjective abstractionism . . . which has nothing to say about the true characteristics of our new life'. A painting from the world of industry and national reconstruction which met with official approval, on the other hand, was *The Way to Work* (1958) by Konrad Knebel, a contemporary of Metzkes – men and women making their way to the pithead in the cheerless light of dawn, their children tramping along behind them.

Even higher in the Party's estimation stood Walter Womacka, archetypal socialist-realist painter of cheerful men and women at work on collective farms, serving a harmonious society from which conflict has been banished and in which all is sweetness and light. Womacka reached the pinnacle of his influence in the wake of the government's decision to allocate a fixed proportion of the cost of new public buildings to decorative features applied to the finished structure. While director of the Hochschule für bildende Künste Womacka set up a studio for the manufacture of this 'buildings-related art', as it was called, the most conspicuous piece of which, passed by thousands daily, is his monumental seven-metre-high frieze round the four sides of the Haus des Lehrers on the Alexanderplatz, depicting the joys of life under socialism (Ill. 138)

An artist of great facility and technical talent, Womacka also did a painting, in a powerful, thrusting style of expressionist provenance, depicting the demolition in 1995 of the DDR Foreign Ministry building. The occasion had a sour irony for Womacka. For with the destruction of the building went the destruction of the large murals which he himself had been commissioned to paint for it and which repeated pleas had failed to save.

As the generation of Womacka, Metzkes and Knebel, whose adulthood coincided with the birth of the DDR, was expected to invest its energies in the characterisation and consolidation of their state, so older figures of the anti-fascist tradition reminded the world of the barbaric regime that had killed 6 million Jews and turned Europe into a battlefield. For the former concentration camp of Sachsenhausen, north of Berlin, Grzimek did a

138. *Resting During the Harvest* by Walter Womacka, oil on canvas, 1958.

139. Memorial for Buchenwald concentration camp victims by Fritz Cremer, bronze, 1952-8.

moving group of three figures symbolising Death, Mourning and Accusation. Angrier, both cruder and more demonstratively powerful, is the monumental group of figures by Fritz Cremer for the memorial site of Buchenwald, the earliest important piece of socialist-realist sculpture in Germany and still one of the most impressive works in the country (Ill. 139).

Cremer, a gnarled old communist whose career stretched back to the Nazi years, had lived in Berlin since 1929. From the beginning of a divided Germany he enjoyed a prominent status in the cultural life of the DDR and until his death in 1993 had a studio in a surviving wing of the ruined Academy of Arts building near the Brandenburg Gate. Four metres high, grouped like Rodin's *Burghers of Calais*, his Buchenwald figures stand in a prominent position on the former concentration-camp site, symbolising the indomitable human spirit in its fight against oppression, the moment of liberation from the Nazi yoke. It is a statement of the continuity of history, of the conquest of the past by the progressive forces of the present. 'It is my belief', said Cremer, 'that a nation's tragic past can be fully overcome only when that past can find convincing expression in works of art that conform to historical truth.' The official DDR had its own historical truth, which it tried to foist on to Cremer's piece. But the work of art has proved stronger.

In 1963 Kurella was succeeded as cultural supremo by the Party ideologue Kurt Hager, the hard man who presided over many twists and turns of official policy during the following decades and was still in office when his state collapsed in 1989. For as long as Ulbricht remained in power, the term 'relaxation' seemed grotesquely out of place. With Erich Honecker, however, especially in the aftermath of the 8th Party Congress in 1971, the tension seemed to ease. A younger generation of bureaucrats in the Ministry of Culture sought to make their mark by allowing young artists new freedom to express their personalities. Private galleries opened and a state-controlled art market was established, widening the availability of art and improving artists' financial prospects.

Again Berlin attracted the lion's share of attention. In 1976, under the general supervision of Cremer, some sixteen of the best-known painters in the country, including Willi Sitte, Werner Tübke and Walter Womacka, were invited to submit works for a show in the newly completed Palace of the Republic. The motto for the enterprise as a whole was to be a quotation from Lenin: 'Are communists allowed to dream?' Mildly humorous, almost incongruous, as the slogan sounded, it removed in its generality the danger that certain prominent artists might refuse to work to a narrower and more specifically political brief. The outcome, welcomed by the Ministry of Culture and public alike, was a pot-pourri of themes and styles with some interesting, other less interesting exercises in the approved realism but all testifying to a lively art scene which had no need to feel inferior to that in the other part of the city.

Just how wide the range of artistic concerns and styles could be in a society of depressing uniformity is revealed by the work of Heidrun Hegewald, a young painter who came to Berlin in her twenties and whose work from the early 1970s onwards became among the most controversial in the country. At the 9th national exhibition of 1976 she showed a piece called *Child and Parents* (Ill. 140). Here, in the context of the family, to which the state boasted it attached so much importance, was a chilling denial of optimism and guaranteed happiness, of a dynamic social ethic. Everything is in a minor key – Hegewald characterised her thoughts and feelings as being 'not melodious but rather F-sharp minor, dissonant, subdued by history, their tempi governed by politics'. The scene is totally inanimate. A table would normally bring people together but here it separates them, the mother and father in the darkness looking away from each other and from their child, who stands in her desolation facing a chilling emptiness, the only ray of light coming from the half-open door behind her. Pessimism, reproach, human failure, betrayal of the generations to come – much can be read into the painting.

Hegewald's penchant for such dark, negative, sometimes sinister imagery stimulated by the sensation of musical discords persisted in the Dance of Death which she painted as a commission for the new Gewandhaus concert hall in Leipzig in 1981 and which she called *The Dancing Master: A Portrait of Wrong Notes.*

What had sounded in 1971 like an easing of the terms of state cultural policy did not fulfil its promise. But artists could still find subtle ways of giving their works a dimension of inferred meaning over and beyond what the first glance seemed to convey and what, in the case of public commissions, the organs of state thought they were being given. As a writer could publish an allegorical or historical novel that concealed a contemporary message in a non-contemporary, non-realistic cocoon, so an artist could give his picture various layers of meaning. In a few precious cases he could even confound the intentions of his official patron.

140. *Child and Parents* by Heidrun Hegewald, oil on hardboard, 1976.

One such case involves a series of lithographs made in 1980 for the East Berlin *Magistrat* by Dieter Tucholke in the context of the DDR's rediscovery of Prussia. Portrayed in the DDR as a hotbed of rampant militarism, Prussia, its kings and its generals had long been favourite objects of hate. At the same time the East German state claimed to be the true heir of all those who had made the culture of Prussia great – Lessing and Moses Mendelssohn, the Humboldts and Schinkel, Kleist and Hegel, E. T. A. Hoffmann and Fontane. So gradually the image of Prussia was reconstituted. Statues of generals from the War of Liberation, banished from sight during the Soviet occupation, were brought out of cellars and restored to their former sites. Attention was drawn to the Neue Wache, to the Staatsoper and the Zeughaus as master-pieces of German–Prussian architecture. Most revisionist of all, Rauch's great equestrian statue of Frederick the Great, embodiment of Prussia at its noblest but also at its most unlovable, was restored to its old position in the middle of Unter den Linden.

Tucholke, of the same generation as Heidrun Hegewald, watched this metamorphosis with an irony shared by many, and there is a flavour of caricature in his contributions to the campaign of Prussian rehabilitation. The 'portrait' of Frederick the Great shows the King's features broken up into fragments of scenes from his personal biography and from contempo-rary history, with symbolic objects and motifs, all assembled as a collection of attributes – a surrealistic, cogitated, fantastically detailed and meticulously executed 'collage-like assemblage of virtues and vices – chiefly vices, since there was no other choice', as Tucholke called it. The hollowness of the Prussian ideal was on display, and with it the hollowness of the claims of the DDR, its would-be heir.

Similarly wrongfooted by its misjudgement of the situation was the country's central Culture League, the Kulturbund, when it arranged a multi-disciplinary exhibition in 1982 on the theme of Prometheus. The Kulturbund

141. *Jumping Off the Stage* by Harald Metzkes, oil on canvas, 1987.

expected contributions that would show the titan as a vigorous young revolutionary, defying the gods to advance the cause of the people. In the event it found itself confronted with interpretations which found quite different meanings in the subject. Some chose to dwell on Prometheus' punishment and suffering, both physical and mental; others drew an image of the destruction wrought by the curse of the gods, a destruction brought into a contemporary context by analogies to the nuclear disaster threatening the world at that time. Much was pessimistic and highly subjective, 'formalistic' to the point of abstraction. It was an experience from which, over the few years left to it, the Kulturbund never recovered. Nor did it emerge with much to show for its indignant opposition to the Academy of Arts' exhibition of works by the West German avant-garde artist Joseph Beuys in 1988.

The German Democratic Republic collapsed through its inner contradictions and its inability to command the respect, let alone the loyalty of its citizens. In retrospect the events of 1989 have a surging inevitability about them. At the time they seemed like a miracle – rather, a compound series of miracles each incredible in its own way. Perhaps some with the gift of prophecy saw it all coming. Perhaps the one or the other artist had a vision. At all events there is one painting, done two years before the moment arrived, which said it all to anyone with ears to hear and eyes to see – a kind of prescient obituary: Harald Metzkes' *Jumping Off the Stage* (1987) (Ill. 141).

Metzkes, an established Berlin artist who had crossed swords with the regime more than once, found much of his symbolic subject matter in the realm of the theatre and the circus. Here he depicts an open-air performance in which two harlequins have jumped off the back of the stage, dragging the scenery and other actors with them and leaving one bewildered figure behind, while the audience sit in the background and watch the chaotic events in amazement. The stage as a scene of real events yet a medium of illusion; characters who escape in desperation from this pseudo-reality, bringing its flimsy trappings down around their ears; the artist who wilfully destroys the world he has created. Who could fail to read the picture as an uncanny parable?

The Visual Arts in West Berlin

The ruins of West Berlin felt the same as the ruins of East Berlin. The city had survived the Thousand-Year Reich as one, had been bombed as one and now faced defeat and misery as one.

But division, not unity was to be the order of the day, cultural division as well as political division. Artists, moreover, had divisions within their own ranks – conflicting opinions of their public function in a society itself increasingly riven by conflict, and, in the professional context, divergent views on the aesthetic that properly expresses that function. Common to both sides in the immediate post-war years, however, was an acceptance of the mimetic Berlin tradition of painting and sculpture, to which both could appeal for legitimacy when stating their historical credentials.

Anxious to get away from the subservience to political control which they had endured under the Nazis and which they saw re-emerging in the other part of the city, many painters in West Berlin found in the suffocating ruins around them, not the stimulus to a collective anti-war statement, like Dix and Grosz after the First World War, but a call to quiet reflection on private tragedy. Such is a picture of a refugee woman by the sixty-year-old August Wilhelm Dressler, done in 1946 (Ill. 142), a study of the fate of a single human being, the desolate ruins around her portrayed with a sober, almost dispassionate realism bearing no political or social message, making no accusation. For other artists the scene of destruction itself held the meaning, sometimes in the form of a quasi-photographic record, sometimes as a contrived arrangement of bizarre shapes incorporating the occasional familiar landmark that had survived, sometimes (see Karl Hofer's *Ruins by Night*, Ill. 131) as an almost surreal statement about war and humanity.

A Berlin reduced to rubble, the final bequest from the National Socialists to their people, imposed in its most brutal form a confrontation with

142. *Refugee Woman* by August Wilhelm Dressler, oil on canvas, 1946.

history. Their city under occupation, their lives in the hands of others, the Berliners faced a future more uncertain than that of other Germans. The communists never ceased to rub the noses of their subject citizens in the fact of their 'liberation' by the glorious Red Army, keeping the wound of the Nazi past for ever open. The Germans of the West, under a different kind of pressure from their own occupiers, and with a different conception of the place of art in society, patched up the offending part and looked the other way. By the time the two German states were officially constituted and set on their divergent paths, artists in West Berlin, as in the other battered cities of the Federal Republic, were already beginning to question the continued validity of an aesthetic built on destruction and soul-searching demoralisation. They felt that their art, and their personalities, were being sacrificed on the altar of politics.

So a movement gathered pace that led away from reality and representationalism, which were seen as yesterday's values. Abstract and non-representational art, despised by the Nazis, stood for the future. On the one hand it opened up the world of German art to the international modernist scene – France and the United States, above all – to which it had formerly been denied access. More vitally, here was a new freedom with its own intellectual pedigree, beholden to no extrinsic dogma, the artist to be judged *qua* self-defining artist, not as apologist for an ideology or a cause. Paintings became dissociated exercises in colour, like Hans Hartung's *Black on Russet*, while Josef Albers did a series of geometric *Homages to the Square* – squares of different sizes and colours superimposed one on the other.

No painter illustrates more strikingly the progress of non-representationalism in the 1950s than Werner Heldt, leading painter of the modern Berlin scene. A native Berliner, his earliest paintings dating from the 1920s, Heldt dwelt not on the familiar historical or fashionable parts of the city but on the barren buildings of the poorer suburbs, lonely streets, often seen by night, in which a human presence becomes ever rarer. His style grew progressively more basic, more economical, owing something to cubism, a style to match his depressive personality. Time and again he returned to the genre of the view from the window, the dichotomy of inside and outside, a kind of urban still life. In his last years his forms became increasingly abstract, the houses of Berlin unwelcoming, their windows blacked out, life in them – if there is any – reduced to a few flat shapes in cold, cheerless tones (Ill. 143).

But the tradition of realism would never desert Berlin. At the same time as Heldt was tending more and more to abstraction, Karl Hofer, from his influential position as director of the Hochschule für bildende Künste, branded abstraction and modernism as self-indulgent intellectual games, an abdication of the artist's responsibility to deal with things that really matter. The artist had to face, and to communicate with, the public and to respect that people looked to art partly for pleasure and consolation but also for help in understanding life and the world. They did not welcome new problems of comprehension being thrust upon them. Powerful voices from outside Berlin, like those of Dix and Kokoschka, supported the same cause. Kokoschka later made his contribution to the post-war townscapes of Berlin with a panorama of the city from the top of the Springer building in his characteristically vibrant expressionist manner.

143. *Dull Day* by Werner Heldt, oil on canvas, 1953.

A similar bifurcation runs through the world of public sculpture. Historic moments in the city's post-war history were commemorated on the one hand by the gigantic figure of a *Trümmerfrau* in Hasenheide Park, recalling the time when the women slaved to clear the ruins of their city in 1945, and on the other hand by Eduard Ludwig's soaring abstract in front of Tempelhof Airport, reminding the world, through three concrete arcs symbolising the three air corridors to Berlin from the West, of the air-lift of 1948–9 which saved the city from starvation. Abstract too are the metal sculptures of Hans Uhlmann, such as his large steel composition in front of the Deutsche Oper and his abstract *Concerto* for the Hochschule für Musik.

By contrast, the realist tradition reasserted itself with Waldemar Grzimek's large-scale fountain project for the Wittenberg Platz, in the heart of West Berlin. Grzimek, whose controversial Heine monument had stood in East Berlin since 1958, invoked associations of the Baroque Roman world and also of Begas' *Neptune Fountain* opposite the Rotes Rathaus, with his design for two elaborate fountains. One has no figurative content. The other carries an allegorical programme representing the ages of man, in which the scattered figures, all either at ground level or in the sunken basin of the fountain, draw the passer-by into their ambience and invite him to join them in contemplation (Ill. 144).

As a result of its isolated position, West Berlin could survive only with the constant help of Bonn – economic, cultural, moral. Financial and other concessions were introduced in order to attract people, including those in the culture industry, to settle there, while cultural morale was boosted by guest performances from actors and musicians whose presence demonstrated the West's determination to defend the interests of the city. Between 1953 and

144. Fountain in the Wittenbergplatz by Waldemar Grzimek, bronze, 1982–3.

Berlin and its Culture

145. *S-Bahn Station Witzleben* by Hans Stein, oil on canvas, 1964.

1956 many of the paintings, sculptures and other works of arts from Berlin galleries that had been stored underground in various parts of West Germany during the war were brought back to West Berlin, among them famous works like the bust of Nefertiti, various portraits by Dürer and the painting *The Man with the Golden Helmet*, still attributed at the time to Rembrandt. Here they were put on show in new galleries in Dahlem and elsewhere. In order to coordinate these activities the Bundestag created in 1957, as a rival to the Museum Island in East Berlin, the Foundation of Prussian Culture, a body charged with the preservation of the cultural possessions – palaces, museums, historic buildings, with the paintings, sculptures, furniture and other works of art in them – that belonged to the former state of Prussia, which had been dissolved by allied decree in 1947. No fewer than fourteen museums and galleries in West Berlin now came under the Foundation's control.

Recognition of the importance of art for the life of the city led the Senate in the 1950s to institute a programme of commissions, chiefly of townscapes, which would tide artists over uncertain times. After 1961 the need for such practical support became even more pressing, and public corporations and charities, to whom the survival of Berlin was equally vital, put forward their own initiatives. In 1963 the Ford Foundation, followed by the German Academic Exchange Service, financed a programme to attract foreign painters

146. *Gendarmenmarkt* by Karl Oppermann, oil on canvas, 1964.

and sculptors to work for a year as artists-in-residence, stimulating public interest in matters cultural and encouraging local talent. Few of those visitors, however, left any lasting marks of their presence, not least because a year was too short a period for an outsider to penetrate the peculiar problems of the divided city, in particular the highly politicised nature of its public life. Berlin was no place for the artist who wished to retire to contemplate his navel. The situation demanded a statement of political position and social commitment, and the various groups of young artists active in the 1960s and 1970s settled on such topics as the inhumanity of war, the soullessness of high-rise housing projects and the destruction of the environment in the name of commercial progress as means of defining their ethos.

A later acknowledgement of the continuing need for state support of the arts came in 1975, when a disused hospital in Kreuzberg was converted into an arts centre, the Künstlerhaus Bethanien, which provided studios, workshops, exhibition galleries and living accommodation for young artists supported by various grant-giving bodies. But no amount of official sponsorship could restore Berlin to the pre-eminence it had enjoyed before the war, any more than could the fusion of the Hochschule für bildende Künste and the Hochschule für Musik, also in 1975, to form the largest single Academy of Arts in the whole of Germany.

Berlin and its Culture

The Künstlerhaus Bethanien also brings the argument back from the non-representationalism of the late 1950s to the *engagé* realism of painter–poets like Günter Bruno Fuchs, who created a Bohemian colony in the Kreuzberg district, from where, working in the spirit of Zille, they drew their subject matter. 'Berlin from Behind', they called it, as opposed to the Berlin of fashionable cafés and elegant façades, 'Berlin from the Front'.

Whether as a target of social criticism or as a phenomenon of endless historical and pictorial fascination, a scene of throbbing social life and human vitality or a monster that devoured its own children, it was Berlin, the city itself, what it gave and what it took, that commanded artists' attention. Berlin was not, and never had been, a beautiful capital, as Paris, Madrid, Prague and Vienna are beautiful capitals. Nor does it readily induce a lyrical mode. But its characteristic corners, the variety of the ethnic and regional communities that had settled there, and the ways of its citizens, offered a wealth of raw material for the critical artistic imagination. The S-Bahn, characteristic feature of the landscape since the beginning of the century and symbol of

147. *Street with Underpass* by Louise Rösler, oil on hardboard, 1962.

148. *We Were Like a Museum Exhibit* by Wolf Vostell, silk screen print, 1965.

an urban unity now irrevocably ruptured, became a particularly relevant motif (Ill. 145).

Sometimes, indeed, the artist could act as a chronicler and interpreter of the past, recording a state of affairs that now no longer exists, as Otto Nagel had walked through the Berlin rubble to capture in his sketch book the ruins of 1945. Beginning in 1963 Karl Oppermann, a graduate of the Berlin Hochschule, painted a large number of energetic pictures of the city, East and West, in a style reminiscent of Max Liebermann and Lovis Corinth, in which the reality of the moment was portrayed as the product of events in the recent past – the present explained as the outcome of history. Take the famous trinity of buildings surrounding the Gendarmenmarkt square in East Berlin – the French Church, Schinkel's Schauspielhaus and the German Church. They were gutted in 1943 and left as shells until the 1970s. Oppermann shows the flames engulfing the French Church in the foreground and spreading towards the other two buildings in the pale distance. The original neo-classical façades are still visible; the hand of war is about to destroy them; twenty years later, a sombre *memento mori*, the ruins still display their history. Yet in the foreground there also lies a branch in leaf, sign of life and survival. Past, present and future – another thirty years and the whole square was restored – share a common reality (Ill. 146).

Conversion of the concrete presence of the city into abstract forms leading in a quite different direction from the work of Hans Stein and Karl Oppermann during the same years characterises the late paintings of Louise Rösler, an artist banned by the Nazis as decadent, who lost her Berlin studio in an air-raid in 1943 yet returned after the war to make the city once more the centre of her work. In the 1930s her style had been more or less representational. Now, in the 1960s, she condensed her memories and her new impressions into a highly charged non-representational kaleidoscope of geometric shapes and colours in which the dominant formal control is exerted

by arcs and curves of varying proportions and intensities (Ill. 147). To the younger generation the city was a demon, a hostage to base instincts and commercial greed, a willing victim of the soulless values of technology and scientific hubris. To Louise Rösler it was a place of excitement and stimulation – almost the Berlin of the 1920s again.

That the taste of these 1920s still had its appeal showed itself in 1967 with the opening of a new Berlin art gallery. The Brücke Museum, a charming little building in Dahlem designed by Werner Düttmann, is devoted to the works of the expressionist artists of the Brücke movement – above all Erich Heckel and Karl Schmidt-Rottluff – who dominated Berlin painting in the years of the First World War and the Republic that followed.

But the Berlin of the 1920s was not the Berlin recognised by the young post-Second World War 'critical realists', the generation of the student revolts of 1967-8. Their perception of their city issued in irony and black humour, which found expression in the techniques of collage and montage, whose scope for social comment had long been demonstrated by men like Otto Dix and John Heartfield. Drug culture and pop art joined the scene. The most palpable of all Berlin realities, the Wall, dominated the minds of Kreuzberg artists who had deliberately chosen to live in its brutal shade – men like Rainer Fetting, with paintings called *Van Gogh at the Wall, Sun Setting over East Berlin* or simply *Wall* (see Ill. 149). Wolf Vostell, an artist born at the beginning of the Nazi era, linked the Wall to other violent moments in recent history, such as the East German workers' uprising of 17 June 1953 and the assassination of Lee Harvey Oswald, killer of President John F. Kennedy, setting them in savage counterpoint against the Auschwitz trials of 1965 in a chilling montage called *We Were Like a Museum Exhibit* (Ill. 148).

As committed as Fetting to the city of Berlin, topographically and emotionally, in the 1970s and 1980s was the artist who signs herself G. L. Gabriel. Gabriel had her first one-woman show in Kreuzberg in 1979 at the age of twenty-one, exhibiting large-format compositions in mixed techniques executed with strong, swift strokes. *Blue Bridge* (1986), a monochrome study of the eighteenth-century Jungfernbrücke in east Berlin, is in part an evocation of the spirit of a famous landmark but beyond this an exercise in the identification of the basic geometric forms that make up the bridge's structure – a picture on its way, so to speak, from atmospheric representation to reductionist abstraction.

As to the public's response to art, much depended on the degree to which artists and gallery organisers were prepared to take people into their confidence. Some saw art as communication and were at pains to help the consumer understand the message; others regarded their activity as unconditional and self-justifying, and affected to care little about what others thought of it. Special shows, moreover, always attracted greater attention than permanent exhibitions, and in the unique political climate of Berlin art could readily be made to serve non-artistic ends. Such had been the function back in 1960 of 'Berlin – Centre of Freedom in Art', an event directed against the imposed art of socialist realism in the DDR, and an attraction to citizens of the East at a time when they could still move freely across the city. Right down to the moment in 1989 when the two halves of the city were reunited, a great deal of the cultural – and not only cultural – policy of West Berlin was conducted with one eye on the East and how the hold of the communist regime on its captive subjects could be loosened.

Musical Life in West Berlin

On 18 May 1945, a mere nine days after the German surrender, Leopold Ludwig conducted a concert of operatic music in the hall of the radio building. A week later the Berlin Philharmonic re-formed under Leo Borchardt to give a symphony concert in a cinema still left standing. Fully staged opera returned at the beginning of September with a performance of Beethoven's *Fidelio* by the Städtische Oper under Ludwig in its temporary home, the Theater des Westens, with a cast containing three of the greatest singers of the day – Erna Berger, Peter Anders and Josef Greindl.

It was not a work chosen at random. 'O what joy to breathe the air of freedom!' sing the prisoners in chorus, as they emerge into the daylight from the dungeons to which the tyrant has condemned them. There will have been no one in the audience who did not find himself watching his own liberation from tyranny in twentieth-century Germany.

After their first concert the members of the Berlin Philharmonic Orchestra reassembled to plan its future. Like the Vienna Philharmonic – the earliest to claim this status – it had always been unique among orchestras in being a self-governing body, engaging its own personnel, choosing its own repertoire and appointing its own conductor. From its foundation in 1882 down to this moment it had had just three, all very different from each other: Hans von Bülow, passionate, eccentric, champion of the 'moderns' Wagner and Brahms; Arthur Nikisch, the spellbinder, producer of luxuriant textures; and Wilhelm Furtwängler, idealist intent on conveying the spiritual meaning of the music. But Furtwängler's willingness to continue conducting under the Nazi regime now made him *persona non grata* and, until cleared by an allied deNazification tribunal in 1947, he was forbidden to perform in public. In his place came the remarkable Sergiu Celibidache, a young Romanian who brought with him a wide repertoire which the orchestra especially welcomed and which, to general consternation, he conducted entirely by heart.

Prominent in the orchestra's early post-war programmes was the music that had been banned by the Nazis. For instead of destroying their scores of Mendelssohn, Mahler, Schoenberg and other Jewish composers as ordered, the orchestra had hidden them in the cellars of the old Philharmonie, their concert hall. The Philharmonie had been bombed in 1944 but the orchestral parts were only waiting to be unearthed from the rubble. There was no shortage of guest conductors prepared to return to Berlin to help restore cultural morale during these early post-war years – Bruno Walter, Otto Klemperer, Eugen Jochum, Karl Böhm among others.

Popular as Celibidache had been, nothing could match the emotional reception given to Furtwängler when he returned to conduct the Berlin Philharmonic in May 1947. When he and his orchestra were joined later that year by Yehudi Menuhin – the first Jewish musician to appear in Germany after the end of the war – the occasion was heralded as a public gesture of forgiveness and reconciliation, albeit a gesture resented in quarters where the thought of forgiveness was still utterly remote.

The Berlin Philharmonic, for its own part, adopted from the beginning a firm pro-Western stance in a political situation becoming increasingly polarised. It made a tour of Great Britain with Furtwängler in 1948 but to the approval of the Western allies refused to play in East Berlin. It had no wish to imply that it was indifferent to what was developing in the other part of its city.

The four occupying powers played a considerable part in the way cultural life developed in Germany after the end of the war. Each had its own view of what should be permitted and promoted in the strained reality of that historical moment. Each brought its own cultural values to bear on the task of rehabilitation and exercised the right of censorship over what could be published in its zone, what art exhibitions could be held and what plays and films could be shown. Each power, moreover, took the opportunity to publicise its own national culture within its zone of occupation, encouraging a regeneration of cultural values in terms of its own particular ideals.

But in Berlin all four cultures – American, British, French and Russian – were accessible under one roof, so to speak. People could move freely across sector boundaries and enjoy a wider cultural experience than the inhabitants of any other city in the country. A particularly discerning and sophisticated concert-going public emerged. The Russians brought with them Shostakovich, Prokofiev and Khatchaturian, the British introduced Britten, Walton and Tippett, and the Americans the symphonies of Roy Harris, Walter Piston and William Schuman. This interplay between cosmopolitan stimulus, a critical public and an experimentally minded generation of young composers contributed to the rapid revival of a vigorous musical life.

In 1946 a second symphony orchestra was formed in West Berlin under the auspices of RIAS, the radio station in the American sector of the city, to which the Hungarian conductor Ferenc Fricsay was appointed in 1949.

Fricsay left his mark on Berlin musical life during these early post-war years but his growing reputation as a conductor of contemporary music took him away from the city more often than the public liked. Berlin audiences and musicians had a particularly close relationship to their conductors and expected a near-exclusive commitment on their part in return for public esteem and loyalty. But international pressures, especially from the United States, were working in the opposite direction, and Fricsay, who left the RIAS Symphony Orchestra (later the Berlin Radio Symphony Orchestra, now the German Symphony Orchestra of Berlin, under Vladimir Ashkenasy) in 1953, was one of the first to feel them. The following year the Berlin Philharmonic passed into the hands of the man who embodied to perfection the concept of the conductor as international jet-setter – Herbert von Karajan.

Over the thirty-five years of Karajan's reign the Berlin Philharmonic Orchestra's concerts were at the centre of the city's musical life. Not that the orchestra was ever his one and only commitment. He had the musical directorship of La Scala, Milan to attend to, and that of the Vienna Staatsoper. Then there was the annual Salzburg Festival, not to speak of the numerous guest appearances to which he travelled in his private plane. 'Karajan here, Karajan there,' mocked the cabaret comedian Günter Neumann, with a nod towards Rossini's *Barber of Seville*. In fact, as time went by, he gave more and more concerts in Berlin, spent more and more time with the orchestra, at home and on tours abroad, and demanded total loyalty from his musicians. This was all the more necessary in the face of the challenging modern works he introduced into the repertoire – symphonies by Prokofiev and Shostakovich, Britten's *War Requiem*, works by Schoenberg, Alban Berg, Luigi Nono, Penderecki and many others. Arguably he moulded his players into a more complete, more sensitive, more beautiful instrument than any of his predecessors – one of the great orchestras of the world.

But their relationship ended unhappily – perhaps inevitably so. What to Karajan appeared as infringements of the maestro's natural authority were to the orchestra's members the assertion of their constitutional rights. One much publicised squabble concerned Karajan's proposal to appoint a woman to the ranks of what had from the beginning been a male preserve, which the orchestra intended to keep so. In 1984 he accused the Chamber Orchestra, a select body of players drawn from the members of the full orchestra, of accepting private engagements to the detriment of his own performances, and demanded that the Chamber Orchestra be disbanded – which, of course, it was not. In 1989 he peremptorily declared that he would conduct only six of the customary twelve annual symphony concerts and handed in his resignation, set round with allegations that the orchestra, as a corporate institution, had failed to fulfil its obligations towards him. He died three months later – at the time the musician with the most classical recordings to his name in the world, vilified by some as a showman but revered by far more as one of the great conductors of all time. His successor, Claudio Abbado, is still the orchestra's principal conductor.

The Berlin Philharmonic cast a long shadow and the other orchestras that emerged in the post-war years could establish an independent personality only by staking out particular areas of activity for themselves. The Radio

Berlin and its Culture

Symphony Orchestra, serving the needs of radio in a semi-educational role, had an obligation to offer an especially wide repertoire in which contemporary music figured prominently, an emphasis retained when they later extended their activities from the broadcasting studio to the concert hall. Lorin Maazel was their principal conductor from 1964 to 1975.

Different again, humbler perhaps, geared to ensuring that the broad concert-going public had access to the familiar classics that were in constant demand – Beethoven's Fifth Symphony, Schubert's 'Unfinished' Symphony, Mendelssohn's Violin Concerto, Tchaikovsky's *Pathétique* – was the Symphonisches Orchester Berlin, founded in 1949. In no way intimidated by the aura that surrounded the 'Karajan Circus', as the Berlin Philharmonic in its new tent-like Philharmonie building was disrespectfully dubbed, the SOB also found an educational role for itself, giving concerts in schools, showing the children how instruments worked and explaining how a symphony orchestra functioned.

Domestic music-making had always been a characteristic feature of German social life, and sharing in the musical recovery after the end of the war were amateur choral societies that had been a feature of musical life in Berlin since the nineteenth century, and on whom the preservation of the oratorio and cantata tradition rested. There was the Philharmonic Choir, for instance, founded the same year as the Philharmonic Orchestra and conducted in the 1920s by Otto Klemperer, among others, and the much travelled Choir of St Hedwig's Cathedral, the largest oratorio choir in the city. Most venerable and most prestigious is the Singakademie, established in 1791. Eternally remembered for its revival of Bach's *St Matthew Passion* under Mendelssohn in 1829, the Singakademie always cultivated sacred music as its special domain but has more recently also turned its attention to complex secular works.

In the years immediately before the Second World War Berlin had two publicly owned opera houses (the Kroll Opera had closed its doors in 1931) – the Deutsche Oper or Städtische Oper in Charlottenburg and the Staatsoper on Unter den Linden. In addition there were the Komische Oper in the Friedrichstrasse (now gone), and the Theater des Westens, still standing in the Kantstrasse, both serving in general the 'lighter' side of the operatic repertoire. The Deutsche Oper and the Staatsoper were both destroyed in the war and both rebuilt, now, however, no longer complementary institutions in a single context but rivals in a divided city, the one beholden to the West, the other to the East. The power of history lay with the latter, Knobelsdorff's noble classicistic building for Frederick the Great, which had seen men like Spontini, Meyerbeer and Richard Strauss in control of its destinies. The Städtische Oper dated only from 1912 but during the 1920s, under Bruno Walter and Carl Ebert, its Mozart productions had come to be regarded as among the finest in the country.

In the post-war years, however, its activities could not be divorced from political realities. The situation of West Berlin was anomalous and precarious but nothing could be allowed to threaten its survival or impair its well-being, and the federal government ensured that the city's museums, theatres and concert halls received the backing they needed to fulfil their public function. This need to assert the city's cultural personality underlay the institution, as early as 1951, of two international festivals, one devoted to the cinema, the other – the Berliner Festwochen – to drama, music, ballet and the visual arts.

So the Städtische Oper, soon to receive back its first name of Deutsche Oper, quickly became an institution to embody the resurgence of the cultural life of West Berlin and the determination of the stubborn, self-confident population to assert their corporate identity. It owed its rapid return to eminence after 1945 chiefly to the enterprise of Heinz Tietjen and Ferenc Fricsay. Tietjen, an operatic producer of great experience, one-time director of the Bayreuth Festival, had been General Administrator of the Prussian State Theatres, including the Staatsoper, since 1927 but had no desire to stay in the East after the end of the war. In 1948 he was joined as General Music Director by Fricsay, who also took over the RIAS Symphony Orchestra the following year. Matching his work with the orchestra, Fricsay's special contribution to Berlin operatic life in the early post-war years lay in his introduction of modern classics into the repertoire – works by his compatriots Bartók and Kódaly but also Britten's *Peter Grimes* and *Albert Herring*, Menotti's *The Consul* and Honegger's *Joan of Arc at the Stake*. Shortly before his death he returned to conduct the performance of *Don Giovanni* which inaugurated the new, rebuilt Deutsche Oper in September 1961, four weeks after the Berlin Wall had gone up.

One of the most controversial of the Städtische Oper's premières during its last years in the Theater des Westens was Hans Werner Henze's *König Hirsch* in 1956. The complex libretto by Heinz von Kramer utterly baffled both critics and public, as did the dissonant avant-garde music, and interruptions from the auditorium almost brought the performance to a halt. The work was withdrawn. Presented in a radically revised form seven years later, it proved a great success. Another première of Henze's, *The Young Lord*, to a libretto by Ingeborg Bachmann, given by the same company in its new house in 1965, was welcomed without reservation.

König Hirsch was performed under the aegis of Carl Ebert, director of the Städtische Oper during the late Weimar years and of the Glyndebourne Festival at its foundation in 1934. Back at the Städtische Oper from 1954 to 1961 after periods in Turkey and California, Ebert spiced the classical repertoire with a number of modern works – not only Henze but also Blacher and, in 1959, Schoenberg's masterpiece *Moses und Aron*. The modernisation of the repertoire continued over the five years, 1965–70, that Lorin Maazel was musical director, while controversy over modern productions reached a climax in the 1980s and early 1990s with the work of Götz Friedrich, the present *Intendant*, whose *Ring des Nibelungen*, the four parts of which were given between 1983 and 1985, was one of Berlin's great operatic events of the decade. Today's musical director is Raphael Frühbeck de Burgos.

As capital of Prussia, and even more compellingly as capital of the German empire through the days of the Kaiser, the Weimar Republic and National Socialism, Berlin had always been a prize for performing musicians to covet. But it had never been able to make a comparable claim on the nation's composers. Those who had served successive Kings of Prussia – Graun and Carl Philipp Emanuel Bach at the court of Frederick the Great, Spontini under Friedrich Wilhelm III, Meyerbeer under Friedrich

Wilhelm IV, Richard Strauss in the days of Kaiser Wilhelm II – came in the first instance as producers of opera, directors of orchestras, instrumentalists to encourage chamber music or as general factotums. Most of them also composed but they were not primarily appointed as composers, and, as most unmistakably with Spontini and Meyerbeer, their best work arose elsewhere. Moreover almost all, as far as the Prussian capital was concerned, were mere birds of passage. Similarly in the twentieth century men such as Schreker and Schoenberg, Busoni and Hindemith, came to Berlin not to compose but to teach.

The situation had not changed in the post-war world. A city – semi-city – living on its nerves in the front line of the Cold War could appeal to the artist who saw cultural activity as political activity, and his art as a contribution to a political cause – literature, painting, cinema, the representational arts. The tradition of music teaching and scholarship, too, led by the venerable Hochschule für Musik, continued unbroken. But music as emotional expression, music the supremely irrational, abstract art, did not feel at its ease in such a world, in a Berlin where rationality prevailed over emotionalism, scepticism over faith.

In the wider European context, furthermore, the post-war decades are an epigonal age – some would say we are still in that age. The first thirty years of the century were a period of revolution and upheaval, of new philosophies of music and new ideologies. Busoni, Schoenberg, Stravinsky, Bartók, Hindemith, Alban Berg, the impact of jazz – such forces had transformed the world of music. In their wake came imitators, composers looking for some unexplored corner to examine, some way of declaring a distinguishable personality. Technique takes precedence, salvation is sought in systems, emotion surrenders to intellect, the spontaneous utterance to the pondered construct. The range of experience becomes narrower, less and less is 'said' in the music or the poem or the painting, and the cry goes up, amplified by the publicity mechanisms of festivals, competitions and prizes, for 'originality' at all costs.

So perhaps it is to nobody's surprise that one can venture the observation – only a slight exaggeration, if at all – that, during the forty years of the divided city, West Berlin nurtured only one composer with a personality that has impressed itself on the outside world. And he too came initially as a teacher – Boris Blacher, a prominent figure on the Berlin musical scene from the 1930s until his death in 1975.

Blacher, who in the late 1920s had been a student at the Berlin Hochschule of which he was to become director from 1953 to 1970, was a musical jack-of-all-trades, a master of styles and techniques who characterised himself as one 'who composed now in this manner, now in that, as the fancy took him'. He first drew attention to himself in the 1930s with chamber music in the spirit of Neue Sachlichkeit – bright, brittle, intellectual pieces with strong rhythms, sometimes jazzy, which share the worlds of Stravinsky and Hindemith, sometimes also Satie and Milhaud. The 1940s took him into opera, most strikingly with his *Prussian Fairy-Tale* (1949), a witty treatment of the satirical Hauptmann von Köpenick story, and also produced Orchestral Variations on a Theme of Paganini, a Concerto for Jazz Orchestra and a group of pieces for the Modern Jazz Quartet.

Down to this point Blacher's idiom had been part-tonal, albeit highly chromatic, part-atonal. After joining the teaching staff of the Hochschule in 1948, he experimented with serialism, polyrhythms and other innovative techniques, some of which went into the ballet music he wrote for the Städtische Oper in the 1950s – *Lysistrata*, *Hamlet*, *The Moor of Venice*. An experiment of Dadaist extraction was his *Abstract Opera No. I*, with text by Werner Egk. There was no story, no context, merely a series of unrelated situations and moods, with titles such as Love, Angst, Panic; and the 'text' consisted not of sentences but of syllables in a meaningless jumble of vocalises – 'lo-bu-da', 'na-bu-ung' – with an occasional incongruous observation like 'Weather is fine', while Blacher's music expressed in its own way the spirit of the mood in question. The music has a certain entertainment value but like so much of Blacher's immense output – fourteen operas, sixteen ballet scores, a mass of orchestral and chamber music – it has a strong whiff of the production line and suffers from its sheer competence and ingenuity. In 1960 he set up an electronic studio in the Technical University in which, searching for new timbres, he explored the potentialities of *musique concrète*, of combinations of synthetic and conventional musical sound, of the super-imposition of live music on recorded tapes.

Yet in his teaching – Gottfried von Einem (for a number of whose operas he wrote the libretto), Aribert Reimann and Giselher Klebe were among his pupils – Blacher permitted experimentation only once the historical funda-mentals had been learnt. 'It goes without saying', he told an interviewer, 'that any young composer must first acquaint himself with the great works of the past and study in detail the technique of the classical and pre-classical com-posers, together with that of modern masters.' So the students who passed through Blacher's hands were each allowed their own style and viewed their individual musical language as one among many.

This variety found enthusiastic expression in incidental music for stage productions. Here novelty and experimentation came into their element, stimulated by a flourishing theatrical culture that stretched from conventional to fringe, recalling the days of the Weimar Republic when Weill, Edmund Meisel and Theo Mackeben were providing stage music for Brecht and Piscator. A handful of instrumentalists, in varying combinations – a far cry from the classical orchestra of Mendelssohn's *A Midsummer Night's Dream* music or Grieg's *Peer Gynt* – could provide what was needed to underscore the action in classical and modern plays in a tonal, atonal, serial or any other idiom. Nor was this a task left to hacks. Hans Werner Henze did music for Giraudoux's *Sodom and Gomorrah*, while Blacher, who in his early years had supplied music for silent films, wrote scores for Piscator's dramatisation of *War and Peace* and for Wedekind's Lulu dramas, and provided taped music for Oscar Fritz Schuh's productions at the Theater am Kurfürstendamm. But such music, a species of *Gebrauchsmusik*, rarely outlived the occasion for which it was written.

Berlin, a settlement on the eastern fringes of the Germanic world, an ethnic melting-pot for immigrants from north, south, east and west, devel-oped its cultural personality on the hoof. It survived less by principles than by pragmatism. Yet certain features of personality have come to be recog-nised as characteristic of the Berliners, and the tendencies of their culture –

what it valued and promoted, as what it distrusted and played down – move in parallel. Irony, scepticism, detachment, non-sentimentality – qualities at home in the city of rationalism and the Enlightenment.

Thus as one may be entitled to see a spiritual unity behind the coincidence of these qualities, the rise of Neue Sachlichkeit and *Gebrauchsmusik*, and the assumption by Berlin of the cultural leadership of the country in the 1920s, so the return of this musical idiom to prominence from the 1950s and 1960s onwards may reflect a predisposition to such values. Many contemporary composers share a cool, detached approach to their craft, both those writing for conventional instruments and those using synthesisers and other electronic tools. Serialism and jazz still have their adherents, like the prolific Giselher Klebe, composer of the comic opera *Figaro Sues for Divorce* and Franz Werfel's *Jakobovsky and the Colonel*, while in more 'conservative' circles the voice of Hindemith can still be heard – as, indeed, it could in the work of Blacher, with whom many of the next generation studied. Characteristic of most of this music, and also reminiscent of the avant-garde music of the 1920s, is a high degree of dissonant intellectuality and technical complexity, accompanied by a penchant for a contrapuntal style and a derogation of anything that might savour of emotionalism. Even its lyricism, steely and precise, speaks more to the head than to the heart.

The Capital of the DDR and Its Music

> Music in our Republic exists against a background of social realism. It is an art of reality, an objective art, an art for the working men and women of our country, not for an elite of specialists or connoisseurs, as it was in the twenties. Of course, every artist speaks about what moves him. But he knows that there is a step that must needs take him from the personal to the collective. Socialist music boldly points the way forward, revealing new knowledge about man and the world.

In other words, music was no more able than the other arts to shirk a responsibility to help build the communist utopia. Such axioms could have been put forward in the 1920s by Hanns Eisler, Max Butting, Hermann Scherchen or any member of the Novembergruppe, not excluding Kurt Weill. In fact they are the words of the veteran East German composer Ernst Hermann Meyer in 1987. The sentiments and the terminology never changed.

In reality, of course, there is no such thing as 'socialist music'. There is music put to socialist texts, or music composed for socialist functions and celebrations, but it is the texts and functions that are socialist, not the music. Therefore music, whether in the context of composition or of performance, has to be bound into the activities of bodies and institutions that declare themselves devoted to the cause of socialism. At that moment music becomes an applied art, receiving its *raison d'être* from sources outside itself. Organisations, educational and recreational, need to be created as contexts within which it can be cultivated and studied.

This institutionalisation fed the strengths of a society whose structures were the creatures of centralised planning. The DDR government knew full well the power of music and how it could be harnessed to their interests, from marching songs and brass band music for the army to ditties for use in infants' schools. The Free German Youth movement had its own choirs and orchestras, so did individual schools, where, through the performance of 'school operas' like the Brecht–Weill *Jasager*, socialist principles of collective responsibility could be illustrated. Workers were encouraged to form their own regional orchestras and choral societies under the aegis of the trade union organisation.

In 1957 the first Festival of Drama and Music was held in Berlin as a showpiece of socialist achievement to rival the Festwochen in West Berlin. 'It is the aim of these Berliner Festtage', said Oberbürgermeister Friedrich Ebert in his opening address, 'to bring art to the mass of the working people and the mass of the working people to art.' An annual Festival of Political Songs followed and, in 1976, the first Music Biennale. As an answer to the Berlin Philharmonic Orchestra, the Berlin Symphony Orchestra, originally dating from 1924, was refounded in 1952 but never, even under Kurt Sanderling, who took over as chief conductor in 1960, reached the heights of its illustrious rival.

To link the world of school music with the professional world a new Academy of Music was founded in 1950 for the training of the country's young musicians, since the partition of the city had left the old Hochschule für Musik, founded by Joachim in 1869, in the British sector of Charlottenburg. The opportunity was not lost, however, to make clear that the new DDR Hochschule aimed to produce not just musicians but socialist musicians. Prominent among the early teachers of socialist composition were Rudolf Wagner-Régeny, whose career went back to the 1920s and who, despite his left-wing sympathies, had managed to live through the Third Reich in Berlin, and Hanns Eisler.

Eisler was himself the model of a socialist musician. A native of Leipzig, he studied with Schoenberg in Vienna in the years following the First World War and in the early 1920s composed a number of highly chromatic, dissonant pieces of piano and chamber music under the influence of serialism. He moved to Berlin in 1925, joined the Communist Party and abandoned the intellectualism of the avant-garde New Music for a commitment to 'music for the masses', music as a weapon in the class struggle. 'The initial stage in the cultivation of music by the proletariat', he wrote, 'is characterised, not by the achievement of what the bourgeoisie calls "a high level of culture", but by a marked predisposition towards the usefulness of music.' From the final years of the Weimar Republic come the marching songs and other pieces for the Workers' Musical Association and similar bodies which bear the hallmark of Eisler's style and personality. In musical terms this personality showed itself in a preference for strongly rhythmic pieces in minor keys, which came across as expressions of unflinching defiance and an iron will. For those who heard him, on stage and in recordings, they are songs as inseparable from the booming voice of Ernst Busch as negro spirituals are from Paul Robeson.

Eisler met Brecht in 1930 and at once began the collaboration that was to last until Brecht's last plays and poems. It may often seem, on the evidence of *Die Dreigroschenoper* and *Mahagonny*, that Brecht's ideal musical collaborator was Kurt Weill. Certainly Eisler never reached the musical heights of those two works, or, for that matter, of *Happy End* and the *Berliner Requiem*. But Brecht required from his musicians and colleagues a subservience, both ideological and aesthetic, that Weill was ultimately not prepared to concede, whereas Eisler, the thoroughgoing communist, was always ready to put himself at the service of the cause. When Brecht said, 'Be reasonable, do it my way,' Eisler did so.

Forced to leave Germany in 1933 on both racial and political counts, Eisler found his way to the USA and supported himself there through the war by teaching and by composing film music. After being arraigned before the House Committee on UnAmerican Activities in 1948, he left, and like Brecht, spent the last fourteen years of his life back in Berlin, composing for Brecht's Berliner Ensemble and continuing to write 'applied music' for all manner of practical uses – including the lamentable DDR national anthem. It is a very large and very uneven output, diverse in style, extraordinary in range but all under the direction of an unbending intellect. His whole musical and intellectual personality is laid out in his largest work, *Deutsche Sinfonie,* an anti-fascist, serialist oratorio to texts by Brecht and Ignazio Silone, composed during his years in exile but first performed only in 1959, in East Berlin.

Two years after Eisler's death in 1962 the East Berlin Academy of Music was renamed Hochschule für Musik 'Hanns Eisler' in his memory. Institutions and their reputation mattered a great deal to the country's self-esteem. The musicological research being carried out in the Humboldt University was given prominence through international conferences and through studies on treasures in the State Library, such as the corpus of music manuscripts collected in the eighteenth century by Princess Anna Amalia of Prussia. But the musical organisation that mattered the most to East Berlin, the institution to which the state looked to uphold its musical prestige in international company, was the Staatsoper, today under the musical direction of Daniel Barenboim.

The opera house in Unter den Linden fell to an air-raid in February 1945. But so noble an institution, so rich in tradition, even a tradition the East preferred to dismiss as feudalistic, could not be allowed to founder. A temporary home was prepared for it in the Admiralspalast, a theatre in the Friedrichstrasse formerly given over to operettas and revues, and in September 1945, four months after the end of the war, the company re-emerged with a performance of Gluck's *Orphée et Euridice.* A core of established soloists was still in the city – Peter Anders, Erna Berger, Erich Witte, Rita Streich, Gottlob Frick – and week by week, under the general administration of Ernst Legal, the last controller of the Kroll Opera, the repertoire grew – *Rigoletto, Eugene Onegin, Madame Butterfly, The Tales of Hoffmann, Die Entführung aus dem Serail.* Furtwängler returned in 1947 to conduct *Die Zauberflöte, Der fliegende Holländer* and *Tristan und Isolde,* and gave a number of symphony concerts with the opera orchestra. Modern works were taken up – Hindemith's *Mathis der Maler* in 1948, Gottfried von Einem's *Dantons Tod* in 1949 – while the ballet company reassembled in 1946 and added its own works to the programme. Among the guest conductors attracted to the city were Joseph Keilberth, Hans Knappertsbusch and Georg Solti. Surrounded by ruins, recovery proceeded apace.

In the early years after the war the Staatsoper fashioned its own artistic policies within the framework sanctioned by the Soviet occupying power. But with the proclamation of the German Democratic Republic it passed into the direct control of the state, which saw it as an institution devoted to the greater glory, not of art, but of the Republic. 'In its artistic work', ran the official bulletin, 'the Berlin Staatsoper firmly pledges itself to the principles of socialist music theatre.'

Just such a piece of socialist music theatre was given its first public performance by the Staatsoper, still in its temporary home in the Admiralspalast, in 1951, one of the most intriguing premières in the opera's history – *Die Verurteilung des Lukullus* ('The Condemnation of Lucullus'), text by Brecht, music by Paul Dessau.

Dessau, a former student at the Klindworth-Scharwenka conservatoire and a soldier during the First World War, was the third in the triumvirate of Brecht's leading composers, alongside Weill and Eisler. Jewish by birth and left wing in political tendency, like them, Dessau had made his name among the avant-garde of the late 1920s and worked in various opera houses, including the Städtische Oper under Bruno Walter. Exiled in 1933, he arrived in the USA in 1939, where for nine years he scraped a living by writing film scores, by copying and by teaching. Here he developed his mature musical language, at which he arrived through the disciplines of Schoenberg's dodecaphonic system. Here, too, he met Brecht, with whom he developed an immediate rapport, setting his poems and writing the music for *Mother Courage*, *Der gute Mensch von Sezuan* and other plays. In 1948 both men declared their allegiance to East Berlin, where both died and were buried within a few yards of each other – Brecht in 1956, Dessau over twenty years later.

Seeking a subject for his first opera, Dessau lighted on an earlier radio play of Brecht's on the Roman general Lucullus, a commander who is condemned by a people's court for having waged imperialist war. The audience, invited to identify with Lucullus' legionaries, are left to draw the parallel with the two German wars of the twentieth century. Initially the opera, both text and music, fell foul of an anti-intellectual, 'anti-formalist' campaign being waged by the Party. The custodians of orthodoxy went so far as to pack the theatre at a preview with louts instructed to boo and whistle. But the genuine spectators did not allow themselves to be cowed and applauded enthusiastically. 'Dessau's music', said Brecht, 'is far simpler than that of, say, Richard Strauss. Any unprejudiced audience can enjoy it, especially one that has come looking for enjoyment.' And indeed, its astringent harmonic style and vivacious rhythms, often putting one in mind of Stravinsky, raise few hurdles to its immediate accessibility.

Over the last dozen years of his life Dessau wrote four more operas, including an allegorical, fairy-tale work *Lancelot*, with a text by Heiner Müller, and *Einstein*, to a witty libretto by the young DDR poet Karl Mickel. *Einstein*, a work, like Brecht's *Galileo* and Kipphardt's *Oppenheimer*, that faces the predicament of the scientist divided by his loyalty to science and his loyalty to society, is a fascinating piece. Its narrative substance is Einstein's career from his expulsion by the Nazis from Germany in 1933 to his death in the USA in 1955, with the threat of nuclear war looming in the background. Flanking this life story are commentaries on the action from the traditional German clown figure, Hans Wurst. And it is Hans Wurst, as Chorus, who has the last word, dancing at the end of the opera on the edge of a gigantic knife to symbolise Einstein's fate. The diversity of the characters is met by a panoply of musical styles, from twelve-tone serialism to jazz and taped interludes, and including parodies of Bach and Mozart – a virtual number opera held together by a dynamic creative will of expressionist intensity.

The question might be asked of the three composers most intimately associated with him: Is there life after Brecht? For Weill the mere question is impertinent. For Eisler the short answer would probably have to be: Not a long life. And Dessau? A more esoteric composer, he stands somewhere between them in the lineage of Stravinsky and Hindemith, with an avant-garde, pre-Brecht career in an old Berlin, like Weill, and a final independent flourish of stage works and *Gebrauchsmusik* in a new Berlin thirty years later. It is a life – personal, professional, artistic – profoundly representative of the twentieth century.

All Dessau's operas after *Lukullus* had their première in the capital's leading house. After almost ten years of exile in the Admiralspalast (since renamed the Metropol-Theater) the Staatsoper returned to its home in Unter den Linden, which was ceremonially reopened in its former glory in 1955 with a historic performance of Wagner's *Meistersinger*. It was to have been conducted by Erich Kleiber, returning to the podium he had been forced to leave twenty years earlier. But when he learnt that the communists had not restored the inscription above the portico commemorating Frederick the Great, the building's original patron, Kleiber cancelled his engagement in disgust. In the event the celebratory *Meistersinger* was conducted by Franz Konwitschny, with a famous cast containing Josef Herrmann as Sachs, Erich Witte as Stolzing and the young Theo Adam as Pogner. *Der Rosenkavalier, Don Giovanni, Fidelio, Eugène Onegin, Wozzeck* and other classics soon followed, the opera orchestra resumed its programme of symphony concerts and the ballet returned. The first complete *Ring des Nibelungen* was given in 1957.

Two further sets of activities sprang from the rehabilitated Staatsoper. One was the resumption of events in the Apollosaal, the beautiful little Rococo concert hall in the opera building, now restored to its former splendour, where solo recitals, chamber music and chamber operas were given. Monteverdi's *L'incoronazione di Poppea* and Kurt Schwaen's *Leonce und Lena* were performed here, and on one interesting evening in the 1977–8 season two expressionist one-act pieces, congenial bedfellows, shared the stage – Hindemith's *Hin und zurück* and Kurt Weill's *Der Zar lässt sich photographieren*. In a different context the Apollosaal became the venue for events staged by the Hermann-Duncker-Ensemble, a Workers' Choral Association whose performances of opera the Staatsoper undertook to supervise, lending some of its own singers for the principal roles.

But the events of 13 August 1961 made it hard to sustain such gestures. The hundreds of singers, orchestral players, dancers, technicians and actors who lived in West Berlin but worked in the East – 70 per cent of the Staatsoper's personnel were affected – found themselves suddenly locked out. Horst Stein, General Music Director, happened to be conducting in

Hamburg on the fateful day. He immediately sent in his resignation, without going back. Leading singers like Gerhard Stolze and Gerhart Unger, making guest appearances abroad at that same moment, also stayed where they were. A hard time followed as the Staatsoper desperately combed the DDR's provincial houses and those of neighbouring Eastern-bloc countries for replacements and stepped up the training of young musicians in its own academies.

Yet under the direction of Max Burghardt, then of Hans Pischner, the new house quickly succeeded in adding contemporary works to its repertoire in the 1960s and 1970s. Some were by state-sponsored DDR composers whose music has hardly penetrated beyond the confines of their own country – Jean Kurt Forest's *Flowers of Hiroshima* (after the novel by Edita Morris) and *Der arme Konrad* ('Poor Conrad', from the play by Friedrich Wolf), Ernst Hermann Meyer's *Reiter der Nacht* ('Riders in the Night', dealing with apartheid in South Africa), Robert Hanell's *Esther*. Since opera was expected to serve the same ideological goals as theatre, the subject matter of such works tended to deal with a revolutionary situation or exalt a revolutionary hero, from whatever national or historical background. Such calculations underlay the decision to commission and mount the world première of *Joe Hill*, an opera on the American trade unionist and folksinger by Alan Bush, the prolific English composer of left-wing music rarely heard in his own country.

Some of these performances, however, were of more durable works, many, again in deference to political realities, from the Soviet Union and other socialist countries – Prokofiev's *The Story of a Real Man* and *The Fiery Angel* and Shostakovich's *The Nose* (after Gogol but originally disowned by the Soviet authorities) in the 1960s and *Katerina Ismailova* in 1973, the year of the fourth Berlin Music Biennale, with the composer present. Another import was Werner Egk's *Peer Gynt*, a work which had the unusual distinction of being acceptable both to Hitler, at the time of its composition, and now to the communist German state. Egk's *The Government Inspector*, to the tale by Gogol, was included in the repertoire for 1975, the climax of which was a performance of Penderecki's *The Devils of Loudon*. The ballet company, too, looked east, adding to modern classics like Stravinsky's *Rite of Spring* and Ravel's *Daphnis and Chloë*, Bartók's *Miraculous Mandarin* and two ballets by Khatchaturian – *Gayaneh* and *Spartacus*. The Staatsoper claimed that in the thirty years from the end of the war to 1975 it had put on a grand total of 182 operas.

The re-establishment of the Berlin Staatsoper after the Second World War, however revolutionary the accompanying declaration of principles, signified the restoration of a link with the past. East Berlin's second opera house, which opened at the end of 1947 with Johann Strauss' *Die Fledermaus*, was a venture new in intent, though not in name – the Komische Oper, which took over the Metropol-Theater in the Behrenstrasse, the revue theatre where the legendary Fritzi Massary had had her triumphs in the early decades of the century (the old Komische Oper in the Friedrichstrasse had been destroyed in an air-raid in 1945). In charge of the new enterprise, virtually its creator, both in concept and in practical reality, was Walter Felsenstein.

Felsenstein, a native of Vienna, had been at the Berlin Schiller-Theater throughout the war. Envisaging an *opéra comique* of the kind familiar in France and Italy but new to Germany, he gained approval for his project from the Soviet authorities, whom he promised an international repertoire of 'light' operas, starting with the operettas of Johann Strauss and Offenbach and extending to the classical *opere buffe* of Mozart, Rossini and Donizetti, then on to Mussorgsky's *Sorochintsy Fair*, Orff's *Die Kluge* and Britten's *Albert Herring*. 'I would regard my project as fulfilled', he said, 'if, after years in this theatre, we succeeded in performing *Falstaff* exactly as Verdi had imagined it.'

First and foremost a man of the theatre, for whom music was a means to a dramatic end, Felsenstein undertook a radical reformulation of the ethos of opera in a Marxist spirit, aiming at a 'realistic music-theatre', as he called it, presented in twentieth-century terms. Primacy lay with the significance of the text, as he interpreted it. Everything is therefore sung in German. In Johann Strauss' *Gipsy Baron* and Weber's *Freischütz* he emphasised the elements of class conflict and presented *The Marriage of Figaro* as a socio-revolutionary drama. When the question of his successor arose, the obvious name being that of his assistant Götz Friedrich, he objected on the ground that Friedrich was not sufficiently committed to socialism. Shortly afterwards Friedrich left the Komische Oper altogether and made his own controversial career in the West.

Felsenstein, who died in 1975, has had a lasting influence on the interpretation of opera in Germany. But over and above this, in the context of a divided city, he stands alongside the painters Heinrich Ehmsen and Karl Hofer, the sculptor Waldemar Grzimek, the architect Hans Scharoun and early DEFA film directors like Wolfgang Staudte in trying to believe, into the 1950s, that although the political facts pointed implacably in the opposite direction, some kind of cultural unity could still be retained in Berlin and in Germany as a whole. His career reflected this. In 1945 he had directed at the reopened Hebbel-Theater in West Berlin; the following year he moved east. That the Komische Oper happened to be close to the sector border at the Brandenburg Gate, he said to his assembled company in 1952 – a time when it still made sense to think such thoughts – was a geographical accident, 'but that its influence transcends the partition of the city is a fact acknowledged in Germany and beyond. It is, moreover, a factor relevant to the cultural policies of the country as a whole.' The events of 13 August 1961 shattered the illusion once and for all.

Although the majority of the DDR's leading directors – Wolfgang and Matthias Langhoff, Manfred Karge, the Swiss Benno Besson – confined themselves to 'straight' theatre, Felsenstein was not alone in turning his attention to opera. Ruth Berghaus, wife of Paul Dessau, moved freely from one genre to the other, arousing controversy wherever she went. As well as producing her husband's operas she did Richard Strauss' *Elektra* at the Staatsoper in 1967 and *The Barber of Seville* the following year, directed the première of Heiner Müller's *Zement* at the Berliner Ensemble in 1973, then returned to the Staatsoper with Siegfried Matthus' setting of Rilke's *Cornet* in 1985.

Of the younger generation around Felsenstein, two stand out, producers indebted to the Komische Oper for their early experience but who have since gone far beyond its confines. Götz Friedrich distinguished himself as early as 1958 with his productions of *The Tales of Hoffmann* and Benjamin Britten's *Albert Herring* at the Théâtre des Nations festival in Paris and went on in the 1960s to tackle works as different as Richard Strauss' *Salome*, Janáček's *Jenufa* and, in 1970, *Porgy and Bess*. In 1972 he left the DDR and in 1981 became General Administrator of the Deutsche Oper in West Berlin. England remembers him for his *Ring des Nibelungen* at Covent Garden in 1989–91 and for his *Elektra* in 1997. His erstwhile colleague Harry Kupfer, who joined the Komische Oper from Dresden the same year that Friedrich went to the Deutsche Oper, and is its director today, continued the line of self-consciously Marxist productions in the 1980s – *Così fan tutte*, *The Magic Flute*, *Boris Godunov* and the première of Siegfried Matthus' *Judith* in 1985.

As in literature the foundations of recovery after the Second World War were laid by those of the older generation returning from exile or emerging from 'inner emigration', so too it was the generation of composers in their forties and fifties on whom the musical reputation of the DDR was made to rest. These composers, almost by definition, were politically committed to the socialist state in which they had chosen to live. But there was no musical 'point zero', as in literature, no musical grounds for writing off the past and making 1945 the moment for a new beginning. If a composer wished, for his personal development, to experiment with new techniques, he would need no justification from without. On the other hand, in the public context music, like the other arts, was viewed as an applied art, a practical function, and the style chosen would be that which best promoted that function. 'Music', said Paul Dessau, 'is mental effort, not relaxed enjoyment. To write new music, a contemporary music that reflects our life in socialism, can never be an easy matter, for the challenge is to adopt an unequivocal attitude to the problems of our age.'

A long way from this world but still the music of a committed socialist émigré who also returned to the DDR in 1948, this time from London, is the work of Ernst Hermann Meyer. Barely known as a composer in 1933, when, at the age of twenty-eight, he fled Berlin for London, Meyer spent the next fifteen years in England, writing occasional film scores, training choirs for the Workers' Educational Association and conducting. He also made a name for himself with his research, based on Marxist principles, into early English chamber music down to Purcell, publishing a book on the subject in 1946. Back after the war in his native Berlin, where he lived until his death in 1988, he gave himself over to composition, conveying his commitment to the East German regime in particular through choral settings of socialist and anti-fascist texts.

Meyer, together with Max Butting, Wagner-Régeny, Kurt Schwaen and the others of the old guard of socialist musicians, worked through into the 1960s and 1970s, a time of political consolidation when the old concentration on the anti-fascism born of war had given way to the aim of building a new society in which the initiative had passed to the younger generation. Composers, no less than other workers in the culture industry, were expected to contribute to the image of a socialist culture. Music, as a non-representational art – music in its own absolute terms, that is, not bound by thoughts of a pre-existing text or the requirements of a specific function – had a greater chance than the other arts to avoid giving offence to suspicious bureaucrats intent on tracking down 'formalistic' tendencies. Nevertheless the most trivial of circumstances might influence the official attitude towards a particular work or a particular artist, and composers, with an uneasy eye on the fate of Shostakovich, had to expect interference with their activities at any time. It was an experience not unknown to the most outstanding figure of the younger generation, the most substantial composer to come out of the DDR during the forty years of its existence – Siegfried Matthus.

Born in East Prussia in 1934, Matthus studied with Wagner-Régeny at the East Berlin Hochschule für Musik and with Hanns Eisler, and subsequently settled in the city. Much of his output is in large forms – six operas, concertos for various instruments, choral and vocal music – and his first opera, *Der letzte Schuss* ('The Final Shot'), produced by Götz Friedrich at the Komische Oper in 1967, at once established him as a composer to be reckoned with. In the 1970s and 1980s he cultivated a free, athematic style, a full-blooded expressive musical language in which he became more and more expansive.

This language, atonal, often harsh and dissonant, owing a debt to serialism and recalling Alban Berg in its emotional but unsentimental lyrical moments, is strikingly displayed in Matthus' dramatic settings of passages from Hölderlin's *Hyperion* for baritone and orchestra (1979), an impressive prelude to his three operatic works of the 1980s. The first of these, which Matthus called an 'operatic vision', is a one-act dramatisation of Rilke's *Weise von Liebe und Tod des Cornets Christoph Rilke*, the famous little epic of love and war that had so deeply moved the soldiers of the war of 1914–18. First performed at the reopening of the Dresden opera house in 1985, reminiscent in spirit of Britten's *War Requiem*, grim, intense, the dissonances intensified by the stark orchestration, the work has great dramatic power. So, too, has the opera *Judith*, in its own way also a portrayal of love and war. Based on Hebbel's sado-masochistic tragedy, *Judith* was the outstanding event of the 29th East Berlin Festtage of 1985, its mastery acknowledged by public and critics alike. Modern opera has little to set alongside the passion of the terrifying climax of the work, as Judith slays her seducer Holofernes and is then raped by one of her own people as they plunder Holofernes' camp.

A further opera, *Count Mirabeau*, set in the French Revolution, with an intellectually demanding libretto by the composer, was produced at the Staatsoper in 1989, a few months before the Berlin Wall came down. Matthus' conception of opera locates the meaning of the drama at its profoundest in the music; who better than the composer himself, therefore, to say what form the libretto should take? As he wrote it, he would already anticipate the music that he would come to set to it – like Wagner. At the same time that libretto has to have its own intellectual validity and a degree of autonomy – unlike Wagner. Although their musical languages are hardly compatible, there is a good deal in this philosophy of opera that links Matthus with Michael Tippett.

Count Mirabeau confirmed Matthus' status as the leading East German composer of the day. The 'East' has since lost its meaning. His standing was already acknowledged across the Wall when he was commissioned to write a work for the centennial of the Berlin Philharmonic Orchestra in 1982 – the Concerto for Trumpet, Percussion and Orchestra. A united Berlin and a united Germany now provide his true ambience.

POSTSCRIPT

After a summer of rumbling discontent in the German Democratic Republic in 1989, with an ever-growing number of its citizens clamouring to be allowed to leave the land of 'actually existing socialism', the largest anti-government protest meeting ever seen in the country took place on 4 November in the wide open space of the Alexanderplatz. Television cameras relayed the scene to East and West. Three days later the regime of Erich Honecker collapsed and the government resigned.

On 9 November the people, the *Volk*, breached the Berlin Wall and surged into the once forbidden territory of West Berlin. A year later, on 3 October 1990, the German Democratic Republic officially merged with the Federal Republic of Germany and lost its independent existence. Berlin, it was announced, would again be the capital of the Republic and again the seat of government. The DDR, it seemed, 'had perished as though it had never been', perished in a bloodless revolution that had liberated 17 million souls from totalitarianism.

What, beyond the patent material and political consequences, has unification, reunification, meant – the sudden, breathtaking events which the Germans prosaically, almost apologetically, call *die Wende*, 'the U-turn'? And where do these events, as viewed from East and West, leave the cultural life of the country – or countries, for a declaration on a piece of paper cannot overnight create a unity out of two communities that have been facing in different directions for forty years?

The closer the identification of culture with the mechanisms of the state, the more incisive will be the changes wrought in cultural life by developments – economic, political, social – within the state. The revolutionary events of 1989 and 1990 led to the disappearance of the East German state from the map, and with it went the parasitic structures of a state-controlled culture – censorship of the spoken and written word, the commissioning of socialist works of art, culture leagues, associations of writers and the whole bureaucratic infrastructure. For the artist of the East there was no longer a Party line to toe – though nor, ironically, was there any longer a *raison d'être* for the art and literature that had sought subtle ways of escaping from the throttling authority of the *apparatchiks*. The sources of resentment and the subjects of protest had vanished overnight. The jibes of cabaret had to be recycled. The familiar ugly landmarks of the East German state, reassuring in their ugliness, were no longer there. The presentation of life in the discredited society of the immediate past, moreover, its corruption, its moral bankruptcy, its betrayal of the socialist ideals in which it claimed to find its legitimisation, had already passed from the writer to the television journalist and the newspaper reporter.

The discussion of the actual manner of reunification, the remarkable urgency with which the two Germanies became politically one, the conflict between what East and West thought was happening or should happen, the dichotomy in the East between impatience for material gain and a return to the idealistic vision of a single *Volk* – such issues swirled round what was put forward as a merger but turned out to be a takeover. Günter Grass was one who called for an initial period of cohabitation between East and West Germany because they had grown too far apart over the last forty years to be instantly reunited. There was no considered reason, after the first euphoric moments had passed, why the citizens of the East should rush into the arms of the West or why the West should hasten to embrace them. In the arts, moreover – take particularly the theatre and the performing arts, or in Berlin the sudden availability of duplicate sets of museum specialists (East and West), the personnel of two Academies of Arts (East and West) and so on – many were manifestly redundant and faced with dismissal.

With a similar view of past and present Christa Wolf also hoped for the retention of what had become characteristic of the East, with all its faults and failures: 'Allow us to clear it up ourselves,' she pleaded. To pretend that those forty years had never existed would be an affront to history. Even Heiner Müller, while affecting not to care whether there is one Germany or two, trying to immerse himself in purely literary matters, conceded that the *Wende* imposed a change of function on the writer, a change he based on the premiss: 'There is no dialogue between art and politics.' There never had been in the old DDR – it had been a monologue delivered by politics. But Müller must have had Brecht turning in his grave.

That indeed there was, and is, much to 'clear up', as Christa Wolf put it, has been savagely revealed by the cumulative demonstration of the activities of the State Security Service, the Stasi, and the thousands of petty – sometimes not so petty – Judases prepared to help in its dirty work. From the beginning the Stasi made a deliberate set at cultural circles, enticing writers and intellectuals into its web with the prospect of preferment and favour, such as trips abroad or access to hard currency.

It surprised no one that men of declared allegiance like Hermann Kant and the officials of state organisations such as the Kulturbund should have been willing to betray their fellow-citizens. But as more and more of the Stasi files were made public, murky episodes come to light in the behaviour of figures who had throughout the DDR years preserved apparently untarnished reputations. Christa Wolf, for one, was called to account, and as recently as 1996 the body charged with the handling of the files released compromising evidence against Erwin Strittmatter, one of the most popular and successful DDR novelists, whose involvement in such matters came as an unwelcome shock. It remains in any case an uncomfortable reality that the East German state survived for as long as it did, not only through the blackmail and repression exercised by the regime but through the tacit consent of its citizens to be thus blackmailed and repressed.

149. *Wall* by Rainer Fetting,
acrylic on canvas, 1980.

With the demise of the DDR and of the social system that sustained its culture went the consignment to history of vital moments of tension which had become symbolical points of attraction for writers – artists and film makers also – in both East and West, events such as the workers' uprising of 17 June 1953 and the erection on 13 August 1961 of the Berlin Wall. The Wall had been a gruesome obscenity. But, as the obstacle that had kept East and West, Warsaw Pact and Nato apart for four decades and prevented the Cold War from turning hot, it had a meaning beyond that of an inhuman incursion into the lives of the Berliners on both sides. Its removal accompanied the collapse of communism in Eastern Europe but left its former victims with the need to find new defining parameters in its place.

Indeed, one of the most striking reactions of the East Germans to the collapse of their state was the sense of bewilderment and insecurity that arose with the sudden disappearance of all the unnatural restraints that had conditioned their personal and social lives for so long. Decisions had to be taken individually that had formerly been decreed by central authority; responsibilities had to be assumed for matters in which one had previously had no say; the familiar monolithic structures of bureaucracy, that is of collective buck-passing, were no longer there to offer the protection of their comforting anonymity. The whole ethos of society, of work, of work in society, had changed. As the people needed, and still need, time to adjust to this new ethos, so writers who find their raw material in society also need to let the situation settle before bringing their imagination to bear upon the potentialities, the problems and the tensions within it.

The young, in particular, those who never knew a Berlin without a Wall or a Germany without barbed wire and death strips, and had long seen through the hollowness of back-scratching socialism, East German style, found no sense of direction in the new order, no constructive role models to adopt – though no shortage of destructive ones. The awareness of liberation, of the passing of a tyranny, could not outweigh the corrosive dissatisfaction and resentment at what was happening to them after 'their' revolution, a time when decisions on their future were being patronisingly taken by others – as they always had been. *Plus ça change . . .*

As time goes on, the pressures of coalescence must needs win the day. The demonstrators of 1989 in the Alexanderplatz paraded against the *ancien régime* with placards reading 'Wir sind das Volk' – '*We* are the People'. Later, proclaiming their proud new sense of national solidarity, they changed their slogan to 'Wir sind Ein Volk' – 'We are One People'. Until 1989 storytellers, dramatists or film makers who took the physical and psychological horrors of the Wall as their subject matter were confronting the present. Today they are dealing with history.

Whether writers will still choose to write about this particular item of history remains to be seen. They will in any case find no shortage of political, moral and environmental problems in their united country, and in Europe and the world as a whole, with which to take issue. Reiner Kunze and Wolf Biermann, among many, had found no difficulty in engaging their minds with the controversies that exercised the West after they arrived there as DDR refugees in the 1970s, and those issues have not gone away.

But disposing of the detritus of the DDR itself was to uncover its own problems. In 1990 Christa Wolf published 'Was bleibt' ('What's Left'), a short story centred on the activities of the Stasi. Actually she had written it in 1979, and this is the time in which its sinister events take place. But she kept it out of sight until, a decade later, the Stasi had been destroyed – and with it, one might say, the immediate need for her book. Self-incrimination through silence.

A fierce argument broke out in East and West. What right, ran the indignant accusation, had intellectuals like Christa Wolf, who had enjoyed perks and privileges under a hated and repressive regime, to claim, now that the danger had passed, that their conscience was clear and that they had not betrayed both their calling and their fellows by failing to speak out against evil and injustice? 'By keeping quiet', wrote Reiner Kunze, who was expelled from the country in 1976, 'most of those who stayed were sending us into exile time and again.' Justification of a lack of civil courage was even sought in a comparison between the tyranny of the Nazis and the totalitarianism of the DDR to bolster a plea that to have spoken up for freedom of expression would have meant harassment or imprisonment – as in the early Ulbricht era it certainly did. But such pusillanimity, ran the counter-argument, destroyed any claims that DDR intellectuals might make for respect and equality in a unified country. Socialism, in any case, had been exposed as a false god – a fact that left-wing intellectuals in the West, backers of the wrong horse, also had to face.

Attitudes also divided along generation lines. Where Horst Brasch, Deputy Minister of Culture, clung to the DDR to the end, his son, Thomas, defected to pursue his career as a writer in the West. So did Hans Noll, son of the popular anti-fascist novelist Dieter Noll. The most radical of the younger generation rejected all left-wing politics, in East and West alike, pronounced post-war literature – all bourgeois literature, indeed – dead and sounded yet another 'Stunde null'. What had started in 1933, they argued, had never really stopped. Only now, in 1990, could the definitive break be made. It is a characteristically German 'crisis of the intellectuals'.

A classic recent example of what is still at stake in this latest episode of the German saga of 'coming to terms with the past' involves the German PEN Club.

Like the State Museums in Berlin, the Prussian Academy of Arts and other institutions bifurcated by the political division of the city, the PEN Club had split into East and West sections. In 1996 the West section met to discuss a formal invitation to the East to reunite. Many speakers drew attention to the extensive infiltration of the East PEN by Stasi informers and found it impossible to share a platform with such corrupt elements. Günter Grass, on the other hand, supported by Walter Jens, threatened to resign if the motion to merge the two bodies were not wholeheartedly approved, arguing that West German writers had no moral right to condemn their colleagues in the East who had been forced to live under a dictatorship, while they themselves had been spared such an ordeal. Although in the event the motion was carried, almost a third of those present voted against, showing how deep feelings run on such issues and throwing the whole future of the German PEN Club into confusion.

Reunification was a national matter. No citizen of either of the two Germanies, from Munich to Mecklenburg, from the Oder to the Rhine, could escape its consequences, the positive and the optimistic – surely predominant – yet no less the problematical and the painful, still by no means overcome nearly a decade later. But, as at so many moments in the past, Berlin, both metropolitan master and vicarious victim, was destined to become a microcosm of the opportunities and pressures, the joys and the responsibilities, that confronted the new nation. A new nation, yes, with formidable economic power and political influence, yet a nation that was to receive back – could it ever really have been doubted, even in Bonn? – its old imperial–republican–totalitarian capital. And that capital, in its turn, epicentre of the Cold War, regained its former pride and sense of importance as the embodiment of the open, self-confident, liberal tradition on which the future should rest.

The new situation thus reveals two interlocking but distinguishable aspects. One is that of the future of Berlin in its restored representative function. Announcing a plan for a new capital does not make a new capital overnight. At the same time the centre of the federal government has to set the tone for the development of the country as a whole, in the interests both of its own *amour propre* and of its image on the international scene. Ministries and government agencies have already identified the spots in the city's historic centre – many of them in the former East Berlin – in which they propose to set up their headquarters, sometimes in buildings surviving from imperial Prussia or the Nazi era, sometimes in offices yet to be built. The Bundestag will move into the old Reichstag building, totally redesigned internally by Norman Foster but externally looking much as it has always done. On the edge of the Tiergarten nearby a new government quarter is to be built – a meeting-place for the Bundesrat (the second chamber, consisting of representatives of the sixteen provincial *Länder*), a new office for the Federal President and a new Federal Chancellery. Foreign embassies will eventually move here, and strenuous efforts are being made to expand the activities of manufacturing industry, especially those serving the new electronic media. Above all, there will have to be a huge building programme to accommodate an extended urban infrastructure and provide housing for thousands of new residents, in government service and the private sector alike.

The second, related aspect is that of the inner social and cultural character of Berlin itself – of how, as a single entity, it will address its public and evolve a new personality. No doubt there will be wistful glances cast back at the Golden Twenties – though the few surviving witnesses of those days are now in their nineties. In the years immediately following the Second World War, too, there had been writers who envisaged a return to the values of the Weimar Republic and the reassertion, at least in intellectual and cultural terms, of the unity that was then slipping away from them.

Now, fifty years on, in a pluralistic society from which the political hostility between East and West has finally gone, substance and quality in the arts have become the criteria for survival. Darwinian principles were left to take care of the commercial sector. But state sponsorship of culture also had to be fought for, especially at a time when the material and social costs of reunification were reaching a level almost beyond comprehension. If a subsidised cultural enterprise, whatever its esteem, appeared 'surplus to requirements', the authorities would not hesitate to withdraw their support. In 1993, for example, they closed the Schiller-Theater in Charlottenburg, a respected house whose progressive tradition went back to 1906, for just that reason.

One consequence of the decades of partition – a painful necessity at the time, now, ironically, a source of strength – was the creation of rival, parallel cultural and educational institutions to reflect the antagonistic philosophies, East and West, of the communities they served. With reunification the ministries, the Party cadres and the other trappings of DDR government vanished at a stroke. But at the same time the new city found itself in possession of a double cultural legacy. To be sure, most of the institutions of the former East had to be sanitised, 'decommunised', before they could find a place in the total scheme of things. Schools and colleges had to be depoliticised, the teachers who for two generations had been presenting the curriculum in the light – or obfuscation – of Marxism–Leninism now had to teach to a different agenda. Active Party members formerly in positions of influence were removed and their places taken by men from the West. Resentment and apprehension soured the atmosphere in many an august state institution of the former DDR. Much of what happened – and the ripples are still being felt – was not very pretty but it was not less inevitable for that.

But the richness of the joint legacy is impressive. Today Berlin has three fully fledged universities, three university teaching hospitals and a total of seventeen institutions awarding university degrees. There are three classical opera houses, nine symphony orchestras, over 300 mainstream and fringe theatres and twenty-four species of that most characteristic Berlin animal, cabaret.

No less impressive is the corpus of Berlin's museums and art galleries, state-administered and private. It has now become possible to restore the unity of the state collections which were dispersed during and after the Second World War. Three principal sites have been designated for their exhibition: the five houses of the Museum Island, stretching from the Altes Museum to the Bode-Museum, together with the Zeughaus; the gallery at Dahlem, in the west of the city, hitherto the repository of most of the greatest paintings from the Prussian state collections; and an impressive complex of new buildings within the Kulturforum centred on the Kemper-Platz, where the Philharmonie concert hall and the Prussian State Library also stand.

From the beginning – from 1830, to be exact, when classical statuary and Renaissance paintings from the collection of King Friedrich Wilhelm III went on public display in Schinkel's Altes Museum – the state museums had been conceived on a grand scale as statements of Prussian glory, exhibitions through which the citizens could share a pride in their kingdom. The state of Prussia was formally dissolved in 1947. But a reunified Berlin, by marshalling the cultural energies unique to a capital city, can do much to restore an experience of former greatness.

'We Are One People,' the demonstrators had chanted in 1989. They are not. Yet. Still today most of those who live in the eastern boroughs of the city work in the East, have their friends in the East and relax in the East. Likewise those in the West. The East does not look or feel like the West. The 'alternative' culture of Prenzlauer Berg has a different personality from that of Kreuzberg. It is proving easier to rebuild Schinkel's Bauakademie on its original site, or to reassemble the physical surroundings of the Pariser Platz and the Brandenburg Gate, than to restore the psychological and spiritual unity of the city. And in 1990 not everyone, either in the two Germanies or abroad, welcomed the prospect of reunification, for there was much to be apprehensive about, even to fear.

But the Unification Treaty stated: 'The capital of Germany is Berlin.' Except for the occasional stretch of concrete deliberately left standing – 'lest we forget' – the Wall has long been dismantled. Although psychological barriers take longer to break down than physical barriers, the direction of history is unmistakable and centuries of a common culture will assert themselves. 'What belongs together will grow together,' said Willy Brandt. And nestling at the heart of that culture, in the catchword from the popular song, Berlin is still Berlin – 'Berlin bleibt doch Berlin'.

SOURCES

CHAPTER II: THE AGE OF THE REFORMATION

(p. 14) The passage from Trithemius is in his *Opera historica*, II, 480. (p. 15) On Karl Barth see R. H. Bainton, *Here I Stand: A Life of Martin Luther*, New York, 1950, 64. (p. 26) 'The only reason for building churches . . .': in the Weimarer Ausgabe of Luther's works (1883 ff) 10, I, 1, Hälfte, 252).

CHAPTER III: THE CONSOLIDATION OF PRUSSIA

(p. 29) 'in order that We . . .': in *Corpus constitutionum Marchicarum*, Berlin/Halle, 1737, I, II, col. 31. (p. 35) For the quote from Pöllnitz see *The Memoirs of Charles-Lewis, Baron de Poelnitz*, London, 1745, I, 130. (p. 38) For the quote from Queen Sophie Charlotte see H. Ostwald, *Berlin und die Berlinerinnen*, Berlin, 1911, 19. (p. 48) For the quote from Spener see R. Glatzer (ed.), *Berliner Leben 1648–1806*, Berlin, 1956, 70. (p. 51) The quote from J. A. R. Marriott is in his *The Evolution of Prussia*, Oxford, 1915, 101. (p. 52) Klose's *Berliner Briefe* are in the Berlin periodical *Der Bär* XI, 1885. (p. 53) Eckenberg's playbill is reproduced in R. Freydank, *Theater in Berlin*, Berlin, 1988, 49.

CHAPTER IV: THE AGE OF ENLIGHTENMENT

(p. 59) The quote from Mirabeau is in Glatzer, *op. cit.*, 279. For August Friedrich Julius Knüppeln see W. Schneider, *Berlin: Eine Kulturgeschichte in Bildern und Dokumenten*, Leipzig/Weimar, 1980, 174. The quotations from James Harris, first Earl of Malmesbury, are in his *Diaries and Correspondence,* London, 1844, I, 123, 124 and 97–8. (p. 62) The passage from Moses Mendelssohn is in his *Gesammelte Schriften*, Leipzig, 1863, III, 355. (p. 64) 'After the *Oedipus* of Sophocles . . .': in Lessing's 17th Literaturbrief. (p. 64) 'If a tragedy . . .' is from Lessing's *Theatralische Bibliothek* (*Sämtliche Werke*, ed. K. Lachmann and F. Muncker, VII, 68); on the reception of *Miss Sara Sampson* see D. Hildebrandt, *Lessing*, Munich/Vienna, 1979, 174. (p. 65) On Herder's letter to Gleim see G. Hillen, *Lessing-Chronik*, Munich, 1979, 125; (p. 66) 'A tame horse . . .': see *Geschichte der deutschen Literatur vom 18. Jahrhundert bis zur Gegenwart*, ed. V. Zmegac, Königstein, 1979, I/1, 106. The quote from Schönemann is in Freydank, *op. cit.*, 80. (p. 67) The announcement of Koch's performance is in Freydank, *op. cit.*, 99. (p. 70) Voltaire's remark on La Barbarina is in L. Schneider, *Geschichte der Oper in Berlin*, Berlin, 1919, 61. The quote from Lessing (Lessing and Mylius, *Beiträge zur Historie und Aufnahme des Theaters*) is given in Glatzer, *op. cit.*, 245. (p. 72) 'Only the French . . .': cf. W. Kothe, *Friedrich der Grosse als Musiker*, Berlin,

1869, 17. (p. 73) On J. S. Bach's visit to Sanssouci see H.-G. Ottenberg, *Carl Philipp Emanuel Bach*, Oxford, 1987, 50–1. (p. 74) The quotes from Burney are in his *The Present State of Music in Germany*, London, 1773, II, 150, 203. Brahms' remark is quoted in A. W. Thayer's *Beethoven*, trans. Krehbiel, III, 20 (p. 75) Nicolai, *ed. cit.*, 396. The remarks on Reichardt by Goethe and Schiller are in W. Salmen, *Johann Friedrich Reichardt*, Freiburg/Zurich, 1963, 83. (p. 76) The quotes from König are in Glatzer, *op. cit.* 'What a prospect . . .': quoted in Schneider, *op. cit.*, 172. (p. 81) 'Nothing gets cleaned or swept . . .': see Glatzer, *op. cit.*, 268. (p. 88) 'He is an artist . . .': from Goethe's *Dichtung und Wahrheit* (Berliner Ausgabe XIII, 634).

CHAPTER V: ROMANTICISM

(p. 90) 'Romanticism was a manner of thinking . . .': cf. H. Brunschwig, *La Crise de l'état prussien à la fin du 18e. siècle*, Paris, 1947, 219. (p. 93) 'Romantic literature . . .': in Friedrich Schlegel's *Fragmente* in the *Athenaeum* I, 2 (1798). Goethe's classic–romantic antithesis is in his *Gespräche mit Eckermann*, 2 April 1829. (p. 96–7) The quotation from Thomas Mann is in *Deutschland und die Deutschen* (1945); that by Nietzsche is from a letter to Georg Brandes, 27 March 1888; that by Jean Paul is quoted in *Kunst in Berlin*, exhibition catalogue 1987, 192. (p. 103) Schiller's letter to Körner is dated 28 May 1804. (p. 104) The quote from Madame de Staël is given in *Stadtbilder, Berlin in der Malerei vom 17. Jahrhundert bis zur Gegenwart*, exhibition catalogue 1987, 96.

CHAPTER VI: REALISM AND REVOLUTION

(p. 114) 'Generally speaking . . .': from Johann David Friedrich Rumpf, *Berlin Fremdenführer*, 1826: see Schneider, *op. cit.*, 234. (p. 119) 'It had to teach dancing . . .': see M. Jacobs in *In Tyrannos*, ed. H. J. Rehfisch, London, 1944, 193. (p. 124) 'Since 1815 . . .': from Alexis, 'Berlin in seiner neuen Gestaltung' in Brockhaus' *Conservations-Lexikon der Gegenwart*, 1838, 453–63. (p. 134) 'A real poet . . .': cf. *Heine in Berlin*, ed. G. Wolf, Berlin, 1980, 275; Rahel's description of Heine, *ibid.*, 279. (p. 141) For the quote from Spontini see C. Bouvet, *Spontini*, London, 1930, 69, and for that from Hoffmann, *Gruss an Spontini*, 1820. (p. 143) Meyerbeer's letter of 5 February 1845 is in H. and G. Becker, *Giacomo Meyerbeer. A Life in Letters*, London, 1989, 100. (p. 147) Goethe's letter to Zelter is dated 2 May 1820. The anecdote about the *St Matthew Passion* is related by Eduard Devrient in *Meine Erinnerungen an Felix Mendelssohn-Bartholdy*, Leipzig, 1869. (p. 150) Berlioz' comment is in his *Mémoires*, Paris, 1878, II, 118–19. (p. 151) Berlioz, *ibid.* (p. 151) 'After the third act . . .': in Charlotte Birch-Pfeiffer, letter to Feodor Wehl, 6 November 1847.

CHAPTER VII: THE SELF-ASSURANCE OF EMPIRE

(p. 153–4) For the remark by Marx see W. Blumenberg, 'Ein unbekanntes Kapitel aus Marx's Leben' (*International Review of Social History*, 1956, 83). (p. 154) For the quote from Clausewitz see G. Barraclough, *Factors in German History*, Oxford, 1946, 118; for the quote from Bismarck see H. Kathe, *Preussen zwischen Mars und Musen*, Munich/Berlin, 1993, 355. (p. 160–1) For the quote from Caroline Bauer's *Aus meinem Bühnenleben*, see P. Bloch and W. Grzimek, *Das Klassische Berlin*, Frankfurt/Berlin/Vienna, 1978, 390–1. (p. 169) The quote from Jules Huret is from his *En Allemagne: Rhin et Westphalie*, Paris, 1907, 12; on the quote from Wilhelm II see Bloch and Grzimek, *op. cit.*, 279. (p. 176) The quote by Menzel is in Karl Scheffler, *Adolph Menzel*, Berlin, 1938, 9. (p. 180) Klinger's description of his work is in *Kunst in Berlin, op. cit.*, 314. (p. 181) For the quote by Richard Dehmel see R. Widerra, *Hans Baluschek*, Berlin, 1947, 18. (p. 183) For Liebermann's remark on the Nazis see J. Wulf, *Die bildenden Künste im Dritten Reich*, Frankfurt/Berlin/Vienna, 1983, 34. (p. 192) 'Realism embraces life . . .': see P. Demetz, *Theodor Fontane. Formen des Realismus*, Frankfurt/Berlin, 1964, 218. 'The grand style . . .': see F. Kummer, *Deutsche Literaturgeschichte des 19. Jahrhunderts*, Dresden, 1909, 623. (p. 194) The quotation from Thomas Mann is the final sentence of his essay 'Der alte Fontane'. (p. 198–9) The quotation from Brahm is in Freydank, *op. cit.*, 328. (p. 200) 'For me . . .': see Freydank, *op. cit.*, 331, note 5; for the quote from Hauptmann see his *Gedanken über das Bemalen der Statuen*, 1887 (Centenar Ausgabe VI, 896) (p. 200) For the quotation from the *Berliner Börsen-Courier* see Freydank, *op. cit.*, 331. (p. 204) For Strauss' letter to Schoenberg see *Berliner Leben 1900–1914*, ed. D. and R. Glatzer, Berlin, 1986, I, 565. (p. 204) Butting's quote is in *Berliner Leben 1900–1914, ed. cit.*, 564; 'As the music started up . . .': Hauptmann, *Das Abenteuer meiner Jugend*, see *Berliner Leben 1870–1900*, 233. (p. 205–6) 'Having provided oneself . . .': see O. Schrenk, *Berlin und die Musik*, Berlin, 1940, 44. (p. 206) For the quotes by Bülow see *Berliner Leben 1870–1900, ed. cit.*, 248; the anecdote of Richard Strauss conducting is in *Paul Dessau. Aus Gesprächen*, Leipzig, 1974, 125; for the quotation from the *Berliner Tageblatt* see *Berliner Leben 1870–1900, ed. cit.*, 240. (p. 207) For the quotation from Tchaikovsky see A. Orlova, *Tchaikovsky. A Self-Portrait*, Oxford, 1990, 341. 'Military discipline and respect . . .': see W. Jansen and R. Lorenzen, *Possen, Piefke und Posaunen*, Berlin, 1987, 114.

CHAPTER VIII: THE YEARS OF THE WEIMAR REPUBLIC

(p. 210) 'This is more than just a lost war . . .': from Walter Gropius, *The Scope of Total Architecture*, London, 1962, 19. (p. 211) The quotes from Zuckmayer are from his *Als wär's ein Stück von mir*, Vienna, 1966, 311 ff. (p. 212) Tucholsky's letter to Hasenclever is dated 11 April 1933. (p. 214) For the quote from the Werkbund see H.-W. Kruft, *A History of Architectural Theory*, London, 1994, 581, note 43. (p. 220) The quote from Käthe Kollwitz is in her *Aus meinem Leben*, Munich, 1961, 86. (p. 224) 'Expressionism believes in the all-possible . . .': see *Expressionism: Der Kampf um eine literarische Bewegung*, ed. P. Raabe, Munich, 1965, 136. (p. 228) For the quote from Benn see his Introduction to *Lyrik des expressionistischen Jahrzehnts*, Munich, 1962, 11. (p. 233) For the quote from Rilke see *LiteraturOrt Berlin*, ed. G. Rühle, Berlin, 1994, 37. (p. 234) for the quote from Hofmannsthal see *LiteraturOrt Berlin, ed. cit.*, 30; on the quote from Jünger see *LiteraturOrt Berlin ed. cit.*, 163. On Spengler see R. Taylor, *The Intellectual Tradition of Modern Germany*, London, 1973, II, 125. (p. 236) For the quote from Walter Benjamin see *LiteraturOrt Berlin, ed. cit.*, 65. (p. 237) 'All great poems . . .': from Brecht, 'Kurzer Bericht über 400 junge Lyriker', 1927. (p. 238) Tucholsky on Brecht is in Tucholsky's *Gesammelte Werke 1907–1932*, Reinbek, 1960–1, II, 1062. (p. 241) Fallada's remark is in *LiteraturOrt Berlin, ed. cit.*, 154. (p. 243) The quotation from Döblin comes in 'Mein Buch *Berlin Alexanderplatz*', 1932. (p. 246) 'The theatre should not just play . . .': cf. M. Ley-Piscator, *The Piscator Experiment*, New York, 1967, 61. (p. 257) The quote from Busoni is from a letter of 1918 to Gisella Selden-Groth quoted in H. H. Stuckenschmidt, *Ferruccio Busoni,* trans. S. Morris, London, 1970, 65. (p. 261) The Hindemith quote is in I. Kemp, *Hindemith*, Oxford, 1970, 23.

CHAPTER IX: NAZI BERLIN

(p. 262) Döblin's remark is in his 'Abschied und Wiederkehr' (*Die Zeitlupe*, Olten/Freiburg, 1962, 202). (p. 263) On the quote from Romain Rolland see R. Taylor,

Literature and Society in Germany 1918–1945, Brighton, 1980, 291. (p. 264) 'Those who start by burning books . . .': from Heine's drama *Almansor*. (p. 266–7) The quote from Göring is in P. O. Rave, *Kunstdiktatur im Dritten Reich*, Hamburg, 1949, 31. (p. 267) For the quote from Goebbels see J. Wulf, *Theater und Film im Dritten Reich*, Frankfurt, 1983, 320. (p. 268) On Emil Jannings see Wulf, *op. cit.*, 365; for the quote from the *Lokal-Anzeiger* see Wulf, *op. cit.*, 442. For the quote from the *Völkischer Beobachter* see Wulf, *op. cit.*, 391. (p. 274) 'In the beginning . . .': on Troost see Kruft, *op. cit.*, 391. (p. 275) 'The spiritual renewal . . .': see J. Wulf, *Die bildenden Künste in Dritten Reich*, Frankfurt, 1983, 195; 'Only when the artist . . .': *ibid.*, 111. (p. 275) For the quote from Göring see Rave, *op. cit.*, 23. (p. 281) 'One day . . .': in O. Nagel, *Berliner Bilder*, Berlin, 1970, 23. (p. 282) 'To us . . .': see *Entartete Musik*, Exhibition catalogue, London, 1995, 8; on Goebbels' address to the Reichsmusiktage see *Entartete Musik*, 10. 'The challenge facing us . . .': see J. Wulf, *Musik im Dritten Reich*, Frankfurt, 1983, 139. (p. 283) 'I am firmly resolved . . .': see L. P. Lochner, *Fritz Kreisler*, London, 1957, 227. (p. 285) 'It is a sad moment . . .': quoted in *Musik im Dritten Reich, ed. cit.*, 197–8, 'a man who utterly despises sport': quoted in H. G. Heister and H. G. Klein, *Musik und Musikpolitik im faschistischen Deutschland*, Frankfurt, 1984, 121.

CHAPTER X: TWO BERLINS

(p. 288) 'No one believed . . .: from Günther Weisenborn, *Der gespaltene Horizont*, Berlin, 1982, 251–2. For the quote from Huchel see K. Wagenbach, *Vaterland, Muttersprache. Deutsche Schriftsteller und ihr Staat seit 1945*, Berlin, 1979, 111; for the quote from Dix see J. Hermand, *Kultur im Wiederaufbau*, Munich, 1986, 111. (p. 291) For the quote from Friedrich Luft see his *Stimme der Kritik* I, Berlin, 1965, 16. (p. 294) The quote from Scharoun is in *Die Metropole*, ed. J. Boberg et al., Munich, 1986, II, 304. (p. 295) The quote from Mies van der Rohe is in W. Blaser, *Mies van der Rohe. The Art of Structure*, London, 1965, 6. (p. 302) The quote from Benn is in *LiteraturOrt Berlin, ed. cit.*, 54. (p. 304) 'The strength of documentary theatre . . .': see *Positionen des Dramas*, ed. H. L. Arnold and T. Buck, Munich, 1977, 230. (p. 305) Luft's review of Weiss' *Marat/Sade* is in *Die Welt*, 30 April 1964. (p. 312) 'What these poets have to say . . .': cf. H. C. Buch, *Kritische Wälder*, 1972, 116. (p. 313–14) 'Every single "and" . . .': see R. H. Thomas and W. van der Will, *The German Novel and the Affluent Society*, Manchester, 1968, x; on Adorno see *Kultur und Gesellschaft* I, ed. R. Tiedemann, Frankfurt, 1977, 30. (p. 315) The quotation from Schnurre is from the Preface to his collection *Man sollte dagegen sein*, Olten/Freiburg, 1960. (p. 317) 'A novel is a version of reality . . .': from Johnson's *Vorschläge zur Prüfung eines Romans*, Frankfurt, 1973; 'Where reality is known . . .': from an interview in *Konkret*, January 1962, 19. (p. 318) 'I prefer to keep the wound open': cf. Grass, *Dokumente zur politischen Wirkung*, 1971 97. (p. 323) 'When Germany comes to be reunited . . .': letter from Brecht to Helene Weigel, 21 April 1949. (p. 331) 'The ice-age of no dialogue . . .': see Müller, *Theatermaschine*, trans. M. von Henning, London, 1995, xiv. (p. 338) 'Progressive writers . . .': see *Dokumente der Sozialistischen Einheitspartei Deutschlands. Beschlüsse und Erklärungen des Zentralsekretariats und des Parteivorstandes*, Berlin, 1950, II, 191. (p. 344) The quote from Uwe Kolbe is from L. Cohn-Pfister in *Germanic Review* 67, Vol. 4, 1992, 156. Thomas Mann's letter to Hans Rodenberg of DEFA is dated 7 Februrary 1955. (p. 349) 'Confused, frivolous . . .': see R. Schenk, *Das 2. Leben der Filmstadt Babelsberg*, Berlin, 1994, 203. (p. 353) For the quotation by Mattheuer see *Auftragskunst der DDR 1949–1990*, ed. M. Flacke, Munich/Berlin, 1995, 9. (p. 354) For the quotations from the Politbureau committee see *Auftragskunst, ed. cit.*, 21. (p. 355) For the comments on Metzkes see *Auftragskunst, ed. cit.*, 29, note 88. (p. 357) For the quotation by Cremer see *Auftragskunst, ed. cit.*, 116, note 4. (p. 359) The quotation by Tucholke is in *Auftragskunst, ed. cit.*, 288. (p. 377) 'Music in our Republic . . .': in *Studien zur Berliner Musikgeschichte*, Berlin, 1989, 20. (p. 378) The quotation from Eisler is from his *Musik und Politik. Schriften 1924–1948*, Leipzig, 1973, 212.

(p. 380) 'In its artistic work . . .': from *Deutsche Staatsoper/Deutsche Demokratische Republik*, Berlin, 1973, final page. (p. 380) The quotation from Brecht is in W. Otto, *Die Lindenoper*, Berlin, 1980, 203. (p. 383) 'I would regard my project . . .': Felsenstein's words are in C. Hasche, T. Schölling and J. Fiebach, *Theater in der DDR*, Berlin, 1994, 13. Felsenstein, *ibid.*, 24. (p. 384) 'Music is mental effort . . .': from *Paul Dessau. Aus Gesprächen*, Berlin, 1974, 12.

POSTSCRIPT

Reiner Kunze's remark (p. 389) is quoted in *'Es geht nicht um Christa Wolf'. Der Literaturstreit im vereinten Deutschland*, ed. T. Anz, Munich, 1991, 12.

BIBLIOGRAPHY

GENERAL

These are broad cultural surveys and works on the background history of Berlin, most with further bibliographies. Among standard reference books are *The New Grove Dictionary of Music and Musicians*, London, 1980; *Die Musik in Geschichte und Gegenwart*, Kassel, 1949–; U. Thieme and F. Becker (eds), *Allgemeines Lexikon der bildenden Künstler*, Leipzig, 1907–50; *Neue Deutsche Biographie*, Berlin, 1971–; W. Kosch, *Deutsches Literatur-Lexikon*, Bern, 1966–; W. Kosch, *Deutsches Theater-Lexikon*, Klagenfurt/Vienna, 1953.

Die Bau- und Kunstdenkmale in der DDR: Hauptstadt Berlin, Berlin, 1983

R. Bauer, *Berlin. Illustrierte Chronik bis 1870*, Berlin, 1988

E. Berckenhagen, *Berliner und Märkische Gläser*, Darmstadt, 1956

——, *Die Malerei in Berlin vom 13. bis zum ausgehenden 18. Jahrhundert*, Berlin, 1964

Berlin im Bild seiner Maler, exhibition catalogue, Charlottenburg, Berlin, 1984

Berlin 1945–1989: Jahr für Jahr, Berlin, 1995

H. Börsch-Supan, *Die Kunst in Brandenburg–Preussen*, Berlin, 1980

D. Clelland (ed.), *Berlin. An Architectural History*, London, 1983

W. Doede, *Berlin. Kunst und Künstler seit 1870*, Recklinghausen, 1961

R. Freydank, *Theater in Berlin*, Berlin, 1988

J. F. Geist and K. Kürvers, *Das Berliner Mietshaus*, 3 vols, Munich, 1980, 1984, 1989

W. Grzimek, *Deutsche Bildhauer des zwanzigsten Jahrhunderts*, Munich, 1969

W. Haftmann, *Malerei im zwanzigsten Jahrhundert*, Munich, 1979

W. Haus, *Geschichte der Stadt Berlin*, Berlin, 1992

C. W. Haxthausen and H. Suhr (eds), *Berlin. Culture and Metropolis*, Minneapolis, 1991

W. Hegemann, *Das steinerne Berlin*, Brunswick, 1988

H. Herzfeld, *Berlin. Brennpunkt deutschen Schicksals*, Berlin, 1960

W. Hinderer (ed.), *Geschichte der politischen Lyrik in Deutschland*, Stuttgart, 1978

——, *Geschichte der deutschen Lyrik*, Stuttgart, 1983

S. Hinz, *Innenraum und Möbel*, Berlin, 1976

J. Huret, *En Allemagne. Berlin*, Paris, 1909

Juden in Berlin. Ein Lesebuch, Berlin, 1988

E. Kaeber, *Beiträge zur Berliner Geschichte*, Berlin, 1964

H. Kathe, *Preussen zwischen Mars und Musen*, Berlin, 1993

W. Kiaulehn, *Berlin. Schicksal einer Weltstadt*, Berlin, 1980

A. F. J. Knüppeln, *Charakteristik von Berlin*, Philadelphia, 1785

H. Kotschenreuther, *Berlin im Bild seiner Maler. XVIII. bis XX. Jahrhundert*, Berlin, 1965

M. Krammer, *Berlin im Wandel der Jahrhunderte*, Berlin, 1965

Kunst in Berlin, exhibition catalogue, Berlin, 1987

H. Kunz, *Musikstadt Berlin*, Berlin, 1956

L. Löffler, *Berlin und der Berliner*, Berlin, 1856

H. Ludwig (ed.), *Erlebnis Berlin. 300 Jahre Berlin im Spiegel seiner Kunst*, Berlin, 1979

H. Mackowsky, *Häuser und Menschen im alten Berlin*, Berlin, 1923

I. Materna and W. Ribbe (eds). *Berlin: Geschichte in Daten*, Munich, 1996

H. Müther, *Berlins Bautradition*, Berlin, 1956

M. Osborn, *Berlins Aufstieg zur Weltstadt*, Berlin, 1929

H. Ostwald, *Berlin und die Berlinerin*, Berlin, 1911

——, *Kultur- und Sittengeschichte Berlins*, Berlin, 1924

Preussen, Versuch einer Bilanz, exhibition catalogue, Gropius-Bau, Berlin, 1981

P. O. Rave, *Berlin in der Geschichte seiner Bauten*, Berlin, 1966

A. Read and D. Fisher, *Berlin. The Biography of a City*, London, 1994

A. Reissner, *Berlin 1695–1945*, London, 1984

W. Ribbe (ed.), *Geschichte Berlins*, Munich, 1987

——, (ed.), *Berlinische Lebensbilder*, Berlin, 1986

——, and W. Schäche (eds), *Baumeister – Architekten – Stadtplaner*, Berlin, 1987

——, and J. Schmädeke, *Kleine Berlin-Geschichte*, 3rd edn, Berlin, 1994

G. Rühle (ed.), *LiteraturOrt Berlin*, Berlin, 1994

C. Sachs, *Musikgeschichte der Stadt Berlin bis zum Jahre 1800*, Berlin, 1908

G. Schade, *Berliner Porzellan*, Leipzig, 1978

K. Scheffler, *Berlin – Ein Stadtschicksal*, Berlin, 1989

W. Scheffler, *Berlins Goldschmiede*, Berlin, 1968

O. Schenker, *Berlin und die Musik*, Berlin, 1940

H. Schmitz, *Berliner Eisenkunstguss*, Munich, 1917

W. Schneider and W. Gottschalk, *Berlin, Eine Kulturgeschichte in Bildern und Dokumenten*, Leipzig/Weimar, 1980

H. Seeger and U. Bökel, *Musikstadt Berlin*, Leipzig, 1974

H. Spiero, *Das poetische Berlin*, Munich, 1911–12

Stadtbilder. Berlin in der Malerei vom 17. Jahrhundert bis zur Gegenwart, exhibition catalogue, Berlin Museum, Berlin, 1987

W. Stechele, *Berlin und die deutsche Dichtung*, Berlin, 1927

W. Stresemann, *Philharmonie und Philharmoniker*, Berlin, 1979

W. Süss (ed.), *Hauptstadt Berlin*, 2 vols, Berlin, 1994, 1995

G. Wahnrau, *Berlin, Stadt der Theater*, Berlin, 1957

I. Wallace, *Berlin*, Oxford, 1993

A. Weissmann, *Berlin als Musikstadt*, Leipzig, 1911

F. Wendland, *Berlins Gärten und Parke*, Frankfurt/Berlin/Vienna, 1979

W. Wendland, *700 Jahre Kirchengeschichte Berlins*, Leipzig, 1930

I. Wirth, *Maler sehen eine Stadt. Malerei und Graphik aus drei Jahrhunderten*, Berlin, 1963

SPECIFIC PERIODS

The following is a selection of works on literature, painting, music and the other arts arranged, albeit with a certain degree of overlap, to correspond to the individual chapters of the book. Many of these works – those that deal with particular genres or individuals, for example – inevitably have a scope that goes beyond the specific context of Berlin but it would have been unhelpful to exclude them when they contain substantial information on the culture of Berlin itself.

Chapters I and II

F. L. Carsten, *The Origins of Prussia*, Oxford, 1954; R. Kötzschke, *Geschichte der ostdeutschen Kolonisation*, Munich, 1937; F. Berckenhagen, *Die Malerei in Berlin vom 13. bis zum ausge-*

henden 18. Jahrhundert, Berlin, 1964; M. Tosetti, *St Marien zu Berlin*, Berlin, 1974; *Die Nikolaikirche zu Berlin*, Märkisches Museum, Berlin, n.d.; A. Elschenbroich (ed.), *Deutsche Literatur des 16. Jahrhunderts*, Munich/Vienna, 1981; H. Kathe, *op. cit.*; W. Stammler, *Der Totentanz*, Munich, 1948; *450 Jahre Reformation*, ed. L. Stern and H. Steinmetz, Berlin, 1967

Chapter III

Berliner Leben 1648–1806, ed. R. Glatzer, Berlin, 1956; C. Sachs, *Musik und Oper am kurbrandenburgischen Hof*, Berlin, 1910; B. Haendcke, *Deutsche Kultur im Zeitalter des dreissigjährigen Krieges*, Leipzig, 1906; E. Berckenhagen, *op. cit.*; R. Petras, *Berliner Plastik im 18. Jahrhundert*, Berlin, 1954; H. Hettner, *Geschichte der deutschen Literatur im 18. Jahrhundert*, Berlin/Weimar, 1979; R. Pascal, *German Literature in the Sixteenth and Seventeenth Centuries*, London, 1968; G. Hoffmeister, *German Baroque Literature*, New York, 1977; E. Faden, *Berlin im Dreissigjährigen Krieg*, Berlin, 1927; H.-A. Koch, *Das deutsche Singspiel*, Stuttgart, 1974; H. Schultz, *Berlin 1650–1800. Sozialgeschichte einer Residenz*, Berlin, 1987

Chapter IV

E. M. Batley, *Catalyst of Enlightenment. Gotthold Ephraim Lessing*, Bern, 1990; *Berliner Leben, ed. cit.*; H.-J. Kadatz and G. Murza, *Georg Wenzeslaus von Knobelsdorff*, Leipzig, 1983; *Studien zur Berliner Musikgeschichte vom 18. Jahrhundert bis zur Gegenwart*, ed. T. Ebert-Obermeier, Berlin, 1989; W. Otto, *Die Lindenoper*, Berlin, 1980; E. Redslob, *Barock und Rokoko in den Schlössern von Berlin und Potsdam*, Berlin, 1954; D. Hildebrandt, *Lessing*, Munich/Vienna, 1979; H. Knobloch, *Herr Moses in Berlin*, Berlin, 1993; H.-G. Ottenberg, *Carl Philipp Emanuel Bach*, Leipzig, 1982; G. P. Gooch, *Frederick the Great*, London, 1947; H. Hettner, *op. cit.*; H. Schultz, *Berlin 1650–1800*, Berlin, 1987; G. B. Volz, *Aus der Zeit Friedrichs des Grossen*, Berlin, 1908; E. E. Helm, *Music at the Court of Frederick the Great*, Oklahoma, 1960; P. Paret (ed.), *Frederick the Great. A Profile*, New York, 1973; W. Ritzel, *Gottfried Ephraim Lessing*, Stuttgart, 1966; R. Herz, *Berliner Barock*, Berlin, 1928; *Friedrich II. und die Kunst*, exhibition catalogue, Potsdam, 1986; H. Reuther, *Barock in Berlin*, Berlin, 1969; J. Ziechmann (ed.), *Panorama der friderizianischen Zeit*, Bremen, 1985; C. Dahlhaus and L. Finscher (eds), *Die Musik des 18. Jahrhunderts*, Regensburg, 1985

Chapter V

Berliner Leben 1806–1847, ed. R. Köhler and W. Richter, Berlin, 1954; I. Drewitz, *Berliner Salons*, Berlin, 1979; G. Wolf (ed.), *Heine in Berlin*, Berlin, 1980; H. Scurla, *Begegnungen mit Rahel*, Berlin, 1978; *Studien zur Berliner Musikgeschichte, ed. cit.*; J. Füst (ed.), *Henriette Herz*, Berlin, 1850; W. Otto, *Die Lindenoper, ed. cit.*; M. Lüthi, *Märchen*, Stuttgart, 1964; S. Prawer (ed.), *The Romantic Period in Germany*, London, 1970; J. Maass, *Kleist*, Bern/Zurich, 1977; J. Barzun, *Classic, Romantic and Modern*, New York, 1961; R. Benz and A. von Schneider, *Die Kunst der deutschen Romantik*, Munich, 1939; H. Schrade, *Deutsche Maler der Romantik*, Cologne, 1967; A. Einstein, *Music in the Romantic Era*, London, 1947; E. Istel, *Die Blütezeit der musikalischen Romantik in Deutschland*, Leipzig/Berlin, 1921

Chapter VI

E. Kaeber, *Berlin 1848*, Berlin, 1948; P. Weiglin, *Berliner Biedermeier*, Bielefeld/Leipzig, 1942; P. Bloch and W. Grzimek, *Das klassische Berlin*, Frankfurt/Berlin/Vienna, 1978; E. Börsch-Supan, *Berliner Baukunst nach Schinkel 1840–1870*, Munich, 1977; *Karl Friedrich Schinkel 1781–1841*, exhibition catalogue, Berlin, 1982; *Studien zur Berliner Musikgeschichte, ed. cit.*; W. Otto, *Die Lindenoper, ed. cit.*; J. Klein, *Geschichte der deutschen Novelle von Goethe bis zur*

Gegenwart, Berlin, 1966; *Berliner Biedermeier von Blechen bis Menzel*, exhibition catalogue, Bremen, 1967; W. Jansen and R. Lorenzen, *Possen, Piefke und Posaunen. Sommertheater und Gartenkonzerte in Berlin*, Berlin, 1987; G. Hermann, *Das Biedermeier im Spiegel seiner Zeit*, Berlin, 1913; A. Rosenberg, *Die Berliner Malerschule 1819–1879*, Berlin, 1879; H. E. Jacob, *Felix Mendelssohn and His Times*, London, 1963; F. Sengle, *Biedermeierzeit*, Stuttgart, 1971–80

Chapter VII

Berliner Leben 1870–1900, ed. R. Glatzer, Berlin, 1963; P. Bloch and W. Grzimek, *op. cit.*; *Studien zur Berliner Musikgeschichte*, *ed. cit.*; P. de Mendelssohn, *Zeitungsstadt Berlin*, Berlin, 1959; W. Otto, *Die Lindenoper, ed. cit.*; R. Pfefferkorn, *Die Berliner Sezession*, Berlin, 1972; C. Forderer, *Die Grosstadt im Roman*, Wiesbaden, 1992; W. Rothe, *Die Grosstadtlyrik vom Naturalismus bis zur Gegenwart*, Stuttgart, 1981; K. Scheffler, *Adolf Menzel*, Berlin, 1955; J. Schutte, *Lyrik des deutschen Naturalismus*, Stuttgart, 1976; A. Lange, *Das wilhelminische Berlin*, Berlin, 1967; P. Demetz, *Formen des Realismus; Theodor Fontane*, Frankfurt/Berlin/Vienna, 1973; K. H. Bröhan, *Kunst der Jahrhundertwende und der zwanziger Jahre I: Berliner Sezessionisten*, Berlin, 1973; K. S. Guthke, *Gerhart Hauptmann*, Göttingen, 1961; *100 Jahre Deutsches Theater Berlin*, Berlin, 1983; P. Czerny and H. P. Hofmann, *Der Schlager*, Berlin, 1968; B. Förster, *Musiker im bunten Rock*, Berlin, 1962; H. Aust, *Literatur des Realismus*, Stuttgart, 1977; G. Kaiser, *Gottfried Keller*, Frankfurt, 1981

Chapter VIII

Berliner Leben 1900–1914, ed. D. and R. Glatzer, Berlin, 1986; *Berliner Leben 1914–1918*, ed. D. and R. Glatzer, Berlin, 1983; *Studien zur Berliner Musikgeschichte. Musikkultur der zwanziger Jahre*, Berlin, 1989; E. Roters (ed.), *Berlin 1910–1933. Die visuellen Künste*, Berlin, 1983; B. Gilliam (ed.), *Music and Performance during the Weimar Republic*, Cambridge, 1944; *Expressionisten: Die Avantgarde in Deutschland 1905–1920*, exhibition catalogue, Berlin, 1986; F. Henneberg, *Des grosse Brecht-Liederbuch*, Berlin/Frankfurt, 1984; R. Taylor, *Kurt Weill*, London 1991; J. Willett, *The Weimar Years*, London, 1984; J. Schebera, *Damals im Romanischen Café*, Leipzig, n.d.; J. Willett, *The Theatre of Erwin Piscator*, London, 1978; G. Skelton, *Paul Hindemith*, London, 1975; H. H. Stuckenschmidt, *Schoenberg*, London, 1977; A. Beaumont, *Busoni the Composer*, London, 1985; P. Heyworth, *Otto Klemperer, His Life and Times*, Cambridge, 1983; P. Raabe (ed.), *Expressionismus. Der Kampf um eine literarische Bewegung*, Munich, 1965; P. Selz, *German Expressionist Painting*, Berkeley/Los Angeles, 1957; K. Bullivant (ed.), *Culture and Society in the Weimar Republic*, Manchester, 1977; R. Taylor, *Literature and Society in Germany 1918–1945*, Brighton, 1980; *Realismus und Sachlichkeit. Aspekte deutscher Kunst*, exhibition catalogue, Berlin, 1974; H. Jähner, *Künstlergruppe Brücke*, Berlin, 1984; H. Kliemann, *Die Novembergruppe*, Berlin, 1969; K. Riha (ed.), *Dada Berlin*, Stuttgart, 1977; J. L. Styan, *Max Reinhardt*, Cambridge, 1982; W. Jacobsen, A. Kaes and H. H. Prinzler, *Geschichte des deutschen Films*, Stuttgart, 1993

Chapter IX

Art and Power: Europe under the Dictators 1930–1945, exhibition catalogue, London, 1995; F. K. Prieberg, *Musik im NS-Staat*, Frankfurt, 1982; J. Wulf, *Die bildenden Künste im Dritten Reich*, Frankfurt/Berlin/Vienna, 1983; J. Wulk, *Musik im Dritten Reich*, Frankfurt/Berlin/Vienna, 1983; J. Wulf, *Presse und Funk im Dritten Reich*, Frankfurt/Berlin/Vienna, 1983; J. Wulf, *Theater und Film im Dritten Reich*, Frankfurt/Berlin/Vienna, 1983; J. Wulf, *Literatur und Dichtung im Dritten Reich*, Frankfurt/Berlin/Vienna, 1983; H.-W. Heister and H.-G. Klein, *Musik und Musikpolitik im faschistischen Deutschland*, Frankfurt, 1984; H. Brenner, *Die Kunstpolitik des Nationalsozialismus*, Reinbek, 1963; D. Strothmann, *Nationalsozialis-*

tische Literaturpolitik, Bonn, 1963; H. Denkler and K. Prüm, *Die deutsche Literatur im Dritten Reich*, Stuttgart, 1976; R. Taylor, *op. cit.*; B. Hinz, *Die Malerei im deutschen Faschismus*, Munich, 1974; U. Pring (ed.), *Kunst in Berlin von 1930 bis 1960*, exhibition catalogue, Berlin, 1980; W. Schäche, *Architektur und Städtebau in Berlin zwischen 1933 und 1945*, Berlin, 1991; H. R. Klieneberger, *The Christian Writers of the Inner Emigration*, The Hague/Paris, 1968; R. Grimm and J. Hermand (eds), *Exil und Innere Emigration*, Frankfurt, 1972; M. Meyer, *The Politics of Music in the Third Reich*, New York/Bern/Frankfurt, 1991

Chapter X

General and West Berlin

A. Steinhage and T. Flemming (eds), *Berlin 1945–1989. Die Ereignisse in der geteilten Stadt*, Berlin, 1995; *Berlin: Literary Images of a City*, London symposium, 1989; H. H. Stuckenschmidt, *Twentieth Century Music*, London, 1969; J. Hermand, *Kultur im Wiederaufbau. Die Bundesrepublik 1945–1965*, Munich, 1986; J. Hermand, *Die Kultur der Bundesrepublik Deutschland*, Munich, 1988; F. Luft, *Stimme der Kritik*, Berlin, 1965; W. Sebald, *A Radical Stage. Theatre in Germany in the 1970s and 1980s*, New York/Oxford/Munich, 1988; M. Reich-Ranicki, *Deutsche Literatur in West und Ost*, Munich, 1963; A. Williams, S. Parkes and R. Smith (eds), *German Literature at a Time of Change*, London, 1991; H.-G. Pflaum and H. H. Prinzler, *Film in der Bundesrepublik Deutschland*, Munich, 1992; M. Durzak (ed.), *Deutsche Gegenwartsliteratur*, Stuttgart, 1981; H. Kreimeier, *Kino und Filmindustrie in der Bundesrepublik Deutschland*, Kronberg, 1973; R. H. Thomas and W. van der Will, *The German Novel and the Affluent Society*, Manchester, 1968; W. Hinck, *Das moderne Drama in Deutschland*, Göttingen, 1973; M. Patterson, *German Theatre Today*, London, 1976; W. Ismayr, *Das politische Theater in Westdeutschland*, Meisenheim, 1977; K. H. Hilzinger, *Die Dramaturgie des dokumentarischen Theaters*, Tübingen, 1976; W. Kolneder et al. (eds), *Das GRIPS-Theater*, Berlin, 1979; P. Iden, *Die Schaubühne am Halleschen Ufer*, Munich, 1979; M. Durzak, *Der deutsche Roman der Gegenwart*, Stuttgart, 1979; W. M. Lüdke, *Literatur und Studentenbewegung*, Opladen, 1977; J. Held, *Kunst und Kunstpolitik in Deutschland 1945–49*, Berlin, 1981; U. Prinz and W. J. Stock (eds), *Gefühl und Härte. Neue Kunst aus Berlin*, exhibition catalogue, Munich, 1982; U. Prinz and E. Roters, *Kunst in Berlin von 1960 bis heute*, Berlin, 1979; H. Klotz, *Die neuen Wilden in Berlin*, Stuttgart, 1984; W. Grzimek, *op. cit.*; H. Raum, *Die bildende Kunst der BRD und Westberlins*, Leipzig, 1977; K. Thomas, *Zweimal deutsche Kunst nach 1945*, Cologne, 1985; H. Pongs, *Dichtung im gespaltenen Deutschland*, Stuttgart, 1966; O. Knörrich, *Die deutsche Lyrik der Gegenwart*, Stuttgart, 1978; P. Hutchinson, *Literary Presentations of Divided Germany*, Cambridge, 1977; C. Innes, *Modern German Drama*, Cambridge, 1979; M. Kane (ed.), *Socialism and the Literary Imagination*, New York/Oxford, 1991; W. Jacobsen, A. Kaes and H. H. Prinzler, *Geschichte des deutschen Films*, Stuttgart, 1993

East Berlin

H. J. Geerdts (ed.), *Literatur der DDR*, Stuttgart, 1972; J. Flores, *Poetry in East Germany*, New Haven/London, 1971; H. Gebhardt, *Kabarett heute*, Berlin, 1987; J. H. Reid, *Writing Without Taboos. The New East German Literature*, New York/Oxford/Munich, 1990; M. Butting, *Musikgeschichte, die ich miterlebte*, Berlin, 1955; R. Wagner-Régeny, *Begegnungen*, Berlin, 1968; K. Volker, *Bertolt Brecht*, Munich, 1976; J. Willett, *The Theatre of Bertolt Brecht*, London, 1959; F. Henneberg, *op. cit.*; W. Emmerich, *Kleine Literaturgeschichte der DDR*, Stuttgart, 1994; *Das zweite Leben der Filmstadt Babelsberg 1946–92*, ed. Filmmuseum Potsdam, Berlin, 1994; C. Hasche, T. Schölling and J. Fiebach, *Theater in der DDR*, Berlin, 1994; H.-J. Schmitt, *Einführung in Theorie, Geschichte und Funktion der DDR-Literatur*,

Stuttgart, 1975; H. Koch, *Kulturpolitik in der Deutschen Demokratischen Republik*, Berlin, 1976; W. Schivelbusch, *Sozialistisches Drama nach Brecht*, Darmstadt, 1974; F. Trommler, *Sozialistische Literatur in Deutschland*, Stuttgart, 1976; U. Berger and G. Deicke, *Lyrik der DDR*, Berlin/Weimar, 1974; M. Flacke (ed.), *Auftragskunst der DDR 1949–1990*, Munich/Berlin, 1995; M. Flacke (ed.), *Auf der Suche nach dem verlorenen Staat. Die Kunst der Parteien und Massenorganisation der DDR*, Berlin, 1994; U. Kuhirt, *Kunst der DDR 1945–1959*, Leipzig, 1982; W. Kurth, *Berliner Landschaftsmalerei*, Berlin, 1958; T. Hörnigk, *Christa Wolf*, Göttingen, 1989

ILLUSTRATION CREDITS

Stadtmuseum Berlin: 1 (Christel Lehmann), 2 (Christel Lehmann), 3 (Hans-Joachim Bartsch, Berlin), 10 (Hans-Joachim Bartsch, Berlin), 13, 14 (Hans-Joachim Bartsch, Berlin), 15 (Hans-Joachim Bartsch, Berlin), 18 (Hans-Joachim Bartsch, Berlin), 19, 22 (Christel Lehmann), 23 (Christel Lehmann), 24 (Christel Lehmann), 28 (Christel Lehmann), 29, 41 (Roman März, Berlin), 43 (Christel Lehmann), 44 (Hans-Joachim Bartsch, Berlin), 53 (Hans-Joachim Bartsch, Berlin), 54, 63 (Christel Lehmann), 68 (Hans-Joachim Bartsch, Berlin), 71 (Hans-Joachim Bartsch, Berlin), 76 (Hans-Joachim Bartsch, Berlin), 79 (Christel Lehmann), 89 (Hans-Joachim Bartsch, Berlin), 91, 119 (Klaus Göken, 1992), 126, 129 (Hans-Joachim Bartsch, Berlin), 130, 131 (Hans-Joachim Bartsch, Berlin), 147 (Hans-Joachim Bartsch, Berlin), 149 (Hans-Joachim Bartsch, Berlin).

Landesbildstelle Berlin: 4, 21a and b, 70, 81 (Johannes Böse), 100, 102, 123, 132, 137.

Brandenburgisches Landesamt für Denkmalpflege: 5 (Renate Worel), 7, 12 (Udo E. Hänel), 37, 73 (Meßbildarchiv 1935), 74 (Meßbildarchiv 1904), 77 (Meßbildarchiv 1921), 80 (Meßbildarchiv c. 1920).

Bildarchiv Foto Marburg: 8, 16, 17, 20, 25, 72, 98.

AKG London: 11, 124.

Staatliche Museen zu Berlin – Preußischer Kulturbesitz: 26 (Kunstgewerbemuseum. Fotoarchiv Schloß Köpenick), 34 (Kupferstichkabinett. Foto Jörg P. Anders), 36 (Kupferstichkabinett. Foto Jörg P. Anders), 39 (Kunstgewerbemuseum. Fotoarchiv Schloß Köpenick), 40. (Gemäldegalerie. Foto Jörg P. Anders), 48 (Kunstgeweerbemuseum. Foto Hans-Joachim Bartsch), 51 (Kupferstichkabinett – Sammlung der Zeichnungeng und Druckgraphik), 52 (Kupferstichkabinett. Foto Jörg P. Anders), 57 (Kupferstichkabinett. Foto Jörg P. Anders), 59 (Kupferstichkabinett. Foto Jörg P. Anders), 61 (Nationalgalerie. Foto Jörg P. Anders), 65 (Nationalgalerie. Foto Klaus Göken), 69 (Kupferstichkabinett. Foto Jörg P. Anders), 86 (Nationalgalerie), 87 (Kupferstichkabinett. Foto Jörg P. Anders), 90 (Nationalgalerie. Foto Klaus Göken. 1993), 105 (© DACS 1997 Kupferstichkabinett. Foto Jörg P. Anders), 109 (Nationalgalerie. Foto Jens Ziehe, Berlin 1995), 110 (© DACS 1997 Nationalgalerie. Foto Klaus Göken, 1992),127 (Nationalgalerie. Foto Klaus Göken 1993), 136 (Nationalgalerie), 138 (Nationalgalerie), 140 (Nationalgalerie).

Stiftung Preußische Schlößer und Gärten, Berlin-Brandenburg: 27, 32, 33, 38, 56.

Deutsches Historisches Museum Berlin: 30.

Verwaltung der Staatlichen Schlößer und Gärten, Schloß Charlottenburg: 35, 42, 66 (Foto Jörg P. Anders).

Akademie der Khnste, Berlin: 45, 88 (Kraushaar).

Bildarchiv Preußischer Kulturbesitz Berlin: 46 (Kunstbibliothek, Berlin), 47 (Nationalgalerie), 49 (Nationalgalerie. Foto Klaus Göken, Berlin), 65 (Nationalgalerie. Foto Klaus Göken), 83 (Nationalgalerie), 84 (Nationalgalerie. Foto Jörg P. Anders), 85 (Nationalgalerie. Foto Klaus Göken), 96 (Nationalgalerie. Foto G. Stenzel 1993), 104 (© DACS 1997 Nationalgalerie. Foto

Klaus Göken, 1993), 106 (© DACS 1997 Nationalgalerie. Foto Klaus Göken), 112 (Nationalgalerie. Foto Jörg P. Anders), 113 (© DACS 1997. Nationalgalerie/Jörg P. Anders), 115 (© DACS 1997. Nationalgalerie – Gemeinsame Erwerbung des Vereins der Freunde der Landes Berlin 1996), 116 (© DACS 1997. Nationalgalerie/Klaus Göken, Berlin 1992), 128 (Nationalgalerie. Foto Klaus Göken, 1992).

Arthothek Joachim Blauel: 50.

Hamburger Kunsthalle Foto Elke Walford: 55.

Rheinisches Bildarchiv: 62 (Wallraf-Richartz-Museum, Köln).

Niedersächsiches Landesmuseum, Landesgalerie Hannover: 64.

Musikinstrumenten-Museum des Staatlichen Instituts für Musikforschung Preußischer Kulturbesitz, Berlin: 67 (© Jürgen Liepe).

Courtesy Frederic J. Schwartz: 75.

Brigitte Taylor: 82, 97, 111 (Rudolph Belling © DACS 1997), 134, 135, 144.

Nationalgalerie Berlin: 92.

Sächsische Landesbibliothek Dresden/Deutsche Fotothek: 93, 139.

Theodor-Fontane-Archiv Potsdam: 94.

Ullstein: 99 (Rolf Köhler), 117.

Staatsgalerie Stuttgart: 107.

Brücke-Museum: 108 (© DACS 1997).

Allen Memorial Art Museum, Oberlin College, Ohio; Charles F. Olney Fund, 1950: 114.

Fundaciòn Colecciòn Thyssen-Bornemisza, Madrid: 118 (© DACS 1997), 120 (© DACS 1997).

Berlinische Galerie: 125, 148.

Stiftung Ostdeutsche Galerie, Regensburg: 142.

Sprengel Museum, Hannover: 143.

INDEX